WITHDRAWN

Restoration Comedy

EDITED BY

A. NORMAN JEFFARES

Professor of English Literature
University of Leeds

Volume I

THE FOLIO PRESS
LONDON
ROWMAN AND LITTLEFIELD
TOTOWA, NEW JERSEY
1974

© Copyright The Folio Society Limited 1974

First published in the United States 1974
by Rowman and Littlefield, Totowa, N.J.

Folio Press ISBN 0 85067 030 6

Library of Congress Cataloging in Publication Data
Jeffares, Alexander Norman, comp. Restoration comedy.
'A Folio Press publication.'
CONTENTS: v. 1. Killigrew, T. The parson's wedding –
Sedley, C. The mulberry garden – Etherege, G.
She would if she could. (etc.)
1. English drama (Comedy) 2. English drama – Restoration.
I. Title.
PR1248.J4   822'.052   73–19769
Rowman and Littlefield ISBN 0–87471–476–1

PRINTED IN GREAT BRITAIN
by W & J Mackay Limited, Chatham

COMPLETE CONTENTS

COMPLETE ILLUSTRATIONS

Volume 1
Thomas Killigrew
Sir Charles Sedley
A Scene from *She Would If She Could*
A Scene from *Sir Martin Mar-All*
William Wycherley
A Scene from *The Man of Mode*

Volume 2
Thomas Durfey
A Scene from *The Plain Dealer*
Mrs Aphra Behn
John Dryden
Mrs Elizabeth Barry
Anthony Leigh

Volume 3
Thomas Betterton
Thomas Shadwell
William Congreve
Colley Cibber
Sir John Vanbrugh
Mrs Anne Bracegirdle

Volume 4
Robert Wilks as Sir Harry Wildair in *The Constant Couple*
A Scene from *The Way of the World*
Colley Cibber as Lord Foppington
A Scene from *The Recruiting Officer*
George Farquhar
Sir Richard Steele

GENERAL INTRODUCTION

The twenty-four plays included in this collection of Restoration comedies have been chosen not only because they represent the work of the best writers in this genre, or mark particular aspects of its development, but also because they are amusing in themselves. Their humour is as varied as the personalities of their authors, who included fashionable men about town writing with elegant ease, professional authors, theatre managers, and actors with an awareness of what makes a good acting part; others, with a dash of amateur soldiering or architecture, remind us of the multiple talents that created these dashing comedies. Their humour varies from the frank, open coarseness of Killigrew to Etherege's gaiety, and from Dryden's satiric guile, Wycherley's sombre sardonic view of life, Mrs Behn's exuberant delight in farce, Shadwell's Jonsonian characters in action, Vanbrugh's comic sense of man's genius for self-deception, Congreve's wit, Farquhar's fun, and Cibber's easy going ridicule to Steele's sentimentality.

It has often been held that Restoration Comedy burst upon the English stage once the cork of Puritanism had been removed in 1660. Charles the Second and his almost conscientiously worldly and witty Court patronized a theatre which catered for aristocratic taste, in intrigue, in fashionable conversation, in the merry-go-round of sex, marriage and adultery, even in the highflown nonsense of heroic plays and lachrymose tragedies.

The monarch, no doubt full of memories of France, realised a capital city needs drama, and encouraged the revival of the theatre as a vital feature of metropolitan life. The theatres had been closed by the Puritans in 1642. Sir William Davenant and Thomas Killigrew were issued patents to form companies of players and erect theatres, and, the patents once issued in August 1660, the two companies were soon in action. By November, Davenant's Company, known as the Duke of York's Servants, was playing in the old theatre in Salisbury Court, Killigrew's Company, known as the King's Players, opening in a theatre in Bear Yard converted hastily from a tennis court in Vere Street. Plays were also performed by other companies at the Red Bull and the Cockpit Theatre, but their managers, John Rhodes and George Jolly, had

eventually, in view of the patents granted to Killigrew and Davenant, to transfer themselves to the provinces.

Davenant was able to move his company into the Duke's Theatre
in Lincoln's Inn Fields by June 1661 – a theatre used by the Duke's
Players for ten years before their move to yet another new theatre,
the magnificent theatre designed by Wren at Dorset Gardens,
which had a frontage on the Thames and indeed could be reached
by boat. The King's Players moved into the Theatre Royal (known
as the King's House, it was situated in Bridges Street, in Drury
Lane) in May 1663. Killigrew's management of this company,
though merry and jovial, was decidedly inefficient, and at one period
the company was controlled by some of its actors – with the Lord
Chamberlain's approval. By 1682 the two companies had united,
using the Drury Lane theatre as their headquarters, but in 1695
some of the actors and actresses were licensed by the Lord Chamberlain to form a new company. Thomas Betterton, Elizabeth Barry
and Anne Bracegirdle brought this company to Lincoln's Inn
Field's, and opened very successfully with *Love for Love*, Congreve's
close friend Anne Bracegirdle playing the heroine. Congreve com-
bined with Vanbrugh in forming another new company with
Betterton in 1704 and this company transferred its work to the
Queen's or Haymarket Theatre.

Though there were only two theatres (and from 1682 to 1695
only one) in London and their season ran for a little less than nine
months, and though strong competition emerged towards the end
of the seventeenth century from what we might call variety shows,
rope-dancing, acrobatic performances, puppet shows and the like,
the theatres provided for their audiences a surprising number of
new plays as well as tried Elizabethan and Jacobean favourites,
there being an average of about ten new plays a year.

One of the main attractions of the restored theatres must have
been the presence of actresses on their stages, the patents granted
to Killigrew and Davenant having firmly stipulated that only
women should play women's parts. Another was the use of movable
scenery. Neither were completely novel. Actresses in French companies had played on the English boards before the Commonwealth, and both actresses and scenery (following on the earlier
innovations of Inigo Jones in court masques) had graced Sir William

Davenant's pre-Restoration production of *The Siege of Rhodes* in 1656, for which (as well as for private performances of opera) he had the permission of the authorities.

The actresses were physically attractive, and had to be capable of acting aristocratic parts. Cheerful impertinence and pert wit were probably characteristic of them, and we can see a certain conventionality of approach on the part of the dramatists to women's roles which was probably conditioned by a need to create parts suitable for the individual women who were enrolled in the companies. The private lives of many of the actresses provided matter of interest for the audience – liaisons with their admirers could lead to handsome settlements from keepers or even to marriage. The king's relationships with Nell Gwynn and Moll Davis were notorious.

The reaction against the Puritans' sexual repression was strong, and no less so on the stage and in the green-rooms and auditoriums than in the Court itself, or in the Parks, coffee-houses, restaurants and houses of the Town. Thus the frequent writing-in of episodes for women dressed as men or boys, the 'breeches parts' – of which Sylvia's escapade in *The Recruiting Officer* is a good example – obviously delighted the audience in this period of sexual freedom. Indeed the theatre itself was a dangerous place for a woman of genuine virtue to attend. Not only would she be suspected of seeking an intrigue – in the midst of the courtesans and whores who frequented the theatre – but she had also the problem, as Olivia hypocritically put it in *The Plain Dealer*, of how she should react to 'all the hideous obscenity she hears at nasty plays'.

Though the new sliding scenery, set probably in grooves, provided a new visual entertainment, and, together with the large forestage, allowed a fluidity of action as well as an admirable flexibility, the presentation of comedies cannot have always been impeccable, as we learn from Pepys's complaints about actors not knowing their parts. There were obvious difficulties, however, since plays had short runs and the actors were often hardworked. (On rare occasions some of them were distressingly drunk.) And there was always the problem presented by the audience, ready to interrupt, even to hiss and hurl oranges if the play was not to their taste. On the other hand, a good actor or actress could fill a theatre (and the success of the heroic tragedies probably depended as much on the merits of individual actors as on the superb spectacles the managers created to carry the plays' absurd bombast), and if the aristocratic play-goers approved a play they could persuade the Town to fall in with their views 'as the rest of the pack does', in the words of John Dennis, 'with the eager cry of the staunch and the trusty beagles'. If, that is, they were not, like Sparkish in *The Country Wife*, 'louder than the players' because they thought they spoke more wit than that evinced by the author's characters. Indeed many of the play-goers must have found as much drama in the behaviour of some of the young men about Town amusing themselves in the theatre as in the actions of the comedies. For the theatres opened in the afternoon, after dinner, and quarrels easily arose, behaviour being freer, no doubt under the influence of drink, while witty or would-be witty comments and interruptions flourished. An example of this is Sir Charles Sedley's reaction to Orrery's play *The General*, admittedly a heroic play, where the general, commanded to rescue his rival remarks 'Well, I'll save my rival and make her confess, that I deserve, while he do but possess'. 'Why, what, pox', remarked Sedley, 'Would he have him have more, or what is there more to be had of a woman than the possessing her?'

Such an audience, bent on other pursuits besides listening to the plays – gossiping, quarrelling, flirting – was ready to 'run and ramble', as Gatty put it in Etherege's *She Would If She Could*, 'from one playhouse, to the other playhouse, and if they like neither the play nor the women, they seldom stay any longer than the combing of their periwigs, or a whisper or two with a friend; and then they cock their caps, and out they strut again'. It was not an audience where good taste always flourished: it certainly had, however, a strong taste for laughter, and this often fed upon farce and coarseness. What is perhaps surprising about the comedies is the amount of wit, elegance and wisdom – however worldly – that balanced the satire which could easily lapse into cheap cynicism.

And beneath much of the persiflage ran the deep seriousness of some comic writers, who felt an obvious unease about the nature of the sophisticated, witty society they portrayed. Others, of course, were content merely to mirror its insouciant irreverence.

The writers, however, were not merely concerned with their

contemporary situation. Indeed the comedies of the Restoration stage were not completely new. Shadwell's plays, for instance, strongly resemble those of Ben Jonson, as *The Squire of Alsatia* demonstrates. Shadwell added some of the standard ingredients of his time, but he built upon an earlier Jonsonian achievement. Beaumont and Fletcher, too, exercised an influence on Restoration writers of comedy, possibly a more powerful influence than that of Jonson, who, like Shakespeare, seemed to Restoration taste rough, obsolete or, at least, old-fangled. Indeed Shakespeare had to be adapted, to be made palatable for contemporary taste, Dryden's use of *Antony and Cleopatra* for *All for Love* being paralleled by Sir William Davenant's use of *Measure for Measure* and *Much Ado about Nothing* for *The Law against Lovers*. The pedantic side of Jonson did not appeal in an age when knowledge from books was regarded as inferior to that which the life of the Town imparted. Dryden remarked significantly of Jonson's Truewit that he would be a fine gentleman, 'but in a university'. This healthy attitude to pedantry, however, did not prevent playwrights from plundering classical authors, notably Plautus and Terence, where their comic material was likely to amuse a Restoration audience.

There were other sources for them to rifle. Spanish comedies of intrigue provided a profusion of plots and characters. Moreto's *No puede Ser*, for instance, was translated, acted – and damned – under the English title of *Tarugo's Wiles, or, The Coffee-House*. In this collection it re-appears in much more effective guise, in *Sir Courtly Nice*, written at the request of Charles the Second by John Crowne who did not know of the existence of *Tarugo's Wiles* when he began to write his own comedy.

Inevitably French influence on the English comic writers was strong. Molière, whose plays began to be staged in France in 1660, was frequently rifled for material, as were Paul Scarron, Pierre and Thomas Corneille and Philippe Quinault. Molière's attempt to show women as rational beings in *L'Ecole des Maris* was echoed, for instance, in Sir Charles Sedley's comedy *The Mulberry Garden*. Another obvious echo of Molière occurs in Dryden's *Sir Martin Mar-all*, where Molière's *L'Etourdi* (as well as Quinault's *L'Amant indiscret*) provided the basis for a Jonsonian play of intrigue with the classical servant steering his obtuse master through various absurd situations. Italian drama, especially the *Commedia dell'arte* characters, also re-appeared in Restoration writers' work, one example being Edward Ravenscroft's *The London Cuckolds*, which draws on *La Galosia partorere cativi effette* for one of its scenes.

Often English writers would blend two or three different foreign plays into one of their own plots, or make use of specific scenes or draw upon particular characters for parts of their own comedies. But the basic material was more easily available. The world of the Court, and of London, provided the very stuff of comedy in what was, whatever its moral lapses, a brilliantly sophisticated and hedonistic period of fashionable life, when enjoyment reigned in a fierce re-action against a previous period of enforced puritanism.

The relationship between author and audience can be seen in the prologues and epilogues, without which no play could be considered complete. In these the poetic wit of the dramatists or their friends was given its head; often the prologue or epilogue was a kind of essay – they were written sometimes for the first performance, sometimes for the printed text, and sometimes an extra one was written for a later performance; they could relate to the play or to some event of the day; they could be expository or self-justificatory (witness Mrs Behn's attack on male vanity in *The Lucky Chance*) and they could extol the virtues of patronage. As Professor Nicoll has remarked, in most of the verses 'the tone is a familiar one, as of friend talking to friend, or wit to wit; intimacy is of their being'. What he says of the prologues and epilogues (the dedications are another matter, often fulsome in their formal praise and apt for the satire in Wycherley's jest of dedicating *The Plain Dealer* to Lady B——, who was actually Mother Bennet, a well-known London procuress) is true of many of the comedies themselves.

We can catch the tone of Restoration society from Etherege's plays, especially in his two last comedies. They have a light-hearted ease, a sense of the absurdity of life, and an acute awareness of the mode of the times. This emerges clearly in the conversation of the characters. Etherege's heroes and heroines talk wittily, amusingly, intelligently; the playboys grown libertine pursue and give no quarter to over-willing women. In *She Would If She Could*, for in-stance, Sir Oliver Cockwood and Sir Joslin Jolly, a ridiculous elderly pair of gentlemen, frolic almost innocently, so convincing is the naturalness, indeed the speed of their conversation, just as the situations between Sir Oliver and his wife, both hypocrites of a different kind, are carried out of the audience's moral judgement by the instinctive non-stop inventiveness of their selfishly motivated interchanges. Yet Etherege could take a deeper view of life. Sir Frederick Frollick in *The Comical Revenge*, his first play, was a mixture of ceremonial control and gay grotesquerie leading to Courtall and Freeman in *She Would If She Could*, his next play; they find life dull without a variety of intrigues, and they are succeeded by the more sinister figure of Dorimant in *The Man of Mode*. Dorimant treats society with mocking irony, but this remorseless Don Juan is himself overcome by the poetic justice of falling in love with Harriet.

Love was always possible, even if marriage was not. And marriage did not depend upon love; the emphasis of fathers was laid firmly upon fortune when they planned the future of their children at the end of the seventeenth century. Family fortunes mattered, and marriage was an obvious means of augmenting them. These loveless marriages could easily lead to unhappiness and to adultery. The comedies which finally marry off the lovers happily in the fifth act after four acts of suspense while they free themselves from the plans of their parents or their guardians, or while they free themselves from entanglements with other persons, particularly elderly suitors, are, in effect, often romantic and unrealistic. But then the art of the comic writer is to match his characters to his audience so that there is a suspense of reason, of judgment, and, instead, sympathy for the lovers caught in a tangle of situations. And good care is usually taken to sort out some satisfactory financial arrangements before the end of the play.

The most savage satire upon sexual permissiveness in the period was provided by Wycherley, notably in *The Country Wife* and *The Plain Dealer*. Wycherley's own position is hard to establish: he seems to have enjoyed the Town and yet to have been very well aware of the contrast between its appearances and realities: outward shows of fashionable politeness and good breeding, beneath which lurked inner lusts and machinations. *The Country Wife*, which seemed to Macaulay one of 'the most profligate and heartless of human compositions', did provide comment upon contemporary problems of marriage. True, the action of the play revolved around Horner's pretence of having lost his virility in France, but during the play the whole question of trust and jealousy in married couples is put fairly and squarely before us. There is a heartlessness about Wycherley's characters which would be decidedly chilling were it not for the humour he extracts from the constantly changing situations created by Horner's actions. *The Plain Dealer* developed Wycherley's sombre side further, his propensity to rail at life over-harshly for the convincing dramatic success of his play. The comic scenes depend overmuch on the Widow Blackacre, because Manly protests too savagely and Olivia is too shameless.

How indecent Restoration comedy could be in its sexual intrigues can be seen in Mrs Behn's plays, *The Rover* and *The Lucky Chance*. *The Rover* revolves round sexual conquest, with Hellena, an attractively independent hedonist, gaily winning her part of the sex war by insisting on marriage. The financial aspects of marriage were important to Mrs Behn as she tidied up her plot (lifted, rather typically, from an earlier play, *Thomaso, The Wanderer* written by Thomas Killigrew) and speeded up the amoral romp, which proved very popular with Charles the Second. Mrs Behn, however, did provide some moral comment: cuckolding was not a sufficient end in itself; she had a sharp awareness of the miseries caused by forced marriages, 'fatal' as her character Lady Fulbank described them in *The Lucky Chance*. This comedy turned on the rivalry of youth and age, and made fun of two husbands, one doting and the other grasping: both were City aldermen whose own cheating led to their being cuckolded by the younger men – indeed, as Professor Sutherland has sapiently remarked of Ravenscroft's *The London Cuckolds*, staged in November 1681, the cuckolding of citizens in real life or in comedy had become, when Shaftesbury's faction in the city was at its most violent, almost a patriotic duty – and the old habit of mocking the 'cits' (as townsmen and shopkeepers were contemptuously called) prevailed.

The gentlemen of the Town could be no less ludicrous, as Dryden showed in *The Kind Keeper*, which he said was intended as a satire against the crying sin of keeping. His rake's father gains vicarious pleasure, being himself too old for bedroom pleasures, by procuring for younger men. This bedroom farce ran only three nights before being prohibited, though whether for indecency, or for its exposure of keeping is uncertain. We cannot tell what Dryden left out of the printed version, how many of those 'things which offended on the stage'. Dryden was somewhat consciously playing down to his audience, and yet was aware that he wanted the 'gaiety of humour' which he thought comedy required: he expressed his dislike of writing comedies on several occasions and in his preface to *An Evening's Love* (1668) defended his characters by remarking that vicious persons were not happy 'but only as Heaven makes sinners so': the rakes were reclaimed from vice by marriage, 'for then enjoying what they desire in one, they cease to pursue the love of many'. Pepys called this particular comedy of Dryden's very smutty, and his comments are among the most interesting made on comedy by contemporary playgoers. He delighted, for instance, in Dryden's *Sir Martin Mar-all* regarding it as 'the most entire piece of mirth that certainly ever was writ', whereas he had disliked the farcical elements in Etherege's first play *The Comical Revenge* which he described as 'very merry, but only so by gesture, not wit at all' and 'beneath the house'. But a judicious mixture of farce and wit often gave a play its lasting appeal.

Farce was used by Colley Cibber in *Love's Last Shift* as a foil to the serious love affair in which Amanda reclaims her errant husband Loveless. Cibber hurls Amanda's woman into the drunken embraces of Snap, Loveless's servant, in the cellar while Loveless meets Amanda upstairs. Cibber realised, however, the comic value of fops and feeble old men who provided him with his own best acting parts, and his Sir Novelty Fashion is one of the best of his kind. The success of such characters obviously depended upon their being comic in themselves. Cibber's skill in creating them was continued by Vanbrugh, very directly in *The Relapse*, which he wrote as a continuation of and satiric comment on *Love's Last Shift*. Sir Novelty becomes Lord Foppington (Cibber acted both parts) and is even more affected and amusing. To the long list of English comic characters is added Sir Tunbelly Clumsey, whose attitude to his lively daughter Hoyden is crassly insensitive.

Vanbrugh produced a different kind of insensitivity in his next play, *The Provoked Wife*, that of Sir John Brute, whose conduct shows us how unhappy an ill-assorted marriage could be. The play was attacked by the Rev. Jeremy Collier in his famous *Short View of the*

Immorality and Profaneness of the English Stage (1698). Collier's morality no doubt expressed the feelings of many – there had been complaints before he wrote – when he queried the convention of the comic writers that a fine gentleman was 'a fine whoring, swearing, smutty, atheistical man'. He censured, among others, Dryden, Wycherley and Congreve, and his strictures were themselves rapidly counter-attacked. Among the replies were Edward Filmer's *A Defence of Dramatic Poetry*, and John Dennis's *The Usefulness of the Stage*, while Vanbrugh himself weighed in with *A Short Vindication of the Relapse and the Provok'd Wife, by the Author*.

Congreve made the mistake, in his *Amendments of Mr Collier's False and Imperfect Citations*, of being flippant; he found Collier's adverse criticism irritating and reacted over-strongly to it. Nonetheless his arguments had sense in them. He held that the satiric representation of well-bred people was allowable if their manners were ridiculous, and that plays should not be attacked because they included words taken from the Scriptures. (Collier had a capacity for finding irreverence abounding and often very far-fetchedly.) Congreve also argued that passages should not be judged out of their contexts and, perhaps the most important of his arguments, that the author's own ideas should not be confused with those of the characters he exposes on the stage for their foolishness.

Congreve's own *Love for Love*, produced three years before the publication of Collier's pamphlet, was his most popular work. His essay concerning humour in comedy, written in the same year, shows why he was so successful when he gave the audience the kind of entertainment that was certain to please them. He realised that comedy needed more than farce or the merely grotesque. He was as ready to laugh as anybody, he wrote, and as easily diverted with an object truly ridiculous, but at the same time he didn't like seeing things that forced him to entertain low thoughts of his own nature:

'I don't know how it is with others but I confess freely to you I could never look long upon a monkey without very mortifying reflections, though I never heard anything to the contrary, why that creature is not originally of a different species. As I don't think humour exclusive of wit, neither do I think it inconsistent with folly; but I think the follies should be only such as men's humours may

incline them to; and not follies entirely abstracted from both humour and nature.'

He ended the essay with a defence of English eccentricity which
he believed was owed to the great freedom, privilege and liberty
enjoyed by the common people of England. *Love for Love* applied his
ideas brilliantly: it is a series of stock situations – courtships, one of
which turns out happily, the other ending in anticlimax or even
disaster, the feigned madness of Valentine, an obsession with
astrology on the part of Foresight, and affected wit. To these
ingredients Congreve added Ben, the sailor, his speech spiced with
nautical terms, who finally returns to the sea disgusted by the
behaviour of the women, both sophisticated and unsophisticated,
and Foresight, 'an illiterate old fellow, peevish and positive,
superstitious, and pretending to understand astrology, palmistry,
physiognomy, omens, dreams etc.' Sir Sampson Legend's irascible,
exclamatory and peremptory speech is a good piece of characteriza-
tion. Congreve used Valentine's madness as a means of satirising
many aspects of contemporary life, but the whole tone of the play is
satirical: there are, for instance, many satirical remarks on women
throughout. But there are also very serious implications in its action.
Those who do not pretend, ultimately succeed; for instance, Angelica and Valentine reach their happiness when she lays aside her
apparent coldness and he his apparent madness. Tattle and Miss
Frail, who are full of pretence, suffer for their folly by marrying each
other unwittingly; being both in disguise, thinking they were deceiving Angelica and Valentine respectively into marrying them.
And Sir Sampson and Foresight are shown up for their foolishness.
For his vanity in supposing Angelica will marry him, Sir Sampson is
in his own words 'cullied, bubbled, jilted, woman-bobbed at last'
and Foresight is cuckolded. The play succeeds because the action is
speedy, the plot clear, the speech of the characters matches their idio-
syncratic natures, and because farce, wit and humour are well mixed.

The taste of the audience was changing. And though Congreve
described what seemed to him the success of his own next play, *The
Way of the World* (it was in fact a comparative failure when it was
produced), as almost beyond his expectation, he realised 'but little
of it was prepared for that general taste' which seemed to him, as he

wrote the Dedication for the published version of the play, 'now to be predominant in the palates of our audience.' A comment of his that his play had been acted two or three days before some hasty judges could find the leisure 'to distinguish between the character of a Witword and a Truewit' does point to a flaw in *The Way of the World*; it is over-complex. The play now seems to us the supreme achievement in its genre: witty, refined, delicate and subtle, it must have been in many ways above the heads of an audience reaching out for sentimentality and the more obvious sweep of comic action such as we find in Colley Cibber's extremely popular *The Careless Husband*, produced in 1705, a play which made no great demands on the audience, and gave them a more optimistic answer to the problems of a threatened marriage. Cibber had progressed from *Love's Last Shift* in the Epilogue to which he had cynically described the fashion:

> *He's lewd for above four acts, gentlemen.*
> *For faith, he knew, when once he'd changed his fortune,*
> *And reformed his vice, 'twas time – to drop the curtain.*

But in *The Careless Husband* he gives Lord Morelove a speech which records the shift in vogue and the effect of Collier's *Short View* on it:

'Plays now indeed one need not be so much afraid of, for since the late short-sighted View of 'em, vice may go on and prosper, the stage hardly dare show a vicious person speaking like himself, for fear of being called profane for exposing him.'

Congreve, however, was independent of fashion. Expressing his own attitudes in *The Way of the World*, he was presenting brilliant, poised conversation, and taking a cool glance at the foibles of a highly artificial society. And he was presenting in the relationship of Mirabell and Millamant an approach to marriage which sought to avoid the dangers and abuses of conventional matches. There is a case for individual dignity here, for integrity, and not a little idealism. Congreve sought for genuine sensibility in personal relationships to offset the illusions and the dangerous degradation which he was concerned to expose as part of the way of that particular world of the Town which he knew so well. He had no wish to write of the new kind of society which was developing even before the turn of the century.

It was high time for Farquhar to shift the action of comedy out of London. He set *The Recruiting Officer* in Salisbury and *The Beaux Stratagem* in Lichfield and in doing so gave comedy new dimensions. In each play there are new subjects – the country dwellers at home. They had been the butts of the Town's humour for over-long, and Farquhar, led to the provinces on his own recruiting tours, had no intention of repaying the kindness he had received there by making the Town merry at the expense of the country gentlemen; as he pointed out reassuringly to his friends around the Wrekin in the Epistle Dedicatory to *The Recruiting Officer*, he was writing a comedy not a libel and, whilst he held to nature, no person of any character in their country could suffer by being exposed.

Farquhar, as we can judge by his earlier *The Constant Couple* had a kindly attitude to his characters. Sir Harry Wildair was no doubt a flattering self-portrait, but Lady Lurewell, who could so easily have become a termagant, is instead treated with skill and subtlety, and her desire for revenge upon the male sex for the betrayal she suffered in her youth is given a light, easy treatment typical of Farquhar's humour. His comedies have a sparkle about them, a rare speed of action and they still succeed impressively. It is, however, also true that *The Beaux Stratagem*, for all its dashing gaiety, carried discussion of the problems of incompatibility in marriage further than any of the Restoration dramatists had yet dared. Vanbrugh's *The Provoked Wife* showed the virtual impossibility of either party remarrying and so the references to divorce are vague. Lady Brute thinks a court of chancery in heaven would free her from Sir John and Bellinda replies that it would need a House of Lords. But it was not till *The Beaux Stratagem* that we have a case for the dissolution of marriage argued with feeling (no doubt because Farquhar's own marriage was unhappy), on the lines of Milton's divorce tracts. The ending of the play separates Mrs Sullen from her aptly named husband. What will happen to her is left to our imagination. Thanks to Archer's handing over what was stolen from Sullen's study she has her fortune of ten thousand pounds again; she and Sullen have virtually gone through an unmarrying ceremony, and Sullen talks of his divorce. As they lead the country dance at the end of the play Archer is giving Mrs Sullen his hand. Significantly it is Archer, the lady's would-be lover (whose own financial position was solved by the ten thousand pounds

given him by Aimwell), who pronounces the final lines on the parting of the Sullens and the marriage of Aimwell and Dorinda:

> *Both happy in their several states we find,*
> *Those parted by consent and those conjoined,*
> *Consent if mutual saves the lawyer's fee,*
> *Consent is law enough to set you free.*

Farquhar's characters are easier, indeed more convincingly human
than some of their wittier predecessors. By the time of Steele the
change is complete. Steele wrote that Etherege's *The Man of Mode*
was a perfect contradiction to good manners, good sense, and common honesty; he regarded Ravenscroft's *The London Cuckolds* as the
most rank play that ever succeeded; and his own plays, lively and
amusing borrowings and inventions, were full of domestic virtue.

The shift in sensibility is clearly shown in Steele's treatment of
the merchants, the 'cits' who had been the objects of mirth in many
a Restoration comedy. Mr Sealand in *The Conscious Lovers* has a self-
confidence and dignity when he asserts the importance and the
achievements of his class:

'I know the town and the world – and give me leave to say, that
we merchants are a species of gentry, that have grown into the world
this last century, are as honourable, and almost as useful, as you
landed folks, that have always thought yourselves so much above
us . . . '

Amusing an aristocratic audience had given place to reflecting –
and shaping – the views of a new middle class. Cynicism bowed to
sententiousness, worldly wit gave way to worthy wisdom, and the
comedy of sex was completely swamped by a flood of sentimentality.

CONTENTS OF VOLUME ONE

Contents

ILLUSTRATIONS IN
VOLUME ONE

A GENERAL NOTE ON THE TEXT

In this edition the base texts are those of the first editions, the only exception being *The Constant Couple* where, since Farquhar incorporated additional material, the text of the third edition has been used in preference. Spelling has been regularized and modernized throughout, but the original punctuation has been retained to as large an extent as possible because the natural breaks in speech were often indicated more clearly by playwrights and their contemporary typesetters in the early editions than by subsequent texts with punctuation regularized to accord with later practice. Any additions, as opposed to emendations, made by the present editor for the sake of clarification are clearly differentiated by being enclosed within ⟨ ⟩.

Catchwords and the long 's' have been abandoned, as have the heavy capitalization and the italics of the originals. Full points after terms such as Mr, Mrs and St have been omitted. Contracted past tenses of verbs have been expanded, as have contracted names in stage directions and speech prefixes. Similarly the form '*Ex.*' has been printed '*Exit*' or '*Exeunt*' in full, but superfluous directions such as '*Manet*' and '*Manent*' have been omitted. '*Exit*' has been amended to '*Exeunt*' where necessary. Some variant spellings have been made consistent: 'hark'ee' for 'harky', 'hark'e' or 'heark'e'; 'd'ye' for 'd'ee', 'de'e' or 'd'e'; 'aye' for 'ay', 'ey' or 'I'; 'o'clock' for 'a'clock' or 'a clock'; 'Egad' for 'I gad', 'Igad' or 'I ga'd', and similarly with 'Ecod'; 'pshaw' for 'p'shaw' or 'p'sha', 's'death' for ''sdeath', and the same for parallel exclamations. 'I'faith' has been adopted as the normal spelling, 'bye' for 'b'w'y' and 'than', where necessary, for 'then'. 'W' replaces the occasional 'VV' of some copy texts. The form 'O' has been used where there is no following punctuation, otherwise the form 'Oh'. The punctuation and capitalization of 'Ha! Ha! Ha!' or 'ha, ha, ha.' and the like have been regularized, even where it involves amending a preceding punctuation mark to a full point. The copy texts' use of capital or lower case initial letters after dashes (which are sometimes preceded by a comma, semi-colon or colon) has been followed as closely as possible, except that, where the meaning or general direction of a speech alters after a dash, a capital letter is used: where the sense runs on, lower case is adopted.

At times the copy texts' use of exclamation marks precludes their being followed by a capital letter. On these occasions lower case has been adopted, as in *The Mulberry Garden* (Vol. I, p. 173): 'But who, alas! such love, or health can show?' In some cases the copy text has been followed where a capital letter succeeds a colon or semi-colon, but when a sentence which closes a speech ends with a comma, semi-colon or colon, a full stop has generally been silently substituted. Dashes preceding speeches have been omitted. Reported speech has normally been indicated by single inverted commas and the use of hyphens has been regularized. Expressions such as 'a foot' or 'no body', which originally appeared as two words, are printed as one. The spelling of French phrases, except where clearly intended to indicate eccentricity, has been regularized. The occasional use of the form 'Act the First' has been amended to 'Act I', and, in the instances where 'End of the First Act' has been printed (apparently haphazardly), it has been omitted. Marginal brackets indicating triple rhymes have also been deleted.

The form 'Dramatis Personae' has been used throughout for the lists of characters, and, since they do not appear in all plays, the names of the original actors, where they were printed, have been omitted, though reference is made to outstanding performers in the individual introductions. The positioning of preliminary matter has been made consistent, the present editor's introduction being followed, where relevant, by dedication, author's preface, dramatis personae, prologue and text. Epilogues, where occasionally placed at the beginning of plays, have been moved to the end.

Only in the positioning of stage directions has some liberty been taken. In the original texts, these were often printed in the right-hand margin or, particularly in the case of directions such as '*aside*', at the end of the speech to which they refer. In this edition, such directions have been moved to their relevant place. In the textual notes the line numbering includes all headings, stage directions, etc.

A note on the text of each play is provided, and where departures (including changes in punctuation or major re-positioning of stage directions) other than silent corrections of the kind described above, have been made from the copy text, these are recorded. Where the present editor's emendations have been anticipated by other editors, these are also recorded in the textual notes by way of acknowledgement (even though such emendations do not have authorial authority), and details of the editions consulted for such alterations are listed in the 'Abbreviations' cited.

Footnotes have been supplied where meanings seemed difficult or ambiguous, or where amplification seemed called for, but these have been kept to a minimum.

The editor wishes to record his appreciation of the help he has received from Mr David I. Masson of the Brotherton Collection, University of Leeds, as well as from Mr D. G. Neill of the Bodleian Library, Professor Shirley Strum Kenny, Professor Carl J. Stratman CSV, and Mr Brian Rawson, Editorial Director of the Folio Society. He has also received valuable advice and aid from colleagues in the School of English at the University of Leeds: Miss Audrey Stead, Mr Brian Scobie and Mr John Horden, Director of the Institute of Bibliography in the School. He also wishes to thank the Keeper of the Brotherton Collection, University of Leeds, and the Trustees of the British Library for permission to use the copy texts employed in this edition.

THE PARSON'S WEDDING

by Thomas Killigrew

INTRODUCTION

Thomas Killigrew (1612–1683), the fourth son of Sir Robert Killigrew, was a brother of Sir William Killigrew and Dr Henry Killigrew. He was known as a merry droll. His liking for drama began early for, according to Pepys, he used to hang around the Red Bull, an unroofed theatre in Clerkenwell, and 'when the man cried to the boys, "Who will go and be a devil, and he shall see the play for nothing?" then would he go in, and be a devil upon the stage and so get to see plays'. He became page of honour to Charles the First in 1632, and was arrested in 1642 for taking up arms on behalf of the king. Released two years later, he then joined Prince Charles and became English Resident in Venice in 1647, a position he relinquished in 1652. He travelled in Italy and Spain and at the Restoration became a courtier, holding various offices at Court, and being regarded as Charles the Second's Court jester. In 1673 he became Master of the Revels. By a Royal Grant, Killigrew and Sir William Davenant were empowered to establish two companies of players in August 1660, Killigrew becoming manager of the Theatre in Bear Yard which opened in November 1660, and later of the Theatre Royal in Bridges Street. When this theatre was burned down, Killigrew was responsible for the erection of the second Theatre Royal. He died at Whitehall in March 1683.

Two of Killigrew's plays, *The Prisoners* and *Claracilla*, had been produced in the late sixteen-thirties at the Cockpit Theatre. To judge from references to events in 1639–40 in the text of *The Parson's Wedding*, it is possible that he had written this comedy by 1642, but it was not licensed as a new play until 3 November 1663. Had he written it before the theatres were closed in 1642 – and some of the stage directions suggest it was written with a platform stage such as that of the Cockpit in mind – it is likely that the disturbed nature of the general situation militated against a new and expensive play being staged, and its content was likely to cause trouble in a period of puritanism. When it was first published in 1664, the title page announced it had been written at Basle, and Killigrew probably rewrote or revised it there.

When first produced, on 5 or 6 October 1664, at the King's House (the first Drury Lane Theatre, in Bridges Street) it had an all female cast. Being 'a bawdy loose play' it succeeded very well. It was staged again in 1672 at the Lincoln's Inn Fields theatre by the King's Company, and again all the parts were played by actresses.

The Parson's Wedding employed some stock comic situations, notably in the case where Careless and Wild pretend they have married Lady Wild and her niece. There are parallels in Barry's comedy *Ram Alley* (1611), Marmion's *The Antiquary* (1641) and Christopher Bullock's *Woman is a Riddle* (1717). Again, the trickery practised on the parson, which probably stems from Italian fiction, is similar to that in Brome's *Novella* (1632), Howard's *The Six Days' Adventure* (1671), and in Durfey's *Squire Oldsapp* (1675) and *Trick for Trick* (1678), based on John Fletcher's *Monsieur Thomas* (1619).

The play is full of bawdiness, and its humour is robust and ribald. The lively sex warfare in which Careless and Wild are matched against Lady Wild and Mistress Pleasant is set off by the darker side of the play, the coarse and obvious indecency of the parson and the lechery of Lady Love-all, the 'old stallion-hunting widow'. The play is realistic in its portrayal of some aspects of the swinging London of the day, and it is certainly both anti-romantic and anti-platonic in its outspokenness.

Thomas Killigrew

The
Parson's Wedding

A COMEDY

The Scene London

Written at Basil in Switzerland:
by Thomas Killigrew

Dedicated to the
Lady Ursula Bartu,
Widow

LONDON

Printed by J.M. for Henry Herringman, and are to be
sold at his shop at the sign of the Blue Anchor, in
the lower Walk of the New Exchange.

1663

DRAMATIS PERSONAE

⟨MEN⟩

Mr Careless	A gentleman, and a wit.
Mr Wild	A gentleman, nephew to the widow ⟨Lady Wild⟩.
Mr Jolly	An humorous gentleman, and a courtier.
Captain	A leading wit, full of designs.
Parson	A wit also, but over-reached by the captain and his wanton.
Mr Constant ⎱ *Mr Sadd* ⎰	Two dull suitors to the lady widow and Mistress Pleasant.

⟨WOMEN⟩

Lady Wild	A rich (and somewhat youthful) widow.
Mistress Pleasant	A handsome young gentlewoman, of a good fortune.
Mrs Secret	Her (indifferent honest) woman.
Lady Love-all	An old stallion-hunting widow.
Faithful	Her (errant honest) woman.
Mistress Wanton	The captain's livery punk, married to the parson by confederacy.

Bawd, Servants, Drawers, Fiddlers.

ACT ONE

SCENE I

Enter the Captain in choler, and Wanton.

CAPTAIN No more, I'll sooner be reconciled to want, or sickness, than that rascal; a thing, that my charity made sociable; one, that when I smiled would fawn upon me, and wag his stern, like starved dogs; so nasty, the company cried foh upon him; he stunk so of poverty, ale, and bawdry. So poor and despicable, when I relieved him, he could not avow his calling, for want of a cassock, but stood at corners of streets, and whispered gentlemen in the ear, as they passed, and so delivered his wants like a message which being done, the rogue vanished, and would dive at Westminster like a dabchick, and rise again at Temple Gate; the ingenuity of the rascal, his wit being snuffed by want, burned clear then, and furnished him with a bawdy jest or two, to take the company; but now the rogue shall find he has lost a patron.

WANTON As I live, if I had thought you would have been in such a fury, you should never have known it.

CAPTAIN Treacherous rogue, he has always railed against thee to me, as a danger his friendship ought to give me warning of; and nightly cried, 'Yet look back, and hunt not, with good nature and the beauties of thy youth, that false woman; but hear thy friend, that speaks from sad experience'.

WANTON Did he say this?

CAPTAIN Yes, and swears ye are as insatiate as the sea, as covetous, and as ungrateful: that you have your tempest too; and calms, more dangerous than it.

WANTON Was the slave so eloquent in his malice?

CAPTAIN Yes, faith, and urged, you (for your part) were never particular, and seldom sound.

WANTON Not sound? Why, he offered to marry me, and swore he thought I was chaste, I was so particular; and proved it, that consent was full marriage, by the first institution, and those that love, and lie together, and tell, have fulfilled all ceremonies now.

CAPTAIN Did he offer to marry thee?

WANTON Yes, yes.

CAPTAIN If ever then I deserved from thee, or if thou be'st dear to thyself, as thou hast anything thou hop'st shall be safe or sound about thee, I conjure thee, take my counsel; marry him, to afflict him.

WANTON Marry him?

CAPTAIN If I have any power I shall prevail; thou know'st he has a fat benefice, and leave me to plague him, till he give it me to be rid of thee.

WANTON Will you not keep me then?

CAPTAIN I keep thee? Prithee, wilt thou keep me? I know not why men are such fools to pay? We bring as much to the sport, as women; keep thee? I'd marry thee as soon; why? That's wedding sin; no, no keeping I, that you are not your own, is all that prefers you before wives.

WANTON I hope this is not real.

CAPTAIN Art thou such a stranger to my humour? Why I tell thee, I should hate thee if I could call thee mine, for I loathe all women within my knowledge, and 'tis six to four if I knew thy sign I'd come there no more; a strange mistress makes every night anew, and these are your pleasing sins; I had as lief be good, as sin by course.

WANTON Then I am miserable.

CAPTAIN Not so, if you'll be instructed, and let me pass like a stranger when you meet me.

WANTON But have you these humours?

CAPTAIN Yes faith; yet if you will observe them, though you marry him, I may perchance be your friend; but you must be sure to be coy; for to me the hunting is more pleasure than the quarry.

WANTON But if I observe this, will you be my friend hereafter?

CAPTAIN Firm as the day; [*the Parson calls within*] hark, I hear him; I knew he would follow me, I gave him a small touch that wakened his guilt; resolve to endear yourself to him, which you may easily do, by taking his part when I have vexed him; no dispute, resolve it, or as I live here I disclaim thee for ever.

WANTON 'Tis well, something I'll do. [*Exit Wanton*]

CAPTAIN Open the door, I say, and let me in; your favourite and his tithes, shall come no more here.

Enter Parson.

PARSON Yes, but he shall; 'tis not you, nor your braced drum, shall fright me hence, who can command the souls of men; I have read divine Seneca; thou know'st nothing but the earthly part, and canst cry to that, 'Faces about'.★

CAPTAIN Thou read Seneca? Thou steal his cover, to clothe thee, naked and wicked, that for money wouldst sell thy share of the Twelve, and art allowed by all that know thee, fitter to have been Judas, than Judas was for his treachery.

PARSON Rail, do rail, my illiterate captain, that can only abuse by memory; and should I live thou could'st read my sentence, I should never die.

CAPTAIN No ungrateful, live till I destroy thee; and thankless wretch, did all my care of thee deserve nothing but thy malice, and treacherous speaking darkly still? With thy fine, 'No, not he', when any malicious discourse was made of me, and by thy false faint, 'No, faith'; confess, in thy denials, whilst thy smiling excuses stood a greater and more dangerous evidence against me, than my enemies' affidavits could have done.

PARSON I'll lie for never a lean soldier of you all.

CAPTAIN I have, for thee, slave, when I have been wondered at for keeping company with such a face; but they were such as know thee not; all which thy looks deceived, as they did me; they are so simple they'd cozen a jury, and a judge that had wit would swear thou lied'st, shouldst thou confess what I know to be true, and award Bedlam for thee; 'tis so strange and so new a thing, to find so much rogue lodge at the sign of the fool.

PARSON Leave this injurious language, or I'll lay off my cassock, for nothing shall privilege your bragger's tongue, to abuse me, a gentleman, and a soldier ancienter then thyself.

CAPTAIN Yes, thou wer't so; and now I think on't, I'll recount the cause, which, it may be, thou hast forgot, through the variety of sins; it was a hue and cry that followed thee a scholar, and found thee a soldier.

PARSON Thou liest; thou, and scandal have but one tongue, hers dwells with thy coward's teeth.

★ 'Faces about': a military command.

CAPTAIN Oh! Do you rage? Nay, I'll put the cause in print too, I am but a scurvy poet, yet I'll make a ballad shall tell how like a faithful disciple you followed your poor whore, till her martyrdom in the suburbs.*

PARSON I'll be revenged for this scandal.

CAPTAIN Then shall succeed, thy flight from the university, disguised into captain only the outside was worse buff, and the inside more atheist, than they furnished with an insolent faith, uncharitable heart, envious, as old women, cruel and bloody as cowards; thus armed at all points, thou went'st out, threatening God, and trembling at men.

PARSON I'll be revenged, thou poor man of war, I'll be revenged.

Enter Wanton.

WANTON And why so bitter? Whose house is this? Who dares tell this story?

CAPTAIN Why sweet? Hath he not treacherously broke into our cabinet, and would have stolen thee thence? By these hilts, I'll hang him; and then I can conclude my ballad with, 'Take warning all Christian people by the same': I will, you lean slave; I'll prosecute thee, till thou art fain to hide in a servitor's gown again, and live upon crumbs with the robin red-breasts that haunt the hall, your old mess-mates; do you snarl? I'll do't, I will, and put thee to fight with the dogs for the bones that but smell of meat; those that your hungry students have polished with their teeth.

WANTON If you do this, good captain, lieutenant, and company (for all your command, I think, is within your reach) I say, if you dare do this, I shall sing a song of one that bade stand, and made a carrier pay a dear rent† for a little ground, upon his Majesty's highway.

CAPTAIN How now, Mistress Wanton? What's this? What's this?

PARSON This? 'Tis matter for a jury, I'll swear, and positively, I'll hang thee, I'll do't, by this hand, let me alone to swear the jury out of doubt.

---

* suburbs: The suburbs were frequented by prostitutes and a 'suburbian' was a cant term for a prostitute.

† bade stand: . . . a dear rent: a Bidstand was a term for a highwayman, the dear rent an allusion to highway robbery.

CAPTAIN But you are in jest, Mistress Wanton, and will confess (I hope) this is no truth.

WANTON Yes Sir, as great a truth, as that you are in your unpaid-for scarlet; fool! Didst think, I'd quit such a friend, and his stayed fortune, to rely upon thy dead pay, and hopes of a second covenant?

CAPTAIN His fortune? What is't? Th'advowson* of Tyburn Deanery?

PARSON No, nor rents brought in by long staff-speeches, that asks alms with frowns, till thy looks and speech have laid violent hands upon men's charity.

WANTON Let him alone, I'll warrant, he'll never be indicted for drawing anything but his tongue, against a man.

CAPTAIN Very good.

PARSON Dear Mrs Wanton, you have won my heart, and I shall live to dote upon you for abusing this impetuous captain; will you listen to my old suit? Will you marry me, and vex him? Say, dare you do't, without more dispute?

CAPTAIN 'Twas a good question; she that dares marry thee dares do anything; she may as safely lie with the great bell upon her, and his clapper is less dangerous than thine.

WANTON Why, I pray?

CAPTAIN What a miserable condition wilt thou come to? His wife cannot be an honest woman; and if thou should'st turn honest, would it not vex thee to be chaste and paxat,† a saint without a nose? What calendar will admit thee, by an incurable slave that's made of rogues' flesh, consider that.

WANTON Why, that's something yet; thou hast nothing but a few fears, and a little old fame to trust to, and that scarce thatches your head.

CAPTAIN Nay then I see thou'rt base, and this ⟨is⟩ plot (not accident), and now I do not grudge him thee; go together, 'tis pity to part you, whore and parson, as consonant.

WANTON As whore and captain.

CAPTAIN Take her, I'll warrant her a breeder, I'll prophesy she shall lie with thy whole congregation, and bring an heir to thy

* advowson: the right of presentation to a benefice.
† paxat: poxed, probably an affected pronunciation, as in a pax take ye.

parish, one that thou may'st enclose the common by his title, and recover it by Common Law.

PARSON That's more than thy dear dam could do for thee, thou son of a thousand fathers, all poor soldiers, rogues, that ought* mischiefs, no midwives for their birth; but I cry thee mercy, my patron has an estate of old iron by his side, with the farm of old ladies he scrapes a dirty living from.

WANTON He earn from an old lady? Hang him, he's only wicked in his desires; and for adultery he cannot be condemned, though he should have the vanity to betray himself; God forgive me for belying him so often as I have done; the weak-chinned slave hired me once to say, I was with child by him.

CAPTAIN This is pretty, farewell; and may the next pig thou farrow'st have a promising face, without the dad's fool or gallows in't, that all may swear, at first sight, 'That's a bastard'; and it shall go hard but I'll have it called mine; I have the way, 'tis but praising thee, and swearing thou art honest before I am asked: you taught me the trick.

PARSON Next levee I'll preach against thee, and tell them what a piece you are; your drum and borrowed scarf shall not prevail, nor shall you win with charms half-ell-long, (hight ferret riband)† the youth of our parish, as you have done.

CAPTAIN No, lose no time, prithee study and learn to preach, and leave railing against the surplice, now thou hast preached thyself into linen; adieu, Abigal, adieu, heir apparent to Sir Oliver Marre-text;‡ to church, go, I'll send a beadle shall sing your Epithalamium.

PARSON Adieu, my captain of a tame band, I'll tell your old lady how you abused her breath, and swore you earned your money harder than those that dig in the mines for't. [*Exit Captain*] A fart, fill thy sail, captain of a galley foist.§ He's gone, come sweet, let's to church immediately, that I may go and take my revenge; I'll make him wear thin breeches.

---

* ought: owed.   † ferret riband: ferret, a tape of cotton or silk.
‡ Sir Oliver Marre-text: from *As you Like it*.
§ galley foist: a pleasure boat, or one used on particular days for pomp or for state occasions, a city barge used when the Lord Mayor went to Westminster to be sworn in.

WANTON But if you should be such a man as he says you are, what would my friends say, when they hear I have cast myself away?

PARSON He says? Hang him, lean, mercenary, provant* rogue; I knew his beginning when he made the stocks lousy, and swarmed so with vermin we were afraid he would have brought that curse upon the country. He says? But what's matter what he says? A rogue, by sire and dam; his father was a broad fat pedlar, a what-do-you-lack, Sir, that haunted good houses, and stole more than he bought; his dam was a gypsy, a pilfering canting sibyl in her youth, and she suffered in her old age for a witch; poor Strom-well,† the rogue was a perpetual burthen to her, she carried him longer at her back than in her belly; he dwelt there, till she lost him one night in the great frost upon our common, and there he was found in the morning candied in ice: a pox of their charity that thawed him, you might smell a rogue then in the bud, he is now run away from his wife.

WANTON His wife?

PARSON Yes, his wife; why, do you not know he's married according to the rogues' liturgy?‡ A left-handed bridegroom; I saw him take the ring from a tinker's dowager.

WANTON Is this possible?

PARSON Yes, most possible, and you shall see how I'll be revenged on him; I will immediately go seek the ordinance against reform-adoes.

WANTON What ordinance?

PARSON Why, they do so swarm about the Town, and are so destructive to trade and all civil government, that the state has declared, no person shall keep above two colonels and four cap-tains, (of what trade soever) in his family; for now the war is done, broken breech, wood-monger, ragman, butcher, and link-boy, (comrades that made up the ragged regiment in this holy war) think to return and be admitted to serve out their times again.

* provant: supported by government.
† Stromwell: a beggar's child born in straw.
‡ rogues' liturgy: beggars were married by their patricio or hedge priest with special rites of their own.

WANTON Your ordinance will not touch the captain, for he is a known soldier.

PARSON He a captain? An apocryphal modern one, that went convoy once to Brainford with those troops that conducted the contribution-puddings in the late holy war, when the City ran mad after their russet levites,* apron-rogues, with horn hands; hang him, he's but the sign of a soldier; and I hope to see him hanged for that commission, when the king comes to his place again.

WANTON You abuse him, now he's gone; but, –

PARSON Why? Dost thou think I fear him? No wench, I know him too well for a cowardly slave, that dares as soon eat his fox,† as draw it in earnest; the slave's noted to make a conscience of nothing but fighting.

WANTON Well, if you be not a good man, and a kind husband –

PARSON Thou knowest the proverb, as happy as the parson's wife, during her husband's life.

SCENE II

Enter Mistress Pleasant, Widow Wild her aunt, and Secret, her woman, above in the music room, as dressing her, a glass, a table, and she in her night clothes.

PLEASANT Secret, give me the glass, and see who knocks.

WIDOW Niece, what, shut the door? As I live this music was meant to you, I know my nephew's voice.

PLEASANT Yes, but you think his friend's has more music in't.

WIDOW No faith, I can laugh with him, or so, but he comes no nearer than my lace.

PLEASANT You do well to keep your smock betwixt.

WIDOW Faith, wench, so wilt thou and thou beest wise, from him and all of them, and be ruled by me, we'll abuse all the sex, till they put a true value upon us.

PLEASANT But dare you forbid the travelled gentlemen, and abuse

---

* levites: slang word for clergymen.
† his fox: a cant word for a sword.

them and your servant, and swear, with me, not to marry in a
twelve-month, though a lord bait the hook, and hang out the
sign of a Court cupid, whipped by a country widow; then I believe
we may have mirth cheaper then at the price of ourselves, and
some sport with the wits that went to lose themselves in France.

WIDOW Come, no dissembling, lest I tell your servant, when he
returns, how much you're taken with the last new fashion.

SECRET Madam, 'tis almost noon, will you not dress yourself
today?

WIDOW She speaks as if we were boarders; prithee, wench, is not
the dinner our own, sure my cook shall lay by my own roast till
my stomach be up.

PLEASANT But there may be company, and they will say, we take
too long time to trim. Secret give me the flowers my servant sent
me, he sware 'twas the first the wench made of the kind.

WIDOW But when he shall hear you had music sent you today,
'twill make him appear in his old clothes.

PLEASANT Marry, I would he would take exception, he should not
want ill usage to rid me of his trouble; as I live, custom has made
me so acquainted with him, that I now begin to think him not
so displeasing, as at first; and if he fall not out with me, I must
with him, to secure myself. Sure, aunt, he must find sense and
reason absent, for when a question knocks at his head, the answer
tells that there is nobody at home; I asked him, th'other day, if he
did not find a blemish in his understanding, and he swore a great
oath, 'Not he'; I told him 'twas very strange, for fool was so
visible an eye-sore, that neither birth nor fortune could reconcile
to me.

WIDOW Faith, methinks his humour is good, and his purse will
buy good company, and I can laugh and be merry with him sometimes.

PLEASANT Why, pray, aunt, take him to yourself, and see how
merry we will be; I can laugh at anybody's fool, but mine own.

WIDOW By my troth, but that I have married one fool already,
you should not have him. Consider, he asks no portion, and yet
will make a great jointure; a fool with these conveniences, a kind
loving fool, and one that you may govern, makes no ill husband;
niece, there are other arguments too, to bid a fool welcome, which

you will find without teaching; think of it, niece; you may lay out your affection to purchase some dear wit, or judgment of the City, and repent, at leisure a good bargain, in this fool.

PLEASANT Faith, aunt, fools are cheap in the butchery, and dear in the kitchen; they are such unsavoury insipid things that there goes more charge to the sauce than the fool is worth, ere a woman can confidently serve him, either to her bed or board; then if he be a loving fool, he troubles all the world a days, and me all night.

SECRET Friendship-love, Madam, has a remedy for that.

PLEASANT See if the air of this place has not inclined Secret to be a bawd already. No, Secret, you get no gowns that way, upon my word; if I marry, it shall be a gentleman that has wit and honour, though he has nothing but a sword by his side; such a one naked is better than a fool with all his trappings, bells and baubles.

WIDOW Why, as I live, he's a handsome fellow, and merry; mine is such a sad soul, and tells me stories of lovers that died in despair, and of the lamentable end of their mistresses (according to the ballad) and thinks to win me by example.

PLEASANT Faith mine talks of nothing but how long he has loved me; and those that know me not, think I am old, and still finds new causes, (as he calls them) for his love; I asked him the other day if I changed so fast or no.

WIDOW But what thinkest thou, Secret; my nephew dances well, and has a handsome house in the Piazza.★

PLEASANT Your nephew? Not I, as I live; he looks as if he would be wooed; I'll warrant you, he'll never begin with a woman till he has lost the opinion of himself; but since you are so courteous, I'll speak to his friend, and let him know how you suffer for him.

WIDOW Him! Marry God bless all good women from him; why, he talks as if the dairymaid and all her cows could not serve his turn; then they wear such bawdy-breeches, 'twould startle an honest woman to come in their company, for fear they should break, and put her to count from the fall of them; for I'll warrant, the year of the Lord would sooner out of her head than such a sight.

PLEASANT I am not such an enemy now to his humour as to your

★ the Piazza: an open arcade built by Inigo Jones in 1633–34, on the north and east sides of Covent Garden.

nephew's. He rails against our sex, and thinks by beating down
the price of women to make us despair of merchants; but if I had
his heart-strings tied on a true-lover's-knot, I would so firk him
till he found physic in a rope.

SECRET He's a scurvy-tongued fellow, I'm sure of that; and if I
could have got a staff, I had marked him.

WIDOW What did he do to thee, Secret?

PLEASANT Why, he swore, he had a better opinion of her than to
think she had her maidenhead; but if she were that fool, and had
preserved the toy, he swore he would not take the pains of fetching it, to have it; I confess, I would fain be revenged on them,
because they are so blown up with opinion of their wit.

WIDOW As I live, my nephew travels still; the sober honest Ned
Wild will not be at home this month.

PLEASANT What say you? Will you abuse them and all the rest,
and stand to my first proposition?

WIDOW Yes, faith, if it be but to bury my servant, Sadd; for he
cannot last above another Fall. And how, think you, will your
servant take it?

PLEASANT Mine! O God help me, mine's a healthy fool, I would
he were subject to pine and take things unkindly; there were some
hope to be rid of him; for I'll undertake to use him as ill as anybody.

WIDOW As I live, I am easily resolved; for if I would marry, I
know neither who nor what humour to choose.

SECRET By my troth, Madam, you are hard to please; else the
courtier might have served turn.

WIDOW Serve turn! Prithee what haste, Secret? That I should put
myself to bed with one I might make a shift with; when I marry,
thou shalt cry, aye, marry, Madam; this is a husband without
blushing wench, and none of your so-so husbands; yet he might
half overcome my aversion, I confess.

PLEASANT Overcome! I think so, he might have won a city his
way; for when he saw you were resolved he should not eat with
you, he would set himself down as if he meant to besiege us, and
had vowed never to rise till he had taken us in; and because our
sex forbade force, he meant to do it by famine; yet you may stay,
and miss a better market; for hang me, I am of Secret's opinion;

he had but two faults, a handsome fellow, and too soon denied.

WIDOW 'Tis true, he was a handsome fellow, and a civil, that I shall report him; for as soon as it was given him to understand, I desired he would come no more, I never saw him since, but by chance.

PLEASANT Why did you forbid him?

WIDOW There were divers exceptions; but that which angered me then, was, he came with the king's letters patents, as if he had been to take up a wife for his Majesty's use.

PLEASANT Alas! Was that all? Why, 'tis their way at Court, a common course among them, and was it not one the king had a great care of? When my mother was alive, I had such a packet from the Court directed unto me, I bid them pay the post, and make the fellow drink, which he took as ill as I could wish, and has been ever since such a friendly enemy.

WIDOW Nay, as I live, she was for the captain too; his scarf and feather won her heart.

SECRET Truly, Madam, never flatter yourself; for the gentleman did not like you so well as to put you to the trouble of saying, no.

PLEASANT Lord, how I hated and dreaded that scarf and buff-coat?

SECRET Why, Mistress Pleasant, a captain is an honourable charge.

WIDOW Prithee, Secret, name them no more, colonel and captain, commissioner, free-quarters, ordnance and contribution; when Buff utters these words, I tremble and dread the sound; it frights me still when I do but think on them; cuds body, they're twigs of the old rod, wench, that whipped us so lately.

PLEASANT Aye, aye, and they were happy days, wench, when the captain was a lean, poor, humble thing, and the soldier tame, and durst not come within the City, for fear of a constable and a whipping-post; they know the penal statutes give no quarter; then Buff was out of countenance, and skulked from ale-house to ale-house, and the City had no militia but the sheriff's men; in those merry days, a bailiff trod the streets with terror, when all the chains in the city were rusty, but Mr Sheriff's, when the people knew no evil but the constable and his watch; now every committee has as much power, and as little manners, and examines with as much ignorance, impertinence and authority, as a constable in the king's key.

WIDOW [*people talking without*] See, who's that so loud?

SECRET The men you talked of, newly come to Town. —

[*Exeunt Omnes*]

SCENE III

Enter Jack Constant, Will Jolly, Sadd, and a Footman, they comb their heads, and talk.

JOLLY Remember our covenants, get them that can, all friends; and be sure to dispatch the plot, to carry them into the country, lest the brace of new-come monsieurs get them.

CONSTANT Those flesh-flies? I'll warrant thee from them, yet 'twas foolishly done of me to put on this gravity; I shall break out, and return to myself if you put me to a winter's wooing.

SADD A little patience does it; and I am content to suffer anything till they're out of Town: Secret says, they think my pale face proceeds from my love.

JOLLY Does she? That shall be one hint to advance your designs, and my revenge; for so she be cozened I care not who does it, for scorning me, who (by this hand) loved her parlously.

FOOTMAN Sir, what shall I do with the horses?

SADD Carry them to Brumsted's.*

FOOTMAN What shall I do with your worship's.

JOLLY Mine? Take him, hamstring him, kill him, anything to make him away, lest having such a conveniency I be betrayed to another journey into the country. Gentlemen, you are all welcome to my country-house; Charing Cross, I am glad to see thee, with all my heart.

CONSTANT What? Not reconciled to the country yet?

SADD He was not long enough there to see the pleasure of it.

JOLLY Pleasure? What is't called? Walking or hawking, or shooting at butts?

CONSTANT You found other pleasures, or else the story of the meadow is no gospel.

* Brumsted's: presumably either a tavern or a livery stable.

JOLLY Yes, a pox upon the necessity. Here I could as soon have taken the cow, as such a milkmaid.

SADD The wine and meat's good, and the company.

JOLLY When, at a Tuesday-meeting the country comes in to a match at two shillings rubbers, where they conclude at dinner what shall be done this Parliament, railing against the Court and Pope, after the old Elizabeth-way of preaching, till they are drunk with zeal; and then the old knight of the shire from the board's end, in his coronation breeches, vies clinches* with a silenced minister, a rogue that railed against the Reformation merely to be eased of the trouble of preaching.

CONSTANT Nay, as I live, now you are to blame, and wrong him, the man's a very able man.

JOLLY You'll be able to say so, one day, upon your wife's report; I would he were gelded, and all that hold his opinion: by this good day, they get more souls than they save.

SADD And what think you of the knight's son? I hope he's a fine gentleman, when his green suit, and his blue stockings are on; and the welcomest thing alive to Mrs Abigail;† but Tib and Tom in the stock.‡

JOLLY Who, Mr Jeoffry? Hobinol§ the second; by this life, 'tis a very veal, and he licks his nose like one of them; by his discourse you'll guess he had eaten nothing but hay; I wonder he doth not go on all four too, and hold up his leg when he stales; he talks of nothing but the stable. The cobbler's blackbird at the corner has more discourse; he has not so much as the family-jest, which these Coridons use to inherit; I posed him in *Booker's Prophesies*,‖ till he confessed he had not mastered his almanac yet.

CONSTANT But what was that you whispered to him in the hall?

* clinches: repartee involving word-play or punning.
† Mrs Abigail: generic name for a maidservant from Abigail in Beaumont and Fletcher's *The Scornful Lady*.
‡ Tib and Tom in the stock: terms in the game of gleek; Tib is ace of trumps, Tom the knave of trumps.
§ Hobinol: from foolish Hobbinol in Spenser's *The Shepheardes Calendar* (1579).
‖ *Booker's Prophesies*: John Booker (1601/3–1667), a Mancunian who served as apprentice to an haberdasher, later became clerk to aldermen in London, and was renowned as an astrologer. The first number of his Almanack, *Telescopium Uranium*, was published in 1631.

JOLLY Why, the butler and I, by the intercession of March beer, had newly reconciled him to his dad's old cod-piece corslet, in the hall; which, when his zeal was up, he would needs throw down, because it hung upon a cross.

CONSTANT But what think you of my neighbour? I hope her charity takes you.

JOLLY Yes, and her old waiting-woman's devotion; she sighed in the pew behind me; a Dutch skipper belches not so loud, or so sour; my lady's miserable sinner, with the white eyes, she does so squeeze out her prayers; and so wring out, 'Have mercy upon us'; I warrant her, she has a waiting-woman's sting in her conscience; she looks like a dirty souled bawd.

CONSTANT Who is this, my Lady Freedom's woman that he describes?

JOLLY The same, the independent lady, I have promised to send her a cripple or two by the next carrier; her subject husband would needs show me his house one morning; I never visited such an hospital, it stunk like Bedlam, and all the servants were carrying poultices, juleps, and glisters, and several remedies for all diseases, but his; the man sighed to see his estate crumbling away; I counselled him either to give or take a ounce of ratsbane, to cure his mind.

CONSTANT She is my cousin; but he made such a complaint to me, I thought he had married the company of Surgeons' Hall; for his directions to me for several things for his wife's use, were fitter for an 'pothecaries-shop than a lady's closet.

JOLLY I advised him to settle no jointure, but her old stills, and a box of instruments upon her; she hates a man with all his limbs; a wooden-leg, a crutch and *fistula in ano*, wins her heart; her gentleman-usher broke his leg last dog-days, merely to have the honour to have her set it, a foul rank rogue, and so full of salt humours, that he posed a whole college of old women with a gangrene; which spoiled the jest, and his ambling before my lady, by applying a handsaw to his gartering place; and now the rogue wears booted bed-staves, and destroys all the young ashes to make him legs.

SADD I never saw such a nasty affection; she would ha' done well in the incurable; a hand-maid to have waited on the cripples.

JOLLY She converses with naked men, and handles all their members though never so ill affected, and calls the fornication charity; all her discourse to me was flat bawdry, which I could not chide, but spoke as flat as she, till she rebuked me, calling mine beastliness, and hers, natural philosophy; by this day, if I were to marry, I would as soon have chosen a drawn whore out of mine own hospital, and cure the sins of her youth, as marry a she-chirurgeon; one that for her sins in her first husband's days cures all the crimes of her sex in my time. I would have him call her Chiron, the centaur's own daughter; a chirurgeon by sire and dam, Apollo's own colt, she's red-haired too, like that bonny beast with the golden mane and flaming tail.

SADD You had a long discourse with her, Jolly; what was't about?

JOLLY I was advising her to be divorced, and marry the man in the almanack;* 'twould be fine pastime for her to lick him whole.

SADD By this day, I never saw such a mule as her husband is, to bear with her madness; the house is a good house, and well furnished.

JOLLY Yes, but 'tis such a sight to see great French beds full of found children, sons of batchelors, priests' heirs, Bridewell orphans; there they lie by dozens in a bed, like sucking rabbits in a dish, or a row of pins; and then they keep a whole dairy of milch-whores to suckle them.

SADD She is successful, and that spoils her, and makes her deaf to counsel; I bad him poison two or three, to disgrace her; for the vanity and pride of their remedies make those women more diligent than their charity.

JOLLY I asked him why he married her; and he confessed, if he had been sound he had never had her.

CONSTANT He confessed, she cured him of three claps before he married her.

JOLLY Yes, and I believe some other member (though then ill affected) pleaded more than his tongue; and the rogue is like to find her business still, for he flies at all; my God, I owe thee thanks for many things; but 'tis not the least, I am not her husband, nor

---

* the man in the almanack: the figure of a man in old almanacks, surrounded by the twelve signs of the Zodiac, each sign beside the part of the body governed by it.

a country gentleman, whither I believe you cannot easily seduce
me again, unless you can persuade London to stand in the country;
to Hyde Park, or so, I may venture upon your lady-fair days, when
the filly foals of fifteen come kicking in, with their manes and tails
tied up in ribands, to see their eyes roll and neigh, when the
spring makes their blood prick them; so far I am with you by the
way of a country gentleman and a beer-drinker.

SADD For all this dislike, Master Jolly, your greatest acquaintance
lies amongst country gentlemen.

JOLLY Aye, at London, there your country gentlemen are good
company, where to be seen with them is a kind of credit; I come
to a mercer's shop in your coach; 'Boy, call your master'; he
comes bare, I whisper him, 'Do you know the Constants and the
Sadds of Norfolk?' 'Yes, yes', he replies, and strokes his beard;
'They are good men' cry I, 'Yes, yes'; 'No more, cut me off three
suits of satin', he does it, and in the delivery whispers, 'Will these
be bound?'* 'Pish, drive on coachman, speak with me tomorrow'.

CONSTANT And what then?

JOLLY What then? Why, come again next day.

SADD And what if the country gentleman will not be bound?

JOLLY Then he must fight.

SADD I would I had known that before I had signed your bond, I
would have set my sword sooner than my seal to it.

JOLLY Why, if thou repent there's no harm done, fight rather than
pay it.

SADD Why, do you think I dare not fight?

JOLLY Yes, but I think thou hast more wit than to fight with me;
for if I kill thee, 'tis a fortune to me, and others will sign in fear;
and if thou should'st kill me, anybody that knows us would
swear 'twere very strange, and cry, there's God's just judgement
now upon that lewd youth, and thou procurest his hangman's
place at the rate of thy estate.

CONSTANT By this hand, he is in the right; and for mine I meant
to pay when I signed; hang it, never put good fellows to say,
'prithee give me a hundred pounds'.

SADD 'Tis true, 'tis a good ganty† way of begging; yet, for being
killed, if I refuse it, would there were no more danger in the

* bound: paid for in the sense of being bought on credit.   † ganty: smart.

widow's unkindness, than in your fighting; I would not mistrust my design.

JOLLY Why aye, there's a point now in nicety of honour, I should kill you for her; for, you know I pretended first; and it may be if I had writ sad lines to her, and hid myself in my cloak, and haunted her coach, it may be in time she would have sought me; not I, by this hand, I'll not trouble myself for a wench, and married widows are but customary authorized wenches.

CONSTANT Being of that opinion, how cam'st thou to think of marrying one?

JOLLY Why, faith, I know not, I thought to rest me, for I was run out of breath with pleasure, and grew so acquainted with sin, I would have been good for variety; in these thoughts, 'twas my fortune to meet with this widow, handsome, and of a clear fame.

CONSTANT Did'st love her?

JOLLY Yes, faith? I had love, but not to the disease that makes men sick; and I could have loved her still, but that I was angry to have her refuse me for a fault I told her of myself, so I went no more.

SADD Did she forbid you but once?

JOLLY Faith, I think I slipped a fair opportunity, a handsome wench, and three thousand pounds *per annum* in certainty, besides the possibility of being saved.

CONSTANT Which now you think desperate?

Widow and Pleasant looking out at a window.

PLEASANT That is you; cross or pile,★ will you have him yet or no?
WIDOW Peace, observe them.
JOLLY Faith no, I do not despair, but I cannot resolve.

Enter Wild, Careless, and the Captain, going in haste, he comes in at the middle door.

WIDOW Who are those?
CARELESS Captain, whither in such haste? What defeated? Call you this a retreat, or a flight from your friends?
PLEASANT Your nephew, and his governor, and his friend! Here will be a scene, sit close, and we may know the secret of their hearts.

★ cross or pile: heads or tails, *croix ou pile.*

WIDOW They have not met yet since they returned, I shall love this bay window.

CAPTAIN Prithee let me go, there's mischief a-boiling; and if thou shakest me once more thou wilt jumble a lie together I have been hammering this hour.

CARELESS A pox upon you, a-studying lies?

CAPTAIN Why, then they are no lies, but something in the praise of an old lady's beauty, what do you call that?

They spy each other.

JOLLY Who are those?

SADD I'st not the captain, and my friend?

Jolly salutes them, then he goes to the Captain to embrace him, the Captain stands in a French posture, and slides from his old way of embracing.

JOLLY Ned Wild? Tom Careless? What ail'st thou, dost thou scorn my embraces?

CAPTAIN I see you have never been abroad, else you would know how to put a value upon those whose careful observation brought home the most exquisite garb and courtship that Paris could sell us.

JOLLY A pox on this fooling, and leave off ceremony.

CAPTAIN Why then agreed, off with our masks, and let's embrace like the old knot. [*they embrace*]

JOLLY Faith, say, where have you spent these three years' time? In our neighbour France? Or have you ventured o'er the Alps, to see the seat of the Caesars?

SADD And can tell us (ignorant, doomed to walk upon our own land) how large a seat the goddess fixed her flying Trojans in.

CONSTANT Yes, yes, and have seen, and drunk (perhaps) of Tiber's famous stream.

JOLLY And have been where Aeneas buried his trumpeter,* and his nurse;† Tom looks as if he had sucked the one, and had a battle sounded by the other, for joy to see our nation ambitious not to be understood or known when they come home.

CAPTAIN So, now I'm welcome home, this is freedom, and these

* his trumpeter: Misenus (*Aeneid*, VI, 160–165).
† his nurse: Caieta (*Aeneid*, VII, 1–4).

are friends, and with these I can be merry; for gentlemen, you must give me leave to be free too.

JOLLY So you will spare us miserable men, condemned to London, and the company of a Michaelmas term, and never travelled those countries that set mountains on fire a purpose to light us to our lodging.

WILD Why this is better than to stay at home, and lie by hearsay, wearing out yourselves and fortunes like your clothes, to see her that hates you for being so fine, than appearing at a play dressed like some part of it, while the company admire the mercers' and the tailors' work, and swear they have done their parts to make you fine gentlemen.

CARELESS Than leap out of your coach, and throw your cloak over your shoulder, the casting-nets to catch a widow, while we have seen the world, and learned her customs.

CAPTAIN Yes, Sir, and returned perfect monsieurs.

SADD Yes, even to their diseases; I confess my ignorance; I cannot amble, nor ride like Saint George at Waltham.*

JOLLY Yet, upon my conscience, he may be as welcome with a trot, as the other with his pace; and faith, Jack, (to be a little free) tell me, dost thou not think thou had'st been as well to pass here, with that English nose [*the Captain has a patch over his nose*] thou carried'st hence, as with the French tongue thou hast brought home?

CAPTAIN It is an accident, and to a soldier 'tis but a scar; 'tis true, such a sign upon Mr Jolly's face had been as ill as a Red Cross,† and 'Lord have mercy upon us', at his lodging door, to have kept women out of Court.

JOLLY For ought you know of the Court.

CAPTAIN I know the Court, and thee, and thy use, and how you serve but as the handsomest movables, a kind of implement above stairs, and look much like one of the old Court-servants in the hangings.

WILD But that they move, and look fresher, and your apparel more modern.

CARELESS Yet, faith, their office is the same, to adorn the room,

---

* Saint George at Waltham: the sign of a popular inn at Edmonton.
† Red Cross: the sign of the plague.

and be gazed on: alas! He's sad, courage man, these riding
clothes will serve thee at the latter day.

CAPTAIN Which is one of their grievances, for nothing troubles
them more than to think they must appear in a foul winding
sheet, and come undressed.

JOLLY Gentlemen, I am glad to find you know the Court; we know
a traveller too, especially when he is thus changed and exchanged,
as your worships, both in purse and person, and have brought
home foreign visages and inscriptions.

CONSTANT Why that's their perfection, their ambition to have it
said, there go those that have profitably observed the vices of
other countries, and made them their own; and the faults of
several nations, at their return, are their parts.

JOLLY Why there's Jack Careless, he carried out as good stable
manners* as any was in Suffolk, and now he is returned with a
shrug, and a trick to stand crooked, like a scurvy bow unbent,
and looks as if he would maintain oil and salads against a chine of
beef; I knew a great beast of this kind, it haunted the Court much,
and would scarcely allow us (fully reduced to civility) for serving
up mutton in whole joints.

CONSTANT What, silent?

SADD Faith, the captain is in a study.

JOLLY Do, do, con the rivers and towns perfectly, Captain; thou
may'st become intelligencer to the people, and lie thy two sheets
a week in Corrantoes† too.

CONSTANT And could you not make friends at Court, to get their
pictures cut ugly, in the corner of a map, like the old navigators.

JOLLY We'll see, we'll see.

Enter Widow and Pleasant above.

WIDOW I'll interrupt them; servant, you're welcome to Town;
how now, nephew? What, dumb? Where are all our travelled
tongues?

JOLLY Servant! Who doth she mean? By this hand, I disclaim the
title.

---

* stable manners: here native, courteous manners.

† Corrantoes: a coranto was an early printed paper giving foreign news, from
French *courant*. The first was *A Currant of Generall Newes* (1622).

PLEASANT Captain, Secret has taken notes, and desires you would instruct her in what concerns a waiting-woman, and an old lady.

CAPTAIN Very good, yet this shall not save your dinner.

WIDOW Nay, while you are in this humour I'll not sell your companies; and though Master Jolly be incensed, I hope he will do me the favour to dine with me.

JOLLY Faith, lady, you mistake me if you think I am afraid of a widow; for I would have the world know I dare meet her anywhere, but at bed. [*Exit Jolly*]

WILD No more aunt, we'll come; and if you will give us good meat, we'll bring good humours, and good stomachs. [*Widow shuts the curtain*]

CARELESS By this day I'll not dine there, they take a pleasure to raise a spirit that they will not lay, I'll to Bank's.★

CAPTAIN A pox forbid it, you shall not break company, now you know what we are to do after dinner.

CARELESS I will consent, upon condition you forbid the spiritual nonsense the age calls platonic love.†

CAPTAIN I must away too; but I'll be there at dinner, you will join in a plot after dinner.

WILD Anything, good, bad, or indifferent, for a friend and mirth. [*Exeunt all but the Captain*]

CAPTAIN I must go and prevent the rogue's mischief, with the old lady. [*Exit Captain*]

★ Bank's: a well known ordinary.
† platonic love: this became fashionable at Court in the 1630s. Davenant's masque *The Temple of Love* (1634) dealt with this as did his *The Platonic Lovers* (1636).

ACT TWO

SCENE I

Enter Jolly, and the old Lady Love-all.

LOVE-ALL Away, unworthy, false, ungrateful; with what brow darest thou come again into my sight, knowing how unworthy you have been, and how false to love?

JOLLY No, 'tis you are unworthy, and deserve not those truths of love I have paid here; else you would not believe every report that envy brings, and condemn, without hearing me, whom you have so often tried and found faithful.

LOVE-ALL Yes, till I too credulous had pity on your tears; till I had mercy you durst not be false.

JOLLY Nor am not yet.

LOVE-ALL What dost thou call false? Is there a treachery beyond what thou hast done; when I had given my fame, my fortune, myself, and my husband's honour, all in one obligation, a sacrifice to that passion; which thou seemest to labour with despair of, to tell and brag of a conquest o'er a woman, fooled by her passion, and lost in her love to thee, unworthy; – [*she turns away her head*]

JOLLY By this day, 'tis as false as he that said it; hang him, son of a batchelor; a slave that envying my fortune in such a happiness as your love, and chaste embraces, took this way to ruin it; come, dry your eyes, and let the guilty weep; if I were guilty I durst as soon approach a constable drunk, as come here; you know I am your slave.

LOVE-ALL You swore so, and honour made me leave to triumph over your miseries.

JOLLY Do you repent that I am happy? If you do, command my death.

LOVE-ALL Nay, never weep, nor sit sadly, I am friends, so you will only talk and discourse; for 'tis your company I only covet.

JOLLY No, you cannot forgive, because you have injured me; 'tis right woman's justice; accuse first, and harder to reconcile when they are guilty, than when they are innocent, or else you would not turn from me thus.

LOVE-ALL You know your youth hath a strong power over me;

turn those bewitching eyes away; I cannot see them with safety of mine honour.

JOLLY Come you shall not hide your face, there's a charm in it against those that come burned with unchaste fires; for let but your eyes or nose drop upon his heart it would burn up, or quench it straight.

LOVE-ALL No cogging, you have injured me; and now though my love plead, I must be deaf, my honour bids me; for you will not fear again to prove unworthy when you find I am so easy to forgive — [*Jolly kisses her, and she shoves him away with her mouth*] Why, you will not be uncivil.

JOLLY ⟨*aside*⟩ So, the storm is laid, I must have those pearls — she shoved me away with her mouth, I'll to her again.

LOVE-ALL Where are you? What do you take me for? [*still as he offers to touch her, she starts as if he plucked up her coats*] Why you will not be uncivil?

JOLLY Uncivil! By thy chaste self, I cannot, chick; thou hast such a terror, such a guard in those eyes, I dare not approach thee, nor can I gaze upon so much fire; prithee, sirrah, let me hide me from their power here.

LOVE-ALL You presume upon the weakness of our sex; what shall I say or do? Tyrant love!

JOLLY There's a charm in those pearls; pull them off; if they have a frost in them, let me wear them, and then we are both safe.

LOVE-ALL I would you had taken them sooner, I had then been innocent, and might with whiteness have worn my love which I shall ne'er out-live.

JOLLY Dear, do not too fast pour in my joys, lest I too soon reach my heaven.

LOVE-ALL Begone then, lest we prove (having gained that height) this sad truth in love; the first minute after noon is night.

JOLLY Part now? The gods forbid; take from me first this load of joys you have thrown upon me; for 'tis a burthen harder to bear than sadness; I was not born till now, this my first night in which I reap true bliss.

LOVE-ALL No, no; I would it had been your first night, then your falsehood had not given argument for these tears; and I hate myself to think I should be such a foolish fly, thus again to approach your dangerous flame.

JOLLY Come, divert these thoughts; I'll go see your closet.

LOVE-ALL No, no, I swear you shall not.

JOLLY You know, I am going out of Town for two days.

LOVE-ALL When you return, I'll show it you; you will forget me else when you are gone, and at Court.

JOLLY Can your love endure delays? Or shall business thee from hence remove? These were your own arguments; come, you shall show it me.

LOVE-ALL Nay, then I perceive what unworthy way your love would find; ye gods, are all men false?

JOLLY As I live, you shall stay; come, you ought to make me amends for slandering of me; hang me, if ever I told; and he that reports it is the damnedst rogue in a country, come, I say. – [*he pulls her bodkin, that is tied in a piece of black bobbin*]

LOVE-ALL Ah! As I live, I will not, I have sworn; do not pull me, I will not be damned; I have sworn. – [*he pulls her and says this*]

JOLLY As I live, I'll break your bodkin then, a weeping tyrant! Come; by this good day, you shall be merciful.

LOVE-ALL Why, you will not be uncivil; you will not force me, will you? As I live, I will not.

JOLLY Nay, and you be wilful, I can be stubborn too. [*he pulls still*]

LOVE-ALL Hang me, I'll call aloud, why Nan! Nay, you may force me; but, as I live, I'll do nothing.   [*Exeunt ambo*]

SCENE II

Enter Captain.

CAPTAIN A pox upon you, are you earthed? The rogue has got her necklace of pearl; but I hope he will leave the rope to hang me in, how the pox came they so great? I must have some trick to break his neck, else the young rogue will work me out; 'tis an excellent old lady, but I dare not call her so; yet would she were young enough to bear, we might do some good for our heirs, by leaving such a charitable brood behind; she's a woman after the first kind; 'tis but going in to her and you may know her; then she'll oblige so readily, and gives with greater thanks than others receive, takes it so kindly to be courted. I am now to oblige her (as she calls it) by professing young Wild's love, and desiring an assurance; she's sensible of his sufferings, which though it be false, and beyond my commission, yet the hopes of such a new young thing that has the vogue of the Town, for handsomest, 'twill so tickle her age, and so blow up her vanity, to have it said, 'He is in love with her', and so endear her to me for being the means that the parson's malice will be able to take no root; – She comes, I must not be seen. –   [*Goes out the back*]

Enter Love-all, and Jolly.

LOVE-ALL Give me that letter, I'll swear you shall not read it.

JOLLY Take it, I'll away, what time shall I call you, in the evening? There's a play at Court tonight.

LOVE-ALL I would willingly be there, but your ladies are so censorious, and malicious to us young ladies, in the Town, especially to me, because the wits are pleased to afford me a visit, or so; I could be content else to be seen at Court; pray what humour is the queen of? The captain of her guard I know.

JOLLY The queen? [*the Captain knocks*] Who's that knocks at the back door. –

LOVE-ALL Smooth my band, I know not, go down that way, and look you be not false; if you should be false, I'll swear, I should spoil myself with weeping.

JOLLY Farewell, in the evening I'll call you.   [*Exit Jolly*]

LOVE-ALL Who's there? Captain?

⟨Re-enter Captain⟩

Where have you been all this while; I might sit alone, I see, for you, if I could not find conversation in books. [*she takes a book in her hand and sits down*]

CAPTAIN Faith, Madam, friends newly come to Town engaged me, and my stay was civility rather than desire. What book's that?

LOVE-ALL I'll swear he was a witch that writ it; for he speaks my thoughts as if he had been within me; the original, they say, was French.

CAPTAIN Oh, I know it, 'tis *The Accomplished Woman*,* yourself, he means by this, while you are yourself.

LOVE-ALL Indeed, I confess, I am a great friend to conversation, if we could have it without suspicion; but the world's so apt to judge, that 'tis a prejudice to our honour now to salute a man.

CAPTAIN Innocence, Madam, is above opinion, and your fame's too great to be shook with whispers.

LOVE-ALL You are ever civil, and therefore welcome; pray, what news is there now in Town? For I am recluded here; unless it be yours, I receive no visits; and I'll swear, I charged the wench today not to let you in; I wonder she let you come.

CAPTAIN Faith, Madam, if it had been my own business I should not have ventured so boldly; but the necessity that forces me to come concerns my friend, against whom if your mercy be now bounded with those strict ties of honour, and cold thoughts which I have ever found guard your heart, my friend, a young and handsome man, is lost, is lost in his prime, and falls like early blossoms; but methinks you should not prove the envious frost to destroy this young man, this delicate young man, that has whole bundles of boys in his breeches; yet if you be cruel, he and they die, as useless as open arses† gathered green.

LOVE-ALL [*She must be earnest in her looks all the time she speaks; desirous to know who he speaks of*] Good Captain, out with the particular what way can my charity assist him; you know by experience I cannot be cruel, remember how I fetched you out of a swoon, and laid you in my own bed.

CAPTAIN That act preserved a life, that has always been laboured in your service; and I dare say, your charity here will find as fruitful a gratitude.

LOVE-ALL But, I hope, he will not be so uncivil as you were; I'll swear, I could have hanged you for that rape, if I would have followed the law; but I forgave you upon condition you would do so again; but what's this young man you speak of?

CAPTAIN Such is my love to you and him, that I cannot prefer

* *The Accomplished Woman*: published in 1656, it was originally in French 'since made English by the Honourable Walter Montague'.
† open arses: medlars.

mine own particular before your contents; else I'd have poisoned him ere I'd have brought him to your house.

LOVE-ALL Why, I pray?

CAPTAIN Because, he's young, handsome, and of sound parts; that I'm sure will ruin me here.

LOVE-ALL His love may make all these beauties, else I have an honour will defend me against him, were he as handsome as young Wild.

CAPTAIN Why aye, there it is; that one word has removed all my fears and jealousies with a despair; for that's the man whose love, life and fortune, lies at your feet; and if you were single, by lawful ways he would hope to reach what now he despairs of.

LOVE-ALL Let him not despair, love is a powerful pleader, and youth and beauty will assist him; and if his love be noble I can meet it; for there's none that sacrifices more to friendship-love, than I.

CAPTAIN My friend's interest makes me rejoice at this; dare you trust me to say this to him, though it be not usual, pray speak; nay, you are so long still a-resolving to be kind: remember, charity is as great a virtue as chastity, and greater, if we will hear nature plead; for the one may make many maids, the other can but preserve one: but I know you will be persuaded, let it be my importunity that prevailed. Shall I bring him hither one evening?

LOVE-ALL Why do you plead thus? Pray be silent, and when you see him, tell him he has a seat here, and I – [*she turns away*]

CAPTAIN Out with it, what is't? Shall he call you mistress? And his platonic?

LOVE-ALL Away, away; me?

CAPTAIN No niceness, is't a match?

LOVE-ALL Lord, would I were as worthy as willing (pray tell him so) he shall find me one of the humblest mistresses that ever he was pleased to honour with his affections.

CAPTAIN Dare you write this to him, and honour me with bearing it? I confess, I am such a friend to friendship-love too that I would even bring him on my back to a midnight's meeting.

LOVE-ALL If you will stay here, I'll go in and write it. – [*she's going out and he calls her*]

CAPTAIN Madam, I forgot to ask your ladyship one question.

LOVE-ALL What was't?

CAPTAIN There happened a business last night betwixt Mr Wild and one Jolly, a courtier that brags extremely of your favour; I swear, if it had not been for friends that interposed themselves there had been mischief, for Mr Wild was extreme zealous in your cause.

LOVE-ALL Such a rascal I know; villain, to bring my name upon the stage, for a subject of his quarrels, I'll have him cudgelled.

CAPTAIN And I'll swear, he deserved it; for the quarrel ended in a bet of a buck-hunting-nag, that sometime today he would bring a necklace and chain of pearl of yours (not stolen, but freely given) to witness his power.

LOVE-ALL Did the vain rascal promise that?

CAPTAIN Yes, but we laughed at it.

LOVE-ALL So you might; and, as I live, if the necklace were come from stringing I'd send them both to Mr Wild, to wear as a favour, to assure him I am his, and to put the vain slave out of countenance.

CAPTAIN Aye marry, such a timely favour were worth a dozen letters, to assure him of your love, and remove all the doubts the others' discourse may put into his head; and faith I'd send him the chain now, and in my letter promise him the necklace, he'll deserve such a favour.

LOVE-ALL I'll go in and fetch it immediately, will you favour me to deliver it.

CAPTAIN I'll wait upon your ladyship.

LOVE-ALL [*she goes and he follows her, she turns and bids him stay*] I'll swear you shall not go in, you know I forswore being alone with you.

CAPTAIN Hang me, I'll go in; does my message deserve to wait an answer at the door?

LOVE-ALL Aye, but you'll be naught.*

CAPTAIN Oh, ne'er trust me if I break.

LOVE-ALL If you break some such forfeit you'll lose; well, come in for once.

CAPTAIN You are so suspicious.

LOVE-ALL I'll swear, I have reason for't, you are such another man.   [*Exeunt*]

* naught: naughty.

SCENE III

Enter Wanton and Bawd.

WANTON Is he gone?

BAWD Yes, he's gone to the old lady's, high with mischief.

WANTON Fare him well, easy fool, how the trout strove to be tickled, [*she plays with a wedding ring upon her finger*] and how does this ring become me? Ha! They are fine kind of things these wedding rings.

BAWD Besides the good custom of putting so much gold in 'em, they bring such conveniences along.

WANTON Why aye, now I have but one to please; and if I please him, who dares offend me? And that wife's a fool that cannot make her husband one.

BAWD Nay, I am absolutely of opinion, it was fit for you to marry; but whether he be a good husband or no.

WANTON A pox of a good husband, give me a wise one; they only make the secure cuckolds, the cuckold in grain; for dye a husband that has wit but with an opinion thou art honest, and see who dares wash the colour out; now your fool changes with every drop, dotes with confidence in the morning and at night, jealous even to murder, and his love (Lord help us) fades like my gredaline petticoat.*

BAWD This is a new doctrine.

WANTON 'Tis a truth, wench, I have gained from my own observations, and the paradox will be maintained. Take wise men for cuckolds, and fools to make them; for your wise man draws eyes and suspicion with his visit, and begets jealous thoughts in the husband, that his wife may be overcome with his parts; when the fool is welcome to both, pleaseth both, laughs with the one, and lies with the other, and all without suspicion; I tell thee, a fool that has money is the man. The wits and the we's, which is a distinct parreal of wit bound by itself, and to be sold at Wit-hall, or at the sign of the King's Head in the Butchery; these wise things will make twenty jealous, ere one man a cuckold; when

---

* gredaline petticoat: probably a crumpled or puckered petticoat, from French *grediller*, or also from *gris de lin*, flax grey.

the family of fools will head a parish ere they are suspected.

BAWD Well, I see one may live and learn; and if he be but as good at it, now you are his own, as he was, when he was your friend's friend, (as they call it) you have got one of the best hiders of such a business in the Town; Lord, how he would sister you at a play!

WANTON Faith, 'tis as he is used at first; if he get the bridle in's teeth he'll ride to the devil; but if thou beest true, we'll make him amble ere we have done; the plot is here, and if it thrive I'll alter the proverb, 'The parson gets the children', to, 'The parson fathers them'.

BAWD Anything that may get rule; I love to wear the breeches.

WANTON So do we all, wench. Empire? 'Tis all our aim; and I'll put my ranting Roger* in a cage but I'll tame him; he loves already, which is an excellent ring in a fool's nose, and thou shalt hear him sing. –

Happy only is that family, that shows
A cock that's silent, and a hen that crows.

BAWD Do this, I'll serve you for nothing; the impetuous slave had wont to taunt me for beating of my husband, and would sing that song in mockery of me.

WANTON In revenge of which, thou (if thou wilt be faithful) shalt make him sing.

Happy ⟨only⟩ is that family, that shows
A cock that's silent, and a hen that crows.   [*Exeunt*]

SCENE IV

Enter Parson, Love-all, and Faithful.

LOVE-ALL Go, you are a naughty man; do you come hither to rail against an honest gentleman? I have heard how you fell out, you may be ashamed on't, a man of your coat.

PARSON What? To speak truth and perform my duty? The world cries out you are a scabbed sheep, and I come to tar you, that is, give you notice how your fame suffers i'th'opinion of the world.

* ranting Roger: a nickname for a curate from Sir Roger, the curate in *The Scornful Lady*.

LOVE-ALL My fame, sirrah? 'Tis purer than thy doctrine, get thee out of my house.

FAITHFUL You uncivil fellow, do you come hither to tell my lady of her faults, as if her own levite could not discern 'em?

LOVE-ALL My own levite? I hope he's better bred than to tell me of my faults.

FAITHFUL He finds work enough to correct his dearly beloved sinners.

PARSON And the right worshipful my lady, and yourself, they mend at leisure.

LOVE-ALL You are a saucy fellow, sirrah, to call me sinner in my own house; get you gone with – your 'Madam, I hear', and 'Madam I could advise, but I am loath to speak'; take heed, the world talks, and thus with dark sentences put my innocence into a fright, with 'you know what you know good Mistress Faithful'; so do I, and the world shall know too thou hast married a whore.

PARSON Madam, a whore?

FAITHFUL No, Sir, 'tis not so well as a madam-whore, 'tis a poor whore, a captain's cast whore.

LOVE-ALL Now bless me, marry a whore? I wonder any man can endure those things, what kind of creatures are they?

PARSON They're like ladies, but that they are handsomer; and though you take a privilege to injure me, yet I would advise your woman to tie up her tongue, and not abuse my wife.

LOVE-ALL Fie, art thou not ashamed to call a whore, wife? Lord bless us, what will not these men do when God leaves them! But for a man of your coat to cast himself away upon a whore, come wench, let's go and leave him! I'll swear, 'tis strange, the state doth not provide to have all whores hanged or drowned.

FAITHFUL Aye, and 'tis time they look into it, for they begin to spread so, that a man can scarce find an honest woman in a coun-try; they say, they're voted down now, 'twas moved by that charitable member that got an order to have it but five miles to Croydon, for ease of the market-women.*

LOVE-ALL Aye, aye, 'tis a blessed Parliament.

[Exeunt Love-all and Faithful]

* market-women: whores were reputed to ply their trade in the suburbs, notably Croydon.

PARSON That I have played the fool, is visible; this comes of rash-
ness; something I must do to set this right, or else she'll hate, and
he'll laugh at me.

I must not lose him, and my revenge too,

Something that's mischief, I am resolved to do.   [*Exit Parson*]

SCENE V

Enter Wild and Careless.

WILD Now is the parson's wife so contemptible?

CARELESS No, but I'm so full of that resolution to dislike the sex,
that I will allow none honest, none handsome; I tell thee, we must
beat down the price with ourselves, court none of 'em; but let
their maidenheads and their faces lie upon their hands, till they're
weary of the commodity, then they'll haunt us to find proper
chapmen to deal for their ware.

WILD I like this, but 'twill be long a-doing, and it may be ere they
be forced to sell, our bank will be exhausted, and we shall not be
able to purchase.

CARELESS Aye, but we'll keep a credit, and at three six months,*
thou and the captain shall be my factors.

WILD You had best have a partner, else such an undertaking would
break a better back than yours.

CARELESS No partners in such commodities, your factor that
takes up maidenheads, 'tis upon his own account still.

WILD But what course will you take to purchase this trade with
women?

CARELESS I am resolved to put on their own silence and modesty,
answer 'forsooth', swear nothing but 'God's nigs', and hold
arguments of their own cold tenets, as if I believed there were no
true love below the line, then sigh when 'tis proper, and with
forced studies betray the enemy, who seeing my eye fixed on her,
her vanity thinks I am lost in admiration, calls and shakes me ere
I wake out of my design, and being collected, answer out of purpose. Love, divinest? Yes, who is it that is mortal and does not, or
which amongst all the senate of the gods, can gaze upon those

* three six months: possibly at 3% for six months.

eyes, and carry thence the power he brought? This will start her.

WILD Yes, and make her think thee mad.

CARELESS Why that's my design; for then I start too, and rub my eyes, as if I walked, then sigh and strangle a yawn, till I have wrung it into tears, with which I rise, as if o'ercome with grief; then kiss her hands, and let fall those witnesses of faith and love, bribed for my design. This takes; for who would suspect such a devil as craft and youth to live together?

WILD But what kind of women do you think this will take?

CARELESS All kind of women, those that think themselves handsome; it being probable, concludes it real; and those that are handsome in their opinion, that small number will believe it, because it agrees with their wishes.

WILD And when you are gone, it may be they sigh, and their love breaks out into paper, and what then?

CARELESS What then? Why then I'll laugh, and show thee their letters, and teach the world how easy 'tis to win any woman.

WILD This is the way, and be sure to dislike all, but her you design for; be scarce civil to any of the sex besides.

CARELESS That's my meaning, but to her that I mean my prey, all her slave; she shall be my deity; and her opinion my religion.

WILD And while you say it thus to one, I'll talk freer than a privileged fool, and swear as unreasonably as losing gamesters, and abuse thee for thinking to reclaim a woman by thy love, call them all bowls thrown that will run where they will run, and lovers like fools run after them, crying, 'Rub, and fly, for me';* I believe none fair, none handsome, none honest, but the kind.

CARELESS We must make the captain of our plot, lest he betray us; this will gain us some revenge upon the lovers to whom I grudge the wenches, not that I believe they're worth half the cost they pay for them; and we may talk, but 'tis not our opinion can make them happier, or miserable.

Enter Jolly.

WILD Jolly, Will, where hast thou been? We had such sport with

---

* crying, 'Rub . . .' : a term in bowls; when the bowl is retarded or diverted by an impediment or obstacle some players call out 'Rub' to the bowl as if it could hear them and stop.

the parson of our town, he's married this morning to Wanton.

JOLLY Who? The captain's wench? He's in a good humour then; as you love mirth, let's find him, I have news to blow his rage with, and 'twill be mirth to us, to see him divided betwixt the several causes of his anger, and lose himself in his rage while he disputes, which is the greater; [*here he pulls out the pearl*]* your opinion, gentlemen; is this, or his wench, the greater loss?

CARELESS What hast thou there? Pearl! They're false, I hope.

JOLLY Why do you hope so?

CARELESS Because I am thy friend, and would be loath to have thee hanged for stealing.

JOLLY I will not swear they are honestly come by; but I'll be sworn, there's neither force nor theft in't.

WILD Prithee, speak out of riddles, here's none but your friends.

JOLLY Faith, take it, you have heard the captain brag of an old lady, which he thinks he keeps close in a box; but I know where hangs a key can let a friend in, or so: from her, my brace of worthies, whose wits are dulled with plenty, this morning, with three good words, and four good deeds, I earned this toy.

CARELESS The mirth yet, we will all share; I am in pain till we find him, that we may vex his wit that he presumes so much on.

WILD Let's go, let's go, I will desire him to let me see his wench; I will not understand him if he says she's gone.

CARELESS I'll beg of him, for old acquaintance sake, to let me see his old lady.

JOLLY Hark, I hear his voice. –

CAPTAIN ⟨*off stage*⟩ Which way?

CARELESS The game plays itself; begin with him, Ned, while we talk, as if we were busy, we'll take our cue.

WILD When I put off my hat.

Enter Captain.

CAPTAIN S'blood, I thought you had been sunk, I have been hunting you these four hours. Death, you might ha'left word where you went; and not put me to hunt like Tom Fool. 'Tis well you are at London, where you know the way home.

WILD Why in choler? We have been all this while searching you;

* *pearl*: used collectively.

come, this is put on to divert me for claiming your promise, I must see the wench.

CAPTAIN You cannot adad, adad you cannot.

WILD I did not think you would have refused such a kindness.

CARELESS What's that?

WILD Nothing, a toy, he refuses to show me his wench.

CARELESS The devil he does; what have we been thus long comrades, and had all things in common, and must we now come to have common wenches particular? I say, thou shalt see her, and lie with her too, if thou wilt.

JOLLY What? In thy dumps, brother, call to thy aid thy two-edged wit; the captain sad? 'Tis prophetic, I'd as lief have dreamed of pearl,* or the loss of my teeth; yet if he be musty, I'll warrant thee, Ned, I'll help thee to a bout; I know his cloak, his long cloak that hides her; I am acquainted with the parson, he shall befriend thee.

CAPTAIN 'Tis very well, gentlemen; but none of you have seen her yet?

WILD Yes, but we have, by thyself, by thy anger, which is now bigger than thou; by chance we crossed her, coming from church, leading in her hand the parson, to whom she swore she was this day married.

JOLLY And our friendships were now guiding us to find thee out, to comfort thee after the treachery of thy levite. Come, bear it like a man, there are more wenches, what hast thou spied? – [*the Captain gives no answer, but peeps on Jolly's hat*]

WILD His pearl, I believe.

CAPTAIN Gentlemen, I see you are merry; I'll leave you; I must go a little way, to enquire about a business.

WILD H'as got a sore eye, I think.

CAPTAIN I will only ask one question, and return.

CARELESS No faith, stay, and be satisfied.

JOLLY Do, good brother, for I believe there is no question that you now would ask, but here's an oracle can resolve you.

CAPTAIN Are those pearl true?

JOLLY Yes?

* dreamed of pearl: such dreams were supposed to signify fears, a loss of one's teeth or a quarrel among friends.

CAPTAIN And did not you steal them?

JOLLY No.

CARELESS Nor he did not buy them with ready money; but took them upon mortgage of himself to an old lady.

JOLLY Dwelling at the sign of the Buck in Broad Street;* are you satisfied, or must I play the oracle still?

CAPTAIN No, no, I am satisfied.

JOLLY Like jealous men, that take their wives at it, are you not?

CAPTAIN Well, very well, 'tis visible, I am abused on all hands; but gentlemen, why all against me?

CARELESS To let you see your wit's mortal, and not proof against all.

WILD The parson hath shot it through with a jest.

CAPTAIN Gentlemen, which of you, faith, had a hand in that?

JOLLY Faith, none; only a general joy, to find the captain over-reached.

CAPTAIN But do you go sharers in the profit, as well as in the jest?

JOLLY No faith, the toy's mine own.

CAPTAIN They are very fine, and you may afford a good penny-worth, will you sell them?

JOLLY Sell them? Aye, where's a chapman?

CAPTAIN Here, I'll purchase them.

JOLLY Thou? No, no, I have barred thee, by and main,† for I am resolved not to fight for them; that excludes thy purchase by the sword; and thy wench has proved such a loss, in thy last adventure of wit, that I'm afraid, it will spoil thy credit that way too.

CAPTAIN Gentlemen, as a friend, let me have the refusal, set your price.

WILD He's serious.

CARELESS Leave fooling.

JOLLY Why if thou could'st buy them, what would'st thou do with them.

CAPTAIN They're very fair ones, let me see them, methinks they should match very well with these.

JOLLY These, which?

* Broad Street: then in a fashionable district, now one occupied largely by offices, it runs from London Wall to Threadneedle Street.
† by and main: entirely.

OMNES Which?

CARELESS They are true.

CAPTAIN Yes, but not earned with a pair of stolen verses, of, 'I was not born till now, this my first night', and so forsooth; nor given as a charm against lust.

CARELESS What means all this?

JOLLY What? Why 'tis truth, and it means to shame the devil; by this good day, he repeats the same words with which I gathered pearls.

WILD Why then we have two to laugh at.

CARELESS And all friends hereafter, let's fool altogether.

CAPTAIN Gentlemen with the fine wits, and my very good friends do you, or you, or he think I'll keep you company, to make you laugh, but that I draw my honey from you too?

CARELESS Come, come, the captain's in the right.

CAPTAIN Yes, yes, the captain knows it, and dares tell you, your wit, your fortune, and his face, are but my ploughs; and I would have my fine monsieur know, who, in spite of my counsel, will be finer than his mistress, and appears before her so curiously built she dares not play with him for fear of spoiling him; and to let him know the truth I speak, to his fair hands I present this letter, but withal give him to understand, the contents belong to me.

WILD [*reads the letter*] The pearl are sent to me.

CAPTAIN I deny that, unless you prove you sent me; for the letter begins, 'Sir, this noble gentleman, the bearer, whom you are pleased to make the messenger of your love', and so forth; 'and now you should do well to enquire for that noble gentleman, and take an account of him how he has laid out your love, and it may be he'll return you pearl for it; and now gentlemen, I dare propose a peace, at least a cessation of wit (but what is defensive) till such time as the plot which is now in my head be effected, in which you have all your shares.

WILD So she knows I have not the pearl, I am content.

CAPTAIN She'll quickly find that, when she sees you come not tonight, according to my appointment, and hears I have sold the pearl.

JOLLY Here then ceaseth our offensive war.

CAPTAIN I'll give you counsel worth two ropes of pearl.

CARELESS But the wench, how came the parson to get her?

CAPTAIN Faith 'tis hard to say which laboured most, he, or I, to make that match, but the knave did well; there it is (if you assist) I mean to lay the scene of your mirth tonight, for I am not yet fully revenged upon the rogue; for that I know him miserable is nothing, till he believe so too; Wanton and I have laid the plot.

JOLLY Do you hold correspondence?

CAPTAIN Correspondence? I tell thee the plots we laid to draw him on would make a comedy.

Enter a Servant.

SERVANT Sir, the ladies stay dinner.   ⟨*Exit*⟩

CAPTAIN And as we go I'll tell you all the story, and after dinner, be free from all engagements, as we promised thee; and follow but your directions, I'll warrant you mirth and a pretty wench.

OMNES Agreed, anything that breeds mirth is welcome.

JOLLY Not a word at the widow's, let them go on quietly, and steal their wedding too.

CAPTAIN I heard a bird sing, as if it were concluded amongst the couples.

WILD They have been long about it; my coz is a girl deserves more haste to her bed, he has arrived there by carriers' journeys.

CARELESS But that I hate wooing, by this good day, I like your aunt so well, and her humour, she should scarce be thrown away upon pale-face, that has sighed her into a wedding ring, and will but double her jointure.

CAPTAIN Why aye, thus it should be, pray let us make them the seat of the war all dinner, and continue united and true among ourselves, then we may defy all foreign danger.

JOLLY And with full bowls let us crown this peace, and sing, 'Wit, without war, no mirth doth bring'.   [*Exeunt*]

SCENE VI

Enter Parson and Wanton.

WANTON Was she deaf to your report?

PARSON [*walks troubled up and down*] Yes, yes.

WANTON And Ugly, her Abigail, she had her say too?

PARSON Yes, yes.

WANTON And do you walk here biting your nails: do you think I'll be satisfied with such a way of righting me?

PARSON What would'st have me do?

WANTON Have you no gall? Be abused and laughed at by a dull captain, that a strict muster would turn fool? You had wit, and could rail, when I offended you, and none so sudden, none so terrible, none so sure in his revenge, when I displease you.

PARSON Something I'll do.

WANTON Do it then, or I shall curse that e'er I saw you. Death, let the sign of my lady, an out-of-fashion whore, that has paid for sin, ever since yellow starch★ and wheel farthingales were cried down, let her abuse me, and say nothing? If this passes –

PARSON As Christ bless me, but I did, sweetheart: and if it were not church livings are mortal, and they are always hitting me in the teeth with a man of your coat, she should find I am no church man within, nor Mr Parson but in my coat; come to dinner, and after dinner I'll do something.

WANTON I shall do something will vex somebody.

Enter Bawd.

BAWD Will you please to come to dinner? The company stays.

PARSON Come, let's go in.

WANTON No, I must walk a little to digest this breakfast, the guests else will wonder to see I am troubled.

PARSON Come, let this day pass in mirth, spite of mischief, for luck's sake. [*Exit Parson*]

WANTON I'll follow you, and do what I can to be merry.

BAWD Why, he stands already.

WANTON Peace, let me alone, I'll make him jostle, like the miller's mare, and stand like the dun cow, till thou may'st milk him.

BAWD Pray break him of his miserableness, it is one of the chief exceptions I have against him; he reared a puppy once, till it was ten days old, with three hap'worth of milk, and then with his own

★ yellow starch: invented by Anne Turner (1576–1615) who was hanged for the murder of Sir Thomas Overbury: she wore a ruff stiffened by it on her execution day.

dagger slew it, and made me dress it: blessed myself to see him eat it, and he bid me beg the litter, and swore it was sweeter and wholesomer than sucking rabbits, or London pigs, which he called Bellmen's issue.

PARSON [*calls within*] Why sweetheart.

WANTON Hark, he calls me, we must humour him a little, he'll rebel else.

SCENE VII

Enter (at the windows) the Widow and Master Careless, Mistress Pleasant and Master Wild, Captain, Master Sadd, Constant, Jolly, Secret, a table and knives ready for oysters.

WIDOW You're welcome all, but especially Master Jolly; no reply, with 'I thank your ladyship'.

PLEASANT [*speaks to Master Jolly*] I beseech you, Sir, let us never be better acquainted.

JOLLY I shall endeavour, lady, and fail in nothing that is in my power to disoblige you; for there is none more ambitious of your ill opinion than I.

PLEASANT I rejoice at it, for the less love, the better welcome still.

WIDOW And as ever you had an ounce of love for the widow, be not friends among yourselves.

WILD Aunt, though we were at strife when we were along, yet now we unite like a politic state against the common enemy.

PLEASANT The common enemy, what is that?

WILD Women, and lovers in general.

WIDOW Nay, then we have a party, niece, claim; quickly, now is the time, according to the proverb; 'Keep a thing seven years, and then if thou hast no use on't throw't away.'

PLEASANT Agreed, let's challenge our servants; by the love they have professed, they cannot in honour refuse to join with us; and see where they come. –

Enter Sadd and Constant, and meet Secret, she whispers this to Sadd.

SECRET Sir, tis done.

SADD Be secret and grave, I'll warrant our design will take as we can wish.

CONSTANT Sweet Mistress Pleasant.

WIDOW Servant Sadd.

SADD Madam.

WIDOW We are threatened to have a war waged against us, will you not second us?

SADD With these youths we'll do enough, Madam.

WIDOW I'll swear my servant gave hit for hit this morning, as if he had been a master in the noble science of wit.

PLEASANT Mine laid about him with spick and span new arguments, not like the same man, his old sayings and precedents laid by.

WIDOW Thus armed, then, we'll stand and defy them.

WILD Where's your points? Sure aunt, this should be your wedding day, for you have taken the man for better for worse.

WIDOW No, nephew, this will not prove the day that we shall either give or take a ring.

CARELESS Hang me, if I know you can go back again with your honour.

WILD Or in justice refuse him liberty, that has served out his time; either marry him or provide for him, for he is maimed in your service.

WIDOW Why servant Sadd? You'll arm; my nephew has thrown the first dart at you.

CAPTAIN Hast hit, hast hit?

WILD No, Captain, 'twas too wide.

CAPTAIN Too wide? Marry he's an ill marksman that shoots wider than a widow.

JOLLY We are both in one hole, Captain; but I was loath to venture my opinion, lest her ladyship should think I was angry; for I have a good mind to fall upon the widow.

PLEASANT You're a constant man, Master Jolly; you have been in that mind this twelve-month's day.

CONSTANT You are in the right, Madam; she has it to show under his hand, but she will not come in the list with him again; she threw him the last year.

WIDOW Come, shall we eat oysters? Who's there? Call for some wine, Master Jolly; you are not warm yet, pray be free, you are at home.

JOLLY Your ladyship is merry.

WIDOW You do not take it ill, to have me assure you you are at home here?

WILD [*oysters not brought in yet*] Such another invitation (though in jest) will take away Master Sadd's stomach.

SADD No, faith, Ned, though she should take him, it will not take away my stomach; my love is so fixed I may wish my wishes, but she shall never want them to wait upon hers.

PLEASANT A traitor, bind him, has pulled down a side; profess your love thus public?

JOLLY Aye by my faith, continue Master Sadd, give it out you love, and call it a new love, a love never seen before, we'll all come to it as your friends.

SADD Gentlemen, still I love; and if she to whom I thus sacrifice will not reward it, yet the worst malice can say, is, I was unfortunate and misfortune not falsehood made me so.

JOLLY In what chapter shall we find this written, and what verse? You should preach with a method, Master Sadd.

WIDOW Gentlemen, if ever he spoke so much dangerous sense before (either of love or reason) hang me.

SADD Madam, my love is no news where you are; know, your scorn has made it public; and though it could gain no return from you; yet others have esteemed me for the faith and constancy I have paid here.

PLEASANT Did not I foretell you of his love? I foresaw this danger, shall I never live to see wit and love dwell together?

CAPTAIN I am but a poor soldier, and yet never reached to the honour of being a lover; yet from my own observations, Master Sadd, take a truth; 'tis a folly to believe any woman loves a man for being constant to another, they dissemble their hearts only; and hate a man in love worse than a wencher.

JOLLY And they have reason; for if they have the grace to be kind, he that loves the sex may be theirs.

CARELESS When your constant lover, if a woman have a mind to him, and be blessed with so much grace to discover it; he, out of the noble mistake of honour hates her for it, and tells it perchance, and preaches reason to her passion, and cries, 'Miserable beauty, to be so unfortunate as to inhabit in so much frailty'.

CAPTAIN This counsel makes her hate him more than she loved before; these are troubles, those that love are subject to, while we look on and laugh, to see both thus slaved while we are free.

CARELESS My prayers still shall be, 'Lord deliver me from love'.

CAPTAIN 'Tis plague, pestilence, famine, sword, and sometimes sudden death.

SADD Yet I love, I must love, I will love, and I do love.

CAPTAIN In the present tense.

WIDOW No more of this argument, for love's sake.

CAPTAIN By any means, Madam, give him leave to love, and you are resolved to walk tied up in your own arms, with your love as visible in your face, as your mistress's colours in your hat; that any porter at Charing Cross may take you like a letter at the carrier's, and having read the superscription, deliver Master Sadd to the fair hands of Mistress or my Lady such-a-one, lying at the sign of the hard heart.

PLEASANT And she, if she has wit (as I believe she hath) will scarce pay the post for the packet.

WIDOW Treason, how now niece, join with the enemy? [*they give the Captain wine*]

CAPTAIN A health, Ned, what shall I call it?

CARELESS To Master Sadd, he needs it that avows himself a lover.

SADD Gentlemen, you have the advantage, the time, the place, the company; but we may meet when your wits shall not have such advantage as my love.

PLEASANT No more of love, I am so sick on't.

CONSTANT By your pardon, mistress, I must not leave love thus unguarded, I vow myself his follower.

JOLLY Much good may love do him, give me a glass of wine here; Will, let them keep company with the blind boy,* give us his mother, and let them preach again; hear that will, he has good luck, persuades me 'tis an ugly sin to lie with a handsome woman.

CAPTAIN A pox upon my nurse, she frighted me so when I was young with stories of the devil, I was almost fourteen ere I could

* the blind boy: Cupid, son of Venus.

prevail with reasons to unbind my reason, it was so slaved to faith and conscience; she made me believe wine was an evil spirit, and fornication was like the whore of Babylon, a fine face, but a dragon under her petticoats; and that made me have a mind to peep under all I met since.

WIDOW Fie, fie, for shame, do not talk so; are you not ashamed to glory in sin, as if variety of women were none.

JOLLY Madam, we do not glory in fornication; and yet I thank God, I cannot live without a woman.

CAPTAIN Why, does your ladyship think it a sin to lie with variety of handsome women? If it be, would I were the wickedest man in the company.

PLEASANT You have been marked for an indifferent sinner that way Captain.

CAPTAIN Who I? No faith, I was a fool, but and I were to begin again, I would not do as I have done. I kept one; but if ever I keep another, hang me; nor would I advise any friend of mine to do it.

JOLLY Why, I am sure 'tis a provident and safe way; a man may always be provided and found.

PLEASANT Fie upon this discourse.

CAPTAIN Those considerations betrayed me, a pox; it is a dull sin to travel, like a carrier's horse, always one road.

WIDOW Fie, Captain, repent for shame, and marry.

CAPTAIN Your ladyship would have said, 'Marry, and repent'; no, though it be not the greatest pleasure, yet it is better than marrying; for when I am weary of her, my unconstancy is termed virtue, and I shall be said to turn to grace. Beware of women, for better or worse; for our wicked nature, when her sport is lawful, cloys straight; therefore, rather than marry keep a wench.

JOLLY Faith, he is in the right, for 'tis the same thing in number and kind; and then the sport is quickened, and made poignant with sin.

CAPTAIN Yet 'tis a fault, faith, and I'll persuade all my friends from it; especially here where any innovation is dangerous; 'twas the newness of the sin that made me suffer in the opinion of my friends; and I was condemned by all sorts of people; not that I sinned, but that I sinned no more.

CARELESS Why aye, hadst thou been wicked in fashion, and privily lain with everybody, their guilt would have made them protect thee; so that to be more wicked is to be innocent, at least safe; a wicked world, Lord help us.

CAPTAIN But being particular to her, and not in love, nor subject to it, taking an antidote every morning, before I venture into those infectious places where love and beauty dwell; this enraged the maiden beauties of the time, who thought it a prejudice to their beauties to see me careless, and securely pass by their conquering eyes; my name being found amongst none of those that decked their triumphs. But from this 'tis easy to be safe, for their pride will not let them love, nor my leisure me. Then the old ladies that pay for their pleasures; they, upon the news, beheld me with their natural frowns, despairing when their money could not prevail; and hated me when they heard that I for my pleasure would pay as large as they.

JOLLY Gentlemen, take warning; a fee from every man; for by this day, there's strange counsel in this confession.

WIDOW Captain, you forget to pledge Mr Careless; here, will you not drink a cup of wine. Who's there? Bring the oysters.

CAPTAIN Yes, Madam, if you please.

WILD Proceed, Captain.

PLEASANT Fie, Mr Wild, are you not ashamed to encourage him to this filthy discourse.

CAPTAIN A glass of wine then; and I'll drink to all the new married wives that grieve to think, at what rate their fathers purchase a little husband. These when they lie thirsting for the thing they paid so dear for.

Enter a Servant with oysters.

CARELESS These, methinks, should be thy friends, and point thee out as a man for them.

CAPTAIN Yes, till the faithful nurse cries; 'Alas, Madam, he keeps such a one, he has enough at home'; then she swells with envy and rage against us both, calls my mistress ugly, common, unsafe; and me, a weak secure fool.

JOLLY These are strange truths, Madam.

WIDOW Aye, aye, but these oysters are a better jest.

CAPTAIN But she's abused that will let such reason tame her desire, and a fool in love's school; else she would not be ignorant that variety is such a friend to love, that he which rises a funk coward from the lady's bed would find new fires at her maid's; nor ever yet did the man want fire, if the woman would bring the fuel.

PLEASANT For God's sake, leave this discourse.

WIDOW The captain has a mind we should eat no oysters.

WILD Aunt, we came to be merry, and we will be merry, and you shall stay it out; proceed Captain.

WIDOW Fie Captain, I'm ashamed to hear you talk thus: marry, then you will have a better opinion of women.

CAPTAIN Marry! Yes, this knowledge will invite me, it is a good encouragement, is it not think you? What is your opinion? Were not these marriages made in heaven? By this good day, all the world is mad, and makes haste to be fooled, but we sour: and I hope there's none of us believes there has any marriages been made in heaven, since Adam.

JOLLY By my faith, 'tis thought the devil gave the ring thereto.

WIDOW Nephew, I'll swear I'll be gone.

CAPTAIN [*he points to Sadd*] Hold her, Ned, she goes not yet; there's a fourth kind of women that concerns her more than all the rest, *ecce signum* – She is one of those who, clothed in purple, triumph over their dead husbands; these will be caught at first sight, and at first sight must be catched; 'tis a bird that must be shot flying, for they never sit; if a man delay they cool, and fall into considerations of jointure, and friends' opinion; in which time, if she hears thou keepest a wench, thou had'st better be a beggar in her opinion; for then her pride, it may be, would betray her to the vanity of setting up a proper man; (as they call it) but for a wencher no argument prevails with your widow; for she believes they have spent too much that way, to be able to pay her due benevolence.

WIDOW As I live, I'll be gone if you speak one word more of this uncivil subject.

JOLLY Captain, let me kiss thy cheek, for that widow; you understand this, widow? I say no more; here Captain, here's to thee; as it goes down, a pox of care.

WIDOW Jesus! Mr Jolly, have you no observations of the Court, that are so affected with this of the Town?

CONSTANT Faith, they say, there's good sport there, sometimes.

PLEASANT Mr Jolly is afraid to let us partake of his knowledge.

JOLLY No faith, Madam.

CAPTAIN By this drink, if he stay till I have eaten a few more, I'll describe it.

JOLLY What should I say, 'tis certain the Court is the bravest place in the kingdom, for sport, if it were well looked to, and the game preserved fair; but as 'tis, a man may sooner make a set in the Strand. And it will never be better, whilst your divine lovers inhabit there.

CARELESS Let the king make me master of the game.

CAPTAIN And admit us laity-lovers.

JOLLY I would he would; for as 'tis, there's no hopes amongst the ladies; besides, 'tis such an example to see a king and queen good, husband and wife, that to be kind will grow out of fashion.

CAPTAIN Nay, that's not all, for the women grow malicious, because they are not courted; nay, they bred all the last mischiefs, and called the king's chastity a neglect of them.

JOLLY Thou art in the right; an Edward, or a Harry, with seven queens in buckram, that haught* among the men, and stroked the women, are the monarchs they wish to bow to; they love no tame princes, but lions in the forest.

CAPTAIN Why, and those were properly called the fathers of their people, that were indeed akin to their nobility; now they wear out their youth and beauty, without hope of a monumental ballad, or trophy of a libel that shall hereafter point at such a lord, and cry 'That is the royal son of such a one.'

JOLLY And these were the ways that made them powerful at home; for the City is a kind of tame beast; you may lead her by the horns any whither, if you but tickle them in the ear sometimes. Queen Bess, of famous memory, had the trick on't; and I have heard them say, 'In eighty eight', ere I was born, as well I can remember, 'she rode to Tilbury on that bonny beast, the Mayor'.

CAPTAIN I would I might counsel him; I'd so reform the Court.

* haught: were haughty.

CARELESS Never too soon; for now, when a stranger comes in, and spies a covey of beauties, would make a falconer unhood, before he can draw his leash he is warned that's a marked partridge; and that, and every he, has by their example a particular she.

WILD By this light, the six fair maids stand like the working-days in the Almanac; one with 'A' scored upon her breast, that is as much to say, I belong to such a lord; the next with 'B' for an elder brother; 'C' for such a knight; 'D' possessed with melancholy, and at her breast you may knock an hour ere you get an answer, and then she'll tell you there's no lodging there; she has a constant fellow courtier that has taken up all her heart to his own use: in short, all are disposed of, but the good mother; and she comes in like the Sabbath, at the week's end; and I warrant her make anyone rest that comes at her.

CARELESS Aye marry; but if she were like the Jews' Sabbath, it were somewhat; but this looks like a broken commandment, that has had more work done upon her, than all the week besides.

CAPTAIN And what think you, is not this finely carried? You that are about the king, counsel him, if he will have his sport fair, he must let the game be free, as it has been in former ages; then a stranger that has wit, good means, and handsome clothes, no sooner enters the privy chamber, and beats about with three graceful legs,★ but he springs a mistress that danced as well as he, sung better, as free as fair; those at first sight could speak, for wit is always acquainted: these fools must be akin ere they can speak; and now the friends make the bargain, and they go to bed ere they know why.

JOLLY Faith, he's in the right, you shall have a buzzard now hover and beat after a pretty wench, till she is so weary of him she's forced to take her bed for covert, and find less danger in being trussed than in flying.

CAPTAIN And what becomes of all this pudder, after he has made them sport for one night, to see him touse the quarry, he carries her into the country, and there they two fly at one another till they are weary.

CARELESS And all this mischief comes of love and constancy; we shall never see better days till there be an Act of Parliament

★ three graceful legs: three bows.

against it; enjoining husbands not to till their wives, but change and lay them fallow.

JOLLY A pox, the women will never consent to it; they'll be tilled to death first.

WIDOW Gentlemen, you are very bold with the sex.

CAPTAIN Faith, Madam, it is our care of them; why you see they are married at fourteen, yield a crop and a half, and then die, 'tis merely their love that destroys 'em; for if they get a good husbandman, the poor things yield their very hearts.

PLEASANT And do you blame their loves, gentlemen?

JOLLY No, not their love, but their discretion; let them love, and do, a God's name; but let them do with discretion.

WILD But how will you amend this?

JOLLY Instead of two beds and a physician; I'd have the state prescribe two wives and a mistress.

WILD Ho! It will never be granted; the state is made up of old men, and they find work enough with one.

JOLLY We will petition the lower House, there are young men, and (if it were but to be factious) would pass it, if they thought the upper House would cross it; besides, they ought to do it, Death! They provide against cutting down old trees, and preserving highways and post-horses, and let pretty wenches run to decay?

CARELESS Why may it not come within the Statute of Depopulation? As I live, the state ought to take care of those pretty creatures; be you judge, Madam; is't not a sad sight to see a rich young beauty, with all her innocence and blossoms on, subject to some rough rude fellow, that ploughs her; and esteems and uses her as a chattel, till she is so lean, a man may find as good grass upon the common, where it may be she'll sit coughing with sunk eyes, so weak that a boy (with a dog) that can but whistle, may keep a score of them?

WIDOW You are strangely charitable to our sex, on a sudden.

CAPTAIN I know not what they are; but for my part, I'll be a traitor ere I'll look on, and see beauty go thus to wrack; it is enough, custom has made us suffer them to be enclosed; I am sure, they were created common, and for the use of man, and not intended to be subject to jealousy and choler, or to be bought or sold, or let for term of lives or years, as they are now, or else sold at outcries;* 'Oh! yes; who'll give most take her.'

WIDOW Why do not some of you, excellent men, marry, and mend all these errors, by your good example?

JOLLY Because we want fortunes, to buy rich wives, or keep poor ones, and be loath to get beggars, or whores, as well as I love 'em.

PLEASANT Why, are all their children so that have no fortune think you?

JOLLY No, not all; I have heard of Whittington and his cat, and others, that have made fortunes by strange means; but I scarce believe my son would rise from hope, a halfpenny, and a lamb-skin;† and the wenches commonly having more wit and beauty than money, foreseeing small portions, grow sad, and read romances, till their wit spy some unfortunate merit like their own, without money too, and they two sigh after one another, till they grow mysterious in colours, and become a proverb for their constancy; and when their love has worn out the cause, marry in the end a new couple, then grown ashamed of the know-ledge they so long hunted, at length part, by consent, and vanish into Abigail and governor.

WIDOW Well gentlemen, excuse me for this one time; and if ever I invite you to dinner again, punish me with such another dis-course, in the meantime let's go in and dine, meat stays for us.

CAPTAIN Faith Madam, we were resolved to be merry; we have not met these three years till today, and at the Bear‡ we meant to have dined; and since your ladyship would have our company, you must pardon our humour; here Mistress Sadd, here's the widow's health to you.

[*Exeunt Omnes*]

---

* outcries: auctions.
† hope . . . lambskin: from the proverb about Ralph Thornton, a Newcastle merchant: 'At the west gate came Thornton in/With a hop, a halfpenny and a lamb's-skin.'
‡ the Bear: a well known tavern at the Southwark end of the old London Bridge.

ACT THREE

SCENE I

Enter all from dinner.

WIDOW Nephew, how do you dispose of yourself this afternoon?

WILD We have a design we must pursue, which will rid you of all this troublesome company; and we'll make no excuse, because you peeped into our privacies today.

CARELESS Your humble servant, ladies; gentlemen, we'll leave you to pursue your fortunes. [*Exit Careless*]

JOLLY Farewell widow, may'st thou live unmarried till thou run'st away with thyself. [*Exit Jolly*]

CAPTAIN No, no, when that day comes, command the humblest of your servants. [*Exit Captain*]

WILD Farewell aunt; sweet Mistress Pleasant, I wish you good fortune. [*Exit Wild*]

WIDOW Farewell, farewell gentlemen; [*she speaks aside*] niece, now if we could be rid of these troublesome lovers too, we would go see a play.

PLEASANT Rid of them? Why, they are but now in season; as I live, I would do as little to give mine content as any she in Town, and yet I do not grudge him the happiness of carrying me to a play.

WIDOW Aye, but the world will talk, because they pretend; and then we shall be sure to meet my nephew there, and his wild company, and they will laugh to see us together.

PLEASANT Who will you have? Tim the butler, or Formal your gentleman usher? I would take Philip the foreman of the shop as soon.

WIDOW Let's mask ourselves, and take Secret, and go alone by water.

PLEASANT Yes, and follow her like one of my aunts of the suburbs; it is a good way to know what you may yield in a market; for I'll undertake, there are those shall bid for you before the play will be done.

SECRET As I live, Madam, Mistress Pleasant is in the right; I had such a kindness offered me once, and I came to a price with him in knavery; and hang me, if the rogue was not putting the earnest of his affection into my hand.

WIDOW Let's go to the Glass House* then.

PLEASANT I'll go to a play with my servant, and so shall you; hang opinion, and we'll go to the Glass House afterwards; it is too hot to sup early.

SECRET Pray Madam go, they say 'tis a fine play, and a knight writ it.

PLEASANT Pray let Secret prevail, I'll propose it to the lovers; in the meantime go you, and bid the coachman make ready the coach.

SECRET [*whispers Sadd*] 'Twill take. ⟨*to Widow*⟩ Alas, Madam, he's sick, poor fellow, and gone to bed, he could not wait at dinner.

WIDOW Sick?

PLEASANT Why, see how all things work for the young men, either their coach, or afoot; Mr Constant, what think you of seeing a play this afternoon? Is it not too hot to venture, this infectious time?

CONSTANT Fie, Madam, there's no danger, the Bill† decreased twenty last week.

SADD I swear, they say, 'tis a very good play today.

WIDOW Shall we go, niece?

PLEASANT Faith 'tis hot, and there's nobody but we.

SADD Does that hinder? Pray Madam, grudge us not the favour of venturing yourself in our company.

WIDOW Come, leave this ceremony, I'll go in, and put on my mask; Secret shall bring you yours;

PLEASANT No, I'll go, and put it on within.   [*Exeunt Omnes*]

SCENE II

Enter Wild, Careless, Captain and Jolly.

CARELESS By this day, you have nettled the widow.

WILD The captain neglected his dinner for his mirth, as if he had forgot to eat.

JOLLY When did he oversee his drinking so?

---

* Glass House: probably the Glass House in Broad Street, where Venetian glass was made. There was another in Blackfriars.

† the Bill: the weekly Bill of Mortality. These were issued from 1538 to 1837.

CAPTAIN Gentlemen, still it is my fortune to make your worships merry.

WILD As I live, Captain, I subscribe, and am content to hold my wit as tenant to thee; and tonight I'll invite you to supper, where it shall not be lawful to speak till thou has victualled thy man of war.

CAPTAIN Shall's be merry? What shall we have?

WILD Half a score dishes of meat, choose them yourself.

CAPTAIN Provide me then the chines fried, and the salmon calvered, a carp, and black sauce, red-deer in the blood, and an assembly of woodcocks, and jacksnipes, so fat you would think they had their winding sheets on; and upon these, as their pages, let me have wait your Sussex wheat-ear, with a feather in his cap; over all which let our countryman, General Chine of Beef, command: I hate your French *potage*, that looks as the cook-maid had more hand in it than the cook.

WILD I'll promise you all this.

CARELESS And let me alone to cook the fish.

CAPTAIN You cook it? No, no, I left an honest fellow in Town, when I went into Italy, Signior Ricardo Ligones, one of the ancient house of the Armenian Ambassadors; if he be alive he shall be our cook.

WILD Is he so excellent at it?

CAPTAIN Excellent? You shall try, you shall try; why, I tell you, I saw him once dress a shoeing-horn, and a joiner's apron, that the company left pheasant for it.

WILD A shoeing-horn?

CAPTAIN Yes, a shoeing-horn; marry, there was garlic in the sauce.

WILD Is this all you would have?

CAPTAIN This, and a bird of paradise, to entertain the rest of the night, and let me alone to cook her.

WILD A bird of paradise, what's that?

CAPTAIN A girl of fifteen, smooth as satin, white as her Sunday apron, plump, and of the first down: I'll take her with her guts in her belly, and warm her with a country dance or two, then pluck her, and lay her dry betwixt a couple of sheets; there pour into her so much oil of wit as will make her turn to a man, and stick into her heart three corns of whole love, to make her taste of what she is doing, then having strewed a man all over her, shut the door, and leave us, we'll work ourselves into such a sauce as you can never surfeit on, so poignant and yet no hogough;* take heed of a hogough, your onion and woman make the worst sauce; this shook together by an English cook (for your French seasoning spoils many a woman) and there's a dish for a king.

WILD For the first part, I'll undertake.

CARELESS But this for supper; Captain, no more of this now; this afternoon, as you are true to the petticoat, observe your instructions, and meet at Ned's house in the evening.

OMNES We will not fail.

CAPTAIN I must write to Wanton, to know how things stand at home, and to acquaint her how we have thrived with the old lady today.

WILD Whither will you go to write?

CAPTAIN To thy house, 'tis hard by, there's the Fleece.

JOLLY Do, and in the meantime I'll go home and dispatch a little business, and meet you.

WILD Make haste then.

JOLLY Where shall I meet you?

WILD Whither shall we go till it be time to attend the design.

CARELESS Let's go to Court for an hour.

JOLLY Do, I'll meet you at the queen's side.

WILD No, prithee, we are the monsieurs new come over; and if we go fine they will laugh at us, and think we believe ourselves so; if not, then they will abuse our clothes, and swear we went into France only to have our cloaks cut shorter.

CARELESS Will you go see a play?

CAPTAIN Do, and thither I'll come to you, if it be none of our gentlemen poets, that excuse their writings with a prologue that professes they are no scholars.

JOLLY On my word this is held the best penned of the time, and he has writ a very good play; by this day, it was extremely applauded.

CAPTAIN Does he write plays by the day; indeed a man would ha' judged him a labouring poet.

JOLLY A labouring poet? By this hand he's a knight; upon my

* hogough: *haut-goût*, a highly flavoured relish or savoury.

recommendation venture to see it; hang me if you be not extremely well satisfied.

CARELESS A knight and write plays? It may be, but 'tis strange to us; so they say there are other gentlemen poets without land or Latin; this was not ordinary; prithee when was he knighted?

JOLLY In the north, the last great knighting, when 'twas God's great mercy we were not all knights.

WILD I'll swear, they say, there are poets that have more men in liveries, than books in their studies.

CAPTAIN And what think you, gentlemen, are not these things to start a man? I believe 'tis the first time you have found them lie at the sign of the Page, Foot-men and Gilded Coaches; they were wont to lodge at the Thin Cloak, they and their muses made up the family; and thence sent scenes to their patrons, like boys in at windows, and one would return with a doublet, another with a pair of breeches, a third with a little ready money; which, together with their credit with a company, in three terms you rarely saw a poet repaired.

JOLLY This truth nobody denies.

WILD Prithee let us resolve what we shall do, lest we meet with some of them: for it seems they swarm, and I fear nothing like a dedication, though it be but of himself; for I must hear him say more than either I deserve or he believes; I hate that in a poet, they must be dull, or all upon all subjects; so that they can oblige none but their muse.

JOLLY I perceive by this you will not see the play; what think you of going to Sim's,★ to bowls, till I come?

CARELESS Yes, if you will go to see that comedy; but there is no reason we should pay for our coming in, and Act Two; like some whose interest in the timber robs them of their reason, and they run as if they had stolen a bias.

WILD Resolve what you will do, I am contented.

CARELESS Let's go walk in the Spring Garden.†

★ Sim's: Simon Wadloe was the landlord of the Devil Tavern in Ben Jonson's day: the tavern was situated between Temple Bar and the Middle Temple Gate.
† Spring Garden: between St James's Park and Charing Cross, a garden laid out by Charles I as a bowling green, so-called because of a spring which wet anyone who walked above it. The New Spring Garden was at Vauxhall.

WILD I'll do it for company, but I had as lief be rid in the Horse-market, as walk in that fools' fair; where neither wit nor money is, nor sure to take up a wench; there's none but honest women.

CAPTAIN A pox on't, what should we do there? Let's go and cross the field to Pike's,★ her kitchen is cool winter and summer.

CARELESS I like that motion well, but we have no time, and I hate to do that business by half; after supper, if you will, we'll go and make a night on't.

CAPTAIN Well, I must go write, therefore resolve of somewhat; shall I propose an indifferent place where 'tis probable we shall all meet.

OMNES Yes.

CAPTAIN Go you before to the Devil,† and I'll make haste after.

CARELESS Agreed, we shall be sure of good wine there and in *fresco*, for he is never without patent snow.‡

WILD Patent snow, what doth that project hold?

JOLLY Yes, faith, and now there is a commission appointed for toasts against the next winter.

WILD Marry, they are wise, and foresaw the Parliament, and were resolved their monopolies should be no grievance to the people.

CAPTAIN Farewell, you will be sure to meet.

OMNES Yes, yes.   [*Exeunt Omnes*]

SCENE III

Enter Wanton and her Maid, with her lap full of things.

WANTON Bid them ply him close and flatter him, and rail upon the old lady and the captain; and, do you hear, give him some hints to begin the story of his life, do it handsomely, and you shall see how the sack will clip his tongue.

MAID I warrant you, I'll fit him.

WANTON When he is in his discourse, leave him and come down into the parlour, and steal away his box with the false rings that stands by his bedside; I have all his little plate here already.

MAID Make you haste, I'll warrant you I'll dress him.   [*Exeunt*]

★ Pike's: Pike Garden in Southwark.   † the Devil: the Devil Tavern.
‡ patent snow: for cooling drink.

SCENE IV

Enter the Captain, with a letter in his hand, and his Boy to him with a candle, his going to write the superscription.

BOY Sir, the Lady Love-All passed by even now.

CAPTAIN The Lady Love-All? Which way went she.

BOY To the rich lady the widow, where your worship dined.

CAPTAIN 'Tis no matter; here, carry this letter, and bring an answer to the Devil quickly; and tell her we'll stay there till the time be fit for the design. [*Exeunt*]

SCENE V

Enter Careless, Wild, and a Drawer, at the Devil.

CARELESS Jack, how goes the world? Bring us some bottles of the best wine.

DRAWER You shall, Sir; your worship is welcome into England.

CARELESS Why look you, who says a drawer can say nothing, but 'Anan, anan, Sir'? Score a quart of sack in the half-moon.*

DRAWER Your worship is merry; but I'll fetch you that, Sir, shall speak Greek,† and make your worship prophesy, you drank none such in your journey.

WILD Do it then, and make a hole in this angel‡ thou may'st creep through; [*gives him an angel*] who is't that peeps, a fiddler? Bring him by the ears.

Enter the Tailor that pipes.

TAILOR A tailor, an't like your worship.

CARELESS A tailor? Hast thou a stout faith?

TAILOR I have had, an't like your worship; but now I am in despair.

CARELESS Why then thou art damned; go, go home, and throw thyself into thine own hell, it is the next way to the other.

TAILOR I hope your worship is not displeased.

---

* the half-moon: a room in the tavern. † speak Greek: be merry, get drunk.
‡ angel: a gold coin worth about ten shillings, last coined by Charles I. It bore a device of St Michael killing a dragon.

CARELESS What dost do here? A tailor without faith, dost come to take measure of ours?

TAILOR No, I come to speak with one Master Jolly, a courtier, a very fine-spoken gentleman, and a just compter, but one of the worst paymasters in the world.

WILD [*aside* ⟨*to Careless*⟩] As thou lovest me, let's keep him here till he comes, and make him valiant with sack that he may urge him till he beats him; we shall have the sport, and be revenged upon the rogue for dunning a gentleman in a tavern.

CARELESS ⟨*to Wild*⟩ I'll charge him: ⟨*to Tailor*⟩ here drink, poor fellow, and stay in the next room till he comes.

TAILOR I thank your worship, but I am fasting; and if it please your worship to call for a dozen of manchets* that I may eat a crust first, then I'll make bold with a glass of your sack.

WILD Here, here, drink in the meantime, fetch him some bread.

TAILOR Will your worship have me drink all this vessel of sack?

CARELESS Yes, yes, off with't, 'twill do you no harm. [*the Tailor drinks*]

WILD Why do you not take some order with that Jolly to make him pay thee?

TAILOR I have petitioned him often, but can do no good.

CARELESS A pox upon him, petition him, his heart is hardened to ill, threaten to arrest him; nothing but ⟨a⟩ serjeant can touch his conscience.

TAILOR Truly, gentlemen, I have reason to be angry, for he uses me ill, when I ask him for my money.

JOLLY [*speaks within*] Where is Master Wild, and Master Careless?

TAILOR I hear his voice.

JOLLY Let the coach stay.

Enter Jolly.

How now, who would he speak with?

WILD Do not you know?

JOLLY Yes, and be you judge if the rogue does not suffer deservedly; I have bid him any time this twelve month but send his wife, and I'll pay her, and the rogue replies, nobody shall lie with his wife but himself.

* manchets: small loaves of fine wheaten bread.

CARELESS Nay, if you be such a one.

TAILOR No more they shall not, I am but a poor man.

JOLLY By this hand, he's drunk.

TAILOR Nay then, I arrest you in mine own name at his Majesty's suit.

WILD As I live, thou shalt not beat him.

JOLLY Beat him? I'll kiss him, I'll pay him, and carry him about with me, and be at the charge of sack to keep him in the humour. [*he hugs the quart-pot*]

TAILOR Help, rescue, I'll have his body, no bail shall serve.

Enter Drawer.

DRAWER Sir, yonder is a gentleman would speak with you; I do not like his followers.

JOLLY What are they, bailiffs?

DRAWER Little better.

JOLLY Send him up alone, and stand you ready at the stair's feet.

CARELESS How* can that be?

JOLLY It is the scrivener at the corner, pick a quarrel with him for coming into our company; the drawers will be armed behind them, and we will so rout the rascals; take your swords, and let him sleep.

CARELESS What scrivener?

JOLLY Cropp the Brownist,† he that the ballad was made on.

CARELESS What ballad?

JOLLY Have not you heard of the scrivener's wife that brought the blackamoor from the Holy Land, and made him a Brownist; and in pure charity lay with him, and was delivered of a magpie; a pied prophet; which when the elect saw, they prophesied, if it lived, 'twould prove a great enemy to their sect; for the midwife cried out, ''Twas born a bishop, with tippet and white-sleeves'; at which the zealous mother cried, 'Down with the idol'; so the midwife and she in pure devotion killed it.

WILD Killed it? What became of them?

JOLLY Why, they were taken and condemned, and suffered under

---

* How: Kentish dialect for 'Who'.

† Brownist: a follower of Robert Browne (1549–1630), an extreme Puritan, who loathed bishops and was generally anti-authoritarian in his views.

a catholic sheriff, that afflicted them with the litany all the way
from Newgate to the gallows, which in roguery he made to be
set up altar-wise too, and hanged them without a psalm.

WILD But how took they that breach of privilege?

JOLLY I know not, Gregory* turned them off, and so they des-
cended, and became Brown martyrs.

WILD And is the husband at door now?

JOLLY Yes, yes, but he's married again to a rich widow at Wapping,
a wench of another temper, one that you cannot please better
than by abusing him; I always pick quarrels with him, that she
may reconcile us, the peace is always worth a dinner, at least.
Hark, I hear him. –

⟨*Enter Cropp*⟩

Save you Mr Cropp, you are come in the nick to pledge a health.

CROPP No, Sir, I have other business, shall I be paid my money,
or no?

JOLLY [*drinks*] Yes.

CROPP Sir?

JOLLY You asked whether you should be paid your money, or no,
and I said, 'Yes'.

CROPP Pray, Sir be plain.

CARELESS And be you so, Sir; how durst you come into this
room, and company, without leave?

CROPP Sir, I have come into good lords' company, ere now.

CARELESS It may be so, but you shall either fall upon your knees,
and pledge this health, or you come no more into lords' company,
no, by these hilts.

CROPP 'Tis idolatry; do, martyr me, I will not kneel, nor join in
sin with the wicked. [*they tug him and make him kneel*]

JOLLY Either kneel, or I'll tear thy cloak, which by the age and
looks, may be that which was writ for† in the time of the primitive
church.

CROPP Pay me, and I'll wear a better; it would be honestlier done,

---

* Gregory: Gregory Brandon, the hangman. His son Richard succeeded him
before 1640, and died in 1649.
† writ for: St Paul asked Timothy to bring a cloak he had left behind at
Troas. II Timothy, IV, 13.

than to abuse this, and profane the text; a text that shows your bishops in those days wore no lawn sleeves; and you may be ashamed to protect him that will not pay his debts; the cries of the widow come against you for it.

JOLLY Remember, sirrah, the dinners and suppers, fat venison and good words, I was fain to give you, christening your children still, by the way of brokage; count that charge, and how often I have kept you from fining for sheriff, and thou art in my debt; then I am damned for speaking well of thee so often against my conscience, which you never consider.

CROPP I am an honest man, Sir.

JOLLY Then ushering your wife, and Mistress Ugly her daughter, to plays and masques at Court; you think these courtesies deserve nothing in the hundred; 'tis true, they made room for themselves with their dagger elbows; and when Spider your daughter laid about her with her breath, the devil would not have sat near her.

CROPP You did not borrow my money with this language.

JOLLY No, sirrah; then I was fain to flatter you, and endure the familiarity of your family, and hear (nay fain sometimes to join in) the lying praises of the holy sister that expired at Tyburn.

CROPP Do, abuse her, and be cursed; 'tis well known she died a martyr; and her blood will be upon some of you, 'tis her orphan's money I require; and this is the last time I'll ask it, I'll find a way to get it. [*he offers to go, and Jolly stays him*]

JOLLY Art serious? By that light, I'll consent, and take it for an infinite obligation if thou wilt teach the rest of my creditors that trick; 'twill save me a world of labour; for, hang me if I know how to do't.

CROPP Well, Sir, since I see your resolution, I shall make it my business.

CARELESS Prithee, let's be rid of this fool.

CROPP Fool? Let him pay the fool his money, and he'll be gone.

JOLLY No, Sir, not a farthing; 'twas my business to borrow it, and it shall be yours to get it in again; nay, by this hand, I'll be feasted too, and have good words; nay, thou shalt lend me more ere thou get'st this again.

CROPP I'll lay my action upon you.

JOLLY Your action you rogue, lay two.

CARELESS Lay three for battery; [*they kick him and thrust him out of the room.* ⟨*As they go, Careless looks back*⟩] what have we here? A she-creditor too? Who would she speak with?

Enter Faithful, Wild and Careless return and meet her.

WILD She looks as if she had trusted in her time.

CARELESS Would you speak with any here, old gentlewoman?

FAITHFUL My business is to Mr Jolly.

CARELESS From yourself, or are you but a messenger?

FAITHFUL My business, Sir, is from a lady.

CARELESS From a lady? From what lady, pray? Why so coy?

FAITHFUL From a lady in the Town.

CARELESS Hoh! Hoh! From a lady in the Town; is it possible I should have guessed you came from a lady in the suburbs, or some country-madam, by your riding face?

Enter Jolly again.

JOLLY I think we have routed the rascals. Faithful? What makes thy gravity in a tavern?

FAITHFUL Sport, it seems, for your saucy companions.

JOLLY Ho, ho, mull,* ho; no fury, Faithful.

FAITHFUL 'Tis well, Sir; my lady presents her service to you, and hath sent you a letter, there's my business.

CARELESS Prithee, who is her lady?

JOLLY The Lady Love-all.

CARELESS Oh, oh, does she serve that old lady? God help her.

FAITHFUL God help her: pray for yourself, Sir, my lady scorns your prayers.

JOLLY Faithful, come hither; prithee is thy lady drunk?

FAITHFUL Drunk, Sir?

JOLLY Aye, drunk, or mad, she'd never writ this else; she requires me, here, to send back by you the pearl she gave me this morning; which sure she'd never do if she were sober; for you know, I earned them hard.

FAITHFUL I know? What do I know? You will not defame my lady, will you?

CARELESS By no means, this is by way of counsel; fie, give a thing,

* mull: a heifer, cow; hence wench.

and take a thing;* if he did not perform, he shall come at night, and pay his scores.

FAITHFUL 'Tis well, Sir; is this your return for my lady's favours? Shall I have the pearl, Sir?

JOLLY No; and tell her 'tis the opinion of us all, he that opens her stinking oyster is worthy of the pearl.

FAITHFUL You are a foul-mouthed fellow, sirrah; and I shall live to see you load a gallows, when my lady shall find the way to her own again.

JOLLY If she miss, there are divers can direct her, you know; adieu, Faithful, do you hear? Steal privately down by the back door, lest some knavish boy spy thee, and call thine age, bawd.

[*Exit Faithful*]

CARELESS Prithee, who is this thing?

JOLLY 'Tis my lady's waiting-woman, her bawd, her she confessor, herself at second hand; her beginning was simple and below stairs, till her lady finding her to be a likely promising bawd; secret as the key at her girdle, obedient as her thoughts, those virtues raised her from the flat petticoat, and kercher, to the gorget† and bum-roll;‡ and I remember 'twas good sport at first, to see the wench perplexed with her metamorphosis; she since has been in love with all the family, and now sighs after the levite; and if he forsake her too, I prophesy, a waiting-woman's curse will fall upon her, to die old, despised, poor, and out of fashion.

Enter Captain.

CAPTAIN Why do you not hang out a painted cloth? And take two pence a piece, and let in all the tame fools at door, those sons of wonder that now gape, and think you mad.

CARELESS 'Tis no matter what they think, madness is proper here; are not taverns Bacchus his temples, the place of madness, does not the sign of madness hang out at the door?

JOLLY While we within possess our joys and cups, as full of pleasure as weeping Niobe's afflicted eyes were swelled with grief and

---

* give . . . thing: a proverbial saying: 'Give a thing and take a thing/To wear the devil's golden ring'.

† gorget: an embroidered wimple.

‡ bum-roll: the equivalent of a Victorian bustle.

tears; blessing on the cause that made our joys thus complete; for see Plutus in our pockets, Mars by our sides, Bacchus in our head, self-love in our hearts, and change of virgins in our arms, beauties whose eyes and hearts speak love and welcome; no rigid thinkers, no niggard beauties that maliciously rake up their fire in green sickness to preserve a spark that shall flame only in some dull day of marriage; let such swear and forswear, till (of the whole parish) they love each other least, whilst we wisely set out our cobwebs in the most perspicuous places to catch these foolish flies.

CARELESS He's in the right; dost think we retreated hither to beat a bargain for a score of sheep, or dispute the legality of votes, and weigh the power of prerogative and Parliament, and club for concluding sack, or read the Fathers here, till we grow costive, like those that have worn their suffering elbows bare, to find a knowledge to perplex 'em? A pox on such brain-breaking thoughts; avoid them, and take with me into thy hand a glass of eternal sack, and prophesy the restoration of senses, and the fall of a lover from grace, which our dear friend, Mr Jolly, will prove to whom the Lady Love-all (by Faithful lately departed) sent for the pearl you wot of.

CAPTAIN But, I hope, he had the grace to keep them.

JOLLY No, no; I'm a fool, I.

CAPTAIN Was not my boy here?

JOLLY No, we saw him not.

CAPTAIN A pox of the rogue, he's grown so lazy.

WILD Your boy is come in just now, and called for the key of the back door, there's women with him.

CAPTAIN Oh! That's well, 'tis Wanton; I sent for her, to laugh over the story of the old lady and her pearl; where have you been all this while, sirrah?

Enter Boy.

BOY I could overtake the coach, Sir, no sooner.

CAPTAIN The coach? What coach?

BOY The Lady Love-all's.

CAPTAIN The Lady Love-all's? Why what had you to do with her coach?

BOY I went to give her the letter your worship sent her.

CAPTAIN The letter? What letter?

BOY That your worship gave me.

CAPTAIN That I writ, at Ned's house, to Wanton?

BOY The letter you gave me, Sir, was directed to the Lady Love-all, and she stormed like a mad-woman at the reading of it.

CARELESS Why, thou wilt not beat the boy for thy own fault? What letter was it?

CAPTAIN 'Twas enough, only a relation of the pearl, wherein she finds herself sufficiently abused to Wanton.

JOLLY Now, gentlemen, you have two to laugh at.

CAPTAIN A pox of fooling, let's resolve what to do, there's no denying, for she has all the particulars under my hand.

BOY You must resolve of something, for she's coming, and stayed only till the back door was opened.

CAPTAIN How did she know I was here?

BOY Your worship bade me tell her, you would stay here for her.

CARELESS How came this mistake?

CAPTAIN Why, the devil ought* us a shame it seems. You know I went home to give Wanton an account how we advanced in our design; and when I was writing the superscription, I remember the boy came in and told me the Lady Love-all passed by.

JOLLY And so, it seems, you in pure mistake directed your letter to her.

CARELESS Well, resolve what you'll do with her, when she comes.

CAPTAIN Faith, bear it like men, 'tis but an old lady lost; let's resolve to defy her, we are sure of our pearl; but lest we prolong the war, take the first occasion you can all to avoid the room; when she's alone, I'll try whether she'll listen to a composition.

JOLLY Have you no friends in the close committee?

CAPTAIN Yes, yes, I am an Essex man.†

CARELESS Then get some of them to move, it may be voted no letter.

JOLLY Aye, aye; and after 'tis voted no letter, then vote it false, scandalous and illegal, and that is in it; they have a precedent for it in the Danish packet, which they took from a foolish fellow, who presuming upon the Law of Nations, came upon an embassy to the king without an order, or pass from both Houses.

* ought: owed.   † an Essex man: a simpleton.

Enter Love-all and Faithful.

LOVE-ALL Sir, I received a letter, but by what accident I know not; for I believe it was not intended me, though the contents concern me.

CAPTAIN Madam, 'tis too late to deny it; is it peace or war you bring? Without dispute, if war, I hang out my defiance; if peace, I yield my weapon into your hands.

LOVE-ALL Are you all unworthy? Your whole sex falsehood? Is it not possible to oblige a man to be loyal? This is such a treachery no age can match; apply yourself with youth and wit to gain a lady's love and friendship only to betray it? Was it not enough you commanded my fortune, but you must wreck my honour too, and instead of being grateful for that charity which still assisted your wants, strive to pay men with injuries, and attempt to make the world believe I pay to lose my fame? [*he smiles*] And then make me the scorned subject of your whore's mirth; base and unworthy, do you smile, false one? I shall find a time for you too, and my vengeance shall find you all.

FAITHFUL Yea, Sir; and you that had such a ready wit to proclaim my lady, whore and me bawd, I hope to see you load a gallows for it.

CAPTAIN Once again, is it peace or war?

LOVE-ALL Peace? I'll have thy blood first, dog; where's my pearl? [*she speaks to Wild*] – You ought to right me, Sir, in this particular; it was to you I sent them.

WILD Madam, I sent not for them.

CAPTAIN No more words; I have them, I earned them, and you paid them.

FAITHFUL You are a foul-mouthed fellow, sirrah.

LOVE-ALL Peace, wench, I scorn their slander, it cannot shake my honour; 'tis too weighty and too fixed for their calumny.

JOLLY I'll be sworn for my part on't, I think it is a great honour; I am sure I had as much as I could carry away in ten nights, and yet there was no miss on't.

CAPTAIN You? I think so; there's no mark of my work, you see, and yet I came after thee, and brought away loads would have sunk a sedan-man.

WILD By this relation she should be a woman of a great fame.

CARELESS Let that consideration, with her condition, and her age, move some reverence, at least to what she was; Madam, I am sorry I cannot serve you in this particular.

[Exeunt Jolly and Careless]

LOVE-ALL I see all your mean baseness, pursue your scorn; come, let's go, wench, I shall find some to right my fame; and though I have lost my opinion, I have gained a knowledge how to distinguish of love hereafter; and I shall scorn you and all your sex, that have not soul enough to value a noble friendship.

WILD Pray, Madam, let me speak with you.

CAPTAIN We'll have no whispering; I said it, and I'll maintain it with my sword.

Enter Drawer.

DRAWER Sir, there's one without would speak with you?

CAPTAIN With me?

DRAWER No, Sir, with Master Wild.

WILD Madam, I'll wait upon you presently.   *[Exit Wild]*

CAPTAIN Madam, I know my company is displeasing to you, therefore I'll take my leave; Drawer, show me another room?

[The Captain makes a turn or two, they look at each other, then he goes out]

LOVE-ALL O Faithful, Faithful; I am most miserably abused, and can find no way to my revenge.

FAITHFUL Madam, I'll give them ratsbane, and speedily too, ere they can tell; for that rascal the captain has a tongue else, will proclaim you, and undo your fame for ever.

LOVE-ALL Aye, aye, my fame, my fame, Faithful; and if it were not for mine honour, (which I have kept unstained to this minute) I would not care.

FAITHFUL This it is; you will still set your affection upon every young thing; I could but tell you on't.

LOVE-ALL Who could have suspected they would have been so false in their loves to me that have been so faithful to them. –

Enter Drawer.

Honest friend, where is Master Wild?

DRAWER The other gentlemen carried him away with them?

LOVE-ALL Are they all gone then?

DRAWER Yes, by this hand; these gentlemen are quickly satisfied; [*aside*] what an ugly whore they have got! How she states it!

LOVE-ALL Come, let's go wench. [*she offers to go*]

DRAWER Mistress, who pays the reckoning?

LOVE-ALL What says he?

FAITHFUL He asks me, who pays the reckoning?

LOVE-ALL Who pays the reckoning? Why, what have we to do with the reckoning?

DRAWER Shut the door, Dick, we'll have the reckoning before you go.

FAITHFUL Why, goodman sauce-box, you will not make my lady pay for their reckoning, will you?

DRAWER My lady? A pox of her title, she'd need of something to make her pass.

FAITHFUL What do you say, sirrah?

DRAWER I say, the gentlemen paid well for their sport; and I know no reason why we should lose our reckoning.

LOVE-ALL What do you take me for, my friend?

DRAWER In troth, I take you for nothing; but I would be loath to take you for that use I think they made shift with you for.

FAITHFUL Madam, this is that rascally captain's plot.

LOVE-ALL Patience, patience. O for a bite at the slave's heart. Friend, mistake me not, my name is Love-all, a lady; send one along with me and you shall have your money.

DRAWER You must pardon me, Madam, I am but a servant; if you be a lady pray sit in an inner room, and send home your woman for the money; the sum is six pounds, and be pleased to remember the waiters.

LOVE-ALL Go Faithful, go fetch the money. O revenge, revenge: shall I lose my honour, and have no revenge.

[*Exeunt Omnes*]

ACT FOUR

SCENE I

Enter Wanton, Captain, Careless and Wild.

WANTON By all that a longing bride hopes for, which I am not,
I am better pleased with this revenge than mine own plot, which
takes as I could wish; I have so anointed my high priest with sack,
that he would have confuted Baal's priest; and now he does so
slumber in his ale, and calls to bed already, swears the sun is
set.

CAPTAIN Faith, wench, her abusing of me made me leave her for
the reckoning.

CARELESS Yes, faith, they have treated her upsey whore* lain
with her, told, and then pawned her.

WANTON Yes, yes, you are fine things; I wonder women can endure you; for me, I expect you worse, and am armed for't.

WILD Faith let's send and release her, the jest is gone far enough;
as I live, I pity her.

WANTON Pity her? Hang her, and rid the country of her, she is
a thing wears out her limbs as fast as her clothes, one that never
goes to bed at all, nor sleeps in a whole skin, but is taken to pieces
like a motion,† as if she were too long; she should be hanged for
offering to be a whore.

CAPTAIN As I live, she is in the right; I peeped once to see what
she did before she went to bed; by this light, her maids were dis-
secting her; and when they had done, they brought some of her
to bed, and the rest they either pinned or hung up, and so she lay
dismembered till morning; in which time, her chamber was
strewed all over, like an anatomy school.

WANTON And when she travels anywhere she is transported with
as great a care, and fear of spoiling, as a juggler's motion, when
he removes from fair to fair.

CARELESS She is a right broken gamester, who, though she lacks
wherewithal to play, yet loves to be looking on.

Enter Wanton's Maid ⟨Bawd⟩.

* upsey whore: in the manner of a whore.　　† motion: a puppet.

BAWD He is awake, and calls for you impatiently, he would fain be in bed, the company is all gone.

WANTON Are you instructed?

BAWD Let me alone, I'll warrant you for my part.

WANTON Farewell then, you are all ready; who plays Master Constable?

CAPTAIN I, I; and Ned Jolly the sumner.*

WANTON Farewell, farewell then.   [Exeunt Wanton and Bawd]

WILD It is a delicate wench.

CARELESS She has excellent flesh, and a fine face; by this light, we must depose the captain from his reign here. [they whisper this]

WILD I like her shrewdly; I hate a wench that is all whore and no company; this is a comedy all day, and a fair at night.

CARELESS I hope to exalt the parson's horn here.

CAPTAIN And what think you? Is it not a sweet sin, this lying with another man's wife?

Wanton above.

WANTON Is Jolly come.

CAPTAIN No, but he'll be here instantly.

WILD Is he abed?

WANTON Yes, yes, and he sleeps as if he had been put to bed by his sexton, with dust to dust, and ashes to ashes.

CAPTAIN And we'll wake him with that shall be as terrible to him as the latter day.

WANTON Let him sleep a while that he may be fresh, else the jest is spoiled; for it is his sense of his disgrace must work my ends.

WILD I'll go home then, and get supper ready, and expect you.

Enter Jolly.

CAPTAIN Do, our scene lies here; who's there, Jolly?

JOLLY Yes.

CAPTAIN Are you fitted?

JOLLY Yes, I have got the Blackfriars' music; I was fain to stay till the last act; and who do you think I saw there?

WILD I know not.

* sumner: a man employed to summon persons to appear in court.

JOLLY Guess.

WILD Prithee, I cannot guess.

JOLLY Your aunt and Mistress Pleasant, and trusty Secret.

WILD What man?

JOLLY The lovers only, so close in a box!

CAPTAIN It will be a match, and there's an end; prithee let them go to't; what is't to us, let's mind our business now, and think on them hereafter.

WANTON A pox upon them for a couple of stalk-hounds; have they killed at last? Why, this is fools' fortune;* it would be long enough ere one that has wit got such a wife.

CAPTAIN No more of this now; have you borrowed the watchmen's coats?

JOLLY Yes, and bills, beards, and constable's staff, and lanthorn; and let me alone to fit him, for the sumner; but when this is done I expect my fee, a tithe night at least; Wanton, I will lie with thee for thy roguery; what are you dumb, you will not refuse me, I hope?

WANTON Not, if I thought thou desired'st it; but I hate to have it desired indifferently, and but so so done neither when 'tis done.

JOLLY I hope you will not disgrace my work, will you?

WANTON Faith, they say thy pleasure lies in thy tongue; and therefore, though I do not give thee leave to lie with me, yet I will give thee as good a thing that will please thee as well.

JOLLY Some roguery I expected.

WANTON No faith, I am serious; and because I will please you both, Master Wild shall lie here, and you shall have leave to say you do, which will please you as well.

JOLLY Faith, and my part is some pleasure, else, 'I have loved, enjoyed, and told', is mistook.

WANTON Aye, but never to love, seldom enjoy, and always tell? Faugh, it stinks, and stains worse than Shoreditch dirt, and women hate and dread men for't; why, I that am a whore professed cannot see youth digest it, though it be my profit and interest. For to be a private whore in this Town starves in the nest like young birds when the old one's killed.

* fools' fortune: proverbial expression, the luck of a fool, or fools have fortune.

CARELESS Excellent girl, 'tis too true Jolly; your tongue has kept many a woman honest.

WANTON Faith, 'tis a truth, this I shall say, you may all better your pleasures by, if you will observe it; I dare say, the fear of telling keeps more women honest than Bridewell hemp; and were you wise men, and true lovers of liberty, now were the time to bring wenching to that perfection no age could ever have hoped; now you may sow such seed of pleasure, you may be prayed for hereafter; now, in this age of zeal and ignorance, would I have you four, in old clothes, and demure looks, present a petition to both Houses, and say, you are men touched in conscience for your share in that wickedness which is known to their worships by the pleasure of adultery, and desire it may be death,* and that a law may be passed to that purpose; how the women will pray for you, and at their own charges rear statues in memory of their benefactors; the young and kind would then haunt your chambers, pray, and present you, and court the sanguine youth, for the sweet sin secured by such a law; none would lose an occasion, nor churlishly oppose kind nature, nor refuse to listen to her summons, when youth and passion calls for those forbidden sweets; when such security as your lives are at stake, who would fear to trust; with this law all oaths and protestations are cancelled; letters and bawds would grow useless too; by instinct the kind will find the kind; and having one nature become of one mind; now we lose an age, to observe and know a man's humour, ere we dare trust him; but get this law, then 'tis, like and enjoy; and whereas now, with expense of time and fortune, you may glean some one mistress amongst your neighbours' wives, you shall reap women whole armfuls as in the common field; there is one small town, wise only in this law; and I have heard them say, that know it well, there has been but one execution this hundred years; yet the same party searched seven years, and could not find an honest woman in the town.

CARELESS An excellent plot, let us about it; ink and paper, dear Wanton, we will draw the petition presently.

* it may be death: Acts against adultery, fornication and incest were passed in Cromwell's parliament. A case was recorded in 1653 of a man of eighty-nine being executed for committing adultery with a woman of more than sixty.

WANTON Will Master Jolly consent too? You must not then, as soon as a handsome woman is named, smile, and stroke your beard, tell him that is next you, you have lain with her; such a lie is as dangerous as a truth, and 'twere but justice to have thee hanged for a sin thou never committed'st, for having defamed so many women.

JOLLY If all those liars were hanged, I believe the scale would weigh down the guilty.

WANTON One rogue hanged, for example, would make a thousand kind girls: if it take it shall be called my law, Wanton's law; then we may go in petticoats again, for women grew imperious and wore the breeches, only to fright the poor cuckolds, and make the fools digest their horns – Are you all ready, shall I open the door?

CAPTAIN Yes.

WILD I'll expect you at my house.

OMNES We'll come, we'll come.

> *[Exit Wild one way, and the rest of the company another]*

CAPTAIN So, knock louder.

They knock within, and the Parson discovered in his bed and the Bawd with him.

PARSON Who's there? What would you have?

CAPTAIN Here's his Majesty's watch, and Master Constable's worship must come in; we have a warrant from the Lords to search for a delinquent.

PARSON You come not here, I'll answer your warrant tomorrow.

JOLLY Break open the door.

PARSON I would you durst.

BAWD Lord! Dear what shall we do?

PARSON Why, sweet, I'll warrant you, art thou not my wife, my rib, bone of my bone? I'll suffer anything ere one hair of thee shall be touched.

BAWD Hark, they break open the door.

PARSON They dare not; why dost thou tremble so? Alas, sweet innocence, how it shakes?

CAPTAIN Break open the door.

PARSON I'll complain to the bishop of this insolence.

BAWD They come, they come, lamb.

⟨*They enter in.*⟩

PARSON No matter sweet; they dare not touch thee; what would you have Mr Constable? You are very rude.

CAPTAIN Read our warrant, and our business will excuse us? ⟨*he delivers the warrant*⟩ Do you know any such person as you find there?

PARSON Yes, Sir, but not by this name; such a woman is my wife, and no Lindabrides;★ we were married today, and I'll justify her my wife the next court day; you have your answer, and may be gone.

JOLLY We must take no notice of such excuses now; if she be your wife, make it appear in court, and she will be delivered unto you.

PARSON If she be my wife Sir? I have wedded her and bedded her, what other ceremonies would you have? Be not afraid, sweetheart.

JOLLY Sir, we can do no less than execute our warrant; we are but servants; and, Master Constable, I charge you in the king's name to do your duty; behold the body of the delinquent.

PARSON Touch her that dares; I'll put my dagger in him. [*he takes his dagger*]. Fear nothing, sweetheart; Master Constable you'll repent this insolence offered to a man of my coat.

BAWD Help, my dearest, will you let me be haled thus? [*here they strive to take her out*]

PARSON Villains, what will you do? Murder, rape.

CAPTAIN Yes, yes, 'tis likely; I look like a ravisher.

JOLLY Hold him, and we'll do well enough with her.

As they go to pull her out of the bed, they discover the Bawd. When they let him go he turns to her, and holds her in his arms

CAPTAIN What have we here, an old woman?

PARSON Let me go, slaves and murderers.

CAPTAIN Let him go.

JOLLY Do any of you know this woman? This is not she we looked for.

PARSON No? Rascal, that mistake shall not excuse you.

JOLLY It is old Goodman what-d'ye-call-him? His wife.

CAPTAIN Hold the candle, and let's see her face.

★ Lindabrides: the name of a lady in *The Mirror of Knighthood* (1585), hence a mistress, a lady-love, and, in cant, a prostitute.

When they hold the candle, she lies in his bosom and his arms about her; she must be as nastily dressed as they can dress her; when he sees her he falls into a maze, and shoves her from him.

JOLLY What have we here, adultery? Take them both, here will be new matter.

PARSON Master Constable, a little argument will persuade you to believe I am grossly abused; sure this does not look like a piece that a man would sin to enjoy, let that then move your pity, and care of my reputation; consider my calling, and do not bring me to a public shame for what you're sure I am not guilty of, but by plot of some villains.

BAWD Dear, will you disclaim me now?

PARSON Oh, impudence!

JOLLY Master Constable, do your duty; take them both away, as you will answer it.

CAPTAIN Give him his cassock, to cover him. [*they put on his cassock and her coat, and lead them away*]

PARSON Why gentlemen, whither will you carry me?

CAPTAIN To the next justice, I think it is Master Wild, he is newly come from travel; it will be a good way, neighbours, to express our respects to him.

PARSON No faith, gentlemen, e'en go the next way to Tyburn, and dispatch the business without ceremony, for ye'll utterly disgrace me; this is that damned captain; my wife is abroad too, I fear she is of the plot.

JOLLY Come, away with 'em.

BAWD Whither will they lead us, dear?

PARSON Oh, oh, impudence! Gentlemen, do not lead us together I beseech you.

CAPTAIN Come, come, lead them together, no ceremonies; your faults are both alike. [*Exeunt Omnes*]

SCENE II

Enter Wanton and Wild.

WANTON You had best brag now, and use me like my Lady What'st-ye-call; but if you do I care not.

WILD Come, y'are a fool, I'll be a faithful friend, and make good conditions for thee before thy husband be quit.

WANTON You must do it now or never. [*Wild sits down with Wanton in his lap*]

WILD Hark, hark, I hear them – What's the news?

Enter Captain, Jolly, Watch, Bawd and Parson.

CAPTAIN We have brought a couple of delinquents before your worship, they have committed a very foul fault.

JOLLY And we have brought the fault along too, that your worship may see it, you will be the better able to judge of the offenders.

PARSON Ha! What do I see? My wife in Master Justice's lap?

WANTON What has the poor fellow done?

CAPTAIN Why Madam, he has been taken abed with this woman, another man's wife.

WANTON In bed with her? And do you raise him to punish him? Master Constable, if you would afflict him, command them to lie together again; is not the man mad?

PARSON This is fine roguery, I find who rules the roast.

WILD Well, to the business; you say, he was taken in bed with another man's wife.

CAPTAIN Yes, and't like your worship.

WILD Make his mittimus★ to the hole at Newgate.

WANTON Sure I have seen this fellow's face. – Friend, have I never seen your face before?

PARSON If I mistake not, I have seen one very like your ladyship's too, she was a captain's cast-whore in the Town. I shall have a time to be revenged.

WILD How now, sirrah? Are you threatening? Away with him.

CAPTAIN I'll fetch a stronger watch, Sir, and return presently.

WILD Do, Master Constable, and give the poor woman something, and set her free; for I dare say 'twas his wickedness, she looks like one that ne'er thought on such a thing.

BAWD God bless your worship, I am innocent; he never left making love till I consented.

Enter Captain in his own shape.

★ mittimus: a warrant of committal to prison.

PARSON O miserable! Miserable!

CAPTAIN How now, what's the news here? My honoured friend, and Master Parson, what makes you here at this time of night? Why I should have thought this a time to have envied you for your fair bride's embraces. Do you give these favours? [*plays with the cord that binds his arms*] Are these your bride-laces?* It's a new way.

PARSON Is it new to you?

WANTON How now Captain?

CAPTAIN Wanton, is this your plot to endear your husband to you?

PARSON No, 'tis thy plot, poor beaten captain, but I shall be revenged.

CAPTAIN Yes, faith, it was my plot, and I glory in't, to undermine my Machiavel, which so greedily swallowed that sweet bait that had this hook.

PARSON 'Tis well.

CAPTAIN But my anger ends not here. Remember the base language you gave me, 'Son of a thousand fathers, Captain of a tame band, and one that got my living by the long staff-speeches'; for which, and thy former treacheries, I'll ruin thee, slave; I'll have no more mercy on thee, than old women on blind puppies; I'll bring you to your commendations in Latin epistles again, nor leave thee anything to live on, no, not bread, but what thou earn'st by raking gentlewomen's names in anagrams; and Master Justice, if ever you'll oblige me, stand to me now, that I may procure the whipping of him from the reverend bench.

PARSON I am undone.

WILD I can do nothing but justice, you must excuse me; I shall only make it appear how fit it is to punish this kind of sin in that coat in time, and to crush such serpents in the shells.

PARSON Mercy, O mercy!

WILD Officers, away with him. [*they pull him away*]

PARSON No mercy? [*the Parson looks very dejected*]

WANTON Yes, upon conditions there may be some mercy.

WILD And these they are – let the watch stay in t'other room. [*Exit Watch*] – First, your wife shall have her liberty, and you yours, as she reports of you; and when you bring her with you,

* bride-laces: lace used to bind sprigs of rosemary at weddings.

you shall be welcome; then you shall not be jealous, that's another point.

CAPTAIN That he shall have a cure for –

WANTON Yes, yes, I'll apply something to his eyes shall cure him of his doubt.

WILD Then you shall ask the captain pardon and your wife; to him you shall allow half your parsonage to maintain her; the deeds are ready within; if you'll sign them, and deliver your wife to our use, she shall discharge you.

PARSON I submit, Sir, but I hope your worship will desire no witness to the use of my wife; the sumner and the watch too; I hope your worship will enjoin them silence.

WANTON You shall not need to fear, I'll have a care of your credit; call in the watch; [*she discovers them*] do you know these faces?

PARSON Ha! Abused?

JOLLY Nay, no flinching, if you do, I betake me to Master Sumner again.

CAPTAIN And I become severe Master Constable in a trice.

PARSON No, no, I submit, and I hope we are all friends; I'm sure I have the hardest part, to forgive.

WANTON And I, before all this company, promise to forget and forgive thee, and am content to take thee again for my dear and mortal husband, now you are tame; but you must see you do so no more, and give yourself to be blind; when it is not fit for you to see; and practise to be deaf; and learn to sleep in time, and find business to call you away when gentlemen come that would be private.

CAPTAIN Why so, now things are as they should be; and when you will obey, you shall command: but when you would be imperious, then I betake me to my constable's staff 'till you subscribe. '*Cedunt armis togae*';★ and if it be false Latin, Parson, you must pardon that too.

JOLLY By this hand, I must have my tithe-night with thee; thou art such a wag; say, when? When wilt thou give me leave? Ha!

WANTON Never.

★ *Cedunt armis togae*: togas give way to arms. An incorrect quotation, reversing the meaning of Cicero's *cedant arma togae, concedat laurea laudi*, let arms give way to the toga, the laurels give way to praise. (*De Officiis*, I, 22, 77) The laurels are those of a triumphant general and the praise is civic praise.

JOLLY Never?

WANTON No, never.

JOLLY D'ye hear, I am none of them that work for charity; either resolve to pay, or I kick down all my milk again.

WANTON What would you have?

JOLLY Give me leave to lie with you.

WANTON No indeed.

JOLLY No?

WANTON No; but rather than quarrel, as I said before, I will give you leave to say you have lain with me.

WILD I am of opinion she owes you nothing now, so Mistress Wanton, take your husband; and to remove all doubts, this night I'll be at the charge of a wedding supper.

PARSON This is better than Newgate hole yet, Bridewell hemp, brown bread and whip-cord.   [*Exeunt Omnes*]

SCENE III

Enter the Widow and Mistress Pleasant, Master Sadd, and Master Constant.

WIDOW By my troth, it was a good play.

PLEASANT And I am glad I am come home, for I am e'en as weary with this walking; for God's sake whereabouts does the pleasure of walking lie? I swear, I have often sought it till I was weary, and yet I could ne'er find it.

A Watch at the Widow's door.

SADD What do these halberds at your door?

WIDOW Halberds, where?

SADD There, at your lodging.

CONSTANT Friend, what would those watchmen have?

WATCHMAN The house is shut up for the sickness* this afternoon.

PLEASANT The sickness?

WATCHMAN Yes forsooth, there's a coachman dead full of the tokens.

SADD Where is the officer?

WATCHMAN He is gone to seek the lady of the house, and some

* the sickness: the plague.

other company that dined here yesterday, to bring her in, or carry her to the pest-house.

WIDOW Ha! What shall we do, niece?

SADD If you please to command our lodging.

PLEASANT It will be too much trouble.

WIDOW Let's go to Love-all's.

PLEASANT Not I, by my faith; it is scarce for our credits to let her come to us.

WIDOW Why? Is she naught?

CONSTANT Faith, Madam, her reputation is not good.

WIDOW But what shall we do then?

CONSTANT Dare you adventure to oblige us?

WIDOW Thank you Sir, we'll go to my nephew's at Covent Garden; he may shift among his acquaintance.

PLEASANT It was well thought on, the Piazza is hard by too.

WIDOW We'll borrow your coach thither, and we'll send it you back again straight.

CONSTANT We'll wait upon you, Madam.

WIDOW This accident troubles me; I am heartily sorry for the poor fellow.

PLEASANT I am sorry too; but pray, aunt, let us not forget ourselves in our grief; I am not ambitious of a red cross* upon the door.

CONSTANT Mistress Pleasant is in the right; for if you stay the officers will put you in.

WIDOW We shall trouble you, Sir, for your coach.   [*Exeunt Omnes*]

SCENE IV

Enter Parson, Captain, Wild, Wanton, Careless and Jolly.

PARSON I am reconciled; and will no longer be an uncharitable churchman; I think this sack is a cooler.

CAPTAIN What? Does it make you to see your error?

PARSON Yes, and consider my man of war; nor will I again dispute his letters of mart, nor call them passes for pirates; I am free.

* a red cross: crosses a foot high were painted on the doors and windows of houses infected by the plague. 'Lord have mercy' was written upon them.

CAPTAIN And welcome, anything but anger is sufferable, and all is jest when you laugh; and I will hug thee for abusing me with thy eyes in their scabbards; but when you rail with drawn eyes, red and naked, threatening a levite's second revenge★ to all that touches your concubine, then I betake me to a dark lanthorn, and a constable's staff, and by help of these Fathers whom I cite I prove my text, women that are kind ought to be free.

PARSON But Captain, is it not lawful for us shepherds to reclaim them?

CAPTAIN A mere mistake; for sin like the sea may be turned out, but will ne'er grow less; and though you should drain this Mistress Doll,† yet the whore will find a place, and perhaps over-flow some maid, till then honest; and so you prove the author of a new sin, and the defiler of a pure temple; therefore I say, while you live, let the whore alone till she wears out; nor is it safe to vamp them,‡ as you shall find, read Ball§ the first and the second.

WILD No more discourse. Strike up fiddlers.

CAPTAIN See, who's that knocks?

A Country Dance.

When they are merry, singing catches and drinking healths, the Widow, Mrs Pleasant and the two Lovers knock at the door.

SERVANT Sir, 'tis Mistress Pleasant, and the two gentlemen that dined there today.

WILD My aunt, and Mistress Pleasant.

JOLLY What a pox makes them abroad at this time of night?

CAPTAIN It may be, they have been a-wenching.

SERVANT Sir, they were upon alighting out of the coach when I came up.

WILD Quickly, Mrs Wanton, you and your husband to bed, there's the key; Mr Parson, you know the way to the old chamber, and to it quickly, all is friends now.

★ levite's second revenge: a reference to the story of the Levite and his concubine in Judges XIX, XX.

† Mistress Doll: a prostitute, from Dol Common in *The Alchemist* (1610).

‡ to vamp them: Montagu Summers, *Restoration Comedy* (1921), p. 382, relates this to *The Whore in Grain*, licensed 26 January 1623/4, 'new vamp'd' at the Red Bull in 1639.

§ Ball: John Ball (1585–1640), a puritan preacher.

PARSON Sweetheart, we'll steal away.

WANTON The devil on them, they have spoiled our mirth.

[Exeunt Parson ⟨and Wanton⟩]

WILD Jack, get you and your company down the back-way into the kitchen, and stay there till we see what this visit means.

[Exeunt Fiddlers]

CAPTAIN Means! What should it mean? It is nothing but the mischievous nature all honest women are endued with, and naturally given to spoil sport: I wonder what fart blew them hither tonight.

WILD Nay, have a little patience, Captain; you and Mr Jolly must sit quiet awhile within, till we know the cause.

CAPTAIN It is but deferring our mirth for an hour, or so.

SERVANT Sir, here's my lady.

WILD Quickly remove those things there: Captain, step in there. –

⟨*Exit Captain*⟩

Enter Widow, Pleasant, Sadd and Constant.

WIDOW Nephew, do you not wonder to see me here, at this time of night?

WILD I know it is not ordinary, therefore I believe 'tis some design: what is it, Mrs Pleasant? Shall I make one?

PLEASANT As I live, Sir, pure necessity; neither mirth nor kindness hath begot this visit.

CARELESS What, is your coach broke?

WIDOW Faith, nephew, the truth is, the sickness is in my house, and my coachman died since dinner.

WILD The sickness?

PLEASANT Aye, as I live, we have been walking since the play; and when we came home we found the watch at the door, and the house shut up.

SADD And a constable gone in search of all those that dined there today, with order to furnish us lodgings in the pest-house.

WIDOW Are you not afraid to receive us?

WILD As I live, the accident troubles me; and I am sorry such a misfortune should beget me this favour; and I could wish myself free from the honour, if the cause were removed too.

PLEASANT As I live, Mr Wild, I must have been forced to have lain with my servant tonight, if you had not received me.

WILD If I thought so, I would carry you out in my arms, I am so much Mr Constant's friend.

PLEASANT But are you more his friend than mine, Mr Wild?

WILD No, but I presume by this he has gained so much interest as he would not be very displeasing to you.

CONSTANT Oh! Your humble servant, Sir.

PLEASANT If I had had a mind to that lodging, I had ne'er come hither; for when I have a mind to it, I'll marry without dispute; for I fear nobody so much as a husband; and when I can conquer that doubt, I'll marry at a minute's warning.

WIDOW No dispute now, can you furnish us with a couple of beds?

WILD Yes, yes.

WIDOW And have you e'er a woman in the house?

WILD My sister's maid is here.

CARELESS Madam, if you resolve to do us this honour, you shall find clean linen, and your beds quickly ready.

WIDOW But where will my nephew and you, Sir, lie tonight?

CARELESS Oh, Madam, we have acquaintance enough in the Town.

WIDOW Well, Sir, we'll accept this courtesy; and when you come into Suffolk you shall command my house.

WILD Prithee call Bess, and bid her bring sheets to make the bed; I'll go and fetch in a pallet, 'tis as good a bed as the other, and if you will stay the removing, we'll set up a bedstead.

PLEASANT No, a pallet, pray; but what shall we do for night-clothes, aunt?

WILD Why, what are those you bought my sister's?

WIDOW Is not that linen gone yet?

CARELESS No faith, Madam, his man forgot it, till the carriers were gone last week.

WILD Will that serve?

PLEASANT Yes, yes, pray do us the favour to let us have it, 'tis but washing of't again.

WILD Nay, if it will serve, discourse no more; I'll fetch the bundle; and prithee fetch the combs and looking-glasses I bought the other day; for other necessaries that want a name the wench shall furnish you with.

WIDOW Nay, but where is she, nephew?

WILD I'll call her, if she be not gone to bed; it is an ignorant young thing, I am to send her to my sister's in the country; I have had such ado to put her in the fashion.

PLEASANT What country is she? Prithee, Mr Wild, let's see her.

WILD I'll call her down.   [*Exit Wild*]

SADD Madam, now we see y'are safe we'll kiss your hands, and wait upon you tomorrow.

WIDOW It must be early then, Sir; for I shall borrow my nephew's coach, and begone betimes into the country to take a little fresh air, and prevent the search.

CONSTANT Pray, Madam, be pleased to command ours.

WIDOW No, Sir, I humbly thank you; my nephew's will hold our company.

CONSTANT Your humble servant, Mistress Pleasant.

SADD Your servant, Madam.

PLEASANT Good night, Mr Constant.

WIDOW Sir, you'll excuse us, we have nobody here to light you down.

CARELESS Madam, I am here your servant as much as those that wear your livery; and this house holds no other; we can be civil, Madam, as well as extravagant.

WIDOW Your humble servant, Mr Careless.

CARELESS Gentlemen, if you'll wait on my lady to her chamber, then I'll wait upon you down.

SADD You oblige us, Sir.   [*Exeunt Omnes*]

SCENE V

Enter Wild, Captain, Wanton, Parson and Jolly.

CAPTAIN The plague?

WILD The plague; as I live, and all my relation is truth, every syllable; but, Mrs Wanton, now must you play your masterpiece; be sure to blush, and appear but simple enough, and all is well; thou wilt pass for as arrant a chambermaid as any is in the parish.

PARSON Hum! New plots?

CAPTAIN Let me put on a petticoat and a muffler, and I'll so chambermaid it, and be so diligent with the clean smock and the chamber-pot: now would I give all the shoes in my shop to lie with 'em both.

WANTON Let me alone to fit them, I can make a scurvy curtsy naturally; remember, I am an Essex woman,* if they ask.

WILD Come, come quickly, take those sweetmeats; bring the great cake and knife, and napkins, for they have not supped; and Captain, make some lemonade,† and send it by the boy to my chamber; and do you hear, Jolly, you must stay till we come, for we must lie with you tonight.

JOLLY We'll stay, but make haste then.

CAPTAIN And bring our cloaks and swords out with you.

WILD I will, I will; but be quiet all.

PARSON Mr Wild, I hope there is no plot in this.

CAPTAIN There's no jealousy, Mr Parson; 'tis all serious upon my life, come away with us. [*Exeunt Omnes*]

SCENE VI

The tiring room, curtains drawn, and they discourse, his chamber, two beds, two tables, looking-glasses, night-clothes, waistcoats, sweet-bags, sweetmeats and wine, Wanton dressed like a chambermaid; all above if the scene can be so ordered

Enter Widow and Mrs Pleasant, Wild and Careless; the Widow and Mrs Pleasant salute Wanton.

WILD Faith, aunt, 'tis the first time I have had the honour to see you in my house; and as a stranger I must salute you.

WIDOW As I live, nephew, I'm ashamed to put you to this trouble.

WILD It is an obligation. – Mrs Pleasant, I know you have not supped; I pray you be pleased to taste these sweetmeats, they are of Sall's doing; but I understand not sweetmeats, the wine I'll answer for; and, in a word, you are welcome: you are *Patrona*, and we your slaves.

* an Essex woman: a simpleton.
† lemonade: this is possibly the earliest occurrence of the word.

CARELESS Good rest, and a pleasing dream, your humble servant
wishes you.

WIDOW Good night, nephew; good night, Mr Careless.

PLEASANT Good night, Mr Careless; your humble servant, Mr
Wild.

[Exeunt Wild and Careless]

WIDOW Why aye, here are men have some wit; by this good night,
had we lain at my servant's, we should have found the laced cap
and slippers that have been entailed upon the family these five
descents, advanced upon the cupboard's head instead of plate.*

[they sit down to undress them]

PLEASANT They are a couple of the readiest youths too; how they
run and do all things with a thought! I love him for sending his
sister, a pretty wench.

WIDOW Pray, let's go to bed; I am weary.

PLEASANT You will not go to bed with all those windows open;
sweetheart, prithee shut them, and bring me hither; – dost understand me? As I live, 'tis a great while since I went to the play.

WIDOW It has been one of the longest days; a year of them would
be an age.

PLEASANT Oh, do you grow weary; you'll break your covenant
ere the year go out.

WIDOW Prithee, shut the windows, and come pin up my hair.

[The curtains are closed]

SCENE VII

*Enter Wild, Jolly, Careless, Captain and Parson, and Fiddlers, and one with
a torch, with their cloaks and their swords, putting them on. Enter Wild's
Man.*

WILD See you wait diligently, and let them want nothing they
call for; come shall we go? 'Tis very late.

CAPTAIN But how does Wanton carry it?

WILD They saluted her; and Mrs Pleasant swore you might see
the country-simplicity in her face.

* we should . . . plate: the men had left food and drink, the servant would
only have put out bed wear.

PARSON A pox upon her, crafty gypsy.

CAPTAIN Why, art not thou glad to see she can be honest when she will?

PARSON I'll show you all a trick, for her, within these few days, or I'll miss my aim.

JOLLY Come, let's go. [*they all offer to go*]

CAPTAIN I have a mind to stay till Wanton comes.

WILD Stay a little then, for 'twill not be long ere they be abed.

CAPTAIN I hear Wanton's voice.

Enter Wanton.

WILD Are they abed?

WANTON Yes, and have so admired you, and Mr Careless, and abused the lovers; well, gentlemen, you are the wits of the time; but if I might counsel, well they might lie alone this night; but it should go hard if I lay not with one of them within a month.

CARELESS Were they so taken with their lodging?

WANTON All that can be said they said, you are the friendliest men, the readiest men, the handsomest men that had wit; and could tell when to be civil, and when to be wild; and Mrs What's-her-name the younger, asked why Mr Wild did not go a wooing to some rich heir; upon her conscience, she said, you would speed.

CARELESS Well, well, there's a time for all things; come let's go. [*they offer to depart*]

WILD Take a light. – Good night, Wanton.

CAPTAIN D'ye hear, d'ye hear; let me speak with you. [*they all come back again*]

WILD What's the business?

CAPTAIN I cannot get hence this night: but your good angels hang at my heels; and if I can prevail, you shall stay.

WILD What to do?

CAPTAIN What to do? Why I'll be hanged if all this company do not guess.

JOLLY Prithee, what should we stay for?

CAPTAIN For the widow, and her niece; are they worth the watching for a night?

WILD Yes, certainly.

CAPTAIN Then take my counsel, and let me give it out y'are married, you have new clothes come home this morning, and there's that you spoke of I'll fetch from the tailor's, and here's a parson shall rather give them his living, than stay for a licence; the fiddlers too are ready to salute 'em.

CARELESS But if they refuse?

JOLLY Which, upon my conscience, they will.

CAPTAIN As you hope, else you are laughed at for missing the widow: Ned, follow my counsel, appear at her chamber window in thy shirt, and salute all that passes by; let me alone to give it out, and invite company and provide dinner; then when the business is known, and I have presented all your friends at Court with ribands,★ she must consent, or her honour is lost, if you have but the grace to swear it, and keep your own counsel.

CARELESS By this hand, he has reason; and I'll undertake the widow.

WILD It will incense them, and precipitate the business which is in a fair way now; and if they have wit, they must hate us for such a treachery.

CAPTAIN If they have wit they will love you; beside, if it come to that, we two will swear we saw you married, and the parson shall be sworn he did it: – priest, will you not swear?

PARSON Yes, anything; what is't, Captain?

WILD If this jest could do it, yet 'tis base to gain a wife so poorly; she came hither too for sanctuary; it would be an uncivil and an unhospitable thing, and look as if I had not merit enough to get a wife without stealing her from herself; then, 'tis in mine own house.

CAPTAIN The better; nay, now I think on't, why came she hither? How do you know the plague is there? All was well at dinner; I'll be hanged if it be not a plot; the lovers too whom you abused at dinner, are joined with them; a trick, a mere trick of wit to abuse us; and tomorrow when the birds are flown, they'll laugh at you, and say, 'Two country ladies put themselves naked into the hands of three travelled City-wits, and they durst not lay hold on them.'

★ ribands: as wedding attire.

CARELESS A pox upon these niceties.

WANTON If they have not some design upon you hang me, why did they talk so freely before me else?

CARELESS Let's but try, we are not now to begin to make the world talk; nor is it a new thing to them to hear we are mad fellows.

CAPTAIN If you get them, are they worth having?

WILD Having? Yes.

CAPTAIN If you miss them the jest is good; prithee, Ned, let me prevail, 'tis but a mad trick.

WILD If we would, how shall we get into the chamber?

WANTON Let me alone for that; I'll put on my country simplicity, and carry in a chamber-pot; then under pretence of bolting the back door I'll open it, and yet I grudge them the sport so honestly; for you wenchers make the best husbands; after you are once married, one never sees you.

CAPTAIN I warrant thee wench.

WANTON No faith, I have observed it, they are still the doting'st husbands, and then retreat and become justices of the peace, and none so violent upon the bench, as they, against us poor sinners; yet I'll do it, for upon my conscience the young gentlewoman will fall upon her back, and thank me.   [*Exit Wanton*]

CAPTAIN Away, go then, and leave your fooling, and in the morning, Ned, get in, and plead naked with your hands in the bed.

PARSON And if they cry, put your lips to their mouths, and stop them.

CAPTAIN Why look you, you have the authority of the church too.

WILD Well, I am resolved; go you about your part, and make the report strong.

CARELESS And d'ye hear? Be sure you set the cook at work, that if we miss we may have a good dinner, and good wine, to drink down our grief.

CAPTAIN Miss? I warrant thee thrive.   [*Exit Captain*]

CARELESS Nay, if I knock not down the Widow, geld me, and come out tomorrow complete uncle, and salute the company, with, 'You are welcome gentlemen, and good morrow nephew Ned.'

WILD Uncle Tom, good-morrow, Uncle Tom.

Enter Wanton.

WANTON All's done, the door is open, and they're as still as
children's thoughts; 'tis time you made you ready, which is, to
put off your breeches, for 'tis almost day; and take my counsel, be
sure to offer force enough, the less reason will serve; especially
you, Master Wild, do not put a maid to the pain of saying,
'Aye'.

WILD I warrant thee, wench; let me alone.

CARELESS We'll in, and undress us, and come again; for we must
go in at the back door.

WILD I'll meet you, is the captain gone? [*Exeunt Wild and Careless*]

WANTON Yes, yes, he's gone.

JOLLY Come Master Parson, let us see the cook in readiness, where
are the fiddlers? What will become of our plot? For the coachman;
Master Sadd and his friend will stink of their jest if this thrive.

PARSON They have slept all night, on purpose, to play all day.

JOLLY When the ribands and points★ come from the Exchange,†
pray see the fiddlers have some, the rogues will play so out of tune
all day else, they will spoil the dancing if the plot do take.

*Enter Wild, and Careless, in their shirts, with drawers under; nightgowns on,
and in slippers.*

WANTON Let's see them in the chamber first, and then I shall go
with some heart about the business; so, so, creep close and quietly;
you know the way, the widow lies in the high bed, and the pallet
is next the door. [*they kneel at the door to go in. She shakes her coats over
'em*]

WILD Must we creep?

WANTON Yes, yes, down upon your knees, always, till you get a
woman, and then stand up for the cause; stay let me shake my
smock over you for luck sake.

⟨*Exeunt Wild and Careless*⟩

JOLLY Why so, I warrant you thrive.

★ ribands and points: for the wedding guests.
† the Exchange: the Royal Exchange, founded by Sir Thomas Gresham,
opened by Queen Elizabeth in January 1570/71. It contained many shops.

PARSON A pox take you, I'll pare your nails when I get you from this place once.

WANTON Sweetheart, sweetheart, off with your shoe.

PARSON Aye, with all my heart, there's an old shoe after you; would I gave all in my shop the rest were furnished with wives too.

JOLLY Parson, the sun is rising, go send in the fiddlers, and set the cook on work, let him chop soundly.

PARSON I have a tithe pig at home, I'll e'en sacrifice it to the wedding.   [*Exit Parson*]

WANTON They will find them in good posture, they may take privy marks if they please; for they said it was so hot they could endure no clothes, and my simplicity was so diligent to lay them naked, and with such 'twists and turns fastened them to the feet, I'll answer for't, they find not the way into them in an hour.

Enter a Servant and Parson.

JOLLY Why then they may pull up their smocks, and hide their faces?

SERVANT Master Jolly, there was one without would speak with you.

JOLLY Who was it?

SERVANT It is the lady that talks so well.

JOLLY They say indeed she has an excellent tongue, I would she had changed it for a face; 'tis she that has been handsome.

PARSON Who? Not the poetess we met at Master Sadd's?

JOLLY Yes, the same.

PARSON Sure she's mad.

JOLLY Prithee tell her I am gone to bed.

SERVANT I have done as well Sir; I told her Mistress Wanton was here, at which discreetly, being touched with the guilt of her face, she threw out a curse or two and retreated.

WANTON Who is this you speak of, I will know who 'tis.

PARSON Why 'tis she that married the Genoway* merchant; they cozened one another.

WANTON Who? Peg Driver, Bugle Eyes?

JOLLY The same, the same.

* Genoway: Genoa.

WANTON Why she is ugly now?

PARSON Yes, but I have known her, by this hand, as fine a wench as ever sinned in Town or suburbs; when I knew her first, she was the original of all the wainscot chambermaids, with brooms, and barefoot madams, you see sold at Temple Bar, and the Exchange.

WANTON Ah! Th'art a divel; how could'st thou find in thy heart to abuse her so? Thou lov'st antiquities too; the very memory that she had been handsome should have pleaded something.

JOLLY 'Was handsome' signifies nothing to me.

WANTON But she's a wit, and a wench of an excellent discourse.

PARSON And as good company as any's i'th Town.

JOLLY Company? For whom? Leather-ears, his Majesty of Newgate watch? There her story will do well, while they louse themselves.

PARSON Well, you are curious now, but the time was, when you have skipped for a kiss.

JOLLY Prithee, Parson, no more of wit, and 'was handsome', but let us keep to this text – and with joy think upon thy little Wanton here, that's kind, soft, sweet and sound; [*he kisses Wanton*] these are epithets for a mistress; nor is there any elegancy in a woman like it; give me such a naked scene, to study night and day; I care not for her tongue, so her face be good; a whore dressed in verse, and set speeches, tempts me no more to that sweet sin, than the statute of whipping can keep me from it; this thing we talked on, which retains nothing but the name of what she was, is not only poetical in her discourse, but her tears and her love, her health, nay her pleasure, were all fictions, and had scarce any live-flesh about her till I administered.

PARSON Indeed 'tis time she sat out, and gave others leave to play; for a reverend whore is an unseemly sight; besides it makes the sin malicious, which is but venial else.

WANTON Sure, he'll make a case of conscience on't; you should do well, sweetheart, to recommend her case to your brethren that attend the committee of affection, that they may order her to be sound and young again, for the good of the Commonwealth.

⟨*Exeunt*⟩

ACT FIVE

SCENE I

Enter Fiddlers, Jolly and Wanton.

JOLLY Oh, are you ready? Are you ready?

FIDDLERS Yes, and't like your worship.

JOLLY And did you bid the cook chop lustily, and make a noise?

FIDDLERS Yes, Sir, he's at it.

WANTON I hear the captain.

Enter Captain.

JOLLY Have you brought clothes and ribands?

CAPTAIN Yes, yes, all is ready; did you hear them squeak yet?

WANTON No, by this light; I think, 'tis an appointment, and we have been all abused.

CAPTAIN Give the fiddlers their ribands, and carry the rest in; Mistress Wanton, you must play my lady's woman today, and mince it to all that come, and hold up your head finely when they kiss you, and take heed of swearing when you are angry, and pledging whole cups when they drink to you.

WANTON I'll warrant you, for my part.

CAPTAIN Go get you in then, and let your husband dip the rosemary.*

JOLLY Is all ready?

CAPTAIN All, all, some of the company are below already, I have so blown it about, one porter is gone to the Exchange, to invite Master Wild's merchant to his wedding, and, by the way to bid two or three fruiterers to send in fruit for such a wedding, another in my lady's name to Sall's, for sweetmeats; I swore at Bradborn in his shop myself, that I wondered he would disappoint Master Wild for his points, and having so long warning; he protested 'twas not his fault, but they were ready, and he would send John with them presently; one of the watermen is gone to the Melon Garden, the other to Cook's at the Bear, for some bottles of his

---

* rosemary: this was much used in weddings (the shrub was said to be useful in love-making) and to wear rosemary was as significant of a wedding as to wear a white favour.

best wine, and thence to Gracious Street,★ to the poulterers, and all with directions to send in provisions for Master Wild's wedding; and who should I meet at door, but Apricock Tom, and Mary, waiting to speak with her young master; they came to beg that they might serve the feast; I promised them they should, if they would cry it up and down the Town, to bring company; for Master Wild was resolved to keep open house.

JOLLY Why then here will be witnesses enough.

CAPTAIN But who should I meet at the corner of the Piazza, but Joseph Taylor;† he tells me, there's a new play at the Friars' today, and I have bespoke a box for Master Wild and his bride.

JOLLY And did not he wonder to hear he was married?

CAPTAIN Yes; but I told him, 'twas a match his aunt made for him, when he was abroad.

JOLLY And I have spread it sufficiently at Court, by sending to borrow plate for such a wedding.

Enter a Servant.

SERVANT There's half a dozen coachfuls of company lighted; they call for the bride-laces and points.

CAPTAIN Let the fiddlers play then, and bid God give them joy, by the name of my Lady Careless and Mistress Wild.

FIDDLER Where shall we play, Sir?

JOLLY Come with us, we'll show you the window.

SCENE II

The Fiddlers play in the tiring room, and the stage curtains are drawn, and discover a chamber, as it was, with two beds and the ladies asleep in them; Master Wild being at Mistress Pleasant's bedside, and Master Careless at the Widow's; the music awakes the Widow

WIDOW Niece, niece, niece Pleasant.

PLEASANT Ha! I hear you, I hear you, what would you have? [*she*

★ Gracious Street: between Cornhill and Eastcheap.

† Joseph Taylor: Taylor (1586?–1653?) was one of the original actors in Shakespeare's plays.

opens the curtain and calls her, she is under a canopy]

WIDOW Do you not hear the fiddlers?

PLEASANT Yes, yes, but you have waked me from the finest dream.

WIDOW A dream, what was't? Some knavery.

PLEASANT Why, I know not, but 'twas merry, e'en as pleasing as some sins; well, I'll lie no more in a man's bed, for fear I lose more than I get.

WIDOW Hark, that's a new tune.

PLEASANT Yes, and they play it well; this is your jaunty nephew; I would he had less of the father in him, I'd venture to dream out my dream with him; in my conscience he's worth a dozen of my dull servant, that's such a troublesome visitant, without any kind of conveniency.

WIDOW Aye, aye, so are all of that kind; give me your subject lover; those you call servants are but troubles, I confess.

PLEASANT What is the difference, pray, betwixt a subject, and a servant lover?

WIDOW Why, one I have absolute power over, the other's at large; your servant lovers are those take mistresses upon trial, scarce give them a quarter's warning before they are gone.

PLEASANT Why, what do your subject lovers do? I am so sleepy.

WIDOW Do? All things for nothing; then they are the diligent'st and the humblest things a woman can employ; nay, I ha' seen ⟨one⟩ of them tame, and run loose about a house; I had one once, by this light, he would fetch and carry, go back, seek out, he would do anything; I think some falconer bred him.

PLEASANT By my troth, I am of your mind.

WIDOW He would come over, for all my friends; but it was the doggedest thing to my enemies, he would sit upon's tail before them, and frown, like John-a-Napes when the Pope is named; he heard me once praise my little spaniel bitch Smut for waiting, and hang me if I stirred for seven years after, but I found him lying at my door.

PLEASANT And what became of him?

WIDOW Faith, when I married he forsook me; I was advised since, that if I would ha' spit in's mouth sometimes he would have stayed.

PLEASANT That was cheap, but 'tis no certain way; for 'tis a general opinion, that marriage is one of the certain'st cures for love that one can apply to a man that is sick of the sighings; yet if you were to live about this Town still, such a fool would do you a world of service; I'm sure Secret will miss him, he would always take such a care of her, ha's saved her a hundred walks for hoods and masks.

WIDOW Yes, and I was certain of the earliest fruits and flowers that the spring afforded.

PLEASANT By my troth, 'twas foolishly done to part with him; a few crumbs of your affection would have satisfied him, poor thing.

WIDOW Thou art in the right; in this Town there's no living without 'em; they do more service in a house for nothing, than a pair of those, what-d'ye-call-'ems, those he-waiting-women, beasts, that custom impose upon ladies.

PLEASANT Is there none of them to be had now, think you? I'd feign get a tame one, to carry down into the country.

WIDOW Faith, I know but one breed of them about the Town that's right, and that's at the Court; the lady that has them brings 'em all up by hand; she breeds some of them from very puppies; there's another wit too in the Town that has of them; but hers will not do so many tricks; good sullen diligent waiters those are which she breeds, but not half so serviceable.

PLEASANT How does she do it? Is there not a trick in't?

WIDOW Only patience, but she has a heavy hand with 'em (they say) at first, and many of them miscarry; she governs them with signs, and by the eye, as Banks* breeds his horse; there are some too that arrive at writing, and those are the right breed, for they commonly betake themselves to poetry; and if you could light on one of them, 'twere worth your money; for 'tis but using of him ill, and praising his verses sometimes, and you are sure of him for ever.

PLEASANT But do they never grow surly, aunt?

WIDOW Not, if you keep them from raw flesh, for they are a kind

---

* Banks: the owner of a famous horse, mentioned by many Elizabethan writers. It could play tricks with cards and dice, and was reputed to have gone up to the roof of St Paul's.

of lion-lovers; and if they once taste the sweet of it, they'll turn to their kind.

PLEASANT Lord, aunt, there will be no going without one this summer into the country; pray let's enquire for one; either a he-one to entertain us, or a she-one to tell us the story of her love; 'tis excellent to bedward, and makes one as drowsy as prayers.

WIDOW Faith, niece, this Parliament has so destroyed 'em, and the platonic humour, that 'tis uncertain whether we shall get one or no; your leading members in the lower House have so cowed the ladies, that they have no leisure to breed any of late; their whole endeavours are spent now in feasting, and winning close commit-tee-men, a rugged kind of sullen fellows, with implacable stomachs and hard hearts, that make the gay things court and observe them, as much as the foolish lovers use to do; yet I think I know one she-lover, but she is smitten in years o'th' wrong side of forty; I am certain she is poor too; and in this lean age for courtiers, she perhaps would be glad to run this summer in our park.

PLEASANT Dear aunt, let us have her; has she been famous? Has she good tales, think you, of knights? Such as have been false or true to love, no matter which.

WIDOW She cannot want cause to curse the sex; handsome, witty, well-born, and poor in Court, cannot want the experience how false young men can be; her beauty has had the highest fame; and those eyes that weep now unpitied have had their envy, and a dazzling power.

PLEASANT And that tongue, I warrant you, which now grows hoarse with flattering the great law-breakers, once gave law to princes; was it not so aunt? Lord, shall I die without begetting one story?

WIDOW Penthesilea,* nor all the cloven knights the poets treat of, yclad in mightiest petticoats, did her excel for gallant deeds; and, with her honour, still preserved her freedom; my brother loved her; and I have heard him swear, Minerva might have owned her language; an eye like Pallas, Juno's wrists, a Venus for shape, and a mind chaste as Diana, but not so rough; never uncivilly cruel, nor faulty kind to any; no vanity, that sees more than lovers pay, nor blind to a gallant passion; her maxim was, he that could love, and tell her so handsomely, was better com-

---

* Penthesilea: a queen of the Amazons, killed by Achilles in the Trojan War.

pany, but not a better lover than a silent man; thus, all passions found her civility, and she a value from all her lovers. But alas, niece, this 'was' (which is a sad word) 'was handsome', and 'was beloved', are abhorred sounds in women's ears. [*the Fiddlers play again*]

PLEASANT Hark, the fiddlers are merry still; will not Secret have the wit to find us this morning, think you?

FIDDLERS God give you joy, Master Careless; God give your ladyship joy, my Lady Wild.

WIDOW What did the fellow say? God give me joy?

PLEASANT As I live, I think so.

FIDDLERS God give you joy, Mistress Pleasant Wild.

WIDOW This is my nephew, I smell him in this knavery.

PLEASANT Why did they give me joy by the name of Mistress Wild? I shall pay dear for a night's lodging if that be so, especially lying alone; by this light, there is some knavery afoot.

All the company confused without, and bid 'God give them joy'.

JOLLY Rise, rise, for shame, the year's afore you.

CAPTAIN Why, Ned Wild, why Tom, will you not rise and let's in? What, is it not enough to steal your wedding overnight, but lock yourselves up in the morning too? All your friends stay for points here, and kisses from the brides.

WILD A little patience, you'll give us leave to dress us?

CARELESS Why, what's a clock, Captain?

The women squeak when they speak.

CAPTAIN It's late.

CARELESS Faith, so it was before we slept.

WIDOW Why, nephew, what means this rudeness? As I live, I'll fall out with you. This is no jest.

WILD No, as I live, aunt. We are in earnest; but my part lies here, and there's a gentleman will do his best to satisfy you; [*they catch the women in their arms*] and sweet Mistress Pleasant, I know you have so much wit as to perceive this business cannot be remedied by denials; here we are, as you see, naked, and thus have saluted hundreds at the window that passed by, and gave us joy this morning.

PLEASANT Joy, of what? What do you mean?

CARELESS [*kisses the Widow*] Madam, this is visible, and you may coy it, and refuse to call me husband; but I am resolved to call you wife, and such proofs I'll bring as shall not be denied.

WIDOW Promise yourself that; see whether your fine wits can make it good; you will not be uncivil?

CARELESS Not a hair but what you give, and that was in the contract before we undertook it; for any man may force a woman's body, but we have laid we will force your mind.

WILD But that needs not, for we know by your discourse last night and this morning, we are men you have no aversion to; and I believe, if we had taken time and wooed hard, this would have come a course; but we had rather win you by wit, because you desired us.

WIDOW 'Tis very well, if it succeed.

CARELESS And, for my part, but for the jest of winning you, and this way, not ten jointures should have made me marry?

WIDOW This is a new way of wooing.

CARELESS 'Tis so, Madam; but we have not laid our plot so weakly (though it were sudden) to leave it in anybody's power but our own to hinder it.

PLEASANT Do you think so?

WILD We are secure enough, if we can be true to ourselves.

CARELESS Yet we submit in the midst of our strength, and beg you will not wilfully spoil a good jest by refusing us. By this hand, we are both sound, and we'll be strangely honest, and never in ill humours, but live as merry as the maids, and divide the year between the Town and the country; what say you, is't a match? Your bed is big enough for two, and my meat will not cost you much; I'll promise nothing but one heart, one purse betwixt us, and a whole dozen of boys, is't a bargain?

WIDOW Not, if I can hinder it, as I live.

WILD Faith, Mistress Pleasant, he hath spoken nothing but reason, and I'll do my best to make it good; come faith, teach my aunt what to do, and let me strike the bargain upon your lips.

PLEASANT No, Sir, not to be half a queen; if we should yield now your wit would domineer for ever; and still in all disputes (though never so much reason on our side) this shall be urged as an argument of your master wit to confute us; I am of your aunt's mind,

Sir; and if I can hinder it, it shall be no match.

WILD Why then know, it is not in your powers to prevent it.

WIDOW Why, we are not married yet.

CARELESS No, 'tis true.

WIDOW By this good light then I'll be dumb for ever here after, lest I light upon the words of marriage by chance.

PLEASANT 'Tis hard, when our own acts cannot be in our own power, gentlemen.

WILD The plot is only known to four, the minister and two that stood for fathers, and a simple country maid that waited upon you last night, which plays your chambermaid's part.

PLEASANT And what will all these do?

WILD Why, the two friends will swear, they gave you; the parson will swear, he married you; and the wench will swear, she put us to bed.

WIDOW Have you men to swear we are married?

PLEASANT And a parson to swear he did it?

BOTH Yes.

WIDOW And a wench that will swear, she put us to bed?

BOTH Yes, by this good light, and witness of reputation.

PLEASANT Dare they or you look us in the face, and swear this?

CARELESS Yes faith, and all but those four know no other but really it is so; and you may deny it, but I'll make Mr Constable put you to bed, with this proof, at night.

WIDOW Pray, let's see these witnesses.

WILD Call in the four only.

[*Exit Careless*]

PLEASANT Well, this shall be a warning to me; I say nothing, but if ever I lie from home again.

WILD I'll lie with you.

PLEASANT 'Tis well; I dare say, we are the first women (if this take) that ever were stolen against their wills.

WILD I'll go call the gentlemen.   [*Exit Wild*]

WIDOW I that have refused a fellow that loved me these seven years, and would have put off his hat, and thanked me to come to bed, to be beaten with watchmen's staves into another's; for by this good light, for ought that I perceive, there's no keeping these out at night.

PLEASANT And unless we consent to be their wives, today, Mr
Justice will make us their whores at night: oh, oh, what would not
I give to come off! Not that I mistake them, but I hate they should
get us thus.

Enter Wild, Jolly, Captain, Careless, Parson, Wanton, with rosemary in
their hands, and points in their hats.

CARELESS Follow. – Will not you two swear we were married last
night?

JOLLY
CAPTAIN } Yes, by this light, will we.

WILD Will not you swear you married us?

PARSON Yea, verily.

CARELESS And come hither, pretty one, will not you swear you
left us all abed last night, and pleased?

WANTON Yes forsooth; I'll swear anything your worship shall
appoint me.

WIDOW But, gentlemen, have you no shame, no conscience; will
you swear false, for sport?

JOLLY By this light, I'll swear, if it be but to vex you: remember
you refused me. [*aside*] That is contrary to covenants though
with my brace of lovers; what will they do with their coachman's
plot? But 'tis no matter, I have my ends; and so they are cozened
I care not who does it.

CAPTAIN And, faith, Madam, I have sworn many times false, to no
purpose; and I should take it ill, if it were mine own case, to have
a friend refuse me an oath upon such an occasion.

PLEASANT And are you all of one mind?

PARSON Verily we will all swear.

PLEASANT Will you verily? What shall we do, aunt? [*laughs*]

WIDOW Do you laugh? By this light, I am heartily angry.

PLEASANT Why, as I live, let's marry them, aunt, and be revenged.

WIDOW Marry, where's the parson?

CAPTAIN Here, here, Mr Parson, come and do your office.

PLEASANT That fellow? No, by my troth, let's be honestly joined,
for luck's sake, we know not how soon we may part.

WILD What shall she do for a parson? Captain, you must run and fetch one.

CAPTAIN Yes, yes; but methinks this might serve turn; by this hand, he's a Marshall, and a Case,* by sire and dam; pray try him, by this light, he comes of the best preaching kind in Essex.

WIDOW Not I, as I live, that were a blessing in the devil's name.

PARSON A pox on your wedding; give me my wife and let me be gone.

CAPTAIN Nay, nay, no choler, parson; the ladies do not like the colour of your beard.

PARSON No, no, fetch another, and let them escape with that trick, then they'll jeer your beard's blue, i'faith.

CARELESS By this hand, he's in the right; either this parson, or take one another's words; to bed now, and marry when we rise.

PLEASANT As I live, you come not here till you are married; I have been nobody's whore yet, and I will not begin with my husband.

WILD Will you kiss upon the bargain, and promise before these witnesses not to spoil our jest, but rise and go to church.

PLEASANT And what will Mr Constant and Mr Sadd say?

CAPTAIN Why, I'll run and invite them to the wedding; and you shall see them expire in their own garters.

JOLLY No, no, ne'er fear't, their jest is only spoiled.

CAPTAIN Their jest, what jest?

JOLLY Faith, now you shall know it, and the whole plot: in the first place, your coachman is well, whose death, we, by the help of Secret, contrived, thinking by that trick to prevent this danger, and carry you out of Town.

CAPTAIN But had they this plot?

JOLLY Yes faith, and see how it thrives; they'll fret like carted bawds† when they hear this news.

---

* a Marshall, and a Case: Two noted Presbyterian divines. Stephen Marshall (1594?–1655) preached the famous sermon on Judges V.23 ('Curse you Meroz . . .') before the House of Commons on 13 February 1641. Thomas Case (1598–1682) was a doctrinaire minister ejected from his living for refusing to conform.
† carted bawds: bawds punished by being carried through the streets in a cart.

PLEASANT Why, aunt; would you have thought Mr Sadd a plotter? Well, 'tis some comfort we have them to laugh at.

WIDOW Nay faith, then, gentlemen, give us leave to rise, and I'll take my venture, if it be but for a revenge on them.

CARELESS Gentlemen, bear witness.

CAPTAIN Come, come away, I'll get the points; I'm glad the coachman's well, the rogue had like to have spoiled our comedy.

[*Exeunt Omnes*]

SCENE III

Enter the Lady Love-all, Master Sadd, and Constant, undressed and buttoning themselves as they go.

SADD Married?

CONSTANT And to them?

LOVE-ALL Aye, married, if you prevent it not; catched with a trick, an old stale trick; I have seen a ballad on't.

SADD We shall go near to prevent 'em. – Boy, my sword.

Enter Captain.

CAPTAIN Whither so fast?

SADD You guess.

CAPTAIN If you mean the wedding, you come too late.

CONSTANT Why, are they married?

CAPTAIN No, but lustily promised.

SADD We may come time enough to be revenged though. –

CAPTAIN Upon whom? Yourselves, for you are only guilty: who carried them thither last night? Who laid the plot for the coach-man?

SADD Why, do they know it?

LOVE-ALL Well, you'll find the poet a rogue, 'tis he that has betrayed you; and if you'll take my counsel, be revenged upon him.

CONSTANT Nay, we were told he did not love us.

CAPTAIN By my life, you wrong him; upon my knowledge the poet meant you should have them.

SADD Why, who had the power to hinder then?

CAPTAIN I know not where the fault lies directly; they say, the

wits of the Town would not consent to't, they claim a right in the
ladies, as orphan-wits.

CONSTANT The wits! Hang 'em in their strong lines.

CAPTAIN Why aye, such a clinch as that has undone you; and upon
my knowledge 'twere enough to hinder your next match.

SADD Why, what have they to do with us?

CAPTAIN I know not what you have done to disoblige them; but
they crossed it; there was amongst 'em too a pair of she-wits,
something stricken in years; they grew in fury at the mention of
it, and concluded you both with an authority out of a modern
author; besides 'tis said, you run naturally into the sixpenny
room* and steal sayings, and a discourse more than your penny-
worth of jests, every term; why, just now, you spit out one jest
stolen from a poor play, that has but two more in five acts; what
conscience is there in't, knowing how dear we pay poets for our
plays?

CONSTANT 'Twas madam with the ill face, one of those whom you
refused to salute the other day, at Chipp's house; a cheesecake
had saved all this.

LOVE-ALL Why do you not make haste about your business, but
lose time with this babbler?

SADD Madam, will you give us leave to make use of your coach?

LOVE-ALL You may command it, Sir; when you have done, send
him to the Exchange, where I'll dispatch a little business, and be
with you immediately.   [*Exeunt all but the Captain*]

CAPTAIN So, this fire's kindled; put it out that can. What would
not I give for a peeper's place at the meeting; I'll make haste, and
it shall go hard but I'll bear my part of the mirth too.   [*Exit*]

SCENE IV

Enter Pleasant, Careless, Wild, Parson, Jolly, Wanton and Secret: the
Fiddlers play as they come in.

PARSON Master Jolly, I find I am naturally inclined to mirth this
day, and methinks my corns ache more than my horns; and to a
man that has read Seneca a cuckold ought to be no grief; especially

* sixpenny room: the cheapest part of the theatre.

in this parish where I see such droves of St Luke's clothing;*
there's little Secret too, th'allay† of waiting-woman, makes me
hope, she may prove metal of the parson's standard. Find a way
to rid me of Wanton, and I'll put in to be chaplain to this merry
family; if I did not inveigle formal Secret, you should hang me; I
know the trick on't; 'tis but praying too, and preaching of the
waiting-woman, then carefully seeing her cushion laid, with her
book and leaf turned down, does it, with a few anagrams, acrostics,
and her name in the register of my Bible: these charm the soft-
souled sinner; then sometimes to read a piece of my sermon, and
tell her, a Saturday, where my text shall be, spells that work more
than philtres.

JOLLY If you can be serious, we'll think of this at leisure. – See how
they eye Wanton.

CARELESS What? Consulting parson? Let us be judges betwixt
you; d'ye hear, Jack, if he offers ready money, I counsel, as a
friend, take it; for, by this light, if you refuse it, your wife will not;
d'ye see those gay petticoats?

PARSON Yes, if you mean my wife's.

CARELESS You know th'are his, and she only wears 'em for his
pleasure; and 'tis dangerous to have a wife under another man's
petticoats; what if you should find his breeches upon hers?

PARSON Are not you married too? Take care that yours does not
wear the breeches, another kind of danger, but as troublesome as
that, or sore eyes; and if she get but a trick of taking as readily as
she's persuaded to give, you may find a horn, at home; I have
seen a cuckold of your complexion; if he had had as much hoof as
horn, you might have hunted the beast by his slat.‡

PLEASANT How fine she is! And, by this light, a handsome wench!
Mr Jolly, I am easier persuaded to be reconciled to your fault,
than any man's I have seen, of this kind; her eyes have more

---

* St Luke's clothing: On 18 October Cuckolds' Fair was held (on St Luke's
Day) in Charlton near Greenwich, whence a procession marched wearing
horns from Cuckolds' Haven on the south bank of the Thames. The origin
of this fair was reputed to be King John's having been discovered in an affair
with a miller's wife. He compensated the miller with a large estate, on condition he toured his lands on St Luke's Day wearing a pair of horns.
† allay: alloy.   ‡ slat: track.

arguments in 'em than a thousand of those that seduce the world; hang me if those quivers be not full of darts; I could kiss that mouth, myself. Is this she my aunt quarrelled with you for?

JOLLY The same, self-same. And by this hand, I was barbarous to her, for your aunt's sake; and had I not scaped that mischief of matrimony, by this light, I had never seen her again; but I was resolved not to quit her, till I was sure of a wife, for fear of what has followed; had I been such an ass as to have left her upon the airy hopes of a widow's oaths; what a case had I been in now? You see, your aunt's provided of a man. Bless him, and send him patience, 'twould have been fine to have seen me walking, and sighing upon cold hunting, seeking my whore again, or forced to make use of some common mercenary thing that sells sin and diseases, crimes, penance and sad repentance together; here's consolation and satisfaction, in Wanton, though a man lose his meal with the widow. And, faith, be free, how do you like my girl; rid thee of her; what does she want now, pray, but a jointure, to satisfy any honest man? Speak your conscience; ladies don't you think a little repentance, hereafter, will serve, for all the small sins that good nature can act with such a sinner?

PARSON Pray, Sir, remember she's my wife; and be so civil to us both, as to forget these things.

JOLLY For that, Jack, we'll understand hereafter, 'tis but a trick of youth, man, and her jest will make us both merry, I warrant thee.

PARSON Pray, Sir, no more of your jests, nor your Jack; remember my coat and calling. This familiarity both with my wife and my-self, is not decent; your clergy with Christian names are scarce held good Christians.

Enter Widow.

WIDOW I wonder at nothing so much as Mr Jolly's mirth, today; where lies his part of the jest? Cozened or refused by all, not a fish that stays in's net.

JOLLY No, what's this? [*Jolly hugs Wanton*] Show me a fairer in all your streams; nor is this my single joy, who am pleased to find you may be cozened; rejoice to see you may be brought to lie with a man for a jest; let me alone to fit you with a trick too.

CARELESS Faith, it must be some new trick; for thou art so beaten at the old one, 'twill neither please thee nor her; besides, I mean to teach her that myself.

PLEASANT I shall never be perfectly quiet in my mind, till I see somebody as angry as myself; yet I have some consolation when I think on the wise plot that killed the coachman, how the plague, red cross and halberd has cut their fingers that designed it, their anger will be perfect. Secret says they are coming, and that the Lady Love-all has given 'em the alarm.

Enter Sadd and Constant.

WILD And see where the parties come, – storms and tempests in their minds, their looks are daggers.

PLEASANT Servant, what? You're melancholy and full of wonder; I see you have met the news.

SADD Yes Madam, we have heard a report that will concern both your judgment and your honour.

PLEASANT Alas, Sir, we're innocent; 'tis mere predestination.

CONSTANT All weddings, Mr Sadd, you know go by chance, like hanging.

PLEASANT And, I thank my stars, I have 'scaped hanging; to ha' been his bride had been both.

CONSTANT This is not like the promise you made us yesterday.

WIDOW Why truly, servant, I scarce know what I do yet; the fright of the plague had so possessed my mind with fear that I could think and dream of nothing, last night, but of a tall black man, that came and kissed me in my sleep, and slapped his whip in mine ears, 'twas a saucy ghost, (not unlike my coachman that's dead) and accused you of having a hand in his murder, and vowed to haunt me till I was married. I told my niece the dream.

PLEASANT Nay, the ghost sighed, and accused Secret and Master Sadd of making him away. Confess, faith, had you a hand in that bloody jest?

WIDOW Fie, servant; could you be so cruel as to join with my woman against me?

CONSTANT 'Tis well, ladies; why a pox do you look at me, this was your subtle plot; a pox on your clerk's wit; you said the jest would beget a comedy when 'twas known, and so I believe 'twill.

SADD Madam, I find you have discovered our design, whose chief
end was, to prevent this mischief which I doubt not, but you'll
both live to repent your share of, before you have done travelling
to the Epsoms, Burbons,* and the Spaws,† to cure those travelled
diseases these knights errant have, with curiosity, sought out for
you; 'tis true, th' are mischiefs that dwell in pleasant countries,
yet those roses have their thorns; and I doubt not, but these
gentlemen's wit may sting as well as please, sometime; and you
may find it harder to satisfy their travelled experience, than to
have suffered our home-bred ignorance.

CARELESS Hark, if he be not fallen into a fit of his cousin; these
names of places he has stolen out of her receipt-book; amongst
all whose diseases, find me any so dangerous, troublesome or
incurable, as a fool, a lean, pale, sighing, coughing fool, that's rich
and poor both, being born to an estate, without a mind or heart
capable to use it, of a nature so miserable he grudges himself
meat; nay, they say, he eats his meals twice, a fellow whose
breath smells of yesterday's dinner, and stinks as if he had eat all
our suppers over again; I would advise you Mr Sadd to sleep with
your mouth open, to air it, or get the brewer to ton it; faugh, an
empty justice, that stinks of the lees and casks, and belches Little-
ton‡ and Ployden's§ cases; dost thou think any woman that has
wit, or honour, would kiss that bung-hole; by this light, his head
and belly look as blue and lank as French rabbits, or stale poultry;
alas, Sir, my lady would have a husband to rejoice with, no green-
tailed lecturer, to stand sentry at his bed's side, while his nasty
soul scours through him, sneaking out at the backdoor. – These,
Sir, are diseases which neither the Spa, or Bath, can cure; your
garters and willow are a more certain remedy.

CONSTANT Well, Sir, I find our plot's betrayed, and we have
patience left; 'tis that damned captain has informed.

SADD Yet 'tis one comfort, Madam, that you have missed that man

* Burbons: Bourbonne-les-Bains.
† Spaws: an older pronunciation of Spas, still in use in northern England.
‡ Littleton: Sir Thomas Littleton (1402–1481), a famous judge and legal
authority, author of *Tenures*.
§ Ployden: Edmund Plowden (1518–1585) a famous jurist, author of *Les
Comentaries* (1571). Versions in English were published later.

of war, that Knight of Finsbury;* his dowager, with ale and switches, would ha' bred a ballad.

PLEASANT Faith, Sir, you see what a difficulty it is, in this age, for a woman to live honest, though she have a proper man to her husband; therefore it behoves us to consider, who we choose.

JOLLY The lady has reason; for being allowed but one, who would choose such weazels as we see daily married, that are all head and tail, crooked, dirty, sold vermin, predestined for cuckolds, painted snails, with houses on their backs, and horns as big as Dutch cows; would any woman marry such? Nay, can any woman be honest, that lets such hod-man-dods† crawl o'er her virgin breast, and belly, or suffer 'em to leave their slimy paths upon their bodies only for jointures? Out, 'tis mercenary and base; the generous heart has only the laws of nature and kindness in her view; and when she will oblige, friend is all the ties that nature seeks, who can both bear and excuse those kind crimes; and I believe, one as poor as the despised captain, and neglected courtier, may make a woman as happy in a friendship as Master Sadd, who has as many faults as we have debts; one, whose father had no more credit with nature, than ours had with fortune; whose soul wears rags as well as the captain's body.

SADD Nay then, I'll laugh; for I perceive, y'are angrier than we; alas, has lost both ventures, Wanton, and the Widow.

JOLLY Both, and neither so unlucky as to be thy wife; thy face is hanged with blacks already, we may see the bells toll in thy eyes; a bride and a wedding shirt? A sexton and a winding sheet? A scrivener to draw up jointures? A parson to make thy will, man; by this light he's as chap-fallen as if he had lain under the table all night.

CARELESS Faith, Master Sadd, he's parlously in the right; ne'er think of marrying in this dull clime, wedlock's a trade you'll ne'er go through with; wives draw bills upon sight, and 'twill not be for your credit to protest 'em; rather follow my counsel, and marry *la Venetiano* for a night and away; a pistole‡ jointure does

---

* Knight of Finsbury: Finsbury Fields, where the militia drilled.
† hod-man-dods: shell-snails, deformed persons.
‡ pistole: a gold coin: if Spanish, then worth about 16 to 18 shillings; if French ,the louis d'or of Louis XIII.

it; then 'tis but repenting in the morning, and leave your woman, and the sin both, i'th' bed; but if you play the fool, like your friends, and marry in serious earnest, you may repent it too, as they do; but where's the remedy?

WIDOW What was't you said, Sir, do you repent?

CARELESS By this hand, Widow, I don't know; but we have pursued a jest a great way. Parson, are you sure we're married.

PARSON Yes, I warrant you, for their escaping.

CARELESS Their escaping? Fool, thou mistak'st me, there's no fear of that; but I would fain know, if there be no way for me to get out of this noose; no hole to hide a man's head in from this wedlock?

PARSON Not any, but what I presume she'll show you anon.

CARELESS Hum! Now do I feel all my fears flowing in upon me; Wanton and Mistress Pleasant both grow dangerously handsome, a thousand graces in each, I never observed before, now, just now, when I must not taste, I begin to long for some of their plums.

WIDOW Is this serious, Sir?

CARELESS Yes truly, Widow, sadly serious; is there no way to get three or four mouthfuls of kisses from the parson's wife?

WIDOW This is sad, Sir, upon my wedding day, to despise me for such a common thing.

SADD As sad, as I could wish; this is a jest makes me laugh. – Common? No Madam, that's too bitter, she's forest only, where the royal chase is as free as fair.

WANTON Were not you a widow today?

SADD Yes faith, girl, and as foolish a one as ever coach jumbled out of joint.

WANTON Stay then till tomorrow, and tell me the difference betwixt us.

SADD I hope, thou'lt prove a she-prophet; could I live to see thee turn honest wife, and she the wanton widow.

WANTON I cannot but laugh, to see how easy it is, to lose or win the opinion of the world; a little custom heals all, or else what's the difference betwixt a married widow and one of us? Can any woman be pure, or worth the serious sighing of a generous heart, that has had above one hand laid upon her? Is there place to write above one lover's name, with honour, in her heart; 'tis indeed for one a royal palace; but if it admits of more, an hospital, or an inn, at best, as well as ours; only off from the road, and less frequented.

PLEASANT Shrewdly urged.

WANTON And though the sins of my family threw me into want, and made me subject to the treachery of that broken faith, to whose perjury I owe all my crimes, yet still I can distinguish betwixt that folly and this honour, which must tell you; 'He or she that would be thought twice so, was never once a lover'.

CONSTANT Parson, thou art fitted; a whore, and apothegms! What sport will she make us under a tree, with a salad, and sayings, in the summer?

WILD Come, Wanton, no fury; you see my aunt's angry.

WANTON So am I, Sir, and yet can calmly reason this truth; married widows, though chaste to the law and custom, yet their second hymens make that which was but dying in the first husband's bed, a stain in the second sheets, where all their kindness and repeated embraces want their value, because they're sullied and have lost their lustre.

SADD By this light, I'll go to school to Wanton, she has opened my eyes, and I begin to believe I have 'scaped miraculously; by this hand, wench, I was within an inch of being married to this danger; for what can we call these second submissions, but a tolerated lawful mercenariness, which though it be a rude and harsh expression, yet your carriage deserves it.

PLEASANT Fie, Master Sadd, pray leave being witty; I fear, 'tis a mortal sin, to begin in the fifth act of your days upon an old subject too, abusing of widows, because they despise you.

WIDOW Alas, niece, let him alone, he may come in, for his share; the Parson, that has so oft received 'em, will not refuse him tithes, there, in charity.

WANTON That, or conveniency, interest, or importunity, may, by your example prevail; but 'tis not fair play, Madam, to turn your lover to the common, as you call it, now he's rid lean in your service; take heed, Mr Careless, and warning Mr Sadd; you see how fit for the scavenger's team your lady leaves her lovers.

CARELESS Such a lecture before I had married would ha' made me have considered of this matter. Dost thou hear Wanton, let us forgive one another, being married, for that folly has made us guilty alike.

WANTON And I would fain know the difference betwixt ours, and a wedding crime, which is worst; to let love, youth and good humour betray us to a kindness, or to be gravely seduced by some aunt or uncle, without consideration of the disparity of age, birth, or persons, to lie down before a jointure; ladies, you may flatter yourselves, but the ingenuous part of the world cannot deny, but such minds, had they been born where our faults are not only tolerated but protected, would have listened to the same things, interest counsels thereto.

CARELESS Parson, what boot betwixt our wives? Either come to a price, or draw off your doxy.

PARSON Propose, propose, here will be mirth anon.

SADD Yes, yes, propose, while I break it to your lady; Madam, you see, here's a proper man to be had, and money to boot – What, dumb?

WANTON No, she's only thinking; faith, Madam, try 'em both tonight, and choose tomorrow.

WILD Come, no more of this; aunt, take my word for your husband, that have had more experience of him than all these; 'tis true, he will long for these girls, as children do for plums; and when h'as done, make a meal upon cheese; and you must not wonder, nor quarrel at what he says in his humour, but judge him by his actions; and when he is in his fit, and raves most, put him into your bed, and fold him close in your arms, aunt; if he does not rise as kind and as good a husband as he that sings psalms best, hang me; why, you're a fool, aunt; a widow, and dislike a longing bridegroom! I thought you had known better; do you love a spurred horse, rather than a duker,* that neighs, and scrapes? I would not say this, but that I know him; let him not go out of your sight, for he's now in season, a ripe mature husband; no delays; if you let him hang longer upon hope his fruit will fall alone.

WIDOW You are merry, Sir; but if I had known this humour – [*she kisses Careless, and he kisses her twice*]

WILD You'd ha' kissed him first; but being ignorant, let me make

* duker: a cringing horse or person.

you blush; come, a kiss, and all's friends. – How now, Sir, again, again, aunt, look to yourself.

CARELESS Um! By this light, sweetheart, and I thank thee; [*kisses her again*] nay widow, there's no jesting with these things – Nay, I am a lion, in my love: aware, puss, if you flatter me, for I shall deceive you.

PARSON Since all are cozened, why should I be troubled at my fortune; faith gentlemen, what will you two give me for a wife, betwixt you?

CONSTANT Faith, they're mischiefs dear bought, though a man get 'em for nothing.

PARSON I'm almost of his mind; and if other people find no more pleasure in a married life then I, upon my wedding day, I'd pass my time in the Piazza, with the mountebank, and let him practise upon my teeth, and draw 'em too ere he persuades the words of matrimony out of my mouth again. Aye, aye, Mr Constant, you may laugh, you ha' missed a wife; would I were in your case, the world should see how cheerfully I should bear such an affliction.

CONSTANT Jack, I ha' made my peace at home, and by seeing others shipwrecked will avoid the danger, and here resolve, never to sigh again for any woman; they're weeds grow in every hedge; and transplanting of 'em thus to our beds gives certain trouble, seldom pleasure, never profit.

Enter Captain.

PARSON See where the enemy comes; now if you be wise, arm, and unite against him, as a common foe; he's come from his old lady, designing a reconciliation; the rogue's provident, and would fain have a nest for his age to rest in; buff and feathers do well in the youth and heat of thirty; but in the winter of old age, captain at threescore, lame and lean, may lie with the almanac out of date.

CAPTAIN The parson's grown witty, and prophesies upon the strength of bride-cake; if I guess aright, thou'lt be hanged; for 'tis a truth, I have been endeavouring to make it appear, her fears were mistaken in me: but I find the witch more implacable than the devil; the waiting-woman is harder to forgive her part, than my lady. Faithful will not be reconciled, the merciless bawd is all fire and sword, no quarter; bless me from an old waiting-woman's wrath; she'll never forgive me the disappointing her of a promise when I was drunk; her lady and she are coming, but in such a fury, I would not have the storm find you in the street; therefore I counsel you to avoid the boys, and take shelter in the next house.

WILD No, let's home, and with all diligence get our dinner, to defend us; and let the porter dispute it at the wicket, till she signs articles of peace.

OMNES Agreed. – [*Careless is kind to the Widow; as he goes out, Wild and Pleasant go together, Jolly and the Parson's wife ⟨Wanton⟩ go together*]

WILD See how they pair now, 'tis not threescore year will part 'em now he has tasted a kiss or two.

JOLLY Parson, I'll be your brideman.

PARSON 'Tis well, Sir, I shall ha' my time too.

JOLLY Aye by this hand; nay, we'll share fairly.

CAPTAIN That's but reason, Wanton; and since he grows tame, use him kindly for my sake.

PARSON Can any of you digest sponge and arsenic?

CAPTAIN Arsenic? What's that?

PARSON An Italian salad,* which I'll dress for you, by Jove, ere I'll walk in my canonical-coat lined with horn; death, if I suffer this, we shall have that damned courtier pluck on his shoes with the parson's musons;† fine i'faith, none but the small levite's brow to plant your shoeing-horn-seed in? – [*as he is going off the Captain stays him*] How now?

CAPTAIN Prithee, Jack, stay, and say something to the gentlemen, by way of epilogue. Thou art a piece of a scurvy poet thyself; prithee oblige the author, and give us a line or two in praise of his play.

PARSON I oblige him? Hang him and all his friends, and hurt nobody; yes, I'm likely to speak for him; you see how I ha' been used today betwixt you, I shall find a time to be revenged; let go my cloak; I have a province, within, of mine own to govern, let me go.

CAPTAIN Who, thy wife? Faith stay, and give them an opportunity; thy pain will be the sooner over: you see 'tis a thing resolved

* Italian salad: slang for poison.
† musons: horns shed by a deer, hence a reference to cuckoldom.

betwixt 'em, and now thou'rt satisfied in the matter, be wise and silent; who knows what good she may do thee another time; I dare say, if she had as many souls in her as she had men, she'd bring thee a cure of herself.

PARSON Let me go, or I shall be as troublesome as you are injurious, for all your titles, Sir.

CAPTAIN Lend me your cloak then, to appear more decent; you'd not ha' me present epilogue in buff,* whoreson dunce, with a red nose.

PARSON Sir, my business is praying, not epilogues.

CAPTAIN With that face? By this light, 'tis a scandal to see it flaming so near the altar; thou look'st as if thou'dst cry 'Tope', in the face of the congregation, instead of 'Amen'.

PARSON Thou'rt an ass, 'tis proper there, 't has zeal and fervour in't, and burns before the altar like the primitive lamps.

CAPTAIN I cry thee mercy; by this light, he'll make it sacrilege anon to steal his nose; thou'lt entitle the altar to that coal; was't not kindled *ex voto*? Nay, I will have your cloak.

PARSON Take it; would 'twere Nessus his shirt,† for you and your poet's sake. [*Exit Parson*]

CAPTAIN What, does the rogue wish 'twere made of nettles?

Captain puts on his cloak, and addresses himself to speak the epilogue, and is interrupted by the Lady Love-all and Faithful her woman, who in haste and full of anger pull him by the cloak.

LOVE-ALL By your favour, Sir; did you see any company pass this way?

The Music plays.

CAPTAIN None, but the three brides, and they are gone just before you. – Hark, the music will guide you.

LOVE-ALL Is it certain then they're married?

* buff: black cloaks were formerly worn by actors speaking prologues and epilogues.

† Nessus his shirt: Nessus, mortally wounded by Hercules, gave Deianira his tunic dipped in blood, telling her it would be a charm against infidelity. Hearing Hercules was in love with Iole, Deianira sent the tunic to him; when he put it on he was seized with dreadful torment when the tunic's venom attacked him.

CAPTAIN Yes, lady, I saw the church's rights performed.

FAITHFUL Why does your ladyship lose time in talking with this fellow; don't you know him, Madam? 'Tis the rascally captain, hid in a black cloak; I know you, sirrah.

LOVE-ALL She has reason; now I mark him better, I should know that false face too; see Faithful, there are those treacherous eyes still.

CAPTAIN Alas, you mistake me, Madam, I am Epilogue now; the captain's within; and as a friend I counsel you, not to incense the gentlemen against the poet, for he knows all your story; and if you anger him he'll put it in a play; but if you'll do friendly offices, I'll undertake, instead of your pearl you lost, to help you to the jewel, the Scotch dictionary will tell you the value of it; let them go alone, and fret not at their loss; stay, and take my counsel, it shall be worth three revenges.

LOVE-ALL Well, what is't, Sir?

CAPTAIN They say, you have a great power over the parson; if you can prevail with him to express his anger in some satiric comedy (for the knave has wit, and they say his genius lies that way), tell him, 'tis expected he should be revenged upon the illiterate courtier that made this play; if you can bring this business about, I may find a way, as Epilogue, to be thankful, though the captain abused you today. Think on't, Stephen★ is as handsome, when the play is done, as Mr Wild was in the scene.

LOVE-ALL There's something of reason in what he says. – But my friend, how shall one believe you; you that were such a rascal today, in buff, is it to be hoped you can be honest only with putting on a black cloak? Well, I'll venture once again; and if I have any power, he shall sting the malicious rascal; and I think he is fit for such a business. I'm sure he has the worst tongue; and a conscience that neither honour nor truth binds; and therefore 'tis to be believed, if he will rail in public he may be even with your poet; I will clothe and feed him and his muse this seven years, but I will plague him: Secret tells me, 'twas your poet too that pawned me, today, in the tavern.

CAPTAIN By my faith, did he; nay 'twas he that told me of your friendship with Jolly.

★ Stephen: Stephen Hamerton, a handsome actor of the time.

LOVE-ALL I wonder the parson has been so long silent; a man of his coat and parts, to be beaten with a pen, by one that speaks sense by rote, like parrots; one that knows not why sense is sense, but by the sound; one that can scarce read, any, not his own hand; well, remember your promise.

CAPTAIN Leave it to me, he is yours; and if our plot take, you shall all have your shares in the mirth; but not the profit of the play; and the parson, more than his tithe, a second day.

LOVE-ALL We will discourse of this some other time; and pray dispatch what 'tis you have to say to this noble company, that I may be gone; for those gentlemen will be in such fury, if I stay; and think, because we are alone, God knows what.

CAPTAIN 'Tis no matter what they think, 'tis not them we are to study now; but these guests, to whom pray address yourself civilly, and beg that they would please to become fathers, and give those brides within; what say you, gentlemen, will you lend your hands to join them; the match you see is made; if you refuse, Stephen misses the wench, and then you cannot justly blame the poet. For you know, they say, that alone is enough to spoil the play. ⟨*Exeunt*⟩

NOTES

The copy text used is that of the first edition of 1663 in the Brotherton Collection, University of Leeds.

Abbreviations
F1 The first folio edition. The title page of this edition, included in the folio edition of Killigrew's *Comedies, and Tragedies*, 1664, is dated 1663.
D Dodsley's *A Select Collection of Old Plays*, IX, 1744
BD *British Drama*, Vol. III, 1810

'Sad' has been regularised to 'Sadd' and, where applicable, 'SCEN.' to 'SCENE'.

9.25   insatiate/unsatiate F1
11.15   'No, not he'/No not he F1
11.17   'No, faith'/No, faith F1
13.32   accident),/accident,) F1
15.7   country. He/country; he F1
15.15   candied/candid F1
17.22   Sure, aunt,/Sure (aunt) F1
19.1   nephew's. He/Nephews, he F1
19.18   Fall. And/Fall, and F1
20.28   rod, wench,/rod (wench) F1
21.7   *Constant, Will Jolly, Sadd/Constant, Will. Sadd, Jolly* F1
22.14   wife's/wives F1
24.13   was't/wa'st F1
25.8   Jolly, your/*Jolly*; your F1
26.9   cam'st/can'st F1
26.13   for variety;/(for variety;) F1
28.2   too/to F1
34.12   letter, I'll swear you/letter I'll swear, you F1
34.32   desire. What/desire, what F1
36.4   and of sound/and sound F1
36.22   let it be . . . prevailed. Shall – emendation in *Restoration Comedy*, ed. M. Summers, 1921/let be . . . prevailed, shall F1
37.21   others'/others F1

39.3 it, now you are his own, as/it now, you are his own; as F1
39.13 wench. Empire?/wench; Empire? F1
39.24 Happy ⟨only⟩ is/Happy only F1
39.24 family, that/family that F1
40.12 your 'Madam, I hear', and 'Madam . . . speak'; . . .
with 'you . . . Faithful';/your Madam, I hear, and
(Madam) . . . speak; . . . with you . . . Faithful; F1
41.3 me. I/me, I F1
41.4 I must . . . to do/F1 sets as prose
43.34 Fool. 'Tis/Fool, 'tis F1
44.24 F1 gives 'Come, bear . . . spied?' to CAPTAIN
44.25 *the Captain/he* F1
44.30 H'as – emendation in *Restoration Comedy*, ed. M. Summers,
1921/Has F1
47.12 CAPTAIN/ *Joll.* F1
47.23 aunt so well, and her humour, she/Aunt so well and her
humour she F1
48.14 passes – emendation in *Restoration Comedy*, ed. M. Summers,
1921/passes. F1
48.15 did, sweetheart:/did (sweetheart:) F1
49.13 with 'I . . . ladyship'./with I . . . ladyship. F1
49.27 party, niece/party Niece F1
50.15 points? Sure/points, sure F1
51.18 and misfortune not falsehood/misfortunate; not false F1
53.13 sinner that/sinner; that F1
53.16 done. I/done, I F1
54.3 innocent, at least/innocent at lest F1
54.7 love and beauty dwell BD/Love Beauty dwells F1
54.20 wine. Who's/wine, who's F1
57.2 of beauties/of a Beauties F1
57.22 beats/beat F1
57.23 springs/spring F1
58.1 husbands/Husband F1
59.30 F1 prints *Exeunt omnes* at the end of Widow's preceding
speech
61.10 F1 prints Secret *whispers Sadd* ''Twill take' as a stage
direction
63.8 CARELESS/CAPT. F1

67.30	F1 prints *Enter Jolly* after his speech
76.21	F1 prints *Exit Captain* before *The Captain makes a turn*
76.34	F1 prints *Enter Drawer* at the end of Love-all's speech
77.23	patience. O/patience, Oh F1
77.30	money. O/money; Oh F1
78.6	priest/priests F1
78.14	women can/women, can F1
80.15	sumner: Summer F1
80.34	youth BD/you, he F1
83.20	*here they . . . her out* BD/F1 prints immediately after *takes his dagger*
84.20	travel; it/travel, it F1
86.5	embraces. Do/embraces, do F1
86.35	in t'other/in the t'other F1
88.18	it/is F1
96.19	Mrs What's-her-name/Mrs (What's-her-name) F1
98.31	hear/here F1
100.8	chop emendation in *Restoration Comedy*, ed. M. Summers, 1921/Chap F1
101.21	scene/Scence F1
101.33	Well, sweetheart,/well (sweet heart) F1
105.5	he BD/and F1
108.16	jointures/joynters F1
110.20	me. [*aside*] That is . . . does it/me [That is . . . does it] *Speaks these words aside* F1
113.17	'Twas madam with/'Twas, Madam, with F1
113.30	*Enter Pleasant . . . /Enter Widow, Pleasant . . .* F1
114.29	wench! Mr/wench, Mr F1
114.31	man's I/man's; I F1
115.3	myself. Is/myself, is F1
115.6	had/had had F1
115.24	will/ill F1
116.29	married. I/married, I F1
116.31	Sadd of . . . away. Confess/Sad; of . . . away confess F1
117.28	cure; your/cure your F1
119.24	too/two F1
121.35	humour –/humour. F1
125.20	way),/way,) F1

THE MULBERRY GARDEN
by Sir Charles Sedley

INTRODUCTION

The Mulberry Garden was first performed on 18 May 1668, and was first published in the same year. Though critics seem to have found it disappointing, the play was a theatrical success. Pepys, who was at the first performance and recorded that he was never less pleased at a new play in his life, did, nonetheless, go to see the play on two other occasions. It was probably revived in 1675 and 1688, when further quarto editions were published. Some of the theatrical success may have been caused by its author's reputation as a wit and his position at court. Sir Charles Sedley was one of 'the merry gang', as Andrew Marvell described the young men who formed the circle of the Court wits, among them the Earls of Rochester and Dorset as well as the slightly older Duke of Buckingham. Sedley, a posthumous child, had grown up in the latter years of the Protectorate, his mother, Sir Henry Savile's daughter, probably being a moderate royalist, a friend of Edmund Waller, and a woman of considerable culture and charm. Charles was sent to Wadham College, Oxford, at a time when Dr Wilkins was Warden; under his tutelage the college was a centre of the new rationalism and experimental philosophy which succeeded Bacon's interest in science and eventuated in the Philosophical Club, itself to evolve into the Royal Society. Several of the Court wits, Sedley, Rochester, Carr Scroope and Gardiner, attended Wadham College, and an effect of the thinking of the *virtuosi*, the enthusiastic followers of the new science, was that reason and scepticism replaced religion and mysticism, notably in the experimental attitude of the Court wits to life. Charles succeeded his brother, Sir William, after the latter died of measles in April 1655/6, and within a year married Katharine Savage, a sister of Sir William's widow. Charles was apparently regarded with some suspicion by the Protector's Council, and was appointed by the provisional government as one of the Commissioners to raise a Militia in 1659.

After the Restoration, Sedley became a friend of the king but, unlike the other wits, 'he never asked the king for any thing'. The Duke of Ormonde described the king's young friends as 'confident young men who abhorred all discourse that was serious, and, in the liberty they assumed in drollery and raillery, preserved no reverence towards God or man, but laughed at all sober men, and even at religion itself'. They were young men reacting against Puritan austerity, and also against Cavalier conventions, and felt themselves to be liberated from the past, creating a new way of life founded upon libertine attitudes of gratifying natural appetites and passions.

Not unnaturally Sedley gained a reputation for being profane and wicked, but we find Pepys fascinated by him, enjoying his conversation at the theatre on several occasions when he sat near him. He recorded one of Sedley's loud comments on a speech in *Altemira* where an ardent lover decided to rescue his rival and hand over his mistress to him:

> I'll save my Rival and make her confess
> That I deserve while he do but possess.

Sedley remarked for the pit 'Why, what, pox, would he have more or what is there to be had more of a woman than the possessing her?'

Sedley's marriage seems to have been happy at first but Lady Katharine subsequently lost her reason, soon after the Restoration, her mania taking the form of a belief that she was a queen. About 1670 Sedley met Ann Ayscough, with whom he went through a form of marriage in 1672. They had two sons. Ann Ayscough successfully helped Sedley to reform his morals and get his finances on a sounder footing. He was 'greatly shocked' when Katharine, his daughter by his legal wife, became a mistress of James, Duke of York, and when, in the winter of 1680, he was nearly killed by the falling roof of a tennis court, this accident turned his attention more firmly to religion. There followed a lapse to easier living, then his conversion by another serious illness in 1686.

After William of Orange became king Sedley realised the change in England – and himself, and became an excellent Parliamentarian. He had first been elected to the House of Commons in 1662, initially supporting the Court party, though he later became a Whig. He was not a member of King James's only parliament, but was elected to King William's second parliament in 1690. Sedley's speeches were detached. 'I will never' he said in the House of Commons on 9 February 1692/3, 'creep into the favour of any sort of men and vote against my judgement'.

During the last decade of the seventeenth century Sedley seems to have been in and out of favour with the Court. He was regarded as the equal of Sir George Etherege by their contemporaries, and now that modern criticism has got over Macaulay's difficulties with the Restoration dramatists his work can be dispassionately assessed and its merits recognised.

Sedley's ability to write good, lively fluent prose appears to advantage in parts of *The Mulberry Garden*. When Olivia, one of Sir John Everyoung's daughters, prefers the Mulberry Garden to the 'long walk at home' we find she puts her idea with an unobtrusive grace and ease of speech:

For in my opinion half a score young men, and fine ladies well dressed, are a greater ornament to a garden than a wilderness of sycamores, orange and lemon trees, and the rustling of rich vests and silk petticoats, better music than the purling of streams, chirping of birds, or any of our country entertainments.

This kind of prose is the better appreciated by a modern audience because it is so much more attractive than the heroic verse spoken by Sir Samuel Forecast's daughters, Althea and Diana, and their lovers, the cavaliers Eugenio and Philander. The contrast between the daughters of Sir Samuel Forecast, the severe puritan, and those of Sir John Everyoung, the jolly cavalier, is not confined to language alone, for Olivia and her sister Victoria are a madcap pair, who were originally to have given the play another name, that of *The Wandering Ladies*. The two brothers, Forecast and Everyoung, have differing views on how to bring up children and beneath its stock situations, its Restoration raffishness, the play contains an echo of Molière's attempt to show women as rational beings in *L'Ecole des Maris* (itself probably founded on Terence's *Adelphi*). Everyoung's two daughters use their liberty to discover in the Mulberry Garden the true nature of the two gallants, Modish and Estridge. Wildish helps in the stirring up of the two coxcombs and Estridge is tricked into marrying the Widow. All of this is part and parcel of Restoration comedy, but Sedley's plot is somewhat shapeless. He intended a contrast between the world of literary convention, as exemplified in the stilted conversation of the other lovers in heroic verse, and the real world of the Restoration. The play's action is set in 1660, the year when, through the action of General Monk, Charles the Second came to his throne and there was ushered in what Dryden called 'a very merry dancing, drinking, laughing, quaffing and unthinking time'. Sedley takes part in the shaping of Restoration comedy, he strives to capture the light, flippant gaiety of the Court, and in Wildish he succeeds in portraying a man who is friendly with puritan and cavalier, who has kept himself 'unengaged', and is representative of the new generation of rational wits and pleasure-seeking men about Town. Unlike Modish and Estridge he posseses true wit, a sense of style and good manners (similar to that which his creator was to display in later life), a potential for better things.

When Olivia and Wildish agree to marry, there is an anticipation of Congreve's brilliance in the scene between Millamant and Mirabell in *The Way of the World*, and the whole play is suddenly lifted out of the ordinary and a more thoughtful note is added than is provided in, say, the cudgelling of Sir Samuel Forecast (realistic and likely to appeal to Restoration audiences which were used to such things happening in real life) or Diana in male attire (an idealistic episode which, like Horatio's support of Eugenio, is less convincing because of its heroic setting). Indeed Sedley is concerned with problems of marriage, and presents, in contrast to the heroic attitude, a new realism which is well put by Olivia:

Nothing venture, nothing win, and for my part I am resolved to allow all innocent liberty. This matrimony is a pill will scarce go down with a young man without gilding.

Sir Charles Sedley

The Mulberry-Garden

A COMEDY

As it is acted by His Majestie's Servants
at the Theatre-Royal

Written by
the Honourable Sir Charles Sedley

LONDON

Printed for H. Herringman, at the Sign of the Blew Anchor
in the Lower Walk of the New Exchange.
1668

THE EPISTLE DEDICATORY

To Her Grace the Duchess of Richmond and Lennox⋆

Madam,

'Tis an unquestioned privilege we authors have of troubling whom-soever we please with an epistle dedicatory, as we call it, when we print a play; kings and princes have never been able to exempt either themselves or their favourites from our persecution. I think your grace (for a person of so great eminence, beauty, indulgence to wit, and other advantages that mark you out to suffer under addresses of this nature) has 'scaped very well hitherto. For I do not remember your name yet made a sanctuary to any of these criminals: but, Madam, your time is come, and you must bear it patiently. All the favour I can show you, is that of a good executioner, which is not to prolong your pain. You see, Madam, here the unhappiness of being born in our time, in which to that virtue and perfection, the Greeks and Romans would have given temples and altars, the highest thing we dare dedicate, is a play or some such trifle. This that I now offer to your grace, you were so kind to when it was in loose sheets, that by degrees you have trained it up to the confidence of appearing in print before you: and I hope you will find it no hard matter to pardon a presumption you have yourself been accessory to, especially in one that is entirely,

Madam

Your grace's devoted and

obedient servant,

CHARLES SEDLEY

⋆ Duchess of Richmond and Lennox: Frances Stuart or Stewart (1648–1702). Many men, notably the king, Buckingham, Anthony Hamilton, John Roettiers and Nathaniel Lee, fell in love with her, but she was thought to have refused all her admirers and, in 1667, she eloped with Charles Stuart, third Earl of Richmond and Lennox.

DRAMATIS PERSONAE

⟨MEN⟩
Sir John Everyoung
Sir Samuel Forecast
Harry Modish
Ned Estridge
Jack Wildish
Snappum
Eugenio
Philander
Horatio

⟨WOMEN⟩
Diana ⎱
Althea ⎰ Forecast's daughters
Widow Brightstone
Victoria ⎱
Olivia ⎰ Everyoung's daughters

Officer and Assistants, Servant to Sir Samuel Forecast, Musicians and Dancers, Prentices, and Sedan-men

PROLOGUE

New poets (like fresh beauties come to Town)
Have all that are decayed to cry 'em down,
All that are envious, or that have writ ill:
For wits and heroes fain would, dying, kill.
Like statesmen in disgrace, they ill endure
A better conduct should our good procure:
As an old sinner, who in's youth has known
Most women bad, dares venture upon none.
Our author, seeing here the fate of plays,
The dangerous rocks upon the coast of praise,
The cruel critic and malicious wit,
Who think themselves undone if a play hit:
And like those wretches who on shipwrecks thrive,
Rage if the vessel do the storm out-live,
By others' loss he stood a while forewarned,
But against tempting hope no man is armed:
Amongst great gamesters, when deep play is seen,
Few that have money but at last come in:
He has known many with a trifling sum,
Into vast fortunes by your favours run:
This gives him confidence to try his fate,
And makes him hope he is not come too late;
If you'll undo him quite, like rooks* begin,
And for this once in cunning let him win:
He hopes the ladies at small faults will wink,
And a new poet, a new servant think.

* rooks: cardsharpers.

ACT ONE

SCENE I

Sir John Everyoung's house stands

Enter Sir John Everyoung, and Sir Samuel Forecast.

EVERYOUNG Well, for all this heat, let's every one govern his own family as he has a mind to't; I never vex myself that your daughters live shut up as if they were in Spain or Italy; nor pray don't you trouble yourself that mine see plays, balls, and take their innocent diversion, as the custom of the country, and their age requires.

FORECAST They are my nieces, as they are your daughters, and I'll tell you, you spoil 'em with your own examples: youth may well be allowed to be stark mad, when they see age so extravagant: is that a dress for my elder brother, and a reverend justice?

EVERYOUNG Yes, and a properer than your little cuffs, black cap, and boots there, for a gentleman.

FORECAST Of eighteen I confess, but not of fifty.

EVERYOUNG Yes, though he were as old as any before the Flood; and for my part I'll not bate a riband for all the whole tribe of you can say: you know yourself every fool would fain be thought wise; and why an old man should not desire to be thought young, I see no reason: as long as I am whole at heart, I'm resolved my clothes shall ne'er betray me.

FORECAST There's no need on't, your face does it sufficiently; come I'm ashamed to see you every day set out thus powdered, and trimmed, like an old player, to act a young prince; your periwig* I like very well, it serves to keep your bald pate warm, but that flirting hat there looks as it were made rather for your wit than your head. Pray which is most *à-la-mode*, right reverend spark? – Points, or laces? Girdle, or shoulder-belts? What say your letters out of France?

EVERYOUNG Lord, what pains you take to quarrel at my dress and mirth, as if age were not tedious enough already, but we must add neglect of ourselves, and moroseness toward others: children

* periwig: periwigs began to come into fashion about 1663.

nowadays are not so fond of their parents, that we need use any art to make 'em hate us.

FORECAST Well, go then, and carry your daughters abroad, and break their bellies with sillabub,* 'tis the greatest kindness you can do 'em now; as you have bred 'em, you may e'en keep 'em to yourself, and save their portions; I believe nobody will be very fond of a Hyde Park filly† for a wife; nor an old boy that looks like a pedlar's pack for a father-in-law: but now I think on't, you are such a spark, they'd lose their reputations with you if they had any.

EVERYOUNG For ought I see good brother, they stand as fair in the opinion of the world as yours, and have done nothing but what I like very well.

FORECAST What do you count it nothing, to be all day abroad, to live more in their coach than at home, and if they chance to keep the house an afternoon, to have the yard full of sedans, the hall full of footmen and pages, and their chambers covered all over with feathers and ribands,‡ dancing and playing at cards with 'em till morning.

EVERYOUNG Why, where's the hurt of all this?

FORECAST O no hurt at all; but if they were my daughters I should be looking for cradles and nurses, I should be sorry to hear Diana or Althea went abroad without some discreet body to look after them, or were at home indeed without employing their time in some piece of huswifery, or at least some good book.

EVERYOUNG You and I shall never hit it, for now I think those women who have been least used to liberty, most apt to abuse it, when they come to't.

FORECAST O this fine believing gentleman, I should laugh heartily to see him a grandfather without a son-in-law.

Enter to them Victoria and Olivia.

VICTORIA Sir if you don't use the coach yourself, my sister and I would go abroad this afternoon.

---

* sillabub: a drink or dish made of cream or milk curdled by the addition of whisky, wine or cider, then sweetened and flavoured.
† Hyde Park filly: a courtesan.
‡ feathers and ribands: probably fops and beaux.

EVERYOUNG Take it children, but don't keep the horses out too late.

FORECAST What! Never ask 'em whither they're going? By your favour I'll put that question to 'em; come hither Victoria, what visits do you intend this afternoon?

VICTORIA None Sir, we were only going a-rambling.

FORECAST A-rambling, methinks that word sounds very prettily i' the mouth of a young maid; next time I ask 'em whither they're going, I believe they'll answer me, 'To drink a bottle or two': but whither pray?

OLIVIA For that Sir we shall take counsel of the weather, either up into the City, or towards the Park.

FORECAST What, none but you two?

OLIVIA We intended to call on my cousins Althea and Diana.

FORECAST They took physic this morning, and are not well, you'll lose your labour.

VICTORIA Sir they sent for us but an hour ago.

FORECAST You had better go without 'em, they are all undressed, to stay for 'em would but make you lose the sweet of the evening.

EVERYOUNG Brother, what are you jealous of them too? I assure you they are no men in women's clothes.

FORECAST I am not jealous of 'em, but since you'd have it so, I'd as lief they'd keep away.

EVERYOUNG And I'd as lief you'd keep away, till you understand yourself better; what? You think your daughters, like your money, never safe, but under lock and key; who would you have 'em converse with, if not with their relations?

FORECAST With those that are a kin to 'em in manners and be-haviour, such as they may learn some goodness of; I see nothing they can learn here but vanity.

VICTORIA Sister they begin to be angry, come let's leave 'em till the storm be over.   [*Exeunt*]

FORECAST What are they gone? I warrant if we had been reading a play, or romance, we should not have been rid of 'em so soon; but I'll spoil their sport at my house.

EVERYOUNG A precious design, and worthy of your gravity! But if you do brother, I'll tell you one thing, you'll go near to spoil a match at cross purposes:* farewell.   [*Exeunt*]

* cross purposes: a game of cross-questions.

SCENE II

Modish his chamber

Enter Henry Modish and Ned Estridge.

MODISH Good-morrow, Ned, I thought I had left you too deep engaged last night to have been here thus early.

ESTRIDGE Why you sneaked away just as the sport began, like a half-bred cock that strikes a stroke or two briskly, and then runs.

MODISH Faith, I had so many irons in the fire for today, I durst not run the hazard of a disorder last night: but you know my heart was with you.

ESTRIDGE You would not have repented it, if your whole body and soul had been with us; Jack Wildish sent for a dozen more of champagne and a brace of such girls, as we should have made honourable love to, in any other place; and Sir John Everyoung was in the pleasantest humour, I'd give a piece I could repeat the satire he made of the country.

MODISH It would be good news to his daughters, for they say, now and then in a morning he is of another mind.

ESTRIDGE That's only while his head aches, they need not fear him; he swears he'll ne'er stir beyond Hyde Park or Coleby's* at farthest, as long as he has an acre left, they shall all come to him: 'tis a pleasant old fellow, he has given me a hundred pounds for my Graybeard, and is to ride himself this day month twice round the Park, against a bay stone-horse† of Wildish's for two hundred more.

MODISH Methought Wildish and you were very intimate, pray how long have you been acquainted?

ESTRIDGE Faith, about a week or so, time's a thing only necessary for the friendship of vulgar spirits: O here comes the gentleman we were speaking of;

Enter Wildish.

now Jack, what small petticoat do you come from?

WILDISH E'en such another as you are going to now with all this

* Coleby's: Coleby was the landlord of the tavern of the Mulberry Garden.
† stone-horse: a stallion.

bravery; those cravats that design the Right Honourable, I'll lay a piece will be rumpled by a worse woman than they were washed, yet afore night.

MODISH Would all the world were of his mind, we young men should pass our time well.

WILDISH O never the better for that; such *monsieurs* as you by your feathers are known to be birds of prey, and though you catch nothing, you scare all; besides, every good man is not acquainted with this principle among you, that you can be in love with nothing but yourselves, and may be jealous of his wife, when indeed you come innocently to take a view of your persons from head to feet in the great glass; comb out your periwig, shake your garnitures,* and be gone.

ESTRIDGE What, dost think we have no other way of entertainment? No discourse, Jack?

WILDISH Yes, a little now and then about their dress, whether their patches be too many or too few, too great or too small, whether her handkerchief be *Point de Venise* or *Rome*;† and having left behind you some proof of your ability in the mode, return to show yourselves at the last act of a play.

MODISH I dare swear, Jack, thy acquaintance puts thee to none of these criticisms, a plain gorget‡ and a black scarf are all their varieties; and 'Are you well mistress?' and 'What company have you kept lately?' thy most familiar questions. But raillery apart. Say it were a man's fortune to prevail upon one of these thou believest so impregnable forts, and to be received where never any but yourself came so near as to be denied; were not that a conquest?

WILDISH As great as that of a place not tenable can be; the present plunder indeed is somewhat, but upon the first siege you must look to be driven out: a lady's heart is a kind of fortification that is easier surprised by being well manned, and makes ever the strongest resistance of itself.

* garnitures: ornaments.
† *Point de Venise* or *Rome*: point, thread lace, named after the place of its manufacture. That of Venice was regarded as rich.
‡ gorget: originally throat armour, later a piece of woman's clothing covering neck and breast.

ESTRIDGE 'Tis true, Modish, for I have still observed, that when one of these persons of honour does a little forget herself, though at first through a secret sympathy, and invincible inclination (as they call it) for one particular man, she ever after loves the whole sex the better for it.

WILDISH Right; for these good creatures, women, are like cats, if once made tame, anyone may play with 'em; if not, there's no coming near 'em.

MODISH Thou thinkest thou hast mauled 'em now; why I tell thee, Jack, a hector is not readier to pick a quarrel with a saucy creditor, and swear he will never pay the rascal, than a man is to have one with his mistress towards the latter end of an amour; especially if it amount to a handsome occasion of leaving her, 'tis the kindest thing she can do then: what think you, Estridge?

ESTRIDGE Faith, I'm of your mind, yet I have known some unconscionable ladies make their servants wait as long for a just exception, and almost as impatiently, as they did for the first favour.

WILDISH Favour and exception, gentlemen, are words I don't meet with in seven years. Where I go, my piece makes my compliment when I come in, and my excuse when I go away; and 'tis ever well taken too: I have all the day to bestow upon my business, the night upon my friends; whilst you are kissing the cards at ombre,* or presenting oranges† at a playhouse.

ESTRIDGE Thou never knew'st it seems what 'twas to be in love then.

WILDISH No faith, I never let the disease run on so far, I always took it in time, and then a bottle of wine or two, and a she-friend is an approved remedy; there are men in the world though, who in that distemper prescribe some serious employment, continual exercise, spare diet, and the like; but they are philosophers, and in my opinion make the remedy worse than the disease.

ESTRIDGE I do confess yours is the pleasantest cure, if it be one;

---

* kissing the cards at ombre: a flirtatious gesture; kissing the cards was the equivalent of kissing the lady playing the card game, a Spanish one which came into fashion in the Restoration period.

† presenting oranges: lovers and husbands often treated mistresses and wives to oranges in the theatre.

but I doubt it only gives a little ease for the present, and like small beer in the morning after a merry bout overnight, doth but make us the worse afterwards.

MODISH Aye now, you talk to him of what he understands, what do you tell him of love for? Who by his own confession never knew what it was.

WILDISH No, but I guess this same love you speak of, gentlemen, to be much like longing in women, a fantastical appetite to some one thing above all others, which if they cannot get, the lover miscarries of his passion, and the lady of her little one; or if they do, are both quickly satisfied, and it becomes for ever after very indifferent, if not loathsome.

ESTRIDGE Well, Modish, I perceive we shall do no good on him, let's take him to the Mulberry Garden,★ and see what the ladies can do.

WILDISH You shall excuse me, I have a small ramble of my own for an hour or two this afternoon: and so your servant.　　　　[*Exit*]

MODISH 'Tis time we were going, I warrant they have walked every foot of the Garden, twice over by this time: they are mad to know, whether their friends in Town have dealt faithfully with 'em of late, concerning the mode.

ESTRIDGE These country ladies for the first month take up their places in the Mulberry Garden, as early as a citizen's wife at a new play.

MODISH And for the most part are as easily discovered; they have always somewhat on, that is just left off by the better sort.

ESTRIDGE They are the antipodes of the Court; for when a fashion sets there, it rises among them.　　　　　　[*Exeunt*]

SCENE III

Enter Victoria and Olivia.

VICTORIA Sister, whatever the matter is, methinks we don't see half the company that used to meet here at nights, when we were last in Town.

OLIVIA 'Tis true, but methinks 'tis much better than the long

★ Mulberry Garden: a pleasure ground on the site of Buckingham Palace.

walk at home: for in my opinion half a score young men, and fine ladies well dressed, are a greater ornament to a garden, than a wilderness of sycamores, orange, and lemon trees; and the rustling of rich vests and silk petticoats, better music than the purling of streams, chirping of birds, or any of our country entertainments: and that I hope the place will afford us yet, as soon as the plays are done.

VICTORIA Sister, what would you give to see Estridge come in now?

OLIVIA 'Tis impossible, he would not miss his devotion to the Park, for all I could give, such an evening as this: besides the two garnitures he brought out of France are soiled, his feather broke, and he has been so out of humour these two days, there's no enduring him; he lost his money too last night I hear; and losing gamesters are but ill company.

VICTORIA Fie sister, you make him a saver* with a look; and fine, in but thinking he is so: you deserve not so complete a servant, but I hope you'll be as obliging to his face, as you are severe to him behind his back.

OLIVIA The only way to oblige most men is to use 'em thus, a little now and then; even to their faces, it gives 'em an opinion of our wit; and is consequently a spur to theirs: the great pleasure of gaming were lost, if we saw one another's hands; and of love, if we knew one another's hearts: there would be no room for good play in the one, nor for address in the other; which are the refined parts of both. But what would you give to see Horatio?

VICTORIA To see Horatio, as I knew him once,
I would all other happiness renounce;
But he is now another's, and my aim
Is not to nourish, but to starve my flame:
I dare not hope my captive to regain,
So many charms contribute to his chain.
Althea's slave, let false Horatio live,
Whilst I for freedom, not for empire strive.

OLIVIA Fie sister, leave this rhyming at least.

Enter to them Estridge and Modish.

* saver: a gaming term, a saver being one who avoids loss without gaining.

ESTRIDGE Ladies, it is our wonder to find anybody here at this time of day, and no less our happiness to meet with you; all the world is at the Park, where we had been ourselves, but that we saw your livery at the gate.

VICTORIA I pray let us not keep you here gentlemen, your mistresses will curse us, and yourselves too, by and by, if the Garden should not fill.

ESTRIDGE If we wish any company, ladies, 'tis for your sakes, not our own.

MODISH For my part I would ne'er desire a garden fuller than this is now; we are two to two, and may be hand to hand when you please.

OLIVIA I don't know what you think, but in my mind the more the merrier, especially in these places.

ESTRIDGE Aye, for show, Madam, but it happens in great companies, as at feasts, we see a great deal, and fall to heartily of nothing, and for the most part rise hungry: and 'tis with lovers, Madam, as with great-bellied women, if they find what they long for, they care not whether there be anything else or no.

VICTORIA What in love already? Sure the air of this place is a great softener of men's hearts.

MODISH How can it choose, having so many lovers' sighs daily mixed with it? But 'twere a much better quality in't, Madam, if it could incline ladies to believe, and look with pity on those flames they raise.

OLIVIA 'Tis too early to make love this two hours. 'Flames' and 'pity' would sound much better in the evening.

MODISH 'Tis not with love, Madam, as with meaner arguments; I might entertain you with my passion for an age, and yet have as much left for anon, as if I had not spoke one word; the sea is easier emptied than a lover's breast.

OLIVIA What say you, Sir, is this your opinion too?

ESTRIDGE Yes faith, Madam, and I think a lover can no more say at once, what he hath to say to his mistress, than a man can eat at once for his whole lifetime.

OLIVIA Nay, if it be so endless, I should beg of my servant, whenever I have one, e'en to keep it to himself for altogether.

ESTRIDGE There you betray your ignorance, with your pardon,

Madam; to see the fair Olivia, and not to love her, is not more impossible, than to love her, and not tell her on't. Silent lovers you may read of, and in romances too, but heavens forbid you should e'er meet with any.

OLIVIA If they knew how little they were like to get by being otherwise, I'm confident I should meet with none else.

ESTRIDGE Well, Madam, I perceive love, like wine, makes our discourse seem extravagant to those that are not wound up to the same height: but had you any spark of what I feel, I should have had another answer.

OLIVIA Why, what answer?

ESTRIDGE Nay, I know not, but some pretty one, that love would have devised for you; no more to be imagined by you now, than what you shall talk of next in your sleep. In the meantime, ladies, will you do us the honour to eat sillabubs?

OLIVIA Sister, let's go, so they'll promise to say nothing but what they think to us when we are there.

MODISH You may do what you please, Ned, but 'tis a liberty I dare not use myself to, for fear of an ill habit.

ESTRIDGE You are very confident of our good opinion, ladies; I believe there are few women in Town would accept of our company on these terms.

VICTORIA Faith, sister, let's bate★ 'em that circumstance, truth is a thing merely necessary for witnesses, and historians, and in these places doth but curb invention, and spoil good company; we will only confine 'em to what's probable.

MODISH Content, and I dare swear 'twill be better for all parties.

[*Exeunt*]

SCENE IV

Sir Samuel Forecast's house

Enter Althea and Diana.

DIANA We two, or none, may of our stars complain,
  Who afford us nothing to share but pain;
  Each bears her own, and th' other's portion too;

★ bate: deduct.

This cruel wonder can high friendship do.

ALTHEA To us how cheap might they have joy allowed,
Since both had had what they on each bestowed!
But yet thy loss I rate above my own,
Fate on thy love till now did never frown:
Philander thee above the world did prize,
Thy parents saw him almost with thy eyes:
All things so prosperous were, thou couldst not guess,
An accident to wound thy happiness.
I wretched maid, have but a passion lost,
Which if none else, my parents would have crossed:
My lowly hopes do but a step descend,
Whilst thine, from their full height do headlong bend:
This hour that promised all, can nothing pay,
And Hymen steals his lighted torch away.

DIANA Ah, dear Althea; let not thou and I
Contend who most exceeds in misery;
It is a dismal strife, since were my own
Less, I'd share thine till they were equal grown.
Curse on ambition, why should honour take
A present back again, that love did make?
On thee Eugenio did his life bestow,
To me Philander did his service vow;
Yet both for honour have those ties despised,
And now are fled, or must be sacrificed.
Unkind Philander, had love filled thy breast
With half those flames thou hast so oft expressed,
They had consumèd in their purer fires
All other thoughts, and thou would'st never mind,
Who were for kings, and who for slaves designed.

ALTHEA The noble sense they show of the sad fate
Of their dear country, sets a higher rate
Upon their love; for who that had a grain
Of honour in him, could endure the reign
Of proud usurpers, whose relentless will,
Is all the law by which men spare or kill;
And his true prince in banishment behold,
Worthy of more than fortune can withhold;

These monstrous with the crimes of prosperous fate,
The other shining in his adverse state,
So that each stroke of fortune does but seem
A step for his heroic mind to climb,
Till he has got above her reach, and then
The virtue she has tried she'll love again?
Though I must truly mourn their ill success,
I could not wish Eugenio had done less.

DIANA Had their high virtue the least doubt endured,
Even with their death it had been cheaply cured:
But this brave act is but to me and you,
A dangerous proof of what before we knew.

ALTHEA Though their true worth to us before were clear,
This act has made it to the world appear;
None ever with that obstinacy loved,
But they were pleased to see their choice approved:
No joy complete to worthy minds can seem,
Which is not heightened by the world's esteem.

DIANA My heart, Althea, does less grieve it has
Ventured its treasure in so loved a cause,
Than that Philander did not let me know
The danger he was like to undergo.

ALTHEA Sister, though laws of decency refuse,
We shining swords and glittering armour use;
Yet a decision of what's right or wrong,
As well as men's, does to our minds belong;
And we best show it when we most approve
Those men that fight in quarrels which we love:
Though they of courage have the ruder part,
The virtue may become a woman's heart,
Though not her hand; and she that bravely dares
Expose her love, sure for her life not cares.
I knew Eugenio must that hazard run,
Nor could consent he should the danger shun;
And had Philander the like thoughts of you,
He without doubt had dealt as freely too.

DIANA I must confess my love could never yield,
That he again should win it in the field:

Let me the greatness of your mind admire,
Whilst I deplore the greatness of my fire,
A fire which lends no light, but that which serves
To show how much what I exposed deserves,
How much he hazards, and how far I am
From venturing him for the whole voice of fame,
Whose danger had I known, my eyes, alas!
Had wept a sea, he would have feared to pass;
But we so long of what is past complain,
As if no further mischief did remain,
As if fate here had her whole malice spent,
And all the arrows from her quiver sent.

ALTHEA When fate would harm where virtue does protect,
She does her guilt and impotence detect;
She can but rob the virtuous of that rest,
She must restore again with interest,
And all the danger of these heroes past,
Must needs consider their high worth at last.

DIANA What we desire, how fain we would believe,
And with that fortune knew not to deceive?
But she profusely to some presents makes,
And as unjustly from some others takes.
I fear she's so much to their worth in debt,
She'll nothing pay, because the whole's too great:
Like tyrants' wealth, her bounties still appear,
Who give to few, what they from many tear.

ALTHEA In the meantime I fear our cruel friends
Will not consult our liking, but their ends:
I know they'll press I should Horatio wed,
And promise thee unto some stranger's bed.

DIANA They may such matches as they please provide,
But here I vow, I'll never be a bride
To any but Philander; in that heart
He taught to love, none else shall have a part.

ALTHEA I the like vow to my Eugenio make,
Which fate's worst malice shan't have power to break;
As trees exposed to storms take deeper root,
Than those that do in peaceful valleys sprout:

So in all noble minds, a virtuous love
By opposition does the firmer prove.
DIANA 'Tis fit, Althea, I now take my leave,
Whilst you prepare Horatio to receive.
ALTHEA Farewell, Diana, and be sure you do
Nothing unworthy of your love and vow.

[Exeunt Diana and Althea severally]

ACT TWO

SCENE I

Enter Sir Samuel Forecast, Althea, Jack Wildish, and Olivia.

FORECAST Daughter, we are much beholding to Horatio, the
portion I can give with you does not deserve a man of past half his
fortune; six thousand pounds a year, an estate well wooded, and
I am told very improvable, it makes me young again to think
on't: Eugenio I never liked, and as things stand now, am right
glad we had no more to do with him; but that I am one whose
affection and goodwill to the state★ has sufficiently manifested
itself, I might be thought to have a hand in their design, and so
have been put in the Tower, and had my fortune seized on:
Eugenio shall never call a child of mine, wife, as long as I live.

WILDISH But, Sir, your zeal to the cause† has put you above those
apprehensions.

FORECAST You say right, Mr Wildish, but we cannot be in this
case too secure; and I am resolved Althea, to take off all suspicion,
shall out of hand marry with Horatio.

ALTHEA Sir, I hope you will allow me some time to dismiss
Eugenio from my thoughts.

WILDISH And, pray Sir, what prejudice, what exception have you
to Eugenio?

FORECAST Originally this only, his father made a purchase of some
land, that lay next hedge to mine, and gave a thousand pounds
more than it was worth, only to buy it over my head: think no
more on him upon my blessing, he is not the man he was; he had
an estate, 'tis now sequestered,‡ he dare not show his head; and
besides, I would not have a son-in-law of his principles, for six
times his fortune; I should be sorry to see any child of mine
soliciting her husband's composition§ at a committee.

★ the state: the Commonwealth, the Republican government.
† the cause: of Republicanism and puritanism, known as the Good Old Cause
by the Puritans.
‡ sequestered: confiscated by the Commonwealth as belonging to a Royalist.
§ soliciting her husband's composition: Royalists could 'compound' for their
loyalty by surrendering part or all of their estates.

ALTHEA Had I once had the relation of a wife to Eugenio, I should have thought nothing a trouble that had become my duty, and could as cheerfully have shared an honourable suffering, as the most flourishing condition.

FORECAST I charge you never receive visit, or message from him more, and tell your sister Diana, 'tis my pleasure she quit all correspondence with Philander. They are both dangerous persons. [*turns to Wildish*] These young wenches, Mr Wildish, have less forecast than pigeons, so they be billing, they look no farther; ne'er think of building their nests, nor what shall become of their little ones.

WILDISH Sir, I think they're i' th' right, let 'em increase and multiply, and for the rest, trust him that set 'em a-work.

FORECAST Mr Wildish, you are a merry gentleman; but I'll tell you, Mistress Althea, as I have given you life, I'll take care you shan't make it miserable.

ALTHEA Sir, the happiness of life lies not in wealth, in title, or in show, but in the mind, which is not to be forced; and we are not the less slaves for being bound in chains of gold: a marriage with Horatio may make me appear happy to the envious world, but like those destructive arts, which, while they seem to aid, consume our native beauties, indeed must prey upon my inward peace.

FORECAST I'll warrant you peace within, and without too; Horatio is a well-natured proper gentleman, and one that loves you.

WILDISH Now there Sir Samuel I'm on your side, for so the fan be played with, the hand kissed; in fine, the passion handsomely discharged, 'tis no great matter who does it. As children cry after their old nurses, but till they are acquainted with their new: so young ladies regret the loss of one servant, but till they have got the same familiarity with another; which, by the way, is seldom long first.

Enter a Servant.

SERVANT Sir, there's a man out of Pater-Noster Row* with stuffs.

* Pater-Noster Row: famous for mercers.

FORECAST Bid him carry 'em into the next room. Come Althea, let's in and look upon 'em.

[*Exeunt Althea, and Sir Samuel*]

OLIVIA We woman are ever sure of your good word, Mr Wildish; when you have a mistress, I hope she'll deserve it from you in particular, and have in perfection all those good qualities you so liberally bestow upon the whole sex, in your discourse.

WILDISH Why, Madam, I thought you had understood raillery; faith I have so good an opinion of the sex I am ashamed to own it but to one of them in private; this is only the way of talking I have got among my companions, where when we meet over a bottle of wine, 'tis held as great a part of wit to rally women handsomely behind their back, as to flatter 'em to their faces.

OLIVIA But why do you make us poor women the subject of your mirth?

WILDISH You are grown of late so uncharitable, and villainous hard-hearted, are encompassed with so many difficulties, as decency, honour, and reputation, that we men that love our pleasure, begin to hate you worse than beggars do a coach with the glasses drawn up,* despair of relief, and fall a railing.

OLIVIA And if some kind-hearted wretch do chance to relieve one of you, like beggars you tell it presently, and send more; I warrant you're fine fellows, a woman is well helped up, that has one of you to her servant.

WILDISH Nay don't put me in among 'em, I am a mere apostate, though not resolute enough to endure the martyrdoms of being continually laughed at by half a score of 'em: all that I have done of late, has been mere compliance, as papists go to church for fear of the penalty.†

OLIVIA Pray, Sir, to what fair saint do we owe your conversion?

WILDISH Faith there are many in the world now would make you guess this half hour, telling you first the colour of her hair, her age, her country, and perhaps the first letter of her name; but I hate that way of fooling – 'tis yourself – whom I love.

---

* glasses drawn up: glazed windows in coaches were a novelty in the Restoration period and were described as a 'new fashion' in 1663.

† penalty: fines imposed on those Roman Catholic recusants who did not attend Anglican services.

OLIVIA Impudent fellow! Don't you expect I should forbid you the house, or at least, for punishment of such rudeness, condemn your guilty passion to eternal silence and despair? What! Men have lived years in deserts for their mistresses' sake, and yet have trembled when they spoke of love; which you venture at with as little ceremony as you'd ask me how I slept last night.

WILDISH I know not what romances order in this case, I ne'er thought it would be mine, and so ha'n't much studied it: but prithee don't baulk a young beginner; 'tis my first fault, and so be not too severe, I shall relapse else beyond redemption.

OLIVIA Well, I'm content for once your ignorance should plead your pardon.

WILDISH Nay Mistress Olivia consider me a little further; I have lost the pleasure of mirth, of wine, and company; all things that were before delightful to me, are no longer so; my life is grown but one continued thought of your fair self: and is a pardon all that I must hope for?

OLIVIA Come, leave your fooling, your old humour does better with you, a thousand times, than this whining love. As there are some perfumes so strong, that they lose that name with most: so compliments may be so gross, that they become injurious.

WILDISH Why here's it now; there are so many cheats in this trade of love too, that like beggars, the true go unrelieved, because we meet with now and then a counterfeit: on my life Mistress Olivia the plenty I have ever lived in, puts me as much out of countenance to ask a charity of this kind, as I could be, should fortune constrain me, to entreat one of the other; and would not trouble you, could my pain admit redress from any but yourself.

OLIVIA Sure, Mr Wildish, you would think I had an excellent opinion of myself, or an implicit faith in whatever you say, should I believe all this now.

WILDISH If I told a chirurgeon, I had broke my leg, do you think he would not take my word?

OLIVIA Yes sure.

WILDISH Why should not you take it then for a wounded heart? They are neither of 'em matters to brag on; and I would no more lead the life of a lover if I were free, than I would that of a sick man if I were well.

OLIVIA Methinks the sick men, as you call 'em, live so like the well, as one can scarce know one from th' other.

WILDISH In your chamber, perhaps; but abroad we find a thousand differences.

OLIVIA As how, I pray?

WILDISH Why, your true lover leaves all company when the sport begins, the table when the bottles are called for, the gaming-house when the cards come up; is more afraid of an engagement, than a lawyer in term-time;* would less miss the last act of a play, the Park, or indeed any abominable old ladies, where he may hope to see the party, than a young wench can Gray's Inn walks,† the first Sunday of her new gown.

OLIVIA What, is this all?

WILDISH Not half: ask him to sup, he has business; or if he promise, 'tis ten to one he fails, and if he sees his mistress, is so transported, that he forgets to send his excuse; if he cannot find her, and so chance to keep his word, sits in such dismal dumps, that he spoils the whole company.

OLIVIA And will you be such an animal for my sake?

WILDISH Faith I'm afraid so, but if not well used, I shall find the way home again.

OLIVIA Whatever you think, Sir, I shall contribute no more to the keeping you my servant, than I did to the making you so.

WILDISH Well, do but use as proper means to keep me your servant, as you have done to make me so, and I am satisfied.

OLIVIA Why, what means?

WILDISH As your beauty bred my affection, so let your kindness nourish it.

OLIVIA Mr Wildish, you have been so pleasant upon this new argument, that I had almost forgot my visit to Diana.

WILDISH I'm upon equal terms with you there; for I have made Ned Estridge and Harry Modish stay this half hour for me at the French House :‡ and so your servant.   [*Exeunt*]

---

* term-time: when court is in session.

† Gray's Inn walks: a piece of ground laid out as a garden with lawns, walks and trees, when Bacon was Treasurer of the Inn, a fashionable promenade.

‡ the French House: probably Chatelain's, a French tavern in Covent Garden.

SCENE II

Enter Althea.

ALTHEA Under what tyranny are women born!
  Here we are bid to love, and there to scorn;
  As if unfit to be allowed a part
  In choosing him, that must have all our heart;
  Or that our liking, like a headstrong beast,
  Were made for nothing, but to be oppressed;
  And below them, in this regard we are,
  We may not fly the cruelty we fear.
  The horse may shake the rider from his back,
  The dog his hated master may forsake;
  Yet nothing of their native worth impair,
  Nor any conscious sting about them bear.
  But if a virgin an escape contrive,
  She must for ever in dishonour live,
  Condemned within herself, despised of all,
  Into worse mischiefs than she fled from, fall.
  Duty commands I should Horatio wed,
  Love does as strongly for Eugenio plead;
  My mind, distracted thus, a storm abides
  Like seas, when winds blow full against their tides.

Enter Horatio.

HORATIO Madam, methinks you look not pleased; I fear
  My hapless passion did too late appear
  For my content; and only now can prove
  The wretched triumph of some elder love.
  But, fair Althea, you were much to blame
  With your own breath to blow a hopeless flame.
  Ah! Had you to its childhood been severe,
  As now to its full growth you cruel are,
  'T had died with half that pain it now must bear:
  Young plants with ease up by the roots we tear;
  But when well grown, the axe must be employed,
  And they with force and labour are destroyed.
ALTHEA Generous Horatio, forbear to blame

Me, as the cruel author of your pain.
How could I know that you my lover were,
Until yourself your passion did declare?
How had it looked in me to have complained
Of thoughts, perhaps, you never entertained?
How could I check, alas, those hopes in you,
Your heart did never harbour, that I knew?
HORATIO Not know, Althea! Why should the same eyes
So slowly see, so suddenly surprise?
The very minute I beheld your face,
You might in mine my growing passion trace.
Now trembling fear did her pale colour spread,
Then springing hope brought back the native red:
Joy may be seen, and grief itself unfold,
And so may love, though it be never told.
In every look my passion was confessed,
And every action my high flame expressed.
As foolish witnesses their cause o'erthrow,
My arts to hide it, did it clearer show.
ALTHEA But as fond parents will not seem to know
A fault they needs must punish when they do;
So I at first was loath to see a crime
In one, I otherwise did so esteem:
For know, Horatio, setting love apart,
None than yourself is deeper in my heart;
Your worth and honour I can value, though
I no requital to your flame allow.
HORATIO You can give all things else above their due,
And yet wrong that which most belongs to you:
Madam, these words, soothe with a cruel art
Where I less feel, and wound a mortal part;
With friendship and esteem you strive in vain,
Kind maid, to ease a lover of his pain:
For where your beauty once has raised a flame,
To offer less, and nothing, are the same.
Love and ambition of their aim denied,
No other way can e'er be satisfied.
ALTHEA You that could faithless to Victoria prove,

Methinks should blush even at the name of love.
Her numerous charms your loud accusers are,
And call Horatio false, as she is fair.
HORATIO You should with pity, not displeasure see
The change that your own self creates in me.
The Roman Senate had their greatness worn
Perhaps till now, had Caesar ne'er been born.
Darius' self could not his Persians blame,
Because that Alexander overcame.
In love like war, some victor still there grows,
Whose spreading empire nothing can oppose.
ALTHEA Countries are fixed, and cannot fly, although
They apprehend a certain overthrow.
Lovers, the force they can't oppose, might shun,
And may with safety and with honour run.
Who then would pity him that stays to die,
When virtue and his duty bid him fly?
HORATIO Althea, in love's wars all heroes are,
Death does less terrible than flight appear;
As gamesters, when they lose, still deeper set,
Helping ill fortune to increase their debt:
So lovers, when a nymph gets half their heart,
Themselves, alas, betray the other part.
ALTHEA Victoria's wrongs my gratitude deter;
Your gifts to me are robberies from her.
HORATIO I came at first, Althea, 'tis most true
With love to her, and but respect to you.
But, ah! how soon within my tortured breast
You of each other's places are possessed!
ALTHEA Beauty, the wrongs of beauty should revenge,
And the fair punish, when the faithless change.
HORATIO I change Althea, but (as pious men
Become blest saints) never to change again.
If none your matchless beauty must adore,
But such alone as never loved before,
You do unjustly, and too high advance
In love th' already too great power of chance:
Since that you should their first affection be,

Let's you their fortune, not their passion see.
ALTHEA It lets me see they falsehood never knew,
     And gives me leave to hope they will be true.
HORATIO Sure none can faithless to such beauty prove;
     He that's in heaven, can no higher move.
ALTHEA A lover's heaven in his fancy lies,
     Which beauty oft neglects, and oft supplies.
HORATIO 'Tis not, Althea, that you question mine,
     But 'tis Eugenio's faith does brighter shine;
     'Tis he that makes Victoria's wrong your pain,
     My love a crime, a virtue your disdain.
     These tales of falsehood, and of former love,
     Reproaches only, where we like not, prove.
ALTHEA Horatio, I am glad your disrespect
     Has turned so soon to justice my neglect:
     You that reproach me with a former love,
     Yourself unfit but for my anger prove.   [*Exit Althea*]
HORATIO O stay a while! Sure you must joy to see
     The torture you're so pleased to work in me;
     Not that I hope I shall your pity find,
     But that the sight may glut your cruel mind.
     Nature inconstant to her own designs,
     To a fair form a cruel temper joins;
     She makes the heedless lover kneel in vain,
     And in love's temple, to adore disdain.   [*Exit Horatio*]

⟨SCENE III⟩

Enter Sir Samuel Forecast and Jack Wildish.

FORECAST When am I to see your fair and wealthy cousin, Mr
     Wildish?
WILDISH This minute if you please, Sir.
FORECAST I doubt you are not stirring in the business, you do not
     lay the necessity of marrying home enough to her: I might have
     got access ere now else, and our counsel have been drawing the
     writings.*

          * writings: marriage contract.

WILDISH It must be done by degrees: if I should have been too forward, it might have caused in her a suspicion of my purpose, and so my worthy friend Sir Samuel have come to her upon some prejudice, which I would not for half her fortune.

FORECAST Pray, Mr Wildish, is she so concerned for her late husband as the world talks?

WILDISH Ten times more; looks upon his picture all day long as earnestly as if she were to copy it; since he died, has used no pocket-handkerchers, but what was made of his old shirts, and wets two a day of 'em with her tears; because he died on a Monday, fasts that day of the week; takes none into her service but Thomases, because 'twas his Christian name, and has now sent into Wales for a Thomas ap Thomas to be her gentleman-usher.

FORECAST 'Tis strange she should so affect his name! What think you then, if you called me Sir Thomas Forecast?

WILDISH Faith, Sir, what you please; but I think it will be altogether needless, and if she should come to discover, it might spoil all, s'light, she might mistrust your particular, if she should find you put a trick upon her in your name.

FORECAST Well, I'll be ruled by you, Mr Wildish, you know her humour best.

WILDISH I can't but think how she'll look upon me when I talk to her of another husband; but I'll venture, Sir Samuel, to serve you. Come let's away, her house is here hard by. [*Exeunt*]

SCENE IV

They enter the Widow's house.

WILDISH I show the way, Sir.

They find her ⟨the Widow⟩ looking upon her husband's picture, and ⟨she⟩ does not see 'em.

FORECAST Excellent woman, she sees us not! O the endless treasure of a virtuous wife! It extends even to our memories, and pictures.

WILDISH [*goes up, and speaks to her*] Madam, here is Sir Samuel Forecast come to wait on you.

WIDOW Sir, I hope you'll pardon me, if I have let my grief employ any part of that time which was due to my acknowledgment for this favour; you were my husband's friend, and as such will ever be most welcome to me; and though his too scrupulous kindness allowed me not the acquaintance, scarce the sight of any man; yet I did always place a value where he gave his esteem, especially, so highly as he did to you.

FORECAST Madam, I am much bound to you for your good opinion, and come to condole with you: your husband was an honest, prudent, and a wealthy gentleman, kept good hours, and even reckonings, loved me well, and we have drank many a dish of coffee★ together.

WIDOW Sir, whilst you repeat his virtues, you do but count my loss, and telling me how good he was, makes me but more sensibly want him.

FORECAST He and I were just of an age, and when we were boys, of a strength.

WIDOW And what of that, Sir?

WILDISH Why, cousin it makes me think that Sir Samuel would make as loving a husband to you, as your last was, and I'll swear it troubles me heartily to see my pretty coz here not yet out of danger of smooth-faced younger brothers, such as marry wives only to keep wenches, and never bring 'em to Town but to pass away some part of their estates.

FORECAST Some such there are; but heaven bless the estate, and widow of my good friend your husband out of such hands.

WILDISH Now I have brought you together, I'll leave you; cousin, you are not afraid to be left alone with Sir Samuel?   [*Exit*]

WIDOW I know his virtue, and my own too well.

FORECAST Don't you find, Madam, business very troublesome?

WIDOW I do indeed, and have the misfortune to be involved in it.

FORECAST Have you many law-suits?

WIDOW But one considerable, which being with a man in power, in these corrupt times, a woman unfriended and unknown as I am, must expect to lose.

★ coffee: the first English coffee-house was opened in 1650; they were at first associated with republicanism. After the Restoration they increased greatly in number.

FORECAST Of what value?

WIDOW Five thousand pounds: I shall have enough left however, to make me happy with a man that loves me.

FORECAST Enough left! Such another word would make me foreswear, not only thee but thy whole sex; five thousand pounds well disposed, why I tell thee, 'tis able to procure us judgments on half the young prodigals of this age; thou and I might live comfortably on the forbearance money,* and let the interest run on.

WIDOW I did but put the worst, not that I doubt my title, if I have common justice.

FORECAST No, thou shalt secure thy title, I am a near kinsman to the judge, and a by-way to his favour.

WIDOW How do you mean?

FORECAST Why I have many times bought a thousand pounds' worth of other men's lands of him for a hundred.

WIDOW I would not corrupt justice for a world.

FORECAST What again widow? Nay then I perceive thou do'st it on purpose to lose my heart: but to say truth, it were unreasonable to expect thy tender years should understand the true worth of money, so far, that for its sake to trample on those unprofitable and foolish principles the honourable beggars of former times governed their lives by: but thou wilt one day know, that age hath its beauties too, as well as youth, and more universally adored.

WIDOW Gravity and wisdom, Sir, I know men may expect, but our sex has no pretence to them.

FORECAST No, wealth and power, widow, which awe the grave and wise; gold and silver are the best red and white; the other, every milkmaid may boast equal with a countess.

Enter Sir John Everyoung, Modish, and Estridge, with Fiddles playing.

WIDOW What rude fellow's that?

EVERYOUNG [*to the music*] Hold, let's parley first. Faith, widow, one that loves you but too well.

WIDOW Love me! Upon what acquaintance? I ne'er saw your face before in my days.

* forbearance money: money paid, in addition to the interest, to a creditor for allowing a loan to be repaid after the stipulated time.

EVERYOUNG And do'st thou like it now?

WIDOW Not so well as yourself, you may be confident.

EVERYOUNG All this shan't cross my honest purpose, I come in mere charity to prevent thy ruin; and if thou be'st not lost to all sense and reason, nay, even all natural appetite, I'll do't.

WIDOW I know no ruin near, this is the worst accident has befallen me a good while.

EVERYOUNG Hear me but out, and thou shalt bless it; can'st thou be such a traitor to flesh and blood, as to count it nothing to be joined to that old trunk there? If he increase or multiply, it must be thy bags; interest, and brokage are his best instruments.

WIDOW You don't consider that all this might be as well applied to your sweet self.

EVERYOUNG Yes, most properly, why 'tis that makes me hate matrimony, and puts me at distance with, 'To have and to hold'; I confess my tick is not good, and I never desire to game for more than I have about me. Now second me.

MODISH The minute you marry, widow, you are not worth a groat, all is your husband's; and if hereafter you shall come to a sense of your unequal choice, and endeavour to repair it in some young and worthy friend; the old gentleman takes pet, turns you over to a tedious suit for alimony, which your friend furnishes you with money to follow, for a while, and in times grows weary of it himself.

ESTRIDGE Then like an old gamester, that has lost all he has upon the square, your only way is to turn rook★ and play upon advantage.

WIDOW Why, do you know these gentlemen?

FORECAST Aye, to my shame, the ringleader of 'em is my brother, there is no remedy but patience.

WIDOW Gentlemen, you talk at a strange rate for the first time; but whomever I marry my virtue will secure him of my constancy.

MODISH Pray Madam, don't profane that honourable name: 'tis mere obstinacy to an old man, a fault methinks you have too ingenious a countenance to be guilty of.

EVERYOUNG If thou should'st be so improvident, as to neglect the

★ rook: cardsharper.

comfort of a gallant, thou'lt never 'scape the scandal, having such a husband.

MODISH If you are precise, Madam, they'll give you your chaplain; if you love business, your lawyer; if you keep a gentleman-usher, you are undone.

ESTRIDGE If you take some honest gentleman (which by my troth I think is your best course) upon the first hard journey, as the world goes now, 'tis ten to one he falls lame of an old bruise.

WIDOW You are very tender of my credit: if you had been as careful, gentlemen, of your own sobriety, I fear I had missed all this good counsel.

EVERYOUNG Oh! Are you edified? It is good counsel then: and for the warmth that ripened us to this care of thee, be thankful, and enquire no further. But brother, methinks you are over-serious for a man that comes a-suitoring.

WIDOW He does not find your mirth take so well.

Enter Wildish apart.

WILDISH S'light here's Sir John Everyoung, he'll spoil all, if I don't take him off instantly.

Wildish goes out, and brings in three of the Widow's maids.

FORECAST Brother, brother, these frolics do you no right in the eye of the world.

EVERYOUNG Hang the world, give me the pretty black-eye of the widow.

A Song.

WILDISH Gentlemen; here's work for you.

EVERYOUNG A muss, a muss!* You see, Wildish, we found the house, though you would not tell us where it was, 'tis dangerous to give a hint to men of our parts. Brother, take your widow, show her that you are so far qualified towards a bridegroom, as to lead a country dance.

WIDOW I'll have no dancing in my house.

FORECAST You see they are a little merry, humour 'em in this, they'll be gone the sooner.

* a muss: a game in which objects are scrambled for, a state of confusion.

WIDOW Well, Sir Samuel Forecast, anything to serve you.

> [*They dance, and Forecast steals away*]

MODISH Sir Samuel gone?

EVERYOUNG Faith then the sport's at the best, let's all be gone: farewell widow, I have done my part: if thou fallest now, say thou had'st fair warning.

> [*Exeunt Omnes*]

ACT THREE

SCENE I

Enter Eugenio, and Philander.

EUGENIO Dear friend, I am in doubt whether I shall
This 'scape, a blessing, or misfortune, call;
Since now I live to hear, Althea must
Be to her duty, or to me unjust.
Ye powers that were so kind, my life to spare,
Oh why was not my love as much your care?
You saved my life, that I might live to feel
Despair can wound as mortally as steel.
My cause till now my antidote has been,
'Gainst all the mischief it could plunge me in;
The strictest prison, I have freedom thought,
And been on scaffolds without terror brought.
But these few words 'Althea is a bride'
More wound my soul, than can the world beside.

PHILANDER Why does Eugenio fancies entertain,
That are Althea's wrongs, and his own pain?
Like boys, who in the dark, strange shapes create
In their own brain, themselves to tremble at:
Despair's the portion of the damned below,
And in a generous mind should never grow;
Trust to Althea's virtue, trust her love,
And you will safe in either of 'em prove.

EUGENIO But sure no friend could so my quiet hate,
As this report, of nothing, to create.

PHILANDER Perhaps her father does no less intend,
And she, a while, her answer may suspend.
Not that her virtue doubts, what it shall do,
But that she may gain time to speak with you:
Every black cloud does not with thunder swell,
Nor every symptom a disease foretell.
Some storms blow over; though thy fate appear
Thus gloomy now, anon it may be clear.

EUGENIO It may, but who can unconcernèd be,

A tempest heard, and his whole wealth at sea?
I with more ease all other harms could bear,
Than of Althea's loss but simply hear.

PHILANDER All that we hear, we are not to believe.

EUGENIO Our hopes do oft'ner, than our fears deceive.

PHILANDER The advantage man o'er beasts in reason gets
He pays with interest in fond conceits;
They cannot fear misfortune till it fall,
And when 'tis gone remember 't not at all:
But man 'gainst his own rest in battle placed,
Feels mischiefs e'er they come, and when they're past.
The smiles of fortune you so false have found,
Methinks, you should not mind her when she frowned:
How would Althea's virtues grieve to find
Themselves suspected in Eugenio's mind!
Like princes murdered on the royal throne,
Where till that minute they had brightest shone.

EUGENIO Sure my Althea cannot disapprove
These fears that spring but from excess of love.
Of love and courage none too much can share.

PHILANDER But 'tis their use, that does their worth declare:
Courage, when brutal, ceases to be brave,
And love, grown jealous, can no merit have.

EUGENIO A higher mark of love there cannot be,
We doubt no lover, whom we jealous see.

PHILANDER So fevers are of life sure proofs we know,
And yet our lives they often overthrow;
Diseases, though well cured, our bodies mar,
And fears, although removed, our loves impair:
True love, like health, should no disorder know.

EUGENIO But who, alas! such love, or health can show?
Our passions, like ourselves, are framed to die,
And have still something they must perish by;
We none (brave friend) for being hapless blame,
But all allow, 'tis baseness to be tame;
He that has raised this tempest in my mind,
Shall in the billows his own ruin find;
I'll fight him instantly, and make him know,

I am not more his rival than his foe.

PHILANDER Thy life, alas (dear friend) 's no longer thine,
Thou hast engaged it in a brave design:
Thy bleeding country, and thy prince's right,
Are th' only quarrels that thy sword should fight,
If you into the tyrant's hands should fall,
'Twould pull a sudden ruin on us all.
Which, if you stir, we may have cause to fear,
Since tyrant's eyes and hands are everywhere.

EUGENIO Now thou hast touched me in the tend'rest part,
Though love possess, honour must rule my heart;
My nation's fate's too great a sacrifice
For me to make, though to Althea's eyes;
No, I am calmed, and happy am to have
A friend so full of temper when I rave,
And hope the gods, whilst I my own neglect,
To fight their quarrel, will my love protect. [*Exeunt*]

SCENE II

⟨A room in Sir John Everyoung's house⟩

Enter Victoria and Olivia.

VICTORIA Sister, I doubt we are a little too free with our servants, this Modish, and his friend Estridge: few plays gain audience by being in print, and fewer women get husbands by being too much known.

OLIVIA But ours are most accomplished *monsieurs*, must be assaulted on all parts ere they'll yield; must have their ears charmed as well as eyes: 'twere ill husbandry in a mercer to be thrifty in his patterns, it often disparages a good stuff; and too great reservedness in one of us, especially at the first, might give a discouragement to our further acquaintance.

VICTORIA Now might I have my wish, I would come all new, nay my voice and name should not be known; where I would be liked, I would have the few charms I am mistress of, make their assault at an instant, all at one time:

For sure Horatio did their power subdue,
By conquering one, ere he another knew.

OLIVIA Fie sister, think no more of him; but to the matter in hand, who ever caught anything with a naked hook? Nothing venture, nothing win, and for my part I am resolved to allow all innocent liberty; this matrimony is a pill will scarce down with a young man without gilding; let Estridge believe I am in love with him, and when he leaves me, he'll find I am not.

Enter to them Wildish.

WILDISH So he will, when he marries you, or I am deceived, Madam.

VICTORIA What, turned eavesdropper, Mr Wildish?

WILDISH No ladies, but your heads are so taken up with these heirs apparent, that you can't see a younger brother when he comes into the room.

OLIVIA Not when our backs are towards him, but otherwise as an elder, anywhere, but before a parson.

WILDISH You are in the right; jointure, and allowance for clothes, have clearly got the better of us: dear Madam, I consider not your portion, but your person; give your estate where you please, so you will but settle your affection upon me, my fate depends upon your answer; and the like artillery of unlanded lovers: but I never repine at that; for fine women, like great tables, though they are maintained by men of fortunes, are ever open to men of parts.

OLIVIA Why now, Wildish, you talk like yourself again; ever since I saw you last, I have been in most terrible apprehension of a whining copy of verses.

WILDISH Expectation you mean, Madam, but 'tis not come to that yet; though I talk a little extravagantly when I see you, I am not so thoroughpaced a lover, but I can express myself in prose.

VICTORIA But you, being a new convert, can't give too many marks of your devotion: and I should mistrust I were not as I ought to be in my servant's heart, if I did not run sometimes in his head, and then verses follow infallibly.

WILDISH Faith, Madam, that's much as the head lies, there are some you may search every cranny over, and not find three rhymes; very good lovers too; and to say truth, 'tis unreasonable a man should be put to seek fresh words to express that to his mistress, which has been as well said already by somebody else; I think 'tis very fair if he set his hand to't, and that I am ready to do to the most passionate copy of verses you can find.

OLIVIA How much love and constancy will you engage for then?

WILDISH [*he gives a paper to Olivia; she gives it to Victoria*] As much as you can find in that paper there.

OLIVIA Sister, here read 'em, I shall put the accent in the wrong place, stop out of time, or one mischief or other, and so put my poor servant into an agony.

VICTORIA [*reads the title*] 'To a very young lady'.

OLIVIA That's I, Wildish: come, you have been dabbling; proceed, sister, I fear 'em not, I have no more pity on a rhyming lover, than on a beggar that begs in a tone.★

VICTORIA Are not these verses somewhat too weak to stand alone?

WILDISH Faith, Madam, I am of your mind, put a tune to 'em, 'tis an easy stanza.

VICTORIA [*sings*]

> Ah Cloris! That I now could sit
> As unconcerned, as when
> Your infant beauty could beget
> No pleasure, nor no pain.
>
> 2
> When I the dawn used to admire,
> And praised the coming day;
> I little thought the growing fire
> Must take my rest away.
>
> 3
> Your charms in harmless childhood lay,
> Like metals in the mine,
> Age from no face took more away,
> Than youth concealed in thine.
>
> 4
> But as your charms insensibly
> To their perfection pressed,
> Fond love as unperceived did fly,
> And in my bosom rest.

★ a tone: possibly a peculiar whining tone adopted by beggars at the time.

5

My passion with your beauty grew,
    And Cupid at my heart,
Still as his mother favoured you,
    Threw a new flaming dart.

6

Each gloried in their wanton part,
    To make a lover he
Employed the utmost of his art,
    To make a beauty she.

7

Though now I slowly bend to love
    Uncertain of my fate,
If your fair self my chains approve,
    I shall my freedom hate.

8

Lovers, like dying men, may well
    At first disordered be,
Since none alive can truly tell
    What fortune they must see.

Enter a Servant.

SERVANT There's an old gentleman below in a chair enquires for
Mr Wildish, as fine as an emperor, my master Sir John is nobody
to him; as he peeped through the glass, I thought it was Sir
Samuel Forecast.

VICTORIA It is impossible it should be he.

WILDISH Yes faith it is ladies, I am privy to the plot.

OLIVIA Good Mr Wildish bring him up, I would give anything to
see him.

WILDISH Do you step into that closet then; for I must swear the
coast is clear: set the door a little open, and you may see him perfectly, his bravery on my word is not designed for this place, and
he is so politic, that he will think your seeing him may be a prejudice to his design.

Wildish goes out, and brings in Sir Samuel Forecast.

WILDISH Sir Samuel, now you shine indeed; my cousin will be

ravished to see you transform yourself thus for her sake.

FORECAST She is a tender piece, and though her discretion helps her to conceal it, in her heart cannot but love a little bravery; I have two laces in a seam more than my brother Everyoung, and a yard more in my cravat.

WILDISH Nay, you are most exact, and in this dress methinks not unlike Sir John.

FORECAST I came only to show myself to you, and am for my widow presently; shall I have your company?

WILDISH I have a little business here, but I'll be with you by that time you are there, I see you came in a chair.

FORECAST Do you think I had a mind to have the boys follow me in the streets? Pray be secret, Mr Wildish, for I would have nobody know I am in this dress, but yourself, and your fair cousin, for a world: and therefore I will make haste from hence, do you follow me according to your promise. [*Exit*]

WILDISH I shall, Sir Samuel.

OLIVIA I never saw a City-bridegroom so frizzed, so laced, so perfumed, and so powdered in my life.

VICTORIA I think verily he was painted too, I vow I should not have known his worship, if you had not given us a hint of his bravery before.

WILDISH Well, I must recover my old knight: farewell ladies.

OLIVIA Pray be here anon, and give us an account of this adventure.

VICTORIA Certainly it must be very pleasant.

WILDISH I shall obey you, ladies. [*Exit Wildish*]

Enter Everyoung, Victoria, and Olivia laughing.

EVERYOUNG Hey-day! What, are the girls mad?

VICTORIA No, Sir, but I think my uncle Forecast's little better.

EVERYOUNG Why, what of him?

OLIVIA He is, Sir, at this time the greatest spark in London, dressed so like you, that if his condition required it, I should think, Sir, he were going to a scrivener to personate you for a good sum.

EVERYOUNG Well, I'll handsel* his new clothes, and put him as

* handsel: inaugurate.

much out of conceit with bravery as ever he was in his life. Boy, call in the three prentices were brought before me for breaking windows last night.

Enter three Prentices.

I suppose, young men, you would not scruple at a small piece of service to the man that should procure your liberties.

OMNES Free us, and command us anything.

EVERYOUNG Well then follow me, and when I show you a certain chair, take the gentleman out of it, and cudgel him; I'll be at a little distance, and if you want help, be ready to assist you: be sure you call him Sir John Everyoung, and tell him of a lady he affronted.

FIRST PRENTICE We shall call him what you please, Sir, and beat him as much as you please.   [*Exeunt*]

⟨SCENE III⟩

Scene changes ⟨to a street⟩

⟨*Enter Everyoung and Prentices meeting*⟩ *Forecast coming by in his chair.*

EVERYOUNG That's the chair.

They take out Forecast, and cudgel him.

FORECAST If you have humanity, if you had women to your mothers, be more merciful, gentlemen, I never injured you, nor saw any of you in my life.

⟨FIRST⟩ PRENTICE I perceive, Sir John Everyoung, you have forgot the affront you did a lady last night.

FORECAST What affront, Sir, what lady?

⟨FIRST⟩ PRENTICE The affront, Sir, was a great affront, and the lady, a great lady, that thinks fit to have you beaten for't.

FORECAST You mistake, gentlemen, you mistake; for as I am a true servant to the state, I never did kindness or injury to any lady since I was in commission.

⟨SECOND⟩ PRENTICE A true servant of the state, and a man in authority! He shall have three kicks more for that.

Enter Estridge and Modish.

ESTRIDGE What, three upon one! Whoe'er he be, the cause becomes a gentleman: let's rescue him at all adventures. [*they draw, the Prentices run away*]

FORECAST Estridge and Modish! Nay then I am utterly undone, I have only 'scaped a little more beating, to be laughed at as long as I live.

ESTRIDGE Sir, we are very happy that our occasions led us this way, since it has given us an opportunity of serving a gentleman, especially oppressed by odds.

FORECAST I shall take some other time, if you will let me know where to wait on you, to give you thanks for this your seasonable assistance: now, gentlemen, my hurts require a chirurgeon. [*he offers to go away*]

MODISH Nay, Sir, take your hat and sword along with you; there they be. [*he looks a little for 'em*] I never heard any man speak so like Sir Samuel Forecast in my life.

ESTRIDGE But he is dressed very like Everyoung, a mere medley between the two brothers; but we'll see who he is before we go.

MODISH Have you received any hurt in your face, that you cover it with your handkercher?

FORECAST A slight one only.

ESTRIDGE I have sympathy-powder* about me, if you will give me your handkercher while the blood is warm, will cure it immediately. [*Modish snatches it off, and discovers him*]

ESTRIDGE Sir Samuel Forecast, why do you hide yourself thus from your friends? We expected nothing for our pains, neither is your hurt so dangerous, but it might endure the air.

MODISH Methinks you should rather have hid yourself from your enemies: but, Sir Samuel, whatever the matter is, I never saw a man so fine in all my life.

FORECAST Now the brokers take all fine clothes, and the gaol all that love 'em; they have helped me to fine beating.

ESTRIDGE Why do you think the rogues would have had more mercy on your high-crowned hat, black cap, and boots.

* sympathy-powder: a remedy reputedly invented by Sir Kenelm Digby.

FORECAST No, but they took me for my brother Everyoung, who it seems, has lately affronted a lady, and I suffer for it.

MODISH The best advice we can give you, is to go home and shift, for fear of more mishaps.

ESTRIDGE Farewell, Sir Samuel.   [*Exeunt omnes*]

ACT FOUR

SCENE I

The Mulberry Garden

Enter Jack Wildish.

WILDISH I was to blame no earlier to use myself to these women of honour, as they call 'em; for now like one that never practised swimming, upon the first occasion I am lost; there are men would have fooled with Olivia, and fooled her too, perhaps by this time, without ever engaging in one serious thought: your good fencer always thrusts in guard, he's but a novice that receives hit for hit: this Modish and Estridge, I know not what to make of their continual visits, methinks love and jealousy come too quick upon a man in one day.

Enter Modish and Estridge.

Here come the men, they are open enough to let me know all at large; but I would fain contrive it, that the ladies might be witnesses of their servants' most invincible secrecy: I'll steal off ere I am seen, and think on't.

Enter Victoria and Olivia, as he goes out he meets 'em.

WILDISH Slip into that arbour, ladies, and trust me for once for a quarter of an hour's diversion.

OLIVIA Pray, sister, let us go, he has somewhat in his head, I'm confident. [*He puts them into an arbour, and meets Modish in a walk*]

WILDISH Your servant, Modish.

MODISH O your servant!

ESTRIDGE Your servant, Mr Wildish.

WILDISH What, is there store of game here, gentlemen?

MODISH Troth little, or none, a few citizens that have brought their children out to air 'em, and eat cheese-cakes.

WILDISH I thought this place had been so full of beauties, that like a pack of hounds in a hare-warren, you could not hunt one for another: what think you of an arbour and a bottle of rhenish.* [*He brings 'em to the next arbour to the ladies*]

* rhenish: Rhine wine.

ESTRIDGE I like the motion well.

WILDISH And how go the ladies? Will they go abroad alone? Are they come to kissing yet?

ESTRIDGE What ladies?

WILDISH Why, Sir John's daughters, the ladies.

MODISH You are merry, Mr Wildish.

WILDISH I should be so indeed, if it were with me as it is with you, gentlemen, that have two such fine women in love with you, and every night sitting up together till morning.

MODISH I go only to entertain Victoria in mere friendship to Ned Estridge; 'tis he that is the happy man.

ESTRIDGE 'Tis a part of friendship that you discharge very willingly, and very effectually, for sometimes we see neither of you in an hour; and then you return, exclaiming against the heat of the weather, and cruelty of your mistress.

WILDISH What, that she kept him a little too hard to't, or so?

MODISH Fie, Wildish, they are women of honour.

WILDISH Well, here's their health, to make 'em amends. And faith they lose none with me, in being civil to an honest gentleman, 'tis the only wealth is left poor women to exercise their good nature with: a friend at Court may get you a place, a general of an army give you an employment, a bishop★ a church-living, and a fair lady a good turn; every one in their way, and I hold him ungrateful that buries an obligation of any sort in silence: besides 'twere mere robbery to your friends, not to let 'em rejoice in your good fortune.

MODISH But say I have made a vow to the contrary; not that there is, or ever was, any such good fortune; and women's favours, like the gifts of fairies, if once spoke of, vanish.

WILDISH O your servant, what say you Estridge? Are you under a vow too, or are the favours you have received, yet, only such as the hope of further obliges you to secrecy for a while? But you are so serious, I doubt you intend to commit matrimony.

ESTRIDGE Not as long as I can have simple fornication for love or money: I am not for those ladies that deal by wholesale, a bit off

---

★ Court . . . bishop: Sedley seems to have forgotten that the action was taking place in the Commonwealth period, when the Court was in exile in France and the bishops in hiding or exile.

the spit serves my turn as well as the whole joint, and methinks has a prettier relish.

WILDISH That is, metaphorically saying, you have sped with your mistress. – My service to you, remembering the bit off the spit. [*drinks to him*] And how, is she buxom? Does she think happiness consists in motion, or in rest? What sect of philosophers is she of?

ESTRIDGE A Pythagorean;* I, Sir, in all these cases say nothing.

WILDISH Nay, you had as good speak out now, and make me your confidant.

MODISH [*takes Estridge aside*] Jack Wildish is an honest fellow, 'tis not a pin's matter what we say to him; and they are two of the prettiest women in Town: it sounds handsomely, to boast some familiarity, you understand me: he knows 'em not, and will never find us out; I'll begin with him – I wonder, Wildish, we could never get you along with us; the ladies have not vowed virginity, they are no such bugbears as you take 'em for.

WILDISH I take 'em for honest women, or which is e'en as bad, pretenders to it.

ESTRIDGE There is no harm in pretending to it, that like a high price, only serves to keep off ill company.

WILDISH Yes, yes, I know what kind of cattle they are, well enough, there's no having a simple kiss amongst 'em without a journey into the country; nor getting 'em abroad without a sister, or a cousin at least, and then they must be at home too by ten o'clock, have the sillabubs, and tarts, brought into the coach to 'em; drink more sugar than wine, and so foul all the glasses, put you to four or five pound charge, and let you see nothing but themselves, that's man's meat for't; I have been once or twice plagued with such animals as these.

MODISH Can'st thou imagine, Wildish, we would fool away our time with such shadows of women as thou describest? We have solid and substantial pleasures.

WILDISH What? A riband, or a lock of hair, I warrant.

MODISH No, two young juicy girls, that stick as close to us, as the bark to the tree, and part as unwillingly from us, as green fruit does from the stone; and all this through the reputation of sober

* A Pythagorean: an ascetic, like the Greek philosopher Pythagoras.

and discreet servants to their pleasure: if such a scandalous fellow
as thou come into the house without our introduction, the ladies
would cry out, 'O my honour!' as far as they could see thee.

WILDISH Methinks, Sir John Everyoung (an old smell-smock as
he is) should take the alarm, and so remove these so juicy girls.

ESTRIDGE I hope you don't think we mean his daughters all this
while? (That were a trick indeed) We speak of two ladies that
shall be nameless.

WILDISH Faith, gentlemen, I can speak of none such, for all my
acquaintance have two or three names apiece, I assure you.

MODISH Well Jack, to return your civility in the last health you
began, here's to all those incomparable ladies, that like Roman
conquerors* have two or three names apiece: but if thou wouldst
leave this rambling, thou wouldst lose nothing by it; there's as
hard drinking in gentlemen's houses nowadays, as at taverns, and
as hot service in many a lady's chamber, as at Gifford's.†

WILDISH But how should a man do to get into reputation? There
are your men of fashion, as well as stuffs, and they go out again
nobody knows how.

MODISH 'Tis true, in the first place you must shake hands with
your old friends, Hoquemore‡ and Burgundy for a while; leave
your Chaste Ling,§ and La Frond's,|| dine with my lord Such-a-
one one day, my Lady What-d'you-call-'em another; and be sure
to talk on't in the next company you come into, drink wine and
water at table, a dish of tea after dinner, like nothing but what is
French, before the ladies; lose your money very much like a
gentleman to 'em in the afternoon, and the work's done.

WILDISH This is a hard chapter.

ESTRIDGE If thou knew'st once the pleasure of such a sprightly
girl as Olivia, the kind quarrels, the fondness, the pretty sullen-
ness after a little absence, which must be charmed out of it with
kisses, and those thousand other devices that make a lover's

* Roman conquerors: probably the habit of successful Roman generals of
adopting a fourth name, such as Africanus or Germanicus, after their cam-
paigns.
† Gifford's: a well-known brothel run by Mrs Gifford.
‡ Hoquemore: hock, from Hochheim on the Main.
§ Chaste Ling: possibly Chatelain's; see note on p. 161.
|| La Frond's: another French establishment, near Chatelain's.

happiness; thou would'st think all this as easy as lying abed in the country in a wet morning.

MODISH Or, if he could but see Victoria's reservedness a little mollified, and brought to hand with a good supper and the fiddles.

ESTRIDGE Or Olivia in her morning dress, with her guitar,* singing to it most enticingly, and then as kind in her discourse, her little breasts swelling and pouting out, as if they came half way to be kissed.

MODISH Or the other's haughty look melted into smiles, the pretty combat of pride and pleasure in her face, at some certain times.

ESTRIDGE My mistress is in the very spring of beauty.

MODISH And mine in the midsummer of perfection.

ESTRIDGE Mine is –

WILDISH Nay gentlemen, one at once, and no quarrelling I beseech you; you are happy men both, and have reason to be in love with your sweet lives, but I thought Victoria had so obstinately doted on her old servant Horatio, that there had been more hope of winning a widow at her husband's funeral, than of any favour for her now.

MODISH People will be talking, but on my word she'll ne'er break her heart for Horatio; I and my fellow-labourer, time, have done his business.

WILDISH You are the great masters of your art, these are the two beauties, that the whole Town runs mad after.

ESTRIDGE We know it, we know it, and it is no small part of our felicity, to have that lord send his coach and six to carry 'em to the Park; this gentleman offering to play at angel-beast† with 'em, though he scarce know the cards, and has no more visible estate than what he may lose at a sitting: a third begging to give 'em the four and twenty violins, which his father in the county hears of and disinherits for, whilst the ladies put 'em off with some slight excuses, and send the whole Town over after us.

WILDISH You have 'em it seems in most excellent order.

MODISH O there's no true pleasure but in your person of quality, the others love all men so well, they can love none best: they are indeed (like your more generous creatures) somewhat hard to

---

* guitar: guitars were extremely popular at the Court of Charles the Second.
† angel-beast: a fashionable card game.

tame, but I have seen a lion as gentle as an ox: time and industry will do anything.

ESTRIDGE Come, drink a glass round.

MODISH I can't get down a drop of this wine more without a frolic.

WILDISH Every man name the woman that has obliged him last, and drink all their healths in a brimmer.

MODISH Content, begin Estridge.

ESTRIDGE Olivia: now, Modish, name yours.

MODISH Victoria, Victoria: we must have your person too, Wildish.

WILDISH Mistress Betty.

MODISH Betty what?

WILDISH Nay faith, I can go no farther, and may very well be mistaken in that too.

ESTRIDGE Here's a lock of hair, shall I dip it for one glass more?

WILDISH Whose is it first?

ESTRIDGE Olivia's, whose should it be? Black as jet, and shining as her eyes: here's her picture too in little.

WILDISH [*steps a little aside, and looks upon it*] O impudence! His sister's picture, he forgot he showed me a month ago; this lock of hair, produced so confidently, frighted me a little, till I saw the colour.

Enter to them Snappum.

SNAPPUM Gentlemen, I beg your pardon for pressing thus rudely into your company; but the business concerns no less than all my fortunes: I have been long a suitor to a rich widow, and have at last prevailed with her to marry me suddenly.

ESTRIDGE What is that to us, Sir?

SNAPPUM Wildish, you'll I hope make my excuse to your friends: coming into the garden about half an hour ago, I lost a bracelet of her hair, wrought with her own hands, so that there is no deceiving her with a counterfeit: a waiter here tells me, he saw one of you take up such a thing.

WILDISH Is this it?

ESTRIDGE That's mine, and composed of hair so dear to me, that I would fight with Hector, the top of your order for least of 'em.

SNAPPUM And I with Hercules for mine: but pray Mr Wildish, let me see it; if it be that I look for, nobody will quarrel for't, for 'tis full of grey hairs, I assure you.

WILDISH Shall he see it?

ESTRIDGE No.

WILDISH I'll make bold for once though. [*shows it him*]

SNAPPUM 'Tis my old woman's.

WILDISH By the mark I'll swear, for 'tis as grizzled as a silver-haired rabbit; I may venture to let him have it, Estridge, I suppose, mayn't I?

ESTRIDGE Yes, yes, now I remember me, I sent mine to have a new string put to it.

[*Snappum goes off, Wildish follows him a little way*]

WILDISH Adieu, Snappum.

SNAPPUM Are any of these gentlemen good bubbles,* Mr Wildish?

WILDISH What do I know, you had best ask 'em.

SNAPPUM No, I thank you, Sir, I can be satisfied on easier terms; but you were always a lover in ingenuity, pray tell me.

[*Exit Snappum*]

WILDISH Away, away.

Wildish returns.

I'm sorry your mistress has grey hairs so young, I doubt you are not kind to her, Estridge.

MODISH Nay, Wildish, don't insult upon a mistake.

Estridge is out of countenance, and looking up and down, sees the women in the next arbour.

ESTRIDGE I think we have neighbours in the next arbour, and fine women they seem to be in their masks.

MODISH Let's entertain 'em – What ladies, come a-padding† for hearts here in your vizards?‡ A pretty device to make a man in love with he can't tell who.

* bubbles: dupes.

† a-padding: to pad was originally to tramp on a road, and later to rob on highways.

‡ vizards: masks, often worn by ladies in the Elizabethan period, came into fashion again after the Restoration, being worn by ladies in the theatre. But their use by women of ill-repute led to ladies ceasing to wear them.

ESTRIDGE What, rob us of our liberties without one word? Not so much as stand and deliver?

OLIVIA If we should rob you of your hearts, gentlemen, 'twere but petty larceny; Victoria and Olivia would never send hue and cry after us.

MODISH You know us, Madam.

OLIVIA Yes, gentlemen, somewhat better than we did this morning, though I always supposed no less.

ESTRIDGE Than what?

OLIVIA Than that you were the vainest coxcombs in the whole Town, fellows that would hate a woman that were kind to you, because she takes from you the pleasure of belying her.

ESTRIDGE Olivia?

OLIVIA The very same, Sir, whose picture you have in your pocket, and about whose hair you had like to have quarrelled so manfully but now; who sends all the Town after you, and puts others off with slight excuses; the obliging lady, whose health you drank by that name.

ESTRIDGE 'Twas another Olivia I meant, one I knew abroad.

VICTORIA And another Victoria that you meant, Modish?

MODISH Right, right, my landlady's daughter at the Cheval d'Or, since gone into a monastery.

OLIVIA The daughters of a French Everyoung, I warrant too.

ESTRIDGE La Jeunesse was their father, which is all one with Everyoung in English.

MODISH On our honours, ladies, we were ever most tender of your dear credits, and are heartily sorry our mistresses light to be of your names.

OLIVIA Pray will you do me favour to let me see my picture, I'm confident 'tis very like me.

ESTRIDGE Your French namesake's you mean, Madam; that maladroit Wildish let it fall and broke the crystal, and I sent it just now away to have a new one put to it, as I hope to be saved, Madam.

MODISH But, Madam, could you think me so senseless, as discourse of you at that rate? Here's Jack Wildish has heard us speak of these wenches a hundred times.

WILDISH [*apart*] S'light, these fellows will lie themselves into credit again, if I haven't a care of 'em instantly; gentlemen I understand no winks, the few lies I'll venture upon I am resolved to keep for my own use.

ESTRIDGE Prithee Wildish help us but this once.

WILDISH No, no, go on, methinks you are in a very fair way; I am a stranger, the ladies won't mind what I say.

OLIVIA Yes, yes, we'll take your word.

WILDISH Why then, ladies, I assure you upon the honour of a gentleman, and by my friendship to those worthy persons I dare answer, they are too much servants, to discourse so long of anything but yourselves: and for the French women you know as much of 'em as I, having never heard tittle of 'em till this minute.

VICTORIA You have brought a very sufficient witness with you gentlemen, we do believe him.

MODISH Ours is not the first good cause has been lost by ill witnesses: but I perceive, ladies, you don't know Jack Wildish, he is the veriest droll in the whole Town; has a hundred of these fetches.

ESTRIDGE [*to Wildish apart*] Pox on't, thou mayest bring all off yet.

WILDISH Faith my conscience won't give me leave to deceive a lady in a friend's behalf, [*aside*] to do it now, and in my own is all I can obtain of it.

ESTRIDGE [*comes up to Wildish*] S'death, Sir –

WILDISH Nay Estridge, no huffing, you know I mind it not, and 'tis uncivil to fright your mistresses.

MODISH But that we are two to one, and scorn advantages, you should not carry it off thus.

WILDISH I should be more afraid if you were three to one: but some other time for these matters.

OLIVIA Never blame Wildish, we were all the while in the next arbour, so that if he had taken your cue never so readily, 't had done you little service.

VICTORIA Gentlemen this matter will bear no more raillery; we are sensible of our honours, and the injury your extravagant discourse might have done us, with any but so worthy a person as Mr Wildish; but he we are confident understands himself too well to have any ill thought of us from your vanity: we can do no less than forbid you our house, and pray forbear it without further ceremony.

[Wildish takes Victoria; Estridge offers to take Olivia, she refuses]

OLIVIA No, Sir, you'll say I come to pick you up in the Garden one time or other.   *[Exeunt Omnes]*

⟨SCENE II⟩

⟨Outside Sir Samuel Forecast's house⟩

Enter Eugenio like an officer, and three more.
Sir Samuel Forecast above.
Enter a Servant.

SERVANT Sir, there are some soldiers below, say they must search your house for some suspicious person.

FORECAST I warrant they mean Eugenio and Philander, I am utterly undone, suspected for a traitor, and all long of those ungracious girls! I am very glad I have got my Christian cloth on again: go and let 'em in.

EUGENIO Sir, I hope you will excuse us, we do but follow our orders, and having searched your house for some dangerous persons will leave it you again in peace: Eugenio and Philander were your sons, and therefore most probably judged to have made your house their sanctuary.

FORECAST My house their sanctuary! I had rather it should be their grave: since they made the state their enemy, I have been so too.

EUGENIO Then you have no thoughts of 'em for your daughters?

FORECAST No, Sir, I assure you: and to remove all doubt, Althea's shortly to be married to Horatio (One that will bid you welcome, Sir, if you please to come to the wedding) and I hope to dispose of Diana ere long to some honest gentleman of our party.

Enter Althea.

FORECAST I command you, on my blessing, to answer all things this gentleman questions you about, precisely, as it were myself.

EUGENIO Sir, you do well, but you must retire a little, whilst we examine your daughters; a man, though never so well meaning himself, can't answer for others.

[Exit Forecast]

EUGENIO Lady, your father here has showed himself a faithful subject to the Commonwealth; it now remains to know what correspondence you entertain with Eugenio and Philander, your former servants.

ALTHEA Upon my honour not the least, we are too strictly watched to have a correspondence with any man, and are too careful of ourselves to hold one with persons so obnoxious.

EUGENIO Are you resolved you never will?

ALTHEA As things are now they never shall.

EUGENIO Must you then marry Horatio?

ALTHEA My father tells me so, and I have hitherto been dutiful.

EUGENIO Horatio's an accomplished gentleman.

ALTHEA He is Sir, and worthy of more happiness than I can bring him to.

EUGENIO [*aside*] By heaven, she loves him. ⟨*aloud*⟩ You loved Eugenio once, and gave vow for vow.

ALTHEA I did perhaps.

EUGENIO A stranger and an enemy as he is I pity him.

ALTHEA 'Tis noble in you, Sir, but we must all obey our fortunes.

EUGENIO [*lets fall his disguise*] And curse 'em too, if they be all like mine,
That love where beauty, and not virtue, shine.
O that the tyrants knew that I were here!
Death does more lovely now than life appear.
Since thou art false, 'tis she alone has charms;
Neglected love rests only in your arms:
When I am dead you may your choice avow
Without reproach, which sure you cannot now:
And I shall want the sense of all my wrongs,
My death both to my rest, and thine belongs.

ALTHEA Can this Eugenio be, and so unkind,
What strange distemper rages in thy mind?
Could once my soul of a base thought allow,
He that believes me false should find me so.

EUGENIO Must you not, Madam, with Horatio wed?

'Tis a belief that your own words have bred.
ALTHEA Forgive my fear, if any word of mine
   Unto that hateful sound seemed to incline:
   Your rude appearance, of a soldier, made
   My tender heart, and very love afraid:
   I durst not speak, what most I did believe,
   But used such words as you would best receive.
EUGENIO Alas, Althea! what you told me here,
   Did not create, although increase, my fear:
   That you must make him happy, is not new,
   Nor did I learn the killing sounds from you;
   The streets are full of it, and everywhere
   I can of nothing but this hymen hear.
ALTHEA 'Tis true, my father does a match design
   'Twixt me and this Horatio, and does join
   Threats to commands, urges th' uncertain state
   Of your affairs, your party, and the fate
   Of such as do a well-formed power invade;
   How they are always conquered or betrayed.
   My beauty fatal to itself the while
   Inflames Horatio, and discourse (like oil)
   Foments the fire: of such a love he tells,
   As would prevail but where your image dwells;
   But still in vain the heart I gave to you,
   The one does threaten, and the other woo.
EUGENIO An absent lover ill maintains the field:
   Does not my image to his presence yield?
ALTHEA I'm sure it ought; reproaches so severe,
   They that deserve 'em not will never bear.
   'Twere just that faith which you so ill deserve,
   For one of nobler thoughts I should reserve.
EUGENIO We oft are made by a too great concern
   (Like too much light) unable to discern.
   The leave I gave to your surprise so late,
   Now for my own distraction I entreat.
   Where there is much of love, there will appear
   Mixed with our boldest hope some little fear.
ALTHEA That fear in a true lover soon would die,

Which to my virtue is an enemy.

EUGENIO Hope is the passion of a calmer breast,
But high concernments are with doubt oppressed.
To few, alas, is such assurance given
Not to fear hell, although they hope for heaven.
I not your virtue, but my fate accuse,
Which still does me with highest rigour use.

ALTHEA Though fate, Eugenio, for misfortune meant,
I would refuse to be the instrument.
That dire necessity it seldom gave
Of harming them, whom we would only save.

EUGENIO But hark, I think I hear a noise of swords.

ALTHEA The sound, alas, no room for doubt affords
You might perhaps be safe in your disguise.

SOLDIERS [*within*] Where are the rest of 'em? Down with the
doors there.

EUGENIO Their sudden coming all such hope denies,
'Tis me they seek, I am betrayed; but yet
Since I can't shun, I'll try to break the net.
This paper will inform your sister where
She may of her unhappy servant hear,
Make him remove, help him to shun that fate
Which does for the unblessed Eugenio wait.

⟨*Enter Horatio and Soldiers.*⟩

My rival in their head! By all the gods,
Horatio, this is an unmanly odds;
Yet if on thee I can but fall revenged,
I life for death most happily have changed.

HORATIO Eugenio here! I thought of nothing less,
But my clear meaning this will best express.

[*He fights on Eugenio's side*]

OFFICER Down with 'em both.

[*The Soldiers prevail, they are taken*]

EUGENIO Sir, let my life the cruel forfeit pay,
And bear not rashly so much worth away.
Horatio was too far by virtue led,
And saved that blood he nobly should have shed:

He being my rival feared the world might say,
He for my hated life this train did lay.
Honour engaged his sword in my defence,
And honour is a kind of innocence.

HORATIO Eugenio leave to intercede for me,
I only grieve I could not rescue thee,
That so thou mightest thy preservation owe
To the same virtue thou so ill didst know:
And I some fitter time might make thee own
The injustice of thy mean aspersion,
To think I came thus rudely to invade
The place where all that I adore is laid;
And then to take my rival in a snare,
Where if I would I knew I could not spare,
Was an affront thou with that life had'st paid,
Which I defended: but revenge shows base,
Which on our honour more dependence has.

EUGENIO Some other time for this dispute we'll take,
Revenge by threatening we the harder make.

OFFICER Come, gentlemen, you must away, my orders press; you
will have time enough to talk of these things in the Tower.

Enter two Soldiers bringing in Sir Samuel.

OFFICER Sir, you must along.

FORECAST Who I! For what?

OFFICER For harbouring Eugenio here, a known enemy to the
state.

FORECAST You brought him with you for ought I know, I ne'er
saw his face, I answered an officer, and two soldiers that came to
search for him even now, and as I thought, gave 'em satisfaction.
But when I heard the clashing of swords, because I would not be
made accessory to anything that might happen, I confess I
retired into a corner of my garret.

OFFICER Sir, this won't satisfy, the receiver is as bad as the thief;
I have found a traitor in your house, and you shall answer it.

FORECAST Eugenio, you are an honest gentleman, pray speak, did I
know anything of your being here?

EUGENIO Not in the least, Sir: but my word I fear will do you little service.

Enter Wildish.

WILDISH What, Sir Samuel, again under persecution? Nay, faith, I can do you no service now, these are a sort of gamesters I dare not meddle withal.

FORECAST I am undone! Here's Eugenio found in my house, and they are carrying him to the Tower.

WILDISH Come, bear up, Sir, if there come a turn, you'll be a great man.

FORECAST I shall be hanged on that side, and to speak my own conscience, I have deserved it.

WILDISH No, to lie in prison for concealing cavaliers, will be great merit; and let me tell you as a friend, there's like to be a turn suddenly, 'tis thought the general* will declare like an honest man, I say no more; therefore carry yourself moderately, this accident may chance to do you good service, if you have the grace to make the right use on't: but how came Eugenio and Horatio of a side?

FORECAST I came but just now among 'em, and know nothing; but 'tis a strange thing a man can't be believed in his own defence: carry me to prison? I'll see what justice's hand they have for't.

OFFICER We shall find hands enough, ne'er fear it.

[*Exeunt Omnes*]

---

* the general: General George Monk, who was instrumental in restoring Charles the Second to the throne in 1660.

ACT FIVE

SCENE I

Enter Philander solus.

PHILANDER 'Tis strange I nothing of Eugenio hear,
  So long an absence may be worth a fear:
  His friendship was not wont to hide from me
  Of his most secret thoughts the new decree.
  I doubt his love impatient of delay,
  Has to Althea found some desperate way,
  His passion could not my slow cure attend,
  On which, alas, he did in vain depend.
  I was to blame, no sooner to provide
  Against deluded hope's unruly tide;
  Which now I fear has borne him on a shelf,
  Where he'll unkindly perish by himself.

Enter Diana in man's clothes.

  Ha! A strange face! Would I had not been seen;
  But 'tis too good for treason to lurk in.
  Sure gentle youth the place you have mistook,
  I cannot be the man for whom you look.
DIANA Philander in your troubled face I read
  Some apprehensions that you are betrayed:
  But when you shall my woeful story hear,
  A juster sorrow will remove your fear.
PHILANDER Thou hast my name, and yet I know thee not,
  Quickly untie sweet youth this painful knot.
DIANA Know you this hand?
PHILANDER Alas it is my own,
  This from Eugenio could be had or none:
  Speak, is he dead? Is this his legacy?
  And has he sent it, gentle youth, by thee?
  Has he Horatio fought? Killing, or slain,
  He almost equally would breed my pain.
DIANA He and Horatio fought, but on a side.
PHILANDER What wonder beyond this can fate provide.

I knew, Eugenio, thou wert always brave,
And that thy love was still thy honour's slave.

DIANA On your friend's part you have the virtue brought,
But 'twas Horatio for Eugenio fought.

PHILANDER Such a prodigious union could not fail.

DIANA A band of soldiers did o'er both prevail.

PHILANDER Is my unhappy friend a prisoner made?

DIANA He is, and close in the White Tower laid:
He bade me tell you so, that you might shun
The desperate hazard that his life must run.

PHILANDER How came he, gentle youth, thus to expose
My life to one whom he so little knows?

DIANA I am his near relation, and have been
Privy to all designs he has been in.
He bids you to remove without delay,
For y' are endangered hourly by your stay:
The soldiers about him a paper took,
Which, though obscurely, of your lodging spoke.

PHILANDER In vain we to that wretch good counsel give,
Resolved to perish, and unfit to live:
When he is gone, what business have I here?
What can again be worth a hope or fear?
The hour he dies this [*pointing his sword*] shall be my relief,
If I could need another wound than grief.

DIANA How can you hope to please Eugenio's ghost,
In killing him whom he esteems the most?
In life our friends we choose, but those we hate
We rather wish companions of our fate:
If I a present to his shade would send,
It should be of his foe, and not his friend.
But yet I hope Eugenio may escape;
Safety has come in an unlooked for shape.

PHILANDER That hope alone makes me consent to live.

DIANA Can you for life no other reason give?

PHILANDER None that, alas! is fit for thee to hear.

DIANA Does then Diana's heart so vile appear?

PHILANDER I hope thou wilt my better genius prove,
Since thus thou know'st my business and my love.

DIANA She tells me you have often filled her ears
    With gentle words, and wet her arms with tears;
    Vowed that your hope and fear, grief, and delight,
    Her frowns or favours only could excite.

PHILANDER Why so I did, sweet youth, and told her true,
    But I'm amazed it should be known by you.

DIANA Of late she has worn a face of discontent,
    That seemed neglected friendship to lament:
    Eugenio to her sister found a way,
    Though various hazards in his passage lay.

PHILANDER Unwisely he the short-lived pleasure sought,
    Too soon 'twas paid for, and too dearly bought;
    Like Orpheus for one poor untimely look,
    He has the hope of all he loved forsook.

DIANA That haste expressed a passion, though to blame:
    Impatience is of love the best extreme.

PHILANDER That heir's accursed, that for a present sum
    Resigns the hope of all he has to come.
    I would Diana to the world prefer,
    And for her venture anything but her.
    But, gentle youth, methinks thou speak'st as though
    Thou mad'st a doubt, whether I loved or no.

DIANA Pray heaven Diana mayn't: your fault was great,
    To think of honour when the day was set
    For Hymen's rites; when nought else could destroy
    Your hopes, which then were ripening into joy,
    You were a traitor to the state declared,
    And in the glittering toils of fate ensnared.

PHILANDER Be witness heaven, and all ye powers above,
    That see our infant passions weakly move,
    Ere they have force into the face to climb,
    Or to one action can our wills incline,
    If ever, for one moment, in my breast
    I gave to any (she inspired not) rest.

DIANA Why did you then such daring projects frame,
    And danger court that not concerned your flame?

PHILANDER 'Tis true, before I knew Diana's charms,
    I courted fame in danger and in arms,

And thought no cause could lasting glory bring,
Like the just quarrel of our injured king.
Eugenio's friendship too that fire improved,
And made me wed that cause I ever loved:
What since I did was on a former score,
My fate she can't condemn, but must deplore.
I was in honour pre-engaged too far,
E'er to retire, and yet to merit her.
But whence could'st thou this hated knowledge gain?
He worse than kills, who makes me live in pain:
Thy beauty, youth, and words do all persuade,
Thou happy in her nearest trust art made.
                    [*Diana here drops a ring, pulling out a handkerchief*]
Ye gods! The ring I to Diana sent!
Do not frail man beyond his nature tempt.
The good thou hast done, I thus forget it all,
And let my vengeance on my rival fall. [*he draws*]
Draw, or I'll leave thee dead upon the ground.
DIANA [*pulls off her periwig*] I dare not draw – and sure you dare not
     wound.
PHILANDER With sudden light I for a while am blind,
     I sought a rival, and a mistress find;
     Where I thought all my rage, my love is due,
     So high a pitch my wishes never flew;
     I am not by degrees to pleasure led,
     Nor slowly made the doubtful steps to tread,
     But in an instant, my exalted mind
     Feels all her hopes set free, and fears confined:
     So kings in battles that they gave for gone,
     Redeem their own and win another crown.
DIANA That faith, which nothing should in question bring,
     From a few words you doubt, and from a ring:
     How can I hope a lasting friendship, where
     So light appearance brings so mean a fear?
PHILANDER Such a surprise a jealous pang might give
     To any breast where so much love does live.
     But why, Diana, in this strange disguise?
     Was it to make me happier by surprise?

DIANA Could I my fear, as well as love o'ercome,
　　You'd been preserved, and never known by whom;
　　Such a concern I would not have betrayed,
　　Till I were surer of your passion made.
PHILANDER What accident ill understood, could prove
　　Of that dire force to make you doubt my love?
　　You needs must know how we were all betrayed,
　　And the hard scape I and Eugenio made;
　　And since, it had been fatal to be seen,
　　So that this chamber my whole world has been.
DIANA What made me doubt, it matters not to know,
　　Let it suffice I do no longer so.
　　The dreadful sword, which at my breast you held,
　　Though with much fear, I with more joy beheld:
　　For he that truly does his rival hate,
　　Declares he loves his mistress at that rate.
PHILANDER Look on thyself, and measure thence my love,
　　Think what a flame so bright a form must move:
　　That knot be confident will ever last,
　　Which passion tied, and reason has made fast.
DIANA Farewell, Philander, think on what I've said,
　　And kindly judge the weakness of a maid.
PHILANDER Thou art too cruel in so short a stay;
　　Thus would I gaze my very sight away.
DIANA Though for your safety nothing was too dear,
　　Now give me leave for my own self to fear.　　　　[*Exit Diana*]
PHILANDER She has appeared like lightning to my sight,
　　Which when 'tis vanished, leaves a darker night.
　　　　　　　　　　　　　　　　　　　　　　[*Exit Philander*]

⟨SCENE II⟩

⟨Outside the Mulberry Garden⟩

Enter Estridge and Modish.

ESTRIDGE 'Twas certainly that rogue Wildish that betrayed us;
　　the arbour and bottle of wine, were his motions.
MODISH Without all peradventure. You saw the ladies, when they

threw us off, took him home with 'em, nothing could be plainer –
What think you if one of us fought him?

ESTRIDGE Why, faith I think we had e'en as good let that alone;
hang him, he'll fight; 'twas only a trick he put upon us, and let's
rail it off, and serve him in his own kind.

MODISH As how?

ESTRIDGE Do you remember a certain cousin of his that Everyoung carried us to, the widow of a rich alderman, who died
suddenly, and left her all he had? This widow he intends for Sir
Samuel Forecast, and I make no question but he is to have a round
sum for his good word. What think you now, if I order it, that one
of us marry this widow, then I hope we are sufficiently revenged?

MODISH But how is't possible?

ESTRIDGE Nothing so easy: her maid has promised me to persuade
her to take a walk in the Mulberry Garden; this is a time there is
little or no company there, 'tis but waiting at the door with a
trusty servant or two, and we may force her whither we please,
and then of her own accord she'll marry either of us.

MODISH Why so?

ESTRIDGE If for no other, for the same reason that men eat horseflesh in a siege; because she can come at nothing else.

MODISH If it were a foolish girl, we might do somewhat with her
indeed; but these widows are like old birds, not to be tamed;
she'll fight and scratch, and fly about, there will be no enduring
her.

ESTRIDGE Fear nothing: when she considers she has no other way
to save her reputation, she'll hear reason.

MODISH Well; but being equal adventurers, how shall we agree
about the prize?

ESTRIDGE He that marries her, shall give the other a statute upon
his estate, for two thousand pounds, a pretty good sum; and will
serve to stop a gap.

MODISH Content, and I wish thee joy of her with all my heart.

ESTRIDGE You shall find me as good a paymaster as her husband
the old alderman would have been: but stand close, here she
comes.

Enter the Widow and her Maid, they seize 'em.

WIDOW Thieves, murderers, villains! What do you mean?

ESTRIDGE Nothing, nothing, but I'll make bold to stop that pretty mouth of thine, widow, for once. [*they carry 'em off*]

MODISH Whither shall we carry 'em?

ESTRIDGE To a little house I have taken a quarter of a mile off for that purpose, where nobody could hear 'em, though they had falconers' or huntsmen's voices.   [*Exeunt*]

⟨SCENE III⟩

⟨In the Tower of London⟩

Enter Sir John Everyoung, and Sir Samuel Forecast.

EVERYOUNG Give you joy, brother, give you joy.

FORECAST Of what?

EVERYOUNG Why, of your Lieutenancy of the Tower: I know you can be here upon no other account, and indeed your fidelity to the public claims no less.

FORECAST Sir, give you joy of your new suit, and fair periwig there.

EVERYOUNG Faith, brother, it sits with no fortune today, what-e'er's the matter, I was never worse put together in all my life, and but to congratulate your advancement, would not have left the company I dined with.

FORECAST I hope to return your kind visit in the Fleet,★ and see your daughters sell ale and cakes there, and your worship with fewer trappings on; for thither your extravagant courses point.

EVERYOUNG May my periwig never know a good day, nor be taken for my own hair again, but come off always with my hat, if it cost me above twelve pounds.†

FORECAST Pox on your hat, and your periwig, can you tell how I shall get out?

★ the Fleet: the Fleet prison, dating from the Norman period, and used for both criminals and debtors.

† periwig . . . hat . . . twelve pounds: twelve pounds was a very high price for a periwig, and only a badly fitting one would come off with the wearer's hat.

EVERYOUNG No more than how you got in; but you are wise, and know business: alas, I know nothing but how to sort ribands, make horse-matches, throw away my money at dice, and keep myself out of the Tower.

FORECAST O my ungracious girls!

EVERYOUNG What of them? Have they broke prison, and taken sanctuary in the arms of some sturdy prentice, fencing-master, brother of the blade, or any other inferior rascal? You were so strict to 'em, I never looked for other.

FORECAST Not so fast; but if you can be serious for a minute, do: they are virtuous, but Eugenio a former servant to Althea, since declared a traitor to the state, was taken in my house; I suspected to have been privy to his being there, and so carried along with him hither: I protested my innocence to the officers, urged my former service, but all would not do.

EVERYOUNG S'light I hope you had more wit! This is the happiest accident that ever befell mortal, for an old notorious Roundhead to be taken for a Cavalier at this time; why I never thought it had been in you; this was a stratagem might have become Machiavelli* himself.

FORECAST Why, what's the matter? All's well I hope.

EVERYOUNG Yes, never better, the general has this day to some persons of quality declared for the king;† all Cavaliers are immediately to have their liberty; therefore make haste to reconcile with Eugenio and Philander: I have an order for the delivery of all such prisoners as are here upon the account of loyalty to their prince.

FORECAST Philander and Eugenio, on my daughter's account, will do me all the service they can, and I hope to make some advantage of this imprisonment.

EVERYOUNG I'll go and release Eugenio, and bring him to you; Horatio is discharged already: though we fall out now and then about trifles, we are brothers, and ought to serve one another in matters of concern. [*Exeunt*]

---

* Machiavelli: Niccolo Machiavelli (1469–1527), Italian author and statesman, regarded as an epitome of ruthless cunning.
† See Introduction, pp. 135–6.

⟨SCENE IV⟩

Enter Victoria, Olivia, and Wildish.

WILDISH You see now, ladies, what fellows you cast your good opinions on: if I said anything that was disrespectful to either of you, it ought to go for nothing, I was merely your decoy in the business.

OLIVIA We are very well satisfied on all hands.

VICTORIA Sure they'll never have the impudence to trouble us again.

OLIVIA Now would I were married to Estridge, that I might plague him soundly.

WILDISH How can you make that a plague, Madam?

OLIVIA A hundred ways: I would never come home till three o'clock in the morning; tumble my own handkercher myself, to make him jealous; break his soundest sleeps in commendation of his bosom-friend, and never leave till I have made 'em quarrel; fold up all manner of papers, like love-letters, and burn 'em just as he comes into th' room.

WILDISH I can tell you how to be revenged on him beyond all this.

OLIVIA Prithee how, Wildish?

WILDISH Why, marry me, make a good wife to me, and let him hang himself for rage.

OLIVIA I am not so inveterate an enemy, I'll forgive him rather: if I were your wife, I must board half a year with a friend in the country, tumble about the other half in most villainous hackneys,* lie two pair of stairs high, and wear black farandine† the whole year about; see you when you had no money to play, and then be kissed out of a ring or a bracelet.

WILDISH I would not use a City widow of five and fifty so, with seven small children: and am I to suffer nothing all this while?

OLIVIA What can you suffer?

---

* hackneys: originally a hackney meant an ambling horse, then a horse kept for hire and subsequently a carriage kept for hire, as here.

† farandine: a cloth, somewhat similar to poplin, invented by Ferrand early in the seventeenth century.

WILDISH Why, the loss of that which is dearer than life, my liberty; be known for a married man, and so put myself out of all capacity, of breaking gold, promising marriage, or any other way of ensuring myself to scrupulous young virgins I shall like hereafter.

OLIVIA That is to be taken from the occasion of playing the rascal: is that all?

WILDISH Not half; if I make but love to a chambermaid, I shall be answered, you have a sweet lady of your own, and why will you wrong her? If I get acquainted with any young woman, after the fourth or fifth visit, be looked upon by her father and mother, worse than the tax-gatherers in a country village; all this you count nothing.

OLIVIA Not to a lover, Wildish.

WILDISH Well, there is no service so desperate, that a gallant man will shrink at, if he like his reward; and to give his hand thus to a woman, in him that rightly understands what he does, is as bold an action as Mucius Scaevola's:* yet that I may use it hereafter where and when I please, upon my dear Olivia I'll venture it.

OLIVIA Softly, when you please, and where I please.

WILDISH Content Madam: will you do us the favour to be a witness?

VICTORIA Well Mr Wildish, I'll dance bare-foot to serve you.
[*Wildish leads off Olivia*]

OLIVIA Hold, hold Wildish, my heart fails me.

WILDISH ⟨*aside*⟩ S'light, I had a qualm too, there's certainly a more than ordinary providence attends me; I shall scape yet, I am now in a twitter, like a gamester upon a great by,† that is heartily afraid he shall lose it, and yet his love to the money won't suffer him to draw stakes. I must have her.

VICTORIA Nay, now you are come thus far, e'en go on.

OLIVIA Well, Wildish, give me thy hand; the first time thou anger'st me, I'll have a gallant; and the next, make thee a cuckold.
[*Exeunt*]

---

* Mucius Scaevola: a Roman who thrust his hand into a fire to prove his courage.
† by: a throw in dice.

⟨SCENE V⟩

⟨A room in Sir Samuel Forecast's house⟩

Enter Horatio and Althea.

HORATIO Madam, you know your father does command,
　That you should shortly give me your fair hand
　Before a priest; but since I find no part
　Goes along with it of your generous heart,
　My mind the charming present can refuse,
　Fearing t'indulge a passion you accuse;
　My joy with your least trouble weighed must still
　Appear, to my own self the greater ill.
ALTHEA Such words as these, Horatio, but heap more
　Upon a debt that was too great before;
　I'm covered with confusion when I weigh
　How much I owe, how little I can pay:
　You may with ease a fairer mistress find,
　And with more ease such worth will make her kind;
　And if I e'er that happy virgin know,
　I'll sue to make her pay you what I owe.
HORATIO To change your thoughts, I will no longer try,
　But with the stream I cannot turn, comply:
　I to Victoria will my suit renew,
　And hope to find an advocate in you.
ALTHEA You may command me, and Victoria's mind
　Is of itself to you too well inclined.
HORATIO All this methinks should your belief persuade,
　I no contrivance with those villains had,
　To take my rival in so mean a way,
　But only came their sudden rage to stay:
　All that confusion, and surprise could do,
　My passion made me apprehend for you.
ALTHEA Horatio's honour does too brightly shine,
　To be accused of such a low design:
　Had you within the bounds of friendship stayed,
　Yourself and me you had both happy made.

HORATIO With ease from friendship we to love are led,
That slippery path who can securely tread?

Enter Sir Samuel Forecast, Sir John Everyoung, and Eugenio.

ALTHEA I see my father, and Eugenio here,
And in all faces sudden joys appear.
[*Forecast, Everyoung, and Horatio seem to discourse*]
EUGENIO Fortune, I pardon thee thy short-lived spite,
I for thy constant temper took a fit,
Th'art kind, and gentle, and 'tis we are blind,
Who do mistrust the ways thou hast designed
To make us blessed, though better than our own.
ALTHEA Can you have joy, and yet Althea none?
EUGENIO May I all misery first undergo,
Ere joy divided from Althea know.
ALTHEA What is this wonder hangs upon thy tongue?
Delay does only to ill news belong.
EUGENIO Madam, your father licenses my flame,
And you alone can now oppose my claim;
That cause which armies did in vain support,
And noblest spirits did, successless, court,
We shining in a bloodless triumph see,
Without the dire effects of victory.
For in the general's breast (the noblest scene)
The fate of England has transacted been:
On Albion's throne he will our monarch place,
Our neighbour's terror, and our nation's grace,
Whilst at his blessed approach, all factious minds
Vanish, like leaves before autumnal winds.
ALTHEA Such truth in love and loyalty you've shown,
What less for both could by just heaven be done?
EUGENIO This happiness, though great, yet is not all,
My dearest friend I soon shall brother call;
Diana must his deathless flame repay.
ALTHEA Fate, to be pardoned, had no other way.
EUGENIO See how your father kindly strives to evade
His former promise to Horatio made.
ALTHEA That work's so nobly in his breast begun,

That a few words will finish what's undone:
Horatio does all happiness despise,
From my obedience, which my love denies.

FORECAST [*to Eugenio*] Horatio has released me of my promise to
him, and seeing your changeless love to one another, was resolved
to have moved it to me, if I had not prevented him.

EUGENIO ⟨*to Horatio*⟩ Such honour, noble youth, I must confess,
Gives wonder equal to my happiness.

HORATIO Althea I resign, my guilty flame
Was too unjust to reach so fair an aim:
Victoria's wrongs did my success oppose,
And my lost passion its own penance grows.
So some offenders are their duty taught
By th'ill effect and nature of their fault.

EUGENIO My apprehensions by these words are cleared,
And I dare love that virtue which I feared.
In love alone this mystery we find,
Men best agree when of a different mind.

HORATIO There now remains but one thing more to do,
'Tis that Philander may be sent for too.
But see he comes.

Enter Philander.

FORECAST ⟨*to Everyoung*⟩ Brother, if your daughter were here, we
might have a dance. ⟨*to Philander*⟩ Sir, you are heartily welcome, I
kept my girl safe for you, she has not been so much as blown upon
since you saw her; I knew honest men would not be always kept
from their own, there would come a time.

PHILANDER Sir, I was ever most obliged to you –
Eugenio here! Then I am doubly blessed,
And only fear to be with joy oppressed.

EUGENIO The joys of friendship well prepare our mind
For the high raptures we in love shall find:
The name of brothers we shall soon obtain.

PHILANDER Friendship so perfect by no name can gain.

Enter Diana.

Fate is at length ashamed, or weary grown

Upon a flame you smiled so long, to frown;
As vessels tossed upon the raging main,
With greater joy the wished-for port obtain;
Our love this short, fierce tempest having passed,
Will joys more high, since less expected, taste.

DIANA But in the storm did you throw nothing out?

PHILANDER Wrong not my love with so unkind a doubt.

Enter Victoria, Olivia, Wildish.

EVERYOUNG Wildish, thou'rt an honest fellow, I'm glad I found thee.

WILDISH Sir, the honest fellow desires to be known to you by another name, having newly married your daughter Olivia.

EVERYOUNG When, pray Mr Wildish?

WILDISH Just now, Sir, the words are scarce out of our mouths.

EVERYOUNG Well, this is a day I could not have been angry if thou hadst got her with child upon a contract; but you might have asked my leave, ere you went about to make me a grandfather.

WILDISH If I had had a good jointure to offer, so I would, but if I do make you a grandfather, 'tis not done maliciously, I'll swear.

HORATIO My guilty cause myself I dare not plead,
But beg your innocence will intercede:
Since all my fault your matchless beauty made,
Your goodness now should my excuse persuade.

ALTHEA I in Victoria will my interest try,
You, and me both, she hardly shall deny.

HORATIO Victoria's mind I cannot hope to move,
Unless a parent's power assist my love;
Her duty will not your commands withstand,
She'll take a worthless servant from your hand.

EVERYOUNG I'm sure she can have no exception to so deserving a person as Horatio; lovers, like spaniels, do but show their metal in a little ranging: though you had a twittering to Althea, you'll make ne'er the worse husband to Victoria. Victoria!

VICTORIA Sir, what's your pleasure?

EVERYOUNG That which will prove yours in the end: I charge you upon my blessing, give Horatio your hand, go and be married with your cousins, and make but one work of it.

VICTORIA Sir, I am all obedience: whoe'er strove
At once against her duty, and her love?

⟨*Enter Modish, Estridge and Widow.*⟩

WILDISH But Estridge, what fine lady have you got there?

ESTRIDGE A certain widow which I have cast myself away upon:
a kinswoman of yours, Wildish, that you formerly designed for the
right worshipful Sir Formal there: do you know her now? – Sir
we made bold with her without your consent.

WILDISH Old acquaintance, in faith, how is't? I have made as bold,
and been as welcome too, as e'er you'll be Sir: but why did you
steal a marriage thus?

WIDOW You know I always loved stolen pleasures, but this marriage stole me; your old knight was uncertain, came on by inches,
this gentleman leapt into the matter, forced me into a coach, and
married me in an instant: I could have been content to have been
a lady, that I might have taken place of my mistress when she
comes to Town. But a bird in the hand –

ESTRIDGE Why, have you a mistress?

WIDOW As sure as you have had a hundred, and now have a
wife.

MODISH I doubt as things go, I shall scarce find you as good a paymaster as the old alderman.

[*Estridge pulls his hand from her, and looks angry*]

WILDISH Nay, never use her ill now, 'twas none of her fault, she
is a very good creature, and one that I placed to personate my
cousin, on purpose to catch Sir Samuel Forecast; you know he
took the forfeiture of a mortgage that concerned a very good
friend of mine, and I was resolved to be revenged of him; if you
will needs run your head into the noose that's prepared for another, who can help it? My cousin is married in Ireland, whither
she went last summer to look after some money, due to her last
husband.

WIDOW I am her housekeeper though, and can bid you welcome
till she returns.

OLIVIA A pretty pert thing, I like her humour, she carries it off
well: but Wildish, you shall visit her no more now we are married.

WILDISH Fear not, Estridge will take order for that.

HORATIO [*to Victoria*] How I do hate myself! That could so long
  At once such beauty and such goodness wrong.
VICTORIA My kindness has forgot you were to blame,
  Your guilt consumed in your reviving flame.
EVERYOUNG Now you are all paired, let's have a dance.

After the dance, a great shout within.

EUGENIO I hear the people's voice in joyful cries
  Like conquering troops o'er flying enemies;
  They seem to teach us in a ruder way
  The honour due to this all-healing day.
PHILANDER Let's part a while, and vie who shall express
  The highest sense of this great happiness.

⟨*Exeunt Omnes*⟩

EPILOGUE

Poets of all men have the hardest game,
Their best endeavours can no favours claim.
The lawyer, if o'erthrown, though by the laws,
He quits himself, and lays it on your cause.
The soldier is esteemed a man of war,
And honour gains, if he but bravely dare.
The grave physician, if his patient die,
He shakes his head, and blames mortality.
Only poor poets their own faults must bear,
Therefore grave judges be not too severe:
Our author humbly hopes to 'scape your rage,
Being no known offender on the stage,
He came by chance, is a mere traveller;
All countries civil unto strangers are:
Yet faith he's armed howe'er your censures go,
And can prevent the harm, though not the blow.
No poet can from this one comfort fall,
The best ne'er pleased, nor worst displeased you all.

NOTES

The copy text used is that of the first edition, of 1668 in the Brotherton Collection, University of Leeds.

Abbreviations

    Q1 The first quarto edition, 1668

    Q2 The second quarto edition, 1675

    Q3 The third quarto edition, 1688

    P *The Poetical and Dramatic Works of Sir Charles Sedley,* ed. V de Sola Pinto, 1928

    D *Restoration Comedies,* ed. Dennis Davison, 1970

The copy text's 'um' has been regularized to 'em'.

137.7	Sedley/Sidley Q1
148.20	years. Where/years, where Q1
149.5	do you/you do Q1
150.30	starve Q2/stave Q1
151.31	than/then Q1
156.7	Q1 prints *Ring* as a stage direction prior to *Exeunt*
160.10	be not/been't Q/ben't D
160.13	Mistress/Mrs Q1
160.24	Mistress/Mrs. Q1
160.35	WILDISH/*Rild.* Q1
161.11	than/then Q1
161.23	than/Then Q1
167.27	WILDISH Q2/WID. Q1
170.9	credit: if/credit, if Q1
171.5	part: if/part, if Q1
175.19	of us: Q3/off: Q1
176.15	to stand alone P/to allone Q1/to allow D
179.14	*Exeunt/Ex. Victoria and Olivia* Q1
182.18	on't/o'nt Q1
190.22	*aside/alowd* Q1
201.35	peradventure. You/peradventure, you Q1
208.14	Ere/E'er D/E're Q1
210.8	Q1 prints *Enter Everyoung, Victoria* . . .
211.7	Sir Formal/Sir, Formal Q1
212.4	Your P/You Q1

SHE WOULD IF SHE COULD

by Sir George Etherege

INTRODUCTION

Not very much is known of the youth of Sir George Etherege (1634–91). His first play *The Comical Revenge; or, Love in a Tub* (1664) was produced when he was about thirty. His next play *She Would if She Could* was staged in 1668, the year he went to Turkey as secretary to Sir Daniel Harvey. He returned to England three years later, and *The Man of Mode*, his last and best comedy, was produced in 1676. There followed a period of his life in which he seems to have been engaged in heavy drinking with his friends, as well as taking part in occasional fights. In 1676 he was involved with the Earl of Rochester and two friends in tossing fiddlers in blankets and skirmishing the watch. One of the party was run through by a pike and the other three absconded. He was knighted, probably in 1680, and probably as the result of marrying a wealthy widow. James the Second sent him to Ratisbon as English minister where he stayed during the king's reign and found the people and the place dreary. He died in Paris in 1691.

Etherege has a lightheartedness in his writing which is engaging. His first play is badly constructed, but it contains Sir Frederick Frollick, a Restoration gallant, easy-going and libertine, who can see through the hypocrisy of others. There is a mixture in this comedy of farce and wit, an echo of fashionable modes, some romantic sentiments and songs. Etherege, in fact, put many of his own interests down on paper and produced a play which attempts to operate on many levels. *She Would if She Could* is a much more competent piece of dramatic writing; though the plot is still not a strong point there is an ease and at times a sharp wit about the conversation of Etherege's young men and women: they are poised and resourceful. Their business is to know what is fashionable, acceptable, polite. In strong contrast to them are the grosser characters, Lady Cockwood, old but eager, a 'ravenous kite', while Sir Oliver Cockwood and Sir Joslin Jolley, the two country knights, are absurd figures of fun in their desire to recapture their youth; the penitential suit of Sir Oliver, the exuberant noisy gusto of Sir Joslin are farcical enough material for any audience to enjoy. Their speech lacks the modish, mannered style of the city dwellers: but it has a suitable rough and tumble vigour about it:

'So, boys, and how do you like the flesh and blood of the Jollies –
Heuk, Sly-girl – and Mad-cap, hey – come, come, you have heard
them exercise their tongues a while; now you shall see them ply
their feet a little: this is a clean-limbed wench, and has neither
spavin, splinter, nor wind-gall; tune her a jig, and play't roundly,
you shall see her bounce it away like a nimble frigate before a fresh
gale – Hey, methinks I see her under sail already.'

The two heroines Ariana and Gatty are a pleasant pair; their
frolic in the Mulberry Garden where they meet Courtall and Freeman is a gay romp, backed up by further meetings, and some com-
monsense, before the final capitulation of ladies and lovers into
marriage. Sentry's part is a good acting role, and her quick realisa-
tion of the advantages of reinforcing the young men's deception at
the end of the play well in keeping with her character.

The play rattles on at a good speed and situation succeeds situation with sufficient variety to carry the slightness of the plot. There
is plenty of the ludicrous in the discovery of one party by the other
in the Bear. In all these contretemps we capture a sense of the free
thought of the young, and the animality of the old. Sir Oliver and
Lady Cockwood are crude in their appetites, whereas Courtall makes
a match with someone intelligent enough to be likely to hold his
interest and his regard. There is a good-humoured atmosphere about
the whole play; the songs contribute to this and the boisterous Sir
Joslin Jolley, with his friend Rakehell, provide a background of the
carousing tavern life of the time.

The play was not well received at first because of what Shadwell
called 'imperfect acting'; he thought the acting 'had like to have
destroyed *She Would if She Could*' which he considered, and he added
he had the authority of 'some of the best judges in England for 't',
the best comedy written since the Restoration of the stage.

A scene from She Would if She Could

She Would if She Could

A COMEDY

Acted at His Highness
the Duke of York's Theatre

Written by George Etherege Esq

LONDON

Printed for H. Herringman, at the Sign of the Blew
Anchor in the lower walk of the New Exchange.
1668

DRAMATIS PERSONAE

⟨MEN⟩

Sir Oliver Cockwood } Two country knights.
Sir Joslin Jolley

Mr Courtall } Two honest gentlemen of the Town.
Mr Freeman

Mr Rakehell   A knight of the industry.
Thomas   Sir Oliver Cockwood's man.
A *Servant* belonging to Mr Courtall.

⟨WOMEN⟩

My Lady Cockwood
Ariana } Two young ladies, kinswomen of Sir Joslin
Gatty   Jolley's.
Mrs Sentry   My Lady Cockwood's gentlewoman.
Mrs Gazette } Two Exchange-women.
Mrs Trinket

Waiters, Fiddlers, and Other Attendants.

ACT ONE

SCENE I

A dining room

Enter Courtall and Freeman, and a Servant brushing Courtall.

COURTALL So, so, 'tis well: let the coach be made ready.

SERVANT It shall, Sir. *[Exit Servant]*

COURTALL Well, Frank, what is to be done today?

FREEMAN Faith, I think we must follow the old trade; eat well, and prepare ourselves with a bottle or two of good burgundy, that our old acquaintance may look lovely in our eyes; for, for ought as I see, there is no hopes of new.

COURTALL Well! This is grown a wicked town, it was otherwise in my memory; a gentleman should not have gone out of his chamber, but some civil officer or other of the game* would have been with him, and have given him notice where he might have had a course or two in the afternoon.

FREEMAN Truly a good motherly woman of my acquaintance t'other day, talking of the sins of the times, told me, with tears in her eyes, that there are a company of higgling rascals, who partly for themselves, but more especially for some secret friends, daily forestall the markets; nay, and that many gentlemen who formerly had been persons of great worth and honour, are of late, for some private reasons, become their own purveyors, to the utter decay and disencouragement of trade and industry.

COURTALL I know there are some wary merchants, who never trust their business to a factor; but for my part, I hate the fatigue, and had rather be bound to back my own colts, and man my own hawks, than endure the impertinencies of bringing a young wench to the lure.

Enter Servant.

SERVANT Sir, there is a gentlewoman below desires to speak with you.

COURTALL Ha, Freeman, this may be some lucky adventure.

* the game: whoremongering.

SERVANT She asked me, if you were alone.

COURTALL And did not you say Aye?

SERVANT I told her, I would go see.

COURTALL Go, go down quickly, and tell her I am. Frank, prithee let me put thee into this closet a while.

FREEMAN Why, may not I see her?

COURTALL On my life thou shalt have fair play, and go halves, if it be a purchase that may with honour be divided; you may overhear all: but for decency's sake, in, in man.

FREEMAN Well, good fortune attend thee.

Enter Mrs Sentry.

COURTALL Mrs Sentry, this is a happiness beyond my expectation.

SENTRY Your humble servant, Sir.

COURTALL I hope your lady's come to Town?

SENTRY Sir Oliver, my lady, and the whole family. Well! We have had a sad time in the country; my lady's so glad she's come to enjoy the freedom of this place again, and I daresay longs to have the happiness of your company.

COURTALL Did she send you hither?

SENTRY O no, if she should but know that I did such a confident trick, she would think me a good one i'faith; the zeal I have to serve you, made me venture to call in my way to the Exchange, to tell you the good news, and to let you know our lodgings are in James Street at the Black Posts, where we lay the last summer.

COURTALL Indeed, it is very obligingly done.

SENTRY But I must needs desire you to tell my lady, that you came to the knowledge of this by some lucky chance or other; for I would not be discovered for a world.

COURTALL Let me alone, I warrant thee.

Enter Servant.

SERVANT Sir Oliver Cockwood, Sir, is come to wait on you.

SENTRY O heaven! My master! My lady, and myself are both undone, undone –

COURTALL S'death, why did you not tell him I was busy?

SENTRY For heaven's sake Mr Courtall, what shall I do?

COURTALL Leave, leave trembling, and creep into the wood-hole★ here.   [*She goes into the wood-hole*]

Enter Sir Oliver.

COURTALL Sir Oliver Cockwood! [*embraces him*]

SIR OLIVER Honest Ned Courtall, by my troth I think thou tak'st me for a pretty wench, thou hug'st me so very close and heartily.

COURTALL Only my joy to see you Sir Oliver, and to welcome you to Town.

SIR OLIVER Methinks, indeed, I have been an age absent, but I intend to redeem the time; and how, and how stand affairs, prithee now? Is the wine good? Are the women kind? Well, faith, a man had better be a vagabond in this Town, than a justice of peace in the country: I was e'en grown a sot for want of gentleman-like recreations; if a man do but rap out an oath, the people start as if a gun went off; and if one chance but to couple himself with his neighbour's daughter, without the help of the parson of the parish and leave a little testimony of his kindness behind him, there is presently such an uproar, that a poor man is fain to fly his country: as for drunkenness, 'tis true, it may be used without scandal, but the drink is so abominable, that a man would forbear it, for fear of being made out of love with the vice.

COURTALL I see, Sir Oliver, you continue still your old humour, and are resolved to break your sweet lady's heart.

SIR OLIVER You do not think me sure so barbarously unkind, to let her know all this; no, no, these are secrets fit only to be trusted to such honest fellows as thou art.

COURTALL Well may I, poor sinner, be excused, since a woman of such rare beauty, such incomparable parts, and of such an un-blemished reputation, is not able to reclaim you from these wild courses, Sir Oliver.

SIR OLIVER To say the truth, she is a wife that no man need be ashamed of, Ned.

COURTALL I vow, Sir Oliver, I must needs blame you, considering how tenderly she loves you.

SIR OLIVER Aye, aye, the more is her misfortune, and mine too

★ wood-hole: recess for storing firewood.

Ned: I would willingly give thee a pair of the best coach-horses in my stable, so thou could'st but persuade her to love me less.

COURTALL Her virtue and my friendship sufficiently secure you against that, Sir Oliver.

SIR OLIVER I know thou wert never married, but has it never been thy misfortune to have a mistress love thee thus entirely?

COURTALL It never has been my good fortune, Sir Oliver, but why do you ask this question?

SIR OLIVER Because then, perchance, thou might'st have been a little sensible what a damned trouble it is.

COURTALL As how, Sir Oliver?

SIR OLIVER Why look thee, thus: for a man cannot be altogether ungrateful, sometimes one is obliged to kiss, and fawn, and toy, and lie fooling an hour or two, when a man had rather, if it were not for the disgrace sake, stand all that while in the pillory pelted with rotten eggs and oranges.

COURTALL This is a very hard case indeed, Sir Oliver.

SIR OLIVER And then the inconvenience of keeping regular hours, but above all, that damned fiend jealousy does so possess these passionate lovers, that I protest, Ned, under the rose★ be it spoken, if I chance to be a little prodigal in my expense on a private friend or so, I am called to so strict an account at night, that for quietness sake I am often forced to take a dose of cantharides† to make up the sum.

COURTALL Indeed, Sir Oliver, everything considered, you are not so much to be envied as one may rashly imagine.

SIR OLIVER Well, a pox of this tying man and woman together, for better, for worse! Upon my conscience it was but a trick that the clergy might have a feeling in the cause.

COURTALL I do not conceive it to be much for their profit, Sir Oliver, for I dare lay a good wager, let'em but allow Christian liberty, and they shall get ten times more by christenings, than they are likely to lose by marriages.

SIR OLIVER Faith, thou hast hit it right, Ned; and now thou talk'st of Christian liberty, prithee let us dine together today, and be swingingly merry, but with all secrecy.

★ under the rose: *sub-rosa*, confidentially.
† cantharides: Spanish fly, an aphrodisiac.

COURTALL I shall be glad of your good company, Sir Oliver.

SIR OLIVER I am to call on a very honest fellow, whom I left here hard by making a visit, Sir Joslin Jolley, a kinsman of my wife's, and my neighbour in the country; we call brothers, he came up to Town with me, and lodgeth in the same house; he has brought up a couple of the prettiest kinswomen, heiresses of a very good fortune: would thou hadst the instructing of 'em a little; faith, if I am not very much mistaken, they are very prone to the study of the mathematics.

COURTALL I shall be beholding to you for so good an acquaintance.

SIR OLIVER This Sir Joslin is in great favour with my lady, one that she has an admirable good opinion of, and will trust me with him anywhere; but to say truth, he is as arrant a sinner as the best of us, and will boggle at nothing that becomes a man of honour. We will go and get leave of my lady; for it is not fit I should break out so soon without her approbation, Ned.

COURTALL By no means, Sir Oliver.

SIR OLIVER Where shall we meet about an hour hence?

COURTALL At the French House★ or the Bear.†

SIR OLIVER At the French House by all means.

COURTALL Agreed, agreed.

SIR OLIVER Would thou could'st bring a fourth man.

COURTALL What think you of Frank Freeman?

SIR OLIVER There cannot be a better – well – Servant, Ned, servant, Ned!   [*Exit Sir Oliver*]

COURTALL Your servant, Sir Oliver. Mrs Sentry!

MRS SENTRY [*in the hole*] Is he gone?

COURTALL Aye, aye! You may venture to bolt now.

MRS SENTRY [*crawling out*] O heavens! I would not endure such another fright.

COURTALL Come, come, prithee be composed.

MRS SENTRY I shall not be myself again this fortnight; I never was in such a taking‡ all the days of my life. To have been found false, and to one who to say truth, has been always very kind and

★ the French House: probably Chatelain's French tavern in Covent Garden.
† the Bear: a tavern in Drury Lane, or, less likely, the Bear at the Bridge foot.
‡ taking: agitated state.

civil to me; but above all, I was concerned for my lady's honour –

COURTALL Come, come – there's no harm done.

MRS SENTRY Ah! Mr Courtall, you do not know Sir Oliver so well as I do, he has strange humours sometimes, and has it enough in's nature to play the tyrant, but that my lady and myself awe him by our policy.

COURTALL Well, well, all's well; did you not hear what a tearing blade Sir Oliver is?

MRS SENTRY Ah! 'tis a vile dissembling man; how fairly he carries it to my lady's face! But I dare not discover him for fear of betraying myself.

COURTALL Well, Mrs Sentry, I must dine with 'em, and after I have entered them with a beer glass or two, if I can I will slip away, and pay my respects to your lady.

MRS SENTRY You need not question your welcome, I assure you, Sir – Your servant, Sir.

COURTALL Your servant, Mrs Sentry, I am very sensible of this favour, I assure you.

MRS SENTRY I am proud it was in my power to oblige you, Sir.

[*Exit Mrs Sentry*]

COURTALL Freeman! Come, come out of thy hole; how hast thou been able to contain?

FREEMAN Faith much ado, the scene was very pleasant; but above all, I admire thy impudence, I could never have had the face to have wheedled the poor knight so.

COURTALL Pish, pish, 'twas both necessary and honest; we ought to do all we can to confirm a husband in the good opinion of his wife.

FREEMAN Pray how long, if without offence a man may ask you, have you been in good grace with this person of honour? I never knew you had that commendable quality of secrecy before.

COURTALL You are mistaken, Freeman, things go not as you wickedly imagine.

FREEMAN Why, hast thou lost all sense of modesty? Dost thou think to pass these gross wheedles on me too? Come, come, this good news should make thee a little merrier: faith, though she be an old acquaintance, she has the advantage of four or five months' absence. S'lid, I know not how proud you are, but I have thought myself very spruce ere now in an old suit, that has been brushed and laid up a while.

COURTALL Freeman, I know in cases of this nature thou art an infidel; but yet methinks the knowledge thou hast of my sincere dealing with my friends should make thee a little more confiding.

FREEMAN What devilish oath could she invent to fright thee from a discovery?

COURTALL Wilt thou believe me if I swear, the preservation of her honour has been my fault, and not hers?

FREEMAN This is something.

COURTALL Why then, know that I have still been as careful to prevent all opportunities, as she has been to contrive 'em; and still have carried it so like a gentleman, that she has not had the least suspicion of unkindness: she is the very spirit of impertinence, so foolishly fond and troublesome, that no man above sixteen is able to endure her.

FREEMAN Why did you engage thus far then?

COURTALL Some conveniences which I had by my acquaintance with the sot her husband, made me extraordinary civil to her, which presently by her ladyship was interpreted after the manner of the most obliging women: this wench came hither by her commission today.

FREEMAN With what confidence she denied it!

COURTALL Nay, that's never wanting, I assure you; now it is expected I should lay by all other occasions, and watch every opportunity to wait upon her; she would by her good will give her lover no more rest, than a young squire that has newly set up a coach, does his only pair of horses.

FREEMAN Faith, if it be as thou say'st, I cannot much blame the hardness of thy heart; but did not the oaf talk of two young ladies?

COURTALL Well remembered, Frank, and now I think on't, 'twill be very necessary to carry on my business with the old one, that we may the better have an opportunity of being acquainted with them. Come, let us go and bespeak dinner, and by the way consider of these weighty affairs.

FREEMAN Well, since there is but little ready money stirring, rather than want entertainment, I shall be contented to play a while upon tick.

COURTALL And I, provided they promise fair, and we find there's hopes of payment hereafter.

FREEMAN Come along, come along.   [*Exeunt*]

SCENE II

Sir Oliver Cockwood's lodging

Enter Lady Cockwood.

LADY COCKWOOD 'Tis too late to repent: I sent her, but yet I cannot but be troubled to think she stays so long; sure if she has so little gratitude to let him, he has more honour than to attempt anything to the prejudice of my affection – O – Sentry, are you come?

Entry Sentry.

SENTRY O Madam! There has been such an accident!

LADY COCKWOOD Prithee do not fright me, wench –

SENTRY As I was discoursing with Mr Courtall, in came Sir Oliver.

LADY COCKWOOD Oh! – I'm ruined – undone for ever!

SENTRY You'll still be sending me on these desperate errands.

LADY COCKWOOD I am betrayed, betrayed – by this false – what shall I call thee?

SENTRY Nay, but Madam – have a little patience –

LADY COCKWOOD I have lost all patience, and will never more have any –

SENTRY Do but hear me, all is well –

LADY COCKWOOD Nothing can be well, unfortunate woman.

SENTRY Mr Courtall thrust me into the wood-hole.

LADY COCKWOOD And did not Sir Oliver see thee?

SENTRY He had not the least glimpse of me –

LADY COCKWOOD Dear Sentry – and what good news?

SENTRY He intends to wait upon you in the afternoon, Madam –

LADY COCKWOOD I hope you did not let him know I sent you.

SENTRY No, no, Madam – I'll warrant you I did everything much to the advantage of your honour.

LADY COCKWOOD Ah Sentry! If we could but think of some lucky plot now to get Sir Oliver out of the way.

SENTRY You need not trouble yourself about that, Madam, he has engaged to dine with Mr Courtall at the French House, and is bringing Sir Joslin Jolley to get your goodwill; when Mr Courtall has fixed 'em with a beer glass or two, he intends to steal away, and pay his devotion to your ladyship.

LADY COCKWOOD Truly he is a person of much worth and honour.

SENTRY Had you but been there, Madam, to have overheard Sir Oliver's discourse, he would have made you bless yourself; there is not such another wild man in the Town; all his talk was of wenching and swearing, and drinking, and tearing.

LADY COCKWOOD Aye, aye, Sentry, I know he'll talk of strange matters behind my back; but if he be not an abominable hypocrite at home, and I am not a woman easily to be deceived, he is not able to play the spark abroad thus, I assure you.

Enter Sir Oliver, and Sir Joslin, Sir Joslin singing.

My dearest dear, this is kindly done of thee to come home again thus quickly.

SIR OLIVER Nay, my dear, thou shalt never have any just cause to accuse me of unkindness.

LADY COCKWOOD Sir Joslin, now you are a good man, and I shall trust you with Sir Oliver again.

SIR JOSLIN Nay, if I ever break my word with a lady, I will be delivered bound to Mrs Sentry here, and she shall have leave to carve me for a capon.

SENTRY Do you think I have a heart cruel enough for such a bloody execution?

SIR JOSLIN Kindly spoke i'faith, girl, I'll give thee a buss for that. [*kisses her*]

LADY COCKWOOD Fie, fie, Sir Joslin, this is not seemly in my presence.

SIR JOSLIN We have all our failings, lady, and this is mine: a right bred greyhound can as well forbear running after a hare when he sees her, as I can mumbling a pretty wench when she comes in my way.

LADY COCKWOOD I have heard indeed you are a parlous* man, Sir Joslin.

SIR JOSLIN I seldom brag, lady, but for a true cock of the game, little Joslin dares match with the best of 'em.

SIR OLIVER Sir Joslin's merry, my dear.

LADY COCKWOOD Aye, aye, if he should be wicked, I know thou art too much a gentleman to offer an injury to thine own dear lady.

SIR JOSLIN Faith, Madam, you must give my brother Cockwood leave to dine abroad to day.

LADY COCKWOOD I protest, Sir Joslin, you begin to make me hate you too; well, you are e'en grown as bad as the worst of 'em, you are still robbing me of the sweet society of Sir Oliver.

SIR JOSLIN Come, come, your discipline is too severe, i'faith lady.

LADY COCKWOOD Sir Oliver may do what he pleases, Sir, he knows I have ever been his obedient lady.

SIR OLIVER Prithee, my dear, be not angry, Sir Joslin was so earnest in his invitation, that none but a clown could have refused him.

SIR JOSLIN Aye, aye, we dine at my uncle Sir Joseph Jolley's, lady.

LADY COCKWOOD Will you be sure now to be a good dear, and not drink, nor stay out late?

SIR JOSLIN I'll engage for all, and if there be no harm in a merry catch or a waggish story –

Enter Ariana and Mrs Gatty.

Ha, ha! Sly-girl and Mad-cap, are you got up? I know what you have been meditating on; but never trouble your heads, let me alone to bring you consolation.

GATTY We have often been beholding to you, Sir; for every time he's drunk, he brings us home a couple of fresh servants.

SIR OLIVER Well, farewell my dear, prithee do not sigh thus, but make thee ready, visit, and be merry.

LADY COCKWOOD I shall receive most satisfaction in my chamber.

SIR JOSLIN Come, come along, brother: farewell one and all, lady and Sly-girl, Sly-girl and Mad-cap, your servant, your servant –

[*Exeunt Sir Oliver and Sir Joslin singing*]

* parlous: perilous.

LADY COCKWOOD [*to Sentry aside*] Sentry, is the new point I brought come home, and is everything in a readiness?

SENTRY Everything, Madam.

LADY COCKWOOD Come, come up quickly then, girl, and dress me.   [*Exeunt Lady Cockwood and Sentry*]

ARIANA Dost not thou wonder, Gatty, she should be so strangely fond of this coxcomb?

GATTY Well, if she does not dissemble, may I still be discovered when I do; didst thou not see how her countenance changed, as soon as ever their backs were turned, and how earnestly she whispered with her woman? There is some weighty affair in hand, I warrant thee: my dear Ariana, how glad am I we are in this Town again.

ARIANA But we have left the benefit of the fresh air, and the delight of the wandering in the pleasant groves.

GATTY Very pretty things for a young gentlewoman to bemoan the loss of indeed, that's newly come to a relish of the good things of this world.

ARIANA Very good, sister!

GATTY Why, hast not thou promised me a thousand times to leave off this demureness?

ARIANA But you are so quick.

GATTY Why, would it not make any one mad to hear thee bewail the loss of the country? Speak but one grave word more, and it shall be my daily prayers thou may'st have a jealous husband, and then you'll have enough of it I warrant you.

ARIANA It may be, if your tongue be not altogether so nimble, I may be conformable; but I hope you do not intend we shall play such mad reaks* as we did last summer?

GATTY S'life, do'st thou think we come here to be mewed up, and take only the liberty of going from our chamber to the dining room, and from the dining room to our chamber again? And like a bird in a cage, with two perches only, to hop up and down, up and down?

ARIANA Well, thou art a mad wench.

GATTY Would'st thou never have us go to a play but with our grave relations, never take the air but with our grave relations?

* reaks: pranks.

To feed their pride, and make the world believe it is in their power to afford some gallant or other a good bargain?

ARIANA But I am afraid we shall be known again.

GATTY Pish! The men were only acquainted with our vizards and our petticoats, and they are wore out long since: how I envy that sex! Well! We cannot plague 'em enough when we have it in our power for those privileges which custom has allowed 'em above us.

ARIANA The truth is, they can run and ramble here, and there, and everywhere, and we poor fools rather think the better of 'em.

GATTY From one playhouse, to the other playhouse, and if they like neither the play nor the women, they seldom stay any longer than the combing of their periwigs, or a whisper or two with a friend; and then they cock their caps, and out they strut again.

ARIANA But whatsoever we do, prithee now let us resolve to be mighty honest.

GATTY There I agree with thee.

ARIANA And if we find the gallants like lawless subjects, who the more their princes grant, the more they impudently crave?

GATTY We'll become absolute tyrants, and deprive 'em of all the privileges we gave 'em –

ARIANA Upon these conditions I am contented to trail a pike under thee – march along girl.

[Exeunt]

ACT TWO

SCENE I

The Mulberry Garden*

Enter Courtall and Freeman.

COURTALL Was there ever a couple of fops better matched than these two knights are?

FREEMAN They are harp and violin, nature has so tuned 'em, as if she intended they should always play the fool in consort.

COURTALL Now is Sir Oliver secure, for he dares not go home till he's quite drunk, and then he grows valiant, insults, and defies his sweet lady; for which with prayers and tears he's forced to feign a bitter repentance the next morning.

FREEMAN What do we here idling in the Mulberry Garden? Why do not we make this visit then?

COURTALL Now art thou as mad upon this trail, as if we were upon a hot scent.

FREEMAN Since we know the bush, why do we not start the game?

COURTALL Gently, good Frank, first know that the laws of honour prescribed in such nice cases, will not allow me to carry thee along with me; and next, hast thou so little wit to think, that a discreet lady that has had the experience of so much human frailty, can have so good an opinion of the constancy of her servant, as to lead him into temptation?

FREEMAN Then we must not hope her ladyship should make us acquainted with these gentlewomen.

COURTALL Thou may'st as reasonably expect, that an old rook† should bring a young snap‡ acquainted with his bubble;§ but advantages may be hereafter made, by my admission into the family.

FREEMAN What is to be done then?

COURTALL Why, look you, thus I have contrived it: Sir Oliver,

---

* the Mulberry Garden: a pleasure ground on the site of the present Buckingham Palace.

† rook: swindler.   ‡ snap: fellow.   § bubble: dupe.

when I began to grow resty,* that he might incline me a little
more to drunkenness, in my ear discovered to me the humour of
his dear friend Sir Joslin: he assured me, that when he was in that
good natured condition, to requite their courtesy, he always carried the good company home with him, and recommended them
to his kinswomen.

FREEMAN Very good!

COURTALL Now after the fresh air has breathed on us a while, and
expelled the vapours of the wine we have drunk, thou shalt return
to these two sots, whom we left at the French House, according
to our promise, and tell 'em, I am a little stayed by some unlucky
business, and will be with 'em presently; thou wilt find 'em tired
with long fight, weak and unable to observe their order, charge
'em briskly, and in a moment thou shalt rout 'em, and with little
or no damage to thyself gain an absolute victory.

FREEMAN Very well!

COURTALL In the meantime I will make my visit to the longing
lady, and order my business so handsomely, that I will be with
thee again immediately, to make an experiment of the good humour of Sir Joslin.

FREEMAN Let's about it.

COURTALL 'Tis yet too early, we must drill away a little time
here, that my excuses may be more probable, and my persecution
more tolerable.

Enter Ariana and Gatty with vizards, and pass nimbly over the stage.

FREEMAN Ha, ha – how wantonly they trip it! There is temptation enough in their very gait, to stir up the courage of an old
alderman: prithee let us follow 'em.

COURTALL I have been so often baulked with these vizard-masks,†
that I have at least a dozen times forsworn 'em; they are a most
certain sign of an ill face, or what is worse, an old acquaintance.

FREEMAN The truth is, nothing but some such weighty reason, is
able to make women deny themselves the pride they have to be
seen.

* resty: restless, restive – or sluggish.
† vizard masks: they fell into disrepute through courtesans using them
habitually.

COURTALL The evening's fresh and pleasant, and yet there is but little company.

FREEMAN Our course will be the better, these deer cannot herd: come, come man, let's follow.

COURTALL I find it is a mere folly to forswear anything, it does but make the devil the more earnest in his temptation.

[*They go after the Women*]

Enter Women again, and cross the stage.

ARIANA Now if these should prove two men-of-war that are cruising here, to watch for prizes.

GATTY Would they had courage enough to set upon us; I long to be engaged.

ARIANA Look, look yonder, I protest they chase us.

GATTY Let us bear away then; if they be truly valiant they'll quickly make more sail, and board us.

[*The Women go out, and go about behind the scenes to the other door*]

Enter Courtall and Freeman.

FREEMAN S'death, how fleet they are! Whatsoever faults they have, they cannot be broken-winded.

COURTALL Sure, by that little mincing step they should be country fillies that have been breathed at course-a-park,★ and barley-break:† we shall never reach 'em.

FREEMAN I'll follow directly, do thou turn down the cross-walk and meet 'em.

Enter the Women, and after 'em Courtall at the lower door, and Freeman at the upper on the contrary side.

COURTALL By your leave, ladies –

GATTY I perceive you can make bold enough without it.

FREEMAN Your servant, ladies –

ARIANA Or any other ladies that will give themselves the trouble to entertain you.

FREEMAN S'life, their tongues are as nimble as their heels.

★ course-a-park: a country game in which a girl challenged a man to chase her.

† barley-break: another country game involving hard running.

COURTALL Can you have so little good nature to dash a couple of bashful young men out of countenance, who came out of pure love to tender you their service?

GATTY 'Twere pity to baulk'em, sister.

ARIANA Indeed, methinks they look as if they never had been flipped* before.

FREEMAN Yes, faith, we have had many a fair course in this paddock, have been very well fleshed, and dare boldly fasten. [*they kiss their hands with a little force*]

ARIANA Well, I am not the first unfortunate woman that has been forced to give her hand, where she never intends to bestow her heart.

GATTY Now, do you think 'tis a bargain already?

COURTALL Faith, would there were some lusty earnest given, for fear we should unluckily break off again.

FREEMAN Are you so wild that you must be hooded thus?

COURTALL Fie, fie, put off these scandals to all good faces.

GATTY For your reputations' sake we shall keep 'em on: s'life we should be taken for your relations, if we durst show our faces with you thus publicly.

ARIANA And what a shame that would be to a couple of young gallants! Methinks you should blush to think on't.

COURTALL These were pretty toys, invented, first merely for the good of us poor lovers to deceive the jealous, and to blind the malicious; but the proper use is so wickedly perverted, that it makes all honest men hate the fashion mortally.

FREEMAN A good face is as seldom covered with a vizard-mask, as a good hat with an oiled case: and yet on my conscience, you are both handsome.

COURTALL Do but remove 'em a little, to satisfy a foolish scruple.

ARIANA This is a just punishment you have brought upon yourselves, by that unpardonable sin of talking.

GATTY You can only brag now of your acquaintance with a farandine† gown, and a piece of black velvet.

COURTALL The truth is, there are some vain fellows whose loose behaviour of late has given great discouragement to the honourable proceedings of all virtuous ladies.

* flipped: whipped.
† farandine: cloth partly made of silk with wool or hair added.

FREEMAN But I hope you have more charity, than to believe us of the number of the wicked.

ARIANA There's not a man of you to be trusted.

GATTY What a shame is it to your whole sex, that a woman is more fit to be a privy counsellor, than a young gallant a lover?

COURTALL This is a pretty kind of fooling, ladies, for men that are idle; but you must bid a little fairer, if you intend to keep us from our serious business.

GATTY Truly you seem to be men of great employment, that are every moment rattling from the eating-houses to the playhouses, from the playhouses to the Mulberry Garden, that live in a perpetual hurry, and have little leisure for such an idle entertainment.

COURTALL Now would not I see thy face for the world; if it should but be but half so good as thy humour, thou would'st dangerously tempt me to dote upon thee, and forgetting all shame, become constant.

FREEMAN I perceive, by your fooling here, that wit and good humour may make a man in love with a blackamoor. That the devil should contrive it so, that we should have earnest business now.

COURTALL Would they would but be so kind to meet us here again tomorrow.

GATTY You are full of business, and 'twould but take you off of your employments.

ARIANA And we are very unwilling to have the sin to answer for, of ruining a couple of such hopeful young men.

FREEMAN Must we then despair?

ARIANA The ladies you are going to, will not be so hard-hearted.

COURTALL [*to Freeman*] On my conscience, they love us, and begin to grow jealous already.

FREEMAN Who knows but this may prove the luckier adventure of the two?

COURTALL Come, come, we know you have a mind to meet us: we cannot see you blush, speak it out boldly.

GATTY Will you swear then, not to visit any other women before that time?

ARIANA Not that we are jealous, but because we would not have you tired with the impertinent conversation of our sex, and come to us dull and out of humour.

COURTALL Invent an oath, and let it be so horrid 'twould make an atheist start to hear it.

FREEMAN And I will swear it readily, and I will not so much as speak to a woman, 'till I speak to you again.

GATTY But are you troubled with that foolish scruple of keeping an oath?

FREEMAN O most religiously!

COURTALL And may we not enlarge our hopes upon a little better acquaintance?

ARIANA You see all the freedom we allow.

GATTY It may be we may be entreated to hear a fiddle, or mingle in a country dance, or so.

COURTALL Well! We are in too desperate a condition to stand upon articles, and are resolved to yield on any terms.

FREEMAN Be sure you be punctual now!

ARIANA Will you be sure?

COURTALL Or else may we become a couple of credulous coxcombs, and be jilted ever after. – Your servants, ladies

[*Exeunt Men*]

ARIANA I wonder what they think of us!

GATTY You may easily imagine; for they are not of a humour so little in fashion, to believe the best: I assure you the most favourable opinion they can have, is that we are still a little wild, and stand in need of better manning.

ARIANA Prithee, dear girl, what dost think of 'em?

GATTY Faith so well, that I'm ashamed to tell thee.

ARIANA Would I had never seen 'em!

GATTY Ha! Is it come to that already?

ARIANA Prithee, let's walk a turn or two more, and talk of 'em.

GATTY Let us take care then we are not too particular in their commendations, lest we should discover we entrench upon one another's inclinations, and so grow quarrelsome.   [*Exeunt*]

SCENE II

Sir Oliver's lodgings

Enter Lady Cockwood and Sentry.

SENTRY Dear Madam, do not afflict yourself thus unreasonably; I dare lay my life, it is not want of devotion, but opportunity that stays him.

LADY COCKWOOD Ungrateful man! To be so insensible of a lady's passion!

SENTRY If I thought he were so wicked. I should hate him strangely – but, Madam.

LADY COCKWOOD Do not speak one word in his behalf, I am resolved to forget him; perfidious mortal, to abuse so sweet an opportunity!

SENTRY Hark, here is somebody coming upstairs.

LADY COCKWOOD Peace, he may yet redeem his honour.

Enter Courtall.

COURTALL Your humble servant, Madam.

LADY COCKWOOD [*starting*] Mr Courtall, for heaven's sake, how came you hither?

COURTALL Guided by my good fortune, Madam – Your servant, Mrs Sentry.

SENTRY Your humble servant, Sir; I protest you made me start too, to see you come in thus unexpectedly.

LADY COCKWOOD I did not imagine it could be known I was in Town yet.

COURTALL Sir Oliver did me the favour to make me a visit, and dine with me today, which brought me to the knowledge of this happiness, Madam; and as soon as I could possibly, I got the freedom to come hither and enjoy it.

LADY COCKWOOD You have ever been extreme obliging, Sir.

SENTRY [*aside*] 'Tis a worthy gentleman, how punctual he is to my directions!

LADY COCKWOOD Will you be pleased to repose, Sir? Sentry, set some chairs.

[*Exit Sentry*]

COURTALL With much difficulty, Madam, I broke out of my company, and was forced by the importunity of one Sir Joslin Jolley, I think they call him, to engage my honour I would return again immediately.

LADY COCKWOOD You must not so soon rob me of so sweet a satisfaction.

COURTALL No consideration, Madam, could take me from you, but that I know my stay at this time must needs endanger your honour; and how often I have denied myself the greatest satisfaction in the world, to keep that unblemished, you yourself can witness.

LADY COCKWOOD Indeed I have often had great trials of your generosity, in those many misfortunes that have attended our innocent affections.

COURTALL Sir Oliver, Madam, before I did perceive it, was got near that pitch of drunkenness, which makes him come reeling home, and unmanfully insult over your ladyship; and how subject he is then to injure you within an unjust suspicion, you have often told me; which makes me careful not to be surprised here.

LADY COCKWOOD Repose yourself a little, but a little, dear Sir: these virtuous principles make you worthy to be trusted with a lady's honour: indeed Sir Oliver has his failings; yet I protest, Mr Courtell, I love him dearly, but cannot be altogether unsensible of your generous passion.

COURTALL [*aside*] Aye, aye, I am a very passionate lover! ⟨*to her*⟩ Indeed this escape has only given me leisure to look upon my happiness.

LADY COCKWOOD Is my woman retired?

COURTALL Most dutifully, Madam.

LADY COCKWOOD Then let me tell you, Sir – yet we may make very good use of it.

COURTALL [*aside*] Now am I going to be drawn in again.

LADY COCKWOOD If Sir Oliver be in that indecent condition you speak of, tomorrow he will be very submissive, as it is meet for so great a misdemeanour; then can I, feigning a desperate discontent, take my own freedom without the least suspicion.

COURTALL This is very luckily and obligingly thought on, Madam.

LADY COCKWOOD Now if you will be pleased to make an assignation, Sir.

COURTALL Tomorrow about ten o'clock in the lower walk of the New Exchange,* out of which we can quickly pop into my coach.

LADY COCKWOOD But I am still so pestered with my woman, I dare not go without her; on my conscience she's very sincere, but it is not good to trust our reputations too much to the frailty of a servant.

COURTALL I will bring my chariot, Madam, that will hold but two.

LADY COCKWOOD O most ingeniously imagined, dear Sir! For by that means I shall have a just excuse to give her leave to see a relation, and bid her stay there till I call her.

COURTALL It grieves me much to leave you so soon, Madam; but I shall comfort myself with the thoughts of the happiness you have made me hope for.

LADY COCKWOOD I wish it were in my power eternally to oblige you, dear Sir.

COURTALL Your humble servant, Madam.

LADY COCKWOOD Your humble servant, sweet Sir.

[*Exit Courtall*]

Sentry – why Sentry – where are you?

Enter Sentry.

SENTRY Here, Madam.

LADY COCKWOOD What a strange thing is this! Will you never take warning, but still be leaving me alone in these suspicious occasions?

SENTRY I was but in the next room, Madam.

LADY COCKWOOD What may Mr Courtall think of my innocent intentions? I protest if you serve me so again, I shall be strangely angry: you should have more regard to your lady's honour.

SENTRY ⟨*aside*⟩ If I stay in the room, she will not speak kindly to me in a week after; and if I go out, she always chides me thus: this is a strange infirmity she has, but I must bear with it; for on my conscience, custom has made it so natural, she cannot help it.

LADY COCKWOOD Are my cousins come home yet?

* the New Exchange: on the south side of the Strand, arranged as an arcade, much frequented by the fashionable.

SENTRY Not yet, Madam.

LADY COCKWOOD Do'st thou know whither they went this evening?

SENTRY I heard them say they would go take the air, Madam.

LADY COCKWOOD Well, I see it is impossible with virtuous counsel to reclaim them; truly they are so careless of their own, I could wish Sir Joslin would remove 'em, for fear they should bring an unjust imputation on my honour.

SENTRY Heavens forbid, Madam!

Enter Ariana and Gatty.

LADY COCKWOOD Your servant, cousins.

ARIANA ⎫
GATTY ⎭ Your servant, Madam.

LADY COCKWOOD How have you spent the cool of the evening?

GATTY As the custom is, Madam, breathing the fresh air in the Park* and Mulberry Garden.

LADY COCKWOOD Without the company of a relation, or some discreet body to justify your reputations to the world – you are young, and may be yet insensible of it; but this is a strange censorious age, I assure you.

Noise of music without.

ARIANA Hark! What music's this?

GATTY I'll lay my life my uncle's drunk, and hath picked us up a couple of worthy servants, and brought them home with him in triumph.

*Enter the music playing, Sir Oliver strutting, and swaggering,
Sir Joslin singing, and dancing with Mr Courtall, and Mr Freeman
in each hand: Gatty and Ariana seeing Courtall and Freeman shriek
and – exeunt.*

SIR JOSLIN Hey-day! I told you they were a couple of skittish fillies, but I never knew 'em boggle at a man before; I'll fetch 'em again I warrant you, boys.

[*Exit after them*]

FREEMAN [*to Courtall*] These are the very self-same gowns and petticoats.

* the Park: St James's Park.

COURTALL Their surprise confirms us it must be them.

FREEMAN S'life, we have betrayed ourselves very pleasantly.

COURTALL Now am I undone to all intents and purposes, for they will innocently discover all to my lady, and she will have no mercy.

SIR OLIVER [*strutting*] Dan, dan, da ra, dan, etc
Avoid my presence, the very sight of that face makes me more impotent than an eunuch.

LADY COCKWOOD Dear Sir Oliver! [*offering to embrace him*]

SIR OLIVER Forbear your conjugal clippings, I will have a wench, thou shalt fetch me a wench, Sentry.

SENTRY Can you be so inhuman to my dear lady?

SIR OLIVER Peace, envy, or I will have thee executed for petty treason; thy skin flayed off, stuffed and hung up in my hall in the country, as a terror to my whole family.

COURTALL What crime can deserve this horrid punishment?

SIR OLIVER I'll tell thee, Ned: 'twas my fortune t'other day to have an intrigue with a tinker's wife in the country, and this malicious slut betrayed the very ditch where we used to make our assignations, to my lady.

FREEMAN She deserves your anger indeed, Sir Oliver: but be not so unkind to your virtuous lady.

SIR OLIVER Thou do'st not know her, Frank; I have had a design to break her heart ever since the first month that I had her, and 'tis so tough, that I have not yet cracked one string on't.

COURTALL You are too unmerciful, Sir Oliver.

SIR OLIVER Hang her, Ned, by wicked policy she would usurp my empire, and in her heart is a very Pharaoh; for every night she's a-putting me upon making brick without straw.

COURTALL I cannot see a virtuous lady so afflicted, without offering her some consolation: [*aside to her*] Dear Madam, is it not as I told you?

LADY COCKWOOD [*to Courtall aside*] The fates could not have been more propitious, and I shall not be wanting to the furthering of our mutual happiness.

Enter Sir Joslin, with Ariana and Gatty in each hand, dancing and singing.

CATCH
This is sly and pretty,
And this is wild and witty;
If either stayed
Till she died a maid,
I 'faith 'twould be great pity.

SIR JOSLIN Here they are, boys, i'faith and now little Joslin's a
man of his word. Heuk! Sly-girl and Mad-cap, to 'em, to 'em,
to 'em, boys, halloo! [*flings 'em to Courtall and Freeman, who kiss their
hands*] What's yonder, your lady in tears, brother Cockwood?
Come, come, I'll make up all breaches. [*he sings*] – 'And we'll all be
merry and frolic'. Fie, fie, though man and wife are seldom in good
humour alone, there are few want the discretion to dissemble it
in company.

Sir Joslin, Sir Oliver, and Lady Cockwood stand talking together.

FREEMAN I knew we should surprise you, ladies.

COURTALL Faith I thought this conjuring to be but a mere jest
till now, and could not believe the astrological rascal had been so
skilful.

FREEMAN How exactly he described 'em, and how punctual he
was in his directions to apprehend 'em!

GATTY Then you have been with a conjurer, gentlemen.

COURTALL You cannot blame us, ladies, the loss of our hearts was
so considerable, that it may well excuse the indirect means we
took to find out the pretty thieves that stole 'em.

ARIANA Did not I tell you what men of business these were, sister?

GATTY I vow I innocently believed they had some pre-engagement
to a scrivener or a surgeon, and wished 'em so well, that I am sorry
to find 'em so perfidious.

FREEMAN Why, we have kept our oaths, ladies.

ARIANA You are much beholding to providence.

GATTY But we are more, sister; for had we once been deluded into
an opinion they had been faithful, who knows into what incon-
veniences that error might have drawn us?

COURTALL Why should you be so unreasonable, ladies, to expect
that from us, we should scarce have hoped for from you? Fie, fie, the
keeping of one's word is a thing below the honour of a gentleman.

FREEMAN A poor shift! Fit only to uphold the reputation of a paltry citizen.

SIR JOSLIN Come, come, all will be well again, I warrant you, lady.

LADY COCKWOOD These are insupportable injuries, but I will bear 'em with an invincible patience, and tomorrow make him dearly sensible how unworthy he has been.

SIR JOSLIN Tomorrow my brother Cockwood will be another man – So, boys, and how do you like the flesh and blood of the Jollies – Heuk, Sly-Girl – and Mad-cap, hey – come, come, you have heard them exercise their tongues a while; now you shall see them ply their feet a little: this is a clean-limbed wench, and has neither spavin, splinter, nor wind-gall;* tune her a jig and play't roundly, you shall see her bounce it away like a nimble frigate before a fresh gale – Hey, methinks I see her under sail already. [*Gatty dances a jig*] Hey my little Mad-cap – here's a girl of the true breed of the Jollies, i'faith – But hark you, hark you, a consultation, gentlemen – Bear up, brother Cockwood, a little: what think you, if we pack these idle huswives to bed now, and retire into a room by ourselves, and have a merry catch, and a bottle or two of the best, and perfect the good work we have so unanimously carried on today?

SIR OLIVER A most admirable intrigue – tan, dan, da, ra, dan; come, come, march to your several quarters: go, we have sent for a civil person or two, and are resolved to fornicate in private.

LADY COCKWOOD This is a barbarous return of all my kindness.

FREEMAN ⎫
COURTALL ⎭ Your humble servant, Madam.

           [*Exeunt Lady Cockwood and Sentry*]

COURTALL Hark you! Hark you! Ladies do not harbour too ill an opinion of us, for faith, when you have had a little more experience of the world, you'll find we are no such abominable rascals.

GATTY We shall be so charitable to think no worse of you, than we do of all mankind for your sakes, only that you are perjured, perfidious, inconstant, ungrateful.

FREEMAN Nay, nay, that's enough in all conscience ladies, and

* spavin, splinter, nor wind-gall: all diseases in horses.

now you are sensible what a shameful thing it is to break one's word, I hope you'll be more careful to keep yours tomorrow.

GATTY Invent an oath, and let it be so horrid –

COURTALL Nay, nay, it is too late for raillery, i'faith, ladies.

GATTY ⎱
ARIANA ⎰ Well, your servant then.

FREEMAN ⎱
COURTALL ⎰ Your servant, ladies.

[Exeunt Ladies]

SIR OLIVER Now the enemy's marched out –

SIR JOSLIN Then the castle's our own boys – Hey.

> And here and there I had her,
> And everywhere I had her,
> Her toy was such, that every touch
> Would make a lover madder.

FREEMAN ⎱
COURTALL ⎰ Hey brave Sir Joslin!

SIR OLIVER Ah my dear little witty Joslin, let me hug thee.

SIR JOSLIN Strike up your obstreperous rascals, and march along before us. *[Exeunt singing and dancing]*

ACT THREE

SCENE I

The New Exchange

Mrs Trinket sitting in a shop, people passing by as in the Exchange.

MRS TRINKET What d'ye buy? What d'ye lack, gentlemen? Gloves, ribbons, and essences; ribbons, gloves, and essences?

Enter Mr Courtall.

Mr Courtall! I thought you had a quarrel to the Change, and were resolved we should never see you here again.

COURTALL Your unkindness indeed, Mrs Trinket, had been enough to make a man banish himself for ever.

Enter Mrs Gazette.

MRS TRINKET Look you, yonder comes fine Mrs Gazette, thither you intended your visit, I am sure.

MRS GAZETTE Mr Courtall! Your servant.

COURTALL Your servant, Mrs Gazette.

MRS GAZETTE This happiness was only meant to Mrs Trinket, had it not been my good fortune to pass by, by chance, I should have lost my share on't.

COURTALL This is too cruel, Mrs Gazette, when all the unkindness is on your side, to rally your servant thus.

MRS GAZETTE I vow this tedious absence of yours made me believe you intended to try an experiment on my poor heart, to discover that hidden secret, how long a despairing lover may languish without the sight of the party.

COURTALL You are always very pleasant on this subject, Mrs Gazette.

MRS GAZETTE And have not you reason to be so too?

COURTALL Not that I know of.

MRS GAZETTE Yes, you hear the good news.

COURTALL What good news?

MRS GAZETTE How well this dissembling becomes you! But now I think better on't, it cannot concern you, you are more a gentleman, than to have an amour last longer than an Easter term with a country lady; and yet there are some I see as well in the country as in the City, that have a pretty way of huswifing a lover and can spin an intrigue out a great deal farther, than others are willing to do.

COURTALL What pretty art have they, good Mrs Gazette?

MRS GAZETTE When tradesmen see themselves in an ill condition, and are afraid of breaking, can they do better than to take in a good substantial partner, to help to carry on their trading?

COURTALL Sure you have been at 'Riddle me, riddle me', lately, you are so wondrous witty.

MRS GAZETTE And yet I believe my Lady Cockwood is so haughty, she had rather give over the vanity of an intrigue, than take in a couple of young handsome kinswomen to help to maintain it.

COURTALL I knew it would out at last; indeed it is the principle of most good women that love gaming, when they begin to grow a little out of play themselves, to make an interest in some young gamester or other, in hopes to rook a favour now and then: but you are quite out in your policy, my Lady Cockwood is none of these, I assure you – Hark you, Mrs Gazette, you must needs bestir yourself a little for me this morning, or else heaven have mercy on a poor sinner.

MRS GAZETTE I hope this wicked woman has no design upon your body already: alas! I pity your tender conscience.

COURTALL I have always made thee my confident, and now I come to thee as to a faithful counsellor.

MRS GAZETTE State your case.

COURTALL Why, this ravenous kite is upon wing already, is fetching a little compass, and will be here within this half hour to swoop me away.

MRS GAZETTE And you would have me your scarecrow?

COURTALL Something of that there is in't, she is still your customer.

MRS GAZETTE I have furnished her and the young ladies with a few fashionable toys since they came to Town, to keep 'em in countenance at a play, or in the Park.

COURTALL I would have thee go immediately to the young ladies, and by some device or other entice 'em hither.

MRS GAZETTE I came just now from taking measure of 'em for a couple of handkerchiefs.

COURTALL How unlucky's this!

MRS GAZETTE They were calling for their hoods and scarfs, and are coming hither to lay out a little money in ribbons and essences: I have recommended them to Mrs Trinket's shop here.

COURTALL This falls out more luckily than what I had contrived myself, or could have done; for here will they be busy just before the door, where we have made our appointment: but if this long-winged devil should chance to truss me before they come.

MRS GAZETTE I will only step up and give some directions to my maid, about a little business that is in haste, and come down again and watch her; if you are snapped, I'll be with you presently, and rescue you I warrant you, or at least stay you 'till more company come: she dares not force you away in my sight; she knows I am great with Sir Oliver, and as malicious a devil as the best of 'em – your servant, Sir.   [*Exit Mrs Gazette*]

Enter Freeman.

COURTALL Freeman! 'Tis well you are come.

FREEMAN Well! What counter-plot? What hopes of disappointing the old, and of seeing the young ladies? I am ready to receive your orders.

COURTALL Faith, things are not so well contrived as I could have wished 'em, and yet I hope by the help of Mrs Gazette to keep my word, Frank.

FREEMAN Nay, now I know what tool thou hast made choice of, I make no question but the business will go well forward; but I am afraid this last unlucky business has so distasted these young trouts, they will not be so easily tickled as they might have been.

COURTALL Never fear it; whatsoever women say, I am sure they seldom think the worse of a man, for running at all, 'tis a sign of youth and high mettle, and makes them rather *piqué*, who shall tame him: that which troubles me most, is, we lost the hopes of variety, and a single intrigue in love is as dull as a single plot in a play, and will tire a lover worse, than t'other does an audience.

FREEMAN We cannot be long without some under-plots in this

Town, let this be our main design, and if we are anything fortunate in our contrivance, we shall make it a pleasant comedy.

COURTALL Leave all things to me, and hope the best: begone, for I expect their coming immediately; walk a turn or two above, or fool a while with pretty Mrs Anvil, and scent your eyebrows and periwig with a little essence of oranges, or jessamine,* and when you see us all together at Mrs Gazette's shop, put in as it were by chance: I protest yonder comes the old haggard,† to your post quickly: s'death, where's Gazette and these young ladies now?

[*Exit Freeman*]

Enter Lady Cockwood, and Sentry.

O Madam, I have waited here at least an hour, and time seems very tedious, when it delays so great a happiness as you bring with you.

LADY COCKWOOD I vow, Sir, I did but stay to give Sir Oliver his due correction for those unseemly injuries he did me last night. Is your coach ready?

COURTALL Yes, Madam: but how will you dispose of your maid?

LADY COCKWOOD My maid! For heaven's sake, what do you mean, Sir? Do I ever use to go abroad without her?

COURTALL 'Tis upon no design, Madam, I speak it, I assure you; but my glass coach broke last night, and I was forced to bring my chariot, which can hold but two.

LADY COCKWOOD O heaven! You must excuse me, dear Sir, for I shall deny myself the sweetest recreations in the world, rather than yield to anything that may bring a blemish upon my spotless honour.

Enter Mrs Gazette.

MRS GAZETTE Your humble servant, Madam. Your servant, Mr Courtall.

LADY COCKWOOD ⎫
and COURTALL ⎬ Your servant, Mrs Gazette.
⎭

MRS GAZETTE I am extreme glad to see your ladyship here, I intended to send my maid to your lodgings this afternoon, Madam, to tell you I have a parcel of new lace come in, the prettiest patterns that ever were seen; for I am very desirous so good a

* jessamine: jasmine, a shrub.   † haggard: untamed fully grown hawk.

customer as your ladyship should see 'em first, and have your choice.

LADY COCKWOOD I am much beholding to you, Mrs Gazette, I was newly come into the Exchange, and intended to call at your shop before I went home.

Enter Ariana and Gatty, ⟨Mrs⟩ Gazette goes to 'em.

COURTALL S'death, here are your cousins too. Now there is no hope left for a poor unfortunate lover to comfort himself withall.

LADY COCKWOOD Will fate never be more propitious?

ARIANA ⎱
GATTY   ⎰ Your servant, Madam.

LADY COCKWOOD I am newly come into the Exchange, and by chance met with Mr Courtall here, who will needs give himself the trouble, to play the gallant, and wait upon me.

GATTY Does your ladyship come to buy?

LADY COCKWOOD A few trifles; Mrs Gazette says she has a parcel of very fine new laces, shall we go look upon 'em?

ARIANA We will only fancy a suit of knots or two at this shop, and buy a little essence, and wait upon your ladyship immediately.

GATTY Mrs Gazette, you are skilled in the fashion, pray let our choice have your approbation.

MRS GAZETTE Most gladly, Madam.

[*All go to the shop to look upon ware, but Courtall and Lady Cockwood*]

COURTALL S'death, Madam, if you had made no ceremony, but stepped into the coach presently, we had escaped this mischief.

LADY COCKWOOD My over-tenderness of my honour, has blasted all my hopes of happiness.

COURTALL To be thus unluckily surprised in the height of all our expectation, leaves me no patience.

LADY COCKWOOD Moderate your passion a little, Sir, I may yet find out a way.

COURTALL O 'tis impossible, Madam, never think on't now you have been seen with me; to leave 'em upon any pretence will be so suspicious, that my concern for your honour will make me so feverish and disordered, that I shall lose the taste of all the happiness you give me.

LADY COCKWOOD Methinks you are too scrupulous, heroic Sir.

COURTALL Besides the concerns I have for you, Madam, you know the obligations I have to Sir Oliver, and what professions of friendship there are on both sides; and to be thought perfidious and ungrateful, what an affliction would that be to a generous spirit!

LADY COCKWOOD Must we then unfortunately part thus?

COURTALL Now I have better thought on't, that is not absolutely necessary neither.

LADY COCKWOOD These words revive my dying joys, dear Sir, go on.

COURTALL I will by and by, when I see it most convenient, beg the favour of your ladyship, and your young kinswomen, to accept of a treat and a fiddle; you make some little difficulty at first, but upon earnest persuasion comply, and use your interest to make the young ladies do so too: your company will secure their reputations, and their company take off from you all suspicion.

LADY COCKWOOD The natural inclination they have to be jigging, will make them very ready to comply: but what advantage can this be to our happiness, dear Sir?

COURTALL Why, first, Madam, if the young ladies, or Mrs Gazette have any doubts upon their surprising us together, our joining company will clear 'em all; next, we shall have some satisfaction in being an afternoon together, though we enjoy not that full freedom we so passionately desire.

LADY COCKWOOD Very good, Sir.

COURTALL But then lastly, Madam, we gain an opportunity to contrive another appointment tomorrow, which may restore us unto all those joys we have been so unfortunately disappointed of today.

LADY COCKWOOD This is a very prevailing argument indeed; but since Sir Oliver believes I have conceived so desperate a sorrow, 'tis fit we should keep this from his knowledge.

COURTALL Are the young ladies secret?

LADY COCKWOOD They have the good principles not to betray themselves, I assure you.

COURTALL Then 'tis but going to a house that is not haunted by the company, and we are secure, and now I think on't, the Bear in Drury Lane is the fittest place for our purpose.

LADY COCKWOOD I know your honour, dear Sir, and submit to your discretion – Have you gratified your fancies, cousins?

To them Ariana, Gatty, and Gazette from the shop.

ARIANA We are ready to wait upon you, Madam.

GATTY I never saw colours better mingled.

MRS GAZETTE How lively they set off one another, and how they add to the complexion!

LADY COCKWOOD Mr Courtall, your most humble servant.

COURTALL Pray, Madam, let me have the honour to wait upon you and these young ladies, till I see you in your coach.

LADY COCKWOOD Your friendship to Sir Oliver would engage you in an unnecessary trouble.

ARIANA Let not an idle ceremony take you from your serious business, good Sir.

GATTY I should rather have expected to have seen you, Sir, walking in Westminster Hall, watching to make a match at tennis, or waiting to dine with a Parliament man, than to meet you in such an idle place as the Exchange is.

COURTALL Methinks, ladies, you are well acquainted with me upon the first visit.

ARIANA We received your character before, you know, Sir, in the Mulberry Garden upon oath.

COURTALL [*aside*] S'death, what shall I do? Now out comes all my roguery.

GATTY Yet I am apt to believe, sister, that was some malicious fellow that wilfully perjured himself, on purpose to make us have an ill opinion of this worthy gentleman.

COURTALL Some rash men would be apt enough to enquire him out, and cut his throat, ladies, but I heartily forgive him whosoever he was; for on my conscience 'twas not so much out of malice to me, as out of love to you he did it.

MRS GAZETTE He might imagine Mr Courtall was his rival.

COURTALL Very likely, Mrs Gazette.

LADY COCKWOOD Whosoever he was, he was an unworthy fellow I warrant him; Mr Courtall is known to be a person of worth and honour.

ARIANA We took him for an idle fellow, Madam, and gave but very little credit to what he said.

COURTALL 'Twas very obliging, lady, to believe nothing to the disadvantage of a stranger – What a couple of young devils are these?

LADY COCKWOOD Since you are willing to give yourself this trouble.

COURTALL I ought to do my duty, Madam.

[Exeunt all but Ariana and Gatty]

ARIANA How he blushed, and hung down his head!

GATTY A little more had put him as much out of countenance, as a country clown is when he ventures to compliment his attorney's daughter. *[They follow]*

SCENE ⟨II⟩

Sir Oliver's dining room

Enter Sir Joslin and Servant severally.

SIR JOSLIN How now old boy! Where's my brother Cockwood today?

SERVANT He desires to be in private, Sir.

SIR JOSLIN Why? What's the matter, man?

SERVANT This is a day of humiliation, Sir, with him for last night's transgression.

SIR JOSLIN I have business of consequence to impart to him, and must and will speak with him – So, ho! Brother Cockwood!

SIR OLIVER *[without]* Who's that, my brother Jolly?

SIR JOSLIN The same, the same, come away, boy.

SIR OLIVER *[without]* For some secret reasons I desire to be in private, brother.

SIR JOSLIN I have such a design on foot as would draw Diogenes out of his tub to follow it; therefore I say, come away, come away.

⟨*Sir Oliver*⟩ *entering in a nightgown and slippers.*

SIR OLIVER There is such a strange temptation in thy voice, never stir.

SIR JOSLIN What in thy gown and slippers yet! Why, brother, I have bespoke dinner, and engaged Mr Rakehell, the little smart gentleman I have often promised thee to make thee acquainted withal, to bring a whole bevy of damsels in sky, and pink, and flame-coloured taffetas. Come, come, dress thee quickly, there's to be Madam Rampant, a girl that shines, and will drink at such a rate, she's a mistress for Alexander, were he alive again.

SIR OLIVER How unluckily this falls out! Thomas, what clothes have I to put on?

SERVANT None but your penitential suit, Sir, all the rest are secured.

SIR OLIVER O unspeakable misfortune! That I should be in disgrace with my lady now!

SIR JOSLIN Come, come, never talk of clothes, put on anything, thou hast a person and a mien will bear it out bravely.

SIR OLIVER Nay, I know my behaviour will show I am a gentleman; but yet the ladies will look scurvily upon me, brother.

SIR JOSLIN That's a jest i'faith! He that has *terra firma* in the country, may appear in anything before 'em.

⟨*sings*⟩ For he that would have a wench kind,
　　　　Ne'er smugs up himself like a ninny;
　　　　But plainly tells her his mind,
　　　　And tickles her first with a guinea.

Hey boy –

SIR OLIVER I vow thou hast such a bewitching way with thee!

SIR JOSLIN How lovely will the ladies look when they have a beer glass in their hands!

SIR OLIVER I now have a huge mind to venture; but if this should come to my lady's knowledge.

SIR JOSLIN I have bespoke dinner at the Bear, the privat'st place in Town: there will be no spies to betray us, if Thomas be but secret, I dare warrant thee, brother Cockwood.

SIR OLIVER I have always found Thomas very faithful; but faith 'tis too unkind considering how tenderly my lady loves me.

SIR JOSLIN Fie, fie, a man and kept so much under correction by a busk★ and a fan!

SIR OLIVER Nay, I am in my nature as valiant as any man, when once I set out; but i'faith I cannot but think how my dear lady will be concerned when she comes home and misses me.

SIR JOSLIN A pox upon these qualms.

★ busk: a corset.

SIR OLIVER Well, thou hast seduced me; but I shall look so untowardly.

SIR JOSLIN Again art thou at it? In, in, and make all the haste that may be, Rakehell and the ladies will be there before us else.

SIR OLIVER Well, thou art an errant devil – hey – for the ladies, brother Jolly.

SIR JOSLIN Hey for the ladies, brother Cockwood.

[*Exeunt singing* – 'For he that would, etc']

SCENE III

The Bear

[*without*] Ho Francis, Humphrey, show a room there!

Enter Courtall, Freeman, Lady Cockwood, Ariana, Gatty and Sentry.

COURTALL Pray, Madam, be not so full of apprehension; there is no fear that this should come to Sir Oliver's knowledge.

LADY COCKWOOD I were ruined if it should, Sir! Dear, how I tremble! I never was in one of these houses before.

SENTRY [*aside*] This is a bait for the young ladies to swallow; she has been in most of the eating-houses about Town to my knowledge.

COURTALL O Francis!

Enter Waiter.

WAITER Your worship's welcome, Sir; but I must needs desire you to walk into the next room, for this is bespoke.

LADY COCKWOOD Mr Courtall, did not you say, this place was private?

COURTALL I warrant you, Madam. What company dines here, Francis?

WAITER A couple of country knights, Sir Joslin Jolley and Sir Oliver Cockwood, very honest gentlemen.

LADY COCKWOOD Combination to undo me!

COURTALL Peace, Madam, or you'll betray yourself to the waiter.

LADY COCKWOOD I am distracted! Sentry, did not I command thee to secure all Sir Oliver's clothes and leave nothing for him to put on, but his penitential suit, that I might be sure he could not stir abroad today?

SENTRY I obeyed you in everything, Madam; but I have often told you this Sir Joslin is a wicked seducer.

ARIANA If my uncle sees us, sister, what will he think of us?

GATTY We come but to wait upon her ladyship.

FREEMAN You need not fear, you chickens are secure under the wings of that old hen.

COURTALL Is there to be nobody, Francis, but Sir Oliver and Sir Joslin?

WAITER Faith, sir, I was enjoined secrecy; but you have an absolute power over me: coming lately out of the country, where there is but little variety, they have a design to solace themselves with a fresh girl or two, as I understand the business. [*Exit Waiter*]

LADY COCKWOOD O Sentry! Sir Oliver disloyal! My misfortunes come too thick upon me.

COURTALL [*aside*] Now is she afraid of being disappointed on all hands.

LADY COCKWOOD I know not what to do, Mr Courtall, I would not be surprised here myself, and yet I would prevent Sir Oliver from prosecuting his wicked and perfidious intentions.

ARIANA Now shall we have admirable sport, what with her fear and jealousy.

GATTY I lay my life she routs the wenches.

Enter Waiter.

WAITER I must needs desire you to step into the next room; Sir Joslin and Sir Oliver are below already.

LADY COCKWOOD I have not power to move a foot.

FREEMAN We will consider what is to be done within, Madam.

COURTALL Pray, Madam, come; I have a design in my head which shall secure you, surprise Sir Oliver, and free you from all your fears.

LADY COCKWOOD It cannot be, Sir.

COURTALL Never fear it: Francis, you may own Mr Freeman and I are in the house, if they ask for us; but not a word of these ladies, as you tender the wearing of your ears.   [*Exeunt*]

Enter Sir Joslin, Sir Oliver, and Waiter.

SIR JOSLIN Come, brother Cockwood prithee be brisk.

SIR OLIVER I shall disgrace myself for ever, brother.

SIR JOSLIN Pox upon care, never droop like a cock in moulting time; thou art spark enough in all conscience.

SIR OLIVER But my heart begins to fail me when I think of my lady.

SIR JOSLIN What, more qualms yet?

SIR OLIVER Well, I will be courageous: but it is not necessary these strangers should know this is my penitential suit, brother.

SIR JOSLIN They shall not, they shall not. Hark you old boy, is the meat provided? Is the wine and ice come? And are the melodious rascals at hand I spoke for?

WAITER Everything will be in readiness, Sir.

SIR JOSLIN If Mr Rakehell, with a coach full or two of vizard-masks and silk petticoats, call at the door, usher 'em up to the place of execution.

WAITER You shall be obeyed Sir.   [*Exit Waiter*]

Enter Rakehell.

SIR JOSLIN Ho, here's my little Rakehell come! Brother Cock-wood let me commend this ingenious gentleman to your acquaintance; he is a knight of the industry,★ has many admirable qualities, I assure you.

SIR OLIVER I am very glad, Sir, of this opportunity to know you.

RAKEHELL I am happy, Sir, if you esteem me your servant. Hark you, Sir Joslin, is this Sir Oliver Cockwood in earnest?

SIR JOSLIN In very good earnest I assure you; he is a little fantastical now and then, and dresses himself up in an odd fashion: but that's all one among friends, my little Rakehell.

SIR OLIVER Where are the damsels you talked of, brother Jolley? I hope Mr Rakehell has not forgot 'em.

RAKEHELL They are arming for the rancounter.†

SIR JOSLIN What, tricking and trimming?

RAKEHELL Even so, and will be here immediately.

SIR OLIVER They need not make themselves so full of temptation; my brother Jolley and I can be wicked enough without it.

SIR JOSLIN The truth is, my little Rakehell, we are both mighty

★ a knight of the industry: a sharper.   † rancounter: contest.

men at arms, and thou shalt see us charge anon to the terror of the ladies.

RAKEHELL Methinks that dress Sir Oliver is a little too rustical for a man of your capacity.

SIR OLIVER I have an odd humour, Sir, now and then; but I have wherewithal at home to be as spruce as any man.

RAKEHELL Your periwig is too scandalous, Sir Oliver, your black cap and border* is never wore but by a fiddler or a waiter.

SIR JOSLIN Prithee, my little Rakehell, do not put my brother Cockwood out of conceit of himself; methinks your calotte† is a pretty ornament, and makes a man look both polite and politic.

RAKEHELL I will allow you, 'tis a grave ware, and fit for men of business, that are every moment bending of their brows, and scratching of their heads, every project would claw out another periwig; but a lover had better appear before his mistress with a bald pate: 'twill make the ladies apprehend a favour, stop their noses, and avoid you: s'life, love in a cap is more ridiculous than love in a tub, or love in a pipkin.

SIR OLIVER I must confess your whole head is now in fashion; but there was a time when your calotte was not so despicable.

RAKEHELL Here's a peruke, Sir.

SIR OLIVER A very good one.

RAKEHELL A very good one? 'Tis the best in England. Pray, Sir Joslin, take him in your hand, and draw a comb through him, there is not such another frizz‡ in Europe.

SIR JOSLIN 'Tis a very fine one indeed.

RAKEHELL Pray, Sir Oliver, do me the favour to grace it on your head a little.

SIR OLIVER To oblige you, Sir.

RAKEHELL You never wore anything became you half so well in all your life before.

SIR JOSLIN Why, you never saw him in your life before.

RAKEHELL That's all one, Sir, I know 'tis impossible. Here's a beaver, Sir Oliver, feel him; for fineness, substance, and for fashion, the court of France never saw a better; I have bred him but a fortnight, and have him at command already. Clap him on

---

* border: of hair round the forehead.   † calotte: a skull cap.
‡ frizz: mass of small curls.

boldly, never hat took the fore-cock and the hind-cock at one motion so naturally.

SIR OLIVER I think you have a mind to make a spark of me before I see the ladies.

RAKEHELL Now you have the mien of a true cavalier, and with one look may make a lady kind, and a hector* humble: and since I named a hector, here's a sword, Sir: *sa, sa, sa,*† try him, Sir Joslin, put him to't, cut through the staple, run him through the door, beat him to the hilts, if he breaks, you shall have liberty to break my pate, and pay me never a groat of the ten for't.

SIR JOSLIN 'Tis a very pretty weapon indeed, Sir.

RAKEHELL The hilt is true French-wrought, and *dorée* by the best workman in France. This sword and this castor,‡ with an embroidered button and loop, which I have to vary him upon occasion, were sent me out of France for a token by my elder brother, that went over with a handsome equipage, to take the pleasure of this campaign.

SIR OLIVER Have you a mind to sell these things, Sir?

RAKEHELL That is below a gentleman; yet if a person of honour or a particular friend, such as I esteem you, Sir Oliver, take at any time a fancy to a band, a cravat, a velvet coat, a vest, a ring, a flageolet or any other little toy I have about me, I am good-natured, and may be easily persuaded to play the fool upon good terms.

Enter Freeman.

SIR JOSLIN Worthy Mr Freeman!

SIR OLIVER Honest Frank, how cam'st thou to find us out, man?

FREEMAN By mere chance, Sir; Ned Courtall is without writing a letter, and I came in to know whether you had any particular engagements, gentlemen.

SIR OLIVER We resolved to be in private; but you are men without exception.

FREEMAN Methinks you intended to be in private indeed, Sir Oliver. S'death, what disguise have you got on? Are you grown grave since last night, and come to sin *incognito*?

* hector: a bully.   † *sa, sa, sa*: a challenging cry in a duel, from *ça, ça*.
‡ castor: the beaver referred to before.

SIR OLIVER Hark you in your ear, Frank, this is my habit of humiliation, which I always put on the next day after I have transgressed, the better to make my pacification with my incensed lady –

FREEMAN Ha, ha, ha –

RAKEHELL Mr Freeman, your most humble servant, Sir.

FREEMAN O my little dapper officer! Are you here?

SIR JOSLIN Ha, Mr Freeman, we have bespoke all the jovial entertainment that a merry wag can wish for, good meat, good wine, and a wholesome wench or two; for the digestion, we shall have Madam Rampant, the glory of the Town, the brightest she that shines, or else my little Rakehell is not a man of his word, Sir.

RAKEHELL I warrant you she comes, Sir Joslin.

SIR JOSLIN [*sings*]

> And if she comes, she shall not 'scape,
> If twenty pounds will win her;
> Her very eye commits a rape,
> 'Tis such a tempting sinner.

Enter Courtall.

COURTALL Well said, Sir Joslin, I see you hold up still, and bate not an ace of your good humour.

SIR JOSLIN Noble Mr Courtall!

COURTALL Bless me, Sir Oliver, what are you going to act a droll?* How the people would throng about you, if you were but mounted on a few deal boards in Covent Garden now!

SIR OLIVER Hark you, Ned, this is the badge of my lady's indignation for my last night's offence; do not insult over a poor sober man in affliction.

COURTALL Come, come, send home for your clothes; I hear you are to have ladies, and you are not to learn at these years, how absolutely necessary a rich vest and a peruke are to a man that aims at their favours.

SIR OLIVER A pox on't, Ned, my lady's gone abroad in a damned jealous melancholy humour, and has commanded her woman to secure 'em.

COURTALL Under lock and key?

---

* a droll: a reference to the Italian puppet plays at Covent Garden.

SIR OLIVER Aye, aye, man, 'tis usual in these cases, out of pure love in hopes to reclaim me, and to keep me from doing myself an injury by drinking two days together.

COURTALL What a loving lady 'tis!

SIR OLIVER There are sots that would think themselves happy in such a lady, Ned; but to a true bred gentleman all lawful solace is abomination.

RAKEHELL Mr Courtall, your most humble servant, Sir.

COURTALL Oh! My little knight of the industry, I am glad to see you in such good company.

FREEMAN Courtall, hark you, are the masking-habits which you sent to borrow at the playhouse come yet?

COURTALL Yes, and the ladies are almost dressed: this design will add much to our mirth, and give us the benefit of their meat, wine and music for our entertainment.

FREEMAN 'Twas luckily thought of.

Music.

SIR OLIVER Hark, the music comes.

SIR JOSLIN Hey, boys – let 'em enter, let 'em enter.

Enter Waiter.

WAITER An't please your worships, there is a mask of ladies without, that desire to have the freedom to come in and dance.

SIR JOSLIN Hey! Boys –

SIR OLIVER Did you bid 'em come *en masquerade* Mr Rakehell?

RAKEHELL No; but Rampant is a mad wench, she was half a dozen times a-mumming in private company last Shrovetide, and I lay my life she has put 'em all upon this frolic.

COURTALL They are mettled girls, I warrant them, Sir Joslin, let 'em be what they will.

SIR JOSLIN Let 'em enter, let 'em enter, ha boys –

Enter Music and the Ladies in an antic, ★ *and then they take out, my Lady Cockwood, Sir Oliver, the Young Ladies, Courtall and Freeman, and Sentry, Sir Joslin, and dance a set dance.*

SIR OLIVER O my little rogue! Have I got thee? How I will turn and wind, and feague† thy body!

★ an antic: fancy dress   † feague: whip (like a top), or, to do the business of.

SIR JOSLIN Mettle on all sides, mettle on all sides, i'faith; how swimmingly would this pretty little ambling filly carry a man of my body!

[*sings*]   She's so bonny and brisk,
          How she'd curvet and frisk,
          If a man were once mounted upon her!
          Let me have but a leap
          Where 'tis wholesome and cheap,
          And a fig for your person of honour.

SIR OLIVER 'Tis true, little Joslin, i'faith.

COURTALL They have warmed us, Sir Oliver.

SIR OLIVER Now am I as rampant as a lion, Ned, and could love as vigorously as a seaman that is newly landed after an East India voyage.

COURTALL Take my advice, Sir Oliver, do not in your rage deprive yourself of your only hope of an accommodation with your lady.

SIR OLIVER I had rather have a perpetual civil war, than purchase peace at such a dishonourable rate. A poor fiddler, after he has been three days persecuted at a country wedding, takes more delight in scraping upon his old squeaking fiddle, than I do in fumbling on that domestic instrument of mine.

COURTALL Be not so bitter, Sir Oliver, on your own dear lady.

SIR OLIVER I was married to her when I was young, Ned, with a design to be baulked, as they tie whelps to the bell-weather; where I have been so butted, 'twere enough to fright me, were I not pure mettle, from ever running at sheep again.

COURTALL That's no sure rule, Sir Oliver; for a wife's a dish, of which if a man once surfeit, he shall have a better stomach to all others ever after.

SIR OLIVER What a shape is here, Ned! So exact and tempting, 'twould persuade a man to be an implicit sinner, and take her face upon credit.

SIR JOSLIN Come, brother Cockwood, let us get 'em to lay aside these masking fopperies, and then we'll feague 'em in earnest: give us a bottle, waiter.

FREEMAN Not before dinner, good Sir Joslin –

SIR OLIVER Lady, though I have out of drollery put myself into this contemptible dress at present, I am a gentleman, and a man of courage, as you shall find anon by my brisk behaviour.

RAKEHELL Sir Joslin! Sir Oliver! These are none of our ladies, they are just come to the door in a coach, and have sent for me down to wait upon 'em up to you.

SIR JOSLIN Hey – Boys, more game, more game! Fetch 'em up, fetch 'em up.

SIR OLIVER Why, what a day of sport will here be, Ned?

[*Exit Rakehell*]

SIR JOSLIN They shall all have fair play, boys.

SIR OLIVER And we will match ourselves, and make a prize on't, Ned Courtall and I, against Frank Freeman and you brother Jolley, and Rakehell shall be judge for gloves and silk stockings, to be bestowed as the conqueror shall fancy.

SIR JOSLIN Agreed, agreed, agreed.

COURTALL ⎫
⎬ A match, a match.
FREEMAN ⎭

SIR OLIVER Hey, boys!

Lady Cockwood counterfeits a fit.

SENTRY [*pulling off her mask*] O heavens! My dear lady! Help, help!

SIR OLIVER What's here? Sentry and my lady! S'death, what a condition am I in now, brother Jolley! You have brought me into this *premunire*:* for heaven's sake run down quickly, and send the rogue and whores away. Help, help! O help! Dear Madam, sweet lady!

[*Exit Sir Joslin, Sir Oliver kneels down by her*]

SENTRY O she's gone, she's gone!

FREEMAN Give her more air.

COURTALL Fetch a glass of cold water, Freeman.

SIR OLIVER Dear Madam, speak, sweet Madam speak.

SENTRY Out upon thee for a vile hypocrite! Thou art the wicked author of all this; who but such a reprobate, such an obdurate sinner as thou art, could go about to abuse so sweet a lady?

SIR OLIVER Dear Sentry, do not stab me with thy words, but stab me with thy bodkin rather, that I may here die a sacrifice at her feet, for all my disloyal actions.

* premunire: predicament.

SENTRY No, live, live, to be a reproach and a shame to all rebellious husbands; ah, that she had but my heart! But thou hast bewitched her affection; thou should'st then dearly smart for this abominable treason.

GATTY So, now she begins to come to herself.

ARIANA Set her more upright, and bend her a little forward.

LADY COCKWOOD Unfortunate woman! Let me go, why do you hold me? Would I had a dagger at my heart, to punish it for loving that ungrateful man.

SIR OLIVER Dear Madam, were I but worthy of your pity and belief.

LADY COCKWOOD Peace, peace, perfidious man, I am too tame and foolish – were I every day at the plays, the Park, and Mulberry Garden, with a kind look secretly to indulge the unlawful passion of some young gallant; or did I associate myself with the gaming madams, and were every afternoon at my Lady Brief's and my Lady Meanwell's at ombre and quebas,* pretending ill luck to borrow money of a friend, and then pretending good luck to excuse the plenty to a husband, my suspicious demeanour had deserved this; but I who out of a scrupulous tenderness to my honour, and to comply with thy base jealousy, have denied myself all those blameless recreations, which a virtuous lady might enjoy, to be thus inhumanely reviled in my own person, and thus unreasonably robbed and abused in thine too!

COURTALL Sure she will take up anon, or crack her mind, or else the devil's in't.

LADY COCKWOOD Do not stay and torment me with thy sight; go, graceless wretch, follow thy treacherous resolutions, do, and waste that poor stock of comfort which I should have at home, upon those your ravenous cormorants below: I feel my passion begin to swell again. [*she has a little fit again*]

COURTALL Now will she get an absolute dominion over him, and all this will be my plague in the end.

SIR OLIVER [*running up and down*] Ned Courtall, Frank Freeman, Cousin Ariana, and dear cousin Gatty, for heaven's sake join all, and moderate her passion – Ah Sentry! Forbear thy unjust reproaches, take pity on thy master! Thou hast a great influence over her, and I have always been mindful of thy favours.

* quebas: a card game.

SENTRY You do not deserve the least compassion, nor would I speak a good word for you, but that I know for all this, 'twill be acceptable to my poor lady. Dear Madam, do but look up a little, Sir Oliver lies at your feet an humble penitent.

ARIANA How bitterly he weeps! How sadly he sighs!

GATTY I dare say he counterfeited his sin, and is real in his repentance.

COURTALL Compose yourself a little, pray, Madam; all this was mere raillery, a way of talk, which Sir Oliver being well-bred, has learned among the gay people of the Town.

FREEMAN If you did but know, Madam, what an odious thing it is to be thought to love a wife in good company, you would easily forgive him.

LADY COCKWOOD No, no, 'twas the mild correction which I gave him for his insolent behaviour last night, that has encouraged him again thus to insult over my affections.

COURTALL Come, come, Sir Oliver, out with your bosom secret, and clear all things to your lady; is it not as we have said?

SIR OLIVER Or may I never have the happiness to be in her good grace again; and as for the harlots, dear Madam, here is Ned Courtall and Frank Freeman, that have often seen me in company of the wicked; let 'em speak, if they ever knew me tempted to a disloyal action in their lives.

COURTALL On my conscience, Madam, I may more safely swear, that Sir Oliver has been constant to your ladyship, than that a girl of twelve years old has her maidenhead this warm and ripening age.

Enter Sir Joslin.

SIR OLIVER Here's my brother Jolley too can witness the loyalty of my heart and that I did not intend any treasonable practice against your ladyship in the least.

SIR JOSLIN Unless feaguing 'em with a beer glass be included in the statute. Come, Mr Courtall, to satisfy my lady, and put her in a little good humour, let us sing the catch I taught you yesterday, that was made by a country vicar on my brother Cockwood and me.

[*They sing*] Love and wenching are toys,

Fit to please beardless boys,
Th'are sports we hate worse than a leaguer;
When we visit a miss
We still brag how we kiss,
But 'tis with a bottle we feague her.

SIR JOSLIN Come, come, Madam, let all things be forgot; dinner is ready, the cloth is laid in the next room, let us in and be merry; there was no harm meant as I am true little Joslin.

LADY COCKWOOD Sir Oliver knows I can't be angry with him, though he plays the naughty man thus; but why, my dear, would y' expose yourself in this ridiculous habit, to the censure of both our honours?

SIR OLIVER Indeed, I was to blame to be over-persuaded; I intended dutifully to retire into the pantry, and there civilly to divert myself at backgammon with the butler.

SIR JOSLIN Faith, I must even own, the fault was mine, I enticed him hither, lady.

SIR OLIVER How the devil, Ned, came they to find us out here!

COURTALL No bloodhound draws so sure as a jealous woman.

SIR OLIVER I am afraid Thomas has been unfaithful: prithee, Ned, speak to my lady, that there may be a perfect understanding between us, and that Sentry may be sent home for my clothes that I may no longer wear the marks of her displeasure.

COURTALL Let me alone, Sir Oliver. [*he goes to my Lady Cockwood*] How do you find yourself, Madam, after this violent passion?

LADY COCKWOOD This has been a lucky adventure, Mr Courtall; now am I absolute mistress of my own conduct for a time.

COURTALL Then shall I be a happy man, Madam: I knew this would be the consequence of all, and yet could not I forbear the project.

SIR OLIVER [*to Sir Joslin*] How didst thou shuffle away Rakehell and the ladies brother?

SIR JOSLIN I have appointed 'em to meet us at six o'clock at the new Spring Garden.*

SIR OLIVER Then will we yet, in spite of the stars that have crossed us, be in conjunction with Madam Rampant, brother.

COURTALL Come, gentlemen, dinner is on the table.

* the new Spring Garden: at Vauxhall; the old garden was at Charing Cross.

SIR JOSLIN Ha! Sly-girl and Mad-cap, I'll enter you, i'faith; since
you have found the way to the Bear, I'll feague you.

[*sings*]   When we visit a miss,
          We still brag how we kiss;
          But 'tis with a bottle we feague her.

[*Exeunt singing*]

ACT FOUR

SCENE I

A dining room

Enter Lady Cockwood.

LADY COCKWOOD A lady cannot be too jealous of her servant's love, this faithless and inconstant age: his amorous carriage to that prating girl today, though he pretends it was to blind Sir Oliver, I fear will prove a certain sign of his revolted heart; the letters I have counterfeited in these girls' names will clear all; if he accept of that appointment, and refuses mine, I need not any longer doubt.

Enter Sentry.

Sentry, have the letters and message been delivered, as I directed?

SENTRY Punctually, Madam; I knew they were to be found at the latter end of a play, I sent a porter first with the letter to Mr Courtall, who was at the King's House,* he sent for him out by the door-keeper, and delivered it into his own hands.

LADY COCKWOOD Did you keep on your vizard, that the fellow might not know how to describe you?

SENTRY I did, Madam.

LADY COCKWOOD And how did he receive it?

SENTRY Like a traitor to all goodness, with all the signs of joy imaginable.

LADY COCKWOOD Be not angry, Sentry, 'tis as my heart wished it: what did you do with the letter to Mr Freeman? For I thought fit to deceive 'em both, to make my policy less suspicious to Courtall.

SENTRY The porter found him at the Duke's House,† Madam, and delivered it with like care.

* the King's House: the Theatre Royal. This was the building in Bridges Street, destroyed by fire in 1672, and rebuilt in 1673. It lay between Drury Lane and Bridges Street.
† the Duke's House: Davenant's theatre (the Theatre Royal being Killigrew's). This was in Lincoln's Inn Fields, opened in 1661.

LADY COCKWOOD Very well.

SENTRY After the letters were delivered, Madam, I went myself to the playhouse, and sent in for Mr Courtall, who came out to me immediately; I told him your ladyship presented your humble service to him, and that Sir Oliver was going into the City with Sir Joslin, to visit his brother Cockwood, and that it would add much more to your ladyship's happiness, if he would be pleased to meet you in Gray's Inn walks★ this lovely evening.

LADY COCKWOOD And how did he entertain the motion?

SENTRY Bless me! I tremble still to think upon it! I could not have imagined he had been so wicked; he counterfeited the greatest passion, railed at his fate, and swore a thousand horrid oaths, that since he came into the playhouse he had notice of a business that concerned both his honour and fortune; and that he was an undone man, if he did not go about it presently; prayed me to desire your ladyship to excuse him this evening, and that to-morrow he would be wholly at your devotion.

LADY COCKWOOD Ha, ha, ha! He little thinks how much he has obliged me.

SENTRY I had much ado to forbear upbraiding him with his ingratitude to your ladyship.

LADY COCKWOOD Poor Sentry! Be not concerned for me, I have conquered my affection, and thou shalt find it is not jealousy has been my counsellor in this. Go, let our hoods and masks be ready, that I may surprise Courtall, and make the best advantage of this lucky opportunity.

SENTRY I obey you, Madam. [*Exit Sentry*]

LADY COCKWOOD How am I filled with indignation! To find my person and my passion both despised, and what is more, so much precious time fooled away in fruitless expectation: I would poison my face, so I might be revenged on this ungrateful villain.

Enter Sir Oliver.

SIR OLIVER My dearest!

LADY COCKWOOD My dearest dear! Prithee do not go into the City tonight.

★ Gray's Inn walks: famous as a place of assignation.

SIR OLIVER My brother Jolley is gone before, and I am to call him at Counsellor Trott's chamber in the Temple.

LADY COCKWOOD Well, if you did but know the fear I have upon me when you are absent, you would not seek occasions to be from me thus.

SIR OLIVER Let me comfort thee with a kiss; what should'st thou be afraid of?

LADY COCKWOOD I cannot but believe that every woman that sees thee must be in love with thee, as I am; do not blame my jealousy.

SIR OLIVER I protest I would refuse a countess rather than abuse thee, poor heart.

LADY COCKWOOD And then you are so desperate upon the least occasion, I should have acquainted you else with something that concerns your honour.

SIR OLIVER My honour! You ought in duty to do it.

LADY COCKWOOD Nay, I knew how passionate you would be presently; therefore you shall never know it.

SIR OLIVER Do not leave me in doubt, I shall suspect everyone I look upon; I will kill a common council man or two before I come back, if you do not tell me.

LADY COCKWOOD Dear, how I tremble! Will you promise me you will not quarrel then? If you tender my life and happiness, I am sure you will not.

SIR OLIVER I will bear anything rather than be an enemy to thy quiet, my dear.

LADY COCKWOOD I could wish Mr Courtall a man of better principles, because I know you love him, my dear.

SIR OLIVER Why, what has he done?

LADY COCKWOOD I always treated him with great respect, out of my regard to your friendship; but he, like an impudent man as he is, today misconstruing my civility, in most unseemly language, made a foul attempt upon my honour.

SIR OLIVER Death, and hell, and furies, I will have my pumps,* and long sword!

LADY COCKWOOD Oh, I shall faint! Did not you promise me you would not be so rash?

      * pumps: light shoes.

SIR OLIVER Well, I will not kill him, for fear of murdering thee, my dear.

LADY COCKWOOD You may decline your friendship, and by your coldness give him no encouragement to visit our family.

SIR OLIVER I think thy advice the best for this once indeed; for it is not fit to publish such a business: but if he should be ever tempting or attempting, let me know it, prithee, my dear.

LADY COCKWOOD If you moderate yourself according to my directions now, I shall never conceal anything from you, that may increase your just opinion of my conjugal fidelity.

SIR OLIVER Was ever man blessed with such a virtuous lady! [*aside*] Yet cannot I forbear going a-ranging again. Now must I to the Spring Garden to meet my brother Jolley and Madam Rampant.

LADY COCKWOOD Prithee, be so good to think how melancholy I spend my time here; for I have joy in no company but thine, and let that bring thee home a little sooner.

SIR OLIVER Thou hast been so kind in this discovery, that I am loath to leave thee.

LADY COCKWOOD I wish you had not been engaged so far.

SIR OLIVER Aye, that's it: farewell my virtuous dear.

[*Exit Sir Oliver*]

LADY COCKWOOD Farewell, my dearest dear. I know he has not courage enough to question Courtall; but this will make him hate him, increase his confidence of me, and justify my banishing that false fellow our house; it is not fit a man that abused my love, should come hither, and pry into my actions; besides this will make his access more difficult to that wanton baggage.

Enter Ariana and Gatty with their hoods and masks.

Whither are you going, cousins?

GATTY To take the air upon the water, Madam.

ARIANA And for variety, to walk a turn or two in the new Spring Garden.

LADY COCKWOOD I heard you were gone abroad with Mr Courtall and Mr Freeman.

GATTY For heaven's sake, why should your ladyship have such an ill opinion of us?

LADY COCKWOOD The truth is, before I saw you, I believed it merely the vanity of that prating man; Mr Courtall told Mrs Gazette this morning, that you were so well acquainted already, that you would meet him and Mr Freeman anywhere, and that you had promised 'em to receive and make appointment by letters.

GATTY O impudent man!

ARIANA Now you see the consequence, sister, of our rambling; they have raised this false story from our innocent fooling with 'em in the Mulberry Garden last night.

GATTY I could almost foreswear ever speaking to a man again.

LADY COCKWOOD Was Mr Courtall in the Mulberry Garden last night?

ARIANA Yes, Madam.

LADY COCKWOOD And did he speak to you?

GATTY There passed a little harmless raillery betwixt us; but you amaze me, Madam.

ARIANA I could not imagine any man could be thus unworthy.

LADY COCKWOOD He has quite lost my good opinion too: in duty to Sir Oliver, I have hitherto showed him some countenance; but I shall hate him hereafter for your sakes. But I detain you from your recreations, cousins.

GATTY We are very much obliged to your ladyship for this timely notice.

ARIANA ⎫
GATTY ⎬ Your servant, Madam.   [*Exeunt Ariana and Gatty*]

LADY COCKWOOD Your servant, cousins – in the Mulberry Garden last night! When I sat languishing, and vainly expecting him at home: this has incensed me so, that I could kill him. I am glad these girls are gone to the Spring Garden, it helps my design; the letters I have counterfeited, have appointed Courtall and Freeman to meet them there, they will produce 'em, and confirm all I have said: I will daily poison these girls with such lies as shall make their quarrel to Courtall irreconcilable, and render Freeman only suspected; for I would not have him thought equally guilty: he secretly began to make an address to me at the Bear, and this breach shall give him an opportunity to pursue it.

Enter Sentry.

SENTRY Here are your things, Madam.

LADY COCKWOOD That's well: O Sentry! I shall once more be happy; for now Mr Courtall has given me an occasion, that I may without ingratitude check his unlawful passion, and free myself from the trouble of an intrigue, that gives me every day such fearful apprehensions of my honour.

[*Exeunt Lady Cockwood and Sentry*]

SCENE II

New Spring Garden

Enter Sir Joslin, Rakehell, and Waiter.

WAITER Will you be pleased to walk into an arbour, gentlemen?

SIR JOSLIN By and by, good Sir.

RAKEHELL I wonder Sir Oliver is not come yet.

SIR JOSLIN Nay, he will not fail I warrant thee, boy; but what's the matter with thy nose, my little Rakehell?

RAKEHELL A foolish accident; jesting at the Fleece★ this afternoon, I mistook my man a little, a dull rogue that could not understand raillery, made a sudden repartee with a quart-pot, Sir Joslin.

SIR JOSLIN Why dids't not thou stick him to the wall, my little Rakehell?

RAKEHELL The truth is, Sir Joslin, he deserved it; but look you, in case of a doubtful wound, I am unwilling to give my friends too often the trouble to bail me; and if it should be mortal, you know a younger brother has not wherewithal to rebate the edge of a witness, and mollify the hearts of a jury.

SIR JOSLIN This is very prudently considered indeed.

RAKEHELL 'Tis time to be wise, Sir; my courage has almost run me out of a considerable annuity. When I lived first about this Town, I agreed with a surgeon for twenty pounds a quarter to cure me of all the knocks, bruises, and green wounds I should

★ the Fleece: a tavern in York Street, Covent Garden, where many quarrels originated, according to Pepys and John Aubrey.

receive, and in one half year the poor fellow begged me to be released of his bargain, and swore I would undo him else in lint and balsam.

Enter Sir Oliver.

SIR JOSLIN Ho! Here's my brother Cockwood come –

SIR OLIVER Aye, brother Jolley, I have kept my word, you see; but 'tis a barbarous thing to abuse my lady, I have had such a proof of her virtue, I will tell thee all anon. But where's Madam Rampant, and the rest of the ladies, Mr Rakehell?

RAKEHELL Faith, Sir, being disappointed at noon, they were unwilling any more to set a certainty at hazard; 'tis term-time, and they have severally betook themselves, some to their chamber-practice, and others to the places of public pleading.

SIR OLIVER Faith, brother Jolley, let us even go into an arbour, and then feague Mr Rakehell.

SIR JOSLIN With all my heart, would we had Madam Rampant.
   [*sings*] She's as frolic and free,
        As her lovers dare be,
        Never awed by a foolish punctilio;
        She'll not start from her place,
        Though thou nam'st a black ace,★
        And will drink a beer-glass to Spudilio.†
Hey boys! Come, come, come! Let's in, and delay our sport no longer.   [*Exeunt singing, 'She'll not start from her', etc*]

Enter Courtall and Freeman severally.

COURTALL Freeman!

FREEMAN Courtall, what the devil's the matter with thee? I have observed thee prying up and down the walks like a citizen's wife that has dropped her holy-day pocket-handkercher.

COURTALL What unlucky devil has brought thee hither?

FREEMAN I believe a better-natured devil than yours, Courtall, if a leveret be better meat than an old puss, that has been coursed by most of the young fellows of her country: I am not working my brain for a counter-plot, a disappointment is not my business.

★ black ace: card term.
† Spudilio: the ace of spades in ombre and quadrille.

COURTALL You are mistaken, Freeman: prithee be gone, and leave me the garden to myself, or I shall grow as testy as an old fowler that is put by his shoot, after he has crept half a mile upon his belly.

FREEMAN Prithee be thou gone, or I shall take it as unkindly as a chemist would, if thou should'st kick down his limbec,* in the very minute that he looked for projection.

COURTALL Come, come, you must yield, Freeman, your business cannot be of such consequence as mine.

FREEMAN If ever thou hadst a business of such consequence in thy life as mine is, I will condescend to be incapable of affairs presently.

COURTALL Why, I have an appointment made me, man, without my seeking, by a woman for whom I would have mortgaged my whole estate to have had her abroad but to break a cheese-cake.

FREEMAN And I have an appointment made me without my seeking too, by such a she, that I will break the whole ten commandments, rather then disappoint her of her breaking one.

COURTALL Come, you do but jest, Freeman, a forsaken mistress could not be more malicious than thou art: prithee be gone.

FREEMAN Prithee do thou be gone.

COURTALL S'death! The sight of thee will scare my woman for ever.

FREEMAN S'death! The sight of thee will make my woman believe me the falsest villain breathing.

COURTALL We shall stand fooling till we are both undone, and I know not how to help it.

FREEMAN Let us proceed honestly like friends, discover the truth of things to one another, and if we cannot reconcile our business, we will draw cuts,† and part fairly.

COURTALL I do not like that way; for talk is only allowable at the latter end of an intrigue, and should never be used at the beginning of an amour, for fear of frighting a young lady from her good intentions – yet I care not, though I read the letter, but I will conceal the name.

FREEMAN I have a letter too, and am content to do the same.

* limbec: alembic, distilling flask.
† draw cuts: draw lots (with sticks of different lengths).

COURTALL [*reads*] 'Sir, in sending you this letter, I proceed against the modesty of our sex –'

FREEMAN S'death, this begins just like my letter.

COURTALL Do you read on then –

FREEMAN [*reads*] 'But let not the good opinion I have conceived of you, make you too severe in your censuring of me –'

COURTALL Word for word.

FREEMAN Now do you read again.

COURTALL [*reads*] 'If you give yourself the trouble to be walking in the new Spring Garden this evening, I will meet you there, and tell you a secret, which I have reason to fear, because it comes to your knowledge by my means, will make you hate your humble servant.'

FREEMAN *Verbatim* my letter, hey-day!

COURTALL Prithee let's compare the hands. [*they compare 'em*]

FREEMAN S'death, the hand's the same.

COURTALL I hope the name is not the same too –

FREEMAN If it be, we are finely jilted, faith.

COURTALL I long to be undeceived; prithee do thou show first, Freeman.

FREEMAN No – but both together, if you will.

COURTALL Agreed.

FREEMAN Ariana.

COURTALL Gatty – Ha, ha, ha.

FREEMAN The little rogues are masculine in their proceedings, and have made one another confidents in their love.

COURTALL But I do not like this altogether so well, Frank; I wish they had appointed us several places: for though 'tis evident they have trusted one another with the bargain, no woman ever seals before witness.

FREEMAN Prithee how didst thou escape the snares of the old devil this afternoon?

COURTALL With much ado; Sentry had set me; if her ladyship had got me into her clutches, there had been no getting off without a rescue, or paying down the money; for she always arrests upon execution.*

FREEMAN You made a handsome lie to her woman.

* execution: in the way a debtor's person was seized in default of payment.

COURTALL For all this, I know she's angry; for she thinks nothing a just excuse in these cases, though it were to save the forfeit of a man's estate, or reprieve the life of her own natural brother.

FREEMAN Faith, thou hast not done altogether like a gentleman with her; thou should'st fast thyself up to a stomach now and then, to oblige her; if there were nothing in it, but the hearty welcome, methinks 'twere enough to make thee bear sometimes with the homeliness of the fare.

COURTALL I know not what I might do in a camp, where there were no other woman; but I shall hardly in this Town, where there is such plenty, forbear good meat, to get myself an appetite to horseflesh.

FREEMAN This is rather an aversion in thee, than any real fault in the woman; if this lucky business had not fallen out, I intended with your good leave to have out-bid you for her ladyship's favour.

COURTALL I should never have consented to that, Frank; though I am a little resty at present, I am not such a jade, but I should strain if another rid against me; I have ere now liked nothing in a woman that I have loved at last in spite only, because another had a mind to her.

FREEMAN Yonder are a couple of vizards tripping towards us.

COURTALL 'Tis they, i'faith.

FREEMAN We need not divide, since they come together.

COURTALL I was a little afraid when we compared letters, they had put a trick upon us; but now I am confirmed they are mighty honest.

Enter Ariana and Gatty.

ARIANA We cannot avoid 'em.

GATTY Let us dissemble our knowledge of their business a little, and then take 'em down in the height of their assurance.

COURTALL, FREEMAN Your servant, ladies.

ARIANA I perceive it is as impossible, gentlemen, to walk without you, as without our shadows; never were poor women so haunted by the ghosts of their self-murdered lovers.

GATTY If it should be our good fortunes to have you in love with us, we will take care you shall not grow desperate, and leave the world in an ill humour.

ARIANA If you should, certainly your ghosts would be very malicious.

COURTALL 'Twere pity you should have your curtains drawn in the dead of the night, and your pleasing slumbers interrupted by anything but flesh and blood, ladies.

FREEMAN Shall we walk a turn?

ARIANA By yourselves, if you please.

GATTY Our company may put a constraint upon you; for I find you daily hover about these gardens, as a kite does about a back-side,* watching an opportunity to catch up the poultry.

ARIANA Woe be to the daughter or wife of some merchant-tailor, or poor felt-maker now; for you seldom row to Fox Hall† without some such plot against the City.

FREEMAN You wrong us, ladies, our business has happily succeeded, since we have the honour to wait upon you.

GATTY You could not expect to see us here.

COURTALL Your true lover, Madam, when he misses his mistress, is as restless as a spaniel that has lost his master; he ranges up and down the plays, the Park, and all the gardens, and never stays long, but where he has the happiness to see her.

GATTY I suppose your mistress, Mr Courtall, is always the last woman you are acquainted with.

COURTALL Do not think, Madam, I have that false measure of my acquaintance, which poets have of their verses, always to think the last best, though I esteem you so, in justice to your merit.

GATTY Or if you do not love her best, you always love to talk of her most; as a barren coxcomb that wants discourse, is ever entertaining company out of the last book he read in.

COURTALL Now you accuse me most unjustly, Madam; who the devil, that has common sense, will go a-birding with a clack in his cap?

ARIANA Nay, we do not blame you, gentlemen, everyone in their way; a huntsman talks of his dogs, a falconer of his hawks, a jockey of his horse, and a gallant of his mistress.

* back-side: back premises.   † Fox Hall: spelt Vauxhall from about 1700.

GATTY Without the allowance of this vanity, an amour would soon grow as dull as matrimony.

COURTALL Whatsoever you say, ladies, I cannot believe you think us men of such abominable principles.

FREEMAN For my part, I have ever held it as ungrateful to boast of the favours of a mistress, as to deny the courtesies of a friend.

COURTALL A friend that bravely ventures his life in the field to serve me, deserves but equally with a mistress that kindly exposes her honour to oblige me, especially when she does it as generously too, and with as little ceremony.

FREEMAN And I would no more betray the honour of such a woman, than I would the life of a man that should rob on purpose to supply me.

GATTY We believe you men of honour, and know it is below you to talk of any woman that deserves it.

ARIANA You are so generous, you seldom insult after a victory.

GATTY And so vain, that you always triumph before it.

COURTALL S'death! What's the meaning of all this?

GATTY Though you find us so kind, Mr Courtall, pray do not tell Mrs Gazette tomorrow, that we came hither on purpose this evening to meet you.

COURTALL I would as soon print it, and see a fellow to post it up with the play-bills.

GATTY You have reposed a great deal of confidence in her, for all you pretend this ill opinion of her secrecy now.

COURTALL I never trusted her with the name of a mistress, that I should be jealous of if I saw her receive fruit, and go out of the playhouse with a stranger.

GATTY For ought as I see, we are infinitely obliged to you, Sir.

COURTALL 'Tis impossible to be insensible of so much goodness, Madam.

GATTY What goodness, pray, Sir?

COURTALL Come, come, give over this raillery.

GATTY You are so ridiculously unworthy, that 'twere a folly to reprove you with a serious look.

COURTALL On my conscience, your heart begins to fail you now we are coming to the point, as a young fellow's that was never in the field before.

GATTY You begin to amaze me.

COURTALL Since you yourself sent the challenge, you must not in honour fly off now.

GATTY Challenge! O heavens! This confirms all: were I a man, I would kill thee for the injuries thou hast already done me.

FREEMAN [*to Ariana*] Let not your suspicion of my unkindness make you thus scrupulous; was ever city ill treated, that surrendered without assault or summons?

ARIANA Dear sister, what ill spirit brought us hither? I never met with so much impudence in my life.

COURTALL [*aside*] Hey jilts! They are as good at it already, as the old one i'faith.

FREEMAN Come, ladies, you have exercised your wit enough; you would not venture letters of such consequence for a jest only.

GATTY Letters! Bless me, what will this come to?

COURTALL To that none of us shall have cause to repent I hope, Madam.

ARIANA Let us fly 'em, sister, they are devils, and not men, they could never be so malicious else.

Enter Lady Cockwood and Sentry.

LADY COCKWOOD Your servant, cousins.

COURTALL [*starting*] Ho my Lady Cockwood! My ears are grown an inch already.

FREEMAN This is Madam Matchiavel,★ I suspect, Courtall.

COURTALL Nay, 'tis her plot doubtless: now am I as much out of countenance, as I should be if Sir Oliver should take me making bold with her ladyship.

LADY COCKWOOD Do not let me discompose you, I can walk alone, cousins.

GATTY Are you so uncharitable, Madam, to think we have any business with 'em?

ARIANA It has been our ill fortune to meet 'em here, and nothing could be so lucky as your coming, Madam, to free us from 'em.

GATTY They have abused us in the grossest manner.

ARIANA Counterfeited letters under our hands.

★ Matchiavel: a schemer, from Machiavelli (1469–1527), Italian author and statesman, regarded as an epitome of ruthless cunning.

LADY COCKWOOD Never trouble yourselves, cousins, I have heard this is a common practice with such unworthy men: did they not threaten to divulge them, and defame you to the world?

GATTY We cannot believe they intend anything less, Madam.

LADY COCKWOOD Doubtless, they had such a mean opinion of your wit and honour, that they thought to fright you to a base compliance with their wicked purposes.

ARIANA I hate the very sight of 'em.

GATTY I could almost wish myself a disease, to breathe infection upon 'em.

COURTALL Very pretty! We have carried on our designs very luckily against these young ladies.

FREEMAN We have lost their good opinion for ever.

LADY COCKWOOD I know not whether their folly or their impudence be greater, they are not worth your anger, they are only fit to be laughed at, and despised.

COURTALL A very fine old devil this!

LADY COCKWOOD Mr Freeman, this is not like a gentleman, to affront a couple of young ladies thus; but I cannot blame you so much, you are in a manner a stranger to our family: but I wonder how that base man can look me in the face, considering how civilly he has been treated at our house.

COURTALL The truth is, Madam, I am a rascal; but I fear you have contributed to the making me so: be not as unmerciful as the devil is to a poor sinner.

SENTRY Did you ever see the like? Never trust me, if he has not the confidence to make my virtuous lady accessary to his wickedness.

LADY COCKWOOD Aye Sentry! 'Tis a miracle if my honour escapes, considering the access which his greatness with Sir Oliver has given him daily to me.

FREEMAN Faith, ladies, we did not counterfeit these letters, we are abused as well as you.

COURTALL I received mine from a porter at the King's Playhouse, and I will show it you, that you may see if you know the hand.

LADY COCKWOOD ⟨*aside*⟩ Sentry, are you sure they never saw any of your writing?

COURTALL S'death! I am so discomposed, I know not where I have put it.

SENTRY O Madam! Now I remember myself, Mrs Gatty helped
me once to indite a letter to my sweetheart.

LADY COCKWOOD Forgetful wench! Then I am undone.

COURTALL O here it is – Hey, who's here?

As he has the letter in hand, enter Sir Joslin, Sir Oliver, and Rakehell, all
drunk, with Music.

[*They sing*]
>   She's no mistress of mine
>   That drinks not her wine,
>   Or frowns at my friends' drinking motions;
>   If my heart thou would'st gain,
>   Drink thy bottle of champagne.
>   'Twill serve thee for paint and love-potions.

SIR OLIVER Who's here? Courtall, in my lady's company! I'll
dispatch him presently; help me, brother Jolley. [*he draws*]

LADY COCKWOOD For heaven's sake, Sir Oliver!

COURTALL [*drawing*] What do you mean, Sir?

SIR OLIVER I'll teach you more manners, than to make your
attempts on my lady, Sir.

LADY COCKWOOD⎫
             ⎬ [*they shriek*] O! Murder! Murder!
SENTRY   ⎭

LADY COCKWOOD Save my dear Sir Oliver, O my dear Sir
Oliver.

[*The young ladies shriek and run out, they all draw to part 'em, they*
fight off the stage, she shrieks and runs out]

ACT FIVE

SCENE I

Sir Oliver's dining room

Enter Lady Cockwood. Table and carpet★

LADY COCKWOOD I did not think he had been so desperate in his drink; if they had killed one another, I had then been revenged, and freed from all my fears –

Enter Sentry.

Sentry, your carelessness and forgetfulness some time or other will undo me; had not Sir Oliver and Sir Joslin came so luckily into the garden, the letters had been discovered, and my honour left to the mercy of a false man, and two young fleering† girls: did you speak to Mr Freeman unperceived in the hurry?

SENTRY I did, Madam, and he promised me to disengage himself as soon as possibly he could, and wait upon your ladyship with all secrecy.

LADY COCKWOOD I have some reason to believe him a man of honour.

SENTRY Methinks indeed his very look, Madam, speaks him to be much more a gentleman than Mr Courtall, but I was unwilling before now to let your ladyship know my opinion, for fear of offending your inclinations.

LADY COCKWOOD I hope by his means to get these letters into my own hands, and so prevent the inconveniencies they may bring upon my honour.

SENTRY I wonder, Madam, what should be Sir Oliver's quarrel to Mr Courtall.

LADY COCKWOOD You know how apt he is to be suspicious in his drink; 'tis very likely he thought Mr Courtall betrayed him at the Bear today.

SENTRY Pray heaven he be not jealous of your ladyship, finding you abroad so unexpectedly; if he be, we shall have a sad hand of him when he comes home, Madam.

★ carpet: tablecloth.   † fleering: grinning, sneering.

LADY COCKWOOD I should have apprehended it much myself, Sentry, if his drunkenness had not unadvisedly engaged him in his quarrel; as soon as he grows a little sober, I am sure his fear will bring him home, and make him apply himself to me with all humility and kindness; for he is ever underhand fain to use my interest and discretion to make friends to compound these businesses, or to get an order for the securing his person and his honour.

SENTRY I believe verily, Mr Courtall would have been so rude to have killed him, if Mr Freeman and the rest had not civilly interposed their weapons.

LADY COCKWOOD Heavens forbid! Though he be a wicked man, I am obliged in duty to love him: whither did my cousins go after we came home, Sentry?

SENTRY They are at the next door, Madam, laughing and playing lantre-lou,* with my old Lady Loveyouth and her daughters.

LADY COCKWOOD I hope they will not come home then to interrupt my affairs with Mr Freeman: [*knocking without*] Hark! Somebody knocks, it may be him, run down quickly.

SENTRY I fly, Madam.   [*Exit Sentry*]

LADY COCKWOOD Now if he has a real inclination for my person, I'll give him a handsome opportunity to reveal it.

Enter Sentry and Freeman.

FREEMAN Your servant, Madam.

LADY COCKWOOD O Mr Freeman! This unlucky accident has robbed me of all my quiet; I am almost distracted with thinking of the danger Sir Oliver's dear life is in.

FREEMAN You need not fear, Madam, all things will be reconciled again tomorrow.

SENTRY You would not blame my lady's apprehensions, did you but know the tenderness of her affections.

LADY COCKWOOD Mr Courtall is a false and merciless man.

FREEMAN He has always owned a great respect for your ladyship, and I never heard him mention you with the least dishonour.

LADY COCKWOOD He cannot without injuring the truth, heaven knows my innocence: I hope you did not let him know, Sir, of your coming hither.

* lantre-lou: a card game, sometimes spelled lanterloo; later known as loo.

FREEMAN I should never merit the happiness to wait upon you again, had I so abused this extraordinary favour, Madam.

LADY COCKWOOD If I have done anything unbeseeming my honour, I hope you will be just, Sir, and impute it to my fear; I know no man so proper to compose this unfortunate difference as yourself, and if a lady's tears and prayers have power to move you to compassion, I know you will employ your utmost endeavour to preserve me, my dear Sir Oliver.

FREEMAN Do not, Madam, afflict yourself so much, I dare engage my life, his life and honour shall be both secure.

LADY COCKWOOD You are truly noble, Sir; I was so distracted with my fears, that I cannot well remember how we parted at the Spring Garden.

FREEMAN We all divided, Madam: after your ladyship and the young ladies were gone together, Sir Oliver, Sir Joslin, and the company with them, took one boat, and Mr Courtall and I another.

LADY COCKWOOD Then I need not apprehend their meeting again tonight.

FREEMAN You need not, Madam; I left Mr Courtall in his chamber, wondering what should make Sir Oliver draw upon him, and fretting and fuming about the trick that was put upon us with the letters today.

LADY COCKWOOD Oh! I had almost forgot myself; I assure you, Sir, those letters were sent by one that has no inclination to be an enemy of yours. [*knocking below*] Somebody knocks. [*Exit Sentry*] If it be Sir Oliver, I am undone, he will hate me mortally, if he does but suspect I use any secret means to hinder him from justifying his reputation honourably to the world.

Enter Sentry.

SENTRY O Madam! Here is Mr Courtall below in the entry, discharging a coachman; I told him your ladyship was busy, but he would not hear me, and I find, do what I can, he will come up.

LADY COCKWOOD I would not willingly suspect you, Sir.

FREEMAN I have deceived him, Madam, in my coming hither, and am as unwilling he should find me here, as you can be.

LADY COCKWOOD He will not believe my innocent business with

you, but will raise a new scandal on my honour, and publish it to the whole Town.

SENTRY Let him step into the closet, Madam.

LADY COCKWOOD Quick, Sir, quick, I beseech you, I will send him away again immediately. ⟨*Freeman enters closet*⟩

Enter Courtall.

LADY COCKWOOD Mr Courtall! Have you no sense of honour nor modesty left? After so many injuries, to come into our house, and without my approbation rudely press upon my retirement thus?

COURTALL Pray, Madam, hear my business.

LADY COCKWOOD Thy business is maliciously to pursue my ruin; thou comest with a base design to have Sir Oliver catch thee here, and destroy the only happiness I have.

COURTALL I come, Madam, to beg your pardon for the fault I did unwillingly commit, and to know of you the reason of Sir Oliver's quarrel to me.

LADY COCKWOOD Thy guilty conscience is able to tell thee that, vain and ungrateful man!

COURTALL I am innocent, Madam, of all things that may offend him; and I am sure, if you would but hear me, I should remove the justice of your quarrel too.

LADY COCKWOOD You are mistaken, Sir, if you think I am concerned for your going to the Spring Garden this evening; my quarrel is the same with Sir Oliver, and is so just, that thou deserv'st to be poisoned for what thou hast done.

COURTALL Pray, Madam, let me know my fault.

LADY COCKWOOD I blush to think upon't: Sir Oliver, since we came from the Bear, has heard something thou hast said concerning me; but what it is, I could not get him to discover: he told me 'twas enough for me to know he was satisfied of my innocence.

COURTALL This is mere passion, Madam.

LADY COCKWOOD This is the usual revenge of such base men as thou art, when they cannot compass their ends, with their venomous tongues to blast the honour of a lady.

COURTALL This is a sudden alteration, Madam; within these few hours you had a kinder opinion of me.

LADY COCKWOOD 'Tis no wonder you brag of favours behind my back, that have the impudence to upbraid me with kindness to my face; dost thou think I could ever have a good thought of thee, whom I have always found so treacherous in thy friendship to Sir Oliver? [*knock at the door*]

Enter Sentry.

SENTRY O Madam! Here is Sir Oliver come home.

LADY COCKWOOD O heavens! I shall be believed guilty now, and he will kill us both.

COURTALL [*he draws*] I warrant you, Madam, I'll defend your life.

LADY COCKWOOD Oh! There will be murder, murder; for heaven's sake, Sir, hide yourself in some corner or other.

COURTALL I'll step into that closet, Madam.

SENTRY Hold, hold, Sir, by no means; his pipes and his tobacco-box lie there, and he always goes in to fetch 'em.

LADY COCKWOOD Your malice will soon be at an end: heaven knows what will be the fatal consequence of your being found here.

SENTRY Madam, let him creep under the table, the carpet is long enough to hide him.

LADY COCKWOOD Have you good nature enough to save the life and reputation of a lady?

COURTALL Anything to oblige you, Madam. [*he goes under the table*]

LADY COCKWOOD [*running to the closet*] Be sure you do not stir, Sir, whatsoever happens.

COURTALL Not unless he pulls me out by the ears.

SENTRY Good! He thinks my lady speaks to him.

Enter Sir Oliver.

LADY COCKWOOD My dear Sir Oliver –

SIR OLIVER I am unworthy of this kindness, Madam.

LADY COCKWOOD Nay, I intend to chide you for your naughtiness anon; but I cannot choose but hug thee, and kiss thee a little first; I was afraid I should never have had thee alive within these arms again.

SIR OLIVER Your goodness does so increase my shame, I know not what to say, Madam.

LADY COCKWOOD Well, I am glad I have thee safe at home, I will lock thee up above in my chamber, and will not so much as trust thee downstairs, till there be an end of this quarrel.

SIR OLIVER I was so little myself, I knew not what I did, else I had not exposed my person to so much danger before thy face.

SENTRY 'Twas cruelly done, Sir, knowing the killing concerns my lady has for you.

LADY COCKWOOD If Mr Courtall had killed thee, I was resolved not to survive thee; but before I had died I would have dearly revenged thy murder.

SIR OLIVER As soon as I had recollected myself a little, I could not rest till I came home to give thee this satisfaction, that I will do nothing without thy advice and approbation, my dear: I know thy love makes thy life depend upon mine, and it is unreasonable I should upon my own rash head hazard that, though it be for the justification of thy honour. Uds me I have let fall a China orange★ that was recommended to me for one of the best that came over this year. S'life light the candle, Sentry, 'tis run under the table.

LADY COCKWOOD Oh, I am not well!

Sentry takes up the candle, there is a great knocking at the door, she runs away with the candle.

SENTRY O heaven! Who's that that knocks so hastily?

SIR OLIVER Why, Sentry! Bring back the candle; are you mad to leave us in the dark, and your lady not well? How is it, my dear?

LADY COCKWOOD For heaven's sake, run after her, Sir Oliver, snatch the candle out of her hand, and teach her more manners.

SIR OLIVER I will, my dear.   ⟨*Exit Sir Oliver*⟩

LADY COCKWOOD What shall I do? Was ever woman so unfortunate in the management of affairs!

COURTALL What will become of me now?

LADY COCKWOOD It must be so, I had better trust my honour to the mercy of them two, than be betrayed to my husband: Mr Courtall, give me your hand quickly, I beseech you.

COURTALL Here, here, Madam, what's to be done now?

LADY COCKWOOD I will put you into the closet, Sir.

★ China orange: oranges originally came from China. At the time they were a rarity because of the war's effect upon importation.

COURTALL He'll be coming in for his tobacco-box and pipes.

LADY COCKWOOD Never fear that, Sir.

FREEMAN [*out of the closet door*] Now shall I be discovered; pox on your honourable intrigue, would I were safe at Gifford's.*

LADY COCKWOOD Here, here, Sir, this is the door, whatsoever you feel, be not frighted; for should you make the least disturbance, you will destroy the life, and what is more, the honour of an unfortunate lady.

COURTALL So, so, if you have occasion to remove again, make no ceremony, Madam.

Enter Sir Oliver, Sentry, Ariana, Gatty.

SIR OLIVER Here is the candle, how dost thou, my dear?

LADY COCKWOOD I could not imagine, Sentry, you had been so ill-bred, to run away, and leave your master and me in the dark.

SENTRY I thought there had been another candle upon the table, Madam.

LADY COCKWOOD Good! You thought! You are always excusing of your carelessness; such another misdemeanour –

SIR OLIVER Prithee, my dear, forgive her.

LADY COCKWOOD The truth is, I ought not to be very angry with her at present, 'tis a good natured creature; she was so frighted, for fear of thy being mischiefed in the Spring Garden, that I verily believe she scarce knows what she does yet.

SIR OLIVER Light the candle, Sentry, that I may look for my orange.

LADY COCKWOOD You have been at my Lady Loveyouth's, cousins, I hear.

ARIANA We have, Madam.

GATTY She charged us to remember her service to you.

SIR OLIVER So, here it is, my dear, I brought it home on purpose for thee.

LADY COCKWOOD 'Tis a lovely orange indeed! Thank you, my dear; I am so discomposed with the fright I have had that I would fain be at rest.

SIR OLIVER Get a candle, Sentry: will you go to bed, my dear?

LADY COCKWOOD With all my heart, Sir Oliver: 'tis late, cousins, you had best retire to your chamber too.

* Gifford's: a well-known brothel run by Mrs Gifford.

GATTY We shall not stay long here, Madam.

SIR OLIVER Come, my dear.

LADY COCKWOOD Good night, cousins.

GATTY AND ARIANA Your servant, Madam.

[*Exeunt Sir Oliver, Lady Cockwood and Sentry*]

ARIANA I cannot but think of those letters, sister.

GATTY That is, you cannot but think of Mr Freeman, sister, I perceive he runs in thy head as much as a new gown uses to do in the country, the night before 'tis expected from London.

ARIANA You need not talk, for I am sure the losses of an unlucky gamester are not more his meditation, then Mr Courtall is yours.

GATTY He has made some slight impression on my memory, I confess; but I hope a night will wear him out again, as it does the noise of a fiddle after dancing.

ARIANA Love, like some stains, will wear out of itself, I know, but not in such a little time as you talk of, sister.

GATTY It cannot last longer than the stain of a mulberry at most; the next season out that goes, and my heart cannot be long unfruitful, sure.

ARIANA Well, I cannot believe they forged these letters; what should be their end?

GATTY That you may easily guess at; but methinks they took a very improper way to compass it.

ARIANA It looks more like the malice or jealousy of a woman, than the design of two witty men.

GATTY If this should prove a fetch of her ladyship's now, that is a-playing the loving hypocrite above with her dear Sir Oliver.

ARIANA How unluckily we were interrupted, when they were going to show us the hand!

GATTY That might have discovered all: I have a small suspicion, that there has been a little familiarity between her ladyship and Mr Courtall.

ARIANA Our finding of 'em together in the Exchange and several passages I observed at the Bear, have almost made me of the same opinion.

GATTY Yet I would fain believe the continuance of it is more her desire, than his inclination: that which makes me mistrust him most, is her knowing we made 'em an appointment.

ARIANA If she were jealous of Mr Courtall, she would not be jealous of Mr Freeman too; they both pretend to have received letters.

GATTY There is something in it more than we are able to imagine; time will make it out, I hope, to the advantage of the gentlemen.

ARIANA I would gladly have it so; for I believe, should they give us a just cause, we should find it a hard task to hate them.

GATTY How I love the song I learned t'other day, since I saw them in the Mulberry Garden!

[*She sings*]

> To little or no purpose I spent many days,
> In ranging the Park, the Exchange, and th' plays;
> For ne'er in my rambles till now did I prove
> So lucky to meet with the man I could love.
> Oh! How I am pleased when I think on this man,
> That I find I must love, let me do what I can!
>
> 2
>
> How long I shall love him, I can no more tell,
> Than had I a fever, when I should be well.
> My passion shall kill me before I will show it,
> And yet I would give all the world he did know it;
> But O how I sigh, when I think should he woo me,
> I cannot deny what I know would undo me!

ARIANA Fie, sister, thou art so wanton.

GATTY I hate to dissemble when I need not; 'twould look as affected in us to be reserved now we're alone, as for a player to maintain the character she acts in the tiring-room.

ARIANA Prithee sing a good song.

GATTY Now art thou for a melancholy madrigal, composed by some amorous coxcomb, who swears in all companies he loves his mistress so well, that he would not do her the injury, were she willing to grant him the favour, and it may be is sot enough to believe he would oblige her in keeping his oath too.

ARIANA Well, I will reach thee thy guitar out of the closet, to take thee off of this subject.

GATTY I'd rather be a nun, than a lover at thy rate; devotion is not able to make me half so serious as love has made thee already.

Ariana opens the closet, Courtall and Freeman come out.

COURTALL Ha, Freeman! Is this your business with a lawyer? Here's a new discovery, i'faith!

[Ariana and Gatty shriek, and run out]

FREEMAN Peace, man, I will satisfy your jealousy hereafter; since we have made this lucky discovery, let us mind the present business.

[Courtall and Freeman catch the ladies, and bring them back]

COURTALL Nay, ladies, now we have caught you, there is no escaping till w'are come to a right understanding.

Enter Lady Cockwood and Sir Oliver and Sentry.

FREEMAN Come, never blush, we are as loving as you can be for your hearts, I assure you.

COURTALL Had it not been our good fortunes to have been concealed here, you would have had ill nature enough to dissemble with us at least a fortnight longer.

LADY COCKWOOD What's the matter with you here? Are you mad, cousins? Bless me, Mr Courtall and Mr Freeman in our house at these unseasonable hours!

SIR OLIVER Fetch me down my long sword, Sentry, I lay my life Courtall has been tempting the honour of the young ladies.

LADY COCKWOOD O my dear! *[she holds him]*

GATTY We are almost scared out of our wits; my sister went to reach my guitar out of the closet, and found 'em both shut up there.

LADY COCKWOOD Come, come, this will not serve your turn; I am afraid you had a design secretly to convey 'em into your chamber: well, I will have no more of these doings in my family, my dear; Sir Joslin shall remove these girls tomorrow.

FREEMAN You injure the young ladies, Madam; their surprise shows their innocence.

COURTALL If anybody be to blame, it is Mrs Sentry.

SENTRY What mean you, Sir? Heaven knows I know no more of their being here –

COURTALL Nay, nay, Mrs Sentry, you need not be ashamed to own the doing of a couple of young gentlemen such a good office.

SENTRY Do not think to put your tricks upon me, Sir.

COURTALL Understanding by Mrs Sentry, Madam, that these young ladies would very likely sit and talk in the dining-room an hour before they went to bed, of the accidents of the day, and being impatient to know whether that unlucky business which happened in the Spring Garden, about the letters, had quite destroyed our hopes of gaining their esteem; for a small sum of money Mr Freeman and I obtained the favour of her to shut us up where we might over-hear 'em.

LADY COCKWOOD Is this the truth, Sentry?

SENTRY I humbly beg your pardon, Madam.

LADY COCKWOOD [*aside*] A lady's honour is not safe, that keeps a servant so subject to corruption; I will turn her out of my service for this.

SIR OLIVER ⟨*aside*⟩ Good! I was suspicious their business had been with my lady at first.

LADY COCKWOOD ⟨*aside*⟩ Now will I be in charity with him again, for putting this off so handsomely.

SIR OLIVER Hark you my dear, shall I forbid Mr Courtall my house?

LADY COCKWOOD Oh! By no means, my dear; I had forgot to tell thee, since I acquainted thee with that business, I have been discoursing with my Lady Loveyouth, and she blamed me infinitely for letting thee know it, and laughed exceedingly at me, believing Mr Courtall intended thee no injury, and told me 'twas only a harmless gallantry, which his French breeding has used him to.

SIR OLIVER Faith, I am apt enough to believe it; for on my conscience, he is a very honest fellow. Ned Courtall! How the devil came it about that thee and I fell to '*Sa, sa*,' in the Spring Garden?

COURTALL You are best able to resolve yourself that, Sir Oliver.

SIR OLIVER Well, the devil take me, if I had the least unkindness for thee – prithee let us embrace and kiss, and be as good friends as ever we were, dear rogue.

COURTALL I am so reasonable, Sir Oliver, that I will ask no other satisfaction for the injury you have done me.

FREEMAN Here's the letter, Madam.

ARIANA Sister, look here, do you know this hand?

GATTY 'Tis Sentry's.

LADY COCKWOOD O heavens! I shall be ruined yet.

GATTY She has been the contriver of all this mischief.

COURTALL Nay, now you lay too much to her charge in this; she was but my lady's secretary, I assure you, she has discovered the whole plot to us.

SENTRY What does he mean?

LADY COCKWOOD Will he betray me at last?

COURTALL My lady being in her nature severely virtuous, is, it seems, offended at the innocent freedom you take in rambling up and down by yourselves; which made her, out of a tenderness to your reputations, counterfeit these letters, in hopes to fright you to that reservedness which she approves of.

LADY COCKWOOD [*aside*] This has almost redeemed my opinion of his honour. ⟨*aloud*⟩ Cousins, the little regard you had to the good counsel I gave you, put me upon this business.

GATTY Pray, Madam, what was it Mrs Gazette told you concerning us?

LADY COCKWOOD Nothing, nothing, cousins: what I told you of Mr Courtall, was mere invention, the better to carry on my design for your good.

COURTALL Freeman! Pray what brought you hither?

FREEMAN A kind summons from her ladyship.

COURTALL Why did you conceal it from me?

FREEMAN I was afraid thy peevish jealousy might have destroyed the design I had of getting an opportunity to clear ourselves to the young ladies.

COURTALL Fortune has been our friend in that beyond expectation. [*to the ladies*] I hope, ladies, you are satisfied of our innocence now.

GATTY Well, had you been found guilty of the letters, we were resolved to have counterfeited two contracts under your hands, and have suborned witness to swear 'em.

ARIANA That had been a full revenge; for I know you would think it as great a scandal to be thought to have an inclination for marriage, as we should to be believed willing to take our freedom without it.

COURTALL The more probable thing, ladies, had been only to pretend a promise; we have now and then courage enough to venture so far for a valuable consideration.

GATTY The truth is, such experienced gentlemen as you are, seldom mortgage your persons without it be to redeem your estates.

COURTALL 'Tis a mercy we have 'scaped the mischief so long, and are like to do penance only for our own sins; most families are a wedding behind-hand in the world, which makes so many young men fooled into wives, to pay their fathers' debts: all the happiness a gentleman can desire, is to live at liberty, till he be forced that way to pay his own.

FREEMAN Ladies, you know we are not ignorant of the good intentions you have towards us; pray let us treat a little.

GATTY I hope you are not in so desperate a condition, as to have a good opinion of marriage, are you?

ARIANA 'Tis to as little purpose to treat with us of anything under that, as it is for those kind ladies, that have obliged you with a valuable consideration, to challenge the performance of your promise.

SIR OLIVER Well, and how, and how, my dear Ned, goes the business between you and these ladies? Are you like to drive a bargain?

COURTALL Faith, Sir Oliver, we are about it.

SIR OLIVER And cannot agree, I warrant you; they are for having you take a lease for life, and you are for being tenants at will, Ned, is it not so?

GATTY These gentlemen have found it so convenient lying in lodgings, they'll hardly venture on the trouble of taking a house of their own.

COURTALL A pretty country seat, Madam, with a handsome parcel of land, and other necessaries belonging to't, may tempt us; but for a Town-tenement that has but one poor conveniency, we are resolved we'll never deal.

A noise of music without.

SIR OLIVER Hark! My brother Jolley's come home.

ARIANA Now, gentlemen, you had best look to yourselves, and come to an agreement with us quickly; for I'll lay my life, my uncle has brought home a couple of fresh chapmen that will outbid you.

Enter Sir Joslin with music.

SIR JOSLIN Hey boys!

Dance.

[*sings*]   A catch and a glass,
            A fiddle and a lass,
            What more would an honest man have?
            Hang your temperate sot,
            Who would seem what he's not;
            'Tis I am wise, he's but grave.
What's here? Mr Courtall and Mr Freeman!

SIR OLIVER O man! Here has been the prettiest, the luckiest discovery of all sides! We are all good friends again.

SIR JOSLIN Hark you brother Cockwood, I have got Madam Rampant; Rakehell and she are without.

SIR OLIVER O heavens! Dear brother Jolley, send her away immediately, my lady has such an aversion to a naughty woman, that she will swoon if she does but see her.

SIR JOSLIN Faith, I was hard put to't, I wanted a lover, and rather than I would break my old wont, I dressed up Rampant in a suit I bought

Enter Rakehell ⟨and Rampant⟩.

of Rakehell; but since this good company's here, I'll send her away. My little Rakehell, come hither; you see here are two powerful rivals; therefore for fear of kicking, or a worse disaster, take Rampant with you, and be going quickly.

RAKEHELL Your humble servant, Sir.

[Exeunt Rakehell and Rampant]

COURTALL You may hereafter spare yourself this labour, Sir Joslin; Mr Freeman and I have vowed ourselves humble servants to these ladies.

FREEMAN I hope we shall have your approbation, Sir.

SIR JOSLIN Nay, if you have a mind to commit matrimony, I'll send for a canonical sir shall dispatch you presently.

FREEMAN You cannot do better.

COURTALL What think you of taking us in the humour? Consideration may be your foe, ladies.

ARIANA Come, gentlemen, I'll make you a fair proposition; since

you have made a discovery of our inclinations, my sister and I
will be content to admit you in the quality of servants.

GATTY And if after a month's experience of your good behaviour,
upon serious thoughts, you have courage enough to engage further, we will accept of the challenge, and believe you men of
honour.

SIR JOSLIN Well spoke i'faith, girls; and is it a match, boys?

COURTALL If the heart of man be not very deceitful, 'tis very
likely it may be so.

FREEMAN A month is a tedious time, and will be a dangerous trial
of our resolutions; but I hope we shall not repent before marriage,
whate'er we do after.

SIR JOSLIN How stand matters between you and your lady,
brother Cockwood? Is there peace on all sides?

SIR OLIVER Perfect concord, man: I will tell thee all that has happened since I parted from thee, when we are alone, 'twill make
thee laugh heartily. Never man was so happy in a virtuous and
a loving lady!

SIR JOSLIN Though I have led Sir Oliver astray this day or two, I
hope you will not exclude me the Act of Oblivion,★ Madam.

LADY COCKWOOD The nigh relation I have to you, and the respect I know Sir Oliver has for you, makes me forget all that has
passed, Sir; but pray be not the occasion of any new transgres-
sions.

SENTRY I hope, Mr Courtall, since my endeavours to serve you,
have ruined me in the opinion of my lady, you will intercede for
a reconciliation.

COURTALL Most willingly, Mrs Sentry – faith, Madam, since
things have fallen out so luckily, you must needs receive your
woman into favour again.

LADY COCKWOOD Her crime is unpardonable, Sir.

SENTRY Upon solemn protestations, Madam, that the gentlemen's
intentions were honourable, and having reason to believe the
young ladies had no aversion to their inclinations, I was of opinion
I should have been ill-natured, if I had not assisted 'em in the
removing those difficulties that delayed their happiness.

★ Act of Oblivion: a reference to the Act of Oblivion passed at the Restoration.

SIR OLIVER Come, come, girl, confess how many guineas prevailed upon your easy nature.

SENTRY Ten, an't please you, Sir.

SIR OLIVER S'life, a sum able to corrupt an honest man in office! Faith you must forgive her, my dear.

LADY COCKWOOD If it be your pleasure, Sir Oliver, I cannot but be obedient.

SENTRY ⟨*aside*⟩ If Sir Oliver, Madam, should ask me to see his gold, all may be discovered yet.

LADY COCKWOOD ⟨*aside*⟩ If he does, I will give thee ten guineas out of my cabinet.

SENTRY ⟨*aside*⟩ I shall take care to put him upon't, 'tis fit, that I who have bore all the blame, should have some reasonable reward for't.

COURTALL I hope, Madam, you will not envy me the happiness I am to enjoy with your fair relation.

LADY COCKWOOD Your ingenuity and goodness, Sir, have made a perfect atonement for you.

COURTALL Pray, Madam, what was your business with Mr Freeman?

LADY COCKWOOD Only to oblige him to endeavour a reconciliation between you and Sir Oliver; for though I was resolved never to see your face again, it was death to me to think your life was in danger.

SENTRY What a miraculous come off is this, Madam!

LADY COCKWOOD It has made me so truly sensible of those dangers to which an aspiring lady must daily expose her honour, that I am resolved to give over the great business of this Town, and hereafter modestly confine myself to the humble affairs of my own family.

COURTALL 'Tis a very pious resolution, Madam, and the better to confirm you in it, pray entertain an able chaplain.

LADY COCKWOOD Certainly fortune was never before so unkind to the ambition of a lady.

SIR JOSLIN Come, boys, faith we will have a dance before we go to bed – Sly-girl and Mad-cap, give me your hands, that I may give 'em to these gentlemen, a parson shall join you ere long, and then you will have authority to dance to some purpose: brother

Cockwood, take out your lady, I am for Mrs Sentry.

⟨*sings*⟩ We'll foot it and side it, my pretty little miss,

And when we are aweary, we'll lie down and kiss.

Play away, boys.

They dance.

COURTALL [*to Gatty*] Now shall I sleep as little without you, as I should do with you: Madam, expectation makes me almost as restless as jealousy.

FREEMAN Faith, let us dispatch this business; yet I never could find the pleasure of waiting for a dish of meat, when a man was heartily hungry.

GATTY Marrying in this heat would look as ill as fighting in your drink.

ARIANA And be no more a proof of love, than t'other is of valour.

SIR JOSLIN Never trouble your heads further; since I perceive you are all agreed on the matter, let me alone to hasten the ceremony: come, gentlemen, lead 'em to their chambers; brother Cockwood, do you show the way with your lady. Ha Mrs Sentry!

[*sings*] I gave my love a green-gown

I'th merry month of May,

And down she fell as wantonly,

As a tumbler does at play.

Hey boys, lead away boys.

SIR OLIVER Give me thy hand, my virtuous, my dear;

Henceforwards may our mutual loves increase,

And when we are abed, we'll sign the peace.

[*Exeunt Omnes*]

NOTES

The copy text used is that of the first edition of 1668 in the Brotherton Collection, University of Leeds.

Abbreviations
  Q1 The first quarto edition, 1668–71
  Q2 The second quarto edition, 1693
  Q3 The third quarto edition, 1704
  O1 The first octavo edition, 1700

The variant spelling of Sir Joslin Jolley's surname has been regularised to 'Jolley' throughout.

226.16   family. Well / family : Well Q1
229.34   taking all the days Q3 / taking days Q1
231.13   that she has Q2 / that there has Q1
232.8   stays / stay's Q1
236.19   crave? / crave. Q1
243.18   heaven's / heaven Q1
246.12   ARIANA   } / Ambo Q1
246.13   GATTY
255.23   *All go . . . Cockwood* Q3 / precedes Gazette's speech Q1
262.13   in readiness Q2 / in a readiness Q1
271.32   ladies / lady's Q1
273.9   names Q3 / name Q1
293.18   year. / year ; Q1
293.19   Q1 prints *knock* before Lady Cockwood's speech
297.3   *Ariana and Gatty* / *They* Q1
298.3   bed, of / bed ; of Q1
299.14   put O1 / puts Q1
301.16   swoon O1 / swound Q1

SIR MARTIN MAR-ALL
by John Dryden

INTRODUCTION

John Dryden (1631–1700) was born in Northamptonshire in the vicarage of Aldwinkle All Saints. He attended Westminster School, then went to Trinity College, Cambridge. He married Lady Elizabeth Howard in 1663, became Poet Laureate in 1668 and Historiographer Royal in 1670. At the Revolution, Dryden, having refused to take the oaths, lost his laureateship and a post he had held in the Customs since 1683.

In 1658 he began his literary career with 'Heroic Stanzas' on the death of Cromwell; there followed in 1660 'Astraea Redux' on the return of Charles II. His 'Annus Mirabilis' of 1667 contained a brilliant description of the Fire of London and a prophecy of England's future mercantile greatness. He wrote or collaborated in nearly thirty plays, including comedies, tragi-comedies, heroic tragedies, and operas as well as *All for Love; or, The World Well Lost* (1678), a blank verse adaptation of Shakespeare's *Antony and Cleopatra*. His *Essay on Dramatic Poesy* (1668) was a notable piece of criticism. In the sixteen-eighties Dryden wrote satirical and didactic poems, including 'Absalom and Achitophel' (1681), 'The Medal' (1682), 'Religio Laici' (1682), and 'Mac Flecknoe' (1684), and, after his conversion to Roman Catholicism, 'The Hind and the Panther' (1687). The last part of his life was spent on translating classical authors and paraphrasing tales from Ovid, Boccaccio and Chaucer, which were published in 1699, a year before his death and burial in Chaucer's grave at Westminster Abbey.

Dryden, as befitted a man of letters, knew the taste of his contemporaries and responded to it. He realised their enthusiasm for comedy and though he did not think he himself had any gift for it, indeed felt he lacked 'that gaiety of humour which is required to it', he succeeded in writing many good comedies. He began with *The Wild Gallant* in 1663, an indecent blasphemous play, which contained much farce and repartee, often vulgar. *Sir Martin Mar-all*, first published in 1668, was more humorous. Pepys certainly enjoyed it. He couldn't get into the theatre on 15 August 1667 (probably the first performance), the audience being so large, swollen as it was by the king and his courtiers. The next day he was able to get a place and wrote:

'. . . we saw the new play acted yesterday, 'The Feign Innocdnce, or Sir Martin Marr-all': a play made by my Lord Duke of Newcastle, but, as everybody says, corrected by Dryden. It is the most entire piece of mirth, a complete farce from one end to the other, that certainly ever was writ. I never laughed so much in my life. I laughed till my head [ached?] all the evening and night with the laughing, and at very good wit therein, not fooling.'

He was frequently to see the play and after he thought he had seen it ten times he still had as great pleasure in it. The play obviously appealed enormously to Restoration audiences. It is difficult to trace its history fully, but it seems, according to Colley Cibber, to have retained its popularity to 1690, while John Downes in *Roscius Anglianus* (1708) reported it made more money for the company than any preceding comedy except Etherege's *Love in a Tub*. It was acted in the eighteenth century up to 1728.

The reason for the outstanding success of the play was primarily the suitability of Sir Martin's part for the actor John Nokes, renowned for his 'dumb studious pout', his rolling his 'full eye into such a vacant amazement' and his 'silent perplexity'. The rest of the cast was well chosen, with Cave Underhill as Old Moody, Mrs Norris as Lady Dupe, and Mary Davis as Millisent.

The Duke of Newcastle was supposed to have given Dryden a translation he had made of *L'Etourdi* by Molière, which Dryden used as a basis for *Sir Martin Mar-all*, borrowing also from Philippe Quinault's *L'Amant indiscret*. The play was not ascribed to Dryden until 1688, when it was listed in Gerard Langbaine's *Momus Triumphans; or, The Plagiaries of the English Stage*; Langbaine in a later work, *An Account of the English Dramatick Poets* (1691), remarked that the play was generally ascribed to Dryden though his name was not affixed to it.

The play is Jonsonian in its nature: there is a Jonsonian interest in many odd characters, in everyday subjects, and in sex, all held together by a relatively slight plot, which indeed shows signs of revision and improvisation – notably in the case of Warner the servant suddenly revealing he is a gentleman. The play's morality is dubious: the financial returns from the duplicity of Lady Dupe and Mrs Christian are considerable: Sir Martin is likely to continue in his foolishness, unredeemed by satire; Lord Dartmouth suffers monetary loss. But these were not the preoccupations of Dryden nor of the Duke of Newcastle. They were interested in creating amusing scenes and situations and in satirising eccentricities of human behaviour. Pepy's judgment remains a good one: it is farcical, not all fooling, and it is, at times, very funny indeed.

A scene from Sir Martin Mar-All

Sir Martin Mar-All

or the
Feigned Innocence

A COMEDY

As it was Acted at
His Highness the Duke of York's
Theatre

LONDON

Printed for H. Herringman, at the Sign of the Blue Anchor
in the Lower walk of the New Exchange.
1668

DRAMATIS PERSONAE

⟨MEN⟩
Lord Dartmouth	In love with Mrs Christian.
Mr Moody	The swashbuckler.
Sir Martin Mar-all	A fool.
Warner	His man.
Sir John Swallow	A Kentish knight.

⟨WOMEN⟩
Lady Dupe	The old lady.
Mrs Christian	Her young niece.
Mrs Millisent	The swashbuckler's daughter.
Rose	Her maid.
Mrs Preparation	Woman to the old lady.

Other Servants, Men and Women. A Carrier. Bailiffs.

The Scene Covent Garden.

PROLOGUE

Fools, which each man meets in his dish each day,
Are yet the great regalios* of a play;
In which to poets you but just appear,
To prize that highest which costs them so dear:
Fops in the Town more easily will pass;
One story makes a statutable ass:
But such in plays must be much thicker sown,
Like yolks of eggs, a dozen beat to one.
Observing poets all their walks invade,
As men watch woodcocks gliding through a glade:
And when they have enough for comedy,
They stow their several bodies in a pie:
The poet's but the cook to fashion it,
For, gallants, you yourselves have found the wit.
To bid you welcome would your bounty wrong,
None welcome those who bring their cheer along.

* regalios: objects of delight, entertainments or food.

ACT ONE

⟨SCENE I⟩

Enter Warner solus

WARNER Where the devil is this master of mine? He is ever out of the way when he should do himself good. This 'tis to serve a coxcomb, one that has no more brains than just those I carry for him. Well! Of all fops commend me to him for the greatest; he's so opinioned of his own abilities, that he is ever designing somewhat, and yet he sows his stratagems so shallow, that every daw can pick 'em up: from a plotting fool the Lord deliver me. Here he comes, Oh! It seems his cousin's with him, then it is not so bad as I imagined.

Enter Sir Martin Mar-all, Lady Dupe.

LADY DUPE I think 'twas well contrived for your access to lodge her in the same house with you.

SIR MARTIN MAR-ALL 'Tis pretty well, I must confess.

WARNER [*aside*] Had he plotted it himself, it had been admirable.

LADY DUPE For when her father Moody wrote to me to take him lodgings, I so ordered it, the choice seemed his, not mine.

SIR MARTIN MAR-ALL I have hit of a thing myself sometimes, when wiser heads have missed it. – But that might be mere luck.

LADY DUPE Fortune does more than wisdom.

SIR MARTIN MAR-ALL Nay, for that you shall excuse me; I will not value any man's fortune at a rush,★ except he have wit and parts to bear him out. But when do you expect 'em?

LADY DUPE This tide will bring them from Gravesend. You had best let your man go as from me, and wait them at the stairs in Durham Yard.†

SIR MARTIN MAR-ALL Lord, cousin, what a do is here with your counsel! As though I could not have thought of that myself. I could find in my heart not to send him now – stay a little – I could soon find out some other way.

WARNER A minute's stay may lose your business.

SIR MARTIN MAR-ALL Well, go then, – but you must grant, if he had stayed, I could have found a better way, – you grant it.

★ at a rush: cheaply, at a fig.   † Durham Yard: a landing place on the Thames.

LADY DUPE For once I will not stand with you. –

[Exit Warner]

'Tis a sweet gentlewoman this Mrs Millisent, if you can get her.

SIR MARTIN MAR-ALL Let me alone for plotting.

LADY DUPE But by your favour, Sir, 'tis not so easy, her father has already promised her: and the young gentleman comes up with 'em: I partly know the man, – but the old squire is humoursome, he's stout, and plain in speech and in behaviour; he loves none of the fine Town-tricks of breeding, but stands up for the old Elizabeth way in all things. This we must work upon.

SIR MARTIN MAR-ALL Sure! You think you have to deal with a fool, cousin?

Enter Mrs Christian.

LADY DUPE *[whispers]* O my dear niece, I have some business with you.

SIR MARTIN MAR-ALL Well, Madam, I'll take one turn here i'th Piazzas;* a thousand things are hammering in this head; 'tis a fruitful noddle, though I say it.　　　　*[Exit Sir Martin]*

LADY DUPE Go thy ways for a most conceited fool. – But to our business, cousin: you are young, but I am old, and have had all the love-experience that a discreet lady ought to have; and therefore let me instruct you about the love this rich lord makes to you.

MRS CHRISTIAN You know, Madam, he's married, so that we cannot work upon that ground of matrimony.

LADY DUPE But there are advantages enough for you, if you will be wise and follow my advice.

MRS CHRISTIAN Madam, my friends left me to your care, therefore I will wholly follow your counsel with secrecy and obedience.

LADY DUPE Sweetheart, it shall be the better for you another day: well then, this lord that pretends to you is crafty and false, as most men are, especially in love; – therefore we must be subtle to meet with all his plots, and have countermines against his works to blow him up.

MRS CHRISTIAN As how, Madam?

LADY DUPE Why, girl, he'll make fierce love to you, but you must not suffer him to ruffle you or steal a kiss: but you must weep and

* Piazzas: an arcade in Covent Garden, built by Inigo Jones.

sigh, and say you'll tell me on't, and that you will not be used so; and play the innocent just like a child, and seem ignorant of all.

MRS CHRISTIAN I warrant you I'll be very ignorant, Madam.

LADY DUPE And be sure when he has towsed you, not to appear at supper that night, that you may fright him.   ·

MRS CHRISTIAN No, Madam.

LADY DUPE That he may think you have told me.

MRS CHRISTIAN Aye, Madam.

LADY DUPE And keep your chamber, and say your head aches.

MRS CHRISTIAN Oh, most extremely, Madam.

LADY DUPE And lock the door, and admit of no night visits: at supper I'll ask where's my cousin, and being told you are not well, I'll start from the table to visit you, desiring his lordship not to incommode himself; for I will presently wait on him again.

MRS CHRISTIAN But how, when you are returned, Madam?

LADY DUPE Then somewhat discomposed, I'll say I doubt the measles or smallpox will seize on you, and then the girl is spoiled; saying, 'Poor thing, her portion is her beauty and her virtue'; and often send to see how you do, by whispers in my servants' ears, and have those whispers of your health returned to mine: if his lordship thereupon asks how you do, I will pretend it was some other thing.

MRS CHRISTIAN Right, Madam, for that will bring him further in suspense.

LADY DUPE A hopeful girl! Then will I eat nothing that night, feigning my grief for you; but keep his lordship company at meal, and seem to strive to put my passion off, yet show it still by small mistakes.

MRS CHRISTIAN And broken sentences.

LADY DUPE A dainty girl! And after supper visit you again, with promise to return straight to his lordship: but after I am gone send an excuse, that I have given you a cordial, and mean to watch that night in person with you.

MRS CHRISTIAN His lordship then will find the prologue of his trouble, doubting I have told you of his ruffling.

LADY DUPE And more than that, fearing his father should know of it, and his wife, who is a termagant lady: but when he finds the coast is clear, and his late ruffling known to none but you, he will be drunk with joy.

MRS CHRISTIAN Finding my simple innocence, which will inflame him more.

LADY DUPE Then what the lion's skin has failed him in, the fox's subtlety must next supply, and that is just, sweetheart, as I would have it; for crafty folks' treaties are their advantage: especially when his passion must be satisfied at any rate, and you keep shop to set the price of love: so now you see the market is your own.

MRS CHRISTIAN Truly, Madam, this is very rational; and by the blessing of heaven upon my poor endeavours, I do not doubt to play my part.

LADY DUPE My blessing and my prayers go along with thee.

Enter Sir John Swallow, Mrs Millisent, and Rose her maid.

MRS CHRISTIAN I believe, Madam, here is the young heiress you expect, and with her he who is to marry her.

LADY DUPE Howe'er I am Sir Martin's friend, I must not seem his enemy.*

SIR JOHN SWALLOW Madam, this fair young lady begs the honour to be known to you.

MRS MILLISENT My father made me hope it, Madam.

LADY DUPE Sweet lady, I believe you have brought all the freshness of the country up to Town with you. [*they salute*]

MRS MILLISENT I came up, Madam, as we country-gentlewomen use, at an Easter Term, to the destruction of tarts and cheese-cakes, to see a new play, buy a new gown, take a turn in the Park, and so down again to sleep with my forefathers.

SIR JOHN SWALLOW Rather, Madam, you are come up to the breaking of many a poor heart, that like mine, will languish for you.

MRS CHRISTIAN I doubt, Madam, you are indisposed with your voyage; will you please to see the lodgings your father has provided for you?

MRS MILLISENT To wait upon you, Madam.

LADY DUPE This is the door, – [*in whisper*] there is a gentleman

* his enemy: i.e. Sir John's.

will wait you immediately in your lodging, if he might presume
on your commands.

MRS MILLISENT [*in whisper*] You mean Sir Martin Mar-all: I am
glad he has entrusted his passion with so discreet a person. ⟨*aloud*⟩
Sir John, let me entreat you to stay here, that my father may have
intelligence where to find us.

SIR JOHN SWALLOW I shall obey you, Madam.

[*Exeunt Women*]

Enter Sir Martin.

SIR JOHN SWALLOW Sir Martin Mar-all! Most happily encountered! How long have you been come to Town?

SIR MARTIN MAR-ALL Some three days since, or thereabouts:
but I thank God I am very weary on't already.

SIR JOHN SWALLOW Why what's the matter, man?

SIR MARTIN MAR-ALL My villainous old luck still follows me
in gaming, I never throw the dice out of my hand, but my gold
goes after 'em: if I go to piquet,★ though it be but with a novice
in't, he will picque and repicque, and capot me twenty times together: and which most mads me, I lose all my sets, when I want
but one of up.†

SIR JOHN SWALLOW The pleasure of play is lost, when one loses
at that unreasonable rate.

SIR MARTIN MAR-ALL But I have sworn not to touch either
cards or dice this half year.

SIR JOHN SWALLOW The oaths of losing gamesters are most
minded; they foreswear play as an angry servant does his mistress,
because he loves her but too well.

SIR MARTIN MAR-ALL But I am now taken up with thoughts of
another nature; I am in love, Sir.

SIR JOHN SWALLOW That's the worst game you could have
played at, scarce one woman in an hundred will play with you
upon the square: you venture at more uncertainty than at a
lottery: for you set your heart to a whole sex of blanks.‡ But is
your mistress widow, wife, or maid?

★ piquet: a card game, in which picque, repicque and capot are scoring plays.
† want but one of up: need only one point to win.
‡ blanks: unsuccessful lottery tickets.

SIR MARTIN MAR-ALL I can assure you, Sir, mine is a maid; the heiress of a wealthy family, fair to a miracle.

SIR JOHN SWALLOW Does she accept your service?

SIR MARTIN MAR-ALL I am the only person in her favour.

Enter Warner.

SIR JOHN SWALLOW Is she of Town or country?

WARNER [*aside*] How's this?

SIR MARTIN MAR-ALL She is of Kent, near Canterbury.

WARNER [*aside*] What does he mean? This is his rival –

SIR JOHN SWALLOW Near Canterbury say you? I have a small estate lies thereabouts, and more concernments than one besides.

SIR MARTIN MAR-ALL I'll tell you then, being at Canterbury; it was my fortune once in the cathedral church –

WARNER What do you mean, Sir, to entrust this man with your affairs thus? –

SIR MARTIN MAR-ALL Trust him? Why, he's a friend of mine.

WARNER No matter for that; hark you a word Sir. –

SIR MARTIN MAR-ALL Prithee leave fooling: – and as I was saying – I was in the church when I first saw this fair one.

SIR JOHN SWALLOW Her name, Sir, I beseech you.

WARNER For heaven's sake, Sir, have a care.

SIR MARTIN MAR-ALL Thou art such a coxcomb. – Her name's Millisent.

WARNER Now, the pox take you Sir, what do you mean?

SIR JOHN SWALLOW 'Millisent' say you? That's the name of my mistress.

SIR MARTIN MAR-ALL Lord! What luck is that now! Well Sir, it happened, one of her gloves fell down, I stooped to take it up; and in the stooping made her a compliment. –

WARNER ⟨*aside*⟩ The devil cannot hold him, now will this thick-skulled master of mine, tell the whole story to his rival. –

SIR MARTIN MAR-ALL You'll say, 'twas strange Sir; but at the first glance we cast on one another, both our hearts leaped within us, our souls met at our eyes, and with a tickling kind of pain slid to each other's breast, and in one moment settled as close and warm as if they long had been acquainted with their lodging. I followed her somewhat at a distance, because her father was with her.

WARNER Yet hold Sir –

SIR MARTIN MAR-ALL Saucy rascal, avoid my sight; must you tutor me? So Sir, not to trouble you, I enquired out her father's house, without whose knowledge I did court the daughter, and both then and often since coming to Canterbury, I received many proofs of her kindness to me.

WARNER You had best tell him too, that I am acquainted with her maid, and manage your love underhand with her.

SIR MARTIN MAR-ALL Well remembered i'faith, I thank thee for that, I had forgot it I protest! My *valet de chambre*, whom you see here with me, grows me acquainted with her woman –

WARNER O the devil. –

SIR MARTIN MAR-ALL In fine Sir, this maid being much in her mistress's favour, so well solicited my cause, that in fine I gained from fair Mistress Millisent an assurance of her kindness, and an engagement to marry none but me.

WARNER 'Tis very well! You've made a fair discovery! –

SIR JOHN SWALLOW A most pleasant relation I assure you: you are a happy man Sir! But what occasion brought you now to London?

SIR MARTIN MAR-ALL That was in expectation to meet my mistress here; she writ me word from Canterbury, she and her father shortly would be here.

SIR JOHN SWALLOW She and her father, said you Sir?

WARNER Tell him Sir, for heaven's sake tell him all –

SIR MARTIN MAR-ALL So I will Sir, without your bidding: her father and she are come up already, that's the truth on't, and are to lodge by my contrivance in yon house; the master of which is a cunning rascal as any in Town – him I have made my own, for I lodge there.

WARNER You do ill Sir to speak so scandalously of my landlord.

SIR MARTIN MAR-ALL Peace, or I'll break your fool's head – So that by his means I shall have free egress and regress when I please Sir – without her father's knowledge.

WARNER I am out of patience to hear this. –

SIR JOHN SWALLOW Methinks you might do well, Sir, to speak openly to her father.

SIR MARTIN MAR-ALL Thank you for that i'faith, in speaking to old Moody I may soon spoil all.

WARNER So now he has told her father's name, 'tis past recovery.

SIR JOHN SWALLOW Is her father's name Moody say you?

SIR MARTIN MAR-ALL Is he of your acquaintance?

SIR JOHN SWALLOW Yes Sir, I know him for a man who is too wise for you to over-reach; I am certain he will never marry his daughter to you.

SIR MARTIN MAR-ALL Why, there's the jest on't: he shall never know it: 'tis but your keeping of my counsel; I'll do as much for you mun. –*

SIR JOHN SWALLOW No Sir, I'll give you better; trouble not yourself about this lady; her affections are otherwise engaged to my knowledge – hark in your ear – her father hates a gamester like the devil: I'll keep your counsel for that too.

SIR MARTIN MAR-ALL Nay but this is not all dear Sir John.

SIR JOHN SWALLOW This is all I assure you; only I will make bold to seek your mistress out another lodging. –   [*Exit Sir John*]

WARNER Your affairs are now put into an excellent posture, thank your incomparable discretion – this was a stratagem my shallow wit could ne'er have reached, to make a confident of my rival.

SIR MARTIN MAR-ALL I hope thou art not in earnest man! Is he my rival?

WARNER S'life he has not found it out all this while! Well Sir for a quick apprehension let you alone.

SIR MARTIN MAR-ALL How the devil cam'st thou to know on't? And why the devil didst thou not tell me on't?

WARNER To the first of your devil's I answer, her maid Rose told me on't: to the second I wish a thousand devils take him that would not hear me.

SIR MARTIN MAR-ALL O unparalleled misfortune!

WARNER O unparalleled ignorance! Why he left her father at the waterside, while he led the daughter to her lodging, whither I directed him; so that if you had not laboured to the contrary,

* mun: dialect form of man.

fortune had placed you in the same house with your mistress, without the least suspicion of your rival or of her father: but 'tis well, you have satisfied your talkative humour; I hope you have some new project of your own to set all right again: for my part I confess all my designs for you are wholly ruined; the very foundations of 'em are blown up.

SIR MARTIN MAR-ALL Prithee insult not over the destiny of a poor undone lover, I am punished enough for my indiscretion in my despair, and have nothing to hope for now but death.

WARNER Death is a bug-word,★ things are not brought to that extremity, I'll cast about to save all yet.

Enter Lady Dupe.

LADY DUPE Oh, Sir Martin! Yonder has been such a stir within. Sir John, I fear, smokes your design, and by all means would have the old man remove his lodging; pray God your man has not played false.

WARNER Like enough I have: I am coxcomb sufficient to do it, my master knows that none but such a great calf as I could have done it, such an over-grown ass, a self-conceited idiot as I. –

SIR MARTIN MAR-ALL Nay, Warner, –

WARNER Pray, Sir, let me alone: – what is it to you if I rail upon myself? How could I break my own loggerhead.†

SIR MARTIN MAR-ALL Nay, sweet Warner.

WARNER What a good master have I, and I to ruin him: O beast! –

LADY DUPE Not to discourage you wholly, Sir Martin, this storm is partly over.

SIR MARTIN MAR-ALL As how, dear cousin?

LADY DUPE When I heard Sir John complain of the landlord, I took the first hint of it, and joined with him, saying, if he were such a one, I would have nothing to do with him: in short, I rattled him so well, that Sir John was the first who did desire they might be lodged with me, not knowing that I was your kinswoman.

SIR MARTIN MAR-ALL Pox on't, now I think on't, I could have found out this myself. –

WARNER Are you there again, Sir? – Now as I have a soul. –

★ bug-word: a terrifying word, from bogey, or bugaboo.
† loggerhead: blockhead.

SIR MARTIN MAR-ALL Mum, good Warner, I did but forget myself a little, I leave myself wholly to you, and my cousin; get but my mistress for me, and claim whate'er reward you can desire.

WARNER Hope of reward will diligence beget;

Find you the money, and I'll find the wit.

[Exeunt]

ACT TWO

⟨SCENE I⟩

Enter Lady Dupe, and Mrs Christian.

MRS CHRISTIAN It happened Madam, just as you said it would, but was he so concerned for my feigned sickness?

LADY DUPE So much that Moody and his daughter, our new guests, took notice of the trouble, but the cause was kept too close for strangers to divine.

MRS CHRISTIAN Heaven grant he be but deep enough in love, and then –

LADY DUPE And then thou shalt distill him into gold my girl. Yonder he comes, I'll not be seen: – you know your lesson, child.

[*Exit*]

MRS CHRISTIAN I warrant you.

Enter Lord Dartmouth.

LORD DARTMOUTH Pretty Mistress Christian, how glad am I to meet you thus alone!

MRS CHRISTIAN O the father! What will become of me now?

LORD DARTMOUTH No harm I warrant you, but why are you so 'fraid?

MRS CHRISTIAN A poor weak innocent creature as I am, heaven of his mercy, how I quake and tremble! I have not yet clawed off★ your last ill-usage, and now I feel my old fit come again, my ears tingle already, and my back shuts and opens; aye, just so it began before.

LORD DARTMOUTH Nay, my sweet mistress, be not so unjust to suspect any new attempt: I am too penitent for my last fault, so soon to sin again, – I hope you did not tell it to your aunt.

MRS CHRISTIAN The more fool I, I did not.

LORD DARTMOUTH You never shall repent your goodness to me, but may not I presume there was some little kindness in it, which moved you to conceal my crime?

MRS CHRISTIAN Methought I would not have mine aunt angry with you for all this earthly good. But yet I'll never be alone with you again.

★ clawed off: got rid of.

LORD DARTMOUTH Pretty innocence! Let me sit nearer to you: you do not understand what love I bear you: I vow it is so pure – my soul's not sullied with one spot of sin: were you a sister or a daughter to me, with a more holy flame I could not burn.

MRS CHRISTIAN Nay, now you speak high words – I cannot understand you.

LORD DARTMOUTH The business of my life shall be but how to make your fortune, and my care and study to advance and see you settled in the world.

MRS CHRISTIAN I humbly thank your lordship.

LORD DARTMOUTH Thus I would sacrifice my life and fortunes, and in return you cruelly destroy me.

MRS CHRISTIAN I never meant you any harm, not I.

LORD DARTMOUTH Then what does this white enemy so near me? [*touching her hand gloved*] Sure 'tis your champion, and you arm it thus to bid defiance to me.

MRS CHRISTIAN [*pulling her hand away*] Nay fie my Lord, in faith you are to blame.

LORD DARTMOUTH [*pulls at her glove*] But I am for fair wars, an enemy must first be searched for privy armour, e'er we do engage.

MRS CHRISTIAN What does your lordship mean?

LORD DARTMOUTH I fear you bear some spells and charms about you, and, Madam, that's against the laws of arms.

MRS CHRISTIAN My aunt charged me not to pull off my glove for fear of sunburning my hand.

LORD DARTMOUTH She did well to keep it from your eyes,* [*hugging her bare hand*] but I will thus preserve it.

MRS CHRISTIAN Why do you crush it so? Nay now you hurt me, nay – if you squeeze it ne'er so hard – there's nothing to come out on't – fie – is this loving one – what makes you take your breath so short?

LORD DARTMOUTH The devil take me if I can answer her a word, all my senses are quite employed another way.

MRS CHRISTIAN Ne'er stir my lord, I must cry out –

LORD DARTMOUTH Then I must stop your mouth – this ruby for a kiss – that is but one ruby for another.

MRS CHRISTIAN This is worse and worse.

* eyes: which would burn like the sun.

LADY DUPE [*within*] Why niece, where are you niece?

LORD DARTMOUTH Pox of her old mouldy chops.*

MRS CHRISTIAN Do you hear, my aunt calls? I shall be hanged for staying with you – let me go my lord. [*gets from him*]

Enter Lady Dupe.

LADY DUPE My lord, heaven bless me, what makes your lordship here?

LORD DARTMOUTH I was just wishing for you Madam, your niece and I have been so laughing at the blunt humour of your country gentleman, – I must go pass an hour with him.

[*Exit Lord Dartmouth*]

MRS CHRISTIAN You made a little too much haste; I was just exchanging a kiss for a ruby.

LADY DUPE No harm done; it will make him come on the faster: never full-gorge an hawk you mean to fly: the next will be a necklace of pearl I warrant you.

MRS CHRISTIAN But what must I do next?

LADY DUPE Tell him I grew suspicious, and examined you whether he made not love; which you denied. Then tell him how my maids and daughters watch you, so that you tremble when you see his lordship.

MRS CHRISTIAN And that your daughters are so envious, that they would raise a false report to ruin me.

LADY DUPE Therefore you desire his lordship, as he loves you, of which you are confident, henceforward to forbear his visits to you.

MRS CHRISTIAN But how if he should take me at my word?

LADY DUPE Why, if the worst come to the worst, he leaves you an honest woman, and there's an end on't: but fear not that, hold out his messages, and then he'll write, and that is it my bird which you must drive it to: then all his letters will be such ecstasies, such vows and promises, which you must answer short and simply, yet still ply out of 'em your advantages.

MRS CHRISTIAN But Madam! He's i' th' house, he will not write.

LADY DUPE You fool – he'll write from the next chamber to you.

* chops: jaws.

And rather than fail, send his page post with it upon a hobby-horse: – then grant a meeting, but tell me of it, and I'll prevent him by my being there; he'll curse me, but I care not. When you are alone, he'll urge his lust, which answer you with scorn and anger. –

MRS CHRISTIAN As thus an't please you, Madam? What? Does he think I will be damned for him? Defame my family, ruin my name, to satisfy his pleasure?

LADY DUPE Then he will be profane in's arguments, urge nature's laws to you.

MRS CHRISTIAN By'r Lady, and those are shrewd arguments. But I am resolved I'll stop my ears.

LADY DUPE Then when he sees no other thing will move you, he'll sign a portion to you beforehand. Take hold of that, and then of what you will. [*Exeunt*]

⟨SCENE II⟩

Enter Sir John, Mrs Millisent, and Rose.

SIR JOHN SWALLOW Now fair Mrs Millisent, you see your chamber. Your father will be busy a few minutes, and in the meantime permits me the happiness to wait on you. –

MRS MILLISENT Methinks you might have chose us better lodgings, this house is full; the other we saw first, was more convenient.

SIR JOHN SWALLOW For you perhaps, but not for me: you might have met a lover there, but I a rival.

MRS MILLISENT What rival?

SIR JOHN SWALLOW You know Sir Martin, I need not name him to you.

MRS MILLISENT I know more men besides him.

SIR JOHN SWALLOW But you love none besides him, can you deny your affection to him?

MRS MILLISENT You have vexed me so, I will not satisfy you.

SIR JOHN SWALLOW Then I perceive I am not likely to be so much obliged to you as I was to him.

MRS MILLISENT This is romance, – I'll not believe a word on't. –

SIR JOHN SWALLOW That's as you please: however 'tis believed, his wit will not much credit your choice. Madam, do justice to us both; pay his ingratitude and folly with your scorn; my service with your love. By this time your father stays for me: I shall be discreet enough to keep this fault of yours from him; the lawyers wait for us to draw your jointure: and I would beg your pardon for my absence, but that my crime is punished in itself.   [*Exit*]

MRS MILLISENT Could I suspect this usage from a favoured servant!

ROSE First hear Sir Martin ere you quite condemn him; consider 'tis a rival who accused him.

MRS MILLISENT Speak not a word in his behalf: – methought too, Sir John called him fool.

ROSE Indeed he has a rare way of acting a fool, and does it so naturally, it can be scarce distinguished.

MRS MILLISENT Nay, he has wit enough, that's certain.

ROSE ⟨*aside*⟩ How blind love is!

Enter Warner.

MRS MILLISENT How now, what's his business? I wonder after such a crime, if his master has the face to send him to me.

ROSE How durst you venture hither? If either Sir John or my old master see you.

WARNER Pish! They are both gone out.

ROSE They went but to the next street; ten to one but they return and catch you here.

WARNER Twenty to one I am gone before, and save 'em a labour.

MRS MILLISENT What says that fellow to you? What business can he have here?

WARNER Lord, that your ladyship should ask that question, knowing whom I serve!

MRS MILLISENT I'll hear nothing from your master.

WARNER Never breathe, but this anger becomes your ladyship most admirably; but though you'll hear nothing from him, I hope I may speak a word or two to you from myself, Madam.

ROSE 'Twas a sweet prank your master played us: a lady's well helped up that trusts her honour in such a person's hands: to tell all so, – and to his rival too. [*aside*] Excuse him if thou canst.

WARNER [*aside to Rose*] How the devil should I excuse him? Thou knowest he is the greatest fop in nature. –

ROSE But my lady does not know it; if she did –

MRS MILLISENT I'll have no whispering.

WARNER Alas, Madam, I have not the confidence to speak out, unless you can take mercy on me.

MRS MILLISENT For what?

WARNER For telling Sir John you loved my master, Madam. But sure I little thought he was his rival.

ROSE [*aside*] The witty rogue has taken't on himself.

MRS MILLISENT Your master then is innocent.

WARNER Why, could your ladyship suspect him guilty? Pray tell me, do you think him ungrateful, or a fool?

MRS MILLISENT I think him neither.

WARNER Take it from me, you see not the depth of him. But when he knows what thoughts you harbour of him, as I am faithful, and must tell him, – I wish he does not take some pet, and leave you.

MRS MILLISENT Thou art not mad I hope, to tell him on't; if thou dost, I'll be sworn, I'll forswear it to him.

WARNER Upon condition then you'll pardon me, I'll see what I can do to hold my tongue.

MRS MILLISENT This evening in St James's Park I'll meet him.

WARNER He shall not fail you, Madam.

ROSE [*knock within*] Somebody knocks, – O Madam, what shall we do! 'Tis Sir John, I hear his voice.

WARNER What will become of me?

MRS MILLISENT Step quickly behind that door.

[*He goes out*]

To them Sir John.

MRS MILLISENT You've made a quick dispatch, Sir.

SIR JOHN SWALLOW We have done nothing, Madam, our man of law was not within, – but I must look some writings.*

MRS MILLISENT Where are they laid?

* look some writings: examine them.

SIR JOHN SWALLOW In the portmanteau in the drawing-room. [*is going to the door*]

MRS MILLISENT Pray stay a little, Sir. –

WARNER [*at the door*] He must pass just by me; and if he sees me, I am but a dead man.

SIR JOHN SWALLOW Why are you thus concerned? Why do you hold me?

MRS MILLISENT Only a word or two I have to tell you. 'Tis of importance to you. –

SIR JOHN SWALLOW Give me leave –

MRS MILLISENT I must not before I discover the plot to you.

SIR JOHN SWALLOW What plot?

MRS MILLISENT Sir Martin's servant, like a rogue comes hither to tempt me from his master, to have met him.

WARNER [*at the door*] Now would I had a good bag of gunpowder at my breech to ram me into some hole.

MRS MILLISENT For my part I was so startled at the message, that I shall scarcely be myself these two days.

SIR JOHN SWALLOW O that I had the rascal! I would teach him to come upon such errands.

WARNER ⟨*aside*⟩ O for a gentle composition* now! An arm or leg I would give willingly.

SIR JOHN SWALLOW What answer did you make the villain?

MRS MILLISENT I over-reached him clearly, by a promise of an appointment of a place I named, where I ne'er meant to come: but would have had the pleasure first to tell you how I served him, and then to chide your mean suspicion of me.

SIR JOHN SWALLOW Indeed I wondered you should love a fool. But where did you appoint to meet him?

MRS MILLISENT In Gray's Inn Walks.

WARNER ⟨*aside*⟩ By this light, she has put the change upon him! O sweet womankind, how I love thee for that heavenly gift of lying!

SIR JOHN SWALLOW For this evening I will be his mistress; he shall meet another Penelope than he suspects.

MRS MILLISENT But stay not long away.

SIR JOHN SWALLOW You overjoy me, Madam.   [*Exit*]

* composition: agreement, compromise.

WARNER [*entering*] Is he gone, Madam?

MRS MILLISENT As far as Gray's Inn Walks: now I have time to walk the other way, and see thy master.

WARNER Rather let him come hither: I have laid a plot shall send his rival far enough from watching him e'er long.

MRS MILLISENT Art thou in earnest?

WARNER 'Tis so designed, fate cannot hinder it. Our landlord where we lie, vexed that his lodgings should be so left by Sir John, is resolved to be revenged, and I have found the way. You'll see th' effect on't presently.

ROSE O heavens! The door opens again, and Sir John is returned once more.

Enter Sir John.

SIR JOHN SWALLOW Half my business was forgot; you did not tell me when you were to meet him. Ho! What makes this rascal here?

WARNER 'Tis well you're come, Sir, else I must have left untold a message I have for you.

SIR JOHN SWALLOW Well, what's your business, sirrah?

WARNER We must be private first; 'tis only for your ear.

ROSE ⟨*aside*⟩ I shall admire his wit, if in this plunge he can get off.

WARNER I came hither, Sir, by my master's order. –

SIR JOHN SWALLOW I'll reward you for it, sirrah, immediately.

WARNER When you know all, I shall deserve it, Sir; I came to sound the virtue of your mistress; which I have done so cunningly, I have at last obtained the promise of a meeting. But my good master, whom I must confess more generous than wise, knowing you had a passion for her, is resolved to quit: and, Sir, that you may see how much he loves you, sent me in private to advise you still to have an eye upon her actions.

SIR JOHN SWALLOW Take this diamond for thy good news; and give thy master my acknowledgments.

WARNER [*aside*] Thus the world goes, my masters, he that will cozen you, commonly gets your good will into the bargain.

SIR JOHN SWALLOW Madam, I am now satisfied of all sides; first of your truth, then of Sir Martin's friendship. In short, I find you two cheated each other, both to be true to me.

MRS MILLISENT ⟨*aside*⟩ Warner is got off as I would wish, and the knight over-reached.

Enter to them the Landlord disguised like a carrier.

ROSE How now! What would this carrier have?

WARNER [*aside to her*] This is our landlord whom I told you of; but keep your countenance. –

LANDLORD I was looking here-away for one Sir John Swallow; they told me I might hear news of him in this house.

SIR JOHN SWALLOW Friend, I am the man: what have you to say to me?

LANDLORD Nay, faith Sir, I am not so good a schollard to say much, but I have a letter for you in my pouch: there's plaguy news in't, I can tell you that.

SIR JOHN SWALLOW From whom is your letter?

LANDLORD From your old uncle Anthony.

SIR JOHN SWALLOW Give me your letter quickly.

LANDLORD Nay, soft and fair goes far. – Hold you, hold you. It is not in this pocket.

SIR JOHN SWALLOW Search in the other then; I stand on thorns.

LANDLORD I think I feel it now, this should be who.

SIR JOHN SWALLOW Pluck it out then.

LANDLORD I'll pluck out my spectacles and see first. [*reads*] 'To Mr Paul Grimbard – Apprentice to' – No, that's not for you, Sir, – That's for the son of the brother of the nephew of the cousin of my gossip Dobson.

SIR JOHN SWALLOW Prithee dispatch; dost thou not know the contents on't?

LANDLORD Yes, as well as I do my *Pater noster*.

SIR JOHN SWALLOW Well, what's the business on't?

LANDLORD Nay, no great business; 'tis but only that your worship's father's dead.

SIR JOHN SWALLOW My loss is beyond expression! How died he?

LANDLORD He went to bed as well to see to as any man in England, and when he awakened the next morning –

SIR JOHN SWALLOW What then?

LANDLORD He found himself stark dead.

SIR JOHN SWALLOW Well, I must of necessity take orders for my father's funeral, and my estate; heaven knows with what regret I leave you Madam.

MRS MILLISENT But are you in such haste, Sir? I see you take all occasions to be from me.

SIR JOHN SWALLOW Dear Madam, say not so, a few days will, I hope, return me to you.

To them Sir Martin.

Noble Sir Martin, the welcomest man alive! Let me embrace my friend.

ROSE [*aside*] How untowardly he returns the salute! Warner will be found out.

SIR JOHN SWALLOW Well friend! You have obliged me to you eternally.

SIR MARTIN MAR-ALL How have I obliged you, Sir? I would have you to know I scorn your words; and I would I were hanged, if it be not the farthest of my thoughts.

MRS MILLISENT [*aside*] O cunning youth, he acts the fool most naturally. Were we alone, how we would laugh together?

SIR JOHN SWALLOW This is a double generosity, to do me favours and conceal 'em from me. But honest Warner here has told me all.

SIR MARTIN MAR-ALL What has the rascal told you?

SIR JOHN SWALLOW Your plot to try my mistress for me – you understand me, concerning your appointment.

WARNER Sir, I desire to speak in private with you.

SIR MARTIN MAR-ALL This impertinent rascal, when I am most busy, I am ever troubled with him.

WARNER But it concerns you I should speak with you, good Sir.

SIR MARTIN MAR-ALL That's a good one i'faith, thou knowest breeding well, that I should whisper with a serving-man before company.

WARNER Remember, Sir, last time it had been better –

SIR MARTIN MAR-ALL Peace, or I'll make you feel my double fists: if I don't fright him, the saucy rogue will call me fool before the company.

MRS MILLISENT [*aside*] That was acted most naturally again.

SIR JOHN SWALLOW [*to him*] But what needs this dissembling, since you are resolved to quit my mistress to me?

SIR MARTIN MAR-ALL I quit my mistress! That's a good one i'faith.

MRS MILLISENT [*aside*] Tell him you have forsaken me.

SIR MARTIN MAR-ALL I understand you, Madam, you would save a quarrel; but i'faith I'm not so base: I'll see him hanged first.

WARNER Madam, my master is convinced, in prudence he should say so: but love o'ermasters him; when you are gone perhaps he may.

MRS MILLISENT I'll go then: gentlemen, your servant; I see my presence brings constraint to the company.

[*Exeunt ⟨Mrs⟩ Millisent ⟨and⟩ Rose*]

SIR JOHN SWALLOW I'm glad she's gone; now we may talk more freely; for if you have not quitted her, you must.

WARNER Pray, Sir, remember yourself; did not you send me of a message to Sir John, that for his friendship you had left Mistress Millisent?

SIR MARTIN MAR-ALL Why, what an impudent lying rogue art thou!

SIR JOHN SWALLOW How's this! Has Warner cheated me?

WARNER Do not suspect it in the least: you know, Sir, it was not generous before a lady, to say he quitted her.

SIR JOHN SWALLOW Oh! Was that it?

WARNER That was all: [*aside*] say, 'Yes good Sir John' – or I'll swinge you.

SIR MARTIN MAR-ALL Yes, good Sir John.

WARNER ⟨*aside*⟩ That's well, once in his life he has heard good counsel.

SIR MARTIN MAR-ALL Heigh, heigh, what makes my landlord here? He has put on a fool's coat I think to make us laugh.

WARNER ⟨*aside*⟩ The devil's in him; he's at it again; his folly's like a sore in a surfeited horse; cure it in one place, and it breaks out in another.

SIR MARTIN MAR-ALL Honest landlord i'faith, and what make you here?

SIR JOHN SWALLOW Are you acquainted with this honest man?

LANDLORD [*to Sir Martin, softly*] Take heed what you say, Sir.

SIR MARTIN MAR-ALL Take heed what I say, Sir, why? Who should I be afraid of? Of you, Sir? I say, Sir, I know him, Sir; and I have reason to know him, Sir, for I am sure I lodge in his house, Sir, – nay never think to terrify me, Sir; 'tis my landlord here in Charles Street,* Sir.

LANDLORD Now I expect to be paid for the news I brought him.

SIR JOHN SWALLOW Sirrah, did not you tell me that my father –

LANDLORD Is in very good health, for ought I know, Sir; I beseech you trouble yourself no farther concerning him.

SIR JOHN SWALLOW Who set you on to tell this lie?

SIR MARTIN MAR-ALL Aye, who set you on sirrah? This was a rogue that would cozen us both; he thought I did not know him: down on your marribones† and confess the truth: have you no tongue you rascal?

SIR JOHN SWALLOW Sure 'tis some silenced minister:‡ he's grown so fat he cannot speak.

LANDLORD Why, Sir, if you would know, 'twas for your sake I did it.

WARNER For my master's sake! Why, you impudent varlet, do you think to 'scape us with a lie?

SIR JOHN SWALLOW How was it for his sake?

WARNER 'Twas for his own, Sir; he heard you were th' occasion the lady lodged not at his house, and so he invented this lie; partly to revenge himself of you; and partly, I believe, in hope to get her once again when you were gone.

SIR JOHN SWALLOW Fetch me a cudgel prithee.

LANDLORD O good Sir! If you beat me I shall run into oil immediately.§

WARNER Hang him rogue; he's below your anger: I'll maul him

---

* Charles Street: then a fashionable street in Covent Garden.
† marribones: knees.
‡ silenced minister: the Act of Uniformity, 1662, ordered the use of the *Book of Common Prayer*, thus 'silencing' nonconformist ministers.
§ run into oil: as of olives and other plants, by being beaten in a mortar.

for you – the rogue's so big, I think 'twill ask two days to beat him all over. [*beats him*]

LANDLORD O rogue, o villain Warner! Bid him hold, and I'll confess, Sir.

WARNER Get you gone without replying: must such as you be prating? [*beats him out*]

Enter Rose.

ROSE Sir, dinner waits you on the table.

SIR JOHN SWALLOW Friend will you go along, and take part of a bad repast?

SIR MARTIN MAR-ALL Thank you; but I am just risen from table.

WARNER Now he might sit with his mistress, and has not the wit to find out.

SIR JOHN SWALLOW You shall be very welcome.

SIR MARTIN MAR-ALL I have no stomach, Sir.

WARNER Get you in with a vengeance: you have a better stomach than you think you have. [*pushes him*]

SIR MARTIN MAR-ALL This hungry Diego★ rogue would shame me; he thinks a gentleman can eat like a serving-man.

SIR JOHN SWALLOW If you will not, adieu dear Sir; in anything command me.   [*Exit*]

SIR MARTIN MAR-ALL Now we are alone; han't I carried matters bravely sirrah?

WARNER O yes, yes, you deserve sugar plums; first for your quarrelling with Sir John; then for discovering your landlord, and lastly for refusing to dine with your mistress. All this is since the last reckoning was wiped out.

SIR MARTIN MAR-ALL Then why did my landlord disguise himself, to make a fool of us?

WARNER You have so little brains, that a penn'orth of butter melted under 'em, would set 'em afloat: he put on that disguise to rid you of your rival.

SIR MARTIN MAR-ALL Why was not I worthy to keep your counsel then?

★ Diego: a comic servant in Samuel Tuke's *The Adventures of Five Hours*, 1663.

WARNER It had been much at one: you would but have drunk the secret down, and pissed it out to the next company.

SIR MARTIN MAR-ALL Well I find I am a miserable man: I have lost my mistress, and may thank myself for't.

WARNER You'll not confess you are a fool, I warrant.

SIR MARTIN MAR-ALL Well I am a fool, if that will satisfy you: but what am I the nearer for being one?

WARNER O yes, much the nearer; for now fortune's bound to provide for you; as hospitals are built for lame people, because they cannot help themselves. Well; I have yet a project in my pate.

SIR MARTIN MAR-ALL Dear rogue, what is't?

WARNER Excuse me for that: but while 'tis set a-working you would do well to screw yourself into her father's good opinion.

SIR MARTIN MAR-ALL If you will not tell me, my mind gives me I shall discover it again.

WARNER I'll lay it as far out of your reach as I can possible:
– For secrets are edg'd tools,
And must be kept from children and from fools.

[Exeunt]

ACT THREE

⟨SCENE I⟩

Enter Rose and Warner meeting.

ROSE Your worship's most happily encountered.

WARNER Your ladyship's most fortunately met.

ROSE I was going to your lodging.

WARNER My business was to yours.

ROSE I have something to say to you that –

WARNER I have that to tell you –

ROSE Understand then –

WARNER If you'll hear me –

ROSE I believe that –

WARNER I am of opinion that –

ROSE Prithee hold thy peace a little till I have done.

WARNER Cry you mercy, Mistress Rose, I'll not dispute your ancient privileges of talking.

ROSE My mistress, knowing Sir John was to be abroad upon business this afternoon, has asked leave to see a play: and Sir John has so great a confidence of your master, that he will trust nobody with her, but him.

WARNER If my master gets her out, I warrant her, he shall show her a better play than any is at either of the houses – Here they are: I'll run and prepare him to wait upon her.   [*Exit*]

Enter Old Moody, Mrs Millisent, and Lady Dupe.

MRS MILLISENT My hoods and scarfs there, quickly.

LADY DUPE Send to call a coach there.

MR MOODY But what kind of man is this Sir Martin, with whom you are to go?

LADY DUPE A plain downright country gentleman, I assure you.

MR MOODY I like him much the better for't. For I hate one of those you call a man o'th' Town, one of those empty fellows of mere outside: they've nothing of the true old English manliness.

ROSE I confess, Sir, a woman's in a sad condition, that has nothing to trust to, but a periwig above, and a well-trimmed shoe below.

To them Sir Martin.

MRS MILLISENT This, Sir, is Sir John's friend, he is for your humour, Sir, he is no man o'th' Town, but bred up in the old Elizabeth way of plainness.

SIR MARTIN MAR-ALL Aye, Madam, your ladyship may say your pleasure of me.

To them Warner.

WARNER ⟨*aside*⟩ How the devil got he here before me! 'Tis very unlucky I could not see him first –

SIR MARTIN MAR-ALL But as for painting, music, poetry, and the like, I'll say this of myself –

WARNER I'll say that for him, my master understands none of 'em, I assure you, Sir.

SIR MARTIN MAR-ALL You impudent rascal, hold your tongue: I must rid my hands of this fellow; the rogue is ever discrediting me before company.

MR MOODY Never trouble yourself about it, Sir, for I like a man that –

SIR MARTIN MAR-ALL I know you do, Sir, and therefore I hope you'll think never the worse of me for his prating: for though I do not boast of my own good parts –

WARNER He has none to boast of, upon my faith, Sir.

SIR MARTIN MAR-ALL Give him not the hearing, Sir; for, if I may believe my friends, they have flattered me with an opinion of more –

WARNER Of more than their flattery can make good, Sir; – 'tis true he tells you, they have flattered him; but in my conscience he is the most downright simple-natured creature in the world.

SIR MARTIN MAR-ALL I shall consider you hereafter sirrah; but I am sure in all companies I pass for a *virtuoso*.

MR MOODY *Virtuoso*! What's that too? Is not *virtue* enough without *o so*?

SIR MARTIN MAR-ALL You have reason, Sir!

MR MOODY There he is again too; the Town phrase, a great compliment I wis; you have reason, Sir; that is, you are no beast, Sir.

WARNER [*aside to him*] A word in private, Sir; you mistake this old man; he loves neither painting, music, nor poetry; yet recover yourself, if you have any brains.

SIR MARTIN MAR-ALL Say you so? I'll bring all about again I warrant you – I beg your pardon a thousand times Sir; I vow to Gad I am not master of any of those perfections; for in fine, Sir, I am wholly ignorant of painting, music, and poetry; only some rude escapes★ – but, in fine, they are such, that, in fine, Sir –

WARNER [*aside*] This is worse than all the rest.

MR MOODY By coxbones† one word more of all this gibberish, and old Madge‡ shall fly about your ears: what is this 'in fine' he keeps such a coil with too?

MRS MILLISENT 'Tis a phrase *à-la-mode*, Sir, and is used in conversation now, as a whiff of tobacco was formerly, in the midst of a discourse, for a thinking while.

LADY DUPE In plain English, 'in fine', is in the end, Sir.

MR MOODY But by coxbones there is no end on't methinks: if thou wilt have a foolish word to lard thy lean discourse with, take an English one when thou speakest English; as 'So Sir', and 'Then Sir', and so forth; 'tis a more manly kind of nonsense: and a pox of 'In fine', for I'll hear no more on't.

WARNER [*aside*] He's gravelled, and I must help him out. ⟨*aloud*⟩ Madam, there's a coach at door to carry you to the play.

SIR MARTIN MAR-ALL Which house do you mean to go to?

MRS MILLISENT The Duke's, I think.

SIR MARTIN MAR-ALL It is a damned play, and has nothing in't.

MRS MILLISENT Then let us to the King's.

SIR MARTIN MAR-ALL That's e'en as bad.

WARNER [*aside*] This is past enduring. ⟨*aloud*⟩ There was an ill play set up, Sir, on the posts, but I can assure you the bills are altered since you saw 'em, and now there are two admirable comedies at both houses.

MR MOODY But my daughter loves serious plays.

WARNER They are tragi-comedies, Sir, for both.

SIR MARTIN MAR-ALL I have heard her say she loves none but tragedies.

★ rude escapes: artless performances.   † coxbones: God's bones.
‡ old Madge: his cudgel.

MR MOODY Where have you heard her say so, Sir?

WARNER Sir you forget yourself, you never saw her in your life before.

SIR MARTIN MAR-ALL What not at Canterbury, in the cathedral church there? This is the impudentest rascal –

WARNER Mum, Sir –

SIR MARTIN MAR-ALL Ah Lord, what have I done! As I hope to be saved Sir, it was out before I was aware; for if ever I set eyes on her before this day – I wish –

MR MOODY This fellow is not so much fool, as he makes one believe he is.

MRS MILLISENT [*aside*] I thought he would be discovered for a wit: this 'tis to over-act one's part!

MR MOODY Come away daughter, I will not trust you in his hands, there's more in't than I imagined.

[*Exeunt Mr Moody, Mrs Millisent, Lady Dupe, Rose*]

SIR MARTIN MAR-ALL Why do you frown upon me so, when you know your looks go to the heart of me; what have I done besides a little *lapsus linguae*?

WARNER Why, who says you have done anything? You, a mere innocent.

SIR MARTIN MAR-ALL As the child that's to be born in my intentions; if I know how I have offended myself any more than in one word. –

WARNER But don't follow me however – I have nothing to say to you.

SIR MARTIN MAR-ALL I'll follow you to the world's end till you forgive me.

WARNER I am resolved to lead you a dance then.   [*Exit running*]

SIR MARTIN MAR-ALL The rogue has no mercy in him, but I must mollify him with money.

[*Exit*]

⟨SCENE II⟩

Enter Lady Dupe.

LADY DUPE Truly my little cousin's the aptest scholar, and takes out love's lessons so exactly that I joy to see it: she has got already the bond of two thousand pounds sealed for her portion, which I keep for her; a pretty good beginning: 'tis true, I believe he has enjoyed her, and so let him; Mark Anthony wooed not at so dear a price.

To her Mrs Christian.

MRS CHRISTIAN O Madam, I fear I am a-breeding!

LADY DUPE A taking wench! But 'tis no matter; have you told anybody?

MRS CHRISTIAN I have been venturing upon your foundations, a little to dissemble.

LADY DUPE That's a good child, I hope it will thrive with thee, as it has with me: heaven has a blessing in store upon our endeavours.

MRS CHRISTIAN I feigned myself sick, and kept my bed; my lord, he came to visit me, and in the end I disclosed it to him in the saddest passion.

LADY DUPE This frighted him, I hope, into a study how to cloak your disgrace, lest it should have vent to his lady.

MRS CHRISTIAN 'Tis true; but all the while I subtly drove it, that he should name you to me as the fittest instrument of the concealment; but how to break it to you, strangely does perplex him: he has been seeking you all o'er the house; therefore I'll leave your ladyship, for fear we should be seen together.   [*Exit*]

LADY DUPE Now I must play my part;
Nature, in women, teaches more than Art.

Enter Lord ⟨Dartmouth⟩.

LORD DARTMOUTH Madam, I have a secret to impart,
A sad one too,
And have no friend to trust but only you.

LADY DUPE Your lady or your children sick?

LORD DARTMOUTH Not that I know.

LADY DUPE You seem to be in health.

LORD DARTMOUTH In body, not in mind.

LADY DUPE Some scruple of conscience, I warrant; my chaplain shall resolve you.

LORD DARTMOUTH Madam, my soul's tormented.

LADY DUPE O take heed of despair, my lord!

LORD DARTMOUTH Madam, there is no medicine for this sickness; but only you; your friendship's my safe haven, else I am lost and shipwrecked.

LADY DUPE Pray tell me what it is.

LORD DARTMOUTH Could I express it by sad sighs and groans, or drown it with myself in seas of tears, I should be happy, would, and would not tell.★

LADY DUPE Command whatever I can serve you in, I will be faithful still to all your ends, provided they be just and virtuous.

LORD DARTMOUTH That word has stopped me.

LADY DUPE Speak out, my lord, and boldly tell what 'tis.

LORD DARTMOUTH Then in obedience to your commands; your cousin is with child.

LADY DUPE Which cousin?

LORD DARTMOUTH Your cousin Christian here i'th' house.

LADY DUPE Alas then she has stolen a marriage, and undone herself: some young fellow, on my conscience, that's a beggar; youth will not be advised; well, I'll never meddle more with girls; one is no more assured of 'em than grooms of mules, they'll strike when least one thinks on't: but pray your lordship, what is her choice then for an husband?

LORD DARTMOUTH She is not married that I know of, Madam.

LADY DUPE Not married! 'Tis impossible, the girl does sure abuse you. I know her education has been such, the flesh could not prevail; therefore she does abuse you, it must be so.

LORD DARTMOUTH Madam, not to abuse you longer, she is with child, and I the unfortunate man who did this most unlucky act.

LADY DUPE You! I'll never believe it.

LORD DARTMOUTH Madam, 'tis too true; believe it, and be serious how to hide her shame; I beg it here upon my knees.

LADY DUPE Oh, oh, oh. – [*she faints away*]

LORD DARTMOUTH Who's there? Who's there? Help, help, help.

Enter two Women, Rose, Mrs Millisent.

FIRST WOMAN O merciful God, my lady's gone!

SECOND WOMAN Whither?

FIRST WOMAN To heaven, God knows, to heaven.

★ would, and would not: whether or not.

ROSE Rub her, rub her; fetch warm clothes.

SECOND WOMAN I say, run to the cabinet of quintessence;*
Gilbert's Water,† Gilbert's Water.

FIRST WOMAN Now all the good folks of heaven look down upon
her.

MRS MILLISENT Set her in the chair.

ROSE Open her mouth with a dagger or a key; pour, pour, where's
the spoon?

SECOND WOMAN She stirs, she revives, merciful to us all, what
a thing was this! Speak, lady, speak.

LADY DUPE So, so, so.

MRS MILLISENT Alas, my lord, how came this fit?

LORD DARTMOUTH With sorrow, Madam.

LADY DUPE Now I am better: Bess, you have not seen me thus.

FIRST WOMAN Heaven forfend that I should live to see you so again.

LADY DUPE Go, go, I'm pretty well; withdraw into the next room,
but be near I pray, for fear of the worst.

[They go out]

– My lord, sit down near me I pray, I'll strive to speak a few
words to you, and then to bed, – nearer –, my voice is faint. – My
lord, heaven knows how I have ever loved you; and is this my
reward? Had you none to abuse but me in that unfortunate fond
girl that you know was dearer to me than my life? This was not
love to her, but an inveterate malice to poor me. Oh, oh. – [*faints
again*]

LORD DARTMOUTH Help, help, help.

All the Women again.

FIRST WOMAN This fit will carry her: alas it is a lechery!‡

SECOND WOMAN The balsam, the balsam!

FIRST WOMAN No, no, the chemistry oil of rosemary: hold her
up, and give her air.

MRS MILLISENT Feel whether she breathes, with your hand
before her mouth.

---

* cabinet of quintessence: the medicine cabinet.

† Gilbert's Water: probably distilled water, after a method used by Gilbertus
Anglicus to purify water.

‡ lechery: probably lethargy, unnatural sleep.

ROSE No, Madam, 'tis key-cold.

FIRST WOMAN Look up, dear Madam, if you have any hope of salvation!

SECOND WOMAN Hold up your finger, Madam, if you have any hope of fraternity. O the blessed saints that hear me not, take her mortality to them.

LADY DUPE Enough, so, 'tis well, – withdraw, and let me rest a while; only my dear lord remain.

FIRST WOMAN Pray your lordship keep her from swebbing.*

[*Exeunt Women*]

LORD DARTMOUTH Here humbly once again, I beg your pardon and your help.

LADY DUPE Heaven forgive you, and I do: stand up, my lord, and sit close by me: O this naughty girl! But did your lordship win her soon?

LORD DARTMOUTH No, Madam, but with much difficulty.

LADY DUPE I'm glad on't; it showed the girl had some religion in her, all my precepts were not in vain: but you men are strange tempters; good my lord, where was this wicked act then first committed?

LORD DARTMOUTH In an out-room upon a trunk.

LADY DUPE Poor heart, what shift love makes! O she does love you dearly, though to her ruin! And then what place, my lord?

LORD DARTMOUTH An old waste room, with a decayed bed in't.

LADY DUPE Out upon that dark room for deeds of darkness! And that rotten bed! I wonder it did hold your lordship's vigour: but you dealt gently with the girl. Well, you shall see I love you; for I will manage this business to both your advantages, by the assistance of heaven I will; good my lord help, lead me out.

[*Exeunt*]

⟨SCENE III⟩

Enter Warner, Rose.

ROSE A mischief upon all fools! Do you think your master has not done wisely? First to mistake our old man's humour, then to dis-

* swebbing: swooning.

praise the plays; and lastly, to discover his acquaintance with my mistress: my old master has taken such a jealousy of him, that he will never admit him into his sight again.

WARNER Thou makest thyself a greater fool than he, by being angry at what he cannot help. – I have been angry with him too; but these friends have taken up the quarrel. – [*shows gold*] Look you he has sent these mediators to mitigate your wrath: here are twenty of 'em have made a long voyage from Guinea to kiss your hands: and when the match is made, there are an hundred more in readiness to be your humble servants.

ROSE Rather than fall out with you, I'll take 'em; but I confess it troubles me to see so loyal a lover have the heart of an emperor, and yet scarce the brains of a cobbler.

WARNER Well, what device can we two beget betwixt us, to separate Sir John Swallow and thy mistress?

ROSE I cannot on the sudden tell; but I hate him worse than foul weather without a coach.

WARNER Then I'll see if my project will be luckier than thine. Where are the papers concerning the jointure I have heard you speak of?

ROSE They lie within in three great bags, some twenty reams of paper in each bundle, with six lines in a sheet: but there is a little paper where all the business lies.

WARNER Where is it? Canst thou help me to it?

ROSE By good chance he gave it to my custody before he set out for London. You came in good time, here it is, I was carrying it to him; just now he sent for it.

WARNER So, this I will secure in my pocket: when thou art asked for it, make two or three bad faces, and say, 'twas left behind: by this means he must of necessity leave the Town, to see for it in Kent.

Enter Sir John, Sir Martin, Mrs Millisent.

SIR JOHN SWALLOW 'Tis no matter, though the old man be suspicious; I knew the story all beforehand; and, since then you have fully satisfied me of your true friendship to me – [*to Rose*] Where are the writings?

ROSE Sir, I beg your pardon; I thought I had put 'em up amongst my lady's things, and it seems in my haste I quite forgot 'em, and left 'em at Canterbury.

SIR JOHN SWALLOW This is horribly unlucky? Where do you think you left 'em?

ROSE Upon the great box in my lady's chamber; they are safe enough I'm sure.

SIR JOHN SWALLOW It must be so – I must take post immediately: Madam, for some few days I must be absent; and to confirm you, friend, how much I trust you, I leave the dearest pledge I have on earth, my mistress, to your care.

MRS MILLISENT If you loved me, you would not take all occasions to leave me thus!

WARNER [*aside*] Do, go to Kent, and when you come again, here they are ready for you. [*shows the paper*]

SIR MARTIN MAR-ALL What's that you have in your hand there, sirrah?

WARNER Pox, what ill luck was this! What shall I say?

SIR MARTIN MAR-ALL Sometimes you've tongue enough, what are you silent?

WARNER 'Tis an account, Sir, of what money you have lost since you came to Town.

SIR MARTIN MAR-ALL I'm very glad on't: now I'll make you all see the severity of my fortune, – give me the paper.

WARNER Heaven! What does he mean to do, it is not fair writ out, Sir?

SIR JOHN SWALLOW Besides, I am in haste, another time, Sir.

SIR MARTIN MAR-ALL Pray, oblige me, Sir, – 'tis but one minute: all people love to be pitied in their misfortunes, and so do I: will you produce it, sirrah?

WARNER Dear master!

SIR MARTIN MAR-ALL Dear rascal! Am I master or you? You rogue!

WARNER Hold yet, Sir, and let me read it: – you cannot read my hand.

SIR MARTIN MAR-ALL This is ever his way to be disparaging me, – but I'll let you see, sirrah, that I can read your hand better than you yourself can.

WARNER You'll repent it, there's a trick in't, Sir. –

SIR MARTIN MAR-ALL Is there so, sirrah? But I'll bring you out of all your tricks with a vengeance to you. – How now! What's this? [*reads*] 'A true particular of the estate of Sir John Swallow Knight, lying and situate in, &c.'

SIR JOHN SWALLOW This is the very paper I had lost. [*takes the paper*] I'm very glad on't, it has saved me a most unwelcome journey, – but I will not thank you for the courtesy, which now I find you never did intend me – this is confederacy, I smoke★ it now – Come, Madam, let me wait on you to your father.

MRS MILLISENT Well, of a witty man, this was the foolishest part that ever I beheld.   [*Exeunt Sir John, Millisent, and Rose*]

SIR MARTIN MAR-ALL I am a fool, I must confess it, and I am the most miserable one without thy help, – but yet it was such a mistake as any man might have made.

WARNER No doubt on't.

SIR MARTIN MAR-ALL Prithee chide me! This indifference of thine wounds me to the heart.

WARNER I care not.

SIR MARTIN MAR-ALL Wilt thou not help me for this once?

WARNER Sir, I kiss your hands, I have other business.

SIR MARTIN MAR-ALL Dear Warner!

WARNER I am inflexible.

SIR MARTIN MAR-ALL Then I am resolved I'll kill myself.

WARNER You are master of your own body.

SIR MARTIN MAR-ALL Will you let me damn my soul?

WARNER At your pleasure, as the devil and you can agree about it.

SIR MARTIN MAR-ALL D'ye see the point's ready? Will you do nothing to save my life?

WARNER Not in the least.

SIR MARTIN MAR-ALL Farewell, hard-hearted Warner.

WARNER Adieu soft-headed Sir Martin.

SIR MARTIN MAR-ALL Is it possible?

WARNER Why don't you dispatch, Sir? Why all these preambles?

SIR MARTIN MAR-ALL I'll see thee hanged first: I know thou would'st have me killed, to get my clothes.

WARNER I knew it was but a copy of your countenance;† people in this age are not so apt to kill themselves.

★ smoke: discover.   † a copy of your countenance: a sham.

SIR MARTIN MAR-ALL Here are yet ten pieces in my pocket, take 'em, and let's be friends.

WARNER You know the eas'ness of my nature, and that makes you work upon it so. Well, Sir, – for this once I cast an eye of pity on you, – but I must have ten more in hand, before I can stir a foot.

SIR MARTIN MAR-ALL As I am a true gamester, I have lost all but these, – but if thou'lt lend me them, I'll give 'em thee again.

WARNER I'll rather trust you till tomorrow, once more look up, I bid you hope the best.

Why should your folly make your love miscarry,
Since men first play the fools, and then they marry?

[*Exeunt*]

ACT FOUR

⟨SCENE I⟩

Enter Sir Martin and Warner.

SIR MARTIN MAR-ALL But are they to be married this day in private, say you?

WARNER 'Tis so concluded, Sir, I dare assure you.

SIR MARTIN MAR-ALL But why so soon, and in private?

WARNER So soon, to prevent the designs upon her; and in private, to save the effusion of Christian money.

SIR MARTIN MAR-ALL It strikes to my heart already; in fine, I am a dead man. – Warner.

WARNER Well, go your ways, I'll try what may be done. Look if he will stir now; your rival and the old man will see us together, we are just below the window.

SIR MARTIN MAR-ALL Thou can'st not do't.

WARNER On the peril of my twenty pieces be it.

SIR MARTIN MAR-ALL But I have found a way to help thee out, trust to my wit but once.

WARNER Name your wit, or think you have the least grain of wit once more, and I'll lay it down for ever.

SIR MARTIN MAR-ALL You are a saucy masterly companion, and so I leave you.   [*Exit Sir Martin*]

WARNER Help, help, good people, murther, murther!

Enter Sir John and Moody.

SIR JOHN SWALLOW ⎫
MR MOODY   ⎬ How now, what's the matter?

WARNER I am abused, I am beaten, I am lamed for ever.

MR MOODY Who has used thee so?

WARNER The rogue my master.

SIR JOHN SWALLOW What was the offence?

WARNER A trifle, just nothing.

SIR JOHN SWALLOW That's very strange.

WARNER It was for telling him he lost too much at play; I meant him nothing but well, heaven knows, and he in a cursed damned humour would needs revenge his losses upon me: a' kicked me,

took away my money, and turned me off; but if I take it at his
hands –

MR MOODY By coxnouns* it was an ill-natured part, nay, I
thought no better could come on't, when I heard him at his 'Vow
to Gads', and 'in fines'.

WARNER But if I live I'll cry quittance with him: he had engaged
me to get Mrs Millisent your daughter for him; but if I do not all
that ever I can to make her hate him, a great booby, an over-
grown oaf, a conceited Bartlemew.† –

SIR JOHN SWALLOW Prithee leave off thy choler, and hear me a
little: I have had a great mind to thee a long time, if thou think'st
my service better than his, from this minute I entertain thee.

WARNER With all my heart, Sir, and so much the rather, that I
may spite him with it. – This was the most propitious fate. –

MR MOODY 'Propitious'! And 'fate'! What a damned Scander-bag-
rogue‡ art thou to talk at this rate! Hark you, sirrah, one word
more of this gibberish, and I'll set you packing from your new
service; I'll have neither 'propitious' nor 'fate' come within my
doors. –

SIR JOHN SWALLOW Nay, pray father. –

WARNER Good old Sir be pacified: I was pouring out a little of the
dregs that I had left in me of my former service, and now they are
gone, my stomach's clear of 'em.

SIR JOHN SWALLOW This fellow is come in a happy hour; for
now, Sir, you and I may go to prepare the licence, and in the
meantime he may have an eye upon your daughter.

WARNER If you please I'll wait upon her till she's ready, and then
bring her to what church you shall appoint.

MR MOODY But, friend, you'll find she'll hang an arse, and be very
loath to come along with you, and therefore I had best stay behind,
and bring her myself.

WARNER I warrant you I have a trick for that, Sir: she knows
nothing of my being turned away: so I'll come to her as from Sir

---

* coxnouns: God's wounds.

† Bartlemew: from Bartholomew Cokes, a fool or simpleton, after Squire
Cokes, the fool in *Bartholomew Fair*.

‡ Scander-bag-rogue: a brawling rogue, from Iscander Bey, the Albanian who
frequently fought and defeated the Turks.

Martin, and under pretence of carrying her to him, conduct her to
you.

SIR JOHN SWALLOW My better angel –

MR MOODY By th' mess⋆ 'twas well thought on; well son, go you
before, I'll speak but one word for a dish or two at dinner, and
follow you to the Licence-office. Sirrah – stay you here – till my
return.   [*Exeunt Sir John and Moody*]

WARNER [*solus*] Was there ever such a lucky rogue as I! I had
always a good opinion of my wit, but could never think I had so
much as now I find. I have now gained an opportunity to carry
away Mistress Millisent for my master, to get his mistress by
means of his rival, to receive all his happiness, where he could
expect nothing but misery: after this exploit I will have Lilly†
draw me in the habit of a hero, with a laurel on my temples, and
an inscription below it, 'This is Warner the flower of serving-
men'.

Enter Messenger.

MESSENGER Pray do me the favour to help me to the speech of
Mr Moody.

WARNER What's your business?

MESSENGER I have a letter to deliver to him.

WARNER Here he comes, you may deliver it yourself to him.

Re-enter Moody.

MESSENGER Sir, a gentleman met me at the corner of the next
street, and bid me give this into your own hands.

MR MOODY Stay friend, till I have read it.

MESSENGER He told me, Sir, it required no answer.
                                                    [*Exit Messenger*]

MR MOODY [*reads*] 'Sir, permit me, though a stranger, to give
you counsel; some young gallants have had intelligence, that this
day you intend privately to marry your daughter, the rich heiress;
and in fine, above twenty of them have dispersed themselves to
watch her going out: therefore put it off, if you will avoid mischief, and be advised by Your unknown Servant.'

⋆ mess: mass.
† Lilly: Sir Peter Lely (1618–80), the famous Restoration painter.

By the mackings,★ I thought there was no good in't, when I saw 'in fine' there; there are some Papishes, I'll warrant, that lie in wait for my daughter, or else they are no Englishmen, but some of your French Outalian rogues; I owe him thanks however, this unknown friend of mine, that told me on't. Warner, no wedding today, Warner.

WARNER Why, what's the matter, Sir?

MR MOODY I say no more, but some wiser than some, I'll keep my daughter at home this afternoon, and a fig for all these Outalians.

[*Exit Moody*]

WARNER So, here's another trick of fortune as unexpected for bad, as the other was for good. Nothing vexes me, but that I had made my game cock-sure, and then to be back-gammoned:† it must needs be the devil that writ this letter, he owed my master a spite, and has paid him to the purpose: and here he comes as merry too, he little thinks what misfortune has befallen him, and for my part I am ashamed to tell him.

Enter Sir Martin laughing.

SIR MARTIN MAR-ALL [*laughs again*] Warner, such a jest, Warner.

WARNER What a murrain is the matter, Sir? Where lies this jest that tickles you?

SIR MARTIN MAR-ALL [*laughs again*] Let me laugh out my laugh, and I'll tell thee.

WARNER I wish you may have cause for all this mirth.

SIR MARTIN MAR-ALL Hereafter, Warner, be it known unto thee, I will endure no more to be thy May-game:‡ thou shalt no more dare to tell me, I spoil thy projects, and discover thy designs; for I have played such a prize, without thy help, of my own mother-wit ('tis true I am hasty sometimes, and so do harm; but when I have a mind to show myself, there's no man in England, though I say't, comes near me as to point of imagination) I'll make thee acknowledge I have laid a plot that has a soul in't.

★ mackings: an oath possibly from the Mass or Mary.

† back-gammoned: outdone. There is a possible pun on backgammon player as sodomist.

‡ May-game: object of sport or ridicule.

WARNER Pray, Sir, keep me no longer in ignorance of this rare invention.

SIR MARTIN MAR-ALL Know then, Warner, that when I left thee, I was possessed with a terrible fear, that my mistress should be married: well, thought I to myself, and mustering up all the forces of my wit, I did produce such a stratagem.

WARNER But what was it?

SIR MARTIN MAR-ALL I feigned a letter as from an unknown friend to Moody, wherein I gave him to understand, that if his daughter went out this afternoon, she would infallibly be snapped by some young fellows that lay in wait for her.

WARNER Very good.

SIR MARTIN MAR-ALL That which follows is yet better; for he I sent assures me, that in that very nick of time my letter came, her father was just sending her abroad with a very foolish rascally fellow that was with him.

WARNER And did you perform all this a'God's name? Could you do this wonderful miracle without giving your soul to the devil for his help?

SIR MARTIN MAR-ALL I tell thee man I did it, and it was done by the help of no devil, but this familiar* of my own brain; how long would it have been ere thou couldest have thought of such a project? Martin said to his man, 'Who's the fool now?'

WARNER Who's the fool? Why, who used to be the fool? He that ever was since I knew him, and ever will be so!

SIR MARTIN MAR-ALL What a pox? I think thou art grown envious, not one word in my commendations?

WARNER Faith Sir, my skill is too little to praise you as you deserve; but if you would have it according to my poor ability, you are one that had a knock in your cradle, a conceited lack-wit, a designing ass, a hair-brained fop, a confounded busy-brain, with an eternal wind-mill in it; this in short, Sir, is the contents of your panegyric.

SIR MARTIN MAR-ALL But what the devil have I done, to set you thus against me?

WARNER Only this, Sir, I was the foolish rascally fellow that was

* familiar: a demon or witch associated with a particular person.

with Moody, and your worship was he to whom I was to bring his daughter.

SIR MARTIN MAR-ALL But how could I know this? I am no witch.

WARNER No, I'll be sworn for you, you are no conjurer. Will you go Sir?

SIR MARTIN MAR-ALL Will you hear my justifications?

WARNER [*shoves him*] Shall I see the back of you? Speak not a word in your defence.

SIR MARTIN MAR-ALL This is the strangest luck now –

[*Exit Sir Martin*]

WARNER I'm resolved this devil of his shall never weary me, I will overcome him, I will invent something that shall stand good in spite of his folly. Let me see –

Enter Lord ⟨Dartmouth⟩.

LORD DARTMOUTH Here he is – I must venture on him, for the tyranny of this old lady is unsupportable, since I have made her my confident, there passes not an hour but she has a pull at my purse-strings; I shall be ruined if I do not quit myself of her suddenly: I find now, by sad experience, that a mistress is much more chargeable than a wife, and after a little time too, grows full as dull and insignificant. Mr Warner! Have you a mind to do yourself a courtesy, and me another?

WARNER I think, my lord, the question need not be much disputed, for I have always had a great service for your lordship, and some little kindness for myself.

LORD DARTMOUTH What, if you should propose Mistress Christian as a wife to your master? You know he's never like to compass t'other.

WARNER I cannot tell that my lord –

LORD DARTMOUTH £500 are yours at day of marriage.

WARNER £500 'tis true, the temptation is very sweet, and powerful; the devil I confess has done his part, and many a good murder and treason have been committed at a cheaper rate; but yet –

LORD DARTMOUTH What yet –

WARNER To confess the truth, I am resolved to bestow my master upon that other lady (as difficult as your lordship thinks it)

for the honour of my wit is engaged in it: will it not be the same
to your lordship were she married to any other?

LORD DARTMOUTH The very same.

WARNER Come my lord, not to dissemble with you any longer, I
know where it is that your shoe wrings you: I have observed
something in the house, betwixt some parties that shall be nameless: and know that you have been taking up linen at a much
dearer rate, than you might have had it at any draper's in
Town.

LORD DARTMOUTH I see I have not danced in a net before you.

WARNER As for that old lady, whom hell confound, she is the
greatest jill in nature, cheat is her study, all her joy to cozen, she
loves nothing but herself, and draws all lines to that corrupted
centre.

LORD DARTMOUTH I have found her out, though late: first, I'll
undertake I ne'er enjoyed her niece under the rate of £500 a time;
never was woman's flesh held up so high: every night I find out
for a new maidenhead, and she has sold it me as often as ever
Mother Temple, Bennet, or Gifford,* have put off boiled capons
for quails† and partridges.

WARNER This is nothing to what bills you'll have when she's
brought to bed, after her hard bargain, as they call it; then
crammed capons, pea-hens, chickens in the grease, pottages, and
frigacies, wine from Shatling,‡ and La-fronds,§ with New River,‖
clearer by sixpence the pound than ever God Almighty made it;
then midwife – dry-nurse – wet-nurse – and all the rest of their
accomplices, with cradle, baby-clouts, and bearing-clothes –
possets, caudles,¶ broth, jellies, and gravies; and behind all
these, glisters,** suppositers, and a barbarous pothecary's bill,
more inhumane than a tailor's.

LORD DARTMOUTH I sweat to think on't.

WARNER Well my lord! Cheer up! I have found a way to rid you

---

* Temple, Bennet or Gifford: three notorious brothel keepers.
† quails: courtesans.
‡ Shatling: Chatelain's, a French restaurant in Covent Garden.
§ La-fronds: another French establishment.
‖ New River: a canal carrying pure water to London, hence pure water.
¶ caudles: warm spiced drinks.   ** glisters: used for purging.

of it all, within a short time you shall know more; yonder appears a young lady whom I must needs speak with, please you go in and prepare the old lady and your mistress.

LORD DARTMOUTH Good luck, and £500 attend thee.   [*Exit*]

Enter Millisent and Rose above.

MRS MILLISENT I am resolved I'll never marry him!

ROSE So far you are right, Madam.

MRS MILLISENT But how to hinder it, I cannot possibly tell! For my father presses me to it, and will take no denial: would I knew some way –

WARNER Madam, I'll teach you the very nearest, for I have just now found it out.

ROSE Are you there, Mr Littleplot?

WARNER Studying to deserve thee, Rose, by my diligence for thy lady; I stand here, methinks, just like a wooden Mercury,* to point her out the way to matrimony.

ROSE Or, serving-man-like, ready to carry up the hot meat for your master, and then to fall upon the cold yourself.

WARNER I know not what you call the cold, but I believe I shall find warm work on't: in the first place then I must acquaint you, that I have seemingly put off my master, and entered myself into Sir John's service.

MRS MILLISENT Most excellent!

WARNER And thereupon, but base –

Enter Moody.

MRS MILLISENT Something he would tell us, but see what luck's here!

MR MOODY How now, sirrah? Are you so great there already?

MRS MILLISENT I find my father's jealous of him still!

WARNER Sir, I was only teaching my young lady a new song, and if you please you shall hear it.

[*sings*]   Make ready fair lady tonight,
             And stand at the door below,
             For I will be there

* wooden Mercury: a wooden statue, hence signpost, a go-between in matrimonial affairs.

To receive you with care,
And to your true love you shall go.

MR MOODY Ods bobs this is very pretty.

MRS MILLISENT Aye, so is the lady's answer too, if I could but hit on't.

[*sings*] And when the stars twinkle so bright,
Then down to the door will I creep,
To my love I will fly,
Ere the jealous can spy,
And leave my old daddy asleep.

MR MOODY Bodikins I like not that so well, to cozen her old father; it may be my own case another time.

ROSE O Madam! Yonder's your persecutor returned.

Enter Sir John.

MRS MILLISENT I'll into my chamber to avoid the sight of him as long as I can; Lord! That my old doting father should throw me away upon such an ignoramus, and deny me to such a wit as Sir Martin.   [*Exeunt Mrs Millisent and Rose from above*]

MR MOODY O son! Here has been the most villainous tragedy against you.

SIR JOHN SWALLOW What tragedy? Has there been any blood shed since I went?

MR MOODY No blood shed, but, as I told you, a most damnable tragedy.

WARNER A tragedy! I'll be hanged if he does not mean a stratagem.

MR MOODY Jack Sauce! If I say it is a tragedy, it shall be a tragedy in spite of you, teach your grandam how to piss – what – I hope I am old enough to spout English with you Sir?

SIR JOHN SWALLOW But what was the reason you came not after me?

MR MOODY 'Twas well I did not, I'll promise you, there were those would have made bold with Mistress Bride; an' if she had stirred out of doors, there were whipsters* abroad i' faith, padders† of maidenheads, that would have trussed her up, and picked the

---

* whipsters: debauchers. † padders: robbers.

lock of her affections, ere a man could have said, 'What's this?' But by good luck I had warning of it by a friend's letter.

SIR JOHN SWALLOW The remedy for all such dangers is easy, you may send for a parson; and have the business dispatched at home.

MR MOODY A match, i'faith, do you provide a domine, and I'll go tell her our resolutions, and hearten her up against the day of battle.

SIR JOHN SWALLOW Now I think on't, this letter must needs come from Sir Martin; a plot of his, upon my life, to hinder our marriage.

WARNER I see, Sir, you'll still mistake him for a wit; but I am much deceived, if that letter came not from another hand.

SIR JOHN SWALLOW From whom I prithee?

WARNER Nay, for that you shall excuse me, Sir, I do not love to make a breach betwixt persons that are to be so near related.

SIR JOHN SWALLOW Thou seem'st to imply that my mistress was in the plot.

WARNER Can you make a doubt on't? Do you not know she ever loved him, and can you hope she has so soon forsaken him? You may make yourself miserable, if you please, by such a marriage.

SIR JOHN SWALLOW When she is once mine, her virtue will secure me.

WARNER Her virtue!

SIR JOHN SWALLOW What, do you make a mock on't?

WARNER Not I, I assure you, Sir, I think it no such jesting matter.

SIR JOHN SWALLOW Why, is she not honest?

WARNER Yes in my conscience is she, for Sir Martin's tongue's no slander.

SIR JOHN SWALLOW But does she say to the contrary?

WARNER If one would believe him, which for my part I do not, he has in a manner confessed it to me.

SIR JOHN SWALLOW Hell and damnation! –

WARNER Courage, Sir, never vex yourself, I'll warrant you 'tis all a lie.

SIR JOHN SWALLOW But how shall I be 'ssured 'tis so?

WARNER When you are married you'll soon make trial, whether she be a maid or no.

SIR JOHN SWALLOW I do not love to make that experiment at my own cost.

WARNER Then you must never marry.

SIR JOHN SWALLOW Aye, but they have so many tricks to cheat a man, which are entailed from mother to daughter, through all generations, there's no keeping a lock for that door for which every one has a key.

WARNER As for example, their drawing up their breaths with 'Oh! you hurt me, can you be so cruel?' Then the next day she steals a visit to her lover, that did you the courtesy beforehand, and in private tells him how she cozened you twenty to one; but she takes out another lesson with him to practise the next night.

SIR JOHN SWALLOW All this while miserable I must be their May-game.

WARNER 'Tis well if you escape so; for commonly he strikes in with you, and becomes your friend.

SIR JOHN SWALLOW Deliver me from such a friend that stays behind with my wife, when I gird on my sword to go abroad.

WARNER Aye, there's your man, Sir; besides he will be sure to watch your haunts, and tell her of them, that if occasion be, she may have wherewithal to recriminate: at least she will seem to be jealous of you, and who would suspect a jealous wife?

SIR JOHN SWALLOW All manner of ways I am most miserable.

WARNER But if she be not a maid when you marry her, she may make a good wife afterwards, 'tis but imagining you have taken such a man's widow.

SIR JOHN SWALLOW If that were all; but the man will come and claim her again.

WARNER Examples have been frequent of those that have been wanton, and yet afterwards take up.

SIR JOHN SWALLOW Aye, the same thing they took up before.

WARNER The truth is, an honest simple girl that's ignorant of all things, maketh the best matrimony: there is such pleasure in instructing her, the best is, there's not one dunce in all the sex; such a one with a good fortune. –

SIR JOHN SWALLOW Aye, but where is she, Warner?

WARNER Near enough, but that you are too far engaged.

SIR JOHN SWALLOW Engaged to one that hath given me the earnest of cuckoldom beforehand?

WARNER What think you then of Mrs Christian here in the house? There's £5000 and a better penny.

SIR JOHN SWALLOW Aye, but is she fool enough?

WARNER She's none of the wise virgins, I can assure you.

SIR JOHN SWALLOW Dear Warner, step into the next room, and inveigle her out this way, that I may speak to her.

WARNER Remember above all things, you keep this wooing secret; if it takes the least wind, old Moody will be sure to hinder it.

SIR JOHN SWALLOW Do'st thou think I shall get her aunt's consent?

WARNER Leave that to me.   [*Exit Warner*]

SIR JOHN SWALLOW How happy a man shall I be, if I can but compass this! And what a precipice have I avoided! Then the revenge too is so sweet to steal a wife under her father's nose, and leave 'em in the lurch who has abused me; well, such a servant as this Warner is a jewel.

Enter Warner and Mrs Christian to him.

WARNER There she is, Sir, now I'll go to prepare her aunt.

SIR JOHN SWALLOW Sweet mistress, I am come to wait upon you.

MRS CHRISTIAN Truly you are too good to wait on me.

SIR JOHN SWALLOW And in the condition of a suitor.

MRS CHRISTIAN As how, forsooth?

SIR JOHN SWALLOW To be so happy as to marry you.

MRS CHRISTIAN O Lord, I would not marry for anything!

SIR JOHN SWALLOW Why? 'Tis the honest end of womankind.

MRS CHRISTIAN Twenty years hence, forsooth: I would not lie in bed with a man for a world, their beards will so prickle one.

SIR JOHN SWALLOW [*aside*] Pah, – what an innocent girl it is, and very child! I like a colt that never yet was backed; for so I shall make her what I list, and mould her as I will: Lord! Her innocency makes me laugh my cheeks all wet. – ⟨*to her*⟩ Sweet lady. –

MRS CHRISTIAN I'm but a gentlewoman, forsooth.

SIR JOHN SWALLOW Well then, sweet mistress, if I get your friend's consent, shall I have yours?

MRS CHRISTIAN My old lady may do what she will, forsooth, but by my truly, I hope she will have more care of me, than to marry me yet; Lord bless me, what should I do with a husband?

SIR JOHN SWALLOW Well, sweetheart, then instead of wooing you, I must woo my old lady.

MRS CHRISTIAN Indeed, gentleman, my old lady is married already: cry you mercy forsooth, I think you are a knight.

SIR JOHN SWALLOW Happy in that title only to make you a lady.

MRS CHRISTIAN Believe me, Mr Knight, I would not be a lady, it makes folks proud, and so humorous, and so ill huswifes, forsooth.

SIR JOHN ⟨*aside*⟩ Pah, – she's a baby, the simplest thing that ever yet I knew; the happiest man I shall be in the world; for should I have my wish, it should be to keep school, and teach the bigger girls, and here in one my wish it is absolved.

Enter Lady Dupe.

LADY DUPE By your leave, Sir: I hope this noble knight will make you happy, and you make him.

MRS CHRISTIAN [*sighing*] What should I make him?

LADY DUPE Marry, you shall make him happy in a good wife.

MRS CHRISTIAN I will not marry, Madam.

LADY DUPE You fool!

SIR JOHN SWALLOW Pray, Madam, let me speak with you, on my soul 'tis the pretti'st innocent'st thing in the world.

LADY DUPE Indeed, Sir, she knows little besides her work and her prayers; but I'll talk with the fool.

SIR JOHN SWALLOW Deal gently with her, dear Madam.

LADY DUPE Come, Christian, will not you marry this noble knight?

MRS CHRISTIAN [*sobbingly*] Yes, yes, yes. –

LADY DUPE Sir, it shall be tonight.

SIR JOHN SWALLOW This innocence is a dowry beyond all price.

[*Exeunt Lady Dupe and Mrs Christian*]

Enter Sir Martin, to Sir John, musing.

SIR MARTIN MAR-ALL You are very melancholy methinks, Sir.

SIR JOHN SWALLOW You are mistaken, Sir.

SIR MARTIN MAR-ALL You may dissemble as you please, but Mrs Millisent lies at the bottom of your heart.

SIR JOHN SWALLOW My heart, I assure you, has no room for so poor a trifle.

SIR MARTIN MAR-ALL Sure you think to wheedle me, would you have me imagine you do not love her?

SIR JOHN SWALLOW Love her! Why should you think me such a sot? Love a prostitute, and infamous person!

SIR MARTIN MAR-ALL Fair and soft, Sir John.

SIR JOHN SWALLOW You see I am no very obstinate rival, I leave the field free to you: go on, Sir, and pursue your good fortune, and be as happy as such a common creature can make thee.

SIR MARTIN MAR-ALL This is Hebrew-Greek to me; but I must tell you, Sir, I will not suffer my divinity to be profaned by such a tongue as yours.

SIR JOHN SWALLOW Believe it; whate'er I say I can quote my author for.

SIR MARTIN MAR-ALL Then, Sir, whoever told it you, lied in his throat, d'you see, and deeper than that d'ye see, in his stomach and his guts d'ye see: tell me she's a common person! He's a son of a whore that said it, and I'll make him eat his words, though he spoke 'em in a privy-house.

SIR JOHN SWALLOW What if Warner told me so? I hope you'll grant him to be a competent judge in such a business.

SIR MARTIN MAR-ALL Did that precious rascal say it? – Now I think on't I'll not believe you: in fine, Sir, I'll hold you an even wager he denies it.

SIR JOHN SWALLOW I'll lay you ten to one, he justifies it to your face.

SIR MARTIN MAR-ALL I'll make him give up the ghost under my fist, if he does not deny it.

SIR JOHN SWALLOW I'll cut off his ears upon the spot, if he does not stand to't.

Enter Warner.

SIR MARTIN MAR-ALL Here he comes in pudding-time* to resolve the question: come hither, you lying varlet, hold up your

* pudding-time: a favourable time.

hand at the Bar of Justice, and answer me to what I shall demand.

WARNER What a goodier* is the matter, Sir?

SIR MARTIN MAR-ALL Thou spawn of the old serpent, fruitful in nothing but in lies!

WARNER A very fair beginning this.

SIR MARTIN MAR-ALL Didst thou dare to cast thy venom upon such a saint as Mrs Millisent, to traduce her virtue, and say it was adulterate?

WARNER Not guilty, my lord.

SIR MARTIN MAR-ALL I told you so.

SIR JOHN SWALLOW How, Mr Rascal! Have you forgot what you said but now concerning Sir Martin and Mrs Millisent? I'll stop the lie down your throat, if you dare deny't.

SIR MARTIN MAR-ALL Say you so! Are you there again i'faith?

WARNER Pray pacify yourself, Sir, 'twas a plot of my own devising.

SIR MARTIN MAR-ALL Leave off your winking and your pinking, with a horse-pox t'ye, I'll understand none of it; tell me in plain English the truth of the business: for an' you were my own brother, you should pay for it: belie my mistress! What a pox d'ye think I have no sense of honour?

WARNER What the devil's the matter w'ye? Either be at quiet, or I'll resolve to take my heels, and be gone.

SIR MARTIN MAR-ALL Stop thief there! What did you think to scape the hand of justice? [*lays hold on him*] The best on't is, sirrah, your heels are not altogether so nimble as your tongue. [*beats him*]

WARNER Help! Murder! Murder!

SIR MARTIN MAR-ALL Confess, you rogue, then.

WARNER Hold your heads, I think the devil's in you, – I tell you 'tis a device of mine.

SIR MARTIN MAR-ALL And have you nobody to devise it on but my mistress, the very map of innocence?

SIR JOHN SWALLOW Moderate your anger, good Sir Martin.

SIR MARTIN MAR-ALL By your patience, Sir, I'll chastise him abundantly.

SIR JOHN SWALLOW That's a little too much, Sir, by your favour, to beat him in my presence.

* a goodier: the pox.

SIR MARTIN MAR-ALL That's a good one i'faith, your presence shall hinder me from beating my own servant.

WARNER O traitor to all sense and reason! He's a-going to discover that too.

SIR MARTIN MAR-ALL An' I had a mind to beat him to mummy, he's my own, I hope.

SIR JOHN SWALLOW At present I must tell you he's mine, Sir.

SIR MARTIN MAR-ALL Hey-day! Here's a fine juggling!

WARNER Stop yet, Sir, you are just upon the brink of a precipice.

SIR MARTIN MAR-ALL What is't thou meanest now? – a lord! My mind misgives me I have done some fault, but would I were hanged if I can find it out.

WARNER [aside] There's no making him understand me.

SIR MARTIN MAR-ALL Pox on't, come what will, I'll not be faced down with a lie; I say he is my man.

SIR JOHN SWALLOW Pray remember yourself better; did not you turn him away for some fault lately, and laid a livery of black and blue on his back before he went?

SIR MARTIN MAR-ALL The devil of any fault, or any black and blue that I remember: either the rascal put some trick upon you, or you would upon me.

SIR JOHN SWALLOW Oh, ho! Then it seems the cudgelling and turning away were pure invention; I am glad I understand it.

SIR MARTIN MAR-ALL In fine, it's all so damned a lie. –

WARNER Alas! He had forgot it, Sir, good wits, you know, have bad memories.

SIR JOHN SWALLOW No, no, Sir, that shall not serve your turn, you may return when you please to your old master, I give you a fair discharge, and a glad man I am to be so rid of you: were you thereabouts i'faith? What a snake had I entertained into my bosom? Fare you well, Sir, and lay your next plot better between you, I advise you. [*Exit Sir John*]

WARNER Lord, Sir, how you stand! As you were nipped i'th' head: have you done any new piece of folly, that makes you look so like an ass?

SIR MARTIN MAR-ALL Here's three pieces of gold yet; if I had the heart to offer it thee. [*holds the gold afar off trembling*]

WARNER Noble Sir, what have I done to deserve so great a

liberality? I confess if you had beaten me for your own fault, if you had utterly destroyed all my projects, then it might ha' bin expected that ten or twenty pieces should have been offered by way of recompence and satisfaction. –

SIR MARTIN MAR-ALL Nay, an' you be so full o' your flouts, your friend and servant; who the devil could tell the meaning of your signs and tokens, an' you go to that?

WARNER You are no ass then?

SIR MARTIN MAR-ALL Well, Sir, to do you service, d'ye see, I am an ass in a fair way; will that satisfy you?

WARNER For this once produce those three pieces, I am contented to receive that inconsiderable tribute, or make 'em six and I'll take the fault upon myself.

SIR MARTIN MAR-ALL Are we friends then? If we are, let me advise you. –

WARNER Yet advising. –

SIR MARTIN MAR-ALL For no harm, good Warner: but pray next time make me of your counsel, let me enter into the business, instruct me in every point, and then if I discover all, I am resolved to give over affairs, and retire from the world.

WARNER Agreed, it shall be so; but let us now take breath a while, then on again.

For though we had the worst, those heats were past,
We'll whip and spur, and fetch him up at last.

                                                    [*Exeunt*]

ACT FIVE

⟨SCENE I⟩

Enter Lord ⟨Dartmouth⟩, Lady Dupe, Mrs Christian, Rose, and Warner.

LORD DARTMOUTH Your promise is admirably made good to me, that Sir John Swallow should be this night married to Mrs Christian; instead of that, he is more deeply engaged than ever with old Moody.

WARNER I cannot help these ebbs and flows of fortune.

LADY DUPE I am sure my niece suffers most in't, he's come off to her with a cold compliment of a mistake in his mistress's virtue, which he has now found out, by your master's folly, to be a plot of yours to separate them.

MRS CHRISTIAN To be forsaken when a woman has given her consent!

LORD DARTMOUTH 'Tis the same scorn, as to have a town rendered up, and afterwards slighted.

ROSE You are a sweet youth, Sir, to use my lady so, when she depended on you; is this the faith of *valet de chambre*? I would be ashamed to be such a dishonour to my profession; it will reflect upon us in time, we shall be ruined by your good example.

WARNER As how my dear Lady Ambassadress?

ROSE Why, they say the women govern their ladies, and you govern us: so if you play fast and loose, not a gallant will bribe us for our goodwills; the gentle guinea will now go to the ordinary, which used as duly to steal into our hands at the stairfoot as into Mr Doctor's at parting.

LORD DARTMOUTH Night's come, and I expect your promise.

LADY DUPE Fail with me if you think good, Sir.

MRS CHRISTIAN I give no more time.

ROSE And if my mistress go to bed a maid tonight –

WARNER Hey-day! You are dealing with me, as they do with the bankers, call in all your debts together; there's no possibility of payment at this rate, but I'll coin for you all as fast as I can, I assure you.

LADY DUPE But you must not think to pay us with false money as you have done hitherto.

ROSE Leave off your mountebank tricks with us, and fall to your
business in good earnest.

WARNER Faith, and I will Rose; for to confess the truth, I am a
kind of a mountebank, I have but one cure for all your diseases,
that is, that my Mr may marry Mistress Millisent, for then Sir
John Swallow will of himself return to Mrs Christian.

LORD DARTMOUTH He says true, and therefore we must all be
helping to that design.

WARNER I'll put you upon something, give me but a thinking
time. In the first place, get a warrant and bailiff to arrest Sir John
Swallow upon a promise of marriage to Mistress Christian.

LORD DARTMOUTH Very good.

LADY DUPE We'll all swear it.

WARNER I never doubted your ladyship in the least, Madam –
for the rest we will consider hereafter.

LORD DARTMOUTH Leave this to us.

[Exeunt Lord ⟨Dartmouth⟩, Lady Dupe, Mrs Christian]

Enter Millisent above.

WARNER Rose where's thy lady?

MRS MILLISENT What have you to say to her?

WARNER Only to tell you, Madam, I am going forward in the
great work of projection.

MRS MILLISENT I know not whether you will deserve my thanks
when the work's done.

WARNER Madam, I hope you are not become indifferent to my
master.

MRS MILLISENT If he should prove a fool after all your crying
up his wit, I shall be a miserable woman.

WARNER A fool! That were a good jest i'faith; but how comes
your ladyship to suspect it?

ROSE I have heard, Madam, your greatest wits have ever a touch
of madness and extravagance in them, so perhaps has he.

WARNER There's nothing more distant than wit and folly, yet
like east and west, they may meet in a point, and produce actions
that are but a hair's breadth from one another.

ROSE I'll undertake he has wit enough to make one laugh at him a
whole day together: he's a most comical person.

MRS MILLISENT For all this I will not swear he is no fool; he has still discovered all your plots.

WARNER O Madam, that's the common fate of your Machivilians,★ they draw their designs so subtle, that their very fineness breaks them.

MRS MILLISENT However I'm resolved to be on the sure side, I will have certain proof of his wit before I marry him.

WARNER Madam, I'll give you one, he wears his clothes like a great sloven, and that's a sure sign of wit, he neglects his outward parts; besides, he speaks French, sings, dances, plays upon the lute.

MRS MILLISENT Does he do all this, say you?

WARNER Most divinely, Madam.

MRS MILLISENT I ask no more, then let him give me a serenade immediately; but let him stand in the view, I'll not be cheated.

WARNER He shall do't Madam: [*aside*] but how, the devil knows – for he sings like a screech-owl, and never touched the lute.

MRS MILLISENT You'll see't performed?

WARNER Now I think on't, Madam, this will but retard our enterprise.

MRS MILLISENT Either let him do't, or see me no more.

WARNER Well, it shall be done, Madam; but where's your father? Will he overhear it?

MRS MILLISENT As good hap is, he's below stairs, talking with a seaman, that has brought him news from the East Indies.

WARNER What concernment can he have there?

MRS MILLISENT He had a bastard-son there, whom he loved extremely: but not having any news from him these many years, concluded him dead; this son he expects within these three days.

WARNER When did he see him last?

MRS MILLISENT Not since he was seven years old.

WARNER A sudden thought comes into my head to make him appear before his time; let my master pass for him, and by that means he may come into the house unsuspected by your father, or his rival.

★ Machivilians: those who followed the precepts of Niccolo Machiavelli (1469–1527), the Florentine statesman and author of *The Prince*, which greatly influenced Elizabethan drama – and statecraft.

MRS MILLISENT According as he performs his serenade, I'll talk with you – make haste – I must retire a little.

[*Exit Mrs Millisent from above*]

ROSE I'll instruct him most rarely, he shall never be found out; but in the meantime, what wilt thou do with a serenade?

WARNER Faith, I am a little nonplussed on the sudden, but a warm consolation from thy lips, Rose, would set my wits a-working again.

ROSE Adieu, Warner. [*Exit Rose*]

WARNER Inhumane Rose, adieu. Blockhead Warner, into what a premunire* hast thou brought thyself? This 'tis to be so forward for another – but to be godfather to a fool, to promise and vow he should do anything like a Christian –

Enter Sir Martin.

SIR MARTIN MAR-ALL Why, how now bully, in a brown study? For my good I warrant it; there's five shillings for thee, what, we must encourage good wits sometimes.

WARNER Hang your white pelf: sure, Sir, by your largesse you mistake me for Martin Parker,† the ballad-maker; your covetousness has offended my muse, and quite dulled her.

SIR MARTIN MAR-ALL How angry the poor devil is? In fine thou art as choleric as a cook by a fireside.

WARNER I am overheated, like a gun, with continual discharging my wit: s'life, Sir, I have rarefied my brains for you till they are evaporated; but come, Sir, do something for yourself like a man, I have engaged you shall give to your mistress a serenade in your proper person: I'll borrow a lute for you.

SIR MARTIN MAR-ALL I'll warrant thee, I'll do't man.

WARNER You never learned, I do not think you know one stop.

SIR MARTIN MAR-ALL 'Tis no matter for that, Sir, I'll play as fast as I can, and never stop at all.

WARNER Go to, you are an invincible fool I see; get up into your window, and set two candles by you, take my landlord's lute in your hand, and fumble on't, and make grimaces with your mouth,

* premunire: predicament.
† Martin Parker: the point of the remark is that ballad-makers sold their work in the streets usually for a penny.

as if you sung; in the meantime, I'll play in the next room in the dark, and consequently your mistress, who will come to her balcony over against you, will think it to be you; and at the end of every tune, I'll ring the bell that hangs between your chamber and mine, that you may know when to have done.

SIR MARTIN MAR-ALL Why, this is fair play now, to tell a man beforehand what he must do; gramercy i'faith, boy, now if I fail thee –

WARNER About your business then, your mistress and her maid appear already: I'll give you the sign with the bell when I am prepared, for my lute is at hand in the barber's shop.   [*Exeunt*]

Enter Millisent, Rose, with a candle by 'em above.

ROSE We shall have rare music.

MRS MILLISENT I wish it prove so; for I suspect the knight can neither play nor sing.

ROSE But if he does, you're bound to pay the music, Madam.

MRS MILLISENT I'll not believe it, except both my ears and eyes are witnesses.

ROSE But 'tis night, Madam, and you cannot see 'em; yet he may play admirably in the dark.

MRS MILLISENT Where's my father?

ROSE You need not fear him, he's still employed with that same seaman, and I have set Mrs Christian to watch their discourse, that betwixt her and me Warner may have wherewithal to instruct his master.

MRS MILLISENT But yet there's fear my father will find out the plot.

ROSE Not in the least, for my old lady has provided two rare disguises for the master and the man.

MRS MILLISENT Peace, I hear them beginning to tune the lute.

ROSE And see, Madam, where your true knight Sir Martin is placed yonder like Apollo, with his lute in his hand and his rays about his head.

Sir Martin appears at the adverse window, a tune played; when it is done, Warner rings, and Sir Martin holds.

Did he not play most excellently, Madam?

MRS MILLISENT He played well, and yet methinks he held his
  lute but untowardly.

ROSE Dear Madam, peace; now for the song.

The Song.

Blind love to this hour
Had never like me, a slave under his power.
  Then blest be the dart
  That he threw at my heart,
  For nothing can prove
A joy so great as to be wounded with love.

My days and my nights
Are filled to the purpose with sorrows and frights;
  From my heart still I sigh
  And my eyes are ne'er dry,
  So that Cupid be praised,
I am to the top of love's happiness raised.

My soul's all on fire,
So that I have the pleasure to dote and desire,
  Such a pretty soft pain
  That it tickles each vein;
  'Tis the dream of a smart,
Which makes me breathe short when it beats at my heart.

Sometimes in a pet,
When I am despised, I my freedom would get;
  But straight a sweet smile
  Does my anger beguile,
  And my heart does recall,
Then the more I do struggle, the lower I fall.

Heaven does not impart
Such a grace as to love unto ev'ryone's heart;
  For many may wish
  To be wounded and miss:
  Then blest be love's fire,
And more blest her eyes that first taught me desire.

The song being done, Warner rings again; but Sir Martin continues fumbling, and gazing on his mistress.

MRS MILLISENT A pretty humoured song: – but stay, methinks he plays and sings still, and yet we cannot hear him. – Play louder, Sir Martin, that we may have the fruits on't.

WARNER [*peeping*] Death! This abominable fool will spoil all again. Damn him, he stands making his grimaces yonder, and he looks so earnestly upon his mistress, that he hears me not. [*rings again*]

MRS MILLISENT Ah, ah! Have I found you out, Sir? Now as I live and breathe, this is pleasant, Rose, – his man played and sung for him, and he, it seems, did not know when he should give over. [*Millisent and Rose laugh*]

WARNER They have found him out, and laugh yonder as if they would split their sides. Why, Mr Fool, Oaf, Coxcomb, will you hear none of your names?

MRS MILLISENT Sir Martin, Sir Martin, take your man's counsel, and keep time with your music.

SIR MARTIN MAR-ALL [*peeping*] Ha! What do you say, Madam? How does your ladyship like my music?

MRS MILLISENT O most heavenly! Just like the harmony of the spheres that is to be admired, and never heard.

WARNER You have ruined all by your not leaving off in time.

SIR MARTIN MAR-ALL What the devil would you have a man do when my hand is in! Well o'my conscience I think there is a fate upon me.

Noise within.

MRS MILLISENT Look, Rose, what's the matter.

ROSE 'Tis Sir John Swallow pursued by the bailiffs, Madam, according to our plot; it seems they have dogged him thus late to his lodging.

MRS MILLISENT That's well! For though I begin not to love this fool; yet I am glad I shall be rid on him. [*Exeunt Mrs Millisent, Rose*]

Enter Sir John pursued by three bailiffs over the stage.

SIR MARTIN MAR-ALL Now I'll redeem all again, my mistress shall see my valour, I'm resolved on't. Villains, rogues, poltroons!

What? Three upon one? In fine, I'll be with you immediately.

[*Exit*]

WARNER Why, Sir, are you stark mad? Have you no grain of sense left? He's gone! Now is he as earnest in the quarrel as Cokes among the poppits;* 'tis to no purpose whatever I do for him.

[*Exit Warner*]

Enter Sir John and Sir Martin (having driven away the bailiffs). Sir Martin flourishes his sword.

SIR MARTIN MAR-ALL *Victoria! Victoria!* What heart, Sir John, you have received no harm, I hope?

SIR JOHN SWALLOW Not the least, I thank you Sir for your timely assistance, which I will requite with anything but the resigning of my mistress. – Dear Sir Martin, a good night.

SIR MARTIN MAR-ALL Pray let me wait upon you in Sir John.

SIR JOHN SWALLOW I can find my way to Mrs Millisent without you, Sir, I thank you.

SIR MARTIN MAR-ALL But pray, what were you to be arrested for?

SIR JOHN SWALLOW I know no more than you; some little debts, perhaps, I left unpaid by my negligence: once more good night, Sir.   [*Exit*]

SIR MARTIN MAR-ALL He's an ungrateful fellow; and so in fine, I shall tell him when I see him next –

Enter Warner.

Monsieur Warner, *apropos!* I hope you'll applaud me now, I have defeated the enemy, and that in sight of my mistress; boy, I have charmed her, i'faith, with my valour.

WARNER Aye, just as much as you did e'en now with your music; go, you are so beastly a fool, that a chiding is thrown away upon you.

SIR MARTIN MAR-ALL Fool in your face, Sir; call a man of honour, 'Fool', when I have just achieved such an enterprise – Gad now my blood's up, I am a dangerous person, I can tell you that, Warner.

* poppits: earlier form of puppets, the reference being to Bartholomew Cokes at the puppet show in Act V of *Bartholomew Fair*.

WARNER Poor animal, I pity thee.

SIR MARTIN MAR-ALL I grant I am no musician, but you must allow me for a sword-man, I have beat 'em bravely; and in fine, I am come off unhurt, save only a little scratch i'th'head.

WARNER That's impossible, thou hast a skull so thick, no sword can pierce it; but much good may't d'ye, Sir, with the fruits of your valour: you rescued your rival when he was to be arrested on purpose to take him off from your mistress.

SIR MARTIN MAR-ALL Why, this is ever the fate of ingenious men; nothing thrives they take in hand.

Enter Rose.

ROSE Sir Martin, you have done your business with my lady, she'll never look upon you more; she says, she's so well satisfied of your wit and courage, that she will not put you to any further trial.

SIR MARTIN MAR-ALL Warner, is there no hopes, Warner?

WARNER None that I know.

SIR MARTIN MAR-ALL Let's have but one civil plot more before we part.

WARNER 'Tis to no purpose.

ROSE Yet if he had some golden friends that would engage for him the next time –

SIR MARTIN MAR-ALL Here's a Jacobus and a Carolus★ will enter into bonds for me.

ROSE I'll take their royal words for once. [*she fetches two disguises*]

WARNER The meaning of this, dear Rose?

ROSE 'Tis in pursuance of thy own invention, Warner; a child which thy wit hath begot upon me: but let us lose no time. Help! Help! Dress thy master, that he may be Anthony, old Moody's bastard, and thou his servant has come from the East Indies.

SIR MARTIN MAR-ALL Hey-tarock it† – now we shall have Rose's device too, I long to be at it, pray let's hear more on't.

ROSE Old Moody you must know in his younger years, when he was a Cambridge scholar, made bold with a townsman's daughter

---

★ a Jacobus and a Carolus: gold pieces, then worth twenty shillings.

† Hey-tarock it: possibly Hey, trump it. Tarock is an English name for Tarot cards.

there, by whom he had a bastard whose name was Anthony, whom you Sir Martin, are to represent.

SIR MARTIN MAR-ALL I warrant you, let me alone for Tony: but pray go on, Rose.

ROSE This child in his father's time he durst not own, but bred him privately in the Isle of Ely, till he was seven years old, and from thence sent him with one Bonaventure a merchant for the East-Indies.

WARNER But will not this over-burden your memory, Sir?

SIR MARTIN MAR-ALL There's no answering thee anything, thou think'st I am good for nothing.

ROSE Bonaventure died at Surat within two years, and this Anthony has lived up and down in the Mogul's country unheard of by his father till this night, and is expected within these three days: now if you can pass for him, you may have admittance into the house, and make an end of all the business before the other Anthony arrives.

WARNER But hold, Rose, there's one considerable point omitted; what was his mother's name?

ROSE That indeed I had forgot; her name was Dorothy, daughter to one Draw-water a vintner at the Rose.

WARNER Come, Sir, are you perfect in your lesson? Anthony Moody born in Cambridge, bred in the Isle of Ely, sent into the Mogul's country at seven years old with one Bonaventure a merchant, who died within two years; your mother's name Dorothy Draw-water the vintner's daughter at the Rose.

SIR MARTIN MAR-ALL I have it all *ad unguem*★ – what, do'st think I'm a sot? But stay a little, how have I lived all this while in that same country?

WARNER What country? – Pox, he has forgot already –

ROSE The Mogul's country.

SIR MARTIN MAR-ALL Aye, aye, the Mogul's country! What a devil, any man may mistake a little; but now I have it perfect: but what have I been doing all this while in the Mogul's country? He's a heathen rogue, I am afraid I shall never hit upon his name.

WARNER Why, you have been passing your time there, no matter how.

★ *ad unguem*: precisely, correctly.

ROSE Well, if this passes upon the old man, I'll bring your business about again with my mistress, never fear it; stay you here at the door, I'll go tell the old man of your arrival.   [*Exit Rose*]

WARNER Well, Sir, now play your part exactly, and I'll forgive all your former errors. –

SIR MARTIN MAR-ALL Hang 'em, they were only slips of youth – how peremptory and domineering this rogue is! Now he sees I have need of his service: would I were out of his power again, I would make him lie at my feet like any spaniel.

Enter ⟨Mr⟩ Moody, Sir John, Lord ⟨Dartmouth⟩, Lady Dupe, Mrs Millisent, ⟨Mrs⟩ Christian, Rose.

MR MOODY Is he here already, say'st thou? Which is he?

ROSE That sunburned gentleman.

MR MOODY My dear boy Anthony, do I see thee again before I die? Welcome, welcome.

SIR MARTIN MAR-ALL My dear father, I know it is you by instinct; for methinks I am as like you as if I were spit out of your mouth.

ROSE [*aside to the lord*] Keep it up I beseech your lordship.

LORD DARTMOUTH He's wond'rous like indeed.

LADY DUPE The very image of him.

MR MOODY Anthony, you must salute all this company: this is my Lord Dartmouth, this my Lady Dupe, this her niece Mrs Christian.

SIR MARTIN MAR-ALL [*salutes them*] And that's my sister, methinks I have a good resemblance of her too: honest sister, I must need kiss you sister.

WARNER This fool will discover himself, I foresee it already by his carriage to her.

MR MOODY And now Anthony, pray tell's a little of your travels.

SIR MARTIN MAR-ALL Time enough for that, forsooth father, but I have such a natural affection for my sister, that methinks I could live and die with her: give me thy hand sweet sister.

SIR JOHN SWALLOW She's beholding to you, Sir.

SIR MARTIN MAR-ALL What if she be Sir, what's that to you Sir?

SIR JOHN SWALLOW I hope, Sir, I have not offended you?

SIR MARTIN MAR-ALL It may be you have, and it may be you have not, Sir; you see I have no mind to satisfy you, Sir: what a devil! A man cannot talk a little to his own flesh and blood, but you must be interposing with a murrain to you.

MR MOODY Enough of this, good Anthony, this gentleman is to marry your sister.

SIR MARTIN MAR-ALL He marry my sister! Ods foot, Sir, there are some bastards, that shall be nameless, that are as well worthy to marry her, as any man; and have as good blood in their veins.

SIR JOHN SWALLOW I do not question it in the least, Sir.

SIR MARTIN MAR-ALL 'Tis not your best course, Sir; you marry my sister! What have you seen of the world, Sir? I have seen your hurricanoes, and your calentures,* and your ecliptics, and your tropic lines, Sir, an' you go to that, Sir.

WARNER You must excuse my master, the sea's a little working in his brain, Sir.

SIR MARTIN MAR-ALL And your Prester Johns o'th' East-Indies, and your Great Turk of Rome and Persia.

MR MOODY Lord, what a thing it is to be learned, and a traveller! Bodikins it makes me weep for joy; but, Anthony, you must not bear yourself too much upon your learning, child.

MRS MILLISENT Pray brother be civil to this gentleman for my sake.

SIR MARTIN MAR-ALL For your sake, sister Millisent, much may be done, and here I kiss your hand on't.

WARNER Yet again stupidity?

MRS MILLISENT Nay, pray brother hands off, now you are too rude.

SIR MARTIN MAR-ALL Dear sister, as I am a true East-India gentleman –

MR MOODY But pray, son Anthony, let us talk of other matters, and tell me truly, had you not quite forgot me? And yet I made woundy much of you when you were young.

SIR MARTIN MAR-ALL I remember you as well as if I saw you but yesterday: a fine grey-headed – grey-bearded old gentleman as ever I saw in all my life.

* calentures: fevers.

WARNER [*aside*] Grey-bearded old gentleman! When he was a scholar at Cambridge.

MR MOODY But do you remember where you were bred up?

SIR MARTIN MAR-ALL O yes, Sir, most perfectly, in the Isle – stay – let me see, Oh – now I have it – in the Isle of Silly.★

MR MOODY In the Isle of Ely, sure you mean?

WARNER Without doubt he did, Sir, but this damned Isle of Silly runs in's head ever since his sea-voyage.

MR MOODY And your mother's name was – come pray let me examine you – for that I'm sure you cannot forget.

SIR MARTIN MAR-ALL ⟨*aside*⟩ Warner! What was it Warner?

WARNER Poor Mrs Dorothy Draw-water, if she were now alive, what a joyful day would this be to her?

MR MOODY Who the devil bid you speak, sirrah?

SIR MARTIN MAR-ALL Her name, Sir, was Mrs Dorothy Draw-water.

SIR JOHN SWALLOW I'll be hanged if this be not some cheat.

MRS MILLISENT He makes so many stumbles, he must needs fall at last.

MR MOODY But you remember, I hope, where you were born?

WARNER Well, they may talk what they will of Oxford for an university, but Cambridge for my money.

MR MOODY Hold your tongue you scanderbag rogue you, this is the second time you have been talking when you should not.

SIR MARTIN MAR-ALL I was born at Cambridge, I remember it as perfectly as if it were but yesterday.

WARNER How I sweat for him! He's remembering ever since he was born.

MR MOODY And who did you go over withal to the East-Indies?

SIR MARTIN MAR-ALL ⟨*aside*⟩ Warner!

WARNER 'Twas a happy thing, Sir, you lighted upon so honest a merchant as Mr Bonaventure, to take care of him.

MR MOODY Saucy rascal! This is past all sufferance.

ROSE We are undone Warner, if this discourse go on any further.

LORD DARTMOUTH Pray, Sir, take pity o'th' poor gentleman, he has more need of a good supper, than to be asked so many questions.

★ Isle of Silly: the Scilly Isles, off Cornwall.

SIR JOHN SWALLOW These are rogues, Sir, I plainly perceive it;
    pray let me ask him one question – which way did you come
    home Sir?

SIR MARTIN MAR-ALL We came home by land, Sir.

WARNER That is, from India to Persia, from Persia to Turkey,
    from Turkey to Germany, from Germany to France.

SIR JOHN SWALLOW And from thence, over the narrow seas on
    horseback.

MR MOODY 'Tis so, I discern it now, but some shall smoke for't.
    Stay a little Anthony, I'll be with you presently.   [*Exit Moody*]

WARNER [*aside*] That wicked old man is gone for no good, I'm
    afraid, would I were fairly quit of him.

MRS MILLISENT [*aside*] Tell me no more of Sir Martin, Rose, he
    wants natural sense, to talk after this rate; but for this Warner, I
    am strangely taken with him, how handsomely he brought him
    off?

Enter ⟨Mr⟩ Moody with two cudgels.

MR MOODY Among half a score tough cudgels I had in my chamber,
    I have made choice of these two as best able to hold out.

MRS MILLISENT Alas! Poor Warner must be beaten now for all
    his wit, would I could bear it for him.

WARNER But to what end is all this preparation, Sir?

MR MOODY In the first place, for your worship, and in the next,
    for this East-Indian apostle, that will needs be my son Anthony.

WARNER Why, d'ye think he is not?

MR MOODY No, thou wicked accomplice in his designs, I know he
    is not.

WARNER Who, I his accomplice? I beseech you, Sir, what is it to
    me, if he should prove a counterfeit; I assure you he has cozened
    me in the first place.

SIR JOHN SWALLOW That's likely, i'faith, cozen his own ser-
    vant?

WARNER As I hope for mercy, Sir, I am an utter stranger to him,
    he took me up but yesterday, and told me the story word for
    word as he told it you.

SIR MARTIN MAR-ALL ⟨*aside*⟩ What will become of us two now?
    I trust to the rogue's wit to bring me off.

MR MOODY If thou wou'dst have me believe thee, take one of these two cudgels, and help me to lay it on soundly.

WARNER With all my heart.

MR MOODY Out you cheat, you hypocrite, you imposter! Do you come hither to cozen an honest man? [*beats him*]

SIR MARTIN MAR-ALL Hold, hold, Sir.

WARNER Do you come hither with a lie to get a father, Mr Anthony of East-India? ⟨*beats him*⟩

SIR MARTIN MAR-ALL Hold you inhumane butcher.

WARNER I'll teach you to counterfeit again, Sir.

SIR MARTIN MAR-ALL The rogue will murder me.

[*Exeunt Sir Martin ⟨and Warner⟩*]

MR MOODY A fair riddance of 'em both: let's in and laugh at 'em.

[*Exeunt*]

Enter again Sir Martin, and Warner.

SIR MARTIN MAR-ALL Was there ever such an affront put upon a man, to be beaten by his servant?

WARNER After my hearty salutations upon your backside, Sir, may a man have leave to ask you what news from the Mogul's country?

SIR MARTIN MAR-ALL I wonder where thou hadst the impudence to move such a question to me, knowing how thou hast used me.

WARNER Now, Sir, you may see what comes of your indiscretion and stupidity: I always gave you warning of it, but for this time I am content to pass it by without more words, partly, because I have already corrected you, though not so much as you deserve.

SIR MARTIN MAR-ALL Do'st thou think to carry it off at this rate, after such an injury?

WARNER You may thank yourself for't; nay 'twas very well I found out that way, otherwise I had been suspected as your accomplice.

SIR MARTIN MAR-ALL But you laid it on with such a vengeance, as if you were beating of a stockfish.*

WARNER To confess the truth on't, you had angered me, and I was willing to evaporate my choler; if you will pass it by so, I

* stockfish: dried codfish.

may chance to help you to your mistress: no more words of this business, I advise you, but go home and grease your back.

SIR MARTIN MAR-ALL ⟨*aside*⟩ In fine, I must suffer it at his hands; for if my shoulders had not paid for this fault, my purse must have sweat blood for't: the rogue has got such a hank upon me –

Enter Rose.

WARNER So, so, here's another of our vessels come in after the storm that parted us: what comfort, Rose, no harbour near?

ROSE My lady, as you may well imagine, is most extremely incensed against Sir Martin; but she applauds your ingenuity to the skies. I'll say no more, but thereby hangs a tale.

SIR MARTIN MAR-ALL I am considering with myself about a plot, to bring all about again.

ROSE Yet again plotting! If you have such a mind to't, I know no way so proper for you as to turn poet to *Pugenello.*★

Music plays.

WARNER Hark! Is not that music in your house?

ROSE Yes, Sir John has given my mistress the fiddles, and our old man is as jocund yonder, and does so hug himself to think how he has been revenged upon you.

WARNER Why, he does not know 'twas we, I hope?

ROSE 'Tis all one for that.

SIR MARTIN MAR-ALL I have such a plot; I care not, I will speak an' I were to be hanged for't – shall I speak, dear Warner? Let me now; it does so wamble† within me, just like a clyster,‡ i'faith law, and I can keep it no longer for my heart.

WARNER Well, I am indulgent to you; out with it boldly in the name of nonsense.

SIR MARTIN MAR-ALL We two will put on vizards, and with the help of my landlord, who shall be of the party, go a-mumming there, and by some device of dancing, get my mistress away unsuspected by 'em all.

ROSE What if this should hit now, when all your projects have failed, Warner?

★ *Pugenello*: Punchinello, the equivalent of Punch in the Italian puppet show.
† wamble: roll around unsteadily, feel nausea.   ‡ clyster: a suppository.

WARNER Would I were hanged if it be not somewhat probable: nay, now I consider better on't – exceeding probable, it must take, 'tis not in nature to be avoided.

SIR MARTIN MAR-ALL O must it so, Sir! And who may you thank for't?

WARNER Now am I so mad he should be the author of this device. How the devil, Sir, came you to stumble on't?

SIR MARTIN MAR-ALL Why should not my brains be as fruitful as yours or any man's?

WARNER This is so good, it shall not be your plot, Sir, either disown it, or I will proceed no further.

SIR MARTIN MAR-ALL I would not lose the credit of my plot to gain my mistress; the plot's a good one, and I'll justify it upon any ground of England; an' you will not work upon't, it shall be done without you.

ROSE I think the knight has reason.

WARNER Well, I'll order it however to the best advantage: hark you, Rose. [*whispers*]

SIR MARTIN MAR-ALL If it miscarry by your ordering, take notice 'tis your fault, 'tis well invented I'll take my oath on't.

ROSE I must in to 'em, for fear I should be suspected; but I'll acquaint my lord, my old lady, and all the rest who ought to know it, with your design.

WARNER We'll be with you in a twinkling: you and I, Rose, are to follow our leaders, and be paired tonight –

ROSE To have, and to hold, are dreadful words, Warner; but for your sake I'll venture on 'em. [*Exeunt*]

⟨SCENE II⟩

Enter Lord ⟨Dartmouth⟩, Lady Dupe, and Mrs Christian.

LADY DUPE Nay! Good my lord be patient.

LORD DARTMOUTH Does he think to give fiddles and treatments* in a house where he has wronged a lady? I'll never suffer it.

* treatments: feasting.

LADY DUPE But upon what ground will you raise your quarrel?

LORD DARTMOUTH A very just one, as I am her kinsman.

LADY DUPE He does not know yet why he was to be arrested; try that way again.

LORD DARTMOUTH I'll hear of nothing but revenge.

Enter Rose.

ROSE Yes, pray hear me one word, my lord, Sir Martin himself has made a plot.

MRS CHRISTIAN That's like to be a good one.

ROSE A fool's plot may be as lucky as a fool's handsel;* 'tis a very likely one, and requires nothing for your part, but to get a parson in the next room, we'll find work for him.

LADY DUPE That shall be done immediately; Christian, make haste, and send for Mr Ball the nonconformist, tell him here are two or three angels to be earned.

MRS CHRISTIAN And two or three possets to be eaten: may I not put in that, Madam?

LADY DUPE Surely you may.

[*Exit Mrs Christian*]

ROSE Then for the rest – 'tis only this – Oh! They are here! Pray take it in a whisper; my lady knows of it already.

Enter ⟨Mr⟩ Moody, Sir John ⟨Swallow⟩, ⟨Mrs⟩ Millisent.

MRS MILLISENT Strike up again, Fiddle, I'll have a French dance.

SIR JOHN SWALLOW Let's have the brawls.†

MR MOODY No, good Sir John, no quarrelling among friends.

LADY DUPE Your company is like to be increased, Sir; some neighbours that heard your fiddles are come a-mumming to you.

MR MOODY Let 'em come in, and we'll be jovy;‡ an' I had but my hobby-horse at home –

SIR JOHN SWALLOW What, are they men or women?

LADY DUPE I believe some prentices broke loose.

MRS MILLISENT Rose! Go and fetch me down two Indian-gowns

---

* handsel: a gift inaugurating a ceremony. The luck of a fool's handsel may be a proverb.

† brawls: a dance in which men and women form a ring by holding hands.

‡ jovy: jovial.

and vizard-masks – you and I will disguise too, and be as good a mummery to them as they to us.

[*Exit Rose*]

MR MOODY That will be most rare.

*Enter Sir Martin, Warner, Landlord disguised like a Tony.**

MR MOODY O here they come! Gentlemen-maskers you are welcome – [*Warner signs to the Music for a dance*] He signs for a dance I believe; you are welcome, Mr Music, strike up, I'll make one as old as I am.

SIR JOHN SWALLOW And I'll not be out.

⟨*A Dance.*⟩

LORD DARTMOUTH Gentlemen-maskers, you have had the frolic, the next turn is mine; bring two flute-glasses† and some stools, ho, we'll have the ladies' health.

SIR JOHN SWALLOW But why stools, my lord?

LORD DARTMOUTH That you shall see: the humour is, that two men at a time are hoisted up; when they are above, they name their ladies, and the rest of the company dance about them while they drink: this they call the frolic of the altitudes.

MR MOODY Some highlander's invention, I'll warrant it.

LORD DARTMOUTH Gentlemen-maskers, you shall begin.

They hoist Sir Martin and Warner.

SIR JOHN SWALLOW Name the ladies.

LORD DARTMOUTH They point to Mrs Millisent and Mrs Christian. *Allons touchez! Touchez!*

MR MOODY A rare toping health this: come Sir John, now you and I will be in our altitudes.

While they drink the company dances and sings: they are taken down.

SIR JOHN SWALLOW What new device is this tro?‡

MR MOODY I know not what to make on't.

[*When they are up, the company dances about 'em: then dance off. Tony dances a jig*]

---

* Tony: a fool, clown.   † flute-glasses: so called from their slender shape.
‡ tro: from trow, to trust or think, used occasionally, as here, in questions.

SIR JOHN SWALLOW [*to Tony*] Pray, Mr Fool, where's the rest o' your company? I would fain see 'em again.

LANDLORD Come down and tell 'em so, cudden.★

SIR JOHN SWALLOW I'll be hanged if there be not some plot in't, and this fool is set here to spin out the time.

MR MOODY Like enough: undone! Undone! My daughter's gone, let me down, sirrah.

LANDLORD Yes, cudden.

SIR JOHN SWALLOW My mistress is gone, let me down first.

LANDLORD This is the quickest way, cudden. [*he offers to pull down the stools*]

SIR JOHN SWALLOW Hold! Hold! Or thou wilt break my neck.

LANDLORD And you will not come down, you may stay there, cudden.   [*Exit Landlord dancing*]

MR MOODY O scanderbag villains!

SIR JOHN SWALLOW Is there no getting down?

MR MOODY All this was long of you Sir Jack.

SIR JOHN SWALLOW 'Twas long of yourself to invite them hither.

MR MOODY O you young coxcomb, to be drawn in thus!

SIR JOHN SWALLOW You old sot you, to be caught so sillily!

MR MOODY Come but an inch nearer, and I'll so claw thee.

SIR JOHN SWALLOW I hope I shall reach to thee.

MR MOODY And 'twere not for thy wooden breast-work there.

SIR JOHN SWALLOW I hope to push thee down from Babylon.

Enter Lord ⟨Dartmouth⟩, Lady Dupe, Sir Martin, Warner, Rose, ⟨Mrs⟩ Millisent, veiled, Landlord.

LORD DARTMOUTH How, gentlemen! What quarrelling among yourselves!

MR MOODY Coxnowns! Help me down, and let me have fair play, he shall never marry my daughter.

SIR MARTIN MAR-ALL [*leading Rose*] No, I'll be sworn that he shall not, therefore never repine, Sir, for marriages you know are made in heaven: in fine, Sir, we are joined together in spite of fortune.

ROSE [*pulling off her mask*] That we are indeed, Sir Martin, and these

★ cudden: a fool, feeble-wit.

are witnesses; therefore in fine never repine, Sir, for marriages you know are made in heaven.

OMNES Rose!

WARNER What, is Rose split in two? Sure I ha' got one Rose!

MRS MILLISENT Aye, the best Rose you ever got in all your life. [*pulls off her mask*]

WARNER This amazeth me so much, I know not what to say or think.

MR MOODY My daughter married to Warner!

SIR MARTIN MAR-ALL Well, I thought it impossible any man in England should have over-reached me: sure Warner there was some mistake in this: prithee Billy let's go to the parson to set all right again, that every man may have his own before the matter go too far.

WARNER Well, Sir! For my part I will have nothing farther to do with these women, for I find they will be too hard for us, but e'en sit down by the loss, and content myself with my hard fortune: but, Madam, do you ever think I will forgive you this, to cheat me into an estate of £2000 a year?

SIR MARTIN MAR-ALL And I were as thee, I would not be so served Warner!

MRS MILLISENT I have served him but right for the cheat he put upon me, when he persuaded me you were a wit – now there's a trick for your trick, Sir.

WARNER Nay, I confess you have out-witted me.

SIR JOHN SWALLOW Let me down, and I'll forgive all freely. [*they let him down*]

MR MOODY What am I kept here for?

WARNER I might in policy keep you there, till your daughter and I had been in private, for a little consummation: but for once, Sir, I'll trust your good nature. [*takes him down too*]

MR MOODY And thou wert a gentleman it would not grieve me!

MRS MILLISENT That I was assured of before I married him, by my lord here.

LORD DARTMOUTH I cannot refuse to own him for my kinsman, though his father's sufferings in the late times have ruined his fortunes.

MR MOODY But yet he has been a serving-man.

WARNER You are mistaken, Sir, I have been a master, and besides there's an estate of £800 a year, only it is mortgaged for £6000.

MR MOODY Well, we'll bring it off, and for my part, I am glad my daughter has missed 'in fine', there.

SIR JOHN SWALLOW I will not be the only man that must sleep without a bedfellow tonight, if this lady will once again receive me.

LADY DUPE She's yours, Sir.

LORD DARTMOUTH And the same parson, that did the former execution, is still in the next chamber; what with caudels, wine, and quidding,* which he has taken in abundance, I think he will be able to wheedle two more of you into matrimony.

MRS MILLISENT Poor Sir Martin looks melancholy! I am half afraid he is in love.

WARNER Not with the lady that took him for a wit, I hope.

ROSE At least, Sir Martin can do more than you Mr Warner, for he can make me a lady, which you cannot my mistress.

SIR MARTIN MAR-ALL I have lost nothing but my man, and in fine, I shall get another.

MRS MILLISENT You'll do very well, Sir Martin, for you'll never be your own man, I assure you.

WARNER For my part I had loved you before if I had followed my inclination.

MRS MILLISENT But now I am afraid you begin of the latest, except your love can grow up like a mushroom at a night's warning.

WARNER For that matter never trouble yourself, I can love as fast as any man, when I am nigh possession; my love falls heavy, and never moves quick till it comes near the centre; he's an ill falconer that will unhood before the quarry be in sight.

Love's an high metalled hawk that beats the air,
But soon grows weary when the game's not near.

---

* quidding: possibly chewing tobacco.

EPILOGUE

As country vicars, when the sermon's done,
Run huddling to the Benediction;
Well knowing, though the better sort may stay,
The vulgar rout will run unblessed away:
So we, when once our play is done, make haste
With a short Epilogue to close your taste.
In thus withdrawing we seem mannerly,
But when the curtain's down we peep, and see
A jury of the wits who still stay late,
And in their club decree the poor play's fate;
Their verdict back is to the boxes brought,
Thence all the Town pronounces it their thought.
Thus, gallants, we like Lilly★ can foresee,
But if you ask us what our doom will be,
We by tomorrow will our fortune cast,
As he tells all things when the year is passed.

★ Lilly: William Lilly, an astrologer and maker of almanacs.

NOTES

The copy text used is that of the first edition of 1668 in the Brotherton Collection, University of Leeds.

Abbreviations

Q1 The first quarto edition, 1668
Q2 The second quarto edition, 1668/9
Q3 The third quarto edition, 1678
Q4 The fourth quarto edition, 1691
Q5 The fifth quarto edition, 1697
C Dryden's *Comedies, Tragedies and Operas*, I, 1701
DW *Dramatic Works*, ed. Congreve, II, 1717
L & D *The Works of John Dryden*, ed. Loftus and Dearing, IX, 1966

Occasional lines or groups of lines set as verse in the copy text have been set as prose. The spellings 'Marral' and 'Marrall' have been regularised to 'Mar-all' throughout.

323.5   Q1 places s.p. *La. Dupe* before Sir John
325.28   heaven's / Heaven Q1
326.36   led DW / lead Q1
327.27   how, dear cousin? / how? dear Cousin. Q1
327.29   he Q5 / she Q1
329.33   aunt angry Q2 / Aunt an angry Q1
335.26   him . . . me L & D / him. *Sir John* And . . . me Q1
346.8   out before L & D / before Q1
346.22   child that's to Q3 / child's that Q1
346.34   *Enter Lady Dupe* / *Enter old La.* Q1
348.33   *Mrs Millisent* / *Penelope* Q1
349.15   forfend Q2 / foresend Q1
351.25   set / sent Q1
352.28   love Q1 / are Q1 uncorrected
353.27   point's Q3 / points Q1
357.23   *Re-enter Moody* Q4 / Q1 omits
358.4   Outalian rogues Q3 / Outlion-Rogues Q1
358.27   shalt Q2 / shall Q1
359.18   without giving Q5 / without Q1
359.25   used / use Q1
360.37   difficult Q2 / difficultly Q1

362.17   serving-man-like Q2 / Serving-man like Q1
363.28   grandam Q2 / grandham Q1
364.1   this? / this: Q1
366.23   suitor. Q2 / suitor: Q1
366.29   beards will DW / beards it will Q1
367.33   *Lady Dupe* / *Old Lady* Q1
367.34   Sir Martin, *to* Sir John DW / Sir Martin *and* Sir John Q1
368.21   And I'll make DC / and make Q1
370.13   *aside* L & D / Q1 affixes to previous speech
371.5   an' you Q4 / ou'you Q1
373.17   *Lady Dupe, Mrs Christian*] / La. D. Mill. Chr. Q1
373.18   *Enter Millisent above* L & D / Q1 omits
373.35   one another Q2 / another Q1
374.16   *aside* Q4 / Q1 omits
374.34   your Q4 / her Q1
376.2   who Q2 / who who Q1
377.22   breathe / breath Q1
378.14   Why, Mr Q4 / Why Mr Q1
380.30   his servant L & D / his Q1 / his, Q2
390.25   *allons* L & D / a Lon's Q1
390.25   *touchez! Touchez!* / Touché! Touché! Q1
390.28   *While . . . down* and *When . . . jig* DW / Q1 prints as a
          single direction. DW places the second direction after
          Moody's speech 'I know not what to make on't.'
391.19   coxcomb Q4 / Coxcombs Q1
392.36   have Q5 / hath Q1

THE COUNTRY WIFE
by William Wycherley

INTRODUCTION

William Wycherley (1641–1716) came of a Shropshire family. He lived in France for some time in his teens but returned to England before the Restoration and was a member of the Inner Temple. He served with the navy in 1664. In 1679 he married the Countess of Drogheda who was a wealthy widow. She died two years later, and Wycherley then got in debt and spent some months in prison until James the Second paid his debts. He married just before his death to disinherit his son.

The dates when he wrote his plays cannot be established accurately. His first play was acted in 1671 and published in 1672. This was *Love in a Wood, or St James's Park*, a comedy of intrigue; it was followed by *The Gentleman Dancing-Master* acted in 1672. *The Country Wife* was performed on 12 and 15 January in 1674/5 and *The Plain Dealer* in 1676/7. Wycherley's *Miscellany Poems* were published in 1704 and led to his friendship with Pope. He wrote much verse, which Pope corrected, but this lacked the force and vigour of his prose. This prose is seen at its best in *The Country Wife*, which is Wycherley's most successful play and which was very popular when first performed. The cast was a good one with Charles Hart as Horner and Kynaston as Harcourt, while Mrs Knep played Lady Fidget. The popularity lasted to the middle of the eighteenth century, when it seemed unsuited to the taste of the audience and Garrick's version of it, *The Country Girl* (1766), replaced it. In the nineteenth century Macaulay called it 'one of the most profligate and heartless of human compositions'. Twentieth century critics have found the play intellectually amusing, though the character of Horner has presented them with difficulties.

Wycherley obtained some ideas for the play from other dramatists. Terence probably supplied the plot of the supposedly impotent Horner in his *Eunuchus*, and Molière's *L'École des Maris* and *L'École des Femmes* also provided ideas. But *The Country Wife* has a skilfully constructed plot and its three strands are closely intermeshed throughout. Thus the relationships of Horner with Sir Jasper and Lady Fidget, of Horner with Mr Pinchwife and Margery, of Alithea and Sparkish are set off against each other, give the play a balance and ensure its lively progress. This vivacity is maintained by the

excellent dialogue. It can range from polished wit to brutally deva-
stating simplicity, but each speaker's words are caught up by the
next, and it is this relationship between the end of one actor's speech
and the opening word of the next's reply which makes *The Country
Wife* technically impressive, and gives the play its sureness of touch
and fast tempo.

Wycherley delighted in irony, and the situations of the plot in
which Horner is accepted by Sir Jasper Fidget as impotent lend
themselves to a full employment of it – especially as the ladies realise
the truth. It is hardly edifying but it is extremely funny and
Wycherley extracts all the humour he can from it, exploiting the
farcical possibilities to the full.

Besides the humour there is a serious view of marriage. Horner's
activities show up the stupidities of two kinds of husband: Sir
Jasper who neglects his wife and is gullible; Pinchwife, who is
absurdly jealous and tries to keep his wife ignorant and away from
company, is inept. Lady Fidget, Mrs Dainty Fidget and Mrs
Squeamish are equally exposed for hypocrisy and avid greed for sex.
Mrs Pinchwife provides a foil to the scheming Town ladies in her
naivety and her direct, unsophisticated response to Horner. Not
without reason does he say to her 'Peace, dear idiot' as she is about
to testify to his virility. But against all these victims of lustful sexu-
ality we can see the very different situation of Alithea and Harcourt.
Alithea is mistakenly loyal to Sparkish: he shares in Sir Jasper's
gullibility and, later, Pinchwife's jealousy. Eventually she realises
his true nature and Harcourt's: her relationship to Harcourt, as his
to her, is founded upon an equality of intellect. Though we have no
scene akin to a Millamant-Mirabell treaty, it is possible to see these
two making of marriage something dominated by love rather than
finance or sensuality.

Horner is, of course, a very different character and poses many
problems. On the one hand he seems nothing but a rake without
principle: on the other the ladies respect him as a man of honour, and
he is not despised by the gentlemen. He is the lever by which the
plot is activated, and perhaps he is but Wycherley's instrument for
showing up the hypocrisies and stupidities of the fools, the in-
competent, and the incontinent. He does not make advances to the
virtuous Alithea but it is true he had enough to occupy him in

responding to the other ladies. And in this response he himself tends to become ridiculous, a man dominated by his sexual drives. His attitude is ironic and the play itself remains an outstandingly ironic comment on Restoration attitudes to intrigue and marriage.

William Wycherley

The Country Wife

A COMEDY

Acted at the Theatre Royal

Written by Mr Wycherley

Indignor quidquam reprehendi, non quia crasse
Compositum illepideve putetur, sed quia nuper:
Nec veniam antiquis, sed honorem et praemia posci.
HORAT.*

LONDON

Printed for Thomas Dring, at the Harrow, at the
Corner of Chancery Lane in Fleet Street.

1675

*I hate to see something attacked not because it is clumsy and lacking elegance but because it is contemporary, and not only pardon demanded for the old writers, but also honours and rewards.

Horace, *Epistles*, II, i, 76–78.

DRAMATIS PERSONAE

MEN

Mr Horner
Mr Harcourt
Mr Dorilant
Mr Pinchwife
Mr Sparkish
Sir Jasper Fidget

WOMEN

Mrs Margery Pinchwife
Mrs Alithea
My Lady Fidget
Mrs Dainty Fidget
Mrs Squeamish
Old Lady Squeamish
A Boy
A Quack
Lucy, Alithea's Maid

Waiters, Servants, and Attendants.

The Scene London.

PROLOGUE

Spoken by Mr Hart ⟨Horner⟩.

Poets like cudgelled bullies, never do
At first, or second blow, submit to you;
But will provoke you still, and ne'er have done,
Till you are weary first, with laying on:
The late so baffled scribbler* of this day,
Though he stands trembling, bids me boldly say,
What we, before most plays are used to do,
For poets out of fear, first draw on you;
In a fierce prologue, the still pit defy,
And ere you speak, like Castril,† give the lie;
But though our Bayes's‡ battles oft I've fought,
And with bruised knuckles, their dear conquests bought;
Nay, never yet feared odds upon the stage,
In prologue dare not hector with the age,
But would take quarter from your saving hands,
Though Bayes within all yielding countermands,
Says you confederate wits no quarter give,
Therefore his play shan't ask your leave to live:
Well, let the vain rash fop, by huffing so,
Think to obtain the better terms of you;
But we the actors humbly will submit,
Now, and at any time, to a full pit;
Nay, often we anticipate your rage,
And murder poets for you, on our stage:
We set no guards upon our tiring-room,
But when with flying colours, there you come,
We patiently you see, give up to you,
Our poets, virgins, nay our matrons too.

---

* baffled scribbler: this may refer to Wycherley's *The Gentleman Dancing-Master*
(1672) which was not successful.
† Castril: a character in Ben Jonson's *Alchemist* (1610).
‡ Bayes's: poet's.

ACT ONE

SCENE I

Enter Horner, and Quack following him at a distance.

HORNER [*aside*] A quack is as fit for a pimp, as a midwife for a bawd; they are still but in their way, both helpers of nature. – ⟨*to Quack*⟩ Well, my dear doctor, hast thou done what I desired.

QUACK I have undone you for ever with the women, and reported you throughout the whole Town as bad as an eunuch, with as much trouble as if I had made you one in earnest.

HORNER But have you told all the midwives you know, the orange wenches at the playhouses, the City husbands, and old fumbling keepers of this end of the Town, for they'll be the readiest to report it.

QUACK I have told all the chambermaids, waiting-women, tire-women, and old women of my acquaintance; nay, and whispered it as a secret to 'em, and to the whisperers of Whitehall; so that you need not doubt 'twill spread, and you will be as odious to the handsome young women, as –

HORNER As the smallpox. – Well –

QUACK And to the married women of this end of the Town, as –

HORNER As the great ones; nay, as their own husbands.

QUACK And to the City dames as aniseed Robin★ of filthy and contemptible memory; and they will frighten their children with your name, especially their females.

HORNER And cry 'Horner's coming to carry you away': I am only afraid 'twill not be believed; you told 'em 'twas by an English-French disaster,† and an English-French chirurgeon, who has given me at once, not only a cure, but an antidote for the future, against that damned malady, and that worse distemper, love, and all other women's evils.

QUACK Your late journey into France has made it the more credible, and your being here a fortnight before you appeared in public, looks as if you apprehended the shame, which I wonder you do

★ aniseed Robin: a famous hermaphrodite who sold aniseed-water about the streets during the reigns of James I and Charles I.

† English-French disaster: venereal disease, the French pox.

not: well I have been hired by young gallants to belie 'em t'other way; but you are the first would be thought a man unfit for women.

HORNER Dear Mr Doctor, let vain rogues be contented only to be thought abler men than they are, generally 'tis all the pleasure they have, but mine lies another way.

QUACK You take, methinks, a very preposterous way to it, and as ridiculous as if we operators in physic, should put forth bills to disparage our medicaments, with hopes to gain customers.

HORNER Doctor, there are quacks in love, as well as physic, who get but the fewer and worse patients, for their boasting; a good name is seldom got by giving it oneself, and women no more than honour are compassed by bragging: come, come Doctor, the wisest lawyer never discovers the merits of his cause till the trial; the wealthiest man conceals his riches, and the cunning gamester his play; shy husbands and keepers like old rooks* are not to be cheated, but by a new unpractised trick; false friendship will pass now no more than false dice upon 'em, no, not in the City.

Enter Boy.

BOY There are two ladies and a gentleman coming up. ⟨*Exit Boy*⟩

HORNER A pox, some unbelieving sisters of my former acquaintance, who I am afraid, expect their sense should be satisfied of the falsity of the report.

Enter Sir Jasper Fidget, Lady Fidget, and Mrs Dainty Fidget.

No – this formal fool and women!

QUACK His wife and sister.

SIR JASPER My coach breaking just now before your door Sir, I look upon as an occasional reprimand to me Sir, for not kissing your hands Sir, since your coming out of France Sir; and so my disaster Sir, has been my good fortune Sir; and this is my wife, and sister Sir.

HORNER What then, Sir?

SIR JASPER My lady, and sister, Sir. – Wife, this is Master Horner.

LADY FIDGET Master Horner, husband!

SIR JASPER My lady, my Lady Fidget, Sir.

* rooks: cheats.

HORNER So, Sir.

SIR JASPER Won't you be acquainted with her Sir? [*aside*] So the reportis true, I find by his coldness or aversion to the sex; but I'll play the wag with him. ⟨*to him*⟩ Pray salute my wife, my lady, Sir.

HORNER I will kiss no man's wife, Sir, for him, Sir; I have taken my eternal leave, Sir, of the sex already, Sir.

SIR JASPER [*aside*] Hah, hah, hah; I'll plague him yet. ⟨*to him*⟩ Not know my wife, Sir?

HORNER I do know your wife, Sir, she's a woman, Sir, and consequently a monster, Sir, a greater monster than a husband, Sir.

SIR JASPER A husband; how, Sir?

HORNER So, Sir; but I make no more cuckolds, Sir. [*makes horns*]

SIR JASPER Hah, hah, hah, Mercury, Mercury.★

LADY FIDGET Pray, Sir Jasper, let us be gone from this rude fellow.

MRS DAINTY Who, by his breeding, would think, he had ever been in France?

LADY FIDGET Foh, he's but too much a French fellow, such as hate women of quality and virtue, for their love to their husbands, Sir Jasper; a woman is hated by 'em as much for loving her husband, as for loving their money: but pray, let's be gone.

HORNER You do well, Madam, for I have nothing that you came for: I have brought over not so much as a bawdy picture, new postures, nor the second part of the *École des Filles*; nor –

QUACK [*apart to Horner*] Hold for shame, Sir; what d'ye mean? You'll ruin yourself for ever with the sex –

SIR JASPER Hah, hah, hah, he hates women perfectly I find.

MRS DAINTY What pity 'tis he should.

LADY FIDGET Aye, he's a base rude fellow for't; but affectation makes not a woman more odious to them, than virtue.

HORNER Because your virtue is your greatest affectation, Madam.

LADY FIDGET How, you saucy fellow, would you wrong my honour?

HORNER If I could.

LADY FIDGET How d'ye mean, Sir?

SIR JASPER Hah, hah, hah, no he can't wrong your ladyship's honour, upon my honour; he poor man – hark you in your ear – a mere eunuch.

★ Mercury: used in treatment of venereal disease.

LADY FIDGET O filthy French beast, foh, foh; why do we stay? Let's be gone; I can't endure the sight of him.

SIR JASPER Stay, but till the chairs come, they'll be here presently.

LADY FIDGET No, no.

SIR JASPER Nor can I stay longer; 'tis – let me see, a quarter and a half quarter of a minute past eleven; the council will be late, I must away: business must be preferred always before love and ceremony with the wise, Mr Horner.

HORNER And the impotent, Sir Jasper.

SIR JASPER Aye, aye, the impotent Master Horner, hah, ha, ha.

LADY FIDGET What leave us with a filthy man alone in his lodgings?

SIR JASPER He's an innocent man now, you know; pray stay, I'll hasten the chairs to you. – Mr Horner your servant, I should be glad to see you at my house; pray, come and dine with me, and play at cards with my wife after dinner, you are fit for women at that game yet, hah, ha – [*aside*] 'Tis as much a husband's prudence to provide innocent diversion for a wife, as to hinder her unlawful pleasures; and he had better employ her, than let her employ herself. ⟨*to them*⟩ Farewell. [*Exit Sir Jasper*]

HORNER Your servant Sir Jasper.

LADY FIDGET I will not stay with him, foh –

HORNER Nay, Madam, I beseech you stay, if it be but to see, I can be as civil to ladies yet, as they would desire.

LADY FIDGET No, no, foh, you cannot be civil to ladies.

MRS DAINTY You as civil as ladies would desire.

LADY FIDGET No, no, no, foh, foh, foh.

[*Exeunt Lady Fidget and Mrs Dainty*]

QUACK Now I think, I, or you yourself rather, have done your business with the women.

HORNER Thou art an ass, don't you see already upon the report and my carriage, this grave man of business leaves his wife in my lodgings, invites me to his house and wife, who before would not be acquainted with me out of jealousy.

QUACK Nay, by this means you may be the more acquainted with the husbands, but the less with the wives.

HORNER Let me alone, if I can but abuse the husbands, I'll soon disabuse the wives: stay – I'll reckon you up the advantages, I am like to have by my stratagem: first, I shall be rid of all my old acquaintances, the most insatiable sorts of duns, that invade our lodgings in a morning: and next to the pleasure of making a new mistress, is that of being rid of an old one, and of all old debts; love when it comes to be so, is paid the most unwillingly.

QUACK Well, you may be so rid of your old acquaintances; but how will you get any new ones?

HORNER Doctor, thou wilt never make a good chemist, thou art so incredulous and impatient; ask but all the young fellows of the Town, if they do not lose more time like huntsmen, in starting the game, than in running it down; one knows not where to find 'em, who will, or will not; women of quality are so civil, you can hardly distinguish love from good breeding, and a man is often mistaken; but now I can be sure, she that shows an aversion to me loves the sport, as those women that are gone, whom I warrant to be right:* and then the next thing, is your women of honour, as you call 'em, are only chary of their reputations, not their persons, and 'tis scandal they would avoid, not men: now may I have, by the reputation of an eunuch, the privileges of one; and be seen in a lady's chamber, in a morning as early as her husband; kiss virgins before their parents, or lovers; and may be in short the *passe-partout* of the Town. Now Doctor.

QUACK Nay, now you shall be the doctor; and your process is so new, that we do not know but it may succeed.

HORNER Not so new neither, *probatum est*† Doctor.

QUACK Well, I wish you luck and many patients whilst I go to mine.   [*Exit Quack*]

Enter Harcourt, and Dorilant to Horner.

HARCOURT Come, your appearance at the play yesterday, has I hope hardened you for the future against the women's contempt, and the men's raillery; and now you'll abroad as you were wont.

HORNER Did I not bear it bravely?

DORILANT With a most theatrical impudence; nay more than the orange-wenches show there, or a drunken vizard mask,‡ or a great-bellied actress; nay, or the most impudent of creatures, an ill poet; or what is yet more impudent, a second-hand critic.

* right: loose women, a cant term.   † *probatum est*: it has been proved.
‡ vizard mask: courtesan.

HORNER But what say the ladies, have they no pity?

HARCOURT What ladies? The vizard masks you know never pity a man when all's gone, though in their service.

DORILANT And for the women in the boxes, you'd never pity them, when 'twas in your power.

HARCOURT They say 'tis pity, but all that deal with common women should be served so.

DORILANT Nay, I dare swear, they won't admit you to play at cards with them, go to plays with 'em, or do the little duties which other shadows of men, are wont to do for 'em.

HORNER Who do you call shadows of men?

DORILANT Half-men.

HORNER What boys?

DORILANT Aye your old boys, old *beaux garçons*, who like superannuated stallions are suffered to run, feed, and whinny with the mares as long as they live, though they can do nothing else.

HORNER Well a pox on love and wenching, women serve but to keep a man from better company; though I can't enjoy them, I shall you the more: good fellowship and friendship, are lasting, rational and manly pleasures.

HARCOURT For all that give me some of those pleasures, you call effeminate too, they help to relish one another.

HORNER They disturb one another.

HARCOURT No, mistresses are like books; if you pore upon them too much, they doze you, and make you unfit for company; but if used discreetly, you are the fitter for conversation by 'em.

DORILANT A mistress should be like a little country retreat near the Town, not to dwell in constantly, but only for a night and away; to taste the Town the better when a man returns.

HORNER I tell you, 'tis as hard to be a good fellow, a good friend, and a lover of women, as 'tis to be a good fellow, a good friend, and a lover of money: you cannot follow both, then choose your side; wine gives you liberty, love takes it away.

DORILANT Gad, he's in the right on't.

HORNER Wine gives you joy, love grief and tortures; besides the chirurgeon's wine makes us witty, love only sots: wine makes us sleep, love breaks it.

DORILANT By the world he has reason, Harcourt.

HORNER Wine makes –

DORILANT Aye, wine makes us – makes us princes, love makes us beggars, poor rogues, egad – and wine –

HORNER So, there's one converted. – No, no, love and wine, oil and vinegar.

HARCOURT I grant it; love will still be uppermost.

HORNER Come, for my part I will have only those glorious, manly pleasures of being very drunk, and very slovenly.

Enter Boy.

BOY Mr Sparkish is below, Sir.

HARCOURT What, my dear friend! A rogue that is fond of me, only I think for abusing him.

DORILANT No, he can no more think the men laugh at him, than that women jilt him, his opinion of himself is so good.

HORNER Well, there's another pleasure by drinking, I thought not of; I shall lose his acquaintance, because he cannot drink; and you know 'tis a very hard thing to be rid of him, for he's one of those nauseous offerers at wit, who like the worst fiddlers run themselves into all companies.

HARCOURT One, that by being in the company of men of sense would pass for one.

HORNER And may so to the shortsighted world, as a false jewel amongst true ones, is not discerned at a distance; his company is as troublesome to us, as a cuckold's, when you have a mind to his wife's.

HARCOURT No, the rogue will not let us enjoy one another, but ravishes our conversation, though he signifies no more to't, than Sir Martin Mar-all's★ gaping, and awkward thrumming upon the lute, does to his man's voice, and music.

DORILANT And to pass for a wit in Town, shows himself a fool every night to us, that are guilty of the plot.

HORNER Such wits as he, are, to a company of reasonable men, like rooks to the gamesters, who only fill a room at the table, but are so far from contributing to the play, that they only serve to spoil the fancy of those that do.

★ Sir Martin Mar-all: in Dryden's comedy of this name (1667) Sir Martin pretends to serenade a girl with a lute while his concealed servant sings a song to her. See p. 376 ff.

DORILANT Nay, they are used like rooks too, snubbed, checked, and abused; yet the rogues will hang on.

HORNER A pox on 'em, and all that force nature, and would be still what she forbids 'em; affectation is her greatest monster.

HARCOURT Most men are the contraries to that they would seem; your bully you see, is a coward with a long sword; the little humbly fawning physician with his ebony cane, is he that destroys men.

DORILANT The usurer, a poor rogue, possessed of mouldy bonds, and mortgages; and we they call spendthrifts, are only wealthy, who lay out his money upon new purchases of pleasure.

HORNER Aye, your errantest cheat, is your trustee, or executor; your jealous man, the greatest cuckold; your churchman, the greatest atheist; and your noisy pert rogue of a wit, the greatest fop, dullest ass, and worst company as you shall see: for here he comes.

Enter Sparkish to them.

SPARKISH How is't, sparks, how is't? Well faith, Harry, I must rally thee a little, ha, ha, ha, upon the report in Town of thee, ha, ha, ha, I can't hold i'faith; shall I speak?

HORNER Yes, but you'll be so bitter then.

SPARKISH Honest Dick and Frank here shall answer for me, I will not be extreme bitter by the universe.

HARCOURT We will be bound in ten thousand pound bond, he shall not be bitter at all.

DORILANT Nor sharp, nor sweet.

HORNER What, not downright insipid?

SPARKISH Nay then, since you are so brisk, and provoke me, take what follows; you must know, I was discoursing and rallying with some ladies yesterday, and they happened to talk of the fine new signs in Town.

HORNER Very fine ladies I believe.

SPARKISH Said I, 'I know where the best new sign is'. 'Where?', says one of the ladies. 'In Covent Garden', I replied. Said another, 'In what street?' 'In Russell Street', answered I. 'Lord' says another, 'I'm sure there was ne'er a fine new sign there yesterday'. 'Yes, but there was,' said I again, 'and it came out of France, and has been there a fortnight'.

DORILANT A pox I can hear no more, prithee.

HORNER No hear him out; let him tune his crowd* awhile.

HARCOURT The worst music the greatest preparation.

SPARKISH Nay faith, I'll make you laugh. 'It cannot be', says a third lady. 'Yes, yes', quoth I again. Says a fourth lady –

HORNER Look to't, we'll have no more ladies.

SPARKISH No. – Then mark, mark, now, said I to the fourth, 'Did you never see Mr Horner; he lodges in Russell Street, and he's a sign of a man, you know, since he came out of France', heh, hah, he.

HORNER But the divel take me, if thine be the sign of a jest.

SPARKISH With that they all fell a-laughing, till they bepissed themselves; what, but it does not move you, methinks? Well I see one had as good go to law without a witness, as break a jest without a laugher on one's side. – Come, come sparks, but where do we dine, I have left at Whitehall an earl to dine with you.

DORILANT Why, I thought thou hadst loved a man with a title better, than a suit with a French trimming to't.

HARCOURT Go, to him again.

SPARKISH No, Sir, a wit to me is the greatest title in the world.

HORNER But go dine with your earl, Sir, he may be exceptious; we are your friends, and will not take it ill to be left, I do assure you.

HARCOURT Nay, faith he shall go to him.

SPARKISH Nay, pray gentlemen.

DORILANT We'll thrust you out, if you wo'not. What, disappoint anybody for us?

SPARKISH Nay, dear gentlemen hear me.

HORATIO No, no, Sir, by no means; pray go Sir.

SPARKISH Why, dear rogues.

DORILANT No, no. [*they all thrust him out of the room*]

ALL Ha, ha, ha.

Sparkish returns.

SPARKISH But, sparks, pray hear me; what, d'ye think I'll eat then with gay shallow fops, and silent coxcombs? I think wit as necessary at dinner as a glass of good wine, and that's the reason I never

* crowd: fiddle.

have any stomach when I eat alone. – Come, but where do we dine?

HORNER Even where you will.

SPARKISH At Chateline's.*

DORILANT Yes, if you will.

SPARKISH Or at the Cock.†

DORILANT Yes, if you please.

SPARKISH Or at the Dog and Partridge.‡

HORNER Aye, if you have mind to't, for we shall dine at neither.

SPARKISH Pshaw, with your fooling we shall lose the new play; and I would no more miss seeing a new play the first day, than I would miss sitting in the wits' row; therefore I'll go fetch my mistress and away. [*Exit Sparkish*]

Enter to them Pinchwife.

HORNER Who have we here, Pinchwife?

PINCHWIFE Gentlemen, your humble servant.

HORNER Well, Jack, by thy long absence from the Town, the grumness of thy countenance, and the slovenliness of thy habit; I should give thee joy, should I not, of marriage?

PINCHWIFE [*aside*] Death does he know I'm married too? I thought to have concealed it from him at least. ⟨*to Horner*⟩ My long stay in the country will excuse my dress, and I have a suit of law, that brings me up to Town, that puts me out of humour; besides I must give Sparkish tomorrow five thousand pound to lie with my sister.

HORNER Nay, you country gentlemen rather than not purchase, will buy anything, and he is a cracked title, if we may quibble: well, but am I to give thee joy, I heard thou wert married.

PINCHWIFE What then?

HORNER Why, the next thing that is to be heard, is thou'rt a cuckold.

PINCHWIFE [*aside*] Insupportable name.

HORNER But I did not expect marriage from such a whoremaster as you, one that knew the Town so much, and women so well.

* Chateline's: Chatelain's, a fashionable French restaurant in Covent Garden.
† the Cock: a tavern in Bow Street.
‡ the Dog and Partridge: a tavern in Fleet Street.

PINCHWIFE Why, I have married no London wife.

HORNER Pshaw, that's all one, that grave circumspection in marrying a country wife, is like refusing a deceitful pampered Smithfield jade,* to go and be cheated by a friend in the country.

PINCHWIFE [*aside*] A pox on him and his simile. ⟨*to Horner*⟩ At least we are a little surer of the breed there, know what her keeping has been, whether soiled or unsound.

HORNER Come, come, I have known a clap gotten in Wales, and there are cousins, justices, clerks, and chaplains in the country, I won't say coachmen, but she's handsome and young.

PINCHWIFE [*aside*] I'll answer as I should do. ⟨*to Horner*⟩ No, no, she has no beauty, but her youth; no attraction, but her modesty, wholesome, homely, and huswifely, that's all.

DORILANT He talks as like a grazier† as he looks.

PINCHWIFE She's too awkward, ill-favoured, and silly to bring to Town.

HARCOURT Then methinks you should bring her, to be taught breeding.

PINCHWIFE To be taught; no, Sir, I thank you, good wives, and private soldiers should be ignorant. – [*aside*] I'll keep her from your instructions, I warrant you.

HARCOURT [*aside*] The rogue is as jealous, as if his wife were not ignorant.

HORNER Why, if she be ill-favoured, there will be less danger here for you, than by leaving her in the country; we have such variety of dainties, that we are seldom hungry.

DORILANT But they have always coarse, constant, swingeing stomachs‡ in the country.

HARCOURT Foul feeders indeed.

DORILANT And your hospitality is great there.

HARCOURT Open house, every man's welcome.

PINCHWIFE So, so, gentlemen.

HORNER But prithee, why would'st thou marry her? If she be ugly, ill-bred, and silly, she must be rich then.

PINCHWIFE As rich as if she brought me twenty thousand pound

* Smithfield jade: a worn-out horse sold at Smithfield, a loose woman.
† grazier: a farmer who grazes cattle.
‡ swingeing stomachs: with large appetites.

out of this Town; for she'll be as sure not to spend her moderate portion, as a London baggage would be to spend hers, let it be what it would; so 'tis all one: then because she's ugly, she's the likelier to be my own; and being ill-bred, she'll hate conversation; and since silly and innocent, will not know the difference betwixt a man of one and twenty, and one of forty.

HORNER Nine – to my knowledge; but if she be silly, she'll expect as much from a man of forty nine, as from him of one and twenty: but methinks wit is more necessary than beauty, and I think no young woman ugly that has it, and no handsome woman agreeable without it.

PINCHWIFE 'Tis my maxim, he's a fool that marries, but he's a greater that does not marry a fool; what is wit in a wife good for, but to make a man a cuckold?

HORNER Yes, to keep it from his knowledge.

PINCHWIFE A fool cannot contrive to make her husband a cuckold.

HARCOURT No, but she'll club with a man that can; and what is worse, if she cannot make her husband a cuckold, she'll make him jealous, and pass for one, and then 'tis all one.

PINCHWIFE Well, well, I'll take care for one, my wife shall make me no cuckold, though she had your help Mr Horner; I understand the Town, Sir.

DORILANT [*aside*] His help!

HARCOURT [*aside*] He's come newly to Town it seems, and has not heard how things are with him.

HORNER But tell me, has marriage cured thee of whoring, which it seldom does.

HARCOURT 'Tis more than age can do.

HORNER No, the word is, I'll marry and live honest; but a marriage vow is like a penitent gamester's oath, and entering into bonds, and penalties to stint himself to such a particular small sum at play for the future, which makes him but the more eager, and not being able to hold out, loses his money again, and his forfeit to boot.

DORILANT Aye, aye, a gamester will be a gamester, whilst his money lasts; and a whoremaster, whilst his vigour.

HARCOURT Nay, I have known 'em, when they are broke and

can lose no more, keep a-fumbling with the box in their hands to fool with only, and hinder other gamesters.

DORILANT That had wherewithal to make lusty stakes.

PINCHWIFE Well, gentlemen, you may laugh at me, but you shall never lie with my wife, I know the Town.

HORNER But prithee, was not the way you were in better, is not keeping better than marriage?

PINCHWIFE A pox on't, the jades would jilt me, I could never keep a whore to myself.

HORNER So then you only married to keep a whore to yourself; well, but let me tell you, women, as you say, are like soldiers made constant and loyal by good pay, rather than by oaths and covenants, therefore I'd advise my friends to keep rather than marry; since too I find by your example, it does not serve one's turn, for I saw you yesterday in the eighteenpenny place* with a pretty country wench.

PINCHWIFE [*aside*] How the divel, did he see my wife then? I sat there that she might not be seen; but she shall never go to a play again.

HORNER What dost thou blush at nine-and-forty, for having been seen with a wench?

DORILANT No faith, I warrant 'twas his wife, which he seated there out of sight, for he's a cunning rogue, and understands the Town.

HARCOURT He blushes, then 'twas his wife; for men are now more ashamed to be seen with them in public, than with a wench.

PINCHWIFE [*aside*] Hell and damnation, I'm undone, since Horner has seen her, and they know 'twas she.

HORNER But prithee, was it thy wife? She was exceedingly pretty; I was in love with her at that distance.

PINCHWIFE You are like never to be nearer to her. Your servant gentlemen. [*offers to go*]

HORNER Nay, prithee stay.

PINCHWIFE I cannot, I will not.

HORNER Come you shall dine with us.

PINCHWIFE I have dined already.

* eighteenpenny place: the middle gallery in the theatre, in which whores congregated.

HORNER Come, I know thou hast not; I'll treat thee dear rogue, thou sha't spend none of thy Hampshire money today.

PINCHWIFE [*aside*] Treat me; so he uses me already like his cuckold.

HORNER Nay, you shall not go.

PINCHWIFE I must, I have business at home.   [*Exit Pinchwife*]

HARCOURT To beat his wife, he's as jealous of her, as a Cheapside husband of a Covent Garden wife.★

HORNER Why, 'tis as hard to find an old whoremaster without jealousy and the gout, as a young one without fear or the pox.
As gout in age, from pox in youth proceeds;
So wenching passed, then jealousy succeeds:
The worst disease that love and wenching breeds.   ⟨*Exeunt*⟩

★ Cheapside . . . Covent Garden: a City husband, a fashionable wife.

ACT TWO

SCENE I

*Mrs Margery Pinchwife, and Alithea: Pinchwife peeping behind
at the door.*

MRS PINCHWIFE Pray, sister, where are the best fields and woods,
to walk in in London?

ALITHEA A pretty question; why, sister! Mulberry Garden,★ and
St James's Park;† and for close walks the New Exchange.‡

MRS PINCHWIFE Pray, sister, tell me why my husband looks so
grum§ here in Town? And keeps me up so close, and will not
let me go a-walking, nor let me wear my best gown yesterday?

ALITHEA O he's jealous, sister.

MRS PINCHWIFE Jealous, what's that?

ALITHEA He's afraid you should love another man.

MRS PINCHWIFE How should he be afraid of my loving another
man, when he will not let me see any but himself.

ALITHEA Did he not carry you yesterday to a play?

MRS PINCHWIFE Aye, but we sat amongst ugly people, he would
not let me come near the gentry, who sat under us, so that I could
not see 'em: he told me, none but naughty women sat there,
whom they toused and moused; but I would have ventured for
all that.

ALITHEA But how did you like the play?

MRS PINCHWIFE Indeed I was a-weary of the play, but I liked
hugeously the actors; they are the goodliest properest men, sister.

ALITHEA O but you must not like the actors, sister.

MRS PINCHWIFE Aye, how should I help it, sister? Pray, sister,
when my husband comes in, will you ask leave for me to go
a-walking?

ALITHEA [*aside*] A-walking, hah, ha; Lord, a country-gentle-

★ Mulberry Garden: a pleasure ground on the site where Buckingham Palace
now stands.
† St James's Park: noted for its Mall.
‡ the New Exchange: known for its shops, a fashionable building in the
Strand.
§ grum: glum.

woman's leisure is the drudgery of a foot-post; and she requires as much airing as her husband's horses.

Enter Pinchwife to them.

But here comes your husband; I'll ask, though I'm sure he'll not grant it.

MRS PINCHWIFE He says he won't let me go abroad, for fear of catching the pox.

ALITHEA Fie, the smallpox you should say.

MRS PINCHWIFE O my dear, dear bud, welcome home; why dost thou look so fropish,* who has nangered thee?

PINCHWIFE You're a fool.

[*Mrs Pinchwife goes aside, and cries*]

ALITHEA Faith so she is, for crying for no fault, poor tender creature!

PINCHWIFE What you would have her as impudent as yourself, as errant a jillflirt, a gadder, a magpie, and to say all a mere notorious Town-woman?

ALITHEA Brother, you are my only censurer; and the honour of your family shall sooner suffer in your wife there, than in me, though I take the innocent liberty of the Town!

PINCHWIFE Hark you mistress, do not talk so before my wife, the innocent liberty of the Town!

ALITHEA Why, pray, who boasts of any intrigue with me? What lampoon has made my name notorious? What ill women frequent my lodgings? I keep no company with any women of scandalous reputations.

PINCHWIFE No, you keep the men of scandalous reputations company.

ALITHEA Where? Would you not have me civil? Answer 'em in a box at the plays? In the drawing room at Whitehall? In St James's Park? Mulberry Garden? Or –

PINCHWIFE Hold, hold, do not teach my wife, where the men are to be found; I believe she's the worse for your Town documents already; I bid you keep her in ignorance as I do.

MRS PINCHWIFE Indeed be not angry with her bud, she will tell me nothing of the Town, though I ask her a thousand times a day.

* fropish: peevish, testy.

PINCHWIFE Then you are very inquisitive to know, I find?

MRS PINCHWIFE Not I indeed, dear, I hate London; our place-house in the country is worth a thousand of't, would I were there again.

PINCHWIFE So you shall I warrant; but were you not talking of plays, and players, when I came in? You are her encourager in such discourses.

MRS PINCHWIFE No indeed, dear, she chid me just now for liking the player men.

PINCHWIFE [*aside*] Nay, if she be so innocent as to own to me her liking them, there is no hurt in't – ⟨*to her*⟩ Come my poor rogue, but thou lik'st none better than me?

MRS PINCHWIFE Yes indeed, but I do, the player men are finer folks.

PINCHWIFE But you love none better than me?

MRS PINCHWIFE You are mine own dear bud, and I know you, I hate a stranger.

PINCHWIFE Aye, my dear, you must love me only, and not be like the naughty Town-women, who only hate their husbands and love every man else, love plays, visits, fine coaches, fine clothes, fiddlers, balls, treaties, and so lead a wicked Town-life.

MRS PINCHWIFE Nay, if to enjoy all these things be a Town-life, London is not so bad a place, dear.

PINCHWIFE How! If you love me, you must hate London.

ALITHEA ⟨*aside*⟩ The fool has forbid me discovering to her the pleasures of the Town, and he is now setting her agog upon them himself.

MRS PINCHWIFE But, husband, do the Town-women love the player men too?

PINCHWIFE Yes, I warrant you.

MRS PINCHWIFE Aye, I warrant you.

PINCHWIFE Why, you do not, I hope?

MRS PINCHWIFE No, no, bud; but why have we no player men in the country?

PINCHWIFE Ha – Mrs Minx, ask me no more to go to a play.

MRS PINCHWIFE Nay, why, love? I did not care for going; but when you forbid me, you make me as't were desire it.

ALITHEA [*aside*] So 'twill be in other things, I warrant.

MRS PINCHWIFE Pray, let me go to a play, dear.

PINCHWIFE Hold your peace, I wo'not.

MRS PINCHWIFE Why, love?

PINCHWIFE Why, I'll tell you.

ALITHEA [*aside*] Nay, if he tell her, she'll give him more cause to forbid her that place.

MRS PINCHWIFE Pray, why, dear?

PINCHWIFE First, you like the actors, and the gallants may like you.

MRS PINCHWIFE What, a homely country girl? No bud, nobody will like me.

PINCHWIFE I tell you, yes, they may.

MRS PINCHWIFE No, no, you jest – I won't believe you, I will go.

PINCHWIFE I tell you then, that one of the lewdest fellows in Town, who saw you there, told me he was in love with you.

MRS PINCHWIFE Indeed! Who, who, pray who wast?

PINCHWIFE [*aside*] I've gone too far, and slipped before I was aware; how overjoyed she is!

MRS PINCHWIFE Was it any Hampshire gallant, any of our neighbours? I promise you, I am beholding to him.

PINCHWIFE I promise you, you lie; for he would but ruin you, as he has done hundreds: he has no other love for women, but that, such as he, look upon women like basilisks,★ but to destroy 'em.

MRS PINCHWIFE Aye, but if he loves me, why should he ruin me? Answer me to that: methinks he should not, I would do him no harm.

ALITHEA Hah, ha, ha.

PINCHWIFE 'Tis very well; but I'll keep him from doing you any harm, or me either.

Enter Sparkish and Harcourt.

But here comes company, get you in, get you in.

MRS PINCHWIFE But pray, husband, is he a pretty gentleman, that loves me?

PINCHWIFE In baggage, in. [*thrusts her in: shuts the door*]

★ basilisks: their look was reputed to be fatal.

What all the lewd libertines of the Town brought to my lodging, by this easy coxcomb! S'death I'll not suffer it.

SPARKISH Here Harcourt, do you approve my choice? Dear, little rogue, I told you, I'd bring you acquainted with all my friends, the wits, and – [*Harcourt salutes Alithea*]

PINCHWIFE Aye, they shall know her, as well as you yourself will, I warrant you.

SPARKISH This is one of those, my pretty rogue, that are to dance at your wedding tomorrow; and him you must bid welcome ever, to what you and I have.

PINCHWIFE [*aside*] Monstrous! –

SPARKISH Harcourt how dost thou like her, faith? Nay, dear, do not look down; I should hate to have a wife of mine out of countenance at anything.

PINCHWIFE Wonderful!

SPARKISH Tell me, I say, Harcourt, how dost thou like her? Thou hast stared upon her enough, to resolve me.

HARCOURT So infinitely well, that I could wish I had a mistress too, that might differ from her in nothing, but her love and engagement to you.

ALITHEA Sir, Master Sparkish has often told me, that his acquaintance were all wits and *railleurs*,★ and now I find it.

SPARKISH No, by the universe, Madam, he does not rally now; you may believe him: I do assure you, he is the honestest, worthiest, true-hearted gentleman – A man of such perfect honour, he would say nothing to a lady, he does not mean.

PINCHWIFE ⟨*aside*⟩ Praising another man to his mistress!

HARCOURT Sir, you are so beyond expectation obliging, that –

SPARKISH Nay, egad, I am sure you do admire her extremely, I see't in your eyes. – He does admire you Madam. – By the world, don't you?

HARCOURT Yes, above the world, or, the most glorious part of it, her whole sex; and till now I never thought I should have envied you, or any man about to marry, but you have the best excuse for marriage I ever knew.

ALITHEA Nay, now, Sir, I'm satisfied you are of the society of the wits, and *railleurs*, since you cannot spare your friend, even when

★ *railleurs*: banterers, teases.

he is but too civil to you; but the surest sign is, since you are an enemy to marriage, for that I hear you hate as much as business or bad wine.

HARCOURT Truly, Madam, I never was an enemy to marriage, till now, because marriage was never an enemy to me before.

ALITHEA But why, Sir, is marriage an enemy to you now? Because it robs you of your friend here; for you look upon a friend married, as one gone into a monastery, that is dead to the world.

HARCOURT 'Tis indeed, because you marry him; I see Madam, you can guess my meaning: I do confess heartily and openly, I wish it were in my power to break the match, by heavens I would.

SPARKISH Poor Frank!

ALITHEA Would you be so unkind to me?

HARCOURT No, no, 'tis not because I would be unkind to you.

SPARKISH Poor Frank, no gad, 'tis only his kindness to me.

PINCHWIFE [*aside*] Great kindness to you indeed; insensible fop, let a man make love to his wife to his face.

SPARKISH Come dear Frank, for all my wife there that shall be, thou shalt enjoy me sometimes dear rogue; by my honour, we men of wit condole for our deceased brother in marriage, as much as for one dead in earnest: I think that was prettily said of me, ha Harcourt? – But come Frank, be not melancholy for me.

HARCOURT No, I assure you I am not melancholy for you.

SPARKISH Prithee, Frank, dost think my wife that shall be there a fine person?

HARCOURT I could gaze upon her, till I became as blind as you are.

SPARKISH How, as I am! How!

HARCOURT Because you are a lover, and true lovers are blind, stock blind.

SPARKISH True, true; but by the world, she has wit too, as well as beauty: go, go with her into a corner, and try if she has wit, talk to her anything, she's bashful before me.

HARCOURT Indeed if a woman wants wit in a corner, she has it nowhere.

ALITHEA [*aside to Sparkish*] Sir, you dispose of me a little before your time. –

SPARKISH Nay, nay, Madam let me have an earnest of your obedience, or – go, go, Madam –

Harcourt courts Alithea aside.

PINCHWIFE How, Sir, if you are not concerned for the honour of a wife, I am for that of a sister; he shall not debauch her: be a pander to your own wife, bring men to her, let 'em make love before your face, thrust 'em into a corner together, then leave 'em in private! Is this your Town wit and conduct?

SPARKISH Hah, ha, ha, a silly wise rogue, would make one laugh more than a stark fool, hah, ha: I shall burst. Nay, you shall not disturb 'em; I'll vex thee, by the world. [*struggles with Pinchwife to keep him from Harcourt and Alithea*]

ALITHEA The writings are drawn, Sir, settlements made; 'tis too late, Sir, and past all revocation.

HARCOURT Then so is my death.

ALITHEA I would not be unjust to him.

HARCOURT Then why to me so?

ALITHEA I have no obligation to you.

HARCOURT My love.

ALITHEA I had his before.

HARCOURT You never had it; he wants you see jealousy, the only infallible sign of it.

ALITHEA Love proceeds from esteem; he cannot distrust my virtue, besides he loves me, or he would not marry me.

HARCOURT Marrying you, is no more sign of his love, than bribing your woman, that he may marry you, is a sign of his generosity: marriage is rather a sign of interest, than love; and he that marries a fortune, covets a mistress, not loves her: but if you take marriage for a sign of love, take it from me immediately.

ALITHEA No, now you have put a scruple in my head; but in short, Sir, to end our dispute, I must marry him, my reputation would suffer in the world else.

HARCOURT No, if you do marry him, with your pardon, Madam, your reputation suffers in the world, and you would be thought in necessity for a cloak.

ALITHEA Nay, now you are rude, Sir. – Mr Sparkish, pray come hither, your friend here is very troublesome, and very loving.

HARCOURT [*aside to Alithea*] Hold, hold –

PINCHWIFE D'ye hear that?

SPARKISH Why, d'ye think I'll seem to be jealous, like a country bumpkin?

PINCHWIFE No, rather be a cuckold, like a credulous cit.*

HARCOURT Madam, you would not have been so little generous as to have told him.

ALITHEA Yes, since you could be so little generous, as to wrong him.

HARCOURT Wrong him, no man can do't, he's beneath an injury; a bubble, a coward, a senseless idiot, a wretch so contemptible to all the world but you, that –

ALITHEA Hold, do not rail at him, for since he is like to be my husband, I am resolved to like him: nay, I think I am obliged to tell him, you are not his friend. – Master Sparkish, Master Sparkish.

SPARKISH What, what; now dear rogue, has not she wit?

HARCOURT [*speaks surlily*] Not so much as I thought, and hoped she had.

ALITHEA Mr Sparkish, do you bring people to rail at you?

HARCOURT Madam –

SPARKISH How! No, but if he does rail at me, 'tis but in jest I warrant; what we wits do for one another, and never take any notice of it.

ALITHEA He spoke so scurrilously of you, I had no patience to hear him; besides he has been making love to me.

HARCOURT [*aside*] True damned tell-tale woman.

SPARKISH Pshaw, to show his parts – we wits rail and make love often, but to show our parts; as we have no affections, so we have no malice, we –

ALITHEA He said, you were a wretch, below an injury.

SPARKISH Pshaw.

HARCOURT ⟨*aside*⟩ Damned, senseless, impudent, virtuous jade; well since she won't let me have her, she'll do as good, she'll make me hate her.

ALITHEA A common bubble.

* cit: short for citizen, a term usually applied contemptuously to townsmen and shopkeepers.

SPARKISH Pshaw.

ALITHEA A coward.

SPARKISH Pshaw, pshaw.

ALITHEA A senseless driveling idiot.

SPARKISH How, did he disparage my parts? Nay, then my honour's concerned, I can't put up that, Sir; by the world, brother help me to kill him; [*aside*] I may draw now, since we have the odds of him: – 'tis a good occasion too before my mistress – [*offers to draw*]

ALITHEA Hold, hold.

SPARKISH What, what.

ALITHEA [*aside*] I must not let 'em kill the gentleman neither, for his kindness to me; I am so far from hating him, that I wish my gallant had his person and understanding: ⟨*aloud*⟩ Nay if my honour –

SPARKISH I'll be thy death.

ALITHEA Hold, hold, indeed to tell the truth, the gentleman said after all, that what he spoke, was but out of friendship to you.

SPARKISH How! Say, I am, I am a fool, that is no wit, out of friendship to me.

ALITHEA Yes, to try whether I was concerned enough for you, and made love to me only to be satisfied of my virtue, for your sake.

HARCOURT [*aside*] Kind however –

SPARKISH Nay, if it were so, my dear rogue, I ask thee pardon; but why would not you tell me so, faith.

HARCOURT Because I did not think on't, faith.

SPARKISH Come, Horner does not come, Harcourt, let's be gone to the new play. – Come Madam.

ALITHEA I will not go, if you intend to leave me alone in the box, and run into the pit, as you use to do.

SPARKISH Pshaw, I'll leave Harcourt with you in the box, to entertain you, and that's as good; if I sat in the box, I should be thought no judge, but of trimmings. – Come away Harcourt, lead her down.

                      [*Exeunt Sparkish, Harcourt and Alithea*]

PINCHWIFE Well, go thy ways, for the flower of the true Town fops, such as spend their estates, before they come to 'em, and are cuckolds before they're married. But let me go look to my own freehold – How –

Enter my Lady Fidget, Mrs Dainty Fidget, and Mrs Squeamish.

LADY FIDGET Your servant, Sir, where is your lady? We are come to wait upon her to the new play.

PINCHWIFE New play!

LADY FIDGET And my husband will wait upon you presently.

PINCHWIFE [*aside*] Damn your civility – ⟨*to her*⟩ Madam, by no means, I will not see Sir Jasper here, till I have waited upon him at home; nor shall my wife see you, till she has waited upon your ladyship at your lodgings.

LADY FIDGET Now we are here, Sir –

PINCHWIFE No, Madam.

MRS DAINTY Pray, let us see her.

SQUEAMISH We will not stir, till we see her.

PINCHWIFE [*aside*] A pox on you all – [*goes to the door, and returns*] she has locked the door, and is gone abroad.

LADY FIDGET No, you have locked the door, and she's within.

MRS DAINTY They told us below, she was here.

PINCHWIFE [*aside*] Will nothing do? – ⟨*to them*⟩ Well it must out then, to tell you the truth, ladies, which I was afraid to let you know before, lest it might endanger your lives, my wife has just now the smallpox come out upon her, do not be frightened; but pray, be gone ladies, you shall not stay here in danger of your lives; pray get you gone ladies.

LADY FIDGET No, no, we have all had 'em.

SQUEAMISH Alack, alack.

MRS DAINTY Come, come, we must see how it goes with her, I understand the disease.

LADY FIDGET Come.

PINCHWIFE [*aside*] Well, there is no being too hard for women at their own weapon, lying, therefore I'll quit the field. [*Exit Pinchwife*]

SQUEAMISH Here's an example of jealousy.

LADY FIDGET Indeed as the world goes, I wonder there are no more jealous, since wives are so neglected.

MRS DAINTY Pshaw, as the world goes, to what end should they be jealous.

LADY FIDGET Foh, 'tis a nasty world.

SQUEAMISH That men of parts, great acquaintance, and quality should take up with, and spend themselves and fortunes, in keeping little playhouse creatures, foh.

LADY FIDGET Nay, that women of understanding, great acquaintance, and good quality, should fall a-keeping too of little creatures, foh.

SQUEAMISH Why, 'tis the men of quality's fault, they never visit women of honour, and reputation, as they used to do; and have not so much as common civility, for ladies of our rank, but use us with the same indifferency, and ill-breeding, as if we were all married to 'em.

LADY FIDGET She says true, 'tis an errant shame women of quality should be so slighted; methinks birth – birth, should go for something; I have known men admired, courted, and followed for their titles only.

SQUEAMISH Aye, one would think men of honour should not love no more, than marry out of their own rank.

MRS DAINTY Fie, fie upon 'em, they are come to think cross-breeding for themselves best, as well as for their dogs, and horses.

LADY FIDGET They are dogs, and horses for't.

SQUEAMISH One would think if not for love, for vanity a little.

MRS DAINTY Nay, they do satisfy their vanity upon us sometimes; and are kind to us in their report, tell all the world they lie with us.

LADY FIDGET Damned rascals, that we should be only wronged by 'em; to report a man has had a person, when he has not had a person, is the greatest wrong in the whole world, that can be done to a person.

SQUEAMISH Well, 'tis an errant shame, noble persons should be so wronged, and neglected.

LADY FIDGET But still 'tis an erranter shame for a noble person, to neglect her own honour, and defame her own noble person, with little inconsiderable fellows, foh! –

MRS DAINTY I suppose the crime against our honour, is the same with a man of quality as with another.

LADY FIDGET How! No, sure the man of quality is likest one's husband, and therefore the fault should be the less.

MRS DAINTY But then the pleasure should be the less.

LADY FIDGET Fie, fie, fie, for shame sister, whither shall we ramble? Be continent in your discourse, or I shall hate you.

MRS DAINTY Besides an intrigue is so much the more notorious for the man's quality.

SQUEAMISH 'Tis true, nobody takes notice of a private man, and therefore with him, 'tis more secret, and the crime's the less, when 'tis not known.

LADY FIDGET You say true; i'faith I think you are in the right on't: 'tis not an injury to a husband, till it be an injury to our honours; so that a woman of honour loses no honour with a private person; and to say truth –

MRS DAINTY [*apart to Squeamish*] So the little fellow is grown a private person – with her –

LADY FIDGET But still my dear, dear honour.

Enter Sir Jasper, Horner, Dorilant.

SIR JASPER Aye, my dear, dear of honour, thou hast still so much honour in thy mouth –

HORNER [*aside*] That she has none elsewhere –

LADY FIDGET Oh, what d'ye mean to bring in these upon us?

MRS DAINTY Foh, these are as bad as wits.

SQUEAMISH Foh!

LADY FIDGET Let us leave the room.

SIR JASPER Stay, stay, faith to tell you the naked truth.

LADY FIDGET Fie, Sir Jasper, do not use that word 'naked'.

SIR JASPER Well, well, in short I have business at Whitehall, and cannot go to the play with you, therefore would have you go –

LADY FIDGET With those two to a play?

SIR JASPER No, not with t'other, but with Mr Horner, there can be no more scandal to go with him, than with Mr Tattle, or Master Limberham.★

LADY FIDGET With that nasty fellow! No – no.

SIR JASPER Nay, prithee dear, hear me. [*whispers to Lady Fidget*]

HORNER Ladies. [*Horner, Dorilant drawing near ⟨Mrs⟩ Squeamish, and ⟨Mrs⟩ Dainty*]

★ Mr Tattle . . . Master Limberham: names for gallants in plays by Congreve and Dryden.

MRS DAINTY Stand off.

SQUEAMISH Do not approach us.

MRS DAINTY You herd with the wits, you are obscenity all over.

SQUEAMISH And I would as soon look upon a picture of Adam and Eve, without fig leaves, as any of you, if I could help it, therefore keep off, and do not make us sick.

DORILANT What a divel are these?

HORNER Why, these are pretenders to honour, as critics to wit, only by censuring others; and as every raw peevish, out-of-humoured, affected, dull, tea-drinking, arithmetical fop sets up for a wit, by railing at men of sense, so these for honour, by railing at the Court, and ladies of as great honour, as quality.

SIR JASPER Come, Mr Horner, I must desire you to go with these ladies to the play, Sir.

HORNER I! Sir.

SIR JASPER Aye, aye, come, Sir.

HORNER I must beg your pardon, Sir, and theirs, I will not be seen in women's company in public again for the world.

SIR JASPER Ha, ha, strange aversion!

SQUEAMISH No, he's for women's company in private.

SIR JASPER He – poor man – he! Hah, ha, ha.

MRS DAINTY 'Tis a greater shame amongst lewd fellows to be seen in virtuous women's company, than for the women to be seen with them.

HORNER Indeed, Madam, the time was I only hated virtuous women, but now I hate the other too; I beg your pardon ladies.

LADY FIDGET You are very obliging, Sir, because we would not be troubled with you.

SIR JASPER In sober sadness he shall go.

DORILANT Nay, if he wo'not, I am ready to wait upon the ladies; and I think I am the fitter man.

SIR JASPER You, Sir, no I thank you for that – Master Horner is a privileged man amongst the virtuous ladies, 'twill be a great while before you are so; heh, he, he, he's my wife's gallant, heh, he he; no pray withdraw, Sir, for as I take it, the virtuous ladies have no business with you.

DORILANT And I am sure, he can have none with them: 'tis strange a man can't come amongst virtuous women now, but upon the same terms as men are admitted into the Great Turk's seraglio;* but heavens keep me, from being an ombre player with 'em: but where is Pinchwife – [*Exit Dorilant*]

SIR JASPER Come, come, man; what avoid the sweet society of womankind? That sweet, soft, gentle, tame, noble creature woman, made for man's companion –

HORNER So is that soft, gentle, tame, and more noble creature a spaniel, and has all their tricks, can fawn, lie down, suffer beating, and fawn the more; barks at your friends, when they come to see you; makes your bed hard, gives you fleas, and the mange sometimes: and all the difference is, the spaniel's the more faithful animal, and fawns but upon one master.

SIR JASPER Heh, he, he.

SQUEAMISH O the rude beast.

MRS DAINTY Insolent brute.

LADY FIDGET Brute! Stinking mortified rotten French wether,† to dare –

SIR JASPER Hold, an't please your ladyship; for shame Master Horner your mother was a woman – [*aside*] Now shall I never reconcile 'em. ⟨*to her*⟩ Hark you, Madam, take my advice in your anger; you know you often want one to make up your drolling pack of ombre players; and you may cheat him easily, for he's an ill gamester, and consequently loves play: besides you know, you have but two old civil gentlemen (with stinking breaths too) to wait upon you abroad, take in the third, into your service; the other are but crazy: and a lady should have a supernumerary gentleman-usher, as a supernumerary coach-horse, lest sometimes you should be forced to stay at home.

LADY FIDGET But are you sure he loves play, and has money?

SIR JASPER He loves play as much as you, and has money as much as I.

LADY FIDGET Then I am contented to make him pay for his scurrillity; money makes up in a measure all other wants in men – [*aside*] Those whom we cannot make hold for gallants, we make fine.

---

* Great Turk's seraglio: that of the Sultan of Turkey.
† French wether: a French castrated ram, but here Lady Fidget believes that the French pox leads to impotence.

SIR JASPER [*aside*] So, so; now to mollify, to wheedle him, – ⟨*to him*⟩ Master Horner will you never keep civil company, methinks 'tis time now, since you are only fit for them: come, come, man you must e'en fall to visiting our wives, eating at our tables, drinking tea with our virtuous relations after dinner, dealing cards to 'em, reading plays, and gazettes to 'em, picking fleas out of their shocks* for 'em, collecting receipts, new songs, women, pages, and footmen for 'em.

HORNER I hope they'll afford me better employment, Sir.

SIR JASPER Heh, he, he, 'tis fit you know your work before you come into your place; and since you are unprovided of a lady to flatter, and a good house to eat at, pray frequent mine, and call my wife mistress, and she shall call you gallant, according to the custom.

HORNER Who I? –

SIR JASPER Faith, thou sha't for my sake, come for my sake only.

HORNER For your sake –

SIR JASPER Come, come, here's a gamester for you, let him be a little familiar sometimes; nay, what if a little rude; gamesters may be rude with ladies, you know.

LADY FIDGET Yes, losing gamesters have a privilege with women.

HORNER I always thought the contrary, that the winning gamester had most privilege with women, for when you have lost your money to a man, you'll lose anything you have, all you have, they say, and he may use you as he pleases.

SIR JASPER Heh, he, he, well, win or lose you shall have your liberty with her.

LADY FIDGET As he behaves himself; and for your sake I'll give him admittance and freedom.

HORNER All sorts of freedom, Madam?

SIR JASPER Aye, aye, aye, all sorts of freedom thou can'st take, and so go to her, begin thy new employment; wheedle her, jest with her, and be better acquainted one with another.

HORNER [*aside*] I think I know her already, therefore may venture with her, my secret for hers – [*Horner, and Lady Fidget whisper*]

SIR JASPER Sister cuz, I have provided an innocent playfellow for you there.

           * shocks: poodles.

MRS DAINTY Who he!

SQUEAMISH There's a playfellow indeed.

SIR JASPER Yes sure, what he is good enough to play at cards, blindman's buff, or the fool with sometimes.

SQUEAMISH Foh, we'll have no such playfellows.

MRS DAINTY No, Sir, you shan't choose playfellows for us, we thank you.

SIR JASPER Nay, pray hear me. [*whispering to them*]

LADY FIDGET But, poor gentleman, could you be so generous? So truly a man of honour, as for the sakes of us women of honour, to cause yourself to be reported no man? No man! And to suffer yourself the greatest shame that could fall upon a man, that none might fall upon us women by your conversation; but indeed, Sir, as perfectly, perfectly, the same man as before your going into France, Sir; as perfectly, perfectly, Sir.

HORNER As perfectly, perfectly, Madam; nay, I scorn you should take my word; I desire to be tried only, Madam.

LADY FIDGET Well, that's spoken again like a man of honour, all men of honour desire to come to the test: but indeed, generally you men report such things of yourselves, one does not know how, or whom to believe; and it is come to that pass, we dare not take your words, no more than your tailor's, without some staid servant of yours be bound with you; but I have so strong a faith in your honour, dear, dear, noble Sir, that I'd forfeit mine for yours at any time, dear Sir.

HORNER No, Madam, you should not need to forfeit it for me, I have given you security already to save you harmless, my late reputation being so well known in the world, Madam.

LADY FIDGET But if upon any future falling out, or upon a suspicion of my taking the trust out of your hands, to employ some other, you yourself should betray your trust, dear Sir; I mean, if you'll give me leave to speak obscenely, you might tell, dear Sir.

HORNER If I did, nobody would believe me; the reputation of impotency is as hardly recovered again in the world, as that of cowardice, dear Madam.

LADY FIDGET Nay then, as one may say, you may do your worst, dear, dear, Sir.

SIR JASPER Come, is your ladyship reconciled to him yet? Have you agreed on matters? For I must be gone to Whitehall.

LADY FIDGET Why, indeed, Sir Jasper, Master Horner is a thousand, thousand times a better man, than I thought him: cousin Squeamish, sister Dainty, I can name him now, truly not long ago you know, I thought his very name obscenity, and I would as soon have lain with him, as have named him.

SIR JASPER Very likely, poor Madam.

MRS DAINTY I believe it.

SQUEAMISH No doubt on't.

SIR JASPER Well, well – that your ladyship is as virtuous as any she, – I know, and him all the Town knows – heh, he, he; therefore now you like him, get you gone to your business together; go, go, to your business, I say, pleasure, whilst I go to my pleasure, business.

LADY FIDGET Come then dear gallant.

HORNER Come away, my dearest mistress.

SIR JASPER So, so, why 'tis as I'd have it.   [*Exit Sir Jasper*]

HORNER And as I'd have it.

LADY FIDGET Who for his business, from his wife will run;
Takes the best care, to have her business done.

                                        [*Exeunt Omnes*]

ACT THREE

SCENE I

Alithea, and Mrs Pinchwife.

ALITHEA Sister, what ails you, you are grown melancholy?

MRS PINCHWIFE Would it not make anyone melancholy, to see you go every day fluttering about abroad, whilst I must stay at home like a poor lonely, sullen bird in a cage?

ALITHEA Aye, sister, but you came young, and just from the nest to your cage, so that I thought you liked it; and could be as cheerful in't, as others that took their flight themselves early, and are hopping abroad in the open air.

MRS PINCHWIFE Nay, I confess I was quiet enough, till my husband told me, what pure lives, the London ladies live abroad, with their dancing, meetings, and junketings, and dressed every day in their best gowns; and I warrant you, play at ninepins every day of the week, so they do.

Enter Pinchwife.

PINCHWIFE Come, what's here to do? You are putting the Town pleasures in her head, and setting her a-longing.

ALITHEA Yes, after ninepins; you suffer none to give her those longings, you mean, but yourself.

PINCHWIFE I tell her of the vanities of the Town like a confessor.

ALITHEA A confessor! Just such a confessor, as he that by forbidding a silly ostler to grease the horses' teeth, taught him to do't.

PINCHWIFE Come Mistress Flippant, good precepts are lost, when bad examples are still before us; the liberty you take abroad makes her hanker after it; and out of humour at home, poor wretch! She desired not to come to London, I would bring her.

ALITHEA Very well.

PINCHWIFE She has been this week in Town, and never desired, till this afternoon, to go abroad.

ALITHEA Was she not at a play yesterday?

PINCHWIFE Yes, but she ne'er asked me; I was myself the cause of her going.

ALITHEA Then if she ask you again, you are the cause of her asking, and not my example.

PINCHWIFE Well, tomorrow night I shall be rid of you; and the next day before 'tis light, she and I'll be rid of the Town, and my dreadful apprehensions: come, be not melancholy, for thou sha't go into the country after tomorrow, dearest.

ALITHEA Great comfort.

MRS PINCHWIFE Pish, what d'ye tell me of the country for?

PINCHWIFE How's this! What, pish at the country?

MRS PINCHWIFE Let me alone, I am not well.

PINCHWIFE Oh, if that be all – what ails my dearest?

MRS PINCHWIFE Truly I don't know; but I have not been well, since you told me there was a gallant at the play in love with me.

PINCHWIFE Ha –

ALITHEA That's by my example too.

PINCHWIFE Nay, if you are not well, but are so concerned, because a lewd fellow chanced to lie, and say he liked you, you'll make me sick too.

MRS PINCHWIFE Of what sickness?

PINCHWIFE Oh, of that which is worse than the plague, jealousy.

MRS PINCHWIFE Pish, you jeer, I'm sure there's no such disease in our receipt-book at home.

PINCHWIFE No, thou never met'st with it, poor innocent – [*aside*] well, if thou cuckold me, 'twill be my own fault – for cuckolds and bastards, are generally makers of their own fortune.

MRS PINCHWIFE Well, but pray bud, let's go to a play tonight.

PINCHWIFE 'Tis just done, she comes from it; but why are you so eager to see a play?

MRS PINCHWIFE Faith dear, not that I care one pin for their talk there; but I like to look upon the player men, and would see, if I could, the gallant you say loves me; that's all dear bud.

PINCHWIFE Is that all dear bud?

ALITHEA This proceeds from my example.

MRS PINCHWIFE But if the play be done, let's go abroad however, dear bud.

PINCHWIFE Come have a little patience, and thou shalt go into the country on Friday.

MRS PINCHWIFE Therefore I would see first some sights, to tell my neighbours of. Nay, I will go abroad, that's once.

ALITHEA I'm the cause of this desire too.

PINCHWIFE But now I think on't, who was the cause of Horner's coming to my lodging today? That was you.

ALITHEA No, you, because you would not let him see your handsome wife out of your lodging.

MRS PINCHWIFE Why, O Lord! Did the gentleman come hither to see me indeed?

PINCHWIFE No, no; – You are not the cause of that damned question too, Mistress Alithea? – [*aside*] Well she's in the right of it; he is in love with my wife – and comes after her – 'tis so – but I'll nip his love in the bud; lest he should follow us into the country, and break his chariot-wheel near our house, on purpose for an excuse to come to't; but I think I know the Town.

MRS PINCHWIFE Come, pray bud, let's go abroad before 'tis late; for I will go, that's flat and plain.

PINCHWIFE [*aside*] So! The obstinacy already of a Town-wife, and I must, whilst she's here, humour her like one. ⟨*to Alithea*⟩ Sister, how shall we do, that she may not be seen, or known?

ALITHEA Let her put on her mask.

PINCHWIFE Pshaw, a mask makes people but the more inquisitive, and is as ridiculous a disguise, as a stage-beard; her shape, stature, habit will be known: and if we should meet with Horner, he would be sure to take acquaintance with us, must wish her joy, kiss her, talk to her, leer upon her, and the devil and all; no I'll not use her to a mask, 'tis dangerous; for masks have made more cuckolds, than the best faces that ever were known.

ALITHEA How will you do then?

MRS PINCHWIFE Nay, shall we go? The Exchange will be shut, and I have a mind to see that.

PINCHWIFE So – I have it – I'll dress her up in the suit, we are to carry down to her brother, little Sir James; nay, I understand the Town-tricks: come let's go dress her; a mask! No – a woman masked, like a covered dish, gives a man curiosity, and appetite, when, it may be, uncovered, 'twould turn his stomach; no, no.

ALITHEA Indeed your comparison is something a greasy one: but

I had a gentle gallant, used to say, a beauty masked, like the sun in eclipse, gathers together more gazers, than if it shined out.

[Exeunt]

SCENE ⟨II⟩

Changes to the New Exchange

Enter Horner, Harcourt, Dorilant.

DORILANT Engaged to women, and not sup with us?

HORNER Aye, a pox on 'em all.

HARCOURT You were much a more reasonable man in the morning, and had as noble resolutions against 'em, as a widower of a week's liberty.

DORILANT Did I ever think, to see you keep company with women in vain.

HORNER In vain! No – 'tis, since I can't love 'em, to be revenged on 'em.

HARCOURT Now your sting is gone, you looked in the box amongst all those women, like a drone in the hive, all upon you; shoved and ill-used by 'em all; and thrust from one side to t'other.

DORILANT Yet he must be buzzing amongst 'em still, like other old beetle-headed, liquorish drones; avoid 'em, and hate 'em as they hate you.

HORNER Because I do hate 'em, and would hate 'em yet more, I'll frequent 'em; you may see by marriage, nothing makes a man hate a woman more, than her constant conversation: in short, I converse with 'em, as you do with rich fools, to laugh at 'em, and use 'em ill.

DORILANT But I would no more sup with women, unless I could lie with 'em, than sup with a rich coxcomb, unless I could cheat him.

HORNER Yes, I have known thee sup with a fool, for his drinking, if he could set out your hand that way only, you were satisfied; and if he were a wine-swallowing mouth 'twas enough.

HARCOURT Yes, a man drinks often with a fool, as he tosses with a marker,* only to keep his hand in ure;† but do the ladies drink?

HORNER Yes, Sir, and I shall have the pleasure at least of laying 'em flat with a bottle; and bring as much scandal that way upon 'em, as formerly t'other.

HARCOURT Perhaps you may prove as weak a brother amongst 'em that way, as t'other.

DORILANT Foh, drinking with women, is as unnatural, as scolding with 'em; but 'tis a pleasure of decayed fornicators, and the basest way of quenching love.

HARCOURT Nay, 'tis drowning love, instead of quenching it; but leave us for civil women too!

DORILANT Aye, when he can't be the better for 'em; we hardly pardon a man, that leaves his friend for a wench, and that's a pretty lawful call.

HORNER Faith, I would not leave you for 'em, if they would not drink.

DORILANT Who would disappoint his company at Lewis's, for a gossiping?

HARCOURT Foh, wine and women good apart, together as nauseous as sack and sugar: but hark you, Sir, before you go, a little of your advice, an old maimed general, when unfit for action is fittest for counsel; I have other designs upon women, than eating and drinking with them: I am in love with Sparkish's mistress, whom he is to marry tomorrow, now how shall I get her?

Enter Sparkish, looking about.

HORNER Why, here comes one will help you to her.

HARCOURT He! He, I tell you, is my rival, and will hinder my love.

HORNER No, a foolish rival, and a jealous husband assist their rival's designs; for they are sure to make their women hate them, which is the first step to their love, for another man.

HARCOURT But I cannot come near his mistress, but in his company.

HORNER Still the better for you, for fools are most easily cheated,

* tosses with a marker: possibly meaning drinks with someone by him to keep count of his consumption.
† in ure: in practice.

when they themselves are accessaries; and he is to be bubbled* of his mistress, as of his money, the common mistress, by keeping him company.

SPARKISH Who is that, that is to be bubbled? Faith let me snack, I han't met with a bubble since Christmas: gad; I think bubbles are like their brother woodcocks, go out with the cold weather.

HARCOURT [*apart to Horner*] A pox, he did not hear all I hope.

SPARKISH Come, you bubbling rogues you, where do we sup – Oh, Harcourt, my mistress tells me, you have been making fierce love to her all the play long, hah, ha – but I –

HARCOURT I make love to her?

SPARKISH Nay, I forgive thee; for I think I know thee, and I know her, but I am sure I know myself.

HARCOURT Did she tell you so? I see all women are like these of the Exchange, who to enhance the price of their commodities, report to their fond customers offers which were never made 'em.

HORNER Aye, women are as apt to tell before the intrigue, as men after it, and so show themselves the vainer sex; but hast thou a mistress, Sparkish? 'Tis as hard for me to believe it, as that thou ever hadst a bubble, as you bragged just now.

SPARKISH O your servant, Sir; are you at your raillery, Sir? But we were some of us beforehand with you today at the play: the wits were something bold with you, Sir; did you not hear us laugh?

HARCOURT Yes, but I thought you had gone to plays, to laugh at the poet's wit, not at your own.

SPARKISH Your servant, Sir, no I thank you; gad I go to a play as to a country treat, I carry my own wine to one, and my own wit to t'other, or else I'm sure I should not be merry at either; and the reason why we are so often louder, than the players, is, because we think we speak more wit, and so become the poet's rivals in his audience: for to tell you the truth, we hate the silly rogues; nay, so much that we find fault even with their bawdy upon the stage, whilst we talk nothing else in the pit as loud.

HORNER But, why should'st thou hate the silly poets, thou hast too much wit to be one, and they like whores are only hated by each other; and thou dost scorn writing, I'm sure.

* bubbled: gulled.

SPARKISH Yes, I'd have you to know, I scorn writing; but women, women, that make men do all foolish things, make 'em write songs too; everybody does it: 'tis even as common with lovers, as playing with fans; and you can no more help rhyming to your Phyllis, than drinking to your Phyllis.

HARCOURT Nay, poetry in love is no more to be avoided, than jealousy.

DORILANT But the poets damned your songs, did they?

SPARKISH Damn the poets, they turned 'em into burlesque, as they call it; that burlesque is a hocus-pocus trick, they have got, which by the virtue of *Hictius doctius, topsy turvy*, they make a wise and witty man in the world, a fool upon the stage you know not how; and 'tis therefore I hate 'em too, for I know not but it may be my own case; for they'll put a man into a play for looking asquint: their predecessors were contented to make serving-men only their stage-fools, but these rogues must have gentlemen, with a pox to 'em, nay knights: and indeed you shall hardly see a fool upon the stage, but he's a knight; and to tell you the truth, they have kept me these six years from being a knight in earnest, for fear of being knighted in a play, and dubbed a fool.

DORILANT Blame 'em not, they must follow their copy, the age.

HARCOURT But why should'st thou be afraid of being in a play, who expose yourself every day in the playhouses, and as public places.

HORNER 'Tis but being on the stage, instead of standing on a bench in the pit.

DORILANT Don't you give money to painters to draw you like? And are you afraid of your pictures, at length in a playhouse, where all your mistresses may see you.

SPARKISH A pox, painters don't draw the smallpox, or pimples in one's face; come damn all your silly authors whatever, all books and booksellers, by the world, and all readers, courteous or uncourteous.

HARCOURT But, who comes here, Sparkish?

Enter Pinchwife, and his wife in man's clothes, Alithea, Lucy her maid.

SPARKISH Oh hide me, there's my mistress too.

[Sparkish hides himself behind Harcourt]

HARCOURT She sees you.

SPARKISH But I will not see her, 'tis time to go to Whitehall, and I must not fail the drawing room.

HARCOURT Pray, first carry me, and reconcile me to her.

SPARKISH Another time, faith the king will have supped.

HARCOURT Not with the worse stomach for thy absence; thou art one of those fools, that think their attendance at the king's meals, as necessary as his physicians, when you are more troublesome to him, than his doctors, or his dogs.

SPARKISH Pshaw, I know my interest, Sir, prithee hide me.

HORNER Your servant, Pinchwife, – what he knows us not –

PINCHWIFE [*to his wife aside*] Come along.

MRS PINCHWIFE Pray, have you any ballads, give me sixpenny worth?

CLASP* We have no ballads.

MRS PINCHWIFE Then give me *Covent-Garden-Drollery*,† and a play or two – O here's *Tarugo's Wiles*,‡ and *The Slighted Maiden*,§ I'll have them.

PINCHWIFE [*apart to her*] No, plays are not for your reading; come along, will you discover yourself?

HORNER Who is that pretty youth with him, Sparkish?

SPARKISH I believe his wife's brother, because he's something like her, but I never saw her but once.

HORNER Extremely handsome, I have seen a face like it too; let us follow 'em.

[*Exeunt Pinchwife, Mrs Pinchwife. Alithea, Lucy, Horner, Dorilant following them*]

HARCOURT Come, Sparkish, your mistress saw you, and will be angry you go not to her; besides I would fain be reconciled to her, which none but you can do, dear friend.

SPARKISH Well that's a better reason, dear friend; I would not go

* Clasp: presumably one of the stall holders in the New Exchange.

† *Covent Garden Drollery*: the alternative title was *or a Colection of all the Choice Songs, Poems, Prologues and Epilogues (Sung and Spoken at Courts and Theatres) Never in Print before* (1672). These were collected by R[ichard] B[rome].

† *Tarugo's Wiles*: the alternative title was *or the Coffee House*. This was a comedy by Sir Thomas St Serfe, produced in 1668.

§ *The Slighted Maid*: a comedy by Sir Robert Stapylton, produced in 1663.

near her now, for her's, or my own sake, but I can deny you nothing; for though I have known thee a great while, never go, if I do not love thee, as well as a new acquaintance.

HARCOURT I am obliged to you indeed, dear friend, I would be well with her only, to be well with thee still; for these ties to wives usually dissolve all ties to friends: I would be contented, she should enjoy you a-nights, but I would have you to myself a-days, as I have had, dear friend.

SPARKISH And thou shalt enjoy me a-days, dear, dear friend, never stir; and I'll be divorced from her, sooner than from thee; come along –

HARCOURT [*aside*] So we are hard put to't, when we make our rival our procurer; but neither she, nor her brother, would let me come near her now: when all's done, a rival is the best cloak to steal to a mistress under, without suspicion; and when we have once got to her as we desire, we throw him off like other cloaks.

[*Exit Sparkish, and Harcourt following him*]

Re-enter Pinchwife, Mrs Pinchwife in man's clothes, ⟨Alithea, Lucy, her maid.⟩

PINCHWIFE [*to Alithea*] Sister, if you will not go, we must leave you – [*aside*] The fool her gallant, and she, will muster up all the young saunterers of this place, and they will leave their dear sempstresses to follow us; what a swarm of cuckolds, and cuckold-makers are here? ⟨*to his wife*⟩ Come let's be gone Mistress Margery

MRS PINCHWIFE Don't you believe that, I han't half my belly full of sights yet.

PINCHWIFE Then walk this way.

MRS PINCHWIFE Lord, what a power of brave signs are here! Stay – the Bull's Head, the Ram's Head, and the Stag's Head, dear –

PINCHWIFE Nay, if every husband's proper sign here were visible, they would be all alike.

MRS PINCHWIFE What d'ye mean by that, bud?

PINCHWIFE 'Tis no matter – no matter, bud.

MRS PINCHWIFE Pray tell me; nay, I will know.

PINCHWIFE They would be all bulls', stags', and rams' heads.

[*Exeunt Pinchwife, Mrs Pinchwife*]

Re-enter Sparkish, Harcourt, ⟨to⟩ Alithea, Lucy, at t'other door.

SPARKISH Come, dear Madam, for my sake you shall be reconciled to him.

ALITHEA For your sake I hate him.

HARCOURT That's something too cruel, Madam, to hate me for his sake.

SPARKISH Aye indeed, Madam, too, too cruel to me, to hate my friend for my sake.

ALITHEA I hate him because he is your enemy; and you ought to hate him too, for making love to me, if you love me.

SPARKISH That's a good one, I hate a man for loving you; if he did love you, 'tis but what he can't help, and 'tis your fault not his, if he admires you: I hate a man for being of my opinion, I'll ne'er do't, by the world.

ALITHEA Is it for your honour or mine, to suffer a man to make love to me, who am to marry you tomorrow?

SPARKISH Is it for your honour or mine, to have me jealous? That he makes love to you, is a sign you are handsome; and that I am not jealous, is a sign you are virtuous, that I think is for your honour.

ALITHEA But 'tis your honour too, I am concerned for.

HARCOURT But why, dearest Madam, will you be more concerned for his honour, than he is himself; let his honour alone for my sake, and his. He, he has no honour –

SPARKISH How's that?

HARCOURT But what, my dear friend can guard himself.

SPARKISH O ho – that's right again.

HARCOURT Your care of his honour argues his neglect of it, which is no honour to my dear friend here; therefore once more, let his honour go which way it will, dear Madam.

SPARKISH Aye, aye, were it for my honour to marry a woman, whose virtue I suspected, and could not trust her in a friend's hands?

ALITHEA Are you not afraid to lose me?

HARCOURT He afraid to lose you, Madam! No, no – you may see how the most estimable, and most glorious creature in the world, is valued by him; will you not see it?

SPARKISH Right, honest Frank, I have that noble value for her, that I cannot be jealous of her.

ALITHEA You mistake him, he means you care not for me, nor who has me.

SPARKISH Lord, Madam, I see you are jealous; will you wrest a poor man's meaning from his words?

ALITHEA You astonish me, Sir, with your want of jealousy.

SPARKISH And you make me giddy, Madam, with your jealousy, and fears, and virtue, and honour; gad, I see virtue makes a woman as troublesome, as a little reading, or learning.

ALITHEA Monstrous!

LUCY [*behind*] Well to see what easy husbands these women of quality can meet with, a poor chambermaid can never have such lady-like luck; besides he's thrown away upon her, she'll make no use of her fortune, her blessing, none to a gentleman, for a pure cuckold, for it requires good breeding to be a cuckold.

ALITHEA I tell you then plainly, he pursues me to marry me.

SPARKISH Pshaw –

HARCOURT Come, Madam, you see you strive in vain to make him jealous of me; my dear friend is the kindest creature in the world to me.

SPARKISH Poor fellow.

HARCOURT But his kindness only is not enough for me, without your favour; your good opinion, dear Madam, 'tis that must perfect my happiness: good gentleman he believes all I say, would you would do so, jealous of me! I would not wrong him nor you for the world.

SPARKISH Look you there; hear him, hear him, [*Alithea walks carelessly, to and fro*] and do not walk away so.

HARCOURT I love you, Madam, so –

SPARKISH How's that! Nay – now you begin to go too far indeed.

HARCOURT So much I confess, I say I love you, that I would not have you miserable, and cast yourself away upon so unworthy, and inconsiderable a thing, as what you see here. [*clapping his hand on his breast, points at Sparkish*]

SPARKISH No faith, I believe thou would'st not, now his meaning is plain: but I knew before thou would'st not wrong me nor her.

HARCOURT No, no, heavens forbid, the glory of her sex should fall so low as into the embraces of such a contemptible wretch, the last of mankind – [*embracing Sparkish*] my dear friend here – I injure him.

ALITHEA Very well.

SPARKISH No, no, dear friend, I knew it Madam, you see he will rather wrong himself than me, in giving himself such names.

ALITHEA Do not you understand him yet?

SPARKISH Yes, how modestly he speaks of himself, poor fellow.

ALITHEA Methinks he speaks impudently of yourself, since – before yourself too, insomuch that I can no longer suffer his scurrilous abusiveness to you, no more than his love to me. [*offers to go*]

SPARKISH Nay, nay, Madam, pray stay, his love to you: Lord, Madam, has he not spoke yet plain enough?

ALITHEA Yes indeed, I should think so.

SPARKISH Well then, by the world, a man can't speak civilly to a woman now, but presently she says, he makes love to her: nay, Madam, you shall stay, with your pardon, since you have not yet understood him, till he has made an *éclaircissement** of his love to you, that is what kind of love it is; answer to thy catechism: friend, do you love my mistress here?

HARCOURT Yes, I wish she would not doubt it.

SPARKISH But how do you love her?

HARCOURT With all my soul.

ALITHEA I thank him, methinks he speaks plain enough now.

SPARKISH [*to Alithea*] You are out still. But with what kind of love, Harcourt?

HARCOURT With the best, and truest love in the world.

SPARKISH Look you there then, that is with no matrimonial love, I'm sure.

ALITHEA How's that, do you say matrimonial love is not best?

SPARKISH Gad, I went too far ere I was aware: but speak for thyself Harcourt, you said you would not wrong me, nor her.

HARCOURT No, no, Madam, e'en take him for heaven's sake.

SPARKISH Look you there, Madam.

* *éclaircissement*: elucidation.

HARCOURT Who should in all justice be yours, he that loves you most. [*claps his hand on his breast*]

ALITHEA Look you there, Mr Sparkish, who's that?

SPARKISH Who should it be? Go on Harcourt.

HARCOURT [*points at Sparkish*] Who loves you more than women, titles, or fortune fools.

SPARKISH Look you there, he means me still, for he points at me.

ALITHEA Ridiculous!

HARCOURT Who can only match your faith, and constancy in love.

SPARKISH Aye.

HARCOURT Who knows, if it be possible, how to value so much beauty and virtue.

SPARKISH Aye.

HARCOURT Whose love can no more be equalled in the world, than that heavenly form of yours.

SPARKISH No –

HARCOURT Who could no more suffer a rival, than your absence, and yet could no more suspect your virtue, than his own constancy in his love to you.

SPARKISH No –

HARCOURT Who in fine loves you better than his eyes, that first made him love you.

SPARKISH Aye – nay, Madam, faith you shan't go, till –

ALITHEA Have a care, lest you make me stay too long –

SPARKISH But till he has saluted you; that I may be assured you are friends, after his honest advice and declaration: come pray, Madam, be friends with him.

Enter Pinchwife, Mrs Pinchwife.

ALITHEA You must pardon me, Sir, that I am not yet so obedient to you.

PINCHWIFE What, invite your wife to kiss men? Monstrous, are you not ashamed? I will never forgive you.

SPARKISH Are you not ashamed, that I should have more confidence in the chastity of your family, than you have; you must not teach me, I am a man of honour, Sir, though I am frank and free; I am frank, Sir –

PINCHWIFE Very frank, Sir, to share your wife with your friends.

SPARKISH He is an humble, menial friend, such as reconciles the differences of the marriage bed; you know man and wife do not always agree, I design him for that use, therefore would have him well with my wife.

PINCHWIFE A menial friend – you will get a great many menial friends, by showing your wife as you do.

SPARKISH What then, it may be I have a pleasure in't, as I have to show fine clothes, at a playhouse the first day, and count money before poor rogues.

PINCHWIFE He that shows his wife, or money will be in danger of having them borrowed sometimes.

SPARKISH I love to be envied, and would not marry a wife, that I alone could love; loving alone is as dull, as eating alone; is it not a frank age, and I am a frank person? And to tell you the truth, it may be I love to have rivals in a wife, they make her seem to a man still, but as a kept mistress; and so good night, for I must to Whitehall. Madam, I hope you are now reconciled to my friend; and so I wish you a good night, Madam, and sleep if you can, for tomorrow you know I must visit you early with a canonical gentleman. Good night dear Harcourt.   [*Exit Sparkish*]

HARCOURT Madam, I hope you will not refuse my visit to-morrow, if it should be earlier, with a canonical gentleman, than Mr Sparkish's.

PINCHWIFE [*coming between Alithea and Harcourt*] This gentle-woman is yet under my care, therefore you must yet forbear your freedom with her, Sir.

HARCOURT Must, Sir –

PINCHWIFE Yes, Sir, she is my sister.

HARCOURT 'Tis well she is, Sir – for I must be her servant, Sir. Madam –

PINCHWIFE Come away sister, we had been gone, if it had not been for you, and so avoided these lewd rakehells, who seem to haunt us.

Enter Horner, Dorilant to them.

HORNER How now Pinchwife?

PINCHWIFE Your servant.

HORNER What, I see a little time in the country makes a man turn wild and unsociable, and only fit to converse with his horses, dogs, and his herds.

PINCHWIFE I have business, Sir, and must mind it; your business is pleasure, therefore you and I must go different ways.

HORNER Well, you may go on, but this pretty young gentleman – [*takes hold of Mrs Pinchwife*]

HARCOURT The lady –

DORILANT And the maid –

HORNER Shall stay with us, for I suppose their business is the same with ours, pleasure.

PINCHWIFE [*aside*] S'death he knows her, she carries it so sillily, yet if he does not, I should be more silly to discover it first.

ALITHEA Pray, let us go, Sir.

PINCHWIFE Come, come –

HORNER [*to Mrs Pinchwife*] Had you not rather stay with us? Prithee Pinchwife, who is this pretty young gentleman?

PINCHWIFE One to whom I'm a guardian. [*aside*] I wish I could keep her out of your hands –

HORNER Who is he? I never saw anything so pretty in all my life.

PINCHWIFE Pshaw, do not look upon him so much, he's a poor bashful youth, you'll put him out of countenance. Come away brother. [*offers to take her away*]

HORNER O your brother!

PINCHWIFE Yes, my wife's brother; come, come, she'll stay supper for us.

HORNER I thought so, for he is very like her I saw you at the play with, whom I told you, I was in love with.

MRS PINCHWIFE [*aside*] O jeminy! Is this he that was in love with me, I am glad on't I vow, for he's a curious fine gentleman, and I love him already too. [*to Mr Pinchwife*] Is this he bud?

PINCHWIFE [*to his wife*] Come away, come away.

HORNER Why, what haste are you in? Why won't you let me talk with him?

PINCHWIFE Because you'll debauch him, he's yet young and innocent, and I would not have him debauched for anything in the world. [*aside*] How she gazes on him! The divel –

HORNER Harcourt, Dorilant, look you here, this is the likeness of that dowdy he told us of, his wife, did you ever see a lovelier creature? The rogue has reason to be jealous of his wife, since she is like him, for she would make all that see her, in love with her.

HARCOURT And as I remember now, she is as like him here as can be.

DORILANT She is indeed very pretty, if she be like him.

HORNER Very pretty, a very pretty commendation – she is a glorious creature, beautiful beyond all things I ever beheld.

PINCHWIFE So, so.

HARCOURT More beautiful than a poet's first mistress of imagination.

HORNER Or another man's last mistress of flesh and blood.

MRS PINCHWIFE Nay, now you jeer, Sir; pray don't jeer me –

PINCHWIFE Come, come. [*aside*] By heavens she'll discover herself.

HORNER I speak of your sister, Sir.

PINCHWIFE Aye, but saying she was handsome, if like him, made him blush. [*aside*] I am upon a rack –

HORNER Methinks he is so handsome, he should not be a man.

PINCHWIFE ⟨*aside*⟩ O there 'tis out, he has discovered her, I am not able to suffer any longer. [*to his wife*] Come, come away, I say –

HORNER Nay, by your leave, Sir, he shall not go yet – [*to them*] Harcourt, Dorilant, let us torment this jealous rogue a little.

HARCOURT ⎫
DORILANT ⎭ How?

HORNER I'll show you.

PINCHWIFE Come, pray let him go, I cannot stay fooling any longer; I tell you his sister stays supper for us.

HORNER Does she, come then we'll all go sup with her and thee.

PINCHWIFE No, now I think on't, having stayed so long for us, I warrant she's gone to bed – [*aside*] I wish she and I were well out of their hands – ⟨*to his wife*⟩ Come, I must rise early tomorrow, come.

HORNER Well then, if she be gone to bed, I wish her and you a good night. But pray, young gentleman, present my humble service to her.

MRS PINCHWIFE Thank you heartily, Sir.

PINCHWIFE [*aside*] S'death, she will discover herself yet in spite of me. ⟨*to Horner*⟩ He is something more civil to you, for your kindness to his sister, than I am, it seems.

HORNER Tell her, dear sweet little gentleman, for all your brother there, that you have revived the love I had for her at first sight in the playhouse.

MRS PINCHWIFE But did you love her indeed, and indeed?

PINCHWIFE ⟨*aside*⟩ So, so. ⟨*to her*⟩ Away, I say.

HORNER Nay stay; yes indeed, and indeed, pray do you tell her so, and give her this kiss from me. [*kisses her*]

PINCHWIFE [*aside*] O heavens! What do I suffer; now 'tis too plain he knows her, and yet –

HORNER And this, and this – [*kisses her again*]

MRS PINCHWIFE What do you kiss me for, I am no woman.

PINCHWIFE [*aside*] So – there 'tis out. ⟨*to her*⟩ Come, I cannot, nor will stay any longer.

HORNER Nay, they shall send your lady a kiss too; here Harcourt, Dorilant, will you not? [*they kiss her*]

PINCHWIFE [*aiide*] How, do I suffer this? Was I not accusing another just now, for this rascally patience, in permitting his wife to be kissed before his face? Ten thousand ulcers gnaw away their lips. ⟨*to her*⟩ Come, come.

HORNER Good night dear little gentleman; Madam good night; farewell Pinchwife. [*apart to Harcourt and Dorilant*] Did I not tell you, I would raise his jealous gall.

[*Exeunt Horner, Harcourt, and Dorilant*]

PINCHWIFE So they are gone at last; stay, let me see first if the coach be at this door. [*Exit*]

Horner, Harcourt, Dorilant return.

HORNER What not gone yet? Will you be sure to do as I desired you, sweet Sir?

MRS PINCHWIFE Sweet Sir, but what will you give me then?

HORNER Anything, come away into the next walk.

[*Exit Horner, haling away Mrs Pinchwife*]

ALITHEA Hold, hold, – what d'ye do?

LUCY Stay, stay, hold –

HARCOURT Hold Madam, hold, let him present him, he'll come

presently; nay, I will never let you go, till you answer my question.

Alithea, Lucy struggling with Harcourt, and Dorilant.

LUCY For God's sake, Sir, I must follow 'em.

DORILANT No, I have something to present you with too, you shan't follow them.

Pinchwife returns.

PINCHWIFE Where? – How? – What's become of? Gone – whither?

LUCY He's only gone with the gentleman, who will give him something, an't please your worship.

PINCHWIFE Something – give him something, with a pox – where are they?

ALITHEA In the next walk only, brother.

PINCHWIFE Only, only; where, where?

Exit Pinchwife, and returns presently, then goes out again.

HARCOURT What's the matter with him? Why so much concerned? But dearest Madam –

ALITHEA Pray, let me go, Sir, I have said, and suffered enough already.

HARCOURT Then you will not look upon, nor pity my sufferings?

ALITHEA To look upon 'em, when I cannot help 'em, were cruelty, not pity, therefore I will never see you more.

HARCOURT Let me then, Madam, have my privilege of a banished lover, complaining or railing, and giving you but a farewell reason; why, if you cannot condescend to marry me, you should not take that wretch my rival.

ALITHEA He only, not you, since my honour is engaged so far to him, can give me a reason, why I should not marry him; but if he be true, and what I think him to me, I must be so to him; your servant, Sir.

HARCOURT Have women only constancy when 'tis a vice, and like fortune only true to fools?

DORILANT [*to Lucy, who struggles to get from him*] Thou sha't not stir thou robust creature, you see I can deal with you, therefore you should stay the rather, and be kind.

Enter Pinchwife.

PINCHWIFE Gone, gone, not to be found; quite gone, ten thousand plagues go with 'em; which way went they?

ALITHEA But into t'other walk, brother.

LUCY Their business will be done presently sure, an't please your worship, it can't be long in doing I'm sure on't.

ALITHEA Are they not there?

PINCHWIFE No, you know where they are, you infamous wretch, eternal shame of your family, which you do not dishonour enough yourself, you think, but you must help her to do it too, thou legion of bawds.

ALITHEA Good brother.

PINCHWIFE Damned, damned sister.

ALITHEA Look you here, she's coming.

Enter Mrs Pinchwife in man's clothes, running with her hat under her arm, full of oranges and dried fruit, Horner following.

MRS PINCHWIFE O dear bud, look you here what I have got, see.

PINCHWIFE [*aside rubbing his forehead*] And what I have got here too, which you can't see.

MRS PINCHWIFE The fine gentleman has given me better things yet.

PINCHWIFE Has he so? [*aside*] Out of breath and coloured – I must hold yet.

HORNER I have only given your little brother an orange, Sir.

PINCHWIFE [*to Horner*] Thank you, Sir. [*aside*] You have only squeezed my orange, I suppose, and given it me again; yet I must have a City patience.* [*to his wife*] Come, come away –

MRS PINCHWIFE Stay, till I have put up my fine things, bud.

Enter Sir Jasper Fidget.

SIR JASPER O Master Horner, come, come, the ladies stay for you; your mistress, my wife, wonders you make not more haste to her.

HORNER I have stayed this half hour for you here, and 'tis your fault I am not now with your wife.

* City patience: presumably that of a citizen cuckolded by an aristocrat.

SIR JASPER But pray, don't let her know so much, the truth on't is, I was advancing a certain project to his Majesty, about – I'll tell you.

HORNER No, let's go, and hear it at your house: good night sweet little gentleman; one kiss more, you'll remember me now I hope. [*kisses her*]

DORILANT What, Sir Jasper, will you separate friends? He promised to sup with us; and if you take him to your house, you'll be in danger of our company too.

SIR JASPER Alas gentlemen my house is not fit for you, there are none but civil women there, which are not for your turn; he you know can bear with the society of civil women, now, ha, ha, ha; besides he's one of my family; – he's – heh, heh, heh.

DORILANT What is he?

SIR JASPER Faith my eunuch, since you'll have it, heh, he, he.

[*Exeunt Sir Jasper Fidget, and Horner*]

DORILANT I rather wish thou wert his, or my cuckold: Harcourt, what a good cuckold is lost there, for want of a man to make him one; thee and I cannot have Horner's privilege, who can make use of it.

HARCOURT Aye, to poor Horner 'tis like coming to an estate at threescore, when a man can't be the better for't.

PINCHWIFE Come.

MRS PINCHWIFE Presently bud.

DORILANT Come let us go too: [*to Alithea*] Madam your servant. [*to Lucy*] Good night strapper. –

HARCOURT Madam, though you will not let me have a good day, or night, I wish you one; but dare not name the other half of my wish.

ALITHEA Good night, Sir, for ever.

MRS PINCHWIFE I don't know where to put this here, dear bud, you shall eat it; nay, you shall have part of the fine gentleman's good things, or treat, as you call it, when we come home.

PINCHWIFE [*strikes away the orange*] Indeed I deserve it, since I furnished the best part of it.

The gallant treats, presents, and gives the ball;
But 'tis the absent cuckold, pays for all. 〈*Exeunt*〉

ACT FOUR

SCENE I

In Pinchwife's house in the morning

Lucy, Alithea dressed in new clothes.

LUCY Well – Madam, now have I dressed you, and set you out with so many ornaments, and spent upon you ounces of essence, and pulvilio;* and all this for no other purpose, but as people adorn, and perfume a corpse, for a stinking secondhand grave, such or as bad I think Master Sparkish's bed.

ALITHEA Hold your peace.

LUCY Nay, Madam, I will ask you the reason, why you would banish poor Master Harcourt for ever from your sight? How could you be so hardhearted?

ALITHEA 'Twas because I was not hardhearted.

LUCY No, no; 'twas stark love and kindness, I warrant.

ALITHEA It was so; I would see him no more, because I love him.

LUCY Hey day, a very pretty reason.

ALITHEA You do not understand me.

LUCY I wish you may yourself.

ALITHEA I was engaged to marry, you see, another man, whom my justice will not suffer me to deceive, or injure.

LUCY Can there be a greater cheat, or wrong done to a man, than to give him your person, without your heart, I should make a conscience of it.

ALITHEA I'll retrieve it for him after I am married a while.

LUCY The woman that marries to love better, will be as much mistaken, as the wencher that marries to live better. No; Madam, marrying to increase love, is like gaming to become rich; alas you only lose, what little stock you had before.

ALITHEA I find by your rhetoric you have been bribed to betray me.

LUCY Only by his merit, that has bribed your heart you see against your word, and rigid honour; but what a divel is this honour? 'Tis sure a disease in the head, like the megrim,† or

* pulvilio: a scented powder.   † megrim: migraine.

falling-sickness,★ that always hurries people away to do themselves mischief; men lose their lives by it: women what's dearer to 'em, their love, the life of life.

ALITHEA Come, pray talk you no more of honour, nor Master Harcourt; I wish the other would come, to secure my fidelity to him, and his right in me.

LUCY Will you marry him then?

ALITHEA Certainly, I have given him already my word, and will my hand too, to make it good when he comes.

LUCY Well, I wish I may never stick pin more, if he be not an errant natural, to t'other fine gentleman.

ALITHEA I own he wants the wit of Harcourt, which I will dispense withal, for another want he has, which is want of jealousy, which men of wit seldom want.

LUCY Lord, Madam, what should you do with a fool to your husband, you intend to be honest don't you? Then that husbandly virtue, credulity, is thrown away upon you.

ALITHEA He only that could suspect my virtue, should have cause to do it; 'tis Sparkish's confidence in my truth, that obliges me to be so faithful to him.

LUCY You are not sure his opinion may last.

ALITHEA I am satisfied, 'tis impossible for him to be jealous, after the proofs I have had of him: jealousy in a husband, heaven defend me from it, it begets a thousand plagues to a poor woman, the loss of her honour, her quiet, and her –

LUCY And her pleasure.

ALITHEA What d'ye mean, impertinent?

LUCY Liberty is a great pleasure, Madam.

ALITHEA I say loss of her honour, her quiet, nay, her life sometimes; and what's as bad almost, the loss of this Town, that is, she is sent into the country, which is the last ill usage of a husband to a wife, I think.

LUCY [*aside*] O does the wind lie there? ⟨*to her*⟩ Then of necessity, Madam, you think a man must carry his wife into the country, if he be wise; the country is as terrible I find to our young English ladies, as a monastery to those abroad: and on my virginity, I think they would rather marry a London gaoler, than a high

★ falling sickness: epilepsy.

sheriff of a county, since neither can stir from his employment: formerly women of wit married fools, for a great estate, a fine seat, or the like; but now 'tis for a pretty seat only in Lincoln's Inn Fields, St James's Fields, or the Pall Mall.★

Enter to them Sparkish, and Harcourt dressed like a parson.

SPARKISH Madam, your humble servant, a happy day to you, and to us all.

HARCOURT Amen. –

ALITHEA Who have we here?

SPARKISH My chaplain faith – O Madam, poor Harcourt remembers his humble service to you; and in obedience to your last commands, refrains coming into your sight.

ALITHEA Is not that he?

SPARKISH No, fie no; but to show that he ne'er intended to hinder our match has sent his brother here to join our hands: when I get me a wife, I must get her a chaplain, according to the custom; this is his brother, and my chaplain.

ALITHEA His brother?

LUCY [*aside*] And your chaplain, to preach in your pulpit then –

ALITHEA His brother!

SPARKISH Nay, I knew you would not believe it; I told you, Sir, she would take you for your brother Frank.

ALITHEA Believe it!

LUCY [*aside*] His brother! Hah, ha, he, he has a trick left still it seems –

SPARKISH Come my dearest, pray let us go to church before the canonical hour† is past.

ALITHEA For shame you are abused still.

SPARKISH By the world 'tis strange now you are so incredulous.

ALITHEA 'Tis strange you are so credulous.

SPARKISH Dearest of my life, hear me, I tell you this is Ned Harcourt of Cambridge, by the world, you see he has a sneaking

★ Lincoln's Inn Fields, St James's Fields . . . Pall Mall: all fashionable walks.

† the canonical hour: when marriages could legally be performed, between 8 a.m and noon.

college look; 'tis true he's something like his brother Frank, and
they differ from each other no more than in their age, for they were
twins.

LUCY Hah, ha, he.

ALITHEA Your servant, Sir, I cannot be so deceived, though you
are; but come let's hear, how do you know what you affirm so
confidently?

SPARKISH Why, I'll tell you all; Frank Harcourt coming to me this
morning, to wish me joy and present his service to you: I asked
him, if he could help me to a parson; whereupon he told me, he
had a brother in Town who was in orders, and he went straight
away, and sent him, you see there, to me.

ALITHEA Yes, Frank goes, and puts on a black coat, then tells you,
he is Ned, that's all you have for't.

SPARKISH Pshaw, pshaw, I tell you by the same token, the midwife put her garter about Frank's neck, to know 'em asunder, they
were so like.

ALITHEA Frank tells you this too.

SPARKISH Aye, and Ned there too; nay, they are both in a story.

ALITHEA So, so, very foolish.

SPARKISH Lord, if you won't believe one, you had best try him by
your chambermaid there; for chambermaids must needs know
chaplains from other men, they are so used to 'em.

LUCY Let's see; nay, I'll be sworn he has the canonical smirk, and
the filthy, clammy palm of a chaplain.

ALITHEA Well, most reverend doctor, pray let us make an end of
this fooling.

HARCOURT With all my soul, divine, heavenly creature, when
you please.

ALITHEA He speaks like a chaplain indeed.

SPARKISH Why, was there not, 'soul', 'divine', 'heavenly', in what
he said.

ALITHEA Once more, most impertinent black coat, cease your
persecution, and let us have a conclusion of this ridiculous love.

HARCOURT [aside] I had forgot, I must suit my style to my coat,
or I wear it in vain.

ALITHEA I have no more patience left, let us make once an end of
this troublesome love, I say.

HARCOURT So be it, seraphic lady, when your honour shall think it meet, and convenient so to do.

SPARKISH Gad I'm sure none but a chaplain could speak so, I think.

ALITHEA Let me tell you Sir, this dull trick will not serve your turn, though you delay our marriage, you shall not hinder it.

HARCOURT Far be it from me, munificent patroness, to delay your marriage, I desire nothing more than to marry you presently, which I might do, if you yourself would; for my noble, good-natured and thrice generous patron here would not hinder it.

SPARKISH No, poor man, not I faith.

HARCOURT And now, Madam, let me tell you plainly, nobody else shall marry you by heavens, I'll die first, for I'm sure I should die after it.

LUCY How his love has made him forget his function, as I have seen it in real parsons.

ALITHEA That was spoken like a chaplain too, now you understand him, I hope.

SPARKISH Poor man, he takes it heinously to be ıefused; I can't blame him, 'tis putting an indignity upon him not to be suffered, but you'll pardon me Madam, it shan't be, he shall marry us, come away, pray Madam.

LUCY Hah, ha, he, more ado! 'Tis late.

ALITHEA Invincible stupidity, I tell you he would marry me, as your rival not as your chaplain.

SPARKISH [*pulling her away*] Come, come Madam.

LUCY I pray Madam, do not refuse this reverend divine, the honour and satisfaction of marrying you; for I dare say, he has set his heart upon't, good doctor.

ALITHEA What can you hope, or design by this?

HARCOURT ⟨*aside*⟩ I could answer her, a reprieve for a day only, often revokes a hasty doom; at worst, if she will not take mercy on me, and let me marry her, I have at least the lover's second pleasure, hindering my rival's enjoyment, though but for a time.

SPARKISH Come Madam, 'tis e'en twelve o'clock, and my mother charged me never to be married out of the canonical hours; come, come, Lord here's such a deal of modesty, I warrant the first day.

LUCY Yes, an't please your worship, married women show all their modesty the first day, because married men show all their love the first day.   [*Exeunt Sparkish, Alithea, Harcourt, and Lucy*]

SCENE ⟨II⟩

Changes to a bed-chamber, where appear Pinchwife, Mrs Pinchwife

PINCHWIFE Come tell me, I say.

MRS PINCHWIFE Lord, han't I told it an hundred times over.

PINCHWIFE [*aside*] I would try, if in the repetition of the ungrateful tale, I could find her altering it in the least circumstance, for if her story be false, she is so too. ⟨*to her*⟩ Come how was't baggage?

MRS PINCHWIFE Lord, what pleasure you take to hear it sure!

PINCHWIFE No, you take more in telling it I find, but speak how was't?

MRS PINCHWIFE He carried me up into the house, next to the Exchange.

PINCHWIFE So, and you two were only in the room.

MRS PINCHWIFE Yes, for he sent away a youth that was there, for some dried fruit, and china oranges.

PINCHWIFE Did he so? Damn him for it – and for –

MRS PINCHWIFE But presently came up the gentlewoman of the house.

PINCHWIFE O 'twas well she did, but what did he do whilst the fruit came?

MRS PINCHWIFE He kissed me an hundred times, and told me he fancied he kissed my fine sister, meaning me you know, whom he said he loved with all his soul, and bid me be sure to tell her so, and to desire her to be at her window, by eleven of the clock this morning, and he would walk under it at that time.

PINCHWIFE [*aside*] And he was as good as his word, very punctual, a pox reward him for't.

MRS PINCHWIFE Well, and he said if you were not within, he would come up to her, meaning me you know, bud, still.

PINCHWIFE [*aside*] So – he knew her certainly, but for this confession, I am obliged to her simplicity. ⟨*to her*⟩ But what you stood very still, when he kissed you?

MRS PINCHWIFE Yes I warrant you, would you have had me discovered myself?

PINCHWIFE But you told me, he did some beastliness to you, as you called it, what was't?

MRS PINCHWIFE Why, he put –

PINCHWIFE What?

MRS PINCHWIFE Why he put the tip of his tongue between my lips, and so mousled me – and I said, I'd bite it.

PINCHWIFE An eternal canker seize it, for a dog.

MRS PINCHWIFE Nay, you need not be so angry with him neither, for to say truth, he has the sweetest breath I ever knew.

PINCHWIFE The devil – you were satisfied with it then, and would do it again.

MRS PINCHWIFE Not unless he should force me.

PINCHWIFE Force you, changeling! I tell you no woman can be forced.

MRS PINCHWIFE Yes, but she may sure, by such a one as he, for he's a proper, goodly strong man, 'tis hard, let me tell you, to resist him.

PINCHWIFE ⟨*aside*⟩ So, 'tis plain she loves him, yet she has not love enough to make her conceal it from me, but the sight of him will increase her aversion for me, and love for him; and that love instruct her how to deceive me, and satisfy him, all idiot as she is: love, 'twas he gave women first their craft, their art of deluding; out of nature's hands, they came plain, open, silly and fit for slaves, as she and heaven intended 'em; but damned love – well – I must strangle that little monster, whilst I can deal with him. ⟨*to her*⟩ Go fetch pen, ink and paper out of the next room.

MRS PINCHWIFE Yes bud.   [*Exit Mrs Pinchwife*]

PINCHWIFE [*aside*] Why should women have more invention in love than men? It can only be, because they have more desires, more soliciting passions, more lust, and more of the devil.

Mrs Pinchwife returns.

Come, minx, sit down and write.

MRS PINCHWIFE Aye, dear bud, but I can't do't very well.

PINCHWIFE I wish you could not at all.

MRS PINCHWIFE But what should I write for?

PINCHWIFE I'll have you write a letter to your lover.

MRS PINCHWIFE O Lord, to the fine gentleman a letter!

PINCHWIFE Yes, to the fine gentleman.

MRS PINCHWIFE Lord, you do but jeer; sure you jest.

PINCHWIFE I am not so merry, come write as I bid you.

MRS PINCHWIFE What, do you think I am a fool?

PINCHWIFE ⟨*aside*⟩ She's afraid I would not dictate any love to him, therefore she's unwilling; ⟨*to her*⟩ but you had best begin.

MRS PINCHWIFE Indeed, and indeed, but I won't, so I won't.

PINCHWIFE Why?

MRS PINCHWIFE Because he's in Town, you may send for him if you will.

PINCHWIFE Very well, you would have him brought to you; is it come to this? I say take the pen and write, or you'll provoke me.

MRS PINCHWIFE Lord, what d'ye make a fool of me for? Don't I know that letters are never writ, but from the country to London, and from London into the country; now he's in Town, and I am in Town too; therefore I can't write to him you know.

PINCHWIFE [*aside*] So I am glad it is no worse, she is innocent enough yet. ⟨*to her*⟩ Yes you may when your husband bids you write letters to people that are in Town.

MRS PINCHWIFE O may I so! Then I'm satisfied.

PINCHWIFE Come begin – [*dictates*] 'Sir', –

MRS PINCHWIFE Shan't I say, 'Dear Sir'? You know one says always something more than bare 'Sir'.

PINCHWIFE Write as I bid you, or I will write 'whore' with this penknife in your face.

MRS PINCHWIFE Nay good bud [*she writes*] – 'Sir' –

PINCHWIFE 'Though I suffered last night your nauseous, loathed kisses and embraces' – Write.

MRS PINCHWIFE Nay, why should I say so, you know I told you, he had a sweet breath.

PINCHWIFE Write.

MRS PINCHWIFE Let me but put out, 'loathed'.

PINCHWIFE Write I say.

MRS PINCHWIFE Well then. [*writes*]

PINCHWIFE Let's see what have you writ? [*takes the paper, and reads*] 'Though I suffered last night your kisses and embraces' – Thou impudent creature, where is 'nauseous' and 'loathed'?

MRS PINCHWIFE I can't abide to write such filthy words.

PINCHWIFE Once more write as I'd have you, and question it not, or I will spoil thy writing with this, I will stab out those eyes that cause my mischief. [*holds up the penknife*]

MRS PINCHWIFE O Lord, I will.

PINCHWIFE So – so – Let's see now? [*reads*] 'Though I suffered last night your nauseous, loathed kisses, and embraces'; go on – 'Yet I would not have you presume that you shall ever repeat them' – So – [*she writes*]

MRS PINCHWIFE I have writ it.

PINCHWIFE On then – 'I then concealed myself from your knowledge, to avoid your insolencies' – [*she writes*]

MRS PINCHWIFE So –

PINCHWIFE 'The same reason now I am out of your hands' – [*she writes*]

MRS PINCHWIFE So –

PINCHWIFE 'Makes me own to you my unfortunate, though innocent frolic, of being in man's clothes'. [*she writes*]

MRS PINCHWIFE So –

PINCHWIFE 'That you may for ever more cease to pursue her, who hates and detests you' – [*she writes on*]

MRS PINCHWIFE So–h – [*sighs*]

PINCHWIFE What do you sigh? – 'detests you – as much as she loves her husband and her honour' –

MRS PINCHWIFE I vow husband he'll ne'er believe, I should write such a letter.

PINCHWIFE What he'd expect a kinder from you? Come now your name only.

MRS PINCHWIFE What, shan't I say your most faithful, humble servant till death?

PINCHWIFE No, tormenting fiend; [*aside*] her style I find would be very soft. ⟨*to her*⟩ Come wrap it up now, whilst I go fetch wax and a candle; and write on the backside, 'For Mr Horner'.

[*Exit Pinchwife*]

MRS PINCHWIFE 'For Mr Horner' – So, I am glad he has told me his name; dear Mr Horner, but why should I send thee such a letter, that will vex thee, and make thee angry with me; – well I will not send it – Aye, but then my husband will kill me – for I see plainly, he won't let me love Mr Horner – but what care I for my husband – I won't so I won't send poor Mr Horner such a letter – but then my husband – But oh – what if I writ at bottom, my husband made me write it – Aye but then my husband would see't – Can one have no shift, ah, a London woman would have had a hundred presently; stay – what if I should write a letter, and wrap it up like this, and write upon't too; aye but then my husband would see't – I don't know what to do – But yet y'vads* I'll try, so I will – for I will not send this letter to poor Mr Horner, come what will on't. [*she writes, and repeats what she hath writ*] 'Dear, sweet Mr Horner' – *So* – 'my husband would have me send you a base, rude, unmannerly letter – but I won't' – *so* – 'and would have me forbid you loving me – but I won't' – *so* – 'and would have me say to you, I hate you poor Mr Horner – but I won't tell a lie for him' – *there* – 'for I'm sure if you and I were in the country at cards together', – *so* – 'I could not help treading on your toe under the table' – *so* – 'or rubbing knees with you, and staring in your face, till you saw me' – *very well* – 'and then looking down, and blushing for an hour together' – *so* – 'but I must make haste before my husband comes; and now he has taught me to write letters: you shall have longer ones from me, who am

 dear, dear, poor dear Mr Horner, your most
  humble friend, and servant to command
   till death, Margery Pinchwife.'

Stay I must give him a hint at bottom – *so* – now wrap it up just like t'other – *so* – now write 'For Mr Horner', – but O now what shall I do with it? For here comes my husband.

Enter Pinchwife.

PINCHWIFE [*aside*] I have been detained by a sparkish coxcomb, who pretended a visit to me; but I fear 'twas to my wife. ⟨*to her*⟩ What, have you done?

MRS PINCHWIFE Aye, aye, bud, just now.

    * y'vads: in faith.

PINCHWIFE Let's see't, what d'ye tremble for; what, you would not have it go?

MRS PINCHWIFE Here –

He opens, and reads the first letter.

[*aside*] No I must not give him that, so I had been served if I had given him this.

PINCHWIFE Come, where's the wax and seal?

MRS PINCHWIFE [*aside*] Lord, what shall I do now? Nay then I have it – Pray let me see't, Lord you think me so errand a fool, I cannot seal a letter, I will do't, so I will.

[*Snatches the letter from him, changes it for the other, seals it, and delivers it to him*]

PINCHWIFE Nay, I believe you will learn that, and other things too, which I would not have you.

MRS PINCHWIFE So, han't I done it curiously? [*aside*] I think I have, there's my letter going to Mr Horner; since he'll needs have me send letters to folks.

PINCHWIFE 'Tis very well, but I warrant, you would not have it go now?

MRS PINCHWIFE Yes indeed, but I would, bud, now.

PINCHWIFE Well you are a good girl then, come let me lock you up in your chamber, till I come back; and be sure you come not within three strides of the window, when I am gone; for I have a spy in the street. [*Exit Mrs Pinchwife*]

[*Pinchwife locks the door*]

At least, 'tis fit she think so, if we do not cheat women, they'll cheat us; and fraud may be justly used with secret enemies, of which a wife is the most dangerous; and he that has a handsome one to keep, and a frontier town, must provide against treachery, rather than open force – Now I have secured all within, [*holds up the letter*] I'll deal with the foe without with false intelligence.

[*Exit Pinchwife*]

SCENE ⟨III⟩

Changes to Horner's lodging

Quack and Horner.

QUACK Well Sir, how fadges* the new design; have you not the luck of all your brother projectors, to deceive only yourself at last.

HORNER No, good domine doctor, I deceive you it seems, and others too; for the grave matrons, and old rigid husbands think me as unfit for love, as they are; but their wives, sisters and daughters, know some of 'em better things already.

QUACK Already!

HORNER Already, I say; last night I was drunk with half a dozen of your civil persons, as you call 'em, and people of honour, and so was made free of their society, and dressing rooms for ever hereafter; and am already come to the privileges of sleeping upon their pallets, warming smocks, tying shoes and garters, and the like doctor, already, already doctor.

QUACK You have made use of your time, Sir.

HORNER I tell thee, I am now no more interruption to 'em, when they sing, or talk bawdy, than a little squab French page, who speaks no English.

QUACK But do civil persons, and women of honour drink, and sing bawdy songs?

HORNER O amongst friends, amongst friends; for your bigots in honour, are just like those in religion; they fear the eye of the world, more than the eye of heaven, and I think there is no virtue, but railing at vice; and no sin, but giving scandal: they rail at a poor, little, kept player, and keep themselves some young, modest pulpit comedian to be privy to their sins in their closets, not to tell 'em of them in their chapels.

QUACK Nay, the truth on't is, priests amongst the women now, have quite got the better of us lay confessors, physicians.

HORNER And they are rather their patients, but –

Enter my Lady Fidget, looking about her.

Now we talk of women of honour, here comes one, step behind

* fadges: succeeds.

the screen there, and but observe; if I have not particular privileges, with the women of reputation already, doctor, already.

LADY FIDGET Well Horner, am not I a woman of honour? You see I'm as good as my word.

HORNER And you shall see Madam, I'll not be behindhand with you in honour; and I'll be as good as my word too, if you please but to withdraw into the next room.

LADY FIDGET But first, my dear Sir, you must promise to have a care of my dear honour.

HORNER If you talk a word more of your honour, you'll make me incapable to wrong it; to talk of honour in the mysteries of love, is like talking of heaven, or the deity in an operation of witchcraft, just when you are employing the devil, it makes the charm impotent.

LADY FIDGET Nay, fie, let us not be smutty; but you talk of mysteries, and bewitching to me, I don't understand you.

HORNER I tell you Madam, the word money in a mistress's mouth, at such a nick of time, is not a more disheartening sound to a younger brother, than that of honour to an eager lover like myself.

LADY FIDGET But you can't blame a lady of my reputation to be chary.

HORNER Chary – I have been chary of it already, by the report I have caused of myself.

LADY FIDGET Aye, but if you should ever let other women know that dear secret, it would come out; nay, you must have a great care of your conduct; for my acquaintance are so censorious, (O 'tis a wicked censorious world, Mr Horner) I say, are so censorious, and detracting, that perhaps they'll talk to the prejudice of my honour, though you should not let them know the dear secret.

HORNER Nay Madam, rather than they shall prejudice your honour, I'll prejudice theirs; and to serve you, I'll lie with 'em all, make the secret their own, and then they'll keep it: I am a Machiavel in love Madam.

LADY FIDGET Oh, no Sir, not that way.

HORNER Nay, the devil take me, if censorious women are to be silenced any other way.

LADY FIDGET A secret is better kept I hope, by a single person, than a multitude; therefore pray do not trust anybody else with it, dear, dear Mr Horner. [*embracing him*]

Enter Sir Jasper Fidget.

SIR JASPER How now!

LADY FIDGET [*aside*] O my husband – prevented – and what's almost as bad, found with my arms about another man – that will appear too much – what shall I say? ⟨*to him*⟩ Sir Jasper come hither, I am trying if Mr Horner were ticklish, and he's as ticklish as can be, I love to torment the confounded toad; let you and I tickle him.

SIR JASPER No, your ladyship will tickle him better without me, I suppose, but is this your buying china, I thought you had been at the china house?

HORNER [*aside*] China house, that's my cue, I must take it. ⟨*to Sir Jasper*⟩ A pox, can't you keep your impertinent wives at home? Some men are troubled with the husbands, but I with the wives; but I'd have you to know, since I cannot be your journeyman by night, I will not be your drudge by day, to squire your wife about, and be your man of straw, or scarecrow only to pies and jays; that would be nibbling at your forbidden fruit; I shall be shortly the hackney gentleman-usher of the Town.

SIR JASPER [*aside*] Heh, heh, he, poor fellow he's in the right on't faith, to squire women about for other folks, is as ungrateful an employment, as to tell money for other folks; ⟨*to him*⟩ heh, he, he, ben't angry Horner –

LADY FIDGET No, 'tis I have more reason to be angry, who am left by you, to go abroad indecently alone; or, what is more indecent, to pin myself upon such ill-bred people of your acquaintance, as this is.

SIR JASPER Nay, prithee what has he done?

LADY FIDGET Nay, he has done nothing.

SIR JASPER But what d'ye take ill, if he has done nothing?

LADY FIDGET Hah, hah, hah, faith, I can't but laugh however; why d'ye think the unmannerly toad would come down to me to the coach, I was fain to come up to fetch him, or go without him, which I was resolved not to do; for he knows china very well, and has himself very good, but will not let me see it, lest I should beg some; but I will find it out, and have what I came for yet.

HORNER [*apart to Lady Fidget*] Lock the door Madam –

[*Exit Lady Fidget, and locks the door, followed by Horner to the door*]
So, she has got into my chamber, and locked me out; O the impertinency of womankind! Well Sir Jasper, plain-dealing is a jewel; if ever you suffer your wife to trouble me again here, she shall carry you home a pair of horns, by my Lord Mayor she shall; though I cannot furnish you myself, you are sure, yet I'll find a way.

SIR JASPER [*aside*] Hah, ha, he, at my first coming in, and finding her arms about him, tickling him it seems, I was half jealous, but now I see my folly. ⟨*to him*⟩ Heh, he, he, poor Horner.

HORNER Nay, though you laugh now, 'twill be my turn ere long: O women, more impertinent, more cunning, and more mischievous than their monkeys, and to me almost as ugly – now is she throwing my things about, and rifling all I have, but I'll get into her the back way, and so rifle her for it –

SIR JASPER Hah, ha, ha, poor angry Horner.

HORNER Stay here a little, I'll ferret her out to you presently, I warrant. [*Exit Horner at t'other door*]

SIR JASPER [*calls through the door to his wife, she answers from within*]
Wife, my Lady Fidget, wife, he is coming into you the back way.

LADY FIDGET Let him come, and welcome, which way he will.

SIR JASPER He'll catch you, and use you roughly, and be too strong for you.

LADY FIDGET Don't you trouble yourself, let him if he can.

QUACK [*behind*] This indeed, I could not have believed from him, nor any but my own eyes.

Enter Mrs Squeamish.

SQUEAMISH Where's this woman-hater, this toad, this ugly, greasy, dirty sloven?

SIR JASPER So the women all will have him ugly, methinks he is a comely person; but his wants make his form contemptible to 'em; and 'tis e'en as my wife said yesterday, talking of him, that a proper handsome eunuch, was as ridiculous a thing, as a gigantic coward.

SQUEAMISH Sir Jasper, your servant, where is the odious beast?

SIR JASPER He's within in his chamber, with my wife; she's playing the wag with him.

SQUEAMISH Is she so, and he's a clownish beast, he'll give her no
quarter, he'll play the wag with her again, let me tell you; come,
let's go help her – What, the door's locked?

SIR JASPER Aye, my wife locked it –

SQUEAMISH Did she so, let us break it open then?

SIR JASPER No, no, he'll do her no hurt.

SQUEAMISH No – [*aside*] But is there no other way to get into
'em, whither goes this? I will disturb 'em.

> [*Exit ⟨Mrs⟩ Squeamish at another door*]

Enter Old Lady Squeamish.

OLD LADY SQUEAMISH Where is this harlotry, this impudent
baggage, this rambling tomrig?★ O Sir Jasper, I'm glad to see you
here, did you not see my vile grandchild come in hither just now?

SIR JASPER Yes.

OLD LADY SQUEAMISH Aye, but where is she then? Where is
she? Lord Sir Jasper I have e'en rattled myself to pieces in pursuit
of her, but can you tell what she makes here, they say below, no
woman lodges here.

SIR JASPER No.

OLD LADY SQUEAMISH No – What does she here then? Say if it
be not a woman's lodging, what makes she here? But are you sure
no woman lodges here?

SIR JASPER No, nor no man neither, this is Mr Horner's lodging.

OLD LADY SQUEAMISH Is it so are you sure?

SIR JASPER Yes, yes.

OLD LADY SQUEAMISH So then there's no hurt in't I hope, but
where is he?

SIR JASPER He's in the next room with my wife.

OLD LADY SQUEAMISH Nay if you trust him with your wife, I
may with my Biddy, they say he's a merry harmless man now,
e'en as harmless a man as ever came out of Italy† with a good voice
and as pretty harmless company for a lady, as a snake without his
teeth.

SIR JASPER Aye, aye, poor man.

★ tomrig: tomboy.   † man . . . Italy: a castrated Italian singer.

Enter Mrs Squeamish.

SQUEAMISH I can't find 'em – O are you here, grandmother, I followed you must know my Lady Fidget hither, 'tis the prettiest lodging, and I have been staring on the prettiest pictures.

Enter Lady Fidget with a piece of china in her hand, and Horner following.

LADY FIDGET And I have been toiling and moiling, for the prettiest piece of china, my dear.

HORNER Nay, she has been too hard for me, do what I could.

SQUEAMISH O Lord I'll have some china too, good Mr Horner, don't think to give other people china, and me none, come in with me too.

HORNER Upon my honour I have none left now.

SQUEAMISH Nay, nay I have known you deny your china before now, but you shan't put me off so, come –

HORNER This lady had the last there.

LADY FIDGET Yes indeed Madam, to my certain knowledge he has no more left.

SQUEAMISH O but it may be he may have some you could not find.

LADY FIDGET What d'ye think if he had had any left, I would not have had it too, for we women of quality never think we have china enough.

HORNER Do not take it ill, I cannot make china for you all, but I will have a roll-waggon* for you too, another time.

SQUEAMISH [*to Horner aside*] Thank you dear toad.

LADY FIDGET What do you mean by that promise?

HORNER [*apart to Lady Fidget*] Alas she has an innocent, literal understanding.

OLD LADY SQUEAMISH Poor Mr Horner, he has enough to do to please you all, I see.

HORNER Aye Madam, you see how they use me.

OLD LADY SQUEAMISH Poor gentleman I pity you.

HORNER I thank you Madam, I could never find pity, but from

* roll-waggon: a low wheeled vehicle used for transporting goods.

such reverend ladies as you are, the young ones will never spare a man.

SQUEAMISH Come come, beast, and go dine with us, for we shall want a man at ombre after dinner.

HORNER That's all their use of me Madam you see.

SQUEAMISH [*pulls him by the cravat*] Come sloven, I'll lead you to be sure of you.

OLD LADY SQUEAMISH Alas poor man how she tugs him, kiss, kiss her, that's the way to make such nice women quiet.

HORNER No Madam, that remedy is worse than the torment, they know I dare suffer anything rather than do it.

OLD LADY SQUEAMISH Prithee kiss her, and I'll give you her picture in little, that you admired so last night, prithee do.

HORNER Well nothing but that could bribe me, I love a woman only in effigy, and good painting as much as I hate them – I'll do't, for I could adore the devil well painted. [*Kisses Mrs Squeamish*]

SQUEAMISH Foh, you filthy toad, nay now I've done jesting.

OLD LADY SQUEAMISH Ha, ha, ha, I told you so.

SQUEAMISH Foh a kiss of his –

SIR JASPER Has no more hurt in't, than one of my spaniel's.

SQUEAMISH Nor no more good neither.

QUACK [*behind*] I will now believe anything he tells me.

Enter Pinchwife.

LADY FIDGET O Lord here's a man, Sir Jasper, my mask, my mask, I would not be seen here for the world.

SIR JASPER What not when I am with you.

LADY FIDGET No, no my honour – let's be gone.

SQUEAMISH O grandmother, let us be gone, make haste, make haste, I know not how he may censure us.

LADY FIDGET Be found in the lodging of anything like a man, away.   [*Exeunt Sir Jasper, Lady Fidget, Old Lady Squeamish, Mrs Squeamish*]

QUACK [*behind*] What's here another cuckold – he looks like one, and none else sure have any business with him.

HORNER Well what brings my dear friend hither?

PINCHWIFE Your impertinency.

HORNER My impertinency – why you gentlemen that have got

handsome wives, think you have a privilege of saying anything to your friends, and are as brutish, as if you were our creditors.

PINCHWIFE No Sir, I'll ne'er trust you anyway.

HORNER But why not, dear Jack, why diffide in me,* thou knowest so well.

PINCHWIFE Because I do know you so well.

HORNER Han't I been always thy friend honest Jack, always ready to serve thee, in love, or battle, before thou wert married, and am so still.

PINCHWIFE I believe so you would be my second now indeed.

HORNER Well then dear Jack, why so unkind, so grum, so strange to me, come prithee kiss me dear rogue, gad I was always I say, and am still as much thy servant as –

PINCHWIFE As I am yours Sir. What you would send a kiss to my wife, is that it?

HORNER So there 'tis – a man can't show his friendship to a married man, but presently he talks of his wife to you, prithee let thy wife alone, and let thee and I be all one, as we were wont. What, thou art as shy of my kindness, as a Lombard Street† alderman of a courtier's civility at Locket's.‡

PINCHWIFE But you are over-kind to me, as kind, as if I were your cuckold already, yet I must confess you ought to be kind and civil to me, since I am so kind, so civil to you, as to bring you this, look you there Sir. [*delivers him a letter*]

HORNER What is't?

PINCHWIFE Only a love letter Sir.

HORNER From whom – how, this is from your wife – [*reads*] hum – and hum –

PINCHWIFE Even from my wife Sir, am I not wondrous kind and civil to you, now too? [*aside*] But you'll not think her so.

HORNER [*aside*] Ha, is this a trick of his or hers?

PINCHWIFE The gentleman's surprised I find; what, you expected a kinder letter?

HORNER No faith not I, how could I.

PINCHWIFE Yes yes, I'm sure you did, a man so well made as you

---

* diffide in me: distrust me.

† Lombard Street: street of bankers and goldsmiths, hence a wealthy citizen.

‡ Locket's: a fashionable restaurant.

are must needs be disappointed, if the women declare not their passion at first sight or opportunity.

HORNER But what should this mean? Stay the postscript. [*reads aside*] 'Be sure you love me whatsoever my husband says to the contrary, and let him not see this, lest he should come home, and pinch me, or kill my squirrel'.

[*aside*] It seems he knows not what the letter contains.

PINCHWIFE Come ne'er wonder at it so much.

HORNER Faith I can't help it.

PINCHWIFE Now I think I have deserved your infinite friendship, and kindness, and have showed myself sufficiently an obliging kind friend and husband, am I not so, to bring a letter from my wife to her gallant?

HORNER Aye, the devil take me, art thou, the most obliging, kind friend and husband in the world, ha, ha.

PINCHWIFE Well you may be merry Sir, but in short I must tell you Sir, my honour will suffer no jesting.

HORNER What dost thou mean?

PINCHWIFE Does the letter want a comment? Then know Sir, though I have been so civil a husband, as to bring you a letter from my wife, to let you kiss and court her to my face, I will not be a cuckold Sir, I will not.

HORNER Thou art mad with jealousy, I never saw thy wife in my life, but at the play yesterday, and I know not if it were she or no. I court her, kiss her!

PINCHWIFE I will not be a cuckold I say, there will be danger in making me a cuckold.

HORNER Why, wert thou not well cured of thy last clap?

PINCHWIFE I wear a sword.

HORNER It should be taken from thee, lest thou should'st do thyself a mischief with it, thou art mad, man.

PINCHWIFE As mad as I am, and as merry as you are, I must have more reason from you ere we part, I say again though you kissed, and courted last night my wife in man's clothes, as she confesses in her letter.

HORNER [*aside*] Ha –

PINCHWIFE Both she and I say you must not design it again, for you have mistaken your woman, as you have done your man.

HORNER [*aside*] O – I understand something now – ⟨*to him*⟩ Was that thy wife? Why would'st thou not tell me 'twas she? Faith my freedom with her was your fault, not mine.

PINCHWIFE [*aside*] Faith so 'twas –

HORNER Fie, I'd never do't to a woman before her husband's face, sure.

PINCHWIFE But I had rather you should do't to my wife before my face, than behind my back, and that you shall never do.

HORNER No – you will hinder me.

PINCHWIFE If I would not hinder you, you see by her letter, she would.

HORNER Well, I must e'en acquiesce then, and be contented with what she writes.

PINCHWIFE I'll assure you 'twas voluntarily writ, I had no hand in't you may believe me.

HORNER I do believe thee, faith.

PINCHWIFE And believe her too, for she's an innocent creature, has no dissembling in her, and so fare you well Sir.

HORNER Pray however present my humble service to her, and tell her I will obey her letter to a tittle, and fulfil her desires be what they will, or with what difficulty soever I do't, and you shall be no more jealous of me, I warrant her, and you –

PINCHWIFE Well then fare you well, and play with any man's honour but mine, kiss any man's wife but mine, and welcome –

[*Exit Pinchwife*]

HORNER Ha, ha, ha, doctor.

QUACK It seems he has not heard the report of you, or does not believe it.

HORNER Ha, ha, now doctor what think you?

QUACK Pray let's see the letter – hum [*reads the letter*] 'for – dear – love you' –

HORNER I wonder how she could contrive it! What say'st thou to't, 'tis an original.

QUACK So are your cuckolds too originals: for they are like no other common cuckolds, and I will henceforth believe it not impossible for you to cuckold the Grand Signior amidst his guards of eunuchs, that I say –

HORNER And I say for the letter, 'tis the first love letter that ever was without flames, darts, fates, destinies, lying and dissembling in't.

Enter Sparkish pulling in Pinchwife.

SPARKISH Come back, you are a pretty brother-in-law, neither go to church, nor to dinner with your sister bride.

PINCHWIFE My sister denies her marriage, and you see is gone away from you dissatisfied.

SPARKISH Pshaw, upon a foolish scruple, that our parson was not in lawful orders, and did not say all the Common Prayer, but 'tis her modesty only I believe, but let women be never so modest the first day, they'll be sure to come to themselves by night, and I shall have enough of her then; in the meantime, Harry Horner, you must dine with me, I keep my wedding at my aunt's in the Piazza.*

HORNER Thy wedding, what stale maid has lived to despair of a husband, or what young one of a gallant?

SPARKISH O your servant Sir – this gentleman's sister then – No stale maid.

HORNER I'm sorry for't.

PINCHWIFE [*aside*] How comes he so concerned for her –

SPARKISH You sorry for't, why do you know any ill by her?

HORNER No, I know none but by thee, 'tis for her sake, not yours, and another man's sake that might have hoped, I thought –

SPARKISH Another man, another man, what is his name?

HORNER Nay since 'tis past he shall be nameless. [*aside*] Poor Harcourt I am sorry thou hast missed her –

PINCHWIFE [*aside*] He seems to be much troubled at the match –

SPARKISH Prithee tell me – nay you shan't go brother.

PINCHWIFE I must of necessity, but I'll come to you to dinner.

[*Exit Pinchwife*]

SPARKISH But Harry, what have I a rival in my wife already? But with all my heart, for he may be of use to me hereafter, for though my hunger is now my sauce, and I can fall on heartily without, but the time will come, when a rival will be as good sauce for a married man to a wife, as an orange to veal.

* the Piazza: an arcade on the north and east sides of Covent Garden.

HORNER O thou damned rogue, thou hast set my teeth on edge
with thy orange.

SPARKISH Then let's to dinner, there I was with you again, come.

HORNER But who dines with thee?

SPARKISH My friends and relations, my brother Pinchwife you
see of your acquaintance.

HORNER And his wife.

SPARKISH No gad, he'll ne'er let her come amongst us good fellows,
your stingy country coxcomb keeps his wife from his friends, as
he does his little firkin of ale, for his own drinking, and a gentleman can't get a smack on't, but his servants, when his back is
turned broach it at their pleasures, and dust it away, ha, ha, ha,
gad I am witty, I think, considering I was married today, by the
world, but come –

HORNER No, I will not dine with you, unless you can fetch her
too.

SPARKISH Pshaw what pleasure can'st thou have with women
now, Harry?

HORNER My eyes are not gone, I love a good prospect yet, and
will not dine with you, unless she does too, go fetch her therefore,
but do not tell her husband, 'tis for my sake.

SPARKISH Well I'll go try what I can do, in the meantime come
away to my aunt's lodging, 'tis in the way to Pinchwife's.

HORNER The poor woman has called for aid, and stretched forth
her hand doctor, I cannot but help her over the pale out of the
briars.

[*Exeunt Sparkish, Horner, Quack*]

SCENE ⟨IV⟩

Changes to Pinchwife's house

Mrs Pinchwife alone leaning on her elbow. A table, pen, ink, and paper.

MRS PINCHWIFE Well 'tis e'en so, I have got the London disease,
they call love, I am sick of my husband, and for my gallant; I have
heard this distemper, called a fever, but methinks 'tis liker an
ague, for when I think of my husband, I tremble and am in a cold

sweat, and have inclinations to vomit, but when I think of my gallant, dear Mr Horner, my hot fit comes, and I am all in a fever, indeed, and as in other fevers, my own chamber is tedious to me, and I would fain be removed to his, and then methinks I should be well; ah poor Mr Horner, well I cannot, will not stay here, therefore I'll make an end of my letter to him, which shall be a finer letter than my last, because I have studied it like anything; o sick, sick! [*takes the pen and writes*]

Enter Mr Pinchwife who seeing her writing steals softly behind her, and looking over her shoulder, snatches the paper from her.

PINCHWIFE What writing more letters?

MRS PINCHWIFE O Lord bud, why d'ye fright me so? [*she offers to run out: he stops her, and reads*]

PINCHWIFE How's this! Nay you shall not stir Madam.

⟨*reads*⟩ 'Dear, dear, dear, Mr Horner' – very well – I have taught you to write letters to good purpose – but let's see't. 'First I am to beg your pardon for my boldness in writing to you, which I'd have you to know, I would not have done, had not you said first you loved me so extremely, which if you do, you will never suffer me to lie in the arms of another man, whom I loathe, nauseate, and detest' – Now you can write these filthy words but what follows – 'Therefore I hope you will speedily find some way to free me from this unfortunate match, which was never, I assure you, of my choice, but I'm afraid 'tis already too far gone; however if you love me, as I do you, you will try what you can do, but you must help me away before tomorrow, or else alas I shall be forever out of your reach, for I can defer no longer our' – 'our' – what is to follow 'our' – Speak, what? 'Our journey into the country' I suppose – O woman, damned woman, and love, damned love, their old tempter, for this is one of his miracles, in a moment, he can make those blind that could see, and those see that were blind, those dumb that could speak, and those prattle who were dumb before, nay what is more than all, make these dough-baked, senseless, indocile animals, women, too hard for us their politic lords and rulers in a moment; but make an end of your letter, and then I'll make an end of you thus, and all my plagues together. [*draws his sword*]

MRS PINCHWIFE O Lord, O Lord you are such a passionate man, bud.

Enter Sparkish.

SPARKISH How now what's here to do.

PINCHWIFE This fool here now!

SPARKISH What drawn upon your wife? You should never do that but at night in the dark when you can't hurt her, this is my sister-in-law is it not? [*pulls aside her handkerchief*] Aye faith e'en our country Margery, one may know her, come she and you must go dine with me, dinner's ready, come. But where's my wife, is she not come home yet, where is she?

PINCHWIFE Making you a cuckold, 'tis that they all do, as soon as they can.

SPARKISH What the wedding-day? No, a wife that designs to make a cully of her husband, will be sure to let him win the first stake of love, by the world. But come they stay dinner for us, come I'll lead down our Margery.

MRS PINCHWIFE No – Sir go we'll follow you.

SPARKISH I will not wag without you.

PINCHWIFE This coxcomb is a sensible torment to me amidst the greatest in the world.

SPARKISH Come, come Madam Margery.

PINCHWIFE No I'll lead her my way, [*leads her to t'other door, and locks her in and returns*] what would you treat your friends with mine, for want of your own wife? [*aside*] I am contented my rage should take breath –

SPARKISH I told Horner this.

PINCHWIFE Come now.

SPARKISH Lord, how shy you are of your wife, but let me tell you brother, we men of wit have amongst us a saying, that cuckolding like the smallpox comes with a fear, and you may keep your wife as much as you will out of danger of infection, but if her constitution incline her to't, she'll have it sooner or later by the world, say they.

PINCHWIFE [*aside*] What a thing is a cuckold, that every fool can make him ridiculous – ⟨*to him*⟩ Well Sir – But le me advise you, now you are come to be concerned, because you suspect the

danger, not to neglect the means to prevent it, especially when the greatest share of the malady will light upon your own head, for –
Hows' e'er the kind wife's belly comes to swell.
The husband breeds for her, and first is ill.

ACT FIVE

SCENE I

Pinchwife's house

Enter Pinchwife and Mrs Pinchwife, a table and candle.

PINCHWIFE Come take the pen and make an end of the letter, just as you intended, if you are false in a tittle, I shall soon perceive it, and punish you with this as you deserve, write what was to follow – let's see – [*lays his hand on his sword*] 'You must make haste and help me away before tomorrow, or else I shall be forever out of your reach, for I can defer no longer our' – What follows 'our'? –

MRS PINCHWIFE Must all out then bud? [*Mrs Pinchwife takes the pen and writes*] Look you there then.

PINCHWIFE Let's see – 'For I can defer no longer our – wedding – Your slighted Alithea'. What's the meaning of this, my sister's name to't, speak, unriddle?

MRS PINCHWIFE Yes indeed bud.

PINCHWIFE But why her name to't speak – speak I say?

MRS PINCHWIFE Aye but you'll tell her then again, if you would not tell her again.

PINCHWIFE I will not, I am stunned, my head turns round, speak.

MRS PINCHWIFE Won't you tell her indeed, and indeed.

PINCHWIFE No, speak I say.

MRS PINCHWIFE She'll be angry with me, but I had rather she should be angry with me than you bud; and to tell you the truth, 'twas she made me write the letter, and taught me what I should write.

PINCHWIFE [*aside*] Ha – I thought the style was somewhat better than her own. ⟨*to her*⟩ But how could she come to you to teach you, since I had locked you up alone.

MRS PINCHWIFE O through the keyhole bud.

PINCHWIFE But why should she make you write a letter for her to him, since she can write herself?

MRS PINCHWIFE Why she said because – for I was unwilling to do it.

PINCHWIFE Because what – because.

MRS PINCHWIFE Because lest Mr Horner should be cruel, and refuse her, or ⟨be⟩ vain afterwards, and show the letter, she might disown it, the hand not being hers.

PINCHWIFE [*aside*] How's this? Ha – then I think I shall come to myself again – This changeling could not invent this lie, but if she could, why should she? She might think I should soon discover it – stay – now I think on't too, Horner said he was sorry she had married Sparkish, and her disowning her marriage to me, makes me think she has evaded it, for Horner's sake, yet why should she take this course, but men in love are fools, women may well be so. – ⟨*to her*⟩ But hark you Madam, your sister went out in the morning, and I have not seen her within since.

MRS PINCHWIFE Alack-a-day she has been crying all day above it seems in a corner.

PINCHWIFE Where is she, let me speak with her.

MRS PINCHWIFE [*aside*] O Lord then he'll discover all – ⟨*to him*⟩ Pray hold bud, what d'ye mean to discover me, she'll know I have told you then, pray bud let me talk with her first –

PINCHWIFE I must speak with her to know whether Horner ever made her any promise; and whether she be married to Sparkish or no.

MRS PINCHWIFE Pray dear bud don't, till I have spoken with her and told her that I have told you all, for she'll kill me else.

PINCHWIFE Go then and bid her come out to me.

MRS PINCHWIFE Yes, yes bud –

PINCHWIFE Let me see –

MRS PINCHWIFE ⟨*aside*⟩ I'll go, but she is not within to come to him. I have just got time to know of Lucy her maid, who first set me on work, what lie I shall tell next, for I am e'en at my wit's end –   [*Exit Mrs Pinchwife*]

PINCHWIFE Well I resolve it, Horner shall have her, I'd rather give him my sister than lend him my wife, and such an alliance will prevent his pretensions to my wife sure, – I'll make him of kin to her, and then he won't care for her.

Mrs Pinchwife returns.

MRS PINCHWIFE O Lord bud I told you what anger you would make me with my sister.

PINCHWIFE Won't she come hither?

MRS PINCHWIFE No no, alack-a-day, she's ashamed to look you in the face, and she says if you go in to her, she'll run away downstairs, and shamefully go herself to Mr Horner, who has promised her marriage she says, and she will have no other, so she won't –

PINCHWIFE Did he so – promise her marriage – then she shall have no other, go tell her so, and if she will come and discourse with me a little concerning the means, I will about it immediately, go –

[*Exit Mrs Pinchwife*]

His estate is equal to Sparkish's, and his extraction as much better than his, as his parts are, but my chief reason is, I'd rather be of kin to him by the name of brother-in-law, than that of cuckold –

Enter Mrs Pinchwife.

Well what says she now?

MRS PINCHWIFE Why she says she would only have you lead her to Horner's lodging – with whom she first will discourse the matter before she talks with you, which yet she cannot do; for alack poor creature, she says she can't so much as look you in the face, therefore she'll come to you in a mask, and you must excuse her if she make you no answer to any question of yours, till you have brought her to Mr Horner, and if you will not chide her, nor question her, she'll come out to you immediately.

PINCHWIFE Let her come I will not speak a word to her, nor require a word from her.

MRS PINCHWIFE O I forgot, besides she says, she cannot look you in the face, though through a mask, therefore would desire you to put out the candle.

PINCHWIFE I agree to all, let her make haste –

[*Exit Mrs Pinchwife*]

[*puts out the candle*] There 'tis out. – My case is something better, I'd rather fight with Horner for not lying with my sister, than for lying with my wife, and of the two I had rather find my sister too forward than my wife; I expected no other from her free education, as she calls it, and her passion for the Town – well – Wife and sister are names which make us expect love and duty, pleasure and comfort, but we find 'em plagues and torments, and are equally, though differently troublesome to their keeper; for we have as much ado to get people to lie with our sisters, as to keep 'em from lying with our wives.

Enter Mrs Pinchwife masked, and in hoods and scarves, and a nightgown and petticoat of Alithea's in the dark.

What are you come sister? Let us go then – but first let me lock up my wife, Mrs Margery where are you?
MRS PINCHWIFE Here bud.
PINCHWIFE Come hither, that I may lock you up, get you in, [*locks the door*] come sister where are you now?

Mrs Pinchwife gives him her hand, but when he lets her go, she steals softly on t'other side of him, and is led away by him for his sister Alithea.

SCENE ⟨II⟩

Changes to Horner's lodging

Quack, Horner.

QUACK What all alone, not so much as one of your cuckolds here, nor one of their wives! They use to take their turns with you, as if they were to watch you.
HORNER Yes it often happens, that a cuckold is but his wife's spy and is more upon family duty, when he is with her gallant abroad hindering his pleasure, than when he is at home with her playing the gallant, but the hardest duty a married woman imposes upon a lover is, keeping her husband company always.
QUACK And his fondness wearies you almost as soon as hers.
HORNER A pox, keeping a cuckold company after you have had his wife, is as tiresome as the company of a country squire to a witty fellow of the Town, when he has got all his money.
QUACK And as at first a man makes a friend of the husband to get the wife, so at last you are fain to fall out with the wife to be rid of the husband.
HORNER Aye, most cuckold-makers are true courtiers, when once

a poor man has cracked his credit for 'em, they can't abide to come near him.

QUACK But at first to draw him in are so sweet, so kind, so dear, just as you are to Pinchwife. But what becomes of that intrigue with his wife?

HORNER A pox he's as surly as an alderman that has been bit, and since he's so coy, his wife's kindness is in vain, for she's a silly innocent.

QUACK Did she not send you a letter by him?

HORNER Yes, but that's a riddle I have not yet solved – Allow the poor creature to be willing, she is silly too, and he keeps her up so close –

QUACK Yes, so close that he makes her but the more willing, and adds but revenge to her love, which two when met seldom fail of satisfying each other one way or other.

HORNER What here's the man we are talking of I think.

Enter Pinchwife leading in his wife masked, muffled and in her sister's gown.

HORNER Pshaw.

QUACK Bringing his wife to you is the next thing to bringing a love letter from her.

HORNER What means this?

PINCHWIFE The last time you know Sir I brought you a love letter, now you see a mistress, I think you'll say I am a civil man to you.

HORNER Aye the devil take me will I say thou art the civilest man I ever met with, and I have known some; I fancy, I understand thee now, better than I did the letter, but hark thee in thy ear –

PINCHWIFE What?

HORNER Nothing but the usual question man, is she sound on thy word?

PINCHWIFE What you take her for a wench and me for a pimp?

HORNER Pshaw, wench and pimp, paw* words, I know thou art an honest fellow, and hast a great acquaintance among the ladies, and perhaps hast made love for me rather than let me make love to thy wife –

* paw: improper.

PINCHWIFE Come Sir, in short, I am for no fooling.

HORNER Nor I neither, therefore prithee let's see her face presently, make her show man, art thou sure I don't know her?

PINCHWIFE I am sure you do know her.

HORNER A pox why dost thou bring her to me then?

PINCHWIFE Because she's a relation of mine.

HORNER Is she faith man, then thou art still more civil and obliging, dear rogue.

PINCHWIFE Who desired me to bring her to you.

HORNER Then she is obliging, dear rogue.

PINCHWIFE You'll make her welcome for my sake I hope.

HORNER I hope she is handsome enough to make herself welcome; prithee let her unmask.

PINCHWIFE Do you speak to her, she would never be ruled by me.

HORNER Madam – [*Mrs Pinchwife whispers to Horner*] She says she must speak with me in private, withdraw prithee.

PINCHWIFE [*aside*] She's unwilling it seems I should know all her indecent conduct in this business – ⟨*to them*⟩ Well then I'll leave you together, and hope when I am gone you'll agree, if not you and I shan't agree Sir. –

HORNER ⟨*aside*⟩ What means the fool? – ⟨*to him*⟩ If she and I agree 'tis no matter what you and I do. [*whispers to Mrs Pinchwife, who makes signs with her hand for him to be gone*]

PINCHWIFE In the meantime I'll fetch a parson, and find out Sparkish and disabuse him. ⟨*aside*⟩ You would have me fetch a parson, would you not, well then – Now I think I am rid of her, and shall have no more trouble with her – our sisters and daughters like usurers' money, are safest, when put out; but our wives, like their writings,* never safe, but in our closets under lock and key.

[*Exit Pinchwife*]

Enter Boy.

BOY Sir Jasper Fidget Sir is coming up.

HORNER Here's the trouble of a cuckold, now we are talking of, a pox on him, has he not enough to do to hinder his wife's sport, but he must other women's too. – Step in here Madam.

[*Exit Mrs Pinchwife*]

* writings: marriage settlements.

Enter Sir Jasper.

SIR JASPER My best and dearest friend.

HORNER ⟨*aside*⟩ The old style doctor – ⟨*to him*⟩ Well be short, for I am busy, what would your impertinent wife have now?

SIR JASPER Well guessed i'faith, for I do come from her.

HORNER To invite me to supper, tell her I can't come, go.

SIR JASPER Nay, now you are out faith, for my lady and the whole knot of the virtuous gang, as they call themselves, are resolved upon a frolic of coming to you to-night in a masquerade, and are all dressed already.

HORNER I shan't be at home.

SIR JASPER Lord how churlish he is to women – nay prithee don't disappoint 'em, they'll think 'tis my fault, prithee don't, I'll send in the banquet and the fiddles, but make no noise on't, for the poor virtuous rogues would not have it known for the world, that they go a-masquerading, and they would come to no man's ball, but yours.

HORNER Well, well – get you gone, and tell 'em if they come, 'twill be at the peril of their honour and yours.

SIR JASPER Heh, he, he – we'll trust you for that, farewell –

[*Exit Sir Jasper*]

HORNER Doctor anon you too shall be my guest.
But now I'm going to a private feast.   ⟨*Exit*⟩

SCENE ⟨III⟩

Changes to the Piazza of Covent Garden

Sparkish, Pinchwife.

SPARKISH [*with the letter in his hand*] But who would have thought a woman could have been false to me, by the world, I could not have thought it.

PINCHWIFE You were for giving and taking liberty, she has taken it only Sir, now you find in that letter, you are a frank person, and so is she you see there.

SPARKISH Nay if this be her hand – for I never saw it.

PINCHWIFE 'Tis no matter whether that be her hand or no, I am sure this hand at her desire led her to Mr Horner, with whom I left her just now, to go fetch a parson to 'em at their desire too, to deprive you of her forever, for it seems yours was but a mock marriage.

SPARKISH Indeed she would needs have it that 'twas Harcourt himself in a parson's habit, that married us, but I'm sure he told me 'twas his brother Ned.

PINCHWIFE O there 'tis out and you were deceived not she, for you are such a frank person – but I must be gone – you'll find her at Mr Horner's, go and believe your eyes.   [*Exit Pinchwife*]

SPARKISH Nay I'll to her, and call her as many crocodiles, sirens, harpies, and other heathenish names, as a poet would do a mistress, who had refused to hear his suit, nay more his verses on her. But stay, is not that she following a torch at t'other end of the Piazza, and from Horner's certainly – 'tis so –

Enter Alithea following a Torch,★ *and Lucy behind.*

You are well met Madam though you don't think so; what you have made a short visit to Mr Horner, but I suppose you'll return to him presently, by that time the parson can be with him.

ALITHEA Mr Horner, and the parson Sir. –

SPARKISH Come Madam no more dissembling, no more jilting for I am no more a frank person.

ALITHEA How's this.

LUCY [*aside*] So 'twill work I see –

SPARKISH Could you find out no easy country fool to abuse? None but me, a gentleman of wit and pleasure about the Town, but it was your pride to be too hard for a man of parts, unworthy false woman, false as a friend that lends a man money to lose, false as dice, who undo those that trust all they have to 'em.

LUCY [*aside*] He has been a great bubble by his similes as they say –

ALITHEA You have been too merry Sir at your wedding dinner sure.

SPARKISH What d'ye mock me too?

ALITHEA Or you have been deluded.

★ *a Torch*: a linkboy carrying a torch.

SPARKISH By you.

ALITHEA Let me understand you.

SPARKISH Have you the confidence, I should call it something else, since you know your guilt, to stand my just reproaches? You did not write an impudent letter to Mr Horner, who I find now has clubbed with you in deluding me with his aversion for women, that I might not forsooth suspect him for my rival.

LUCY [*aside*] D'ye think the gentleman can be jealous now Madam –

ALITHEA I write a letter to Mr Horner!

SPARKISH Nay Madam, do not deny it, your brother showed it me just now, and told me likewise he left you at Horner's lodging to fetch a parson to marry you to him, and I wish you joy Madam, joy, joy, and to him too much joy, and to myself more joy for not marrying you.

ALITHEA [*aside*] So I find my brother would break off the match, and I can consent to't, since I see this gentleman can be made jealous. O Lucy, by his rude usage and jealousy, he makes me almost afraid I am married to him, art thou sure 'twas Harcourt himself and no parson that married us.

SPARKISH No Madam I thank you, I suppose that was a contrivance too of Mr Horner's and yours, to make Harcourt play the parson, but I would as little as you have him one now, no not for the world, for shall I tell you another truth, I never had any passion for you, till now, for now I hate you, 'tis true I might have married your portion, as other men of parts of the Town do sometimes, and so your servant, and to show my unconcernedness, I'll come to your wedding, and resign you with as much joy as I would a stale wench to a new cully, nay with as much joy as I would after the first night, if I had been married to you, there's for you, and so your servant, servant. [*Exit Sparkish*]

ALITHEA How was I deceived in a man!

LUCY You'll believe then a fool may be made jealous now? For that easiness in him that suffers him to be led by a wife, will likewise permit him to be persuaded against her by others.

ALITHEA But marry Mr Horner, my brother does not intend it sure; if I thought he did, I would take thy advice, and Mr Harcourt for my husband, and now I wish, that if there be any over-wise woman of the Town, who like me would marry a fool, for fortune, liberty, or title, first that her husband may love play, and be a cully to all the Town, but her, and suffer none but fortune to be mistress of his purse, then if for liberty, that he may send her into the country under the conduct of some housewifely mother-in-law; and if for title, may the world give 'em none but that of cuckold.

LUCY And for her greater curse Madam, may he not deserve it.

ALITHEA Away impertinent – is not this my old Lady Lanterlu's?★

LUCY Yes Madam. [*aside*] And here I hope we shall find Mr Harcourt –

[*Exeunt Alithea, Lucy*]

SCENE ⟨IV⟩

Changes again to Horner's lodging

Horner, Lady Fidget, Mrs Dainty Fidget, Mrs Squeamish,
a table, banquet, and bottles.

HORNER [*aside*] A pox they are come too soon – before I have sent back my new – mistress. All I have now to do, is to lock her in, that they may not see her –

LADY FIDGET That we may be sure of our welcome, we have brought our entertainment with us, and are resolved to treat thee, dear toad.

MRS DAINTY And that we may be merry to purpose, have left Sir Jasper and my old Lady Squeamish quarrelling at home at backgammon.

SQUEAMISH Therefore let us make use of our time, lest they should chance to interrupt us.

LADY FIDGET Let us sit then.

HORNER First that you may be private, let me lock this door, and that, and I'll wait upon you presently.

LADY FIDGET No Sir, shut 'em only and your lips forever, for we must trust you as much as our women.

HORNER You know all vanity's killed in me, I have no occasion for talking.

★ Lady Lanterlu's: the name is from the card game, lanterloo or loo.

LADY FIDGET Now ladies, supposing we had drank each of us our two bottles, let us speak the truth of our hearts.

MRS DAINTY ⎫
SQUEAMISH ⎭ Agreed.

LADY FIDGET By this brimmer, for truth is nowhere else to be found, [*aside to Horner*] Not in thy heart false man.

HORNER [*aside to Lady Fidget*] You have found me a true man I'm sure.

LADY FIDGET [*aside to Horner*] Not every way – ⟨*aloud*⟩ But let us sit and be merry.

I

[*sings*]
 Why should our damned tyrants oblige us to live,
 On the pittance of pleasure which they only give.
  We must not rejoice,
  With wine and with noise;
 In vain we must wake in a dull bed alone.
 Whilst to our warm rival the bottle, they're gone.
  Then lay aside charms,
  And take up these arms.★   ★ *The glasses.*

2
 'Tis wine only gives 'em their courage and wit,
 Because we live sober to men we submit.
  If for beauties you'd pass,
  Take a lick of the glass.
 'Twill mend your complexions, and when they are gone,
 The best red we have is the red of the grape.
  Then sisters lay't on.
  And damn a good shape.

MRS DAINTY Dear brimmer, well in token of our openness and plain-dealing, let us throw our masks over our heads.

HORNER So 'twill come to the glasses anon.

SQUEAMISH Lovely brimmer, let me enjoy him first.

LADY FIDGET No, I never part with a gallant, till I've tried him. Dear brimmer that makest our husbands shortsighted.

MRS DAINTY And our bashful gallants bold.

SQUEAMISH And for want of a gallant, the butler lovely in our eyes, drink eunuch.

LADY FIDGET Drink thou representative of a husband, damn a husband.

MRS DAINTY And as it were a husband, an old keeper.

SQUEAMISH And an old grandmother.

HORNER And an English bawd, and a French chirurgeon.

LADY FIDGET Aye we have all reason to curse 'em.

HORNER For my sake ladies.

LADY FIDGET No, for our own, for the first spoils all young gallants' industry.

MRS DAINTY And the other's art makes 'em bold only with common women.

SQUEAMISH And rather run the hazard of the vile distemper amongst them, than of a denial amongst us.

MRS DAINTY The filthy toads choose mistresses now, as they do stuffs, for having been fancied and worn by others.

SQUEAMISH For being common and cheap.

LADY FIDGET Whilst women of quality, like the richest stuffs, lie untumbled, and unasked for.

HORNER Aye neat, and cheap, and new often they think best.

MRS DAINTY No Sir, the beasts will be known by a mistress longer than by a suit.

SQUEAMISH And 'tis not for cheapness neither.

LADY FIDGET No, for the vain fops will take up druggets, and embroider 'em, but I wonder at the depraved appetites of witty men, they use to be out of the common road, and hate imitation. Pray tell me beast, when you were a man, why you rather chose to club with a multitude in a common house, for an entertainment, than to be the only guest at a good table.

HORNER Why faith ceremony and expectation are unsufferable to those that are sharp bent, people always eat with the best stomach at an ordinary, where every man is snatching for the best bit.

LADY FIDGET Though he get a cut over the fingers – but I have heard people eat most heartily of another man's meat, that is, what they do not pay for.

HORNER When they are sure of their welcome and freedom, for ceremony in love and eating, is as ridiculous as in fighting, falling on briskly is all should be done in those occasions.

LADY FIDGET Well then let me tell you Sir, there is nowhere

more freedom than in our houses, and we take freedom from a young person as a sign of good breeding, and a person may be as free as he pleases with us, as frolic, as gamesome, as wild as he will.

HORNER Han't I heard you all declaim against wild men.

LADY FIDGET Yes, but for all that, we think wildness in a man, as desirable a quality, as in a duck, or rabbit; a tame man, foh.

HORNER I know not, but your reputations frightened me, as much as your faces invited me.

LADY FIDGET Our reputation, Lord! Why should you not think, that we women make use of our reputation, as you men of yours, only to deceive the world with less suspicion; our virtue is like the statesman's religion, the Quaker's word, the gamester's oath, and the great man's honour, but to cheat those that trust us.

SQUEAMISH And that demureness, coyness, and modesty, that you see in our faces in the boxes at plays, is as much a sign of a kind woman, as a vizard-mask in the pit.

MRS DAINTY For I assure you, women are least masked, when they have the velvet vizard on.

LADY FIDGET You would have found us modest women in our denials only.

SQUEAMISH Our bashfulness is only the reflection of the men's.

MRS DAINTY We blush, when they are shamefaced.

HORNER I beg your pardon ladies, I was deceived in you devilishly, but why, that mighty pretence to honour?

LADY FIDGET We have told you; but sometimes 'twas for the same reason you men pretend business often, to avoid ill company, to enjoy the better, and more privately those you love.

HORNER But why, would you ne'er give a friend a wink then?

LADY FIDGET Faith, your reputation frightened us as much, as ours did you, you were so notoriously lewd.

HORNER And you so seemingly honest.

LADY FIDGET Was that all that deterred you?

HORNER And so expensive – you allow freedom you say.

LADY FIDGET Aye, aye.

HORNER That I was afraid of losing my little money, as well as my little time, both which my other pleasures required.

LADY FIDGET Money, foh – you talk like a little fellow now, do such as we expect money?

HORNER I beg your pardon, Madam, I must confess, I have heard that great ladies, like great merchants, set but the higher prizes upon what they have, because they are not in necessity of taking the first offer.

MRS DAINTY Such as we, make sale of our hearts?

SQUEAMISH We bribed for our love? Foh.

HORNER With your pardon, ladies, I know, like great men in offices, you seem to exact flattery and attendance only from your followers, but you have receivers* about you, and such fees to pay, a man is afraid to pass your grants; besides we must let you win at cards, or we lose your hearts; and if you make an assignation, 'tis at a goldsmith's, jeweller's, or china house, where for your honour, you deposit to him, he must pawn his, to the punctual City, and so paying for what you take up, pays for what he takes up.

MRS DAINTY Would you not have us assured of our gallant's love?

SQUEAMISH For love is better known by liberality, than by jealousy.

LADY FIDGET For one may be dissembled, the other not – [*aside*] but my jealousy can be no longer dissembled, and they are telling ripe: [*claps him on the back*] come here's to our gallants in waiting, whom we must name, and I'll begin, this is my false rogue.

SQUEAMISH How!

HORNER So all will out now –

SQUEAMISH [*aside to Horner*] Did you not tell me, 'twas for my sake only, you reported yourself no man?

MRS DAINTY [*aside to Horner*] O wretch! Did you not swear to me, 'twas for my love, and honour, you passed for that thing you do?

HORNER So, so.

LADY FIDGET Come, speak ladies, this is my false villain.

SQUEAMISH And mine too.

MRS DAINTY And mine.

HORNER Well then, you are all three my false rogues too, and there's an end on't.

LADY FIDGET Well then, there's no remedy, sister sharers, let us not fall out, but have a care of our honour; though we get no

* receivers: servants who accept bribes.

presents, no jewels of him, we are savers of our honour, the jewel of most value and use, which shines yet to the world unsuspected, though it be counterfeit.

HORNER Nay, and is e'en as good, as if it were true, provided the world think so; for honour, like beauty now, only depends on the opinion of others.

LADY FIDGET Well Harry Common, I hope you can be true to three, swear, but 'tis to no purpose, to require your oath; for you are as often forsworn, as you swear to new women.

HORNER Come, faith Madam, let us e'en pardon one another, for all the difference I find betwixt we men, and you women, we forswear ourselves at the beginning of an amour, you, as long as it lasts.

Enter Sir Jasper Fidget, and Old Lady Squeamish.

SIR JASPER O my Lady Fidget, was this your cunning, to come to Mr Horner without me; but you have been nowhere else I hope.

LADY FIDGET No, Sir Jasper.

OLD LADY SQUEAMISH And you came straight hither Biddy.

SQUEAMISH Yes indeed, Lady Grandmother.

SIR JASPER 'Tis well, 'tis well, I knew when once they were thoroughly acquainted with poor Horner, they'd ne'er be from him; you may let her masquerade it with my wife, and Horner, and I warrant her reputation safe.

Enter Boy.

BOY O Sir, here's the gentleman come, whom you bid me not suffer to come up, without giving you notice, with a lady too, and other gentlemen –

HORNER Do you all go in there, whilst I send 'em away, and boy, do you desire 'em to stay below till I come, which shall be immediately.

[*Exeunt Sir Jasper, ⟨Old⟩ Lady Squeamish, Lady Fidget, Mrs Dainty, Squeamish*]

BOY Yes Sir.   [*Exit*]

Exit Horner at t'other door, and returns with Mrs Pinchwife.

HORNER You would not take my advice to be gone home, before your husband came back, he'll now discover all, yet pray my dearest be persuaded to go home, and leave the rest to my management, I'll let you down the back way.

MRS PINCHWIFE I don't know the way home, so I don't.

HORNER My man shall wait upon you.

MRS PINCHWIFE No, don't you believe, that I'll go at all; what are you weary of me already?

HORNER No my life, 'tis that I may love you long, 'tis to secure my love, and your reputation with your husband, he'll never receive you again else.

MRS PINCHWIFE What care I, d'ye think to frighten me with that? I don't intend to go to him again; you shall be my husband now.

HORNER I cannot be your husband, dearest, since you are married to him.

MRS PINCHWIFE O would you make me believe that – don't I see every day at London here, women leave their first husbands, and go, and live with other men as their wives, pish, pshaw, you'd make me angry, but that I love you so mainly.

HORNER So, they are coming up – In again, in, I hear 'em:

[*Exit Mrs Pinchwife*]

Well, a silly mistress, is like a weak place, soon got, soon lost, a man has scarce time for plunder; she betrays her husband, first to her gallant, and then her gallant, to her husband.

Enter Pinchwife, Alithea, Harcourt, Sparkish, Lucy, and a Parson.

PINCHWIFE Come Madam, 'tis not the sudden change of your dress, the confidence of your asseverations, and your false witness there, shall persuade me, I did not bring you hither, just now; here's my witness, who cannot deny it, since you must be confronted – Mr Horner, did not I bring this lady to you just now?

HORNER [*aside*] Now must I wrong one woman for another's sake, but that's no new thing with me; for in these cases I am still on the criminal's side, against the innocent.

ALITHEA Pray, speak Sir.

HORNER [*aside*] It must be so – I must be impudent, and try my luck, impudence uses to be too hard for truth.

PINCHWIFE What, you are studying an evasion, or excuse for her, speak Sir.

HORNER No faith, I am something backward only, to speak in women's affairs or disputes.

PINCHWIFE She bids you speak.

ALITHEA Aye, pray Sir do, pray satisfy him.

HORNER Then truly, you did bring that lady to me just now.

PINCHWIFE O ho –

ALITHEA How Sir –

HARCOURT How, Horner!

ALITHEA What mean you Sir, I always took you for a man of honour?

HORNER [*aside*] Aye, so much a man of honour, that I must save my mistress, I thank you, come what will on't.

SPARKISH So if I had had her, she'd have made me believe, the moon had been made of a Christmas pie.

LUCY [*aside*] Now could I speak, if I durst, and solve the riddle, who am the author of it.

ALITHEA O unfortunate woman! A combination against my honour, which most concerns me now, because you share in my disgrace, Sir, and it is your censure which I must now suffer, that troubles me, not theirs.

HARCOURT Madam, then have no trouble, you shall now see 'tis possible for me to love too, without being jealous, I will not only believe your innocence myself, but make all the world believe it – [*apart to Horner*] Horner I must now be concerned for this lady's honour.

HORNER And I must be concerned for a lady's honour too.

HARCOURT This lady has her honour, and I will protect it.

HORNER My lady has not her honour, but has given it me to keep, and I will preserve it.

HARCOURT I understand you not.

HORNER I would not have you.

MRS PINCHWIFE [*peeping in behind*] What's the matter with 'em all.

PINCHWIFE Come, come, Mr Horner, no more disputing, here's the parson, I brought him not in vain.

HARCOURT No Sir, I'll employ him, if this lady please.

PINCHWIFE How, what d'ye mean?

SPARKISH Aye, what does he mean?

HORNER Why, I have resigned your sister to him, he has my consent.

PINCHWIFE But he has not mine Sir, a woman's injured honour, no more than a man's, can be repaired or satisfied by any, but him that first wronged it; and you shall marry her presently, or – [*lays his hand on his sword*]

Enter to them Mrs Pinchwife.

MRS PINCHWIFE ⟨*aside*⟩ O Lord, they'll kill poor Mr Horner, besides he shan't marry her, whilst I stand by, and look on, I'll not lose my second husband so.

PINCHWIFE What do I see?

ALITHEA My sister in my clothes!

SPARKISH Ha!

MRS PINCHWIFE Nay, pray now don't quarrel about finding work for the parson, he shall marry me to Mr Horner; [*to Pinchwife*] for now I believe, you have enough of me.

HORNER Damned, damned loving changeling.

MRS PINCHWIFE Pray sister, pardon me for telling so many lies of you.

HARCOURT I suppose the riddle is plain now.

LUCY No, that must be my work, good Sir, hear me. [*kneels to Pinchwife, who stands doggedly, with his hat over his eyes*]

PINCHWIFE I will never hear woman again, but make 'em all silent, thus – [*offers to draw upon his wife*]

HORNER No, that must not be.

PINCHWIFE You then shall go first, 'tis all one to me. [*offers to draw on Horner, stopped by Harcourt*]

HARCOURT Hold –

*Enter Sir Jasper Fidget, Lady Fidget, ⟨Old⟩ Lady Squeamish,
Mrs Dainty Fidget, Mrs Squeamish.*

SIR JASPER What's the matter, what's the matter, pray what's the matter Sir, I beseech you communicate Sir.

PINCHWIFE Why my wife has communicated Sir, as your wife may have done too Sir, if she knows him Sir –

SIR JASPER Pshaw, with him, ha, ha, he.

PINCHWIFE D'ye mock me Sir, a cuckold is a kind of a wild beast, have a care Sir –

SIR JASPER No sure, you mock me Sir – he cuckold you! It can't be, ha, ha, he, why, I'll tell you Sir. [*offers to whisper*]

PINCHWIFE I tell you again, he has whored my wife, and yours too, if he knows her, and all the women he comes near; 'tis not his dissembling, his hypocrisy can wheedle me.

SIR JASPER How does he dissemble, is he a hypocrite? Nay then – how – wife – sister is he an hypocrite?

OLD LADY SQUEAMISH An hypocrite, a dissembler, speak young harlotry, speak how?

SIR JASPER Nay then – O my head too – O thou libidinous lady!

OLD LADY SQUEAMISH O thou harloting, harlotry, hast thou don't then?

SIR JASPER Speak good Horner, art thou a dissembler, a rogue? Hast thou –

HORNER Soh –

LUCY [*apart to Horner*] I'll fetch you off, and her too, if she will but hold her tongue.

HORNER [*apart to Lucy*] Canst thou? I'll give thee –

LUCY [*to Pinchwife*] Pray have but patience to hear me Sir, who am the unfortunate cause of all this confusion, your wife is innocent, I only culpable; for I put her upon telling you all these lies, concerning my mistress, in order to the breaking off the match, between Mr Sparkish and her, to make way for Mr Harcourt.

SPARKISH Did you so eternal rotten-tooth, then it seems my mistress was not false to me, I was only deceived by you, brother that should have been, now man of conduct, who is a frank person now, to bring your wife to her lover – ha –

LUCY I assure you Sir, she came not to Mr Horner out of love, for she loves him no more –

MRS PINCHWIFE Hold, I told lies for you, but you shall tell none for me, for I do love Mr Horner with all my soul, and nobody shall say me nay; pray don't you go to make poor Mr Horner believe to the contrary, 'tis spitefully done of you, I'm sure.

HORNER [*aside to Mrs Pinchwife*] Peace, dear idiot.

MRS PINCHWIFE Nay, I will not peace.

PINCHWIFE Not till I make you.

Enter Dorilant, Quack.

DORILANT Horner, your servant, I am the doctor's guest, he must excuse our intrusion.

QUACK But what's the matter gentlemen, for heaven's sake, what's the matter?

HORNER O 'tis well you are come – 'tis a censorious world we live in, you may have brought me a reprieve, or else I had died for a crime, I never committed, and these innocent ladies had suffered with me, therefore pray satisfy these worthy, honourable, jealous gentlemen – that – [*whispers*]

QUACK O I understand you, is that all – Sir Jasper, by heavens and upon the word of a physician [*whispers to Sir Jasper*] Sir, –

SIR JASPER Nay I do believe you truly – pardon me my virtuous lady, and dear of honour.

OLD LADY SQUEAMISH What then all's right again.

SIR JASPER Aye, aye, and now let us satisfy him too. [*they whisper with Pinchwife*]

PINCHWIFE An eunuch! Pray no fooling with me.

QUACK I'll bring half the chirurgeons in Town to swear it.

PINCHWIFE They – they'll swear a man that bled to death through his wounds died of an apoplexy.

QUACK Pray hear me Sir – why all the Town has heard the report of him.

PINCHWIFE But does all the Town believe it.

QUACK Pray inquire a little, and first of all these.

PINCHWIFE I'm sure when I left the Town he was the lewdest fellow in't.

QUACK I tell you Sir he has been in France since, pray ask but these ladies and gentlemen, your friend Mr Dorilant, gentlemen and ladies, han't you all heard the late sad report of poor Mr Horner.

ALL LADIES Aye, aye, aye.

DORILANT Why thou jealous fool do'st thou doubt it, he's an errant French capon.

MRS PINCHWIFE 'Tis false Sir, you shall not disparage poor Mr Horner, for to my certain knowledge –

LUCY O hold –

SQUEAMISH [*aside to Lucy*] Stop her mouth –

LADY FIDGET [*to Pinchwife*] Upon my honour Sir, 'tis as true.

MRS DAINTY D'ye think we would have been seen in his company –

SQUEAMISH Trust our unspotted reputations with him!

LADY FIDGET [*aside to Horner*] This you get, and we too, by trusting your secret to a fool –

HORNER Peace Madam, – [*aside to Quack*] well doctor is not this a good design that carries a man on unsuspected, and brings him off safe. –

PINCHWIFE [*aside*] Well, if this were true, but my wife –

Dorilant whispers with Mrs Pinchwife.

ALITHEA Come brother your wife is yet innocent you see, but have a care of too strong an imagination, lest like an overconcerned timorous gamester by fancying an unlucky cast it should come, women and fortune are truest still to those that trust 'em.

LUCY And any wild thing grows but the more fierce and hungry for being kept up, and more dangerous to the keeper.

ALITHEA There's doctrine for all husbands Mr Harcourt.

HARCOURT I edify Madam so much, that I am impatient till I am one.

DORILANT And I edify so much by example I will never be one.

SPARKISH And because I will not disparage my parts I'll ne'er be one.

HORNER And I alas can't be one.

PINCHWIFE But I must be one – against my will to a country wife, with a country murrain to me.

MRS PINCHWIFE [*aside*] And I must be a country wife still too I find, for I can't like a City one, be rid of my musty husband and do what I list.

HORNER Now Sir I must pronounce your wife innocent, though I blush whilst I do it, and I am the only man by her now exposed to shame, which I will straight drown in wine, as you shall your suspicion, and the ladies' troubles we'll divert with a ballet. Doctor where are your maskers.

LUCY Indeed she's innocent Sir, I am her witness, and her end of

coming out was but to see her sister's wedding, and what she
has said to your face of her love to Mr Horner was but the usual
innocent revenge on a husband's jealousy, was it not Madam
speak –

MRS PINCHWIFE [*aside to Lucy and Horner*] Since you'll have
me tell more lies – ⟨*to Pinchwife*⟩ Yes indeed bud.

PINCHWIFE For my own sake fain I would all believe.
Cuckolds like lovers should themselves deceive.
But – [*sighs*] –
His honour is least safe, (too late I find)
Who trusts it with a foolish wife or friend.

A Dance of Cuckolds.

HORNER Vain fops, but court, and dress, and keep a pother,
To pass for women's men, with one another.
But he who aims by women to be prized,
First by the men you see must be despised.

EPILOGUE

Spoken by Mrs Knep ⟨Lady Fidget⟩:

Now you the vigorous, who daily here
O'er vizard-mask, in public domineer,
And what you'd do to her if in place where;
Nay have the confidence, to cry 'Come out',
Yet when she says 'Lead on', you are not stout;
But to your well-dressed brother straight turn round
And cry, 'Pox on her Ned, she can't be sound':
Then slink away, a fresh one to engage,
With so much seeming heat and loving rage,
You'd frighten listening actress on the stage:
Till she at last has seen you huffing come,
And talk of keeping in the tiring-room,
Yet cannot be provoked to lead her home:
Next you Falstaffs of fifty, who beset
Your buckram maidenheads, which your friends get;
And whilst to them, you of achievements boast,
They share the booty, and laugh at your cost.
In fine, you essenced boys, both old and young,
Who would be thought so eager, brisk, and strong,
Yet do the ladies, not their husbands, wrong:
Whose purses for your manhood make excuse,
And keep your Flanders mares for show, not use;
Encouraged by our woman's man today,
A Horner's part may vainly think to play;
And may intrigues so bashfully disown
That they may doubted be by few or none,
May kiss the cards at picquet, ombre, – loo,
And so be thought to kiss the lady too;
But gallants, have a care faith, what you do.
The world, which to no man his due will give,
You by experience know you can deceive,
And men may still believe you vigorous,
But then we women, – there's no cozening us.

NOTES

The copy text used is that of the first edition of 1675 in the Brotherton Collection, University of Leeds.

Abbreviations
   Q1 The first quarto edition, 1675
   Q2 The second quarto edition, 1683
   Q3 The third quarto edition, 1688
   Q4 The fourth quarto edition, 1695
   Q5 The fifth quarto edition, 1695

The form 'Mr Pinchwife' which appears in the copy text for a few
pages following his first entry has been amended to 'Pinchwife', the
form used throughout the rest of the play. The form 'Master
Pinchwife' has been similarly altered.

414.8   wise, Mr / wise Mr Q1
414.9   impotent, Sir / impotent Sir Q1
414.16   game yet, ha / game; yet hah Q1
415.2   next to / next, to Q1
415.11   'em, who / 'em. Who Q1
418.32   'Where?' / where, Q1
418.33   ladies. / ladies? Q1
419.5   lady – / lady, Q1
419.9   France.' / *France*, Q1
419.13   Well I see Q3 / well see Q1
419.26   wo' not. What, . . . us? / wo' not, what . . . us. Q1
419.34   what, d'ye / what d'ye Q1
420.12   sitting Q3 / setting Q1
429.5   *Alithea* / *her* Q1
430.23   not melancholy / not not melancholy Q1
434.20   [*aside*] Will nothing do? / [Will nothing do?] Q1
435.14   birth – birth / birth birth Q1
435.37   No, sure / No sure Q1
437.3   herd / heard Q1
439.34   venture Q2 / venter Q1
440.27   harmless, my / harmless my Q1

444.10   not the cause Q4/not cause Q1
447.25   Yes, but/Yes, But Q1
450.36   bulls', stags' and rams'/Bulls, Stags and Rams Q1
451.24   his. He, he has/his, he, he, has Q1
452.35   see here./see here, Q1
458.5   love I/love, I Q1
458.29   Q1 sets *Horner, Harcourt, Dorilant return* after Horner's
          speech
460.1   therefore/thereforefore Q1
468.30   room./room: Q1
469.32   Write./Write Q1
471.23   comes Q4/come Q1
475.13   take it./take it Q1
475.33   would come Q5/would not come Q1
476.2   Q1 sets *Exit Lady Fidget . . . the door* after Lady Fidget's
          speech
477.15   vile Q5/vil'd Q1
477.16   Yes./Yes, Q1
478.9   Nay, she . . . me, do/Nay she . . . me do Q1
480.18   wont. What,/wont, what Q1
480.31   hers?/hers: Q1
480.32   find; what,/find, what Q1
481.24   no. I/no, I Q1
483.32   with all/withal Q1
485.28   Speak, what?/speak what? Q1
485.28   Q1 prints *The letter concludes* after 'Our journey into'
486.10   come. But/come, but Q1
486.16   world. But/world, but Q1
488.28   *aside* Q4/Q1 omits
488.29   own. But/own, but Q1
489.28   him. I/him, I Q1
489.34   for her./for her, Q1
490.19   talks Q4/talk Q1
492.4   Pinchwife. But/Pinchwife, but Q1
497.18   mistress. All/mistress, all Q1
499.25   imitation. Pray/imitation, pray Q1
502.8   'tis to no Q2/'tis no Q1
504.7   now./now, Q1

504.38   HARCOURT Q5 / HOR. Q1
506.13   libidinous / libinous Q1
508.3   LADY FIDGET / *Old La. Fid.* Q1
508.7   LADY FIDGET / *Old La. Fid.* Q1
508.24   SPARKISH / Eew Q1
508.35   ballet. Doctor / ballet, doctor Q1

THE MAN OF MODE
by Sir George Etherege

INTRODUCTION

Etherege's last comedy, *The Man of Mode*, was probably first produced on 11 March, 1676. Thomas Betterton played Dorimant and Mrs Barry Mrs Loveit. The play, which was particularly well costumed, was successful and continued to be so until 1730, after which it was staged less often. Many outstanding actors and actresses played in it, among them Colley Cibber, Mrs Oldfield, Mrs Bracegirdle, Robert Wilks, and William Pinkethman. Between 1755 and 1775 it was only once revived. When the play was produced by the Prospect Group at the Georgian Theatre at Richmond in Yorkshire, it was announced that no performance had taken place between 1793 and 1965.

The Man of Mode develops Etherege's earlier comedies and achieves a balance between the absurd triviality of Sir Fopling Flutter and the darker sides of Restoration life. Dorimant, for instance, is a difficult character to fathom: he is at once a satiric observer of social shams, and at the same time himself becomes worthy of such satiric observation. Harriet realises this and remarks on his affectation: but while he is good-natured and good-humoured, like his creator, he has a vast capacity for libertinism, akin to that of Horner in Wycherley's *The Country Wife*, and as disturbing.

These three main characters are supported well by the minor ones: Medley, possibly modelled on Sir Charles Sedley; two conventional young lovers, Bellair and Emilia; Loveit the cast mistress, and Bellinda, too much in love with Dorimant; Lady Townley and Lady Woodvill, the one fashionable and the other oldfashioned; and the excellent orange-woman, shoemaker and servants. The whole picture given by the comedy is a vignette of a significant area of Restoration London life: as John Dennis put it 'an agreeable representation of the persons of condition of both sexes, both in Court and Town'. All the world, he remarked, was charmed with Dorimant. This judgment was largely based on a view that the satire of the play was its justification, but it has always roused fierce opposition for its lack of morality from the eighteenth century to our own time. Lamb's defence, that this is a world of fantasy, will hardly suffice. We are being shown the world which Etherege, his friends and the audience knew. It is possible that the Earl of Rochester* provided the model for Dorimant (and many other models for other characters have been suggested, among them, obviously, Etherege himself) and the earl's late reform raises the question of Dorimant's. Is Dorimant really reformed? Has Harriet really tamed this sex-driven Don Juan? Will he play Mirabell to her Millamant? Is he really in love with her? Will he meet Bellinda again? Is he fundamentally lazy and indulgent, more at the mercy of impulse than he himself might wish?

These questions remain unanswered. Dorimant in his mockery of society is ironically treated by Etherege, while Harriet, equally mocking in her view of the current fashion for gallantry, is not. She is, however, also impulsive. Beneath the issues raised, notably by the last act of the play, are the problems of the age with regard to marriage. The dramatists show ideal lovers pairing off by the end of the play: yet the marriages of the time often lacked any ingredient of love: they were built on financial interest, on the matching of estates, on the planning of parents. This is why the conflicts of old and young, as well as lust and love, so often occur in Restoration comedy as well as the contrasts of town and country, foolish fop and true wit. All make up a sufficiently complex pattern for 'genteel comedy', so that, as in Etherege's case, plot can be subordinated to a reflection of a complex society, well aware of itself in the gilt framed mirrors of its elegant drawing rooms, adjusting its wigs, its patches, its witty conversation, its conventions, to cover some of humanity's deficiencies, and managing to find satiric amusement in contemplating some of the absurdities of social life.

---

* He may have stimulated Etherege into writing *The Man of Mode* by his comment in *Session of the Poets* (1675):

> Now Apollo had got gentle George in his eye,
> And frankly confessed that of all men that writ
> There's none had more fancy, sense, judgment and wit;
> But i'the crying sin, idleness, he was so hardened
> That his long seven years' silence was not to be pardoned.

A scene from The Man of Mode

The Man of Mode

or

Sir Fopling Flutter

A COMEDY

Acted at the Duke's Theatre.

By George Etherege Esq

Licensed, 3 June 1676. *Roger L'Estrange.*

LONDON

Printed by F. Macock, for Henry Herringman,
at the Sign of the Blew Anchor in the
Walk of the New Exchange.
1676

⟨DEDICATION⟩

To Her Royal Highness the Duchess*

Madam,

Poets however they may be modest otherwise, have always too good an opinion of what they write. The world when it sees this play dedicated to your Royal Highness, will conclude, I have more than my share of that vanity. But I hope the honour I have of belonging to you, will excuse my presumption. 'Tis the first thing I have produced in your service,† and my duty obliges me to what my choice durst not else have aspired.

I am very sensible, Madam, how much it is beholding to your indulgence, for the success it had in the acting, and your protection will be no less fortunate to it in the printing; for all are so ambitious of making their court to you, that none can be severe to what you are pleased to favour.

This universal submission and respect is due to the greatness of your rank and birth; but you have other illustrious qualities, which are much more engaging. Those would but dazzle, did not these really charm the eyes and understandings of all who have the happiness to approach you.

Authors on these occasions are never wanting to publish a particular of their patron's virtues and perfections; but your Royal Highness's are so eminently known that did I follow their examples, I should but paint those wonders here of which everyone already has the idea in his mind.

Besides, I do not think it proper to aim at that in prose, which is so glorious a subject for verse; in which hereafter if I show more zeal than skill, it will not grieve me much, since I less passionately desire to be esteemed a poet, than to be thought,

Madam,

your Royal Highness's

most humble, most obedient,

and most faithful servant,

GEORGE ETHEREGE

* The Duchess: Mary of Modena, Duchess of York (1658–1718).

† your service: what this was is not known. The Duke of York granted Etherege a pension in 1682, and Etherege was his envoy at Ratisbon from 1685, when the Duke became King James the Second.

DRAMATIS PERSONAE

⟨MEN⟩

Mr Dorimant
Mr Medley
Old Bellair   } Gentlemen.
Young Bellair
Sir Fopling Flutter
Mr Smirk   A parson.
Handy   A valet de chambre.

⟨WOMEN⟩

Lady Townley
Emilia
Mrs Loveit   } Gentlewomen.
Bellinda
Lady Woodvil, and
Harriet her daughter
Pert and *Busy*   Waiting women.

A Shoemaker, An Orange Woman, Three slovenly Bullies, Two Chairmen, Pages, Footmen, etc.

PROLOGUE

By Sir Carr Scroope, Baronet*

Like dancers on the ropes poor poets fare,
Most perish young the rest in danger are;
This (one would think) should make our authors wary,
But gamester-like the giddy fools miscarry.
A lucky hand or two so tempts 'em on,
They cannot leave off play till they're undone.
With modest fears a muse does first begin,
Like a young wench newly enticed to sin:
But tickled once with praise by her good will,
The wanton fool would never more lie still.
'Tis an old mistress you'll meet here tonight,
Whose charms you once have looked on with delight.
But now of late such dirty drabs have known ye,
A muse o'th' better sort's ashamed to own ye.
Nature well-drawn and wit must now give place
To gaudy nonsense and to dull grimace;
Nor is it strange that you should like so much
That kind of wit, for most of yours is such.
But I'm afraid that while to France we go,
To bring you home fine dresses, dance, and show;
The stage like you will but more foppish grow.
Of foreign wares why should we fetch the scum,
When we can be so richly served at home?
For heaven be thanked 'tis not so wise an age,
But your own follies may supply the state.
Though often ploughed, there's no great fear the soil
Should barren grow by the too frequent toil;
While at your doors are to be daily found,
Such loads of dunghill to manure the ground.
'Tis by your follies that we players thrive,
As the physicians by diseases live.
And as each year some new distemper reigns,
Whose friendly poison helps to increase their gains:

* Sir Carr Scroope: A courtier and poet (1649–1680).

So among you, there starts up every day,
Some new unheard-of fool for us to play.
Then for your own sakes be not too severe,
Nor what you all admire at home, damn here.
Since each is fond of his own ugly face,
Why should you, when we hold it, break the glass?

ACT ONE

SCENE I

A dressing room, a table covered with a toilet, clothes laid ready.

Enter Dorimant in his gown and slippers, with a note in his hand made up, repeating verses.

DORIMANT Now for some ages had the pride of Spain
Made the sun shine on half the world in vain.*
[*then looking on the note*] 'For Mrs Loveit'. What a dull insipid thing is a billet-doux written in cold blood, after the heat of the business is over? It is a tax upon good nature which I have here been labouring to pay, and have done it, but with as much regret, as ever fanatic† paid the Royal Aid‡ or church duties;§ 'twill have the same fate I know that all my notes to her have had of late, 'twill not be thought kind enough. Faith women are i' the right when they jealously examine our letters, for in them we always first discover our decay of passion. Hey – Who waits!

HANDY Sir.

DORIMANT Call a footman.

HANDY None of 'em are come yet.

DORIMANT Dogs! Will they ever lie snoring abed till noon.

HANDY 'Tis all one, sir: if they're up, you indulge 'em so, they're ever poaching after whores all the morning.

DORIMANT Take notice henceforward who's wanting in his duty, the next clap he gets, he shall rot for an example. What vermin are those chattering without?

HANDY Foggy‖ Nan the orange-woman, and swearing Tom the shoemaker.

---

* Now . . . vain: The first lines of Waller's 'Of a War with Spain, and a Fight at Sea'.
† fanatic: a dissenter.
‡ Royal Aid: a tax levied by Parliament on behalf of the king.
§ church duties: local duties charged for the parish church's services.
‖ Foggy: fat, gross.

DORIMANT Go; call in that over-grown jade with the flasket* of guts before her, fruit is refreshing in a morning.

[*Exit Handy*]

It is not that I love you less
Than when before your feet I lay.†

Enter Orange Woman ⟨and Handy⟩.

How now double tripe, what news do you bring?

ORANGE WOMAN News! Here's the best fruit has come to Town t'year, Gad I was up before four o'clock this morning, and bought all the choice i'the market.

DORIMANT The nasty refuse of your shop.

ORANGE WOMAN You need not make mouths at it, I assure you 'tis all culled ware.

DORIMANT The citizens buy better on a holiday in their walk to Totnam.‡

ORANGE WOMAN Good or bad 'tis all one, I never knew you commend any thing, Lord would the ladies had heard you talk of 'em as I have done; here bid your man give me an angel.§ [*sets down the fruit*]

DORIMANT Give the bawd her fruit again.

ORANGE WOMAN Well, on my conscience, there never was the like of you. God's my life, I had almost forgot to tell you, there is a young gentlewoman lately come to Town with her mother, that is so taken with you.

DORIMANT Is she handsome?

ORANGE WOMAN Nay, gad there are few finer women I tell you but so, and a hugeous fortune they say. Here eat this peach, it comes from the stone, 'tis better than any Newington‖ y'have tasted.

DORIMANT This fine woman I'll lay my life [*taking the peach*] is some awkward ill-fashioned country toad, who not having above

---

* Flasket: basket.
† It is not . . . lay: The first lines of Waller's 'The Self-banished'.
‡ Totnam: Tottenham, a northern suburb of London.
§ an angel: a gold coin, worth ten shillings.
‖ Newington: A town in Kent after which some varieties of peach were named.

four dozen of black hairs on her head, has adorned her baldness with a large white fruz,* that she may look sparkishly in the forefront of the king's box, at an old play.

ORANGE WOMAN Gad you'd change your note quickly if you did but see her.

DORIMANT How came she to know me?

ORANGE WOMAN She saw you yesterday at the Change,† she told me you came and fooled with the woman at the next shop.

DORIMANT I remember there was a mask observed me indeed. Fooled did she say?

ORANGE WOMAN Aye, I vow she told me twenty things you said too, and acted with her head and with her body so like you.

Enter Medley.

MEDLEY Dorimant my life, my joy, my darling-sin; how dost thou.

ORANGE WOMAN Lord what a filthy trick these men have got of kissing one another! [*she spits*]

MEDLEY Why do you suffer this cartload of scandal to come near you, and make your neighbours think you so improvident to need a bawd?

ORANGE WOMAN Good, now we shall have it, you did but want him to help you; come pay me for my fruit.

MEDLEY Make us thankful for it huswife, bawds are as much out of fashion as gentlemen-ushers;‡ none but old formal ladies use the one, and none but foppish old stagers employ the other, go you are an insignificant brandy bottle.

DORIMANT Nay, there you wrong her, three quarts of canary§ is her business.

ORANGE WOMAN What you please gentlemen.

DORIMANT To him, give him as good as he brings.

ORANGE WOMAN Hang him, there is not such another heathen in the Town again, except it be the shoemaker without.

MEDLEY I shall see you hold up your hand at the bar next sessions

* fruz: A wig of short, curled hair.
† Change: The New Exchange, shops off the Strand.
‡ gentlemen-ushers: male attendants.
§ canary: a sweet wine from the Canary Islands; a pun on 'canarybird', a whore, may be intended.

for murder, huswife; that shoemaker can take his oath you are in fee with the doctors to sell green fruit to the gentry, that the crudities* may breed diseases.

ORANGE WOMAN Pray give me my money.

DORIMANT Not a penny, when you bring the gentlewoman hither you spoke of, you shall be paid.

ORANGE WOMAN The gentlewoman! The gentlewoman may be as honest† as your sisters for ought as I know. Pray pay me Mr Dorimant, and do not abuse me so, I have an honester way of living, you know it.

MEDLEY Was there ever such a resty‡ bawd?

DORIMANT Some jade's tricks she has, but she makes amends when she's in good humour: come, tell me the lady's name, and Handy shall pay you.

ORANGE WOMAN I must not, she forbid me.

DORIMANT That's a sure sign she would have you.

MEDLEY Where does she live?

ORANGE WOMAN They lodge at my house.

MEDLEY Nay, then she's in a hopeful way.

ORANGE WOMAN Good Mr Medley say your pleasure of me, but take heed how you affront my house, God's my life, in a hopeful way!

DORIMANT Prithee peace, what kind of woman's the mother?

ORANGE WOMAN A goodly brave gentlewoman, Lord how she talks against the wild young men o' the Town; as for your part she thinks you an arrant devil, should she see you, on my conscience she would look if you had not a cloven foot.

DORIMANT Does she know me?

ORANGE WOMAN Only by hearsay, a thousand horrid stories have been told her of you, and she believes 'em all.

MEDLEY By the character, this should be the famous Lady Woodvill, and her daughter Harriet.

ORANGE WOMAN The devil's in him for guessing I think.

DORIMANT Do you know 'em.

MEDLEY Both very well, the mother's a great admirer of the forms and civility of the last age.

---

* crudities: undigested matter in the stomach.
† honest: chaste.   ‡ resty: persistent.

DORIMANT An antiquated beauty may be allowed to be out of humour at the freedoms of the present. This is a good account of the mother, pray what is the daughter?

MEDLEY Why, first she's an heiress vastly rich.

DORIMANT And handsome?

MEDLEY What alteration a twelvemonth may have bred in her I know not, but a year ago she was the beautifulest creature I ever saw; a fine, easy, clean shape, light brown hair in abundance, her features regular, her complexion clear and lively, large wanton eyes, but above all a mouth that has made me kiss it a thousand times in imagination, teeth white and even, and pretty pouting lips, with a little moisture ever hanging on them that look like the Province* rose fresh on the bush, ere the morning sun has quite drawn up the dew.

DORIMANT Rapture, mere rapture!

ORANGE WOMAN Nay, gad he tells you true, she's a delicate creature.

DORIMANT Has she wit?

MEDLEY More than is usual in her sex, and as much malice. Then she's as wild as you would wish her, and has a demureness in her looks that makes it so surprising.

DORIMANT Flesh and blood cannot hear this, and not long to know her.

MEDLEY I wonder what makes her mother bring her up to Town, an old doting keeper cannot be more jealous of his mistress.

ORANGE WOMAN She made me laugh yesterday, there was a judge came to visit 'em, and the old man she told me did so stare upon her, and when he saluted her smacked so heartily, who would think it of 'em?

MEDLEY God-a-mercy judge.

DORIMANT Do 'em right, the gentlemen of the long robe† have not been wanting by their good examples to countenance the crying sin o' the nation.

MEDLEY Come, on with your trappings, 'tis later than you imagine.

DORIMANT Call in the shoemaker, Handy.

* Province: Provins, a town near Paris, known for its roses.
† gentlemen of the long robe: lawyers.

ORANGE WOMAN Good Mr Dorimant pay me, gad I had rather give you my fruit than stay to be abused by that foul-mouthed rogue; what you gentlemen say it matters not much, but such a dirty fellow does one more disgrace.

DORIMANT Give her ten shillings, ⟨*to Orange Woman*⟩ and be sure you tell the young gentlewoman I must be acquainted with her.

ORANGE WOMAN Now do you long to be tempting this pretty creature. Well, heavens mend you.

MEDLEY Farewell bog.*

[*Exeunt Orange Woman and Handy*]

Dorimant, when did you see your *pis aller* as you call her, Mrs Loveit.

DORIMANT Not these two days.

MEDLEY And how stand affairs between you?

DORIMANT There has been great patching of late, much ado, we make a shift to hang together.

MEDLEY I wonder how her mighty spirit bears it.

DORIMANT Ill enough on all conscience, I never knew so violent a creature.

MEDLEY She's the most passionate in her love, and the most extravagant in her jealousy of any woman I ever heard of. What note is that?

DORIMANT An excuse I am going to send her for the neglect I am guilty of.

MEDLEY Prithee read it.

DORIMANT No, but if you will take the pains you may.

MEDLEY [*reads*] 'I never was a lover of business, but now I have a just reason to hate it, since it has kept me these two days from seeing you. I intend to wait upon you in the afternoon, and in the pleasure of your conversation, forget all I have suffered during this tedious absence.' This business of yours Dorimant has been with a vizard† at the playhouse, I have had an eye on you. If some malicious body should betray you, this kind note would hardly make your peace with her.

* bog: fat person.
† vizard: a mask, sometimes meaning a whore, particularly one frequenting a playhouse.

DORIMANT I desire no better.

MEDLEY Why, would her knowledge of it oblige you?

DORIMANT Most infinitely; next to the coming to a good understanding with a new mistress, I love a quarrel with an old one,
but the devil's in't, there has been such a calm in my affairs of late,
I have not had the pleasure of making a woman so much as break
her fan, to be sullen, or forswear herself these three days.

MEDLEY A very great misfortune. Let me see, I love mischief well
enough, to forward this business myself, I'll about it presently,
and though I know the truth of what y'ave done, will set her
a-raving. I'll heighten it a little with invention, leave her in a fit o'
the mother,* and be here again before y'are ready.

DORIMANT Pray stay, you may spare yourself the labour, the
business is undertaken already by one who will manage it with as
much address, and I think with a little more malice than you can.

MEDLEY Who i' the devil's name can this be!

DORIMANT Why the vizard, that very vizard you saw me with.

MEDLEY Does she love mischief so well, as to betray herself to
spite another?

DORIMANT Not so neither, Medley, I will make you comprehend
the mystery; this mask for a farther confirmation of what I have
been these two days swearing to her, made me yesterday at the
playhouse make her a promise before her face, utterly to break off
with Loveit, and because she tenders my reputation, and would
not have me do a barbarous thing, has contrived a way to give me
a handsome occasion.

MEDLEY Very good.

DORIMANT She intends about an hour before me, this afternoon,
to make Loveit a visit, and (having the privilege by reason of a
professed friendship between 'em to talk of her concerns) –

MEDLEY Is she a friend?

DORIMANT Oh, an intimate friend!

MEDLEY Better and better, pray proceed.

DORIMANT She means insensibly to insinuate a discourse of me,
and artificially raise her jealousy to such a height, that transported with the first motions of her passion, she shall fly upon me
with all the fury imaginable, as soon as ever I enter; the quarrel

* fit o' the mother: hysteria.

being thus happily begun, I am to play my part, confess and justify all my roguery, swear her impertinence and ill humour makes her intolerable, tax her with the next fop that comes into my head, and in a huff march away, slight her and leave her to be taken by whosoever thinks it worth his time to lie down before her.

MEDLEY This vizard is a spark, and has a genius that makes her worthy of yourself, Dorimant.

Enter Handy, Shoemaker, and Footman.

DORIMANT You rogue there, who sneak like a dog that has flung down a dish, if you do not mend your waiting I'll uncase you, and turn you loose to the wheel of fortune. Handy, seal this and let him run with it presently.

[*Exit Footman*]

MEDLEY Since y'are so resolved on a quarrel, why do you send her this kind note?

DORIMANT To keep her at home in order to the business. [*to the Shoemaker*] How now you drunken sot?

SHOEMAKER Z'bud,★ you have no reason to talk, I have not had a bottle of sack of yours in my belly this fortnight.

MEDLEY The orange woman says, your neighbours take notice what a heathen you are, and design to inform the bishop, and have you burned for an atheist.

SHOEMAKER Damn her, dunghill, if her husband does not remove her, she stinks so, the parish intend to indite him for a nuisance.

MEDLEY I advise you like a friend, reform your life, you have brought the envy of the world upon you, by living above yourself. Whoring and swearing are vices too genteel for a shoemaker.

SHOEMAKER Z'bud, I think you men of quality will grow as unreasonable as the women; you would engross† the sins o' the nation; poor folks can no sooner be wicked, but th'are railed at by their betters.

DORIMANT Sirrah, I'll have you stand i' the pillory for this libel.

SHOEMAKER Some of you deserve it, I'm sure, there are so many

★ Z'bud: S'blood, contraction of God's blood.   † engross: monopolise.

of 'em, that our journeymen nowadays instead of harmless ballads, sing nothing but your damned lampoons.

DORIMANT Our lampoons you rogue?

SHOEMAKER Nay, good master, why should not you write your own commentaries as well as Caesar.

MEDLEY The rascal's read, I perceive.

SHOEMAKER You know the old proverb, ale and history.*

DORIMANT Draw on my shoes, sirrah.

SHOEMAKER Here's a shoe.

DORIMANT Sits with more wrinkles than there are in an angry bully's forehead.

SHOEMAKER Z'bud, as smooth as your mistress's skin does upon her, so, strike your foot in home. Z'bud if e'er a monsieur of 'em all make more fashionable ware, I'll be content to have my ears whipped off with my own paring knife.

MEDLEY And served up in a ragout, instead of coxcombs to a company of French shoemakers for a collation.

SHOEMAKER Hold, hold, damn 'em caterpillars, let 'em feed upon cabbage; come master, your health this morning next my heart now.

DORIMANT Go, get you home, and govern your family better; do not let your wife follow you to the alehouse, beat your whore, and lead you home in triumph.

SHOEMAKER Z'bud, there's never a man i' the Town lives more like a gentleman, with his wife, than I do. I never mind her motions, she never enquires into mine, we speak to one another civilly, hate one another heartily, and because 'tis vulgar to lie and soak together, we have each of us our several settle-bed.

DORIMANT [*to Handy*] Give him half a crown.

MEDLEY Not without he will promise to be bloody drunk.

SHOEMAKER Tope's the word i' the eye of the world, for my master's honour, Robin.

DORIMANT Do not debauch my servants, sirrah.

SHOEMAKER I only tip him the wink, he knows an alehouse from a hovel.   [*Exit Shoemaker*]

DORIMANT My clothes quickly.

* ale and history: This may refer to the proverbial phrase 'truth is in ale as in history'.

MEDLEY Where shall we dine today?

DORIMANT Where you will; here comes a good third man.

Enter Young Bellair.

YOUNG BELLAIR Your servant gentlemen.

MEDLEY Gentle Sir; now will you answer this visit to your honourable mistress? 'Tis not her interest you should keep company with men of sense, who will be talking reason.

YOUNG BELLAIR I do not fear her pardon, do you but grant me yours, for my neglect of late.

MEDLEY Though y'ave made us miserable by the want of your good company; to show you I am free from all resentment, may the beautiful cause of our misfortune, give you all the joys happy lovers have shared ever since the world began.

YOUNG BELLAIR You wish me in heaven, but you believe me on my journey to hell.

MEDLEY You have a good strong faith, and that may contribute much towards your salvation. I confess I am but of an untoward constitution,* apt to have doubts and scruples, and in love they are no less distracting than in religion; were I so near marriage, I should cry out by fits as I ride in my coach 'Cuckold, cuckold' with no less fury than the mad fanatic does 'glory' in Bethlem.†

YOUNG BELLAIR Because religion makes some run mad, must I live an atheist?

MEDLEY Is it not great indiscretion for a man of credit, who may have money enough on his word, to go and deal with Jews; who for little sums make men enter into bonds, and give judgments?‡

YOUNG BELLAIR Preach no more on this text, I am determined, and there is no hope of my conversion.

DORIMANT [*to Handy who is fiddling about him*] Leave your unnecessary fiddling; a wasp that's buzzing about a man's nose at dinner, is not more troublesome than thou art.

HANDY You love to have your clothes hang just, Sir.

DORIMANT I love to be well-dressed Sir: and think it no scandal to my understanding.

* untoward constitution: not religious.
† Bethlem: Bethlehem hospital, an insane asylum, also known as Bedlam.
‡ give judgments: give goods as security.

HANDY Will you use the essence or orange-flower water?

DORIMANT I will smell as I do today, no offence to the ladies' noses.

HANDY Your pleasure Sir.   ⟨*Exit Handy*⟩

DORIMANT That a man's excellency should lie in neatly tying of a ribbon or a cravat! How careful's natu re in furnishing the world with necessary coxcombs.

YOUNG BELLAIR That's a mighty pretty suit of yours Dorimant.

DORIMANT I am glad 't has your approbation.

YOUNG BELLAIR No man in Town has a better fancy in his clothes than you have.

DORIMANT You will make me have an opinion of my genius.

MEDLEY There is a great critic I hear in these matters lately arrived piping hot from Paris.

YOUNG BELLAIR Sir Fopling Flutter you mean.

MEDLEY The same.

YOUNG BELLAIR He thinks himself the pattern of modern gallantry.

DORIMANT He is indeed the pattern of modern foppery.

MEDLEY He was yesterday at the play, with a pair of gloves up to his elbows, and a periwig more exactly curled than a lady's head newly dressed for a ball.

YOUNG BELLAIR What a pretty lisp he has!

DORIMANT Ho, that he affects in imitation of the people of quality of France.

MEDLEY His head stands for the most part on one side, and his looks are more languishing than a lady's when she lolls at stretch in her coach, or leans her head carelessly against the side of a box i' the playhouse.

DORIMANT He is a person indeed of great acquired follies.

MEDLEY He is like many others, beholding to his education for making him so eminent a coxcomb; many a fool had been lost to the world, had their indulgent parents wisely bestowed neither learning nor good breeding on 'em.

YOUNG BELLAIR He has been, as the sparkish word is, brisk upon the ladies already, he was yesterday at my Aunt Townley's, and gave Mrs Loveit a catalogue of his good qualities under the character of a complete gentleman, who according to Sir Fopling, ought to dress well, dance well, fence well, have a genius for love letters, an agreeable voice for a chamber, be very amorous, something discreet, but not over-constant.

MEDLEY Pretty ingredients to make an accomplished person.

DORIMANT I am glad he pitched upon Loveit.

YOUNG BELLAIR How so?

DORIMANT I wanted a fop to lay to her charge, and this is as pat as may be.

YOUNG BELLAIR I am confident she loves no man but you.

DORIMANT The good fortune were enough to make me vain, but that I am in my nature modest.

YOUNG BELLAIR Hark you Dorimant, with your leave Mr Medley, 'tis only a secret concerning a fair lady.

MEDLEY Your good breeding Sir gives you too much trouble, you might have whispered without all this ceremony.

YOUNG BELLAIR [*to Dorimant*] How stand your affairs with Bellinda of late?

DORIMANT She's a little jilting baggage.

YOUNG BELLAIR Nay, I believe her false enough, but she's ne'er the worse for your purpose; she was with you yesterday in a disguise at the play.

DORIMANT There we fell out, and resolved never to speak to one another more.

YOUNG BELLAIR The occasion?

DORIMANT Want of courage to meet me at the place appointed. These young women apprehend loving, as much as the young men do fighting at first; but once entered, like them too, they all turn bullies straight.

Enter Handy to Bellair.

HANDY Sir: your man without desires to speak with you.

YOUNG BELLAIR Gentlemen, I'll return immediately.

[*Exit Young Bellair*]

MEDLEY A very pretty fellow this.

DORIMANT He's handsome, well-bred, and by much the most tolerable of all the young men that do not abound in wit.

MEDLEY Ever well-dressed, always complaisant, and seldom impertinent; you and he are grown very intimate I see.

DORIMANT It is our mutual interest to be so; it makes the women think the better of his understanding, and judge more favourably of my reputation; it makes him pass upon some for a man of very good sense, and I upon others for a very civil person.

MEDLEY What was that whisper?

DORIMANT A thing which he would fain have known, but I did not think it fit to tell him; it might have frighted him from his honourable intentions of marrying.

MEDLEY Emilia, give her due, has the best reputation of any young woman about the Town; who has beauty enough to provoke detraction; her carriage is unaffected, her discourse modest, not at all censorious, nor pretending like the counterfeits of the age.

DORIMANT She's a discreet maid, and I believe nothing can corrupt her but a husband.

MEDLEY A husband?

DORIMANT Yes, a husband; I have known many women make a difficulty of losing a maidenhead, who have afterwards made none of making a cuckold.

MEDLEY This prudent consideration I am apt to think has made you confirm poor Bellair in the desperate resolution he has taken.

DORIMANT Indeed the little hope I found there was of her, in the state she was in, has made me by my advice, contribute something towards the changing of her condition.

Enter Young Bellair.

Dear Bellair, by heavens I thought we had lost thee, men in love are never reckoned on when we would form a company.

YOUNG BELLAIR Dorimant, I am undone, my man has brought the most surprising news i' the world.

DORIMANT Some strange misfortune is befallen your love.

YOUNG BELLAIR My father came to Town last night, and lodges i' the very house where Emilia lies.

MEDLEY Does he know it is with her you are in love?

YOUNG BELLAIR He knows I love, but knows not whom, without some officious sot has betrayed me.

DORIMANT Your Aunt Townley is your confident, and favours the business.

YOUNG BELLAIR I do not apprehend any ill office from her. I have received a letter in which I am commanded by my father to meet him at my aunt's this afternoon; he tells me farther he has made a match for me and bids me resolve to be obedient to his will, or expect to be disinherited.

MEDLEY Now's your time, Bellair, never had lover such an opportunity of giving a generous proof of his passion.

YOUNG BELLAIR As how I pray?

MEDLEY Why hang an estate, marry Emilia out of hand, and provoke your father to do what he threatens; 'tis but despising a coach, humbling yourself to a pair of galoshes, being out of countenance when you meet your friends, pointed at and pitied wherever you go by all the amorous fops that know you, and your fame will be immortal.

YOUNG BELLAIR I could find in my heart to resolve not to marry at all.

DORIMANT Fie, fie, that would spoil a good jest, and disappoint the well-natured Town of an occasion of laughing at you.

YOUNG BELLAIR The storm I have so long expected, hangs o'er my head, and begins to pour down upon me; I am on the rack, and can have no rest till I'm satisfied in what I fear; where do you dine?

DORIMANT At Long's, or Locket's.*

MEDLEY At Long's let it be.

YOUNG BELLAIR I'll run and see Emilia, and infom myself how matters stand; if my misfortunes are not so great as to make me unfit for company, I'll be with you.   [*Exit Young Bellair*]

Enter a Footman with a letter.

FOOTMAN [*to Dorimant*] Here's a letter Sir.

DORIMANT The superscription's right; 'For Mr Dorimant'.

MEDLEY Let's see the very scrawl and spelling of a true-bred whore.

DORIMANT I know the hand, the style is admirable I assure you.

MEDLEY Prithee read it.

DORIMANT [*reads*] 'I told you you dud not love me, if you dud, you would have seen me again ere now; I have no money and am

* Long's, or Locket's: fashionable taverns.

very mallicolly; pray send me a guynie to see the operies. Your servant to command, Molly.'

MEDLEY Pray let the whore have a favourable answer, that she may spark it in a box, and do honour to her profession.

DORIMANT She shall; and perk up i' the face of quality. Is the coach at door?

HANDY You did not bid me send for it.

DORIMANT Eternal blockhead! [*Handy offers to go*] Hey sot. –

HANDY Did you call me, Sir?

DORIMANT I hope you have no just exception to the name, Sir?

HANDY I have sense, Sir.

DORIMANT Not so much as a fly in winter – how did you come Medley?

MEDLEY In a chair!

FOOTMAN You may have a hackney coach if you please, Sir.

DORIMANT I may ride the elephant if I please, Sir; call another chair, and let my coach follow to Long's. 'Be calm ye great parents, etc.'.

[Exit singing]

ACT TWO

SCENE I

Enter my Lady Townley, and Emilia.

LADY TOWNLEY I was afraid Emilia, all had been discovered.

EMILIA I tremble with the apprehension still.

LADY TOWNLEY That my brother should take lodgings i' the very house where you lie.

EMILIA 'Twas lucky, we had timely notice to warn the people to be secret, he seems to be a mighty good-humoured old man.

LADY TOWNLEY He ever had a notable smirking way with him.

EMILIA He calls me rogue, tells me he can't abide me; and does so bepat me.

LADY TOWNLEY On my word you are much in his favour then.

EMILIA He has been very inquisitive I am told about my family, my reputation, and my fortune.

LADY TOWNLEY I am confident he does not i' the least suspect you are the woman his son's in love with.

EMILIA What should make him then inform himself so particularly of me?

LADY TOWNLEY He was always of a very loving temper himself; it may be he has a doting fit upon him, who knows.

EMILIA It cannot be.

Enter Young Bellair.

LADY TOWNLEY Here comes my nephew. Where did you leave your father?

YOUNG BELLAIR Writing a note within. Emilia, this early visit looks as if some kind jealousy would not let you rest at home.

EMILIA The knowledge I have of my rival, gives me a little cause to fear your constancy.

YOUNG BELLAIR My constancy! I vow –

EMILIA Do not vow. Our love is frail as is our life, and full as little in our power, and are you sure you shall outlive this day?

YOUNG BELLAIR I am not, but when we are in perfect health, 'twere an idle thing to fright ourselves with the thoughts of sudden death.

LADY TOWNLEY Pray what has passed between you and your
father i' the garden.

YOUNG BELLAIR He's firm in his resolution, tells me I must
marry Mrs Harriet, or swears he'll marry himself and disinherit
me, when I saw I could not prevail with him to be more indulgent, I dissembled an obedience to his will, which has composed
his passion, and will give us time, and I hope opportunity to
deceive him.

Enter Old Bellair, with a note in his hand.

LADY TOWNLEY Peace, here he comes.

OLD BELLAIR Harry, take this, and let your man carry it for me
to Mr Fourbe's chamber, my lawyer i' the Temple.* [*to Emilia*]
Neighbour, adod I am glad to see thee here, make much of her,
sister, she's one of the best of your acquaintance, I like her
countenance and her behaviour well, she has a modesty that is
not common i' this age, adod, she has.

LADY TOWNLEY I know her value brother, and esteem her
accordingly.

OLD BELLAIR Advise her to wear a little more mirth in her face,
adod she's too serious.

LADY TOWNLEY The fault is very excusable in a young woman.

OLD BELLAIR Nay, adod, I like her ne'er the worse, a melancholy beauty has her charms, I love a pretty sadness in a face
which varies now and then, like changeable colours, into a smile.

LADY TOWNLEY Methinks you speak very feelingly brother.

OLD BELLAIR I am but five and fifty sister you know, an age not
altogether unsensible! Cheer up sweetheart; [*to Emilia*] I have a
secret to tell thee may chance to make thee merry, we three will
make collation together anon, i' the meantime, mum, I can't
abide you, go I can't abide you. Harry, come you must along with
me to my Lady Woodvill's. I am going to slip the boy at a mistress.

YOUNG BELLAIR At a wife sir, you would say.

OLD BELLAIR You need not look so glum, Sir, a wife is no curse
when she brings the blessing of a good estate with her, but an

* the Temple: the centre of the legal profession in London.

idle Town flirt, with a painted face, a rotten reputation, and a crazy fortune, adod is the devil and all, and such a one I hear you are in league with.

YOUNG BELLAIR I cannot help detraction, Sir.

OLD BELLAIR Out, a pise o' their breeches, there are keeping fools* enough for such flaunting baggages, and they are e'en too good for 'em. [*to Emilia*] Remember night, go y'are a rogue, y'are a rogue; fare you well, fare you well, come, come, come along, Sir.

[*Exeunt Old and Young Bellair*]

LADY TOWNLEY On my word the old man comes on apace; I'll lay my life he's smitten.

EMILIA This is nothing but the pleasantness of his humour.

LADY TOWNLEY I know him better than you, let it work, it may prove lucky.

Enter a Page.

PAGE Madam, Mr Medley has sent to know whether a visit will not be troublesome this afternoon?

LADY TOWNLEY Send him word his visits never are so.

EMILIA He's a very pleasant man.

LADY TOWNLEY He's a very necessary man among us women; he's not scandalous i' the least, perpetually contriving to bring good company together, and always ready to stop up a gap at ombre,† then he knows all the little news o' the Town.

EMILIA I love to hear him talk o' the intrigues, let 'em be never so dull in themselves, he'll make 'em pleasant i' the relation.

LADY TOWNLEY But he improves things so much one can take no measure of the truth from him. Mr Dorimant swears a flea or a maggot, is not made more monstrous by a magnifying glass, than a story is by his telling it.

EMILIA Hold, here he comes.

Enter Medley.

LADY TOWNLEY Mr Medley.

MEDLEY Your servant Madam.

LADY TOWNLEY You have made yourself a stranger of late.

---

* keeping fools: men who keep mistresses.
† ombre: a card game, played by three persons.

EMILIA I believe you took surfeit of ombre last time you were here.

MEDLEY Indeed I had my belly full of that termagant Lady Dealer; there never was so unsatiable a carder, an old gleeker* never loved to fit to't like her; I have played with her now at least a dozen times, till she's worn out all her fine complexion, and her tour† would keep in curl no longer.

LADY TOWNLEY Blame her not poor woman, she loves nothing so well as a black ace.

MEDLEY The pleasure I have seen her in when she has had hope in drawing for a matador.‡

EMILIA 'Tis as pretty sport to her, as persuading masks off is to you to make discoveries.

LADY TOWNLEY Pray where's your friend, Mr Dorimant?

MEDLEY Soliciting his affairs, he's a man of great employment, has more mistresses now depending than the most eminent lawyer in England has causes.

EMILIA Here has been Mrs Loveit, so uneasy and out of humour these two days.

LADY TOWNLEY How strangely love and jealousy rage in that poor woman!

MEDLEY She could not have picked out a devil upon earth so proper to torment her, has made her break a dozen or two of fans already, tear half a score points§ in pieces, and destroy hoods and knots‖ without number.

LADY TOWNLEY We heard of a pleasant serenade he gave her t'other night.

MEDLEY A Danish serenade with kettledrums and trumpets.

EMILIA O barbarous!

MEDLEY What, you are of the number of the ladies whose ears are grown so delicate since our operas, you can be charmed with nothing but *flûtes douces*,¶ and French hautboys.**

---

* gleeker: a player of gleek, another card game.
† tour: a crescent-shaped front of false hair.
‡ a black ace . . . matador: the highest trumps in ombre, the black ace and a third card were known as matadors.
§ points: pieces of lace.   ‖ knots: ribbons in bows.
¶ *flûtes douces*: high-pitched flutes.   ** hautboys: oboes.

EMILIA Leave your raillery, and tell us, is there any new wit come forth, songs or novels?

MEDLEY A very pretty piece of gallantry, by an eminent author, called *The Diversions of Bruxelles*★ very necessary to be read by all old ladies who are desirous to improve themselves at questions and commands,† blind-man's buff, and the like fashionable recreations.

EMILIA O ridiculous!

MEDLEY Then there is *The Art of Affectation*,‡ written by a late beauty of quality, teaching you how to draw up your breasts, stretch up your neck, to thrust out your breech, to play with your head, to toss up your nose, to bite your lips, to turn up your eyes, to speak in a silly soft tone of a voice, and use all the foolish French words that will infallibly make your person and conversation charming, with a short apology at the latter end, in the behalf of young ladies, who notoriously wash, and paint, though they have naturally good complexions.

EMILIA What a deal of stuff you tell us?

MEDLEY Such as the Town affords Madam. The Russians hearing the great respect we have for foreign dancing, have lately sent over some of their best balladins, who are now practising a famous ballet which will be suddenly danced at the Bear Garden.§

LADY TOWNLEY Pray forbear your idle stories, and give us an account of the state of love, as it now stands.

MEDLEY Truly there has been some revolutions in those affairs, great chopping and changing among the old, and some new lovers, whom malice, indiscretion, and misfortune, have luckily brought into play.

LADY TOWNLEY What think you of walking into the next room, and sitting down before you engage in this business?

MEDLEY I wait upon you, and I hope (though women are commonly unreasonable) by the plenty of scandal I shall discover, to give you very good content ladies. ⟨*Exeunt*⟩

★ *The Diversions of Bruxelles*: probably an invented title. R. S. Cox, 'Richard Flecknoe and *The Man of Mode*', *Modern Language Quarterly*, xxix, 1968, 183–9, suggests it is Flecknoe's *Treatise of the Sports of Wit*

† questions and commands: a game.

‡ *The Art of Affectation*: also probably invented, though it may refer to *The Gentlewoman's Companion*, 1675.

§ the Bear Garden: an amphitheatre for bear-baiting on Bankside.

SCENE II

Enter Mrs Loveit and Pert.

MRS LOVEIT [*putting up a letter, then pulling out her pocket glass, and looking in it*] Pert.

PERT Madam.

MRS LOVEIT I hate myself, I look so ill today.

PERT Hate the wicked cause on't, that base man Mr Dorimant, who makes you torment and vex yourself continually.

MRS LOVEIT He is to blame indeed.

PERT To blame to be two days without sending, writing, or coming near you, contrary to his oath and covenant; 'twas to much purpose to make him swear; I'll lay my life there's not an article but he has broken, talked to the vizards i' the pit, waited upon the ladies from the boxes to their coaches; gone behind the scenes, and fawned upon those little insignificant creatures, the players; 'tis impossible for a man of his inconstant temper to forbear I'm sure.

MRS LOVEIT I know he is a devil, but he has something of the angel yet undefaced in him, which makes him so charming and agreeable, that I must love him be he never so wicked.

PERT I little thought Madam to see your spirit tamed to this degree, who banished poor Mr Lackwit but for taking up another lady's fan in your presence.

MRS LOVEIT My knowing of such odious fools, contributes to the making of me love Dorimant the better.

PERT Your knowing of Mr Dorimant, in my mind, should rather make you hate all mankind.

MRS LOVEIT So it does, besides himself.

PERT Pray, what excuse does he make in his letter?

MRS LOVEIT He has had business.

PERT Business in general terms would not have been a current excuse for another; a modish man is always very busy when he is in pursuit of a new mistress.

MRS LOVEIT Some fop has bribed you to rail at him; he had business, I will believe it, and will forgive him.

PERT You may forgive him anything, but I shall never forgive him his turning me into ridicule, as I hear he does.

MRS LOVEIT I perceive you are of the number of those fools his wit had made his enemies.

PERT I am of the number of those he's pleased to rally, Madam; and if we may believe Mr Wagfan, and Mr Caperwell, he sometimes makes merry with yourself too, among his laughing companions.

MRS LOVEIT Blockheads are as malicious to witty men, as ugly women are to the handsome; 'tis their interest, and they make it their business to defame 'em.

PERT I wish Mr Dorrimant would not make it his business to defame you.

MRS LOVEIT Should he, I had rather be made infamous by him, than owe my reputation to the dull discretion of those fops you talk of. Bellinda!

Enter Bellinda.

BELLINDA My dear.

MRS LOVEIT [*running to her*] You have been unkind of late.

BELLINDA Do not say unkind, say unhappy!

MRS LOVEIT I could chide you, where have you been these two days?

BELLINDA Pity me rather my dear, where I have been so tired with two or three country gentlewomen, whose conversation has been more insufferable than a country fiddle.

MRS LOVEIT Are they relations?

BELLINDA No, Welsh acquaintance I made when I was last year at St Winifred's,* they have asked me a thousand questions of the modes and intrigues of the Town and I have told 'em almost as many things for news that hardly were so, when their gowns were in fashion.

MRS LOVEIT Provoking creatures, how could you endure 'em?

BELLINDA [*aside*] Now to carry on my plot, nothing but love could make me capable of so much falsehood; 'tis time to begin,

* St Winifred's: St Winifred gave her name to Holywell in Wales, where her well is supposed to have risen where her head fell, cut off by a pagan prince whose advances she had refused.

lest Dorimant should come before her jealousy has stung her; [*laughs and then speaks on*] I was yesterday at a play with 'em, where I was fain to show 'em the living, as the man at Westminster* does the dead; that is Mrs Such-a-one admired for her beauty, this is Mr Such-a-one cried up for a wit; that is sparkish Mr Such-a-one who keeps reverend Mrs Such-a-one, and there sits fine Mrs Such-a-one who was lately cast off by my Lord Such-a-one.

MRS LOVEIT Did you see Dorimant there?

BELLINDA I did, and imagine you were there with him, and have no mind to own it.

MRS LOVEIT What should make you think so?

BELLINDA A lady masked in a pretty *déshabillé* whom Dorimant entertained with more respect, than the gallants do a common vizard.

MRS LOVEIT [*aside*] Dorimant at the play entertaining a mask, O heavens!

BELLINDA [*aside*] Good.

MRS LOVEIT Did he stay all the while?

BELLINDA Till the play was done, and then led her out, which confirms me it was you!

MRS LOVEIT Traitor!

PERT Now you may believe he had business, and you may forgive him too.

MRS LOVEIT Ungrateful perjured man!

BELLINDA You seem so much concerned my dear, I feel I have told you unawares what I had better have concealed for your quiet.

MRS LOVEIT What manner of shape had she?

BELLINDA Tall and slender, her motions were very genteel, certainly she must be some person of condition.

MRS LOVEIT Shame and confusion be ever in her face when she shows it.

BELLINDA I should blame your discretion for loving that wild man my dear, but they say he has a way so bewitching, that few can defend their hearts who know him.

MRS LOVEIT I will tear him from mine, or die i' the attempt.

BELLINDA Be more moderate.

* the man at Westminster: the guide at Westminster Abbey.

MRS LOVEIT Would I had daggers, darts, or poisoned arrows in my breast, so I could but remove the thoughts of him from thence.

BELLINDA Fie, fie, your transports are too violent, my dear. This may be but an accidental gallantry, and 'tis likely ended at her coach.

PERT Should it proceed farther, let your comfort be, the conduct of Mr Dorimant affects, will quickly make you know your rival, ten to one let you see her ruined, her reputation exposed to the Town, a happiness none will envy her but yourself Madam.

MRS LOVEIT Whoe'er she be, all the harm I wish her, is may she love him as well as I do, and may he give her as much cause to hate him.

PERT Never doubt the latter end of your curse Madam!

MRS LOVEIT May all the passions that are raised by neglected love, jealousy, indignation, spite, and thirst of revenge, eternally rage in her soul, as they do now in mine. [*walks up and down with a distracted air*]

Enter a Page.

PAGE Madam, Mr Dorimant –

MRS LOVEIT I will not see him.

PAGE I told him you were within, Madam.

MRS LOVEIT Say you lied, say I'm busy, shut the door; say anything.

PAGE He's here Madam.

Enter Dorimant.

DORIMANT 'They taste of death who do at heaven arrive,
But we this paradise approach alive.'*

[*to Mrs Loveit*] What dancing the galloping nag† without a fiddle?
[*offers to catch her hand, she flings away and walks on. Pursuing her*] I fear this restlessness of the body, Madam, proceeds from an unquietness of the mind. What unlucky accident puts you out of humour; a point ill-washed, knots spoiled i' the making up, hair

---

* They taste . . . alive: The first two lines of Waller's 'Of Her Chamber' with 'who' substituted for the original 'that'.
† galloping nag: a country dance.

shaded awry, or some other little mistake in setting you in order?

PERT A trifle in my opinion, Sir, more inconsiderable than any you mention.

DORIMANT O Mrs Pert, I never knew you sullen enough to be silent, come let me know the business.

PERT The business, Sir, is the business that has taken you up these two days, how have I seen you laugh at men of business, and now to become a man of business yourself!

DORIMANT We are not masters of our own affections, our inclinations daily alter; now we love pleasure, and anon we shall dote on business; human frailty will have it so, and who can help it.

MRS LOVEIT Faithless, inhuman, barbarous man –

DORIMANT ⟨*aside*⟩ Good, now the alarm strikes.

MRS LOVEIT Without sense of love, of honour, or of gratitude, tell me, for I will know, what devil masked she was, you were with at the play yesterday?

DORIMANT Faith I resolved as much as you, but the devil was obstinate, and would not tell me.

MRS LOVEIT False in this as in your vows to me, you do know!

DORIMANT The truth is I did all I could to know.

MRS LOVEIT And dare you own it to my face; hell and furies! [*tears her fan in pieces*]

DORIMANT Spare your fan, Madam, you are growing hot, and will want it to cool you.

MRS LOVEIT Horror and distraction seize you, sorrow and remorse gnaw your soul, and punish all your perjuries to me. [*weeps*]

DORIMANT 'So thunder breaks the cloud in twain,
And makes a passage for the rain'.★
[*turning to Bellinda*] Bellinda, you are the devil that have raised this storm; you were at the play yesterday, and have been making discoveries to your dear.

BELLINDA Y'are the most mistaken man i' the world.

DORIMANT It must be so, and here I vow revenge, resolve to

★ 'So thunder . . . rain': From Matthew Roydon's 'An Elegy, or Friend's Passion, for his Astrophill', with 'breaks' substituted for the original's 'rends'. (This was identified by R. G. Howarth, 'Untraced Quotations in Etherege', *Notes and Queries*, CLXXXVIII, June 1945.)

pursue, and persecute you more impertinently than ever any loving fop did his mistress, hunt you i' the Park,★ trace you i' the Mall,† dog you in every visit you make, haunt you at the plays, and i' the drawing room, hang my nose in your neck, and talk to you whether you will or no, and ever look upon you with such dying eyes, till your friends grow jealous of me, send you out of Town, and the world suspect your reputation. [*in a lower voice*] At my Lady Townley's when we go from hence. [*he looks kindly on Bellinda*]

BELLINDA I'll meet you there.

DORIMANT Enough.

MRS LOVEIT [*pushing Dorimant away*] Stand off, you sha' not stare upon her so.

DORIMANT Good! There's one made jealous already.

MRS LOVEIT Is this the constancy you vowed?

DORIMANT Constancy at my years! 'Tis not a virtue in season, you might as well expect the fruit the autumn ripens i' the spring.

MRS LOVEIT Monstrous principle!

DORIMANT Youth has a long journey to go, Madam, should I have set up my rest at the first inn I lodged at, I should never have arrived at the happiness I now enjoy.

MRS LOVEIT Dissembler, damned dissembler!

DORIMANT I am so I confess, good nature, and good manners corrupt me, I am honest in my inclinations, and would not, wer't not to avoid offence, make a lady a little in years believe I think her young, wilfully mistake art for nature; and seem as fond of a thing I am weary of, as when I doted on't in earnest.

MRS LOVEIT False man.

DORIMANT True woman.

MRS LOVEIT Now you begin to show yourself!

DORIMANT Love gilds us over, and makes us show fine things to one another for a time, but soon the gold wears off, and then again the native brass appears.

MRS LOVEIT Think on your oaths, your vows and protestations, perjured man.

★ the Park: either Hyde Park or St James's Park.
† the Mall: the walk bordering St James's Park.

DORIMANT I made 'em when I was in love.

MRS LOVEIT And therefore ought they not to bind? O impious!

DORIMANT What we swear at such a time may be a certain proof of a present passion, but to say truth, in love there is no security to be given for the future.

MRS LOVEIT Horrid and ungrateful, begone, and never see me more.

DORIMANT I am not one of those troublesome coxcombs, who because they were once well received, take the privilege to plague a woman with their love ever after; I shall obey you, Madam, though I do myself some violence. [*he offers to go, and Mrs Loveit pulls him back*]

MRS LOVEIT Come back, you sha'not go. Could you have the ill nature to offer it?

DORIMANT When love grows diseased the best thing we can do is to put it to a violent death; I cannot endure the torture of a lingering and consumptive passion.

MRS LOVEIT Can you think mine sickly?

DORIMANT Oh, 'tis desperately ill! What worse symptoms are there than your being always uneasy when I visit you, your picking quarrels with me on slight occasions, and in my absence kindly listening to the impertinences of every fashionable fool that talks to you?

MRS LOVEIT What fashionable fool can you lay to my charge?

DORIMANT Why the very cock-fool of all those fools, Sir Fopling Flutter.

MRS LOVEIT I never saw him in my life but once.

DORIMANT The worse woman you at first sight to put on all your charms, to entertain him with that softness in your voice, and all that wanton kindness in your eyes, you so notoriously affect, when you design a conquest.

MRS LOVEIT So damned a lie did never malice yet invent; who told you this?

DORIMANT No matter; that ever I should love a woman that can dote on a senseless caper, a tawdry French ribbon, and a formal cravat.

MRS LOVEIT You make me mad.

DORIMANT A guilty conscience may do much, go on, be the

game-mistress o' the Town, and enter all our young fops as fast as they come from travail.

MRS LOVEIT Base and scurrilous!

DORIMANT A fine mortifying reputation 'twill be for a woman of your pride, wit, and quality!

MRS LOVEIT This jealousy's a mere pretence, a cursed trick of your own devising; I know you.

DORIMANT Believe it and all the ill of me you can, I would not have a woman have the least good thought of me, that can think well of Fopling; farewell, fall to, and much good may do you with your coxcomb.

MRS LOVEIT Stay, O stay, and I will tell you all.

DORIMANT I have been told too much already.   [*Exit Dorimant*]

MRS LOVEIT Call him again.

PERT E'en let him go, a fair riddance.

MRS LOVEIT Run I say, call him again, I will have him called.

PERT The devil should carry him away first, were it my concern.

[*Exit Pert*]

BELLINDA H'as frighted me from the very thoughts of loving men; for heaven's sake, my dear, do not discover what I told you; I dread his tongue as much as you ought to have done his friendship.

Enter Pert.

PERT He's gone, Madam.

MRS LOVEIT Lightning blast him.

PERT When I told him you desired him to come back, he smiled, made a mouth at me, flung into his coach, and said –

MRS LOVEIT What did he say?

PERT 'Drive away', and then repeated verses.

MRS LOVEIT Would I had made a contract to be a witch when first I entertained this greater devil, monster, barbarian; I could tear myself in pieces. Revenge, nothing but revenge can ease me; plague, war, famine, fire, all that can bring universal ruin and misery on mankind, with joy I'd perish to have you in my power but this moment.   [*Exit Mrs Loveit*]

PERT Follow Madam, leave her not in this outrageous passion.

[*Pert gathers up the things*]

BELLINDA H'as given me the proof which I desired of his love, but 'tis a proof of his ill nature too; I wish I had not seen him use her so.
I sigh to think that Dorimant may be,
One day as faithless, and unkind to me.

[*Exeunt*]

ACT THREE

Lady Woodvil's lodgings

Enter Harriet, and Busy her woman.

BUSY Dear Madam! Let me set that curl in order.

HARRIET Let me alone, I will shake 'em all out of order.

BUSY Will you never leave this wildness?

HARRIET Torment me not.

BUSY Look! There's a knot falling off.

HARRIET Let it drop.

BUSY But one pin, dear Madam,

HARRIET How do I daily suffer under thy officious fingers?

BUSY Ah the difference that is between you and my Lady Dapper. How uneasy she is if the least thing be amiss about her?

HARRIET She is indeed most exact! Nothing is ever wanting to make her ugliness remarkable!

BUSY Jeering people say so!

HARRIET Her powdering, painting, and her patching never fail in public to draw the tongues and eyes of all the men upon her.

BUSY She is indeed a little too pretending.

HARRIET That woman should set up for beauty as much in spite of nature, as some men have done for wit.

BUSY I hope without offence one may endeavour to make oneself agreeable.

HARRIET Not, when 'tis impossible. Women then ought to be no more fond of dressing than fools should be of talking; hoods and modesty, masks and silence, things that shadow and conceal; they should think of nothing else.

BUSY Jesu! Madam, what will your mother think is become of you? For heaven's sake go in again.

HARRIET I won't!

BUSY This is the extravagant'st thing that ever you did in your life, to leave her and a gentleman who is to be your husband.

HARRIET My husband! Hast thou so little wit to think I spoke what I meant when I overjoyed her in the country, with a low curtsy and 'What you please, Madam, I shall ever be obedient'.

BUSY Nay, I know not, you have so many fetches.*

HARRIET And this was one, to get her up to London! Nothing else I assure thee.

BUSY Well, the man, in my mind, is a fine man!

HARRIET The man indeed wears his clothes fashionably, and has a pretty negligent way with him, very courtly, and much affected; he bows, and talks, and smiles so agreeably as he thinks.

BUSY I never saw anything so genteel!

HARRIET Varnished over with good breeding, many a blockhead makes a tolerable show.

BUSY I wonder you do not like him.

HARRIET I think I might be brought to endure him, and that is all a reasonable woman should expect in a husband, but there is duty i' the case – and like the haughty Merab,† I 'find much aversion in my stubborn mind,' which 'is bred by being promised and designed'.‡

BUSY I wish you do not design your own ruin! I partly guess your inclinations Madam – that Mr Dorimant –

HARRIET Leave your prating, and sing some foolish song or other.

BUSY I will, the song you love so well ever since you saw Mr Dorimant.

SONG

When first Amintas charmed my heart,
My heedless sheep began to stray;
The wolves soon stole the greatest part,
And all will now be made a prey.

Ah, let not love your thoughts possess,
'Tis fatal to a shepherdess;
The dangerous passion you must shun,
Or else like me be quite undone.

* fetches: tricks.

† Merab: Saul's elder daughter, who was promised to David, but married to Adriel.

‡ find much . . . designed: This is an echo of Cowley's *Davideis* III where Merab is described: 'And much aversion in her stubborn mind/Was bred by being promised and designed'.

HARRIET Shall I be paid down by a covetous parent for a purchase? I need no land; no, I'll lay myself out all in love. It is decreed –

Enter Young Bellair.

YOUNG BELLAIR What generous resolution are you making, Madam?

HARRIET Only to be disobedient, Sir.

YOUNG BELLAIR Let me join hands with you in that –

HARRIET With all my heart, I never thought I should have given you mine so willingly. Here I Harriet –

YOUNG BELLAIR And I Harry –

HARRIET Do solemnly protest –

YOUNG BELLAIR And vow –

HARRIET That I with you –

YOUNG BELLAIR And I with you –

BOTH Will never marry –

HARRIET A match!

YOUNG BELLAIR And no match! How do you like this indifference now?

HARRIET You expect I should take it ill I see!

YOUNG BELLAIR 'Tis not unnatural for you women to be a little angry, you miss a conquest, though you would slight the poor man were he in your power.

HARRIET There are some it may be have an eye like Bart'lomew,* big enough for the whole Fair, but I am not of the number, and you may keep your gingerbread. 'Twill be more acceptable to the lady, whose dear image it wears Sir.

YOUNG BELLAIR I must confess Madam, you came a day after the Fair.†

HARRIET You own then you are in love –

YOUNG BELLAIR I do.

HARRIET The confidence is generous, and in return I could almost find in my heart to let you know my inclinations.

YOUNG BELLAIR Are you in love?

---

* Bart'lomew: a reference to the wildness of Bartholomew Cokes in Jonson's *Bartholomew Fair*.

† Fair: The Fair was held on St Bartholomew's day in Smithfield, on 24 August.

HARRIET Yes, with this dear Town, to that degree, I can scare endure the country in landscapes and in hangings.

YOUNG BELLAIR What a dreadful thing 'twould be to be hurried back to Hampshire!

HARRIET Ah – name it not! –

YOUNG BELLAIR As for us, I find we shall agree well enough! Would we could do something to deceive the grave people!

HARRIET Could we delay their quick proceeding, 'twere well, a reprieve is a good step towards the getting of a pardon.

YOUNG BELLAIR If we give over the game, we are undone! What think you of playing it on booty?

HARRIET What do you mean?

YOUNG BELLAIR Pretend to be in love with one another! 'Twill make some dilatory excuses we may feign, pass the better.

HARRIET Let us do't, if it be but for the dear pleasure of dissembling.

YOUNG BELLAIR Can you play your part?

HARRIET I know not what it is to love, but I have made pretty remarks by being now and then where lovers meet. Where did you leave their gravities?

YOUNG BELLAIR I'th' next room! Your mother was censuring our modern gallant.

Enter Old Bellair and Lady Woodvil.

HARRIET Peace! Here they come, I will lean against this wall, and look bashfully down upon my fan, while you like an amorous spark modishly entertain me.

LADY WOODVIL Never go about to excuse 'em, come, come, it was not so when I was a young woman.

OLD BELLAIR Adod, they're something disrespectful –

LADY WOODVIL Quality was then considered, and not rallied by every fleering* fellow.

OLD BELLAIR Youth will have its jest, adod it will.

LADY WOODVIL 'Tis good breeding now to be civil to none but players and Exchange women,† they are treated by 'em as much above their condition, as others are below theirs.

* fleering: sneering, jeering.

† Exchange women: shopgirls in the New Exchange.

OLD BELLAIR Out a pise on 'em, talk no more, the rogues ha' got an ill habit of preferring beauty, no matter where they find it.

LADY WOODVIL See your son, and my daughter, they have improved their acquaintance since they were within.

OLD BELLAIR Adod methinks they have! Let's keep back and observe.

YOUNG BELLAIR Now for a look and gestures that may persuade 'em I am saying all the passionate things imaginable –

HARRIET Your head a little more on one side, ease yourself on your left leg, and play with your right hand.

YOUNG BELLAIR Thus, is it not?

HARRIET Now set your right leg firm on the ground, adjust your belt, then look about you.

YOUNG BELLAIR A little exercising will make me perfect.

HARRIET Smile and turn to me again very sparkish!

YOUNG BELLAIR Will you take your turn and be instructed?

HARRIET With all my heart.

YOUNG BELLAIR At one motion play your fan, roll your eyes, and then settle a kind look upon me.

HARRIET So.

YOUNG BELLAIR Now spread your fan, look down upon it, and tell the sticks with a finger.

HARRIET Very modish.

YOUNG BELLAIR Clap your hand up to your bosom, hold down your gown. Shrug a little, draw up your breasts, and let 'em fall again, gently, with a sigh or two, etc.

HARRIET By the good instructions you give, I suspect you for one of those malicious observers who watch people's eyes, and from innocent looks, make scandalous conclusions.

YOUNG BELLAIR I know some indeed who out of mere love to mischief are as vigilant as jealousy itself, and will give you an account of every glance that passes at a play, and i'th' Circle!*

HARRIET 'Twill not be amiss now to seem a little pleasant.

YOUNG BELLAIR Clap your fan then in both your hands, snatch it to your mouth, smile, and with a lively motion fling your body

* th'Circle: Either the assembly at Court or, more likely, a circular path, sometimes called the Ring, in Hyde Park, where people walked, rode, and assembled in carriages. See III, iii, p. 568.

a little forwards. So – now spread it; fall back on the sudden, cover your face with it, and break out into a loud laughter – take up! Look grave, and fall a-fanning of yourself – admirably well acted.

HARRIET I think I am pretty apt at these matters!

OLD BELLAIR Adod I like this well.

LADY WOODVIL This promises something.

OLD BELLAIR Come! There is love i'th case, adod there is, or will be; what say you young lady?

HARRIET All in good time Sir, you expect we should fall to, and love as gamecocks fight, as soon as we are set together, adod y'are unreasonable!

OLD BELLAIR Adod sirrah, I like thy wit well.

Enter a Servant.

SERVANT The coach is at the door madam.

OLD BELLAIR Go, get you and take the air together.

LADY WOODVIL Will you not go with us?

OLD BELLAIR Out a pise: adod I ha' business and cannot. We shall meet at night at my sister Townley's.

YOUNG BELLAIR [*aside*] He's going to Emilia. I overheard him talk of a collation. [*Exeunt*]

SCENE II

Enter Lady Townley, Emilia, and Medley.

LADY TOWNLEY I pity the young lovers, we last talked of, though to say truth their conduct has been so indiscreet, they deserve to be unfortunate.

MEDLEY Y'have had an exact account, from the great lady i'th' box down to the little orange-wench.

EMILIA Y'are a living libel, a breathing lampoon; I wonder you are not torn in pieces.

MEDLEY What think you of setting up an office of intelligence for these matters? The project may get money.

LADY TOWNLEY You would have great dealings with country ladies.

MEDLEY More than Muddiman has with their husbands.*

Enter Bellinda.

LADY TOWNLEY Bellinda, what has been become of you! We have not seen you here of late with your friend Mrs Loveit.

BELLINDA Dear creature, I left her but now so sadly afflicted.

LADY TOWNLEY With her old distemper jealousy!

MEDLEY Dorimant has played her some new prank.

BELLINDA Well, that Dorimant is certainly the worst man breathing.

EMILIA I once thought so.

BELLINDA And do you not think so still?

EMILIA No indeed!

BELLINDA O Jesu!

EMILIA The Town does him a great deal of injury, and I will never believe what it says of a man I do not know again for his sake!

BELLINDA You make me wonder!

LADY TOWNLEY He's a very well-bred man.

BELLINDA But strangely ill-natured.

EMILIA Then he's a very witty man!

BELLINDA But a man of no principles.

MEDLEY Your man of principles is a very fine thing indeed.

BELLINDA To be preferred to men of parts by women who have regard to their reputation and quiet. Well were I minded to play the fool, he should be the last man I'd think of.

MEDLEY He has been the first in many ladies' favours, though you are so severe, Madam.

LADY TOWNLEY What he may be for a lover I know not, but he's a very pleasant acquaintance I am sure.

BELLINDA Had you seen him use Mrs Loveit as I have done, you would never endure him more –

EMILIA What he has quarrelled with her again!

BELLINDA Upon the slightest occasion, he's jealous of Sir Fopling.

LADY TOWNLEY She never saw him in her life but yesterday, and that was here.

* Muddiman: Henry Muddiman (1629–1692), author of a newsletter.

EMILIA On my conscience! He's the only man in Town that's her aversion, how horribly out of humour she was all the while he talked to her!

BELLINDA And somebody has wickedly told him –

EMILIA Here he comes.

Enter Dorimant.

MEDLEY Dorimant! You are luckily come to justify yourself – here's a lady –

BELLINDA Has a word or two to say to you from a disconsolate person.

DORIMANT You tender your reputation too much I know Madam, to whisper with me before this good company.

BELLINDA To serve Mrs Loveit, I'll make a bold venture.

DORIMANT Here's Medley the very spirit of scandal.

BELLINDA No matter!

EMILIA 'Tis something you are unwilling to hear, Mr Dorimant.

LADY TOWNLEY Tell him Bellinda whether he will or no!

BELLINDA [*aloud*] Mrs Loveit!

DORIMANT Softly, these are laughers, you do not know 'em.

BELLINDA [*to Dorimant apart*] In a word y'ave made me hate you, which I thought you never could have done.

DORIMANT In obeying your commands.

BELLINDA 'Twas a cruel part you played! How could you act it?

DORIMANT Nothing is cruel to a man who could kill himself to please you; remember five o'clock tomorrow morning.

BELLINDA I tremble when you name it.

DORIMANT Be sure you come.

BELLINDA I sha' not.

DORIMANT Swear you will!

BELLINDA I dare not.

DORIMANT Swear I say.

BELLINDA By my life! By all the happiness I hope for –

DORIMANT You will.

BELLINDA I will.

DORIMANT Kind.

BELLINDA I am glad I've sworn, I vow I think I should ha' failed you else!

DORIMANT Surprisingly kind! In what temper did you leave Loveit?

BELLINDA Her raving was prettily over, and she began to be in a brave way of defying you, and all your works. Where have you been since you went from thence?

DORIMANT I looked in at the play.

BELLINDA I have promised and must return to her again.

DORIMANT Persuade her to walk in the Mall this evening.

BELLINDA She hates the place and will not come.

DORIMANT Do all you can to prevail with her.

BELLINDA For what purpose?

DORIMANT Sir Fopling will be here anon, I'll prepare him to set upon her there before me.

BELLINDA You persecute her too much, but I'll do all you'll ha' me.

DORIMANT [*aloud*] Tell her plainly, 'tis grown so dull a business I can drudge on no longer.

EMILIA There are afflictions in love Mr Dorimant.

DORIMANT You women make 'em, who are commonly as unreasonable in that as you are at play; without the advantage be on your side, a man can never quietly give over when he's weary?

MEDLEY If you would play without being obliged to complaisance Dorimant, you should play in public places.

DORIMANT Ordinaries* were a very good thing for that, but gentlemen do not of late frequent 'em; the deep play is now in private houses.

LADY TOWNLEY [*Bellinda offering to steal away*] Bellinda, are you leaving us so soon?

BELLINDA I am to go to the Park with Mrs Loveit, Madam –

[*Exit Bellinda*]

LADY TOWNLEY This confidence will go nigh to spoil this young creature.

MEDLEY 'Twill do her good Madam. Young men who are brought up under practising lawyers prove the abler council when they come to be called to the bar themselves –

DORIMANT The Town has been very favourable to you this afternoon, my Lady Townley, you use to have an *embarras* of chairs

* Ordinaries: taverns.

and coaches at your door, an uproar of footmen in your hall, and a noise of fools above here.

LADY TOWNLEY Indeed my house is the general rendezvous and next to the playhouse is the common refuge of all the young idle people.

EMILIA Company is a very good thing, Madam, but I wonder you do not love it a little more chosen.

LADY TOWNLEY 'Tis good to have an universal taste, we should love wit, but for variety, be able to divert ourselves with the extravagancies of those who want it.

MEDLEY Fools will make you laugh.

EMILIA For once or twice! But the repetition of their folly after a visit or two grows tedious and unsufferable.

LADY TOWNLEY You are a little too delicate Emilia.

Enter a Page.

PAGE Sir Fopling Flutter, Madam, desires to know if you are to be seen.

LADY TOWNLEY Here's the freshest fool in Town, and one who has not cloyed you yet. Page!

PAGE Madam!

LADY TOWNLEY Desire him to walk up.

⟨*Exit Page*⟩

DORIMANT Do not you fall on him, Medley, and snub him. Soothe him up in his extravagance! He will show the better.

MEDLEY You know I have a natural indulgence for fools, and need not this caution, Sir!

Enter Sir Fopling Flutter, with his Page after him.

SIR FOPLING Page! Wait without.

⟨*Exit Page*⟩

[*to Lady Townley*] Madam, I kiss your hands, I see yesterday was nothing of chance, the *belles assemblées* form themselves here every day. ⟨*to Emilia*⟩ Lady your servant; Dorimant, let me embrace thee, without lying I have not met with any of my acquaintances, who retain so much of Paris as thou dost, the very air thou had'st when the marquise mistook thee i'the Tuilleries, and cried 'Hé Chevalier,' and then begged thy pardon.

DORIMANT I would fain wear in fashion as long as I can, Sir, 'tis a thing to be valued in men as well as baubles.

SIR FOPLING Thou art a man of wit, and understands the Town; prithee let thee and I be intimate, there is no living without making some good man the confident of our pleasures.

DORIMANT 'Tis true! But there is no man so improper for such a business as I am.

SIR FOPLING Prithee! Why hast thou so modest an opinion of thyself?

DORIMANT Why first, I could never keep a secret in my life, and then there is no charm so infallibly makes me fall in love with a woman as my knowing a friend loves her. I deal honestly with you.

SIR FOPLING Thy humour's very gallant or let me perish, I knew a French count so like thee.

LADY TOWNLEY Wit I perceive has more power over you than beauty, Sir Fopling, else you would not have let this lady stand so long neglected.

SIR FOPLING [*to Emilia*] A thousand pardons, Madam, some civilities due of course upon the meeting a long absent friend. The *éclat* of so much beauty I confess ought to have charmed me sooner.

EMILIA The *brillant* of so much good language Sir has much more power than the little beauty I can boast.

SIR FOPLING I never saw anything prettier than this high work on your *point d'Espaigne* –*

EMILIA 'Tis not so rich as *point de Venise* –†

SIR FOPLING Not altogether, but looks cooler, and is more proper for the season. Dorimant, is not that Medley?

DORIMANT The same, Sir.

SIR FOPLING Forgive me Sir in this *embarras* of civilities, I could not come to have you in my arms sooner. You understand an equipage the best of any man in Town I hear.

MEDLEY By my own you would not guess it.

SIR FOPLING There are critics who do not write Sir.

MEDLEY Our peevish poets will scarce allow it.

SIR FOPLING Damn 'em, they'll allow no man wit, who does not

* *point d'Espaigne*: Spanish lace.   † *point de Venise*: Venetian lace.

play the fool like themselves and show it! Have you taken notice of the *calèche*★ I brought over?

MEDLEY O yes! 'T has quite another air, than th' English makes.

SIR FOPLING 'Tis as easily known from an English tumbril, as an Inns of Court man† is from one of us.

DORIMANT Truly there is a *bel air* in *calèches* as well as men.

MEDLEY But there are few so delicate to observe it.

SIR FOPLING The world is generally very *grossier*‡ here indeed.

LADY TOWNLEY He's very fine.

EMILIA Extreme proper.

SIR FOPLING A slight suit I made to appear in at my first arrival, not worthy your consideration ladies.

DORIMANT The pantaloon is very well mounted.

SIR FOPLING The tassels are new and pretty.

MEDLEY I never saw a coat better cut.

SIR FOPLING It makes me show long-waisted, and I think slender.

DORIMANT That's the shape our ladies dote on.

MEDLEY Your breech though is a handful too high in my eye Sir Fopling.

SIR FOPLING Peace Medley, I have wished it lower a thousand times, but a pox on't 'twill not be.

LADY TOWNLEY His gloves are well fringed, large and graceful.

SIR FOPLING I was always eminent for being *bien ganté*.§

EMILIA He wears nothing but what are originals of the most famous hands in Paris.

SIR FOPLING You are in the right Madam.

LADY TOWNLEY The suit.

SIR FOPLING Barroy.‖

EMILIA The garniture.

SIR FOPLING Le Gras –

MEDLEY The shoes!

SIR FOPLING Piccar!

DORIMANT The periwig!

SIR FOPLING Chedreux.

★ *calèche*: a French light carriage.   † Inns of Court man: a lawyer.
‡ *grossier*: crude.   § *bien ganté*: well-gloved.
‖ Barroy: Sir Fopling gives a list of Parisian merchants, of whom Chedreux was well known, and gave his name to a special kind of wig.

LADY TOWNLEY
AND EMILIA } The gloves!

SIR FOPLING Orangerie! You know the smell ladies! Dorimant, I could find in my heart for an amusement to have a gallantry with some of our English ladies.

DORIMANT 'Tis a thing no less necessary to confirm the reputation of your wit, than a duel will be to satisfying the Town of your courage.

SIR FOPLING Here was a woman yesterday –

DORIMANT Mistress Loveit.

SIR FOPLING You have named her!

DORIMANT You cannot pitch on a better for your purpose.

SIR FOPLING Prithee! What is she?

DORIMANT A person of quality, and one who has a rest of reputation enough to make the conquest considerable; besides I hear she likes you too!

SIR FOPLING Methoughts she seemed though very reserved, and uneasy all the time I entertained her.

DORIMANT Grimace and affection; you will see her i'th' Mall tonight.

SIR FOPLING Prithee, let thee and I take the air together.

DORIMANT I am engaged to Medley, but I'll meet you at Saint James's, and give you some information, upon the which you may regulate your proceedings.

SIR FOPLING All the world will be in the Park tonight: ladies, 'twere pity to keep so much beauty longer within doors, and rob the Ring★ of all those charms that should adorn it – Hey Page.

Enter Page, and goes out again.

See that all my people be ready. Dorimant *au revoir.*

MEDLEY A fine-mettled coxcomb.

DORIMANT Brisk and insipid –

MEDLEY Pert and dull.

EMILIA However you despise him gentlemen, I'll lay my life he passes for a wit with many.

DORIMANT That may very well be, nature has her cheats, stums†

★ the Ring: In Hyde Park. See note on Act III, scene i (p. 560).

† stums: stumming wine is renewing it by creating a new fermentation.

a brain, and puts sophisticate dullness often on the tasteless multitude for true wit and good humour. Medley, come.

MEDLEY I must go a little way, I will meet you i' the Mall.

DORIMANT I'll walk through the Garden thither, [*to the women*]
we shall meet anon and bow.

LADY TOWNLEY Not tonight! We are engaged about a business,
the knowledge of which may make you laugh hereafter.

MEDLEY Your servant ladies.

DORIMANT *Au revoir*, as Sir Fopling says.

> [*Exeunt Medley and Dorimant*]

LADY TOWNLEY The old man will be here immediately.

EMILIA Let's expect him i'th' garden. . . .

LADY TOWNLEY Go, you are a rogue.

EMILIA I can't abide you.   [*Exeunt*]

SCENE III

The Mall

Enter Harriet, Young Bellair, she pulling him.

HARRIET Come along.

YOUNG BELLAIR And leave your mother.

HARRIET Busy will be sent with a hue and cry after us; but that's
no matter.

YOUNG BELLAIR 'Twill look strangely in me.

HARRIET She'll believe it a freak of mine, and never blame your
manners.

YOUNG BELLAIR What reverend acquaintance is that she has
met?

HARRIET A fellow-beauty of the last king's time, though by the
ruins you would hardly guess it.   [*Exeunt*]

Enter Dorimant and crosses the stage.
Enter Young Bellair and Harriet.

YOUNG BELLAIR By this time your mother is in a fine taking.

HARRIET If your friend Mr Dorimant were but here now, that
she might find me talking with him.

YOUNG BELLAIR She does not know him but dreads him I hear of all mankind.

HARRIET She concludes if he does but speak to a woman she's undone, is on her knees every day to pray heaven defend me from him.

YOUNG BELLAIR You do not apprehend him so much as she does.

HARRIET I never saw anything in him that was frightful.

YOUNG BELLAIR On the contrary, have you not observed something extreme delightful in his wit and person?

HARRIET He's agreeable and pleasant I must own, but he does so much affect being so, he displeases me.

YOUNG BELLAIR Lord Madam, all he does and says, is so easy and so natural.

HARRIET Some men's verses seem so to the unskilful, but labour i' the one, and affectation in the other to the judicious plainly appear.

YOUNG BELLAIR I never heard him accused of affectation before.

Enter Dorimant and stares upon her.

HARRIET It passes on the easy Town, who are favourably pleased in him to call it humour.

[Exeunt Young Bellair and Harriet]

DORIMANT 'Tis she! It must be she, that lovely hair, that easy shape, those wanton eyes, and all those melting charms about her mouth, which Medley spoke of; I'll follow the lottery, and put in for a prize with my friend Bellair.

Exit Dorimant repeating

'In love the victors from the vanquished fly;
They fly that wound, and they pursue that die.'*

*Enter Young Bellair and Harriet, and after them Dorimant
standing at a distance.*

YOUNG BELLAIR Most people prefer High Park† to this place.

HARRIET It has the better reputation I confess, but I abominate the dull diversions there, the formal bows, the affected smiles,

* 'In love . . . die': ll. 27–28 of Waller's 'To a Friend, of the Different Success of their Loves'.
† High Park: Hyde Park.

the silly by-words, and amorous tweers,★ in passing; here one meets with a little conversation now and then.

YOUNG BELLAIR These conversations have been fatal to some of your sex, Madam.

HARRIET It may be so, because some who want temper have been undone by gaming, must others who have it wholly deny themselves the pleasure of play?

DORIMANT [*coming up gently, and bowing to her. She starts and looks grave*] Trust me, it were unreasonable, Madam.

HARRIET Lord! Who's this?

YOUNG BELLAIR Dorimant.

DORIMANT Is this the woman your father would have you marry?

YOUNG BELLAIR It is.

DORIMANT Her name?

YOUNG BELLAIR Harriet.

DORIMANT I am not mistaken, she's handsome.

YOUNG BELLAIR Talk to her, her wit is better than her face; we were wishing for you but now.

DORIMANT [*to Harriet*] Overcast with seriousness o' the sudden! A thousand smiles were shining in that face but now; I never saw so quick a change of weather.

HARRIET [*aside*] I feel as great a change within; but he shall never know it.

DORIMANT You were talking of play, Madam, pray what may be your stint?

HARRIET A little harmless discourse in public walks, or at most an appointment in a box barefaced at the playhouse; you are for masks, and private meetings; where women engage for all they are worth, I hear.

DORIMANT I have been used to deep play, but I can make one at small game, when I like my gamester well.

HARRIET And be so unconcerned you'll ha' no pleasure in't.

DORIMANT Where there is a considerable sum to be won, the hope of drawing people in, makes every trifle considerable.

HARRIET The sordidness of men's natures I know makes 'em willing to flatter and comply with the rich, though they are sure never to be the better for 'em.

         ★ tweers: leers, glances.

DORIMANT 'Tis in their power to do us good, and we despair not but at some time or other they may be willing.

HARRIET To men who have fared in this Town like you, 'twould be a great mortification to live on hope; could you keep a Lent for a mistress?

DORIMANT In expectation of a happy Easter, and though time be very precious, think forty days well lost, to gain your favour.

HARRIET Mr Bellair! Let us walk, 'tis time to leave him, men grow dull when they begin to be particular.

DORIMANT Y'are mistaken, flattery will not ensue, though I know y'are greedy of the praises of the whole Mall.

HARRIET You do me wrong.

DORIMANT I do not. As I followed you, I observed how you were pleased when the fops cried 'She's handsome, very handsome, by God she is', and whispered aloud your name, the thousand several forms you put your face into; then to make yourself more agreeable, how wantonly you played with your head, flung back your locks, and looked smilingly over your shoulder at 'em.

HARRIET I do not go begging the men's as you do the ladies' good liking with a sly softness in your looks, and a gentle slowness in your bows, as you pass by 'em – as thus Sir – [*acts him*] Is not this like you?

Enter Lady Woodvil and Busy.

YOUNG BELLAIR Your mother Madam. [*pulls Harriet, she composes herself*]

LADY WOODVIL Ah my dear child Harriet.

BUSY ⟨*aside*⟩ Now is she so pleased with finding her again she cannot chide her.

LADY WOODVIL Come away!

DORIMANT 'Tis now but high Mall* Madam, the most entertaining time of all the evening.

HARRIET I would fain see that Dorimant mother, you so cry out of, for a monster, he's in the Mall I hear.

LADY WOODVIL Come away then! The plague is here and you should dread the infection.

YOUNG BELLAIR You may be misinformed of the gentleman?

* high Mall: The most fashionable, most thronged time on the Mall.

LADY WOODVIL O no! I hope you do not know him. He is the prince of all the devils in the Town, delights in nothing but in rapes and riots.

DORIMANT If you did but hear him speak Madam!

LADY WOODVIL Oh! He has a tongue they say would tempt the angels to a second fall.

Enter Sir Fopling with his equipage, six Footmen, and a Page.

SIR FOPLING Hey. Champagne, Norman, La Rose, La Fleur, La Tour, La Verdure. Dorimant –

LADY WOODVIL Here, here he is among this rout, he names him; come away Harriet, come away.

[*Exeunt Lady Woodvil, Harriet, Busy and Young Bellair*]

DORIMANT This fool's coming has spoiled all, she's gone, but she has left a pleasing image of herself behind that wanders in my soul – It must not settle there.

SIR FOPLING What reverie is this! Speak man.

DORIMANT 'Snatched from myself how far behind Already I behold the shore!'*

Enter Medley.

MEDLEY Dorimant, a discovery! I met with Bellair.

DORIMANT You can tell me no news Sir, I know all.

MEDLEY How do you like the daughter?

DORIMANT You never came so near truth in your life, as you did in her description.

MEDLEY What think you of the mother?

DORIMANT Whatever I think of her, she thinks very well of me I find.

MEDLEY Did she know you?

DORIMANT She did not, whether she does now or no I know not. Here was a pleasant scene towards, when in came Sir Fopling, mustering up his equipage, and at the latter named me, and frighted her away.

MEDLEY Loveit and Bellinda are not far off, I saw 'em alight at St James's.†

★ 'snatched from . . . shore': ll. 3–4 of Waller's 'Of loving at first sight'.

† St James's: probably St James's Palace.

DORIMANT Sir Fopling hark you, a word or two, [*whispers*] Look you do not want assurance.

SIR FOPLING I never do on these occasions.

DORIMANT Walk on, we must not be seen together, make your advantage of what I have told you, the next turn you will meet the lady.

SIR FOPLING Hey – follow me all

[*Exeunt Sir Fopling and his equipage*]

DORIMANT Medley, you shall see good sport anon between Loveit and this Fopling.

MEDLEY I thought there was something toward by that whisper.

DORIMANT You know a worthy principle of hers?

MEDLEY Not to be so much as civil to a man who speaks to her in the presence of him she professes to love.

DORIMANT I have encouraged Fopling to talk to her tonight.

MEDLEY Now you are here she will go nigh to beat him.

DORIMANT In the humour she's in, her love will make her do some very extravagant thing doubtless.

MEDLEY What was Bellinda's business with you at my Lady Townley's?

DORIMANT To get me to meet Loveit here in order to an *éclaircissement*; I made some difficulty of it, and have prepared this rancounter to make good my jealousy.

MEDLEY Here they come!

Enter Loveit, Bellinda and Pert.

DORIMANT I'll meet her and provoke her with a deal of dumb civility in passing by, then turn short and be behind her when Sir Fopling sets upon her –
'See how unregarded now
That piece of beauty passes'.★

[*Exeunt Dorimant and Medley*]

BELLINDA How wonderful respectfully he bowed!

PERT He's always over-mannerly when he has done a mischief.

BELLINDA Methoughts indeed at the same time he had a strange despising countenance.

★ 'See how . . . passes': The first lines of Suckling's 'Sonnet 1', with 'see' substituted for the original's 'Do'st see'.

PERT The unlucky look he thinks becomes him.

BELLINDA I was afraid you would have spoke to him my dear.

MRS LOVEIT I would have died first; he shall no more find me the loving fool he has done.

BELLINDA You love him still!

MRS LOVEIT No.

PERT I wish you did not.

MRS LOVEIT I do not, and I will have you think so, what made you hale me to this odious place Bellinda?

BELLINDA I hate to be hulched* up in a coach; walking is much better.

MRS LOVEIT Would we could meet Sir Fopling now.

BELLINDA Lord! Would you not avoid him?

MRS LOVEIT I would make him all the advances that may be.

BELLINDA That would confirm Dorimant's suspicion, my dear.

MRS LOVEIT He is not jealous; but I will make him so, and be revenged a way he little thinks on.

BELLINDA [*aside*] If she should make him jealous, that may make him fond of her again: I must dissuade her from it. ⟨*aloud*⟩ Lord! My dear, this will certainly make him hate you.

MRS LOVEIT 'Twill make him uneasy though he does not care for me; I know the effects of jealousy on men of his proud temper.

BELLINDA 'Tis a fantastic remedy, its operations are dangerous and uncertain.

MRS LOVEIT 'Tis the strongest cordial we can give to dying love, it often brings it back when there's no sign of life remaining; but I design not so much the reviving his, as my revenge.

Enter Sir Fopling and his equipage.

SIR FOPLING Hey! Bid the coachman send home four of his horses, and bring the coach to Whitehall,† I'll walk over the Park – Madam, the honour of kissing your fair hand is a happiness I missed this afternoon at my Lady Townley's!

MRS LOVEIT You were very obliging, Sir Fopling, the last time I saw you there.

SIR FOPLING The preference was due to your wit and beauty.

* hulched: hunched.

† Whitehall: The royal palace across the Park from the Mall.

Madam, your servant, there never was so sweet an evening.

BELLINDA 'T has drawn all the rabble of the Town hither.

SIR FOPLING 'Tis pity there's not an order made, that none but the *beau monde* should walk here.

MRS LOVEIT 'T would add much to the beauty of the place; see what a sort of nasty fellows are coming.

Enter four★ ill-fashioned fellows singing.

'"Tis not for kisses alone, *etc.*'†

MRS LOVEIT Foh! Their periwigs are scented with tobacco so strong –

SIR FOPLING It overcomes our pulvilio‡ – Methinks I smell the coffee-house they come from.

FIRST MAN Dorimant's convenient, Madam Loveit.

SECOND MAN I like the oily buttock with her.

THIRD MAN What spruce prig is that?

FIRST MAN A caravan, lately come from Paris.

SECOND MAN Peace, they smoke.

[*all of them coughing*]

'There's something else to be done, *etc.*'§

[*Exeunt singing*]

Enter Dorimant and Medley.

DORIMANT They're engaged –

MEDLEY She entertains him as if she liked him.

DORIMANT Let us go forward – seem earnest in discourse and show ourselves. Then you shall see how she'll use him.

BELLINDA Yonder's Dorimant my dear.

MRS LOVEIT I see him, [*aside*] he comes insulting; but I will disappoint him in his expectation. [*to Sir Fopling*] I like this pretty nice humour of yours Sir Fopling: ⟨*aside*⟩ with what a loathing eye he looked upon those fellows!

★ four: three are listed in the *dramatis personae* and only three speak; probably a mistake.
† '"Tis not . . . alone': ll.5–8 of an anonymous song 'Tell me no more you love' afterwards made into the ballad 'Love-a-la-Mode, or, the Modish Mistris'.
‡ pulvilio: scented powder.
§ 'There's something . . . done': The seventh line of the song 'Tell me no more you love'.

SIR FOPLING I sat near one of 'em at a play today, and was almost poisoned with a pair of cordivant* gloves he wears.

MRS LOVEIT [*laughs in a loud affected way*] Oh! Filthy cordivant, how I hate the smell!

SIR FOPLING Did you observe, Madam, how their cravats hung loose an inch from their neck, and what a frightful air it gave 'em.

MRS LOVEIT O I took particular notice of one that is always spruced up with a deal of dirty sky-coloured ribbon.

BELLINDA That's one of the walking flajolets† who haunt the Mall o'nights.

MRS LOVEIT Oh! I remember him! H'has a hollow tooth enough to spoil the sweetness of an evening.

SIR FOPLING I have seen the tallest walk the streets with a dainty pair of boxes, neatly buckled on.

MRS LOVEIT And a little footboy at his heels pocket-high, with a flatcap – a dirty face.

SIR FOPLING And a snotty nose –

MRS LOVEIT Oh – odious, there's many of my own sex with that Holborn equipage trig‡ to Gray's Inn Walks;§ and now and then travel hither on a Sunday.

MEDLEY She takes no notice of you.

DORIMANT Damn her! I am jealous of a counterplot!

MRS LOVEIT Your liveries are the finest, Sir Fopling – O that page! That page is the prettily'st dressed – They are all Frenchmen.

SIR FOPLING There's one damned English blockhead among 'em, you may know him by his mien.

MRS LOVEIT Oh! That's he, that's he, what do you call him?

SIR FOPLING Hey – I know not what to call him –

MRS LOVEIT What's your name?

FOOTMAN John Trott, Madam!

SIR FOPLING O insufferable! Trott, Trott! There's nothing so barbarous as the names of our English servants. What countryman are you sirrah?

FOOTMAN Hampshire, Sir?

SIR FOPLING Then Hampshire be your name. Hey, Hampshire!

---

* cordivant: gloves made of cordovan leather.   † flajolets: long tall people.
‡ trig: trip.   § Gray's Inn Walks: gardens at Gray's Inn, in Holborn.

MRS LOVEIT O that sound, that sound becomes the mouth of a man of quality.

MEDLEY Dorimant you look a little bashful on the matter!

DORIMANT She dissembles better than I thought she could have done.

MEDLEY You have tempted her with too luscious a bait. She bites at the coxcomb.

DORIMANT She cannot fall from loving me to that?

MEDLEY You begin to be jealous in earnest.

DORIMANT Of one I do not love.

MEDLEY You did love her.

DORIMANT The fit has long been over.

MEDLEY But I have known men fall into dangerous relapses when they have found a woman inclining to another.

DORIMANT [*to himself*] He guesses the secret of my heart! I am concerned, but dare not show it, lest Bellinda should mistrust all I have done to gain her.

BELLINDA [*aside*] I have watched his look, and find no alteration there. Did he love her some signs of jealousy would have appeared?

DORIMANT I hope this happy evening, Madam, has reconciled you to the scandalous Mall, we shall have you now hankering here again –

MRS LOVEIT Sir Fopling will you walk –

SIR FOPLING I am all obedience Madam –

MRS LOVEIT Come along then – and let's agree to be malicious on all the ill-fashioned things we meet.

SIR FOPLING We'll make a critique on the whole Mall, Madam.

MRS LOVEIT Bellinda you shall engage –

BELLINDA To the reserve of our friends my dear.

MRS LOVEIT No! No! Exceptions –

SIR FOPLING We'll sacrifice all to our diversion –

MRS LOVEIT All – all –

SIR FOPLING All.

BELLINDA All? Then let it be.

[*Exeunt Sir Fopling, Mrs Loveit, Bellinda and Pert laughing*]

MEDLEY Would you had brought some more of your friends, Dorimant, to have been witness of Sir Fopling's disgrace and your triumph –

DORIMANT 'Twere unreasonable to desire you not to laugh at me; but pray do not expose me to the Town this day or two.

MEDLEY By that time you hope to have regained your credit.

DORIMANT I know she hates Fopling, and only makes use of him in hope to work me on again; had it not been for some powerful consideration which will be removed tomorrow morning, I had made her pluck off this mask, and show the passion that lies panting under.

Enter a Footman.

MEDLEY Here comes a man from Bellair, with news of your last adventure.

DORIMANT I am glad he sent him. I long to know the consequence of our parting.

FOOTMAN Sir, my master desires you to come to my Lady Townley's presently, and bring Mr Medley with you. My Lady Woodvil and her daughter are there.

MEDLEY Then all's well Dorimant.

FOOTMAN They have sent for the fiddles and mean to dance! He bid me tell you, Sir, the old lady does not know you, and would have you own yourself to be Mr Courtage. They are all prepared to receive you by that name.

DORIMANT That foppish admirer of quality, who flatters the very meat at honourable tables, and never offers love to a woman below a lady-grandmother.

MEDLEY You know the character you are to act I see!

DORIMANT This is Harriet's contrivance – Wild, witty, love-some, beautiful and young – Come along Medley.

MEDLEY This new woman would well supply the loss of Mrs Loveit.

DORIMANT That business must not end so, before tomorrow sun is set, I will revenge and clear it.

And you and Loveit to her cost shall find,

I fathom all the depths of womankind.

[*Exeunt*]

ACT FOUR

⟨SCENE I⟩

The scene opens with the fiddles playing a country dance

Enter Dorimant, Lady Woodvil, Young Bellair, and Mrs Harriet,
Old Bellair, and Emilia, Mr Medley, and Lady Townley; as having
just ended the dance.

OLD BELLAIR So, so, so! A smart bout, a very smart bout, adod!

LADY TOWNLEY How do you like Emilia's dancing brother.

OLD BELLAIR Not at all! Not at all.

LADY TOWNLEY You speak not what you think I am sure.

OLD BELLAIR No matter for that, go, bid her dance no more, it don't become her, it don't become her, tell her I say so; [*aside*] Adod I love her.

DORIMANT [*to Lady Woodvil*] All people mingle nowadays Madam. And in public places women of quality have the least respect showed 'em.

LADY WOODVIL I protest you say the truth, Mr Courtage.

DORIMANT Forms and ceremonies, the only things that uphold quality and greatness, are now shamefully laid aside and neglected.

LADY WOODVIL Well! This is not the women's age, let 'em think what they will, lewdness is the business now, love was the business in my time.

DORIMANT The women indeed are little beholding to the young men of this age, they're generally only dull admirers of themselves, and make their court to nothing but their periwigs and their cravats, and would be more concerned for the disordering of 'em, though on a good occasion, than a young maid would be for the tumbling of her head or handerchief.

LADY WOODVIL I protest you hit 'em.

DORIMANT They are very assiduous to show themselves at Court well-dressed to the women of quality, but their business is with the stale mistresses of the Town, who are prepared to receive their lazy addresses by industrious old lovers, who have cast 'em off, and made 'em easy.

HARRIET ⟨*to Medley*⟩ He fits my mother's humour so well, a little more and she'll dance a kissing dance with him anon.

MEDLEY Dutifully observed Madam.

DORIMANT They pretend to be great critics in beauty, by their talk you would think they liked no face, and yet can dote on an ill one, if it belong to a laundress or a tailor's daughter; they cry a woman's past her prime at twenty, decayed at four-and-twenty, old and unsufferable at thirty.

LADY WOODVIL Unsufferable at thirty! That they are in the wrong, Mr Courtage, at five-and-thirty, there are living proofs enough to convince 'em.

DORIMANT Aye Madam! There's Mrs Setlooks, Mrs Droplip, and my Lady Loud! Show me among all our opening buds, a face that promises so much beauty as the remains of theirs.

LADY WOODVIL The depraved appetite of this vicious age talks nothing but green fruit, and loathes it when 'tis kindly ripened.

DORIMANT Else so many deserving women, madam, would not be so untimely neglected.

LADY WOODVIL I protest Mr Courtage, a dozen such good men as you, would be enough to atone for that wicked Dorimant, and all the under-debauchees of the Town. [*Harriet, Emilia, Young Bellair, Medley, Lady Townley, break out into laughter*] What's the matter there?

MEDLEY A pleasant mistake, Madam, that a lady has made, occasions a little laughter.

OLD BELLAIR Come, come, you keep 'em idle! They are impatient till the fiddles play again.

DORIMANT You are not weary, Madam?

LADY WOODVIL One dance more! I cannot refuse you Mr Courtage.

> *They dance. After the dance, Old Bellair, singing and dancing*
> *up to Emilia.*

EMILIA You are very active Sir.

OLD BELLAIR Adod sirrah; when I was a young fellow I could ha' capered up to my woman's gorget.

DORIMANT You are willing to rest yourself Madam –

LADY TOWNLEY We'll walk into my chamber and sit down.

MEDLEY Leave us Mr Courtage, he's a dancer, and the young ladies are not weary yet.

LADY WOODVIL We'll send him out again.

HARRIET If you do not quickly, I know where to send for Mr Dorimant.

LADY WOODVIL This girl's head, Mr Courtage, is ever running on that wild fellow.

DORIMANT 'Tis well you have got her a good husband Madam, that will settle it.

[*Exeunt Lady Townley, Lady Woodvil and Dorimant*]

OLD BELLAIR [*to Emilia*] Adod sweetheart be advised, and do not throw thyself away on a young idle fellow.

EMILIA I have no such intention Sir.

OLD BELLAIR Have a little patience! Thou shalt have the man I spake of. Adod he loves thee, and will make a good husband, but no words –

EMILIA But Sir –

OLD BELLAIR No answer – out a pise! Peace! And think on't.

Enter Dorimant.

DORIMANT Your company is desired within Sir.

OLD BELLAIR I go! I go! Good Mr Courtage – fare you well! [*to Emilia*] Go! I'll see you no more.

EMILIA What have I done Sir?

OLD BELLAIR You are ugly, you are ugly! Is she not Mr Courtage?

EMILIA Better words or I sha'nt abide you.

OLD BELLAIR Out a pise – adod, what does she say! Hit her a pat for me there.   [*Exit Old Bellair*]

MEDLEY You have charms for the whole family.

DORIMANT You'll spoil it all with some unseasonable jest, Medley.

MEDLEY You see I confine my tongue, and am content to be a bare spectator, much contrary to my nature.

EMILIA Methinks, Mr Dorimant, my Lady Woodvil is a little fond of you.

DORIMANT Would her daughter were.

MEDLEY It may be you may find her so! Try her, you have an opportunity.

DORIMANT And I will not lose it! Bellair, here's a lady has something to say to you.

YOUNG BELLAIR I wait upon her. Mr Medley we have both business with you.

DORIMANT Get you all together then. [*to Harriet*] That demure curtesy is not amiss in jest, but do not think in earnest it becomes you.

HARRIET Affectation is catching I find; from your grave bow I got it.

DORIMANT Where had you all that scorn, and coldness in your look?

HARRIET From nature Sir, pardon my want of art: I have not learned those softnesses and languishings which now in faces are so much in fashion.

DORIMANT You need 'em not, you have a sweetness of your own, if you would but calm your frowns and let it settle.

HARRIET My eyes are wild and wandering like my passions, and cannot yet be tied to rules of charming.

DORIMANT Women indeed have commonly a method of managing those messengers of love! Now they will look as if they would kill, and anon they will look as if they were dying. They point and rebate their glances, the better to invite us.

HARRIET I like this variety well enough; but hate the set face that always looks as it would say 'Come love me'. A woman, who at plays makes the *doux yeux* to a whole audience, and at home cannot forbear'em to her monkey.

DORIMANT Put on a gentle smile and let me see, how well it becomes you.

HARRIET I am sorry my face does not please you as it is, but I shall not be complaisant and change it.

DORIMANT Though you are obstinate, I know 'tis capable of improvement, and shall do you justice Madam, if I chance to be at Court, when the critiques of the Circle★ pass their judgment; for thither you must come.

HARRIET And expect to be taken in pieces, have all my features examined, every motion censured, and on the whole be condemned to be but pretty, or a beauty of the lowest rate. What think you?

    ★ the Circle: the assembly at Court.

DORIMANT The women, nay the very lovers who belong to the Drawing-room* will maliciously allow you more than that; they always grant what is apparent, that they may the better be believed when they name concealed faults they cannot easily be disproved in.

HARRIET Beauty runs as great a risk exposed at Court as wit does on the stage, where the ugly and the foolish, all are free to censure.

DORIMANT [*aside*] I love her, and dare not let her know it, I fear she'as an ascendant o'er me and may revenge the wrongs I have done her sex. [*to her*] Think of making a party Madam, love will engage.

HARRIET You make me start! I did not think to have heard of love from you.

DORIMANT I never knew what 'twas to have a settled ague yet, but now and then have had irregular fits.

HARRIET Take heed, sickness after long health is commonly more violent and dangerous.

DORIMANT [*aside*] I have took the infection from her, and feel the disease now spreading in me – ⟨*to her*⟩ Is the name of love so frightful that you dare not stand it?

HARRIET 'Twill do little execution out of your mouth on me I am sure.

DORIMANT It has been fatal –

HARRIET To some easy women, but we are not all born to one destiny, I was informed you use to laugh at love, and not make it.

DORIMANT The time has been but now I must speak –

HARRIET If it be on that idle subject, I will put on my serious look, turn my head carefully from you, drop my lip, let my eyelids fall, and hang half o'er my eyes – Thus while you buzz a speech of an hour long in my ear, and I answer never a word! Why do you not begin?

DORIMANT That the company may take notice how passionately I make advances of love! And how disdainfully you receive 'em.

HARRIET When your love's grown strong enough to make you bear being laughed at, I'll give you leave to trouble me with it. Till when pray forbear, Sir.

* the Drawing-room: at Court. The Drawing-room came to signify the assembly itself.

Enter Sir Fopling and others in masks.

DORIMANT What's here? Masquerades?

HARRIET I thought that foppery had been left off, and people might have been in private with a fiddle.

DORIMANT 'Tis endeavoured to be kept on foot still by some who find themselves the more acceptable, the less they are known.

YOUNG BELLAIR This must be Sir Fopling.

MEDLEY That extraordinary habit shows it.

YOUNG BELLAIR What are the rest?

MEDLEY A company of French rascals whom he picked up in Paris and has brought over to be his dancing equipage on these occasions! Make him own himself; a fool is very troublesome when he presumes he is incognito.

SIR FOPLING [*to Harriet*] Do you know me?

HARRIET Ten to one but I guess at you?

SIR FOPLING Are you women as fond of a vizard as we men are?

HARRIET I am very fond of a vizard that covers a face I do not like, Sir.

YOUNG BELLAIR Here are no masks you see, Sir, but those which came with you. This was intended a private meeting, but because you look like a gentleman, if you will discover yourself and we know you to be such, you shall be welcome.

SIR FOPLING [*pulling off his mask*] Dear Bellair.

MEDLEY Sir Fopling! How came you hither?

SIR FOPLING Faith as I was coming late from Whitehall, after the king's *couchée*,★ one of my people told me he had heard fiddles at my Lady Townley's, and –

DORIMANT You need not say any more, Sir.

SIR FOPLING Dorimant, let me kiss thee.

DORIMANT [*whispers*] Hark you, Sir Fopling?

SIR FOPLING Enough, enough, Courtage. A pretty kind of young woman that, Medley, I observed her in the Mall more *éveillée*† than our English women commonly are, prithee what is she?

MEDLEY The most noted coquette in Town; beware of her.

SIR FOPLING Let her be what she will, I know how to take my measures, in Paris the mode is to flatter the prude, laugh at the

★ *couchée*: a reception in the evening.   † *éveillée*: sprightly.

faux-prude, make serious love to the *demi-prude*, and only rally with the coquette. Medley, what think you?

MEDLEY That for all this smattering of the mathematics you may be out in your judgment at tennis.

SIR FOPLING What a *coq-a-l'âne*★ is this? I talk of women and thou answer'st tennis.

MEDLEY Mistakes will be for want of apprehension.

SIR FOPLING I am very glad of the acquaintance I have with this family.

MEDLEY My lady truly is a good woman.

SIR FOPLING Ah! Dorimant, Courtage I would say, would thou hadst spent the last winter in Paris with me. When thou wer't there La Corneus and Sallyes† were the only habitudes we had, a comedian would have been a *bonne fortune*. No stranger ever passed his time so well as I did some months before I came over. I was well received in a dozen families, where all the women of quality used to visit, I have intrigues to tell thee, more pleasant than ever thou read'st in a novel.

HARRIET Write 'em Sir, and oblige us women! Our language wants such little stories.

SIR FOPLING Writing Madam is a mechanic part of wit! A gentleman should never go beyond a song or a billet.

HARRIET Bussy‡ was a gentleman.

SIR FOPLING Who d'Ambois?§

MEDLEY Was there ever such a brisk blockhead?

HARRIET Not d'Ambois, Sir, but Rabutin. He who writ the *Loves of France*.

SIR FOPLING That may be, Madam! Many gentlemen do things that are below 'em. Damn your authors, Courtage, women are the prettiest things we can fool away our time with.

★ *coq-a-l'âne*: piece of nonsense.

† La Corneus and Sallyes: possibly, according to A. W. Verity, *The Works of Sir George Etherege*, 1888, Madame Cornuel and Madame Selles, both minor literary figures of the time.

‡ Bussy: Roger de Rabutin, Comte de Bussy (1618–1693) who wrote the *Histoire Amoreuse des Gaules*.

§ d'Ambois: Bussy d'Ambois, a French adventurer of the sixteenth century, whose deeds were told in Chapman's play *Bussy d'Ambois*.

HARRIET I hope ye have wearied yourself tonight at Court Sir, and will not think of fooling with anybody here.

SIR FOPLING I cannot complain of my fortune there, Madam – Dorimant –

DORIMANT Again!

SIR FOPLING Courtage, a pox on't, I have something to tell thee. When I had made my court within, I came out and flung myself upon the mat under the state★ i'the outward room, i'th' midst of half a dozen beauties who were withdrawn to jeèr† among themselves, as they called it.

DORIMANT Did you know 'em?

SIR FOPLING Not one of 'em by heavens! Not I. But they were all your friends.

DORIMANT How are you sure of that?

SIR FOPLING Why we laughed at all the Town; spared nobody but yourself. They found me a man for their purpose.

DORIMANT I know you are malicious to your power.

SIR FOPLING And faith! I had occasion to show it, for I never saw more gaping fools at a ball or on a birthday.

DORIMANT You learned who the women were.

SIR FOPLING No matter! They frequent the Drawing-room.

DORIMANT And entertain themselves pleasantly at the expense of all the fops who come there.

SIR FOPLING That's their business, faith I sifted 'em and find they have a sort of wit among them – [*pinches a tallow candle*] Ah filthy.

DORIMANT Look he has been pinching the tallow candle.

SIR FOPLING How can you breathe in a room where there's grease frying! Dorimant thou art intimate with my lady, advise her for her own sake and the good company that comes hither to burn wax lights.

HARRIET What are these masquerades who stand so obsequiously at a distance?

SIR FOPLING A set of balladins, whom I picked out of the best in France and brought over, with a *flûte douce* or two, my servants; they shall entertain you.

★ state: canopy.
† jeèr: The copy text's accent is presumably to indicate Sir Fopling pronounces the word with an affected French accent.

HARRIET I had rather see you dance yourself Sir Fopling.

SIR FOPLING And I had rather do it . . . all the company knows it – but Madame –

MEDLEY Come, come! No excuses Sir Fopling.

SIR FOPLING By heavens Medley –

MEDLEY Like a woman I find you must be struggled with before one brings you what you desire.

HARRIET [*aside*] Can he dance?

EMILIA And fence and sing too, if you'll believe him.

DORIMANT He has no more excellence in his heels than in his head. He went to Paris a plain bashful English blockhead, and is returned a fine undertaking French fop.

MEDLEY I cannot prevail.

SIR FOPLING Do not think it want of complaisance, Madam,

HARRIET You are too well-bred to want that Sir Fopling. I believe it want of power.

SIR FOPLING By heavens and so it is. I have sat up so damned late and drunk so cursed hard since I came to this lewd Town, that I am fit for nothing but low dancing now, a *courante*, a *bourrée* or a *menuet*: but St André* tells me, if I will but be regular in one month I shall rise again. [*Sir Fopling endeavours at a caper*] Pox on this debauchery.

EMILIA I have heard your dancing much commended.

SIR FOPLING It had the good fortune to please in Paris. I was judged to rise within an inch as high as the basque† in an entry I danced there.

HARRIET ⟨*aside*⟩ I am mightily taken with this fool, ⟨*to him*⟩ let us sit: here's a seat Sir Fopling.

SIR FOPLING At your feet, Madam; I can be nowhere so much at ease: by your leave gown.

HARRIET AND EMILIA } Ah! You'll spoil it.

SIR FOPLING No matter, my clothes are my creatures. I make 'em to make my court to you ladies, hey –

Dance.

---

* St André: a French dancing master resident in England.

† basque: the skirt of a doublet, or perhaps a reference to a Basque dancer.

Qu'on commence [to an English dancer] English motions. I was
forced to entertain this fellow, one of my set miscarrying – O
horrid! Leave your damned manner of dancing, and put on the
French air: have you not a pattern before you – Pretty well!
Imitation in time may bring him to something.

After the dance enter Old Bellair, Lady Woodvil and
Lady Townley.

OLD BELLAIR Hey adod! What have we here, a mumming?

LADY WOODVIL Where's my daughter – Harriet.

DORIMANT Here, here, Madam! I know not but under these disguises there may be dangerous sparks, I gave the young lady
warning!

LADY WOODVIL Lord! I am so obliged to you, Mr Courtage.

HARRIET Lord! How you admire this man!

LADY WOODVIL What have you to except against him?

HARRIET He's a fop.

LADY WOODVIL He's not a Dorimant, a wild extravagant fellow
of the times.

HARRIET He's a man made up of forms and common places,
sucked out of the remaining lees of the last age.

LADY WOODVIL He's so good a man that were you not engaged –

LADY TOWNLEY You'll have but little night to sleep in.

LADY WOODVIL Lord! 'Tis perfect day –

DORIMANT *[aside]* The hour is almost come, I appointed Bellinda and I am not so foppishly in love here to forget; I am flesh
and blood yet.

LADY TOWNLEY I am very sensible, Madam.

LADY WOODVIL Lord, Madam!

HARRIET Look in what a struggle is my poor mother yonder?

YOUNG BELLAIR She has much ado to bring out the compliment?

DORIMANT She strains hard for it.

HARRIET See, see! Her head tottering, her eyes staring, and her
under-lip trembling –

DORIMANT Now, now, she's in the very convulsions of her
civility. *[aside]* S'death I shall lose Bellinda: I must fright her
hence! She'll be an hour in this fit of good manners else. *[to Lady*
Woodvil] Do you not know, Sir Fopling, Madam?

LADY WOODVIL I have seen that face – O heaven, 'tis the same we met in the Mall, how came he here?

DORIMANT A fiddle in this Town is a kind of fop-call; no sooner it strikes up, but the house is besieged with an army of masquerades straight.

LADY WOODVIL Lord! I tremble Mr Courtage! For certain Dorimant is in the company.

DORIMANT I cannot confidently say he is not, you had best be gone. I will wait upon you; your daughter is in the hands of Mr Bellair.

LADY WOODVIL I'll see her before me. Harriet, come away.

YOUNG BELLAIR Lights! Lights!

LADY TOWNLEY Light down there.

OLD BELLAIR Adod it needs not –

DORIMANT Call my Lady Woodvil's coach to the door quickly.

OLD BELLAIR Stay Mr Medley, let the young fellows do that duty; we will drink a glass of wine together. 'Tis good after dancing! What mumming spark is that?

MEDLEY He is not to be comprehended in few words.

SIR FOPLING Hey! La Tour.

MEDLEY Whither away Sir Fopling?

SIR FOPLING I have business with Courtage –

MEDLEY He'll but put the ladies into their coach and come up again.

OLD BELLAIR In the meantime I'll call for a bottle.

[*Exit Old Bellair*]

Enter Young Bellair.

MEDLEY Where's Dorimant?

YOUNG BELLAIR Stolen home! He has had business waiting for him there all this night, I believe, by an impatience I observed in him.

MEDLEY Very likely, 'tis but dissembling drunkenness, railing at his friends, and the kind soul will embrace the blessing, and forget the tedious expectation.

SIR FOPLING I must speak with him before I sleep!

YOUNG BELLAIR Emilia and I are resolved on that business.

MEDLEY Peace here's your father.

Enter Old Bellair, and Butler with a bottle of wine.

OLD BELLAIR The women are all gone to bed. Fill boy! Mr
Medley begin a health.
MEDLEY To Emilia.
OLD BELLAIR [*whispers*] Out a pise! She's a rogue and I'll not
pledge you.
MEDLEY I know you well.
OLD BELLAIR Adod drink it then.
SIR FOPLING Let us have the new bachique.
OLD BELLAIR Adod that is a hard word! What does it mean Sir?
MEDLEY A catch or drinking song.
OLD BELLAIR Let us have it then.
SIR FOPLING Fill the glasses round, and draw up in a body. Hey!
Music!
[*they sing*] The pleasures of love and the joys of good wine,
           To perfect our happiness wisely we join.
           We to beáuty all day
           Give the sovereign sway,
           And her favourite nymphs devoutly obey.
           At the plays we are constantly making our court
           And when they are ended we follow the sport.
           To the Mall and the Park
           Where we love till 'tis dark;
           Then sparkling champagne
           Puts an end to their reign;
           It quickly recovers
           Poor languishing lovers,
           Makes us frolic and gay, and drowns all our sorrow.
           But alas! We relapse again on the morrow.
              Let every man stand
              With his glass in his hand,
           And briskly discharge at the word of command.
              Here's a health to all those
              Whom tonight we depose.
           Wine and beauty by turns great souls should inspire.
           Present all together; and now boys give fire –
OLD BELLAIR Adod a pretty business and very merry.

SIR FOPLING Hark you Medley, let you and I take the fiddles and go waken Dorimant.

MEDLEY We shall do him a courtesy, if it be as I guess. For after the fatigue of this night, he'll quickly have his belly full: and be glad of an occasion to cry, 'Take away Handy'.

YOUNG BELLAIR I'll go with you, and there we'll consult about affairs Medley.

OLD BELLAIR [*looks at his watch*] Adod, 'tis six o'clock.

SIR FOPLING Let's away then.

OLD BELLAIR Mr Medley, my sister tells me you are an honest man. And adod I love you. Few words and hearty, that's the way with old Harry, old Harry.

SIR FOPLING Light your flambeux. Hey.

OLD BELLAIR What does the man mean?

MEDLEY 'Tis day Sir Fopling.

SIR FOPLING No matter. Our serenade will look the greater

[*Exeunt Omnes*]

SCENE II

Dorimant's lodging, a table, a candle, a toilet, etc. Handy tying up linen

Enter Dorimant in his gown and Bellinda.

DORIMANT Why will you be gone so soon?

BELLINDA Why did you stay out so late?

DORIMANT Call a chair, Handy! What makes you tremble so?

BELLINDA I have a thousand fears about me: have I not been seen think you?

DORIMANT By nobody but myself and trusty Handy.

BELLINDA Where are all your people?

DORIMANT I have dispersed 'em on sleeveless errands. ⟨*Bellinda sighs*⟩ What does that sigh mean?

BELLINDA Can you be so unkind to ask me? – Well – [*sighs*] Were it to do again –

DORIMANT We should do it, should we not?

BELLINDA I think we should: the wickeder man you to make me love so well – will you be discreet now?

DORIMANT I will –

BELLINDA You cannot.

DORIMANT Never doubt it.

BELLINDA I will not expect it.

DORIMANT You do me wrong.

BELLINDA You have no more power to keep the secret, than I had not to trust you with it.

DORIMANT By all the joys I have had, and those you keep in store –

BELLINDA You'll do for my sake what you never did before –

DORIMANT By that truth thou hast spoken, a wife shall sooner betray herself to her husband –

BELLINDA Yet I had rather you should be false in this than in another thing you promised me.

DORIMANT What's that?

BELLINDA That you would never see Loveit more but in public places, in the Park, at Court and plays.

DORIMANT 'Tis not likely a man should be fond of seeing a damned old play when there is a new one acted.

BELLINDA I dare not trust your promise.

DORIMANT You may –

BELLINDA This does not satisfy me. You shall swear you never will see her more.

DORIMANT I will! A thousand oaths – by all –

BELLINDA Hold – you shall not, now I think on't better.

DORIMANT I will swear –

BELLINDA I shall grow jealous of the oath, and think I owe your truth to that, not to your love.

DORIMANT Then, by my love! No other oath I'll swear.

Enter Handy.

HANDY Here's a chair.

BELLINDA Let me go.

DORIMANT I cannot.

BELLINDA Too willingly I fear.

DORIMANT Too unkindly feared. When will you promise me again?

BELLINDA Not this fortnight.

DORIMANT You will be better than your word.

BELLINDA I think I shall. Will it not make you love me less?

[*Fiddles without*]

[*starting*] Hark! What fiddles are these?

DORIMANT Look out Handy!

Exit Handy and returns.

HANDY Mr Medley, Mr Bellair, and Sir Fopling, they are coming up.

DORIMANT How got they in?

HANDY The door was open for the chair.

BELLINDA Lord! Let me fly –

DORIMANT Here, here, down the back stairs. I'll see you into your chair.

BELLINDA No, no! Stay and receive 'em. And be sure you keep your word and never see Loveit more. Let it be a proof of your kindness.

DORIMANT It shall – Handy direct her. [*kissing her hand*] Everlasting love go with thee.

[*Exeunt Bellinda and Handy*]

Enter Young Bellair, Medley, and Sir Fopling.

YOUNG BELLAIR Not abed yet!

MEDLEY You have had an irregular fit Dorimant.

DORIMANT I have.

YOUNG BELLAIR And is it off already?

DORIMANT Nature has done her part gentlemen, when she falls kindly to work, great cures are effected in little time, you know.

SIR FOPLING We thought there was a wench in the case by the chair that waited. Prithee make us a confidence.

DORIMANT Excuse me.

SIR FOPLING *Le sage* Dorimant – was she pretty?

DORIMANT So pretty she may come to keep her coach and pay parish duties if the good humour of the age continue.

MEDLEY And be of the number of the ladies kept by public-spirited men for the good of the whole Town.

SIR FOPLING [*dancing by himself*] Well said Medley.

YOUNG BELLAIR See Sir Fopling dancing.

DORIMANT You are practising and have a mind to recover I see.

SIR FOPLING Prithee Dorimant! Why hast not thou a glass hung up here? A room is the dullest thing without one!

YOUNG BELLAIR Here is company to entertain you.

SIR FOPLING But I mean in case of being alone. In a glass a man may entertain himself–

DORIMANT The shadow of himself indeed.

SIR FOPLING Correct the errors of his motions and his dress.

MEDLEY I find Sir Fopling in your solitude, you remember the saying of the wise man, and study yourself.

SIR FOPLING 'Tis the best diversion in our retirements. Dorimant thou art a pretty fellow and wear'st thy clothes well, but I never saw thee have a handsome cravat. Were they made up like mine, they'd give another air to thy face. Prithee let me send my man to dress thee but one day. By heavens an English man cannot tie a ribbon.

DORIMANT They are something clumsy-fisted –

SIR FOPLING I have brought over the prettiest fellow that ever spread a toilet, he served some time under Merille★ the greatest genie in the world for a *valet d'chambre*.

DORIMANT What he who formerly belonged to the Duke of Candale?†

SIR FOPLING The same, and got him his immortal reputation.

DORIMANT Y'have a very fine brandenburgh‡ on Sir Fopling.

SIR FOPLING It serves to wrap me up, after the fatigue of a ball.

MEDLEY I see you often in it, with your periwig tied up.

SIR FOPLING We should not always be in a set dress, 'tis more *en cavalier* to appear now and then in a *déshabillé*.

MEDLEY Pray how goes your business with Loveit?

SIR FOPLING You might have answered yourself in the Mall last night. Dorimant! Did you not see the advances she made me? I have been endeavouring at a song!

DORIMANT Already!

★ Merille: Valet to the Duke of Orleans, Louis XIV's brother.
† Candale: Louis-Charles-Gaston de Nogaret de Foix (1627–1658), a French general.
‡ brandenburgh: a woollen gown.

SIR FOPLING 'Tis my *coup d'essai* in English, I would fain have thy opinion of it.

DORIMANT Let's see it.

SIR FOPLING Hey page give me my song – Bellair, here thou hast a pretty voice sing it.

YOUNG BELLAIR Sing it yourself Sir Fopling.

SIR FOPLING Excuse me.

YOUNG BELLAIR You learnt to sing in Paris.

SIR FOPLING I did of Lambert* the greatest master in the world: but I have his own fault, a weak voice, and care not to sing out of a *ruelle*.†

DORIMANT A *ruelle* is a pretty cage for a singing fop indeed.

YOUNG BELLAIR [*reads the song*]

> How charming Phillis is, how fair!
> Ah that she were as willing,
> To ease my wounded heart of care
> And make her eyes less killing.
> I sigh! I sigh! I languish now,
> And love will not let me rest,
> I drive about the Park, and bow
> Still as I meet my dearest.

SIR FOPLING Sing it, sing it man, it goes to a pretty new tune which I am confident was made by Baptiste.‡

MEDLEY Sing it yourself Sir Fopling, he does not know the tune.

SIR FOPLING I'll venture.

Sir Fopling sings.

DORIMANT Aye marry! Now 'tis something. I shall not flatter you Sir Fopling, there is not much thought in't. But 'tis passionate and well turned.

MEDLEY After the French way.

SIR FOPLING That I aimed at – does it not give you a lively

* Lambert: Michel Lambert (1610–1696), Louis XIV's master of chamber music, who was also a composer and singer.

† *ruelle*: lady's bedchamber, where receptions were sometimes held in the morning.

‡ Baptiste: Jean Baptiste Lully (1633–1687). Louis XIV's master of court music. He was a composer and director of opera. 'Baptiste', however, could refer to Giovanni Battista Draghi, an Italian musician resident in London.

image of the thing? Slap down goes the glass, and thus we are
at it.

DORIMANT It does indeed. I perceive, Sir Fopling, you'll be the
very head of the sparks, who are lucky in compositions of this
nature.

Enter Sir Fopling's Footman.

SIR FOPLING La Tour, is the bath ready?

FOOTMAN Yes Sir.

SIR FOPLING *Adieu donc mes chers.*   [*Exit Sir Fopling*]

MEDLEY When have you your revenge on Loveit, Dorimant?

DORIMANT I will but change my linen and about it.

MEDLEY The powerful considerations which hindered have been
removed then.

DORIMANT Most luckily this morning, you must along with me,
my reputation lies at stake there.

MEDLEY I am engaged to Bellair.

DORIMANT What's your business.

MEDLEY Ma-tri-mony an't like you.

DORIMANT It does not, Sir.

YOUNG BELLAIR It may in time Dorimant, what think you of
Mrs Harriet?

DORIMANT What does she think of me?

YOUNG BELLAIR I am confident she loves you.

DORIMANT How does it appear?

YOUNG BELLAIR Why she's never well but when she's talking
of you, but then she finds all the faults in you she can. She laughs
at all who commend you, but then she speaks ill of all who do not.

DORIMANT Women of her temper betray themselves by their
over-cunning. I had once a growing love with a lady, who would
always quarrel with me when I came to see her, and yet was never
quiet if I stayed a day from her.

YOUNG BELLAIR My father is in love with Emilia.

DORIMANT That is a good warrant for your proceedings, go on
and prosper, I must to Loveit. Medley, I am sorry you cannot be a
witness.

MEDLEY Make her meet Sir Fopling again in the same place, and
use him ill before me.

DORIMANT That may be brought about I think. I'll be at your aunt's anon and give you joy Mr Bellair.

YOUNG BELLAIR You had not best think of Mrs Harriet too much, without church security there's no taking up there.

DORIMANT I may fall into the snare too. But –
The wife will find a difference in our fate,
You wed a woman, I a good estate.   [*Exeunt*]

SCENE III

Enter the chair with Bellinda, the men set it down and open it.
Bellinda starting.

BELLINDA [*surprised*] Lord! Where am I? In the Mall! Whither have you brought me?

FIRST CHAIRMAN You gave us no directions, Madam?

BELLINDA [*aside*] The fright I was in made me forget it.

FIRST CHAIRMAN We use to carry a lady from the squire's hither.

BELLINDA [*aside*] This is Loveit, I am undone if she sees me.
⟨*aloud*⟩ Quickly carry me away.

FIRST CHAIRMAN Whither an't like your honour?

BELLINDA Ask no questions –

Enter Loveit's Footman.

FOOTMAN Have you seen my lady, Madam?

BELLINDA I am just come to wait upon her –

FOOTMAN She will be glad to see you, Madam. She sent me to you this morning to desire your company, and I was told you went out by five o'clock.

BELLINDA [*aside*] More and more unlucky!

FOOTMAN Will you walk in Madam?

BELLINDA I'll discharge my chair and follow.   [*Exit Footman*]
Tell your mistress I am here. [*gives the Chairmen money*] Take this! And if ever you should be examined, be sure you say, you took me up in the Strand over against the Exchange, as you will answer to Mr Dorimant.

CHAIRMEN We will an't like your honour.   [*Exeunt Chairmen*]
BELLINDA Now to come off, I must on –
  In confidence and lies some hope is left;
  'Twere hard to be found out in the first theft.   [*Exit*]

ACT FIVE

⟨SCENE I⟩

Enter Mrs Loveit and Pert, her woman.

PERT Well! In my eyes Sir Fopling is no such despicable person.

MRS LOVEIT You are an excellent judge.

PERT He's as handsome a man as Mr Dorimant, and as great a gallant.

MRS LOVEIT Intolerable! Is't not enough I submit to his impertinences, but must I be plagued with yours too?

PERT Indeed Madam –

MRS LOVEIT 'Tis false, mercenary malice –

Enter her Footman.

FOOTMAN Mrs Bellinda Madam –

MRS LOVEIT What of her?

FOOTMAN She's below.

MRS LOVEIT How came she?

FOOTMAN In a chair, ambling Harry brought her.

MRS LOVEIT He bring her! His chair stands near Dorimant's door and always brings me from thence – run and ask him where he took her up; go, there is no truth in friendship neither. Women. as well as men, all are false, or all are so to me at least.

PERT You are jealous of her too?

MRS LOVEIT You had best tell her I am. 'Twill become the liberty you take of late. This fellow's bringing of her, her going out by five o'clock – I know not what to think.

Enter Bellinda.

Bellinda, you are grown an early riser I hear!

BELLINDA Do you not wonder my dear, what made me abroad so soon?

MRS LOVEIT You do not use to be so.

BELLINDA The country gentlewomen I told you of (Lord! they have the oddest diversions!) would never let me rest till I promised to go with them to the markets this morning to eat fruit and buy nosegays.

MRS LOVEIT Are they so fond of a filthy nosegay?

BELLINDA They complain of the stinks of the Town, and are never well but when they have their noses in one.

MRS LOVEIT There are essences and sweet waters.

BELLINDA O they cry out upon perfumes they are unwholesome, one of 'em was falling into a fit with the smell of these narolii.*

MRS LOVEIT Methinks in complaisance you should have had a nosegay too.

BELLINDA Do you think, my dear, I could be so loathsome to trick myself up with carnations and stock-gillyflowers? I begged their pardon and told them I never wore any thing but orange flowers and tuberose. That which made me willing to go was, a strange desire I had to eat some fresh nectarines.

MRS LOVEIT And had you any?

BELLINDA The best I ever tasted.

MRS LOVEIT Whence came you now?

BELLINDA From their lodgings, where I crowded out of a coach and took a chair to come and see you my dear.

MRS LOVEIT Whither did you send for that chair?

BELLINDA 'Twas going by empty.

MRS LOVEIT Where do these country gentlewomen lodge, I pray?

BELLINDA In the Strand over against the Exchange.

PERT That place is never without a nest of 'em, they are always as one goes by fleering in balconies or staring out of windows.

Enter Footman.

MRS LOVEIT [*to the Footman*] Come hither. [*whispers*]

BELLINDA [*aside*] This fellow by her order has been questioning the chairmen! I threatened 'em with the name of Dorimant, if they should have told truth I am lost for ever.

MRS LOVEIT In the Strand said you?

FOOTMAN Yes Madam over against the Exchange. [*Exit Footman*]

MRS LOVEIT ⟨*aside*⟩ She's innocent and I am much to blame.

BELLINDA [*aside*] I am so frighted, my countenance will betray me.

MRS LOVEIT Bellinda! What makes you look so pale?

BELLINDA Want of my usual rest, and jolting up and down so long in an odious hackney.

* narolii: essences of orange.

Footman returns.

FOOTMAN Madam! Mr Dorimant!

MRS LOVEIT What makes him here?

BELLINDA [*aside*] Then I am betrayed indeed, h'has broke his word, and I love a man that does not care for me.

MRS LOVEIT Lord! You faint Bellinda!

BELLINDA I think I shall! Such an oppression here on the sudden.

PERT She has eaten too much fruit I warrant you.

MRS LOVEIT Not unlikely!

PERT 'Tis that lies heavy on her stomach.

MRS LOVEIT Have her into my chamber, give her some surfeit-water, and let her lie down a little.

PERT Come, Madam! I was a strange devourer of fruit when I was young, so ravenous –   [*Exeunt Bellinda and Pert leading her off*]

MRS LOVEIT O that my love would be but calm awhile! That I might receive this man with all the scorn and indignation he deserves.

Enter Dorimant.

DORIMANT Now for a touch of Sir Fopling to begin with. Hey – Page – Give positive order that none of my people stir – Let the *canaille* wait as they should do – since noise and nonsense have such powerful charms,

'I that I may successful prove,

Transforms myself to what you love.'*

MRS LOVEIT If that would do, you need not change from what you are, you can be vain and loud enough.

DORIMANT But not with so good a grace as Sir Fopling. Hey, Hampshire – Oh – that sound, that sound becomes the mouth of a man of quality.

MRS LOVEIT Is there a thing so hateful as a senseless mimic?

DORIMANT He's a great grievance indeed to all who like yourself, Madam, love to play the fool in quiet.

MRS LOVEIT A ridiculous animal, who has more of the ape, than the ape has of the man in him.

* 'I that . . . love': ll.5–6 of Waller's 'To the Mutable Fair', with 'I that' substituted for the original's 'and that'.

DORIMANT I have as mean an opinion of a sheer mimic as yourself, yet were he all ape I should prefer him to the gay, the giddy, brisk-insipid noisy fool you dote on.

MRS LOVEIT Those noisy fools, however you despise 'em, have good qualities, which weigh more (or ought at least) with us women, than all the pernicious wit you have to boast of.

DORIMANT That I may hereafter have a just value for their merit, pray do me the favour to name 'em.

MRS LOVEIT You'll despise 'em as the dull effects of ignorance and vanity! Yet I care not if I mention some. First, they really admire us, while you at best but flatter us well.

DORIMANT Take heed! Fools can dissemble too –

MRS LOVEIT They may! But not so artificially as you – There is no fear they should deceive us! Then they are assiduous, Sir, they are ever offering us their service, and always waiting on our will.

DORIMANT You owe that to their excessive idleness! They know not how to entertain themselves at home, and find so little welcome abroad, they are fain to fly to you who countenance 'em as a refuge against the solitude they would be otherwise condemned to.

MRS LOVEIT Their conversation too diverts us better.

DORIMANT Playing with your fan, smelling to your gloves, commending your hair, and taking notice how 'tis cut and shaded after the new way –

MRS LOVEIT Were it sillier than you can make it, you must allow 'tis pleasanter to laugh at others than to be laughed at ourselves though never so wittily. Then though they want skill to flatter us, they flatter themselves so well, they save us the labour! We need not take that care and pains to satisfy 'em of our love which we so often lose on you.

DORIMANT They commonly indeed believe too well of themselves, and always better of you than you deserve.

MRS LOVEIT You are in the right, they have an implicit faith in us which keeps 'em from prying narrowly into our secrets, and saves us the vexatious trouble of clearing doubts which your subtle and causeless jealousies every moment raise.

DORIMANT There is an inbred falsehood in women, which inclines 'em still to them, whom they may most easily deceive.

MRS LOVEIT The man who loves above his quality, does not suffer more from the insolent impertinence of his mistress, than the woman who loves above her understanding does from the arrogant presumptions of her friend.

DORIMANT You mistake the use of fools, they are designed for properties and not for friends, you have an indifferent stock of reputation left yet. Lose it all like a frank gamester on the square, 'twill then be time enough to turn rook,* and cheat it up again on a good substantial bubble.†

MRS LOVEIT The old man and the ill-favoured are only fit for properties indeed, but young and handsome fools have met with kinder fortunes.

DORIMANT They have to the shame of your sex be it spoken. 'Twas this, the thought of this made me by a timely jealousy endeavour to prevent the good fortune you are providing for Sir Fopling – But against a woman's frailty all our care is vain.

MRS LOVEIT Had I not with a dear experience bought the knowledge of your falsehood, you might have fooled me yet. This is not the first jealousy you have feigned to make a quarrel with me, and get a week to throw away on some such unknown inconsiderable slut, as you have been lately lurking with at plays.

DORIMANT Women, when they would break off with a man never want th'address to turn the fault on him.

MRS LOVEIT You take a pride of late in using of me ill, that the Town may know the power you have over me. Which now (as unreasonably as yourself) expects that I (do me all the injuries you can) must love you still.

DORIMANT I am so far from expecting that you should, I begin to think you never did love me.

MRS LOVEIT Would the memory of it were so wholly worn out in me that I did doubt it too! What made you come to disturb my growing quiet?

DORIMANT To give you joy of your growing infamy.

MRS LOVEIT Insupportable! Insulting devil! This from you, the only author of my shame! This from another had been but justice, but from you, 'tis a hellish and inhuman outrage. What have I done?

* rook: sharper, cheat.   † bubble: grill.

DORIMANT A thing that puts you below my scorn, and makes my anger as ridiculous as you have made my love.

MRS LOVEIT I walked last night with Sir Fopling.

DORIMANT You did Madam, and you talked and laughed aloud 'Ha, ha, ha' – O that laugh, that laugh becomes the confidence of a woman of quality.

MRS LOVEIT You who have more pleasure in the ruin of a woman's reputation than in the endearment of her love, reproach me not with yourself, and I defy you to name the man can lay a blemish on my fame.

DORIMANT To be seen publicly so transported with the vain follies of that notorious fop, to me is an infamy below the sin of prostitution with another man.

MRS LOVEIT Rail on, I am satisfied in the justice of what I did, you had provoked me to't.

DORIMANT What I did was the effect of a passion, whose extravagancies you have been willing to forgive.

MRS LOVEIT And what I did was the effect of a passion you may forgive if you think fit.

DORIMANT Are you so indifferent grown?

MRS LOVEIT I am.

DORIMANT Nay! Then 'tis time to part. I'll send you back your letters you have so often asked for: I have two or three of'em about me.

MRS LOVEIT Give 'em me.

DORIMANT You snatch as if you thought I would not – there – and may the perjuries in 'em be mine if ere I see you more. [*offers to go, she catches him*]

MRS LOVEIT Stay!

DORIMANT I will not.

MRS LOVEIT You shall.

DORIMANT What have you to say?

MRS LOVEIT I cannot speak it yet.

DORIMANT Something more in commendation of the fool. Death! I want patience, let me go.

MRS LOVEIT I cannot. [*aside*] I can sooner part with the limbs that hold him.

⟨*to him*⟩ I hate that nauseous fool, you know I do.

DORIMANT Was it the scandal you were fond of then?

MRS LOVEIT Y'had raised my anger equal to my love, a thing you ne'er could do before, and in revenge I did – I know not what I did: – Would you would not think on't any more.

DORIMANT Should I be willing to forget it, I shall be daily minded of it, 'twill be a commonplace for all the Town to laugh at me, and Medley, when he is rhetorically drunk, will ever be declaiming on it in my ears.

MRS LOVEIT 'Twill be believed a jealous spite! Come forget it.

DORIMANT Let me consult my reputation, you are too careless of it. [*pauses*] You shall meet Sir Fopling in the Mall again tonight.

MRS LOVEIT What mean you?

DORIMANT I have thought on it, and you must. 'Tis necessary to justify my love to the world: you can handle a coxcomb as he deserves, when you are not out of humour Madam!

MRS LOVEIT Public satisfaction for the wrong I have done you! This is some new device to make me more ridiculous!

DORIMANT Hear me!

MRS LOVEIT I will not!

DORIMANT You will be persuaded.

MRS LOVEIT Never.

DORIMANT Are you so obstinate?

MRS LOVEIT Are you so base?

DORIMANT You will not satisfy my love?

MRS LOVEIT I would die to satisfy that, but I will not, to save you from a thousand racks, do a shameless thing to please your vanity.

DORIMANT Farewell false woman.

MRS LOVEIT Do! Go!

DORIMANT You will call me back again.

MRS LOVEIT Exquisite fiend! I knew you came but to torment me.

Enter Bellinda and Pert.

DORIMANT [*surprised*] Bellinda here!

BELLINDA [*aside*] He starts! And looks pale, the sight of me has touched his guilty soul.

PERT 'Twas but a qualm as I said, a little indigestion; the surfeit-water did it Madam, mixed with a little mirabilis.★

★ mirabilis: aqua mirabilis, a medicinal drink of spiced wine.

DORIMANT ⟨*aside*⟩ I am confounded! And cannot guess how she came hither!

MRS LOVEIT 'Tis your fortune Bellinda ever to be here, when I am abused by this prodigy of ill nature.

BELLINDA I am amazed to find him here! How has he the face to come near you?

DORIMANT [*aside*] Here is fine work towards! I never was at such a loss before.

BELLINDA One who makes a public profession of breach of faith and ingratitude! I loathe the sight of him.

DORIMANT ⟨*aside*⟩ There is no remedy, I must submit to their tongues now, and some other time bring myself off as well as I can.

BELLINDA Other men are wicked, but then they have some sense of shame! He is never well but when he triumphs, nay! glories to a woman's face in his villainies.

MRS LOVEIT You are in the right Bellinda, but methinks your kindness for me makes you concern yourself too much with him.

BELLINDA It does indeed my dear! His barbarous carriage to you yesterday, made me hope you ne'er would see him more, and the very next day to find him here again, provokes me strangely: but because I know you love him I have done.

DORIMANT You have reproached me handsomely, and I deserve it for coming hither, but –

PERT You must expect it, Sir! All women will hate you for my lady's sake!

DORIMANT [*aside to Bellinda*] Nay, if she begins too, 'tis time to fly! I shall be scolded to death else. ⟨*aloud*⟩ I am to blame in some circumstances I confess; but as to the main, I am not so guilty as you imagine. I shall seek a more convenient time to clear myself.

MRS LOVEIT Do it now! What impediments are here?

DORIMANT I want time, and you want temper.

MRS LOVEIT These are weak pretences!

DORIMANT You never were more mistaken in your life, and so farewell.   [*Dorimant flings off*]

MRS LOVEIT Call a footman! Pert! Quickly, I will have him dogged.

PERT I wish you would not for my quiet and your own.

MRS LOVEIT I'll find out the infamous cause of all our quarrels, pluck her mask off, and expose her bare-faced to the world.

BELLINDA [*aside*] Let me but escape this time, I'll never venture more.

MRS LOVEIT Bellinda! You shall go with me.

BELLINDA I have such a heaviness hangs on me with what I did this morning, I would fain go home and sleep, my dear.

MRS LOVEIT Death! And eternal darkness. I shall never sleep again. Raging fevers seize the world and make mankind as restless all as I am. [*Exit Mrs Loveit*]

BELLINDA I knew him false and helped to make him so? Was not her ruin enough to fright me from the danger? It should have been, but love can take no warning. [*Exit Bellinda*]

SCENE II

Lady Townley's house

Enter Medley, Young Bellair, Lady Townley, Emilia and Chaplain.

MEDLEY Bear up Bellair, and do not let us see that repentance in thine, we daily do in married faces.

LADY TOWNLEY This wedding will strangely surprise my brother when he knows it.

MEDLEY Your nephew ought to conceal it for a time, Madam, since marriage has lost its good name, prudent men seldom expose their own reputations till 'tis convenient to justify their wives'.

OLD BELLAIR [*without*] Where are you all there? Out, adod, will nobody hear?

LADY TOWNLEY My brother, quickly Mr Smirk into this closet. You must not be seen yet. [⟨*Smirk*⟩ *goes into the closet*]

Enter Old Bellair and Lady Townley's Page.

OLD BELLAIR Desire Mr Fourbe to walk into the lower parlour, I will be with him presently – [*to Young Bellair*] Where have you been, Sir, you could not wait on me today?

YOUNG BELLAIR About a business.

OLD BELLAIR Are you so good at business? Adod I have a business too, you shall dispatch out of hand, Sir. Send for a parson, sister; my Lady Woodvil and her daughter are coming.

LADY TOWNLEY What need you huddle up things thus?

OLD BELLAIR Out a pise, youth is apt to play the fool and 'tis not good it should be in their power.

LADY TOWNLEY You need not fear your son.

OLD BELLAIR H'has been idling this morning, and adod I do not like him. [*to Emilia*] How dost thou do sweetheart?

EMILIA You are very severe, Sir, married in such haste!

OLD BELLAIR Go to, thou'rt a rogue, and I will talk with thee anon. Here's my Lady Woodvil come.

Enter Lady Woodvil, Harriet and Busy.

Welcome Madam; Mr Fourbe's below with the writings.*

LADY WOODVIL Let us down and make an end then.

OLD BELLAIR Sister, show the way [*to Young Bellair who is talking to Harriet*] Harry your business lies not there yet! Excuse him till we have done lady, and then adod he shall be for thee. Mr Medley we must trouble you to be a witness.

MEDLEY I luckily came for that purpose, Sir.

[*Exeunt Old Bellair, Medley, Young Bellair, Lady Townley and Lady Woodvil*]

BUSY What will you do Madam?

HARRIET Be carried back and mewed up in the country again, run away here, anything, rather than be married to a man I do not care for. Dear Emilia, do thou advise me!

EMILIA Mr Bellair is engaged you know.

HARRIET I do; but know not what the fear of losing an estate may fright him to.

EMILIA In the desperate condition you are in, you should consult with some judicious man; what think you of Mr Dorimant?

HARRIET I do not think of him at all.

BUSY ⟨*aside*⟩ She thinks of nothing else I am sure –

EMILIA How fond your mother was of Mr Courtage!

HARRIET Because I contrived the mistake to make a little mirth, you believe I like the man.

* writings: marriage contract.

EMILIA Mr Bellair believes you love him.

HARRIET Men are seldom in the right when they guess at a woman's mind, would she whom he loves loved him no better.

BUSY [*aside*] That's e'en well enough on all conscience.

EMILIA Mr Dorimant has a great deal of wit.

HARRIET And takes a great deal of pains to show it.

EMILIA He's extremely well fashioned.

HARRIET Affectedly grave, or ridiculously wild and apish.

BUSY You defend him still against your mother.

HARRIET I would not were he justly rallied, but I cannot hear any one undeservedly railed at.

EMILIA Has your woman learned the song you were so taken with?

HARRIET I was fond of a new thing, 'tis dull at second hearing.

EMILIA Mr Dorimant made it.

BUSY She knows it Madam, and has made me sing it at least a dozen times this morning.

HARRIET Thy tongue is as impertinent as thy fingers.

EMILIA You have provoked her.

BUSY 'Tis but singing the song and I shall appease her.

EMILIA Prithee do.

HARRIET She has a voice will grate your ears worse than a catcall, and dresses so ill she's scarce fit to trick up a yeoman's daughter on a holy day.

*Song by Sir C. S.**

BUSY [*sings*]

As Amoret with Phillis sat
One evening on the plain,
And saw the charming Strephon wait
To tell the nymph his pain.

The threatening danger to remove
She whispered in her ear,
'Ah Phillis, if you would not love,
This shepherd do not hear.

None ever had so strange an art
His passion to convey

* Sir C. S.: possibly Sir Carr Scroope.

Into a listening virgin's heart
And steal her soul away.

Fly, fly betimes, for fear you give
Occasion for your fate.'
'In vain', said she, 'in vain I strive,
Alas! 'tis now too late'.

Enter Dorimant.

DORIMANT 'Music so softens and disarms the mind'.
HARRIET 'That not one arrow does resistance find'.★
DORIMANT Let us make use of the lucky minute then.
HARRIET [*aside turning from Dorimant*] My love springs with my blood into my face, I dare not look upon him yet.
DORIMANT What have we here, the picture of celebrated beauty, giving audience in public to a declared lover?
HARRIET Play the dying fop, and make the piece complete Sir.
DORIMANT What think you if the hint were well improved? The whole mystery of making love pleasantly designed and wrought in a suit of hangings?
HARRIET 'Twere needless to execute fools in effigy who suffer daily in their own persons.
DORIMANT [*to Emilia aside*] Mrs Bride, for such I know this happy day has made you.
EMILIA [*aside*] Defer the formal joy you are to give me, and mind your business with her – ⟨*aloud*⟩ Here are dreadful preparations Mr Dorimant, writings sealing, and a parson sent for –
DORIMANT To marry this lady –
BUSY Condemned she is, and what will become of her I know not, without you generously engage in a rescue.
DORIMANT In this sad condition, Madam, I can do no less than offer you my service.
HARRIET The obligation is not great, you are the common sanctuary for all young women who run from their relations.
DORIMANT I have always my arms open to receive the distressed. But I will open my heart and receive you, where none yet did ever

★ 'Music so . . . find': ll.11 and 12 of Waller's 'Of my Lady Isabella, Playing on the Lute', 'one' being substituted for the original's 'an'.

enter – You have filled it with a secret, might I but let you know it –

HARRIET Do not speak it, if you would have me believe it; your tongue is so famed for falsehood 'twill do the truth an injury. [*turns her head away*]

DORIMANT Turn not away then; but look on me and guess it.

HARRIET Did you not tell me there was no credit to be given to faces? That women nowadays have their passions as much at will as they have their complexions, and put on joy and sadness, scorn and kindness, with the same ease they do their paint and patches – Are they the only counterfeits?

DORIMANT You wrong your own, while you suspect my eyes, by all the hope I have in you, the inimitable colour in your cheeks is not more free from art than are the sighs I offer.

HARRIET In men who have been long hardened in sin, we have reason to mistrust the first signs of repentance.

DORIMANT The prospect of such a heaven will make me persevere, and give you marks that are infallible.

HARRIET What are those?

DORIMANT I will renounce all the joys I have in friendship and in wine, sacrifice to you all the interest I have in other women –

HARRIET Hold – Though I wish you devout, I would not have you turn fanatic – Could you neglect these a while and make a journey into the country?

DORIMANT To be with you I could live there: and never send one thought to London.

HARRIET Whate'er you say, I know all beyond High Park's a desert to you, and that no gallantry can draw you farther.

DORIMANT That has been the utmost limit of my love – But now my passion knows no bounds, and there's no measure to be taken of what I'll do for you from anything I ever did before.

HARRIET When I hear you talk thus in Hampshire, I shall begin to think there may be some little truth enlarged upon.

DORIMANT Is this all – will you not promise me –

HARRIET I hate to promise! What we do then is expected from us, and wants much of the welcome it finds, when it surprises.

DORIMANT May I not hope?

HARRIET That depends on you, and not on me, and 'tis to no purpose to forbid it. [*turns to Busy*]

BUSY Faith Madam, now I perceive the gentleman loves you too, e'en let him know your mind and torment yourselves no longer.

HARRIET Dost think I have no sense of modesty?

BUSY Think, if you lose this you may never have another opportunity.

HARRIET May he hate me, (a curse that frights me when I speak it!) if ever I do a thing against the rules of decency and honour.

DORIMANT [*to Emilia*] I am beholding to you for your good intentions, Madam.

EMILIA I thought the concealing of our marriage from her might have done you better service.

DORIMANT Try her again –

EMILIA What have you resolved, Madam? The time draws near.

HARRIET To be obstinate and protest against this marriage.

Enter Lady Townley, in haste.

LADY TOWNLEY [*to Emilia*] Quickly, quickly, let Mr Smirk out of the closet.

Smirk comes out of the closet.

HARRIET A parson! Had you laid him in here?

DORIMANT I knew nothing of him.

HARRIET Should it appear you did, your opinion of my easiness may cost you dear.

Enter Old Bellair, Young Bellair, Medley and Lady Woodvil.

OLD BELLAIR Out a pise! The canonical hour* is almost passed; sister, is the man of God come?

LADY TOWNLEY He waits your leisure –

OLD BELLAIR By your favour Sir, adod a pretty spruce fellow! What may we call him?

LADY TOWNLEY Mr Smirk! My Lady Biggot's chaplain.

OLD BELLAIR A wise woman! Adod she is. The man will serve for the flesh as well as the spirit. Please you Sir to commission a young couple to go to bed together a God's name? – Harry.

YOUNG BELLAIR Here Sir.

* The canonical hour: the time during which marriages could take place legally.

OLD BELLAIR Out a pise without your mistress in your hand!

SMIRK Is this the gentleman?

OLD BELLAIR Yes Sir!

SMIRK Are you not mistaken Sir?

OLD BELLAIR Adod, I think not Sir.

SMIRK Sure you are Sir?

OLD BELLAIR You look as if you would forbid the banns Mr Smirk, I hope you have no pretension to the lady!

SMIRK Wish him joy Sir! I have done him the good office today already.

OLD BELLAIR Out a pise what do I hear?

LADY TOWNLEY Never storm brother, the truth is out.

OLD BELLAIR How say you Sir! Is this your wedding day?

YOUNG BELLAIR It is Sir.

OLD BELLAIR And adod it shall be mine too, [*to Emilia*] give me thy hand sweetheart, what does thou mean? Give me thy hand I say.

[*Emilia kneels and Young Bellair*]

LADY TOWNLEY Come come, give her your blessing, this is the woman your son loved and is married to.

OLD BELLAIR Ha! Cheated! Cozened! And by your contrivance sister!

LADY TOWNLEY What would you do with her, she's a rogue and you can't abide her.

MEDLEY Shall I hit her a pat for you Sir?

OLD BELLAIR Adod you are all rogues, and I never will forgive you.

LADY TOWNLEY Whither! Whither away?

MEDLEY Let him go and cool awhile!

LADY WOODVIL [*to Dorimant*] Here's a business broke out now Mr Courtage, I am made a fine fool of.

DORIMANT You see the old gentleman knew nothing of it.

LADY WOODVIL I find he did not. I shall have some trick put upon me if I stay in this wicked Town any longer. Harriet! Dear child! Where art thou? I'll into the country straight.

OLD BELLAIR Adod Madam, you shall hear me first –

Enter Mrs Loveit, and Bellinda.

MRS LOVEIT Hither my man dogged him! –

BELLINDA Yonder he stands my dear.

MRS LOVEIT I see him. – [*aside*] And with him the face that has undone me! O that I were but where I might throw out the anguish of my heart, here it must rage within and break it.

LADY TOWNLEY Mrs Loveit! Are you afraid to come forward?

MRS LOVEIT I was amazed to see so much company here in a morning, the occasion sure is extraordinary –

DORIMANT [*aside*] Loveit and Bellinda! The devil owes me a shame today, and I think never will have done paying it.*

MRS LOVEIT Married! Dear Emilia! How am I transported with the news?

HARRIET [*to Dorimant*] I little thought Emilia was the woman Mr Bellair was in love with – I'll chide her for not trusting me with the secret.

DORIMANT How do you like Mrs Loveit?

HARRIET She's a famed mistress of yours I hear –

DORIMANT She has been on occasion!

OLD BELLAIR [*to Lady Woodvil*] Adod Madam I cannot help it.

LADY WOODVIL You need make no more apologies Sir!

EMILIA [*to Mrs Loveit*] The old gentleman's excusing himself to my Lady Woodvil.

MRS LOVEIT Ha, ha, ha! I never heard of anything so pleasant.

HARRIET [*to Dorimant*] She's extremely overjoyed at something.

DORIMANT At nothing, she is one of those hoiting† ladies, who gaily fling themselves about, and force a laugh, when their aching hearts are full of discontent and malice.

MRS LOVEIT O heaven! I was never so near killing myself with laughing – Mr Dorimant! Are you a brideman?

LADY WOODVIL Mr Dorimant! Is this Mr Dorimant, Madam?

MRS LOVEIT If you doubt it, your daughter can resolve you I suppose.

LADY WOODVIL I am cheated too, basely cheated.

OLD BELLAIR Out a pise, what's here more knavery yet!

LADY WOODVIL Harriet! On my blessing come away I charge you.

HARRIET Dear mother! Do but stay and hear me.

* The devil . . . paying it: This is a variation upon the proverbial saying 'The devil owed a shame and now has paid it'.
† hoiting: giddy.

LADY WOODVIL I am betrayed and thou art undone I fear.

HARRIET Do not fear it – I have not, nor never will do anything against my duty – believe me! Dear mother do.

DORIMANT [*to Mrs Loveit*] I had trusted you with this secret but that I knew the violence of your nature would ruin my fortune as now unluckily it has: I thank you Madam.

MRS LOVEIT She's an heiress I know, and very rich.

DORIMANT To satisfy you I must give up my interest wholly to my love, had you been a reasonable woman, I might have secured 'em both, and been happy –

MRS LOVEIT You might have trusted me with anything of this kind, you know you might. Why did you go under a wrong name?

DORIMANT The story is too long to tell you now, be satisfied, this is the business; this is the mask has kept me from you.

BELLINDA [*aside*] He's tender of my honour, though he's cruel to my love.

MRS LOVEIT Was it no idle mistress then?

DORIMANT Believe me a wife, to repair the ruins of my estate that needs it.

MRS LOVEIT The knowledge of this makes my grief hang lighter on my soul; but I shall never more be happy.

DORIMANT Bellinda!

BELLINDA Do not think of clearing yourself with me, it is impossible – Do all men break their words thus?

DORIMANT Th'extravagant words they speak in love; 'tis as unreasonable to expect we should perform all we promise then, as do all we threaten when we are angry – When I see you next –

BELLINDA Take no notice of me and I shall not hate you.

DORIMANT How came you to Mrs Loveit?

BELLINDA By a mistake the chairmen made for want of my giving them directions.

DORIMANT 'Twas a pleasant one. We must meet again.

BELLINDA Never.

DORIMANT Never!

BELLINDA When we do, may I be as infamous as you are false.

LADY TOWNLEY Men of Mr Dorimant's character, always suffer in the general opinion of the world.

MEDLEY You can make no judgment of a witty man from common fame, considering the prevailing faction, Madam.

OLD BELLAIR Adod he's in the right.

MEDLEY Besides 'tis a common error among women, to believe too well of them they know, and too ill of them they don't.

OLD BELLAIR Adod he observes well.

LADY TOWNLEY Believe me, Madam, you will find Mr Dorimant as civil a gentleman as you thought Mr Courtage.

HARRIET If you would but know him better –

LADY WOODVIL You have a mind to know him better! Come away – You shall never see him more –

HARRIET Dear mother stay –

LADY WOODVIL I wo'not be consenting to your ruin –

HARRIET Were my fortune in your power –

LADY WOODVIL Your person is.

HARRIET Could I be disobedient I might take it out of yours and put it into his.

LADY WOODVIL 'Tis that you would be at, you would marry this Dorimant.

HARRIET I cannot deny it! I would, and never will marry any other man.

LADY WOODVIL Is this the duty that you promised?

HARRIET But I will never marry him against your will –

LADY WOODVIL [*aside*] She knows the way to melt my heart. [*to Harriet*] Upon yourself light your undoing.

MEDLEY [*to Old Bellair*] Come Sir, you have not the heart any longer to refuse your blessing.

OLD BELLAIR Adod, I ha'not – Rise and God bless you both – Make much of her Harry, she deserves thy kindness – [*to Emilia*] Adod sirrah I did not think it had been in thee.

Enter Sir Fopling and his Page.

SIR FOPLING 'Tis a damned windy day! Hey Page! Is my periwig right?

PAGE A little out of order, Sir!

SIR FOPLING Pox o' this apartment, it wants an antechamber to adjust oneself in. [*to Mrs Loveit*] Madam! I came from your house and your servants directed me hither.

MRS LOVEIT I will give order hereafter they shall direct you better.

SIR FOPLING The great satisfaction I had in the Mall last night has given me such disquiet since.

MRS LOVEIT 'Tis likely to give me more than I desire.

SIR FOPLING What the devil makes her so reserved? Am I guilty of an indiscretion, Madam?

MRS LOVEIT You will be of a great one, if you continue your mistake, Sir.

SIR FOPLING Something puts you out of humour.

MRS LOVEIT The most foolish inconsiderable thing that ever did.

SIR FOPLING Is it my power?

MRS LOVEIT To hang or drown it, do one of 'em, and trouble me no more.

SIR FOPLING So *fière! Serviteur*, Madam – Medley! Where's Dorimant?

MEDLEY Methinks the lady has not made you those advances today she did last night, Sir Fopling –

SIR FOPLING Prithee do not talk of her.

MEDLEY She would be a *bonne fortune*.

SIR FOPLING Not to me at present.

MEDLEY How so?

SIR FOPLING An intrigue now would be but a temptation to me to throw away that vigour on one which I mean shall shortly make my court to the whole sex in a ballet.

MEDLEY Wisely considered, Sir Fopling.

SIR FOPLING No one woman is worth the loss of a cut in a caper.

MEDLEY Not when 'tis so universally designed.

LADY WOODVIL Mr Dorimant, every one has spoke so much in your behalf, that I can no longer doubt but I was in the wrong.

MRS LOVEIT There's nothing but falsehood and impertinence in this world! All men are villains or fools; take example from my misfortunes. Bellinda, if thou would'st be happy, give thyself wholly up to goodness.

HARRIET [*to Mrs Loveit*] Mr Dorimant has been your God almighty long enough, 'tis time to think of another –

MRS LOVEIT Jeered by her! I will lock myself up in my house and never see the world again.

HARRIET A nunnery is the more fashionable place for such a retreat, and has been the fatal consequence of many a *belle passion*.

MRS LOVEIT Hold heart! Till I get home! Should I answer 'twould make her triumph greater. [*is going out*]

DORIMANT Your hand Sir Fopling –

SIR FOPLING Shall I wait upon you Madam?

MRS LOVEIT Legion of fools, as many devils take thee.

[*Exit Mrs Loveit*]

MEDLEY Dorimant? I pronounce thy reputation clear – and henceforward when I would know anything of woman, I will consult no other oracle.

SIR FOPLING Stark mad, by all that's handsome! Dorimant thou hast engaged me in a pretty business.

DORIMANT I have not leisure now to talk about it.

OLD BELLAIR Out a pise, what does this man of mode do here again?

LADY TOWNLEY He'll be an excellent entertainment within brother, and is luckily come to raise the mirth of the company.

LADY WOODVIL Madam, I take my leave of you.

LADY TOWNLEY What do you mean, Madam?

LADY WOODVIL To go this afternoon part of my way to Hartly.*

OLD BELLAIR Adod you shall stay and dine first! Come we will all be good friends, and you shall give Mr Dorimant leave to wait upon you and your daughter in the country.

LADY WOODVIL If his occasions bring him that way, I have now so good an opinion of him, he shall be welcome.

HARRIET To a great rambling lone house, that looks as it were not inhabited, the family's so small; there you'll find my mother, an old lame aunt, and myself Sir, perched up on chairs at a distance in a large parlour; sitting moping like three or four melancholy birds in a spacious volary.† Does not this stagger your resolution?

DORIMANT Not at all, Madam! The first time I saw you you left me with the pangs of love upon me, and this day my soul has quite given up her liberty.

HARRIET This is more dismal than the country! Emilia! Pity me, who am going to that sad place. Methinks I hear the hateful

* Hartly: Lady Woodvil's estate, or perhaps Hartley Row in Hampshire.
† volary: aviary.

noise of rooks already . . . Kaw, kaw, kaw. . . . There's music
in the worst cry in London! My dill and cucumbers to pickle.

OLD BELLAIR Sister! Knowing of this matter, I hope you have
provided us some good cheer.

LADY TOWNLEY I have brother, and the fiddles too –

OLD BELLAIR Let 'em strike up then, the young lady shall have a
dance before she departs.

Dance.

After the Dance.

So now we'll in, and make this an arrant wedding day.
[*to the pit*] And if these honest gentlemen rejoice,
Adod the boy has made a happy choice.

[*Exeunt Omnes*]

THE EPILOGUE

By Mr Dryden

Most modern wits, such monstrous fools have shown,
They seemed not of heaven's making but their own,
Those nauseous harlequins* in farce may pass,
But there goes more to a substantial ass!
Something of man must be exposed to view,
That, gallants, they may more resemble you.
Sir Fopling is a fool so nicely writ,
The ladies would mistake him for a wit.
And when he sings, talks loud, and cocks; would cry,
'I vow methinks he's pretty company,
So brisk, so gay, so travelled, so refined!
As he took pains to graft upon his kind.'
True fops help nature's work, and go to school,
To file and finish god-a'mighty's fool.
Yet none Sir Fopling him, or him can call;
He's knight o'th'shire,† and represents ye all.
From each he meets, he culls whate'er he can.
Legion's his name, a people in a man.
His bulky folly gathers as it goes,
And, rolling o'er you, like a snowball grows.
His various modes from various fathers follow,
One taught the toss, and one the new French wallow.
His sword-knot, this; his cravat, this designed,
And this, the yard-long snake he twirls behind.
From one the sacred periwig he gained,
Which wind ne'er blew, nor touch of hat profaned.
Another's diving bow he did adore,
Which with a shog‡ casts all the hair before:
Till he with full decorum brings it back,
And rises with a water spaniel shake.

* harlequins: probably a reference to the success of continental players in England.
† knight o'th'shire: representative of a county in Parliament.
‡ shog: shake.

As for his songs (the ladies' dear delight)
Those sure he took from most of you who write.
Yet every man is safe from what he feared,
For no one fool is hunted from the herd.

NOTES

The copy text used is that of the first edition of 1676 in the Brotherton Collection, University of Leeds

Abbreviations
  Q1   The first quarto edition, 1676
  Q2   The second quarto edition, 1684
  Q3   The third quarto edition, 1693
  W   *The Works of Sir George Etherege*, 1704

525.16   ye Q2 / you Q1
529.12   with her head W / with head Q1
529.20   Good, now 1704 ed. / Good now, Q1
532.16   ado, we / Ado we Q1
533.8   misfortune. Let / Misfortune, let Q1
533.30   concerns) – / Concerns) Q1
534.1   begun, I / begun; I Q1
534.14   *Exit Footman* / *Exit* Handy *and* Footman Q1
535.31   world, for W / World for Q1
535.32   honour, Robin Q2 / honour *Robin* Q1
537.24   Ho, that / Ho that Q1
540.3   aunt's / Aunts Q1
542.26   within. Emilia / within, Emilia Q1
543.13   her, sister / her Sister Q1
543.29   meantime, mum Q3 / mean time Mum Q1
543.30   Q1 prints *Enter* Young Bellair after 'Harry, come you'
548.16   of. Q3 / off. Q1
552.28   weary of, as Q2 / weary off, as Q1
552.35   protestations, / Protestations. Q1
554.10   fall to Q2 / fall too Q1
557.16   'which' is printed as a catchword only in Q1; it is incorporated in the second line of the verse in Q2
572.13   not. As / not, as Q1
581.31   Q1 prints *After the dance* . . . *Emilia* after Emilia's speech
585.2   here? Masquerades? / here Masquerades? Q1
585.20   you. This / you, this Q1
585.23   *off his* Q3 / *of his* Q1
586.21   madam is W. / Madam's Q1

587.16   yourself. They / yourself, they Q1
588.20   André / Andrè Q1
588.21   Q1 sets *Sir Fopling endeavours at a caper* at the end of his speech
589.1   [*to an English dancer*] emendation in *The Mode of Mode* Ed. John Conaghan, 1973 / to an English dancer Q1
591.31   hand, / hand. Q1
592.29   errands / Errants Q1
595.28   dress, 'tis / dress 'tis Q1
597.3   Indeed. I / Indeed, I Q1
597.34   Medley, I / Medley I Q1
598.15   squire's / squires Q1
600.3   *Pert, her* / Pert *her*
604.13   spoken. 'Twas / spoken, 'twas Q1
609.11   to 1733 ed. / too Q1
618.15   *fière! Serviteur* / fiere Serviteur Q1